Algorithmic Foundations for Social Advancement

Shin-ichi Minato · Takeaki Uno · Norihito Yasuda ·
Takashi Horiyama · Ken-ichi Kawarabayashi ·
Shigeru Yamashita · Hirotaka Ono
Editors

Algorithmic Foundations for Social Advancement

Recent Progress on Theory and Practice

Springer

Editors
Shin-ichi Minato
Graduate School of Informatics
Kyoto University
Kyoto, Kyoto, Japan

Norihito Yasuda
Innovative Communication Laboratory
NTT Communication Science Laboratories
Soraku-gun, Kyoto, Japan

Ken-ichi Kawarabayashi
Principles of Informatics Research Division
National Institute of Informatics
Chiyoda-ku, Tokyo, Japan

Hirotaka Ono
Graduate School of Informatics
Nagoya University
Nagoya, Aichi, Japan

Takeaki Uno
Principles of Informatics Research Division
National Institute of Informatics
Chiyoda-ku, Tokyo, Japan

Takashi Horiyama
Graduate School of Information Science
and Technology
Hokkaido University
Sapporo, Hokkaido, Japan

Shigeru Yamashita
Graduate School of Information Science
and Engineering
Ritsumeikan University
Kusatsu, Osaka, Japan

ISBN 978-981-96-0670-2 ISBN 978-981-96-0668-9 (eBook)
https://doi.org/10.1007/978-981-96-0668-9

This Springer imprint is published by the registered company Springer Nature Singapore Pte Ltd.
The registered company address is: 152 Beach Road, #21-01/04 Gateway East, Singapore 189721, Singapore

Preface

This book provides an overview of the cutting-edge research conducted as part of the nationwide academic project in Japan, *Algorithmic Foundations for Social Advancement* (AFSA). The primary goal of this project is to systematize innovative foundations in algorithmic theories and techniques, and apply them to solve socially significant real-life problems, thereby driving social transformation and advancement.

A central theme of this book is how algorithmic foundations can be leveraged to contribute to social advancement. One of the major challenges lies in effectively packaging the profound impact of these algorithmic theories and techniques and creating an interface that connects them with real-life problems. Formulating such social problems into well-defined mathematical or computational terms is no trivial task. It requires not only a solid theoretical foundation but also a deep understanding of the application domain itself.

In this project, we have been conducting research on how to formulate societal challenges in ways that can be addressed using algorithmic techniques. At the same time, researchers with deep theoretical expertise have aimed not merely at solving easily approachable problems but at creating new theoretical solutions based on innovative perspectives linked to societal applications. The synergy between deep theoretical understanding and practical problem formulation is the core of this project.

The AFSA project has spanned five years, with more than 50 researchers from various fields collaborating to create and systematize algorithmic theories and techniques that contribute to social advancement. This collaborative effort has resulted in numerous innovative achievements in algorithmic theories and techniques, and this book presents those research accomplishments.

This book is divided into three parts. Part I, comprising Chapter "Overview of Algorithmic Foundations for Social Advancement (AFSA) Project", serves as an introduction, outlining the social context that motivated the AFSA project, the prospective innovations we aimed to achieve, and the organizational framework that supported these goals. Part II discusses how to bridge the gap between algorithmic solutions and social advancement. Chapters "Motivating Problems and Algorithmic Solutions", "ZDDs and Frontier-Based Search for Solving Combinatorial Problems", and "Graphillion: Combinatorial Solver for Graph Problems" present motivating problems that showcase the remarkable performance improvements driven by algorithmic technologies, followed by examples of how interfaces and tools were provided to apply these solutions to real-world challenges. The subsequent Chapters "Interdisciplinary Discussions for Future Computer Science" through "Reframing Problems: Analyzing the Design of Mixed Reality Tools Through the Lens of Fictionality" then focus on interdisciplinary discussions regarding how to formulate real societal issues into a catalog of problems to be addressed. Finally, Part III, spanning Chapters "Solving Rep-tile by Computers: Performance of Solvers and Analyses of Solutions" to "Perpetual Scheduling Under Frequency Constraints", highlights selected topics on the innovative algorithmic foundations developed through the project, focusing on intriguing subjects and the latest ongoing research. These include processing large-scale discrete structures, graph algorithms, discrete optimization, quantum algorithms, and various other topics related to algorithmic foundations. Each chapter of this book has been authored by the project members who contributed to their respective research areas.

As the lead editor, I would like to express my sincere gratitude to the co-editors of this book for their invaluable discussions and contributions during the planning of the book. I also wish to extend my heartfelt thanks to Prof. Jun Kawahara, Dr. Takeru Inoue, Dr. Susumu Hashimoto, Mr. Kazuki Maeyama, Mr. Yuta Yamamoto, Prof. Giulia Punzi, Prof. Francois Le Gall, Prof. Harumichi Nishimura, Prof. Shigeru Yamashita, Prof. Akitoshi Kawamura, Prof. Ryuhei Uehara, and Prof. Suguru Tamaki for their careful reading and insightful feedback during the writing process. My deep appreciation goes to all the project members who dedicated themselves to the success of this endeavor. The AFSA project was made possible through the financial support by the Ministry of Education, Culture, Sports, Science and Technology (MEXT) of Japan, Grant Number 20H05961 to 20H05967, and other related grants, for which I am deeply grateful. Finally, I express my sincere thanks to the editorial office of Springer for providing the opportunity to publish this book.

I hope that this book serves as a valuable resource for researchers, practitioners, and students and that it contributes to further innovation in algorithmic technologies.

Kyoto, Japan

Shin-ichi Minato
Director of the AFSA project

Contents

Part I
Introduction

The first part serves as an introduction, outlining the social context of the project, as well as the proposed concept of *Algorithmic Foundations for Social Advancement*.

Overview of Algorithmic Foundations for Social Advancement (AFSA) Project

Shin-ichi Minato

Abstract Over the last 30 years, since around 1990, significant advancements in integrated circuits, optical communication, and storage device technologies have driven a remarkable increase in computational power. It is expected that the development of algorithmic technologies that leverage the benefits of this substantial improvement in computational capabilities will become a source of competitiveness in the next generation of highly information-driven societies and have a major ripple effect that drives social advancement. In the first chapter of this book, we describe the social and historical background of algorithmic technology and introduce the concept we propose, called Algorithmic Foundations for Social Advancement (AFSA). Additionally, we explain the innovations we aim to achieve through this research project, our vision of research management, and the organizational structure designed to support these research goals.

1 Background: The Social Importance of Algorithmic Technology

With the rapid advancements in integrated circuits, optical communication, and storage devices, personal computers and information communication terminals available to people have achieved an overwhelming 100,000- to 1,000,000-fold improvement in the price–performance ratio over the last 30 years since around 1990. Such a significant technological advancement is unprecedented in human history. For example, the recent boom in deep learning and AI is based on fundamental techniques [21] that had already been started in the 1980s. However, it was only through the overwhelming increase in computational power and the easier acquisition and distribution of big data that these technologies truly blossomed. It is expected that the development of algorithmic technologies that leverage this overwhelming improvement in computational power will become a driving force of competitiveness in the highly

S. Minato (✉)
Graduate School of Informatics, Kyoto University, Yoshida-Honmachi, Kyoto 606-8501, Japan
e-mail: minato@i.kyoto-u.ac.jp

S. Minato et al. (eds.), *Algorithmic Foundations for Social Advancement*,
https://doi.org/10.1007/978-981-96-0668-9_1

information-driven society over the next 10–20 years, leading to ripple effects that will lead to social advancement.

In history, Google's ascent to dominance began with the development of an algorithmic technique called PageRank [3]. This method enabled the automated execution of popular site searches in just a few seconds, tasks previously difficult to perform manually, and became a key driver of its competitive edge. Additionally, mathematical concepts and related algorithmic technologies such as differential privacy [7] and compressed sensing [5, 6] have enhanced the competitiveness of the modern IT giants known as GAFA (Google, Apple, Facebook, and Amazon), contributing to the emergence of a new economic framework. This illustrates that leading the world in the field of algorithms and developing concepts and methods that can drive advancement in next-generation science, technology, and societal construction is essential to maintaining a nation's competitiveness and continuing to be a leading country. Furthermore, with the increased feasibility of innovative hardware technologies like quantum computing devices [2, 22], there is also a demand for advancing theoretical research on foundational algorithms that can leverage the benefits of future innovative devices. To achieve this, it is crucial to strengthen the community of leading researchers in the field of algorithms and to cultivate world-class young and mid-career researchers continuously.

2 Concept of Algorithmic Foundations for Social Advancement

Just as the astronomer Galileo Galilei was also the inventor of the telescope, theory and application were closely linked in the early days of computer technology development. However, in today's highly advanced technological era, the distance between theoretical and applied researchers has grown, as illustrated in Fig. 1, making it difficult to explore both simultaneously deeply. The foundational theories of algorithms and their applied technologies now form distinct research communities, which creates a gap in the intermediate areas where it is harder to produce research publications, making it challenging to cultivate researchers in the gap area. Now, it becomes more critical to provide methodologies and software tools that contribute to practical applications as a research outcome of algorithmic foundations. Thus, we

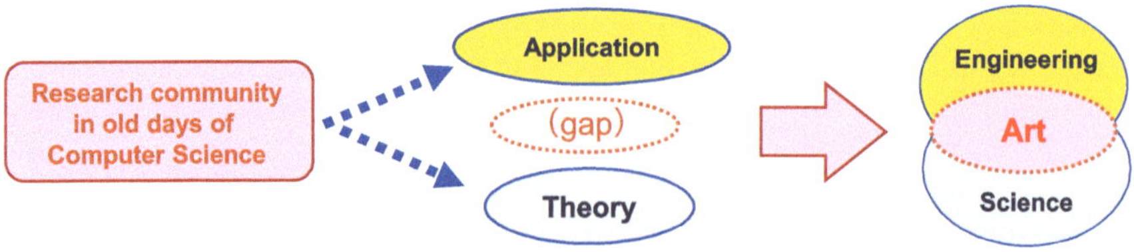

Fig. 1 Research communities in theoretical computer science

Fig. 2 A visual identity of the project

started to organize a research project to form the "Art" layer to bridge Science and Engineering, crossing the gap. Our project logo (Fig. 2) symbolizes this research vision.

While it is essential to provide tools that contribute to real-world applications, these tools must be specialized for individual application problems to be truly utilized. However, over-specialization can lead to a loss of generality, resulting in solutions only useful in isolated cases and hindering long-term academic accumulation.

Considering these challenges, it is necessary to devise some effective method of bridging theory and application, which is considered one of the crucial points for academic transformation. Successful past examples of such efforts include (integer) linear programming (LP/ILP) solvers [8, 12] and matrix computation packages [20]. These tools, which allow problems to be described with concise mathematical formulas and then automatically and efficiently solved, are still widely used today. This success was made possible by demonstrating that various socially important problems could be formulated using concise mathematical models like linear inequalities and matrices. When typical example datasets were made publicly available, researchers competed to develop algorithmic techniques to solve them quickly, leading to significant advancements.

Similar formulation models include Boolean satisfiability (SAT) solvers [1] and Binary Decision Diagram (BDD) [4]/Zero-suppressed Binary Decision Diagram (ZDD) Packages [13, 18], which manipulate Boolean functions and combinatorial sets, respectively. In a broader sense, the instruction sets of microprocessors [9] can also be considered a form of low-level formulation. Additionally, the recent boom in deep machine learning [10] represents a type of formulation for solving pattern recognition problems, while the Ising model [17], which is popular in quantum annealing, serves as a formulation model for solving combinatorial optimization problems.

In the 1990s, a major research project in Japan called *Algorithm Engineering,* led by Ibaraki [11], aimed to apply algorithmic theory to practical engineering applications, demonstrating remarkable foresight that remains relevant even today. However, at that time, it was difficult to produce immediate, transformative societal results due to limited computational power and the effort being primarily driven by theoretical researchers with insufficient connections to the applied research communities.

Later, in the ERATO Minato project [15] carried out in the 2010s, thanks to the significant improvements in computational performance, cutting-edge algorithmic techniques were employed to address real-world engineering problems. Through close collaboration with applied researchers, it achieved breakthrough results in areas such as power grid optimization and big data statistical analysis in life sciences, surpassing the conventional expectations of applied researchers. These individual successes should not just be concluded as isolated incidents but should serve as a foundation for ongoing academic development. Based on this background, a new major research project called *Algorithmic Foundations for Social Advancement* (AFSA) [19] was launched in 2020 to continue these efforts.

In the world, various engineering challenges exist, each of which can be approached through different models and formulations. To truly become a driving force for social advancement through innovative algorithmic foundations, our research project needs to be guided by the following directions:

- Consider problems that involve new concepts and values to promote social advancement.
- Provide algorithm implementations capable of handling the scale and complexity of real-world problems.
- Offer flexibility and usability to adapt to individual problems.
- Possess novelty and usefulness, rather than merely following existing technologies.

We should systematically study such formulations, the theories surrounding them, and techniques for practical applications, as this constitutes what should be called *innovative algorithmic foundation*. We now have access to overwhelmingly advanced computational power, and the emergence of innovative devices like quantum computers is fast approaching. At this opportune time, our research project has been launched.

In recent years, a new academic field known as *e-Science* or the *Fourth Paradigm of Science* has emerged, where information-processing technologies are becoming essential in nearly all scientific fields. The importance of algorithmic techniques, which drive the enhancement of these technologies, is growing significantly. However, at present, interdisciplinary research projects combining informatics with fields such as life sciences, materials science, medicine, and financial engineering are carried out independently, resulting in competition for the limited number of information science researchers, leading to concerns about the fragmentation of human resources.

Research on theories and techniques in the field of algorithms does not require expensive experimental equipment; instead, it is crucial for leading researchers to come together and engage in deep discussions to cultivate new ideas. Maintaining and strengthening a central research community for such exchanges is essential for the future development of information science and technology. This research project aims to establish such a platform, contributing not only to all areas of information science but also, directly and indirectly, to almost all experimental and social sciences.

3 Innovations Our Research Aims to Achieve

The key points for achieving innovations for social advancement in this research domain can be summarized as follows:

- **Research Area**:
  Based on the assumption of dramatically improved computational power and the advent of innovative future devices, we aim to reconstruct and systematize general formulation models that effectively bridge theory and application. Specifically, we will further develop areas of algorithms where our research group has a solid global presence, such as BDD/ZDD packages, SAT solvers, enumeration algorithms, large-scale graph analysis, discrete optimization, and quantum computation theory. These areas will be advanced as integral components of the innovative algorithmic foundation.
- **Research Style**:
  We will implement effective management strategies for large-scale research projects in fields such as algorithm research, which do not require expensive experimental equipment. Leveraging the 10-year achievements initiated by the ERATO Minato Project, which created a research community where theory and application converge to continuously cultivated ideas that became sources of competitiveness, we aim to broadly extend these practices across the entire field of theoretical computer science.
- **Research Output**:
  While achievements in top conferences and journals are undoubtedly important, we will also evaluate the broader societal impact. It includes applications to real-world problems through collaboration with applied researchers, indirect contributions to various other fields of science and technology, the economic ripple effects from practical applications, and the social impact of our outreach efforts toward the general public. All these factors will be actively considered in our evaluations.

With these essential points in mind, we have planned our research project. The field of theoretical computer science, especially in algorithms and computational complexity, has been studied internationally for many years, primarily in Western countries. However, there are several areas where Japanese research groups hold considerable strengths. In this project, we mainly focus on the following three areas, around which we have structured our research groups:

- **Theories and techniques for processing discrete structures to efficiently perform large-scale case analysis and enumeration**:
  This field, which includes techniques such as BDD/ZDD packages, SAT solvers, and enumeration methods, has achieved many results through the ERATO Minato project [15]. While there is highly competitive international research in optimization techniques focused on finding the best single solution, enumeration techniques—aimed at identifying all possible solutions—have recently begun to attract attention. Japanese research groups have maintained a competitive edge in this area.
- **Theories and techniques of algorithms for efficiently processing large graphs and big data**:
  This field, which includes large graphs, machine learning, and discrete optimization, features a group of top young researchers developed through the ERATO

Kawarabayashi project [16], who are competing at the international top level. Significant future development is expected.
- **Theories and techniques for ultra-fast/ultra-parallel algorithms based on non-classical computation models, such as quantum computing**:
  The theory of quantum computing in Japan has a long-standing history, beginning with the ERATO Imai project [14] in 2000. Since then, in the field of quantum computation theory, Japanese research groups have become one of the international leading centers.

Attempts to bridge the algorithm theory researchers with application engineers are frequently made in international research projects. Yet, often, these collaborations do not extend beyond individual studies and do not last long. In international projects, the size of specific research communities is larger than within domestic ones, and breaking out of these frameworks requires more energy. With its relatively small geographical size, Japan offers more frequent opportunities for interaction among leading researchers across various fields of information science than in the international research communities, creating an ideal research environment for algorithm researchers to collaborate closely with applied researchers and build really meaningful algorithmic foundations. However, this does not mean that research activities should be closed within a country. The research community should include top international researchers, and engaging in deep discussions based on the latest technological information is crucial for generating competitive ideas.

4 Organization of AFSA Project

Our research project aims to systematize the recent rapid advances in the theory and techniques of algorithms into an innovative algorithmic foundation that can be widely and freely utilized by scientists and engineers across various fields, thereby establishing it as a fundamental research area that drives social development.

Based on the above objective, we present our vision for managing the research project. In today's highly information-driven society, cutting-edge theories and techniques in algorithms have the potential to impact all scientific fields and serve as a powerful driving force for social development. However, to achieve truly effective research outcomes, it is essential not to proceed with research aimlessly but to strategically define the research direction and allocate resources appropriately. We will advance research in this project by focusing on the following points:

- Conduct research based on new computational models considering recent advances in computational power and future innovative devices. While theoretical computer science has a long history rooted in discrete mathematics, the foundational computational models must adapt appropriately to the latest information-processing environments.

- The progress in big data and AI technologies has deeply integrated information technology into society, significantly altering social structures and ethical perspectives. Therefore, formulating real-world problems based on new social concepts and values is essential to achieve research outcomes that can drive social advancement.
- It is not easy to catch up with or surpass just by following the IT giants and centralized governments of a big country that are investing overwhelming research resources. Therefore, the focus should be on areas where our academic groups have demonstrated strengths. However, since the future is unpredictable, it is essential to avoid over-concentration on existing successful fields and be ready to dynamically allocate resources to new and promising opportunities as they emerge.

Based on the above research management vision, we designed the following project organization. As shown in Fig. 3, our AFSA project consists of six research groups in two categories, A and B. The groups in A (A01 and A02) investigate the interface layer to bridge theory and practice, and the groups in B (B01, B02, B03, and B04) investigate specific theories and techniques to support the interface layer. Each research group consists of six or seven PIs (principal investigators). For the application layer, we have a number of external collaborators affiliated with many kinds of research projects in the specific application domains. Those external researchers and

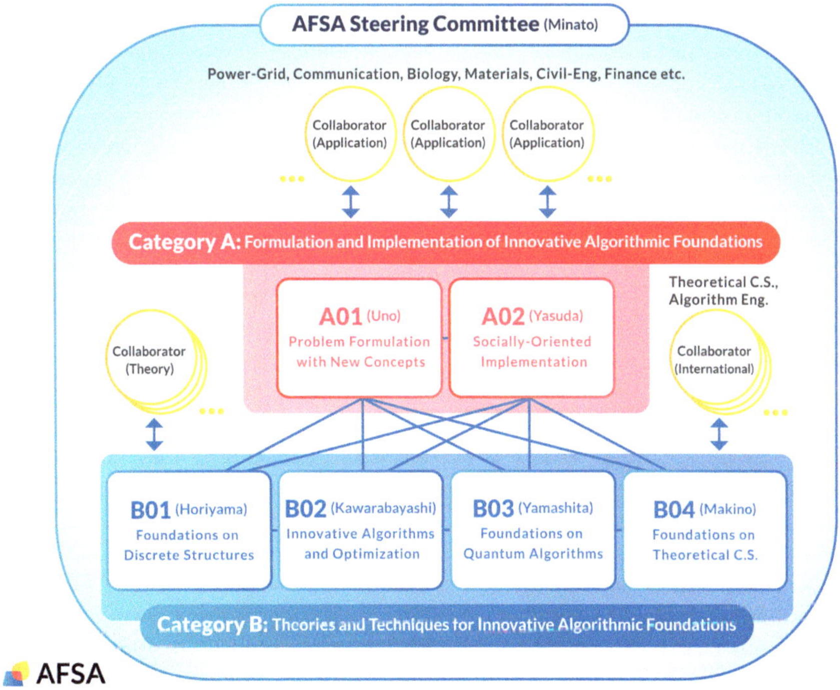

Fig. 3 An organization chart of AFSA project

engineers communicate with AFSA project members through the interface developed by the research groups A01 and A02. The detailed contents of the six research groups are shown below:

- **A01: New Problem Formulation on Next-Generation Informatics and Researches on their Algorithms**:
  Collaborating with researchers in the application layer, this group discusses and formulates a set of new problems to be considered in the future society. We also design efficient algorithms based on a new approach.
- **A02: Socially Oriented Algorithm Implementation**:
  This group implements the algorithms proposed in our project and organizes the algorithmic foundations for social advancement. It provides an interface between theoretical researchers and application engineers.
- **B01: Algorithmic Foundations Based on Large-Scale Discrete Structures**:
  Through the collaboration of theoretical researchers and application engineers, this group tackles how to deal with exponentially large-scale discrete structures and develops innovative design methodologies of efficient algorithms.
- **B02: New Computational Models for Algorithms and Discrete Optimization**:
  This group investigates foundational research topics in the areas of discrete mathematics, combinatorial optimization, machine learning, etc., to develop efficient algorithms for solving very large-scale problems required in our society.
- **B03: Creation of Innovative Foundations to Bridge Theory and Practice of Quantum Algorithms**:
  Combining the knowledge of classical computation and new quantum models, this group constructs useful algorithmic foundations to implement practically efficient quantum computers connected to conventional systems.
- **B04: Exploration and Development of the Basic Theory of Algorithms**:
  This group investigates important problems in theoretical computer science, such as performance assurance, preserving fairness and stability, new computation models, and design methodologies for social requirements.

We also have publicly selected 17 individual research projects based on a call for proposals to work on additional related research topics. It is strongly recommended that they collaborate with at least two different research groups in the AFSA project.

To facilitate collaborative research, we opened two meeting offices in central Tokyo and Kyoto that were dedicated to AFSA project activities. The two offices, Tokyo-Kanda Lab. (Fig. 4) and Kyoto-Teramachi Lab. (Fig. 5), are both located near the central stations of the two big cities so that many researchers in different universities/institutes can easily access one of the offices and frequently meet with each other to have research discussions. Unfortunately, due to the overlap of the first year of launching of the AFSA project and the widespread impact of COVID-19, the project members could not gather closely for discussion. However, we established the two offices as hub centers aiming for the best mix of online and offline activities. Even after easing COVID-19 restrictions, it continues to operate effectively as a hybrid activity hub.

Fig. 4 Tokyo-Kanda laboratory

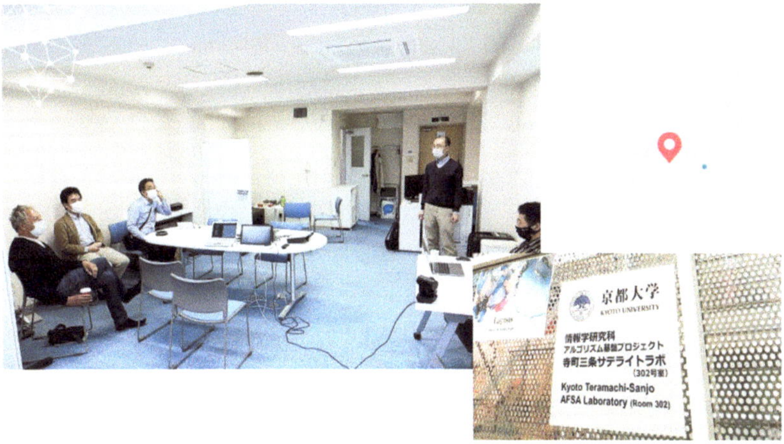

Fig. 5 Kyoto-Teramachi laboratory

5 Concluding Remarks

The AFSA Project is officially scheduled to conclude in March 2025, yet the endeavors of the research community will continue beyond this timeframe. This project will lead an active research community where theoretical insights and practical applications meet together. Our objectives extend beyond generating leading conference papers and journal articles; we also aim to address real-life social problems through collaboration with application research engineers. The algorithmic foundations developed through this project are intended to benefit a broad spectrum of scientific and technological fields, ultimately contributing to future social advancement.

The subsequent chapters of this book will cover the research activities related to this project. In Part II, we first discuss the research topics aimed at bridging algorithmic foundations and real-world social problems, led by the research groups A01 and A02. Part III then presents selected topics in algorithmic foundations, primarily conducted by the research groups in category B.

Acknowledgements This work was supported by MEXT KAKENHI Grant Number 20H05961.

References

1. A. Biere, M. Heule, H. van Maaren, *Handbook of Satisfiability*, vol. 185 (IOS Press, 2009)
2. S. Boixo, T.A.F.M. Spedalieri, N. Chancellor, D.A. Lidar, Experimental signature of programmable quantum annealing. Nat. Commun. **4**(2067) (2013)
3. S. Brin, L. Page, The anatomy of a large-scale hypertextual web search engine. Comput. Netw. ISDN Syst. **30**(1), 107–117 (1998). https://doi.org/10.1016/S0169-7552(98)00110-X. (Proceedings of the Seventh International World Wide Web Conference (WWW1998))
4. R.E. Bryant, Graph-based algorithms for boolean function manipulation. IEEE Trans. Comput. **35**(8), 677–691 (1986). https://doi.org/10.1109/TC.1986.1676819
5. E.J. CandÃÂ¨s, J.K. Romberg, T. Tao, Stable signal recovery from incomplete and inaccurate measurements. Commun. Pure Appl. Math. **59**(8), 1207–1223 (2006). https://doi.org/10.1002/cpa.20124
6. D. Donoho, Compressed sensing. IEEE Trans. Inf. Theory **52**(4), 1289–1306 (2006). https://doi.org/10.1109/TIT.2006.871582
7. C. Dwork, Differential privacy, in *Automata, Languages and Programming (Proc of ICALP2006)*. ed. by M. Bugliesi, B. Preneel, V. Sassone, I. Wegener (Springer, Berlin Heidelberg, Berlin, Heidelberg, 2006), pp. 1–12
8. Gurobi Optimization: Gurobi Optimizer Reference Manual Version 9.1 (2020). https://gurobi.com/
9. J.L. Hennessy, D.A. Patterson, *Computer Architecture: A Quantitative Approach* (Morgan Kaufmann, 2017)
10. G.E. Hinton, R.R. Salakhutdinov, Reducing the dimensionality of data with neural networks. Science **313**(5786), 504–507 (2006)
11. T. Ibaraki et al., Algorithm engineering as a new paradigm : a challenge to hard computation problems. 1998–2001 grant-in-aid for scientific research on priority areas (b), MEXT, Japan (1998). https://kaken.nii.ac.jp/en/grant/KAKENHI-PROJECT-10205101
12. IBM: ILOG CPLEX Optimization Studio V12.10.0 documentation (2019). https://www.ibm.com/jp-ja/products/ilog-cplex-optimization-studio/
13. T. Inoue et al., Graphillion (2013). http://graphillion.org/
14. Japan Science and Technology Agency (JST): ERATO IMAI Quantum Computation and Information Project (2000). https://www.jst.go.jp/erato/en/research_area/completed/irkk_P.html
15. Japan Science and Technology Agency (JST): ERATO MINATO Discrete Structure Manipulation System Project (2009). https://www.jst.go.jp/erato/en/research_area/completed/mrk_P.html

16. Japan Science and Technology Agency (JST): ERATO KAWARABAYASHI Large Graph Project (2011). https://www.jst.go.jp/erato/en/research_area/completed/kkg-p.html
17. T. Kadowaki, H. Nishimori, Quantum annealing in the transverse ising model. Phys. Rev. E **58**(5), 5355 (1998)
18. S. Minato, Zero-suppressed BDDs for set manipulation in combinatorial problems, in *Proceedings of 30th ACM/IEEE Design Automation Conference (DAC'93)* (1993), pp. 272–277
19. S. Minato et al. (2020) Creation and organization of innovative algorithmic foundations for social advancement. 2020-2024 grant-in-aid for transformative research areas, MEXT, Japan (2020). https://afsa.jp/en/
20. C. Moler, J. Little, A history of MATLAB **4**(HOPL) (2020). https://doi.org/10.1145/3386331
21. D.E. Rumelhart, G.E. Hinton, R.J. Williams, Learning representations by back-propagating errors. Nature **323**, 533–536 (1986)
22. V. Silva, *Enter the IBM Q Experience: A One-of-a-Kind Platform for Quantum Computing in the Cloud* (Apress, Berkeley, CA, 2018), pp. 77–141. https://doi.org/10.1007/978-1-4842-4218-6_3

Part II
Bridging Algorithmic Solutions to Social Advancement

In this part, the Chapters "Motivating Problems and Algorithmic Solutions", "ZDDs and Frontier-Based Search for Solving Combinatorial Problems", and "Graphillion: Combinatorial Solver for Graph Problems" first discuss how to effectively package algorithmic technologies and design an interface for practical applications. The subsequent Chapters "Interdisciplinary Discussions for Future Computer Science" through "Reframing Problems: Analyzing the Design of Mixed Reality Tools Through the Lens of Fictionality" then focus on interdisciplinary discussions regarding how to formulate real societal issues into a catalog of problems to be addressed.

Fig. 1 Screenshots of the YouTube animated video [3]

Table 1 The numbers of paths up to $n = 11$

n	Number of paths
1	2
2	12
3	184
4	8,512
5	1,262,816
6	575,780,564
7	789,360,053,252
8	3,266,598,486,981,642
9	41,044,208,702,632,496,804
10	1,568,758,030,464,750,013,214,100
11	182,413,291,514,248,049,241,470,885,236

ends with a calm explanation that state-of-the-art algorithmic technology can solve the same problem in just a few seconds.

The video attracted significant attention, and many people appeared online, attempting to solve the problem themselves. However, when implemented in a straightforward manner, it requires an enormous amount of computation time, just like in the video's story. This enumeration problem has become a well-known example demonstrating the effectiveness of algorithmic techniques. For instance, this problem is featured in one of the beginner-level algorithm guidebooks in the MIT Press Essential Knowledge series [11].

The solution to this problem, using a 2×2 grid graph as an example, is shown in Fig. 2. The task of finding self-avoiding paths from the top-left vertex to the bottom-right vertex can be viewed as a combinatorial problem of selecting which of the 12 edges in the graph to use. If we only enumerate the shortest paths, the path length would be four, where two steps go to the right and the other two go downward. Therefore, it becomes a combination problem of choosing two rightward steps out of four, resulting in six possible paths. In general, for an $n \times n$ grid, the total number of

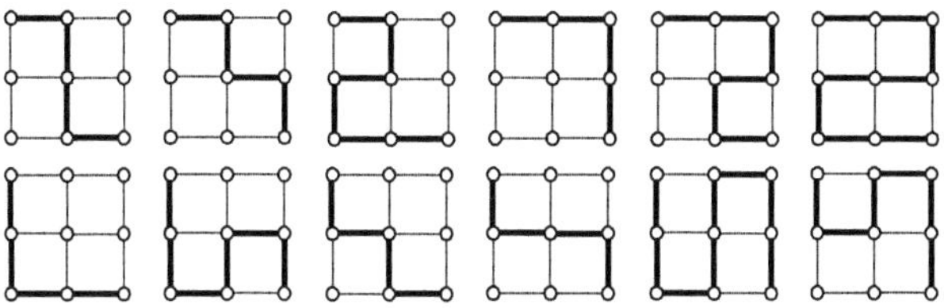

Fig. 2 All self-avoiding paths from the top left to the bottom right in the 2×2 grid graph

shortest paths can be found using the binomial coefficient $\binom{2n}{n}$, which is covered in high school mathematics. However, in this problem, detours are allowed in addition to the shortest paths, so the total number of paths is 12. Allowing detours makes the problem significantly more difficult, and no simple formula or recurrence relation has been found to express the total number of paths. Therefore, the paths must essentially be found through brute-force enumeration. As n increases, the number of solutions grows overwhelmingly, and consequently the time required for enumeration increases dramatically.

Fairy tales involving enormous numbers have existed for a long time (for example, a king rewards a soldier by placing one grain of wheat on the first square of a chessboard, then two grains, four grains, eight grains, and so on). However, these were all problems that could be calculated by hand as long as the formula was known. In contrast, the self-avoiding path enumeration problem, despite its simple form that even children can understand, has no known formula for its solution. Yet, through algorithmic techniques, the computation time can be dramatically reduced from 29 billion years to just a few seconds. A fairy tale based on a problem without a known simple formula, like this one, is unprecedented. This story could only have been created thanks to recent advances in computer science and technology.

2 Binary Decision Trees and Decision Diagrams

Now, let us discuss our approach to solving this problem. We first need to describe the concept of binary decision trees. As mentioned earlier, the path enumeration problem can be viewed as a combinatorial problem of selecting which edges to use from all the edges. As shown in Fig. 3, in the case of $n = 2$, there are nine vertices, including the start s and goal t, and 12 edges labeled e_1 to e_{12}, each with two choices: either use the edge or not. As illustrated in Fig. 4, if edge e_1 is used, we assign $e_1 = 1$, and if it is not used, we assign $e_1 = 0$. By splitting cases for each edge, we can see that the number of possibilities doubles with each additional edge. This process of constructing a graph by dividing cases is the concept of a binary decision tree. Since there are 12 edges, the total number of combinations is $2^{12} = 4096$, each representing a unique combination of edge selections. Among these, only 12 combinations correspond to correct paths, as shown in Fig. 2. In this way, the problem becomes searching through

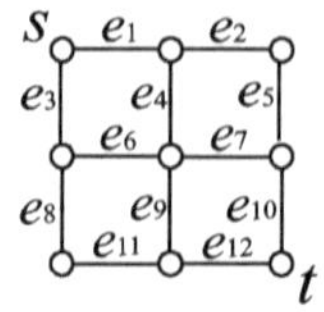

Fig. 3 6 vertices and 12 edges in the 2 × 2 grid graph

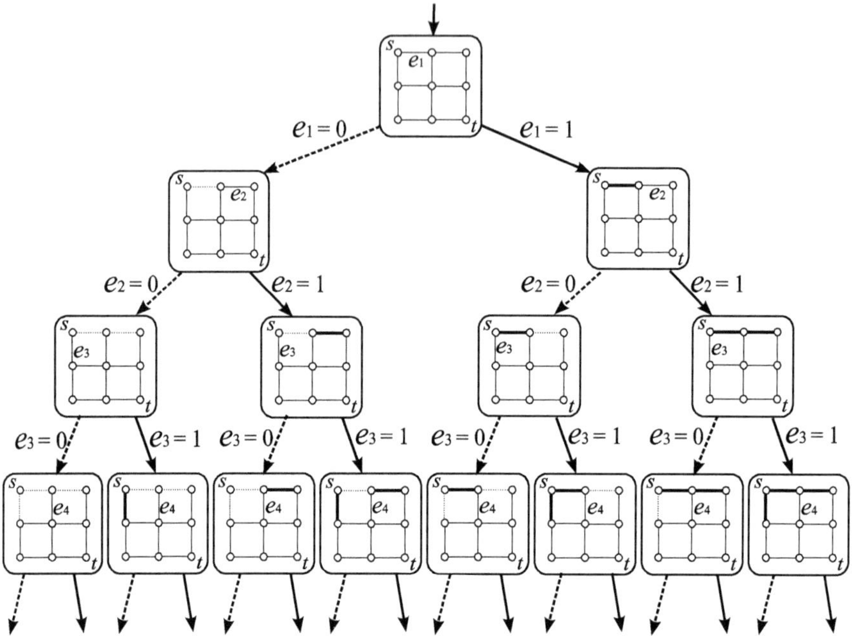

Fig. 4 A binary decision tree for selecting edges

the large binary decision tree of combinations to find the correct set of edges that forms a valid path.

Generating all 4096 possible combinations and then determining the correct ones is clearly inefficient. However, it becomes evident during the decision-making process that the current choice of using or not using certain edges will not result in a valid path. In that case, the process can be interrupted at that point, and the remaining branches can be pruned. In this way, we can repeatedly apply the backtracking method, where one option is chosen, the search proceeds downward, and if it hits a dead end, we backtrack to the previous level and try a different option. This procedure ensures that all solutions will eventually be generated. In a typical backtracking approach, the computation time required is at least proportional to the number of solutions, and depending on the problem, it might take even longer. One might think it would be fast enough if all the solutions could be enumerated in time proportional to the number of solutions. In fact, the animation video assumes that the teacher used this class of algorithm. However, for the path enumeration problem, the number of solutions grows exponentially. Even if a supercomputer could find 20 billion valid paths per second, it would still take 250,000 years to solve a 10×10 grid, meaning the teacher would turn into a robot long before the computation finished.

To solve this problem efficiently, we use the data structure called *decision diagram*. A Binary Decision Diagram (BDD) [1, 2] is a graph representation of a Boolean function, initially developed for VLSI design. As illustrated in Fig. 5a and b, a BDD is derived by reducing a binary decision tree, which represents a decision-making process based on input variables. If we fix the order of the input variables and apply the following two reduction rules: (1) removing redundant nodes (Fig. 6a) and (2) sharing equivalent nodes as much as possible. This reduction process yields a canonical form that compactly and uniquely represents a Boolean function. The compression ratio achieved by using a BDD compared to a decision tree depends on the properties of the Boolean function being represented. In some practical cases, the compression ratios of several dozen to several hundred times can be obtained. (For details, see articles [2, 10].)

A Zero-suppressed Binary Decision Diagram (ZDD) [12] is a variant of the BDD designed for manipulating sets of combinations. An example is shown in Fig. 5c. ZDDs follow special reduction rules that differ from those used in BDDs: (1') Delete all nodes whose arc labeled with 1 directly points to the 0-terminal (Fig. 6b). This reduction rule is particularly effective for representing sparse sets of combinations. For instance, if each item appears in only 1% of the combinations on average, ZDDs can be up to 100 times more compact than ordinary BDDs. Such situations commonly

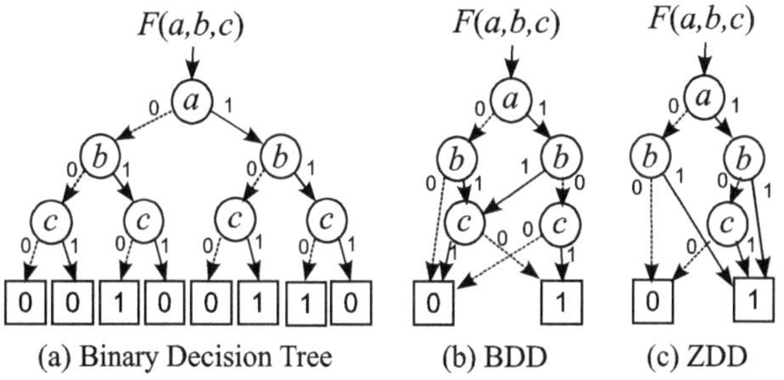

Fig. 5 Binary decision tree, BDDs and ZDDs

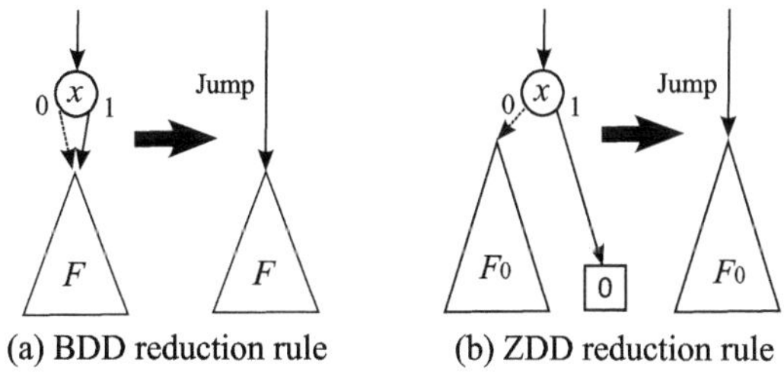

Fig. 6 Reduction rules in BDDs and ZDDs

arise in real-life problems, such as in a supermarket, where the number of items in a customer's basket is usually much smaller than the total number of items on display. ZDD is recognized as one of the most important BDD variants.

3 Knuth's Simpath Algorithm

In 2009, Knuth published the remarkably fast algorithm *Simpath* in his renowned textbook (Vol. 4 Fascicle 1) [10], on page 121 (or page 254 in Vol. 4A), to construct a ZDD corresponding to all self-avoiding s-t paths between two given vertices in a graph. This work is significant because variations of this algorithm can efficiently solve many practical problems. Knuth has made his own source code publicly available on his website, and the program is remarkably fast. For instance, in a 14×14 grid graph (with 420 edges in total), the number of self-avoiding paths between opposite corners is exactly 227449714676812739631826459327989863387613323440 (approximately 2.27×10^{47}). Using the Simpath algorithm, the set of paths can be compressed into a ZDD with only 144759636 nodes, and the computation time is only a few minutes.

Figure 7 illustrates the basic mechanism of the Simpath algorithm. First, we assign a fixed order to all the edges $E = \{e_1, e_2, \ldots, e_m\}$ for the given graph $G = (V, E)$. Then, we construct a binary decision tree from the top down in a breadth-first manner. In the first step, we consider two decisions, 1 and 0, representing whether or not the edge e_1 is included in the s-t path. Two leaf nodes are then created, each holding the current status of the path selection.

In the second step, we visit each leaf node and expand new branches to decide whether the edge e_2 is included in the s-t path. Each new leaf now holds the current status of both e_1 and e_2. This process is repeated sequentially for all leaf nodes at each level k, appending a decision node at the $(k + 1)$-th level for each case. However, branches may be pruned if we detect a contradiction in the current status, such as forming a disjoint component or an unreachable s-t path. In such cases, we assign a value of 0 to the leaf node and do not create further branches from it.

By continuing this process until the m-th level, we construct a complete decision tree that includes all possible s-t paths. We assign a value of 1 to each final leaf node that represents a valid solution. Once the decision tree is built, we apply ZDD reduction rules to each node, from the bottom to the top upward, to obtain a reduced ZDD.

In the above procedure, we can avoid unnecessary expansion by assigning a 0-terminal to any contradicted node (representing a partial pattern that can never form a valid s-t path). However, this alone is insufficient for achieving highly efficient computation. The Simpath algorithm also introduces an additional reduction technique that identifies equivalent nodes at the k-th level. These equivalent nodes, which have identical requirements for the remaining undecided edges to form valid s-t paths, are merged into a single node in the next expansion step. For example, consider the 2×2 grid graph shown in Fig. 8. Suppose it has already been decided whether edges

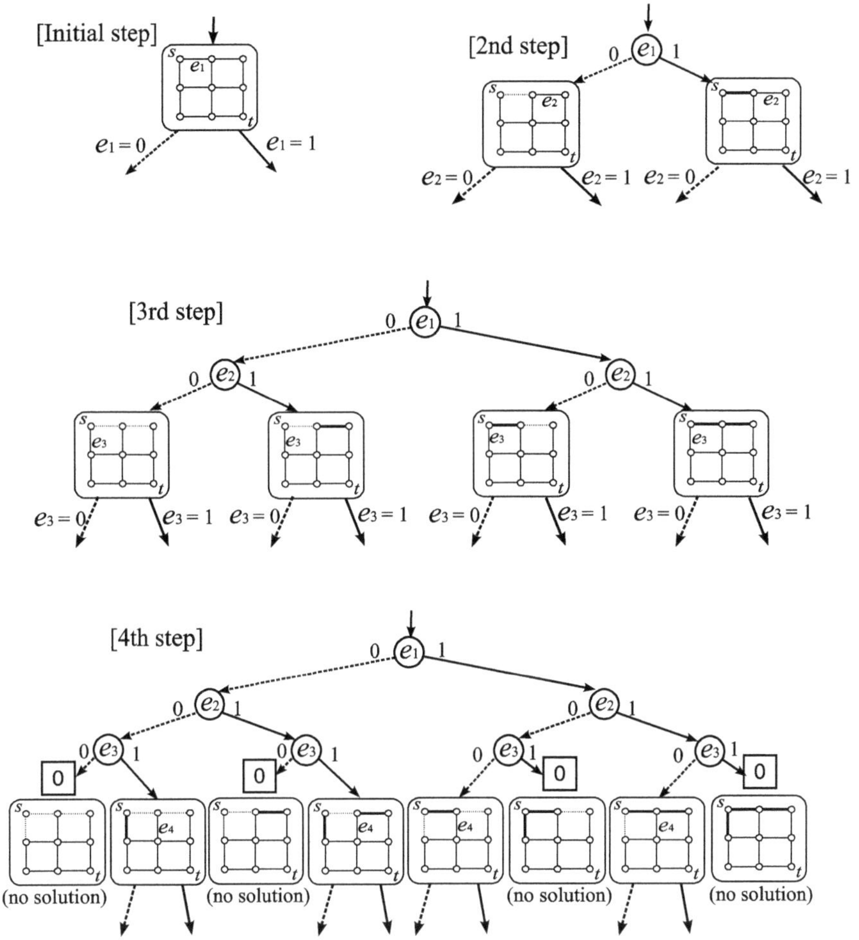

Fig. 7 Example of the execution steps in the Simpath algorithm

e_1 through e_7 are used, and compare two cases: one where (e_3, e_7) are chosen (left), and another where (e_2, e_3, e_4, e_5) are chosen (right). In both cases, we must choose e_8, e_9, e_{10}, and e_{11} among the remaining edges e_8 through e_{12} in order to complete an

Fig. 8 Equivalent patterns at a frontier in the Simpath algorithm

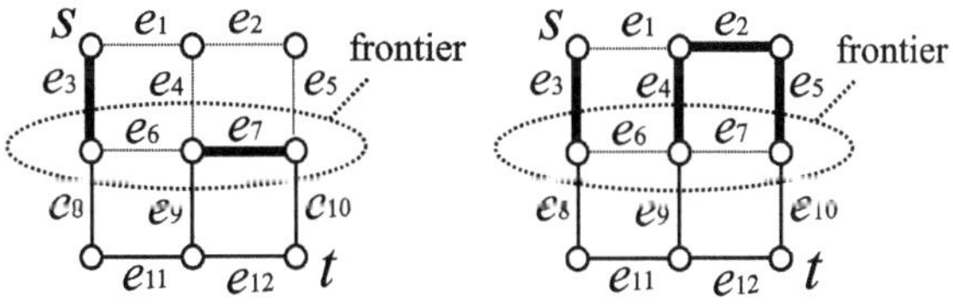

s-t path, and no other possible choices exist. Since the requirements for both patterns are identical, we can merge these two equivalent nodes into a single node.

To check the equivalence of two nodes, we only need to consider the status of a specific set of vertices marked by the dotted circle in the figure. Each vertex in this set is connected to at least one decided edge and one undecided edge. Knuth referred to this set of vertices as the *frontier*. During computation, the frontier moves from the start vertex to the goal vertex. By leveraging dynamic programming to share equivalent states, a compressed ZDD is constructed efficiently. In many cases of the s-t path problem, numerous equivalent nodes arise, significantly reducing computation time. (For further details, please refer to the next chapter.)

As a side note, after the release of our YouTube animation, the author had the opportunity to exchange letters with Prof. Knuth. In his letter, he wrote, "Best wishes to Shin-ichi for 2013. I enjoyed the YouTube video about big numbers and shared it with several friends." Knowing that Prof. Knuth enjoyed our video was incredibly gratifying for both the research project team and the Miraikan members involved in its production. It was a piece of news that delighted all of us.

4 The World Record of This Problem

The video presents the computation results up to $n = 11$, but it is intriguing to explore the largest n for which this problem remains computable. We have continuously improved the algorithm to solve large-scale problems as efficiently as possible. Our research group, Iwashita and colleagues [6], improved Knuth's Simpath algorithm to make it more memory efficient, and using a machine with approximately 500GB of memory, we successfully generated the ZDD for $n = 18$. For $n = 19$ and beyond, memory capacity became insufficient, so they developed a program that does not generate the whole ZDD but generates only one level of ZDD nodes at a time in breadth-first order for counting the number of solutions and successfully enumerated up to $n = 21$. Our group continued the challenge to push the record beyond it. Up to $n = 21$, we used a general-purpose program capable of handling any graph shape. However, by limiting the graph to an $n \times n$ grid graph, we were able to develop specialized algorithms that reduced both computation time and memory usage, allowing us to handle larger graphs. (For details, see references [6, 7].) Through various innovations, our computing power gradually improved, and by the fall of 2013, we could compute up to $n = 26$.

This result was submitted to and officially registered in The *On-Line Encyclopedia of Integer Sequences* (OEIS) [15]. Regardless of its practical use, holding a world record has a certain appeal. For reference, $n = 12$ was first computed by Knuth in 1995. Interestingly, when we visited the site, we found that the YouTube animated video was already linked as a reference. A person from Finland had discovered the video and suggested the link, which was accepted.

Table 2 presents the latest computation results. For values up to $n = 24$, our results match those of a Norwegian research group, confirming the accuracy of the calcu-

Table 2 The world record of the self-avoiding path enumeration problems (A007764 in [15])

n	The number of paths
1	2
2	12
3	184
4	8512
5	1262816
6	575780564
7	789360053252
8	3266598486981642
9	41044208702632496804
10	1568758030464750013214100
11	182413291514248049241470885236
12	64528039343270018963357185158482118
13	69450664761521361664274701548907358996488
14	227449714676812739631826459327989863387613323440
15	2266745568862672746374567396713098934866324885408319028
16	68745445609149931587631563132489232824587945968099457285419306
17	6344814611237963971310297540795524400449443986866480693646369387855336
18	1782112840842065129893384946652325275167838065704767655931452474605826692782532
19	152334497170487999308074281031922969089945425532329455577602986673735506059287756925584 4
20	3962892199823037560207299517133362502106339705739463771515237113377010682364035706704472064940398
21	31374751050137102720420538137382214513103312193698723653061351991346433379389385793965576992246021316463868
22	75597028666734533966151912331522261935310373207240948116739141047951792579274363123498703888331763498727117140443979 2
23	554354293552374770099143184890614379306903799709643313325569586464840084073348855445663869240208757112420600854085134829339 45720
24	1237171223120706475833874486267357083237304198901294353967872708048495169551593048564139455079215303719185802821251228092660030458138679109 4
25	84029748578811334710070837454368091272960542937753835498247426239370284978982152569291785770839709601216256025060273165497184021064940499783756042474 08
26	17369931586279272931175440421236498900372229588288140604663703720910342413276134762789218193498006107082296223143380491348290026721931129627708738890853908108906396

lations. However, we are currently the only group that has successfully computed $n = 26$, and while this number is registered, it has not yet been independently verified. As shown in the table, we can observe that the number of digits in decimal grows approximately at the rate of n^2. In other words, the number of paths increases exponentially with the number of edges, n^2, in the graph. In contrast, using our Simpath algorithm, which is specialized for grid graphs, the number of states on the frontier can be limited to $O(3^n)$. The exponent can be reduced from n^2 to n by utilizing algorithmic techniques, leading to a dramatic speed improvement compared to the naive backtracking method used in the animation video. Although there are still limits as n increases, it is evident that the range of computable problems has expanded significantly. For example, the computation time for $n = 11$ was reduced from 29 billion years to just a few seconds. If important real-life problems fall within this expanded range, the impact of algorithmic techniques becomes highly significant.

5 Application to Practical Problems for Social Advancement

The self-avoiding path enumeration problem featured in the YouTube animated video effectively showcases the fascinating power of algorithmic techniques. However, this problem is not just of puzzle-like interest; it also has practical applications in real-life engineering. Knuth noted that by slightly modifying the Simpath algorithm, ZDDs can be constructed to enumerate not only self-avoiding s-t paths but also Hamiltonian paths, directed paths, and various types of cycles. Moreover, by adjusting the mechanism for storing intermediate states, this method can be applied to various problems, including the enumeration of connected subgraphs, spanning trees/forests, cut sets, and the k-partition problem in graphs. We refer to this breadth-first, top-down dynamic programming approach for constructing ZDDs as the *frontier-based method* [9] and are exploring its application to various real-life problems. For example, path enumeration is crucial in geographic information systems and is also used for dependency analysis in process flow charts, fault analysis of industrial systems, and more.

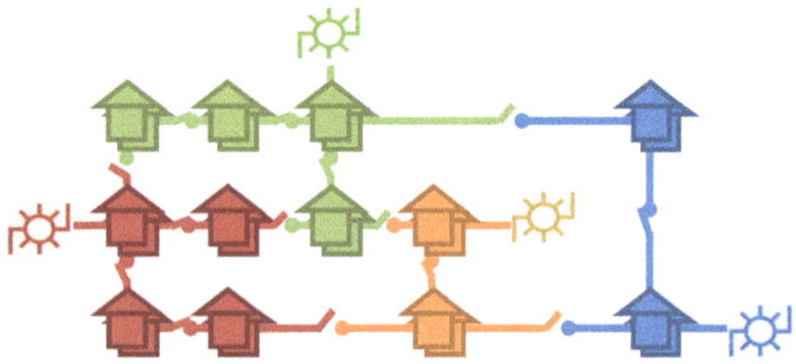

Fig. 9 Example of the electric power distribution network

Inoue et al. [4] discussed its application in the design of electric power distribution systems. Figure 9 shows a small example of the power distribution network. This system operates under the following constraints: each district must be connected to precisely one power substation to prevent outages; different substations must not be directly connected; if the current is too high, the wires may overheat; and if power is transmitted over long distances, the voltage will drop. The objective is to find a combination of switch open/close settings that satisfies all these conditions. The figure shows a simple example with 14 switches, leading to $2^{14} = 16384$ possible patterns, but only 210 of these patterns are topologically correct.

These civil engineering systems are often close to planar graphs, making the frontier-based method highly effective in many cases. They successfully generated a ZDD to enumerate all possible switching patterns in a realistic benchmark of an electric power distribution system with 468 switches. The resulting ZDD represents as many as 10^{60} valid switching patterns, yet the actual size of the ZDD is under 100 MB, and the computation time is around 30 minutes. Once the ZDD is generated, all valid switching patterns are compactly represented, allowing us to efficiently identify patterns with maximum, minimum, or average cost. Additional constraints can also be easily applied to the existing solutions.

In this way, frontier-based methods can be utilized for a wide range of real-life problems, not only in fields directly associated with grid graphs but also in areas such as disaster prevention (e.g., evacuation shelter allocation [16] and reliability analysis of the communication networks [14]), statistical analysis of epidemiological hotspots [5, 13], and the increasingly discussed issue of electoral districting [8], which supports democratic societies. Moreover, this approach has the potential to contribute significantly to advancements in fields like life sciences (e.g., genetic sequence analysis), material sciences, data mining from big data, and machine learning.

6 Concluding Remarks

In this chapter, we presented self-avoiding path enumeration as the motivating problem shown on a YouTube video. Various techniques related to discrete structures and algorithms, such as graph algorithms, combinatorial optimization, data compression, and constraint satisfaction, are believed to be useful for solving real-life problems for social advancement. In the following chapters, we will discuss the algorithmic techniques in more detail.

Acknowledgements This work was partly supported by MEXT KAKENHI Grant Number 20H05961 and 20H05964.

References

1. S.B. Akers, Binary decision diagrams. IEEE Trans. Comput. **C-27**(6), 509–516 (1978). https://doi.org/10.1109/TC.1978.1675141
2. R.E. Bryant, Graph-based algorithms for Boolean function manipulation. IEEE Trans. Comput. **35**(8), 677–691 (1986). https://doi.org/10.1109/TC.1986.1676819
3. S. Doi et al., Time with class! let's count! (the art of 10^{64}–understanding vastness–) (2012). YouTube video, MiraikanChannel. http://www.youtube.com/watch?v=Q4gTV4r0zRs
4. T. Inoue, K. Takano, T. Watanabe, J. Kawahara, R. Yoshinaka, A. Kishimoto, K. Tsuda, S. Minato, Y. Hayashi, Distribution loss minimization with guaranteed error bound. IEEE Trans. Smart Grid **5**(1), 102–111 (2014). https://doi.org/10.1109/TSG.2013.2288976
5. F. Ishioka, J. Kawahara, M. Mizuta, S. Minato, K. Kurihara, Evaluation of hotspot cluster detection using spatial scan statistic based on exact counting. Jpn. J. Stat. Data Sci. Springer **2**(1) (2019). https://doi.org/10.1007/s42081-018-0030-6
6. H. Iwashita, J. Kawahara, S. Minato, ZDD-based computation of the number of paths in a graph. Hokkaido University, Division of Computer Science, TCS Technical Reports, TCS-TR-A-10-60 (2012)
7. H. Iwashita, Y. Nakazawa, J. Kawahara, T. Uno, S. Minato, Efficient computation of the number of paths in a grid graph with minimal perfect hash functions. Hokkaido University, Division of Computer Science, TCS Technical Reports, TCS-TR-A-10-64 (2013)
8. J. Kawahara, T. Horiyama, K. Hotta, S. Minato, Generating all patterns of graph partitions within a disparity bound, in *Proceedings of the 11th International Workshop of Algorithms and Computation (WALCOM2017)* (LNCS 10167, Springer, 2017), pp. 119–131. https://doi.org/10.1007/978-3-319-53925-6_10
9. J. Kawahara, T. Inoue, H. Iwashita, S. Minato, Frontier-based search for enumerating all constrained subgraphs with compressed representation. IEICE Trans. Fundam. **E100–A**(9), 1773–1784 (2017). https://doi.org/10.1587/transfun.E100.A.1773
10. D.E. Knuth, *The Art of Computer Programming: Bitwise Tricks & Techniques; Binary Decision Diagrams*, vol. 4, fascicle 1 (Addison-Wesley, 2009)
11. P. Louridas, *Algorithms* (MIT Press, 2020)
12. S. Minato, Zero-suppressed BDDs for set manipulation in combinatorial problems, in *Proceedings of 30th ACM/IEEE Design Automation Conference (DAC'93)* (1993), pp. 272–277
13. S. Minato, J. Kawahara, F. Ishioka, M. Mizuta, K. Kurihara, A fast algorithm for combinatorial hotspot mining based on spatial scan statistic, in *Proceedings of the 2019 SIAM International Conference on Data Mining, SDM 2019, Calgary, Alberta, Canada, 2–4 May 2019*, ed. by T.Y. Berger-Wolf, N.V. Chawla (SIAM, 2019), pp. 91–99. https://doi.org/10.1137/1.9781611975673.11
14. K. Nakamura, T. Inoue, M. Nishino, N. Yasuda, S. Minato, A fast and exact evaluation algorithm for the expected number of connected nodes: an enhanced network reliability measure, in *IEEE INFOCOM 2023-IEEE Conference on Computer Communications, New York City, NY, USA, 17–20 May 2023* (IEEE, 2023), pp. 1–10. https://doi.org/10.1109/INFOCOM53939.2023.10228897
15. The on-line encyclopedia of integer sequences. https://oeis.org/
16. A. Takizawa, Y. Takechi, A. Ohta, N. Katoh, T. Inoue, T. Horiyama, J. Kawahara, S. Minato, Enumeration of region partitioning for evalcuation planning based on zdd, in *Proceedings of International symposium on Operation Research & its Applications (ISORA2013)* (2014), pp. 64–71

ZDDs and Frontier-Based Search for Solving Combinatorial Problems

Jun Kawahara

Abstract This chapter describes the technical background for solving combinatorial problems using zero-suppressed binary decision diagrams (ZDDs). A ZDD can store a vast number of feasible solutions of a combinatorial problem, such as vertex sets and subgraphs of a given graph. ZDDs enable obtaining many good solutions, random sampling, filtering, and more, rather than just finding a single optimal solution. In this chapter, we describe the definition and characteristics of ZDDs, explain two typical ZDD construction frameworks, and show algorithms that utilize constructed ZDDs.

1 Introduction

A combinatorial problem is a problem of selecting solutions from a finite set of candidates subject to certain conditions, while a combinatorial optimization problem focuses on finding the optimal solution. Many researchers have proposed algorithms for addressing individual combinatorial problems. In addition, there are general-purpose methods that can be applied to many combinatorial problems, such as integer programming and CSP (constraint satisfaction problem) solvers. Recently, a method for solving combinatorial problems using a zero-suppressed binary decision diagram (ZDD) [1], a data structure for representing a family of sets in a compact and efficient manner, has been proposed. A major difference from other methods is that a ZDD can store multiple solutions of a combinatorial problem, allowing not just one solution but multiple good solutions to be obtained. Moreover, ZDDs can perform set operations, enabling the computation of the union of two families of sets, filtering feasible solutions by specified conditions, and uniform random sampling of solutions. By combining these techniques, it is possible to solve combinatorial optimization problems with complex constraints. This chapter describes techniques for combinatorial (optimization) problems using ZDDs.

The organization of this chapter is as follows: Section 2 provides an explanation and examples of combinatorial problems. The definition and characteristics of a ZDD

J. Kawahara (✉)
Graduate School of Informatics, Kyoto University, Yoshida-Honmachi, Kyoto 606-8501, Japan
e-mail: jkawahara@i.kyoto-u.ac.jp

S. Minato et al. (eds.), *Algorithmic Foundations for Social Advancement*,
https://doi.org/10.1007/978-981-96-0668-9_3

are given in Sect. 3. Sections 3.2, 4, and 5 present algorithms for constructing ZDDs. Once a ZDD is constructed, we can perform weight minimization and maximization, filtering solutions, random sampling, and more. These are explained in Sect. 6. A software library using ZDDs, experimental evaluation, and which types of problems ZDDs are most effective for will be described in the next chapter.

2 Combinatorial Problem

Before discussing the formal definition of combinatorial (optimization) problems, we explain the minimum vertex cover problem, the 0-1 knapsack problem, and the minimum weight Hamiltonian cycle problem as examples of combinatorial problems. Many combinatorial problems, including these examples, are known to be NP-hard problems and are considered hard to solve exactly even if the size of the problem (e.g., the number of vertices in the input graph) is only a few hundred. Furthermore, it would be impractical to store a vast number of feasible solutions explicitly and exploit them.

Since the goals of these problems are to find a single minimum or maximum solution, it is appropriate to call them combinatorial *optimization* problems. However, the ZDD-based methods described in this chapter store and utilize not one solution but a large number of solutions. Therefore, we simply call them *combinatorial problems*.

The minimum vertex cover problem is described as follows. A graph $G = (V, E)$ is given, where $V = \{v_1, \ldots, v_n\}$ is a vertex set. Each vertex v_i is assigned a vertex weight w_i. The goal of a vertex cover in G is to find a subset of vertices $V' \subseteq V$ such that for every edge $\{u, w\} \in E$, either $u \in V'$ or $w \in V'$ (or both) is satisfied. The weight of the vertex cover V' is defined as $\sum_{i:v_i \in V'} w_i$, the sum of the weights of all vertices in V'. For example, the set of vertex covers of the graph G_1 in Fig. 1a is $\{\{v_1, v_2, v_3\}, \{v_1, v_2, v_3, v_4\}, \{v_1, v_2, v_4\}, \{v_1, v_3, v_4\}, \{v_1, v_4\}, \{v_2, v_3, v_4\}\}$, which we denote by $\mathcal{V}_1$. Figure 1b) shows the vertex cover $\{v_1, v_4\}$. In the minimum vertex cover problem, when the input is G_1, the vertex cover with the smallest weight is selected from $\mathcal{V}_1$. If the vertex weights are $(w_1, w_2, w_3, w_4) = (5, 2, 4, 8)$, the vertex cover with the smallest weight is $\{v_1, v_2, v_3\}$, and its weight is $5 + 2 + 4 = 11$.

The 0-1 knapsack problem is the following problem. There are n items $1, 2, \ldots, n$. Each item i is given a weight and a value, denoted by w_i and p_i, respectively. Given one knapsack with a capacity of C, a combination of items whose sum of weights is at most C can be packed in the knapsack. The 0-1 knapsack problem is the problem of finding the combination of items that can be packed in the knapsack and that has the largest sum of values. For example, if the items are 1, 2, 3, and 4, their weights are $(w_1, w_2, w_3, w_4) = (3, 4, 7, 10)$, their values are $(p_1, p_2, p_3, p_4) = (6, 4, 8, 9)$, and the knapsack capacity is $C = 12$, then the set of item combinations that can be packed in the knapsack is $\{\emptyset, \{1\}, \{2\}, \{3\}, \{4\}, \{1, 2\}, \{1, 3\}, \{2, 3\}\}$ ($\emptyset$ means that none of the items can be packed in the knapsack). We denote this family of sets by $\mathcal{K}_1$. The item combination with the largest sum of values is $\{1, 3\}$, and its sum of values is $6 + 8 = 14$.

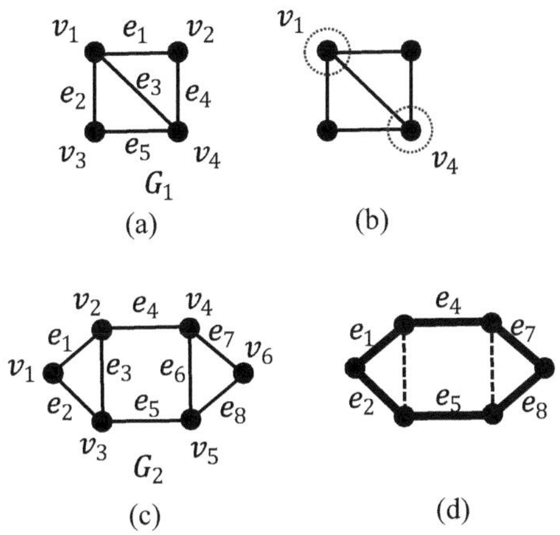

Fig. 1 Examples of graphs. **a** Graph G_1. **b** Example of a vertex cover of G_1. The vertices included in the vertex cover are circled with dotted circles. **c** Graph G_2. **d** Hamiltonian cycle of G_2. Edges included in the Hamiltonian cycle are drawn with thick lines, and edges not included are drawn with dotted lines

The minimum weight Hamiltonian cycle problem is the following problem. A graph $G = (V, E)$ is given, where $E = \{e_1, \dots, e_m\}$ is an edge set. An edge e_i is given an edge weight w_i. A *cycle* in G is a sequence $\{u_0, u_1\}, \{u_1, u_2\}, \dots, \{u_{\ell-1}, u_\ell\}, \{u_\ell, u_0\}$ ($\ell \geq 2$) of edges in E with $u_i \in V$ ($i = 0, 1, \dots, \ell$) and $u_i \neq u_j$ ($i \neq j$). Intuitively, a cycle is a path from a vertex back to its original vertex without passing through the same vertex more than once. A *Hamiltonian cycle* in G is a cycle that includes all vertices in V. For example, the set of (not necessarily Hamiltonian) cycles of graph G_2 in Fig. 1c is $\{\{e_1, e_2, e_3\}, \{e_1, e_2, e_4, e_5, e_6\}, \{e_1, e_2, e_4, e_5, e_7, e_8\}, \{e_3, e_4, e_5, e_6\}, \{e_3, e_4, e_5, e_7, e_8\}, \{e_6, e_7, e_8\}\}$, and only $\{e_1, e_2, e_4, e_5, e_7, e_8\}$ is the Hamiltonian cycle (Fig. 1d). In this chapter, we consider that the order of edges in a cycle is unimportant and we represent a cycle as a set of edges.

As we have seen above, solutions of combinatorial problems are often expressed as a subset $X \subseteq U$ of some set $U = \{x_1, \dots, x_n\}$. This chapter deals with combinatorial problems of this form. From now on, U will be referred to as a *universal set* (also commonly referred to as an underlying set). The universal set is V for the minimum vertex cover problem, $\{1, \dots, n\}$ for the 0-1 knapsack problem, and E for the minimum weight Hamiltonian cycle problem. For a given combinatorial problem, a possible candidate solution that satisfies all the conditions specified in the problem is called a *feasible solution*. For example, the set of all feasible solutions in the vertex cover example above is $\mathcal{V}_1$, and that in the 0-1 knapsack example above is $\mathcal{K}_1$. The set of all feasible solutions of combinatorial problems discussed in this chapter is represented as a family of sets. Hereafter, we refer to it as the *family* of all feasible solutions rather than the set of all feasible solutions.

3 ZDD and Conventional Construction Methods

A ZDD is a data structure that represents a family of sets. It can represent a family of subsets of a universal set compactly and efficiently. In Sects. 4 and 5, we consider representing the family of feasible solutions of a combinatorial problem as a ZDD.

3.1 Definition of ZDD

First, let us explain how a ZDD represents a family of sets. Let $U = \{x_1, \ldots, x_n\}$ be a universal set. We take a ZDD representing the family $\mathcal{V}_1$ of feasible solutions of the minimum vertex cover problem from the previous section as an example. Here, we use x_i instead of v_i. A ZDD representing $\mathcal{V}_1$ is shown in Fig. 2a.

A ZDD is a directed acyclic graph. To avoid confusion between $G = (V, E)$ appearing in a combinatorial problem we consider and a ZDD, the elements of V are called vertices. In contrast, those of a ZDD are called nodes. The elements of E are called edges, whereas they are called arcs in ZDDs. A ZDD has at most two nodes with outdegree 0, called *terminal nodes*. The two terminal nodes are denoted by $\bot$ and $\top$. (In the previous chapter and some literature, **0** and **1** are used instead of $\bot$ and $\top$, respectively.) A ZDD has one node with indegree 0, called the *root node*. Each non-terminal node v is labeled with an element x_i of U. Each non-terminal node has

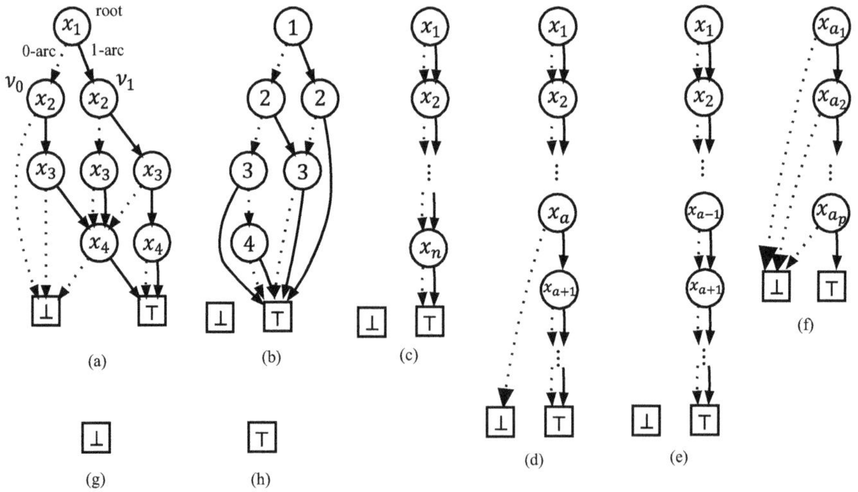

Fig. 2 Examples of ZDDs. **a** ZDD representing $\mathcal{V}_1$. **b** ZDD representing $\mathcal{K}_1$. **c** ZDD representing the power set 2^U. **d** ZDD representing $\mathcal{X}_a$. **e** ZDD representing $\overline{\mathcal{X}}_a$. **f** ZDD representing $\{\{x_{a_1}, x_{a_2}, \ldots, x_{a_p}\}\}$. **g** ZDD $\bot$. **h** ZDD $\top$

two outgoing arcs, called *0-* and *1-arcs*. If an arc of a non-terminal node with label x_i points at another non-terminal node with label x_j, $i < j$ must hold.

A ZDD represents a family of sets in the following sense. Starting from the root of the ZDD in Fig. 2a and following the 1-arc, 0-arc, 1-arc, and 1-arc, we reach $\top$. On this route (we call a path on a ZDD a *route*), a 1-arc is selected at nodes with label x_1, x_3, x_4, and we consider that this route corresponds to the set $\{x_1, x_3, x_4\}$. In general, for a route P from the root to $\top$, if nodes with label $x_{a_1}, x_{a_2}, \ldots, x_{a_p}$ and the 1-arcs outgoing from them are included in P, we consider that P corresponds to the set $\{x_{a_1}, x_{a_2}, \ldots, x_{a_p}\}$. There is a one-to-one correspondence between a route from the root of a ZDD to $\top$ and the corresponding set. The family of sets represented by a ZDD $\mathcal{Z}$ is denoted by $\mathcal{S}_{\mathcal{Z}}$.

A ZDD representing $\mathcal{K}_1$, the family of feasible solutions of the 0-1 knapsack problem in the previous section, is shown in Fig. 2b. Selecting the 1-arc, 0-arc, and 1-arc from the root, we reach $\top$. This route corresponds to the set $\{1, 3\}$. Nodes with label 4 do not appear on the route. In this case, 4 is not included in the set.

We introduce special ZDDs here. Figure 2c shows a ZDD representing a power set 2^U $(= \{X \mid X \subseteq U\})$. The family of sets obtained by collecting all sets of 2^U that contain an element $a \in U$ is denoted by $\mathcal{X}_a$ $(= \{X \mid X \subseteq U, a \in X\})$. The family of sets obtained by collecting all sets of 2^U that do not contain a is denoted by $\overline{\mathcal{X}}_a$ $(= \{X \mid X \subseteq U, a \notin X\})$. ZDDs representing $\mathcal{X}_a$ and $\overline{\mathcal{X}}_a$ are shown in Fig. 2d and e, respectively. A ZDD representing family $\{\{x_{a_1}, x_{a_2}, \ldots, x_{a_p}\}\}$ $(a_1 < a_2 < \cdots < a_p)$, i.e., family consisting of one set, is shown in Fig. 2f. The structure consisting only of $\bot$ is also a ZDD, which represents the empty set $\emptyset$ (or $\{\}$) (Fig. 2g). The structure consisting only of $\top$ is also a ZDD, which represents set $\{\emptyset\}$ (or $\{\{\}\}$), which is distinguished from $\emptyset$ (Fig. 2h).

In this chapter, ZDDs are used to represent the family of all feasible solutions of a combinatorial problem. As described in Sect. 3, the family of feasible solutions (e.g., family of vertex covers) is considered as a family of sets (e.g., family of sets of vertices). The techniques for solving combinatorial problems presented in this (and next) chapter are *not* the kind of algorithms that explore the search space to obtain a solution, but algorithms that construct a ZDD that represents the family of all feasible solutions without omission and duplication.

3.2 Construction of ZDDs by the Reduction Rule

Methods of constructing ZDDs can be classified into three categories: The first is based on the reduction rule. The other two are called bottom-up and top-down methods, which are used depending on the nature of the problem. In this subsection, we describe a method based on the reduction rule. In this method, a complete binary tree with height n ($n = |U|$, the size of the universal set) is first constructed. Since the number of nodes in a complete binary tree with height n is $\Omega(2^n)$, this method is not practical, but the idea of "reduction," which is introduced here, is important and will be explained below. After constructing the complete binary tree, the reduction rule is applied to obtain a ZDD.

We construct a ZDD representing a family $\mathcal{F}$ of sets with the universal set U in the following way. We construct a complete binary tree T with height n (Fig. 3a) with the following properties: we say that a (non-terminal) node at distance $i \in \{0, \ldots, n-1\}$ from the root node of T is at *level* $i+1$. The nodes at level $i+1$ are assigned the label x_{i+1}. The two directed arcs outgoing from each node are a 0-arc and a 1-arc. The nodes corresponding to the leaves of the binary tree are terminal nodes, either $\bot$ or $\top$. If the set corresponding to the route from the root to a terminal node is included in the family $\mathcal{F}$, the terminal is $\top$; if not, the terminal is $\bot$.

The two reduction rules are as follows:

(1) When two equivalent nodes exist, they are merged into one (also called shared). Two nodes are equivalent if they have the same label, their 0-arcs point at the same node, and their 1-arcs point at the same node. In the operation merging two nodes ν and ν', we change the destinations of all the arcs pointing at ν' into ν, and we remove ν' and the arcs outgoing from ν'.
(2) When a 1-arc of a non-terminal node ν points at $\bot$ and a 0-arc of ν points at a node ν', we change the destinations of all the arcs pointing at ν into ν', and we remove ν and the arcs outgoing from ν.

After applying the two reduction rules, the family of sets represented by the ZDD remains the same. A ZDD is called a *reduced* ZDD if the reduction rules are applied as far as possible and no more reduction rules can be applied. A complete binary tree for $\mathcal{V}_1$ is shown in Fig. 3a. First, the multiple $\bot$ and $\top$ are merged into one each. Since nodes ν_a and ν_b in the figure are both labeled x_4, and their 0-arcs (resp., 1-arcs) point at the same node $\bot$ (resp., $\top$), reduction rule (1) can be applied. Since the 1-arc of node ν_c in the figure points at $\bot$, reduction rule (2) can be applied. After applying the two rules, we have the graph shown in Fig. 3b. Further application of the reduction rules as far as possible yields Fig. 2a.

The desired ZDD can be obtained by applying the reduction rules to the complete binary tree. It is easy to check that the resulting ZDD satisfies the properties of a ZDD and represents $\mathcal{F}$.

4 Bottom-Up Construction of ZDDs

In this section, we describe the framework of bottom-up construction of ZDDs. Before explaining it, we describe the recursive structure of ZDDs.

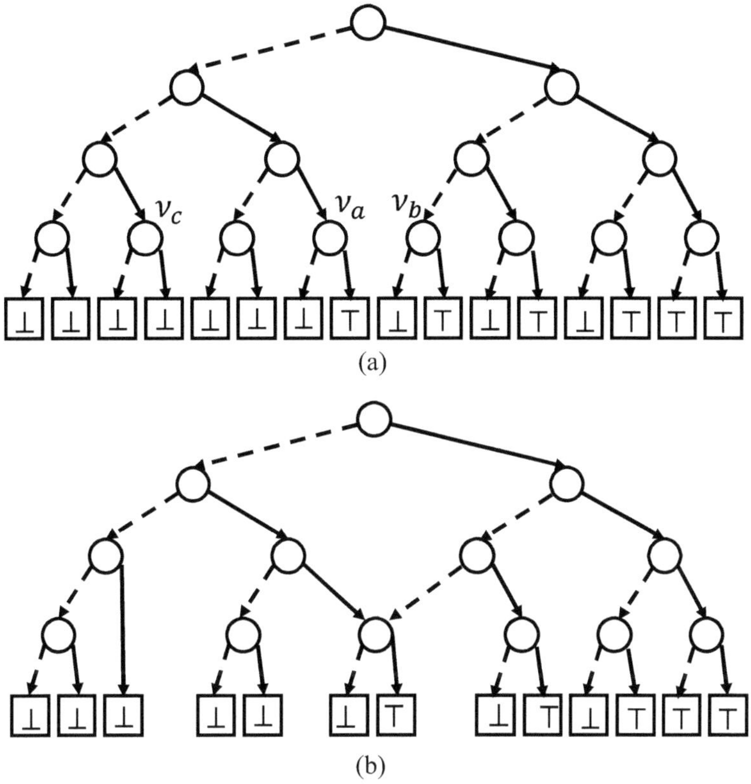

Fig. 3 Example of applying the reduction rules of ZDD. **a** Complete binary tree for $\mathcal{V}_1$. Node labels are omitted. **b** Graph after applying the two reduction rules once each to the complete binary tree. For clarity, $\bot$ and $\top$ are depicted without merging

4.1 Recursive Structure of ZDD

Given a ZDD $\mathcal{Z}$, suppose that the label of the root node of $\mathcal{Z}$ is x_1. For $j = 0, 1$, let ν_j be the node pointed at by the j-arc of the root node (Fig. 2a). Considering all the nodes and arcs reachable from the node ν_j, we obtain a directed acyclic graph. We denote that directed acyclic graph by $\mathcal{Z}_j$ (Fig. 4). Since $\mathcal{Z}_j$ has the root node ν_j, has $\bot$ and $\top$, and satisfies all other ZDD conditions, we can regard $\mathcal{Z}_j$ as a ZDD. Let us consider what family of sets this ZDD represents. First, consider $\mathcal{Z}_0$: the route from the root node ν_0 of $\mathcal{Z}_0$ to $\top$ can be thought of as the route from the root node of $\mathcal{Z}$ through its 0-arc and from there to $\top$. They each represent the same set. Thus, $\mathcal{Z}_0$ is the family of sets obtained by collecting sets in $S_{\mathcal{Z}}$ that do not contain the element

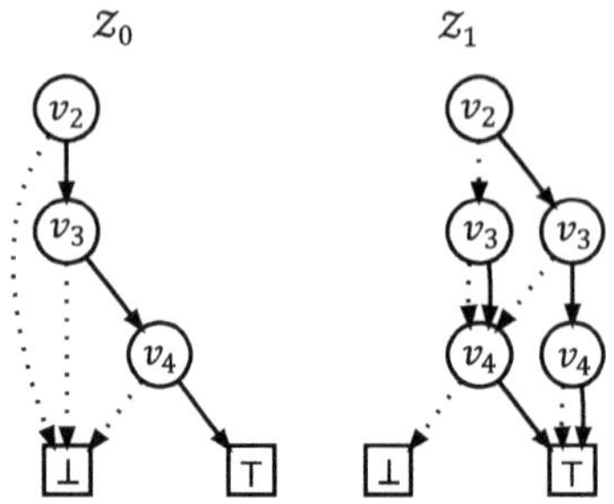

Fig. 4 Recursive structure of ZDD. For $j = 0, 1$, the root node of the ZDD $\mathcal{Z}_j$ is v_j, which is pointed at by the j-arc of the root of $\mathcal{Z}$

x_1. In the same way, $\mathcal{Z}_1$ is the family of sets obtained by collecting sets in $\mathcal{S}_\mathcal{Z}$ that contain the element x_1 and removing x_1 itself from each of them. The following relation holds:

$$\mathcal{S}_\mathcal{Z} = \mathcal{S}_{\mathcal{Z}_0} \cup (\{\{x_1\}\} \sqcup \mathcal{S}_{\mathcal{Z}_1}),$$

where $\mathcal{A} \sqcup \mathcal{B} = \{A \cup B \mid A \in \mathcal{A}, B \in \mathcal{B}\}$ for the two families of sets $\mathcal{A}$ and $\mathcal{B}$. This is the recursive structure of ZDD.

Henceforth, a ZDD composed of all nodes and arcs reachable from v is simply called the "ZDD rooted at v". In some literature, a node v is sometimes identified with the ZDD rooted at v, but in this chapter, we distinguish them.

4.2 *Bottom-Up Construction of ZDDs*

Let us explain the bottom-up construction framework. We take the computation of the intersection of two ZDDs as an example. That is, given two ZDDs $\mathcal{F}$ and $\mathcal{G}$, we describe how to construct a ZDD that represents the intersection $\mathcal{S}_\mathcal{F} \cap \mathcal{S}_\mathcal{G}$ of the families that the two ZDDs represent [1, 2]. We denote this ZDD by $\mathcal{F} \cap \mathcal{G}$. For simplicity, we consider the case where the labels of the root nodes of $\mathcal{F}$ and $\mathcal{G}$ are both x_1. Based on the recursive structure, $\mathcal{F}$ and $\mathcal{G}$ can be represented as follows:

$$\mathcal{S}_\mathcal{F} = \mathcal{S}_{\mathcal{F}_0} \cup (\{\{x_1\}\} \sqcup \mathcal{S}_{\mathcal{F}_1})$$
$$\mathcal{S}_\mathcal{G} = \mathcal{S}_{\mathcal{G}_0} \cup (\{\{x_1\}\} \sqcup \mathcal{S}_{\mathcal{G}_1}).$$

Since the families $\mathcal{S}_{\mathcal{F}_0}$ and $\mathcal{S}_{\mathcal{G}_0}$ are the sets of $\mathcal{S}_\mathcal{F}$ and $\mathcal{S}_\mathcal{G}$ not containing x_1, respectively, all the sets in $\mathcal{S}_{\mathcal{F}_0} \cap \mathcal{S}_{\mathcal{G}_0}$ are included in the family $\mathcal{S}_\mathcal{F} \cap \mathcal{S}_\mathcal{G}$. Similarly, the families $\{\{x_1\}\} \sqcup \mathcal{S}_{\mathcal{F}_1}$ and $\{\{x_1\}\} \sqcup \mathcal{S}_{\mathcal{G}_1}$ are the sets of $\mathcal{S}_\mathcal{F}$ and $\mathcal{S}_\mathcal{G}$ containing x_1. Therefore, all the sets in $\{\{x_1\}\} \sqcup (\mathcal{S}_{\mathcal{F}_1} \cap \mathcal{S}_{\mathcal{G}_1})$ are contained in the family $\mathcal{S}_\mathcal{F} \cap \mathcal{S}_\mathcal{G}$. Hence, the following equation holds:

$$\mathcal{S}_\mathcal{F} \cap \mathcal{S}_\mathcal{G} = (\mathcal{S}_{\mathcal{F}_0} \cap \mathcal{S}_{\mathcal{G}_0}) \cup (\{\{x_1\}\} \sqcup (\mathcal{S}_{\mathcal{F}_1} \cap \mathcal{S}_{\mathcal{G}_1})).$$

The right-hand side of the equation means the ZDD such that the label of the root node of the ZDD is x_1, the 0-arc of the root points at (the root of) $\mathcal{S}_{\mathcal{F}_0} \cap \mathcal{S}_{\mathcal{G}_0}$, and the 1-arc of the root points at (the root of) $\mathcal{S}_{\mathcal{F}_1} \cap \mathcal{S}_{\mathcal{G}_1}$. To compute (construct) $\mathcal{S}_{\mathcal{F}} \cap \mathcal{S}_{\mathcal{G}}$, we recursively compute $\mathcal{S}_{\mathcal{F}_0} \cap \mathcal{S}_{\mathcal{G}_0}$, recursively compute $\mathcal{S}_{\mathcal{F}_1} \cap \mathcal{S}_{\mathcal{G}_1}$, create a new root node with label x_1, and make the destination of the 0- and 1-arcs of the new root node (the roots of) the resulting ZDDs.

In performing this computation, it is more efficient to apply the reduction rule each time: for two ZDDs $\mathcal{Z}_0$ and $\mathcal{Z}_1$, we write $\mathsf{getNode}(x_i, \mathcal{Z}_0, \mathcal{Z}_1)$ as the function that returns a ZDD whose root node label is x_i and whose root 0- and 1-arcs are $\mathcal{Z}_0$ and $\mathcal{Z}_1$, respectively. The operation of $\mathsf{getNode}$ is as follows: if $\mathcal{Z}_1$ is $\bot$, then it returns $\mathcal{Z}_0$ (reduction rule (2)). We check whether a node, say ν, such that the label is x_i and the 0- and 1-arcs of ν are root nodes of $\mathcal{Z}_0$ and $\mathcal{Z}_1$, respectively, has already existed. If it exists, we do not create a new node and return the ZDD rooted as ν. If it does not exist, we create a root node with label x_i whose 0- and 1-arcs point at (the roots of) $\mathcal{Z}_0$ and $\mathcal{Z}_1$, respectively, and return the ZDD.

From the above, $\mathcal{F} \cap \mathcal{G}$ can be computed by recursively computing $\mathcal{F}_0 \cap \mathcal{G}_0$ and $\mathcal{F}_1 \cap \mathcal{G}_1$, letting the resulting ZDDs be $\mathcal{H}_0$ and $\mathcal{H}_1$, respectively, and calling $\mathsf{getNode}(x_1, \mathcal{H}_0, \mathcal{H}_1)$. At the end of the recursion, formulas such as $\emptyset \cap \mathcal{G} = \emptyset$, $\{\emptyset\} \cap \{\emptyset\} = \{\emptyset\}$, and so on, are used. That is, if $\mathcal{F}$ or $\mathcal{G}$ is $\bot$, return $\bot$. If both $\mathcal{F}$ and $\mathcal{G}$ are $\top$, return $\top$. If the label of the root node of $\mathcal{F}$ is not x_1, we just consider $\mathcal{F} = \mathcal{F} \cup (\{\{x_1\}\} \sqcup \emptyset)$ and apply the recursion in the same way.

This method of constructing $\mathcal{F} \cap \mathcal{G}$ in a recursive manner is called a bottom-up construction method. The term "bottom-up" is derived from the operation of constructing a ZDD in the manner that we recursively call the $\cap$ operation over and over again, and create ZDD nodes when returning from the recursive calls, where the root of the ZDD is drawn at the top and the terminals are drawn at the bottom. If we always create a node using the $\mathsf{getNode}$ function, the ZDD obtained by the bottom-up construction method has already been reduced because no node to which the reduction rule can be applied arises.

In addition to the intersection operation $\cap$, bottom-up construction methods can be used for the union set operation $\cup$ and the difference set operation $\setminus$. In general, for a binary operation $\circ$ on families, we write $\mathcal{F} \circ \mathcal{G}$ for the ZDD representing $\mathcal{S}_{\mathcal{F}} \circ \mathcal{S}_{\mathcal{G}}$. For a binary operation $\circ \in \{\cup, \cap, \setminus\}$, the time complexity of computing $\mathcal{S}_{\mathcal{F}} \circ \mathcal{S}_{\mathcal{G}}$ is known to be $\Theta(|\mathcal{F}||\mathcal{G}|)$ theoretically, where $|\mathcal{F}|$ is the number of nodes in ZDD $\mathcal{F}$ [3]. However, it is also known that in many cases appearing in practical applications, it is bounded by $\Theta(|\mathcal{F}| + |\mathcal{G}| + |\mathcal{F} \circ \mathcal{G}|)$; that is, linear time in the sum of the sizes of input and output ZDDs.

4.3 Two Examples of the Bottom-Up Construction

In this subsection, we show two examples of ZDDs using bottom-up construction methods.

Constructing a ZDD from a family of sets

When each set in a family is explicitly given, e.g., as a list, a ZDD representing the family is constructed in the following way. For any subset $X = \{x_{a_1}, \ldots, x_{a_p}\}$ of the universe set, a ZDD representing the family $\{X\}$ consisting of one element is shown in Fig. 2f. We construct a ZDD consisting only of the set for each set in the list. Computing the union $\cup$ of those ZDDs one by one yields a ZDD representing the family. For example, the ZDD representing $\mathcal{V}_1$ is constructed by first computing $\cup$ of the ZDD representing $\{\{x_1, x_2, x_3\}\}$ and the ZDD representing $\{\{x_1, x_2, x_3, x_4\}\}$, and by computing $\cup$ of the obtained ZDD and the ZDD representing $\{\{x_1, x_2, x_4\}\}$, and so on.

Constructing a family of sets representing all vertex covers

Given a graph $G = (V, E)$, we describe how to construct a ZDD for the family of all vertex covers of G by (repetition of) a bottom-up construction method. Recall that the universe set is $V = \{v_1, \ldots, v_n\}$. We focus on an edge $e = \{v_i, v_j\}$ on the graph G. Any vertex cover must contain at least one of v_i and v_j. A subset of 2^V that contains at least one of v_i and v_j is represented by $\mathcal{X}_i \cup \mathcal{X}_j$ ($\mathcal{X}_i$ is defined in Sect. 3.1). Thus, the following formula is a family consisting of the sets containing at least one endpoint of e for every edge $e \in E$:

$$\bigcap_{\{v_i, v_j\} \in E} (\mathcal{X}_i \cup \mathcal{X}_j).$$

This is the family of all vertex covers of G.

The construction of the ZDD representing the above family can be conducted by the operation of the intersection $\cap$ and the union $\cup$ introduced above. Since $\mathcal{X}_i$ can be represented as a ZDD, the ZDD for $\mathcal{X}_i \cup \mathcal{X}_j$ can be obtained. The computation of $\bigcap_{\{v_i, v_j\} \in E}$ can be conducted by repeating $\cap$ of the ZDD operation, and the result obtained is also a ZDD.

In a similar way, the family of independent sets (stable sets) can be computed by

$$\bigcap_{\{v_i, v_j\} \in E} (\overline{\mathcal{X}}_i \cup \overline{\mathcal{X}}_j)$$

and the family of dominating sets can be computed by

$$\bigcap_{v \in V} \left(\mathcal{X}_v \cup \left(\bigcup_{w \in N(v)} \mathcal{X}_w \right) \right),$$

where $N(v)$ is the set of adjacent vertices of v in G. The definitions of independent and dominating sets are omitted.

5 Top-Down Construction of ZDDs

We describe another ZDD construction framework, the top-down construction. The name comes from the process of constructing a ZDD by creating nodes directly from the root (top) of the ZDD toward the terminals (bottom).

This section is organized as follows. Section 5.1 presents a general framework for top-down construction using the 0-1 knapsack problem as an example. In Sects. 5.2–5.4, we show how to construct a ZDD that represents the family of all cycles on a given graph using top-down construction. A subgraph included in the ZDD that the method in Sect. 5.2 constructs may consist of two or more unconnected cycles. Therefore, in Sect. 5.4, we will describe an improved method for constructing a ZDD that represents a family of subgraphs each of which consists of a single cycle. Before explaining this method, we introduce the notion of *frontier-based search* (frontier-based method) for efficient top-down construction of ZDDs in Sect. 5.3. Finally, in Sect. 5.5, we discuss the types of graphs applicable to the frontier-based search.

5.1 Framework of Top-Down Construction

We take the 0-1 knapsack problem as an example to illustrate the top-down construction. First, we create a root node whose label is 1 (corresponding to item 1) and create 0- and 1-arcs outgoing from the root. As the destinations of the 0- and 1-arcs, we create nodes whose label is 2 and 0- and 1-arcs outgoing from them. We create nodes with label $i + 1$ and their 0- and 1-arcs as the destination of the 0- and 1-arcs of nodes with label i ($\in \{1, \ldots, n-1\}$).

In the top-down construction, when we create nodes, we merge nodes if possible. For this purpose, information for the decision is stored into nodes. In the case of the 0-1 knapsack problem, the sum of the weights of the items selected so far is stored into each node. For a node ν, we denote the value by $\nu.\mathrm{w}$. For the root node ν_{root}, we set $\nu_{\mathrm{root}}.\mathrm{w} \leftarrow 0$. For a node ν with label i, we create a node ν_0 as the destination of the 0-arc of ν and set $\nu_0.\mathrm{w} \leftarrow \nu.\mathrm{w}$. Also, we create a node ν_1 as the destination of the 1-arc of ν and set $\nu_1.\mathrm{w} \leftarrow \nu.\mathrm{w} + w_i$.

Two nodes with the same information are merged using the following procedure. When creating a node with label $i + 1$ as the destination of an arc a, we check whether there exists a node with the same value of w labeled $i + 1$ that has already been created, and if such a node, say ν', exists, we do not create a new node and make a point at ν'. Figure 5 shows the merging of nodes for the 0-1 knapsack problem in Sect. 2. In Fig. 5a, node ν_c is not actually created and is merged with node ν_a (Fig. 5b) because the value of w is $\nu_a.\mathrm{w} = 7$ and the value of w of ν_c, which is the destination of the 0-arc of node ν_b, is also 7.

The top-down construction method also performs an operation called *pruning*. When creating a new node ν' as the destination of an arc a of a node ν, if the value of $\nu'.\mathrm{w}$ exceeds the knapsack capacity C, the total sum of items exceeds C without

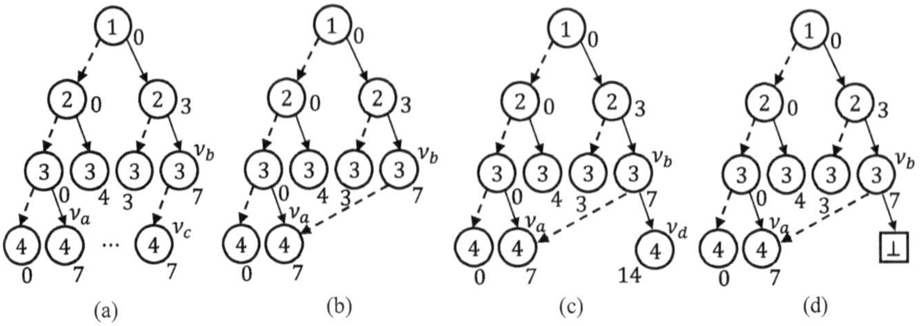

Fig. 5 Example of the top-down construction. The numbers written near the nodes are the w values

adding items thereafter because the weights of the items are all positive. Therefore, any route from v' reaches $\perp$. In this case, instead of creating a new node v', we make the destination of a $\perp$. This operation is called pruning. Figure 5c shows the pruning for the example of the 0-1 knapsack problem in Sect. 2. The value of w of node v_d, which is the destination of the 1-arc of v_b, is 14, which exceeds C. Therefore, pruning is performed and the 1-arc of v_b now points at $\perp$ (Fig. 5d).

The destination of a node with label n is $\perp$ or $\top$. If the value of w exceeds C, it is $\perp$; if not, it is $\top$. In the general framework of top-down construction methods, information is stored into nodes, and nodes are created top-down from the root node to the terminals while performing merging and pruning operations based on the stored information. The information stored in a node is called the *configuration*.

5.2 Construction of a ZDD for the Family of All Cycles: Unconnected Version

For a given graph $G = (V, E)$, we describe how to construct a ZDD representing the family of all cycles on G by a top-down construction method [4–6], which is a generalization of Knuth's Simpath algorithm [5]. (For the sake of illustration, we will discuss cycles that are not necessarily Hamiltonian ones.) The universal set is $E = \{e_1, \ldots, e_m\}$. A cycle must be connected (i.e., not more than one cycle), but we do not consider connectivity first and will impose connectivity condition later. We consider a cycle C on G. The degree with respect to C of all vertices on G is 0 or 2. Conversely, a subgraph of G such that the degrees with respect to C of all vertices on G are 0 or 2 is one or more cycles. If we impose the condition that the subgraph is connected, it becomes one cycle. In this subsection, we describe how to construct a ZDD for the family of subgraphs of G for which the degree of every vertex is 0 or 2. (In the method described here, a subgraph whose degree of every vertex is 0, i.e., $\emptyset$, will also be included in the family of sets represented by the constructed ZDD. We do not describe how to remove it.)

Let us design a top-down construction method for a ZDD representing the family of all cycles of G. The configuration of a node is the degree of each vertex with respect to the edges selected so far (when we say a "degree" below, we mean a degree of the subgraph consisting of the selected edges, not G). For a node ν, the degree of each vertex is stored into ν.deg as an array. The degree of a vertex v is represented by ν.deg[v]. The deg value of the root node is 0 for all vertices. When creating a node as the destination of the 1-arc of a node with label $e_i = \{u, w\}$, the degree of u and w is increased by 1. Therefore, the corresponding deg[u] and deg[w] are increased by 1 each.

Node merging occurs when the labels of two nodes and deg for all vertices are equal. However, since deg for all vertices is rarely equal, node merging rarely occurs in this situation. We will discuss node merging based on a frontier in the next subsection.

5.3 *Improving the Efficiency of the Top-Down Construction: Frontier-Based Search*

The value of deg is used to determine whether the degree in the subgraph of each vertex is 0, 2, or not. For a vertex v, the value of deg[v] is determined at the moment when all edges incident with v are decided to be used or not. At this time, we check whether deg[v] is 0, 2, or not. If deg[v] is neither 0 nor 2, we conduct pruning. If deg[v] is 0 or 2, then the value of deg[v] is never referenced thereafter and there is no need to store deg[v]. Also, for a certain vertex v, if no edge incident with v is determined, the value of deg[v] is 0. Therefore, there is no need to store this value explicitly. Based on this idea, the *frontier* is defined as follows.

Let $i \in \{1, \ldots, m-1\}$. Consider a node ν with label e_{i+1}. (Recall that the input graph is $G = (V, E)$ with $E = \{e_1, \ldots, e_m\}$.) We consider that the 0-arc (resp., 1-arc) of ν represents the situation where we have decided that each of $e_1, \ldots, e_i$ is included in the subgraph, and we are determining that e_{i+1} is not included (resp., included) in the subgraph. In this situation, we call $e_1, \ldots, e_i$ *processed edges* and $e_{i+1}, \ldots, e_m$ *unprocessed edges*. Then, the vertices incident with processed edges are $\{u_j, w_j \mid e_j = \{u_j, w_j\}, j = 1, \ldots, i\}$, and the vertices incident with unprocessed ones are $\{u_j, w_j \mid e_j = \{u_j, w_j\}, j = i+1, \ldots, m\}$. The set of vertices with which both edges are incident is

$$F_i = \{u_j, w_j \mid e_j = \{u_j, w_j\}, j = 1, \ldots, i\} \cap \{u_j, w_j \mid e_j = \{u_j, w_j\}, j = i+1, \ldots, m\}.$$

We define $F_0 = F_m = \emptyset$. In the example of graph G_2, we have $F_0 = \emptyset$. After e_1 is processed, v_1 and v_2 enter the frontier and we have $F_1 = \{v_1, v_2\}$ (Fig. 6a). After e_2 is processed, v_1 leaves the frontier because all edges incident with v_1 have been processed. We have $F_2 = \{v_2, v_3\}$ because v_3 enters the frontier (Fig. 6b). Processing e_3 results in $F_3 = F_2$ because v_2 and v_3 have already been in the frontier (Fig. 6c).

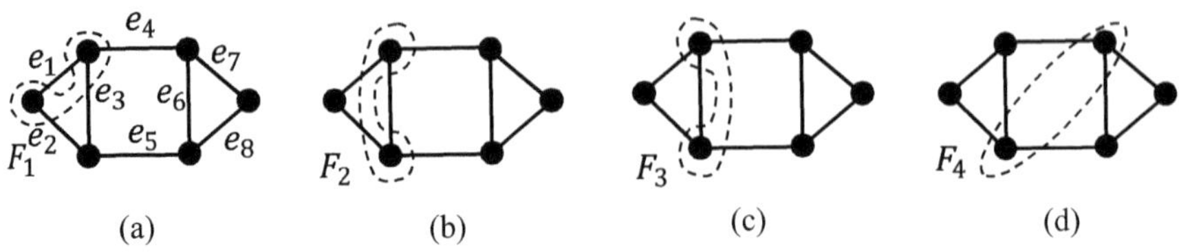

Fig. 6 Transition of the frontier. The vertices surrounded by the dotted curve are the ones on the frontier

After e_4 is processed, v_2 leaves the frontier and we have $F_4 = \{v_3, v_4\}$ (Fig. 6d). Continuing this process, we obtain $F_7 = \{v_5, v_6\}$. After e_8 is processed, v_5 and v_6 leave the frontier and we have $F_8 = \emptyset$.

For a node ν with label e_{i+1}, we store the value $\nu.\mathtt{deg}[v]$ of only vertices $v \in F_i$, and we do not store $\nu.\mathtt{deg}[v']$ for any $v' \notin F_i$. The equivalency of nodes is decided only by this stored information. That is, for nodes ν, ν' with label e_{i+1}, ν and ν' are considered equivalent if and only if $\nu.\mathtt{deg}[u] = \nu'.\mathtt{deg}[u]$ holds for all vertices $u \in F_i$. For example, for two nodes ν_a and ν_b (labeled e_5) in Fig. 7a, we have $F_4 = \{v_3, v_4\}$ and we store only the values of $\mathtt{deg}[v_3]$ and $\mathtt{deg}[v_4]$. Figure 7b and c show the states corresponding to ν_a and ν_b. Since $\nu_a.\mathtt{deg}[v_3] = \nu_b.\mathtt{deg}[v_3] = 1$ and $\nu_a.\mathtt{deg}[v_4] = \nu_b.\mathtt{deg}[v_4] = 1$, ν_b is merged into ν_a.

The initial values of $\mathtt{deg}[v]$ are as follows. Consider the situation where we are creating a node as the destination of an arc of a node ν with label e_i. A vertex $v \in F_{i+1} \setminus F_i$, which does not belong to F_i but belongs to F_{i+1}, is the endpoint of

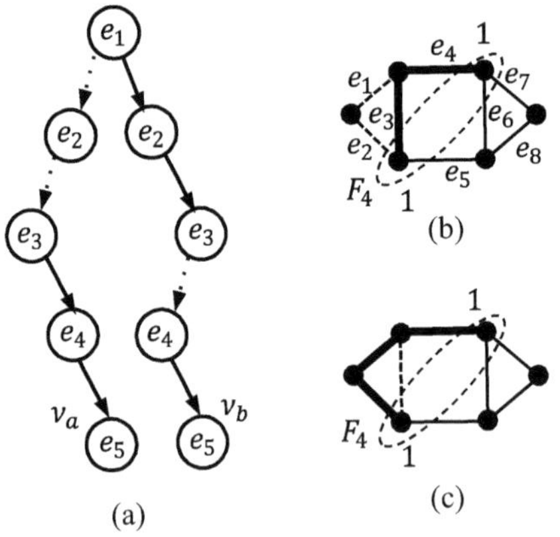

Fig. 7 Example of merging nodes in a top-down construction of a ZDD representing the family of all cycles. Nodes other than the nodes we focus on are omitted. The numbers written near the vertices of the graphs in (**b**) and (**c**) are the values of $\mathtt{deg}$. Bold edges are ones that have been processed and decided to be used, dotted edges are ones that have been processed and decided not to be used, and thin edges are unprocessed ones. We draw processed (resp., unprocessed) edges on the right (resp., left) side of the frontier

e_i. Just before e_i is processed, there is no processed edge incident with v, and by processing e_i, the processed edge gets connected to v for the first time. This situation is called v *entering the frontier*. Immediately after v enters the frontier, we set the value of $\nu.\texttt{deg}[v]$ to 0 and store it into the node. If e_i is used (the arc is a 1-arc), the value of $\nu.\texttt{deg}[v]$ is 1.

The pruning operation is as follows: if the value of $\texttt{deg}[v]$ exceeds 2, pruning is performed. Consider again the situation where we are creating a node as the destination of an arc of a node ν with label e_i. In this case, a vertex $v \in F_i \setminus F_{i+1}$ which belongs to F_i but does not belong to F_{i+1} is the endpoint of e_i and is incident with no other processed edges (because $v \notin F_{i+1}$). Therefore, the degree of v is determined after e_i is processed. This situation is called v *leaving the frontier*. When v leaves the frontier, if the value of $\nu.\texttt{deg}[v]$ is neither 0 nor 2, the degree of v is determined to be neither 0 nor 2. Therefore, pruning is performed. That is, we make the destination of the arc of ν point at $\bot$.

A strict mathematical proof that the above method constructs the correct ZDD is shown in the paper [7]. To construct the family of only all Hamiltonian cycles, rather than (not necessarily Hamiltonian) cycles, simply change "degree 0 or 2" to "degree 2" in the above description, and no modification of the algorithm is necessary except in that part.

5.4 *Construction of a ZDD for the Family of All Cycles: Connected Version*

We describe how to guarantee that subgraphs represented by a constructed ZDD are connected. For simplicity, we assume that the input graph is connected. We store which connected component vertices belong to into each node. Although it is possible to use a data structure such as the disjoint-set forest [8] to store connected components, for the sake of illustration, we represent connected components as numbers $1, \ldots, n$. Vertices with the same number belong to the same connected component, and vertices with different numbers belong to different connected components. For a node ν, let $\nu.\texttt{comp}[v]$ be the number of the connected component that a vertex v on the frontier belongs to. Figure 8a shows an example of connected components and their numbers.

Fig. 8 Example of a connected component becoming isolated. The numbers written near vertices is the value of comp

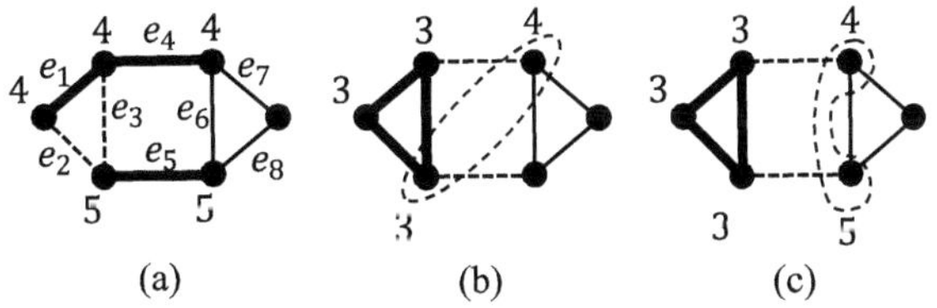

When a vertex v_i enters the frontier, we set $\mathtt{comp}[v_i] \leftarrow i$. For an edge $e_j = \{u, w\}$, when $\mathtt{comp}[u] = \mathtt{comp}[w]$, the value of comp is not updated because u and w has already belonged to the same connected component. When $\mathtt{comp}[u] \neq \mathtt{comp}[w]$, let $c_{\min} = \min\{\mathtt{comp}[u], \mathtt{comp}[w]\}$ and $c_{\max} = \max\{\mathtt{comp}[u], \mathtt{comp}[w]\}$. In this case, the connected components whose numbers are $c_{\min}$ and $c_{\max}$ are integrated into one connected component, and for all vertices v such that $\mathtt{comp}[v] = c_{\min}$, we set $\mathtt{comp}[v] \leftarrow c_{\max}$. For example, in Fig. 8a, when e_6 is used, the value of comp for vertices v_1, v_2, v_4 changes into 5.

The following procedure is used to guarantee that subgraphs represented by a constructed ZDD are connected: when v leaves the frontier, if there exists a vertex u ($\neq v$) on the frontier F_{i+1} such that $\mathtt{comp}[u] = \mathtt{comp}[v]$ holds, it means that the connected component with number $\mathtt{comp}[v]$ is on the frontier F_{i+1}, in which case no pruning is performed. Otherwise, if there is a vertex with degree at least one on F_{i+1}, two or more connected components arise because the connected component with number $\mathtt{comp}[v]$ cannot be connected with any other connected component. In other words, the subgraph is no longer connected. Therefore, in this case, pruning is performed. After the last edge e_m is processed, the frontier F_m becomes empty $\emptyset$. At this point, if pruning has not occurred, then the subgraph is connected. For example, in Fig. 8b, after edge e_5 is processed, vertex v_3 leaves the frontier, resulting in Fig. 8c. Assuming that e_5 is not used, any vertex with number 3, which is the component number of v_3, is not on the frontier except for v_3, and the connected component with number 3 gets isolated from the others. Thus, the moment when a connected component gets isolated can be detected.

We store the values of deg and comp (for vertices on the frontier) into nodes as configuration simultaneously, and we define that two nodes are equivalent if and only if the stored configurations of the two nodes completely coincide. If we update the values and conduct pruning arcs as described above, we can construct a ZDD representing the family of subgraphs that are connected and whose degree is all 0 or 2, i.e., cycles. See the paper [4] for pseudocode of the algorithm.

The complexity of the top-down construction is the multiplication of the time for creating one node and the number of created nodes if we can perform the search of equivalent nodes by using a hash table within a constant time. In the case of (Hamiltonian) cycles, the time for creating one node is $O(\max_i |F_i|)$, and thus the total computation time is $O(\max_i |F_i||\mathcal{H}|)$, where $\mathcal{H}$ is the output ZDD.

5.5 *Constructing ZDDs for Various Types of Subgraphs Using the Frontier-Based Search*

By storing deg and comp into nodes as configuration, we can construct ZDDs for various types of subgraphs, not just (Hamiltonian) cycles. Given two vertices of the input graph, s and t, it is also possible to construct a ZDD representing the family of all s-t paths in the input graph. Pruning is performed when it is determined that the value of deg[s] or deg[t] is not 1. The degrees of all vertices other than s and t are 0 or 2.

Various types of subgraphs can be constructed as ZDDs by storing various information at ZDD nodes other than deg and comp. Specifically, the following conditions can be imposed on subgraphs represented by constructed ZDDs. See also the cited papers for details.

- Vertex degree.
  - Degree of a specified vertex.
  - Number of vertices with a specified degree [9].
- Connectivity of vertices.
  - Condition that two vertices must be included in the same connected component.
  - Condition that two vertices must be included in different components.
- Number of connected components.
- Existence of cycles.
- Condition that the sum of edge weights is greater (or less) than a specified weight.
- Suppose that the family $\mathcal{Z}'$ of subgraphs is given as a ZDD:
  - Condition that each subgraph contains some element of $\mathcal{Z}'$ as a subgraph.
  - Condition that each subgraph contains no element of $\mathcal{Z}'$ as a subgraph.
  - Condition that each subgraph contains no element of $\mathcal{Z}'$ as an induced subgraph [10].
  - Condition that each subgraph contains no element of $\mathcal{Z}'$ as a topological minor [11].

The types of subgraphs that can be handled according to the above conditions are listed below. Individual terms are not explained.

- Path [5]: s-t path, path starting at a specified vertex, path in which both the start and end vertices are not specified, s-t Hamiltonian path, and Steiner path.
- Cycle [5]: (single) cycle, Hamiltonian cycle, and Steiner cycle.
- Tree [6]: tree, forest, spanning tree, spanning forest, rooted spanning forest, and Steiner tree.
- Matching: matching, complete matching, and b-matching.
- Regular graph: k-regular graph, connected k-regular graph, and regular graph of any degree.
- Clique: k-clique, and clique with any number of vertices.
- Degree specified subgraph [9].
- Graph partition [12].
- Bipartite graph.
- Graph characterized by forbidden subgraphs: chordal graph, chordal bipartite graph, d-claw-free graph, interval graph, and proper interval graph [10].
- Graph characterized by forbidden topological minors: planar graph, outerplanar graph, series-parallel graph, and cactus [11].

6 Utilization of ZDDs

A ZDD constructed by the methods described in the previous sections contains all feasible solutions of a combinatorial problem without omission and duplication, which means that the ZDD contains much more information than just the optimal solution. In this section, we describe some techniques using them. The methods presented here are described in [5]. In this section, for a non-terminal node ν of a ZDD, let ν_0 and ν_1 be the nodes pointed at by the 0- and 1-arcs of ν, respectively.

Counting up the solutions

The number of solutions in the family represented by a ZDD can be counted by the following algorithm: the number of solutions in the family represented by a ZDD $\mathcal{Z}$ is the number of routes from the root node ν_{root} of $\mathcal{Z}$ to $\top$. This number can be computed as follows: consider the number of routes from any node ν to $\top$ and denote it by $c(\nu)$. The number of solutions included in the family represented by $\mathcal{Z}$ is $c(\nu_{\text{root}})$. Since all routes from ν to $\top$ pass through either ν_0 or ν_1, the following holds:

$$c(\nu) = c(\nu_0) + c(\nu_1).$$

The number of routes from $\bot$ to $\top$ is zero, and that of routes from $\top$ to $\top$ is one. Therefore, we have $c(\bot) = 0$ and $c(\top) = 1$. For each node, we compute the values of c in the order of nodes closer to the terminals (i.e., the index j of x_j is larger), and finally obtain the value of $c(\nu_{\text{root}})$. The time complexity of this algorithm is linear in the number of nodes of the ZDD.

Uniform random sampling of a solution

We describe a method for uniformly random sampling of a solution from the family of solutions represented by a ZDD. Using the solution counting method described above, we compute the value of c for each node. Uniform random sampling can be thought of as randomly sampling a route from the root node to $\top$. Suppose that we start from the root node, and we are currently on a node ν. We move to the node ν_0 pointed at by the 0-arc of ν with probability $c(\nu_0)/(c(\nu_0) + c(\nu_1))$ and to the node ν_1 pointed at by the 1-arc of ν with probability $c(\nu_1)/(c(\nu_0) + c(\nu_1))$. We repeat this process. Since $c(\bot) = 0$ holds, we will never reach $\bot$ and will certainly reach $\top$. This process yields one route from the root node to $\top$, and the set corresponding to the route is the sampled solution. The time complexity of sampling one solution is $O(|U|)$, where $|U|$ is the number of elements in the universal set.

Solution enumeration

It is also possible to enumerate all the solutions in the family represented by a ZDD. However, since the number of solutions in a family is generally enormous, it is not practical to enumerate all of them. To enumerate the solutions in the family, we search all the paths from the root to $\top$. This is done by the following backtracking method. We first start from the root node ν_{root}. From the root node, we proceed toward the 0-arc of the root and reach the node ν_0 pointed at by the 0-arc. From there, it searches for a route from ν_0 to $\top$ recursively. After that, it returns to ν and next proceeds toward the 1-arc of the root, searching for a route from ν_1 to $\top$ recursively.

Consider a recursive function $\mathsf{enum}(\nu, S)$ that performs this operation (outputs all solutions) (ν is a node of a ZDD, and $S \subseteq U$). Let $\mathcal{Z}$ be the ZDD rooted at ν. The function $\mathsf{enum}(\nu, S)$ outputs each solution in the family represented by $\mathcal{Z}$ plus S. In other words, it outputs $\mathcal{S}_{\mathcal{Z}} \sqcup \{S\}$. The call $\mathsf{enum}(\nu_{\mathrm{root}}, \emptyset)$ returns the desired result.

The behavior of $\mathsf{enum}(\nu, S)$ is as follows: when $\mathsf{enum}(\bot, S)$ is called, it does nothing. When $\mathsf{enum}(\top, S)$ is called, it outputs S. Consider the case where ν is a non-terminal node with label x. The behavior of $\mathsf{enum}(\nu, S)$ in this case is as follows. First, it calls $\mathsf{enum}(\nu_0, S)$ and outputs all the solutions each of which does not contain x. Then, it calls $\mathsf{enum}(\nu_1, S \cup \{x\})$ and outputs all the solutions each of which contains x.

Linear weight minimization and maximization

When each element in the universe set is given a weight, we can compute the solution with the smallest or largest linear weight. A ZDD for a combinatorial problem maintains the family of all feasible solutions, and the various constraints specified as the problem setting are taken into account when constructing the ZDD. Therefore, it is sufficient to select the solution from the family of feasible solutions represented by the ZDD that has the minimum or maximum weight. It can be done in linear time in the number of nodes in the ZDD by the method described below. Since both minimum and maximum can be computed in almost the same way, we discuss the minimum here. For any node ν, let x_i be the label of ν. Let $d(\nu)$ be the linear weight of the solution whose weight is minimum among the solutions represented by the ZDD rooted at ν. The value $d(\nu)$ can be computed as follows.

$$d(\nu) = \min\{d(\nu_0), d(\nu_1) + w_i\},$$

where w_i is the weight of x_i. By setting $d(\bot) = +\infty$, $d(\top) = 0$, $+\infty$ is ignored when taking min. This algorithm can be performed in $O(|\mathcal{F}|)$, where $\mathcal{F}$ is the input ZDD.

Extracting only solutions not containing a specified element

Given a ZDD $\mathcal{Z}$, a ZDD representing the family of solutions that are in $\mathcal{S}_{\mathcal{Z}}$ and do not contain a specified element x_i ($\in U$) can be constructed by a bottom-up construction algorithm. Let $\mathsf{offset}(\nu, x_i)$ be a recursive function that constructs a ZDD representing the family of solutions in the family represented by the ZDD rooted at ν not containing the specified element x_i. If ν is $\bot$ or $\top$, it returns $\bot$ and $\top$, respectively. If ν is a non-terminal node with label x_j, it does the following: if $j > i$, it returns the ZDD rooted at ν, since the family contains no solutions containing x_i. If $j = i$, the ZDD rooted at ν_0 represents the family of solutions that do not contain x_i, it is returned. If $j < i$, the following is computed recursively. We recursively call $\mathsf{offset}(\nu_0, x_i)$ for solutions not containing x_j. Then, we recursively call $\mathsf{offset}(\nu_1, x_i)$ for solutions containing x_j. Let $\mathcal{Z}'_0$ and $\mathcal{Z}'_1$ be the resulting ZDDs of both, respectively. We call $\mathsf{getNode}(x_j, \mathcal{Z}'_0, \mathcal{Z}'_1)$ and return the constructed ZDD.

```
for s in vcs.rand_iter():
    print(s)
```

The enumeration of all the elements (i.e., vertex covers) of `vcs` is as follows. Note again that the following code does not stop when the number of elements of `vcs` is huge.

```
for s in vcs:
    print(s)
```

When executed, the following result is obtained.

```
[2, 1, 3, 4]
[2, 1, 3]
[2, 1, 4]
[2, 3, 4]
[1, 3, 4]
[1, 4]
```

To perform the linear weight minimization or maximization, it is necessary to provide vertex weights. Vertex weights are given by `dict` of Python, where a vertex is a key and a weight is a value. The following example outputs 5 lightest vertex covers in a decreasing order of weights.

```
weights = {1: 5, 2: 2, 3: 4, 4: 8}
count = 5
for s in vcs.min_iter(weights): # if max_iter, output in
                                # an increasing order of weights.
    print(s)
    count -= 1
    if count <= 0:
        break
```

The method for extracting sets that contain or do not contain a specified element is as follows:

```
vcs_i3 = vcs.including(3)
# [[1, 2, 3], [2, 3, 4], [1, 3, 4], [1, 2, 3, 4]]
vcs_e3 = vcs.excluding(3)
# [[1, 4], [1, 2, 4]]
```

The method for extracting sets whose number of vertices is less than, greater than, or equal to a specified number of vertices is as follows:

```
vcs_s3 = vcs.smaller(3) # [[1, 4]]
vcs_l3 = vcs.larger(3) # [[1, 2, 3, 4]]
```

```
vcs_g3 = vcs.graph_size(3)
# [[1, 2, 3], [1, 2, 4], [2, 3, 4], [1, 3, 4]]
```

It is also possible to extract the vertex covers whose weight is less than or equal to a specified value. In the example below, the weights are represented as `weights` and all vertex covers with weights less than 13 are extracted.

```
vcs_s13 = vcs.cost_le(weights, 13) # [[1, 4], [1, 2, 3]]
```

It is also possible to conduct the union and intersection operations. The following example shows how to obtain vertex covers containing vertex 2 or containing vertex 3. The union can be obtained by the | operation.

```
vcs_i23 = vcs.including(2) | vcs.including(3)
# [[1, 2, 3], [1, 2, 4], [2, 3, 4], [1, 3, 4], [1, 2, 3, 4]]
```

The following example obtains all the independent and dominating sets of a graph. The `&` operation can be used to obtain the intersection of two families of sets.

```
iss = VertexSetSet.independent_sets(edges)
dss = VertexSetSet.dominating_sets(edges)
idss = iss & dss # [[1], [4], [2, 3]]
```

Only minimal vertex covers can also be obtained.

```
vcs_minimal = vcs.minimal() # [[1, 4], [1, 2, 3], [2, 3, 4]]
```

2.3 *Family of Subgraphs*

In the previous chapter, we have considered the (Hamiltonian) cycle problem, whose solution sets are (Hamiltonian) cycles. For example, an example of a cycle of graph G_2 in Fig. 1c is $\{e_1, e_2, e_4, e_5, e_7, e_8\}$, which is shown in Fig. 1d, and the family of all (not necessarily Hamiltonian) cycles is $\{\{e_1, e_2, e_3\}, \{e_1, e_2, e_4, e_5, e_6\}, \{e_1, e_2, e_4, e_5, e_7, e_8\}, \{e_3, e_4, e_5, e_6\}, \{e_3, e_4, e_5, e_7, e_8\}, \{e_6, e_7, e_8\}\}$. Recall that a subgraph of a graph in this (and previous) chapter is represented by a set of edges. `GraphSet` is a Python class that represents a set of subgraphs.

To obtain the set of all Hamiltonian cycles of a given graph, the following procedure is used. In the example, we use graph G_2.

```
GraphSet.set_universe([(1, 2), (1, 3), (2, 3), (2, 4),
                       (3, 5), (4, 5), (4, 6), (5, 6)])
hcs = GraphSet.cycles(is_hamilton = True)
# [[(1, 2), (1, 3), (2, 4), (3, 5), (4, 6), (5, 6)]]
```

The variable hcs is an object of the GraphSet class, which represents a set of subgraphs as edge sets. The methods of the GraphSet class are almost the same as those of the VertexSetSet class. In the following example, we randomly sample a Hamiltonian cycle from hcs (although hcs has only one cycle in this example).

```
h_cycle = hcs.choice()
print(h_cycle) # [(1, 2), (1, 3), (2, 4), (3, 5), (4, 6), (5, 6)]
```

The variable h_cycle is a graph, i.e., a list of tuples representing edges. All other methods for VertexSetSet introduced above can be used.

```
hcs.len()
for hc in hcs.rand_iter():
    print(hc)
weights = {(1, 2): 25, (1, 3): 32,...}
for hc in hcs.max_iter(weights):
    print(hc)
hcs2 = hcs.cost_le(weights, 20)
```

Graphillion can handle various types of subgraphs of an input graph. The following are examples of them.

```
connected_components()
cliques()
trees()
forests()
cycles()
paths()
matchings()
perfect_matchings()
induced_graphs()
bipartite_graphs()
```

As an example of usage, consider the following situation. Given a graph, we want to find a path between two specified vertices s and t. However, paths must go through a vertex u, and must not go through vertices v and w. The distance of paths must be at most 25. Among such paths, we select 10 paths uniformly at random and output them. Example code is shown below.

```
# specify the input graph as ''edges''
GraphSet.set_universe(edges)
weights = {...} # omitted
paths = GraphSet.paths(s, t)
s_paths = paths.including(u).excluding(v).
                excluding(w).cost_le(weights, 25)
count = 10
for p in s_paths:
    print(p)
```

Table 1 Experimental results for vertex covers. "TZ *X*" means network (graph) *X* in the Internet Topology Zoo [6]. "M/O" means out of memory (exceeding 64GB). Since grid graphs with odd length have less vertex covers than those with even length, we show the results only for grid graphs with even length

Graph	# Vertices	# Edges	Time	Memory	# Solutions
12×12 grid	144	264	43.5	6280.3 MB	1.6×10^{26}
14×14 grid	196	364	743.2	47792.7 MB	3.4×10^{35}
16×16 grid	256	480	–	M/O	–
TZ Colt	153	191	0.1	24.6 MB	4.0×10^{34}
TZ UsCarrier	158	189	0.2	46.1 MB	2.5×10^{32}
TZ Cogentco	197	245	0.5	98.5 MB	3.4×10^{40}
TZ Kdl	754	899	–	M/O	–

```
    count -= 1
    if count <= 0:
        break
```

3 Performance Evaluation

As mentioned in the previous chapter, NP-hard combinatorial problems are not always solvable even when the problem size is only a few hundred. Graphillion allows us not only to obtain exact optimal solutions of combinatorial problems such as the vertex cover problem and Hamiltonian cycle problem, but also to perform operations described in the previous section, such as extracting multiple solutions in order of decreasing weight.

We present the performance of Graphillion for some graphs. The environment for the computer experiment presented in this section is Intel Core i7-10710U CPU, 64 GB memory, Linux Ubuntu 24.04, and Python 3.10. The version of Graphillion is 1.8. The graphs used in this experiment include complete graphs, grid graphs, and network benchmark graphs provided by the Internet Topology Zoo [6]. We present the results of graphs where we successfully computed the sets of solutions. We assign uniformly random integers ranging from 10 to 100 as weights to each vertex. Although we do not describe the variable order of ZDDs in the previous and this chapter, it is important because it affects the performance of the computation. We adopt the order determined by the method based on graph cuts [1].

We show the results for vertex covers. Given a graph, the code that obtains the set of all the vertex covers of the graph is as follows:

```
vcs = VertexSetSet.vertex_covers(edges)
```

The results of this method are presented in Table 1. The table columns include the input graph name, the number of vertices, the number of edges, the method's execution time (in seconds), the amount of memory used, and the number of solutions. The method's execution time primarily consists of the construction time of the ZDD. For the Internet Topology Zoo data, the method successfully obtained the sets in under 1 s for graphs with fewer than 200 vertices. For the 14×14 grid graph, the method successfully constructed 338752110195939290445247645371206783 solutions in 743.2 s. However, for the 16×16 grid graph, which has 256 vertices and 480 edges, we were unable to obtain the set of solutions due to insufficient memory. Although the sets of solutions obtained are compressed, a significant amount of memory is still required to compute them for larger graphs.

Next, we present the computation times for several methods introduced in the previous section. For the 14×14 grid graph, the `vcs.len()` method, which finds the number of solutions, took 2.24 s. The `vcs.choice()` method, which obtains one solution, and the `vcs.including(v)` method, which extracts only solutions that include a specified element v, both finished within 0.01 s. Obtaining 10 solutions with the minimum weight using the `vcs.min_iter()` method also took less than 0.01 s. The execution time of these methods is negligibly small compared to the time required to construct the set of solutions.

4 Discussion

We discuss the types of problems for which Graphillion is better suited compared to other methods. Graphillion maintains an exact set of feasible solutions for problems with graph sizes ranging from a few hundred to a few thousand vertices. Therefore, Graphillion is useful when exact solutions, rather than approximate ones, are required. Graphillion is also useful when it is necessary to output multiple high-quality solutions for comparison or to generate a large number of solutions through random sampling. For very large graphs, such as those with millions of vertices, it is impractical for Graphillion to function effectively.

In addition, Graphillion can be used for problems that involve enumerating subgraphs of a given graph, or when the nature of the problem requires implicit graph enumeration. Graphillion has been applied to the construction of high-strength test suites for combinatorial interaction testing [9], the development of structured Naïve Bayes classifiers for detecting anomalous paths in graphs [2], the evaluation of low-latency network topologies [7], and other similar tasks.

Graphillion has the potential to be applied to graph problems where the solution space cannot be expressed using linear inequalities and where complex constraints must be considered. One example of such a problem is the representation of the set of rooted spanning forests in the optimization of switch configurations in a power distribution network [5].

5 Conclusion

In this chapter, we introduced Graphillion, a Python library designed to solve combinatorial problems on graphs. Graphillion can be used to solve combinatorial problems such as the minimum vertex cover problem, where a solution is a set of vertices for a given graph. It can also solve problems like the Hamiltonian cycle problem, where the solution is a subgraph of a given graph. Graphillion is still under development and is expected to evolve as a powerful tool for solving a wide range of graph problems.

References

1. J. Kawahara, B. Fifield, K. Imai, C.T. Kenny, The essential role of empirical validation in legislative redistricting simulation. Stat. Public Policy **7**(1), 52–68 (2020)
2. A. Choi, N. Tavabi, A. Darwiche, Structured features in Naive Bayes classification, in *Proceedings of the AAAI Conference on Artificial Intelligence*, vol. 30, no. 1 (Mar 2016)
3. A.A. Hagberg, D.A. Schult, P. Swart, J.M. Hagberg, Exploring network structure, dynamics, and function using networkx, in *The 7th Python in Science Conference* (2008), pp. 11–15
4. T. Inoue, H. Iwashita, J. Kawahara, S. Minato, Graphillion: software library for very large sets of labeled graphs. Int. J. Softw. Tools Technol. Transf. **18**(1), 57–66 (2016)
5. T. Inoue, K. Takano, T. Watanabe, J. Kawahara, R. Yoshinaka, A. Kishimoto, K. Tsuda, S. Minato, Y. Hayashi, Distribution loss minimization with guaranteed error bound. IEEE Trans. Smart Grid **5**(1), 102–111 (2014)
6. S. Knight, H.X. Nguyen, N. Falkner, R. Bowden, M. Roughan, The Internet topology zoo. IEEE J. Select. Areas Commun. **29**(9), 1765–1775 (2011)
7. M. Koibuchi, I. Fujiwara, F. Chaix, H. Casanova, Towards ideal hop counts in interconnection networks with arbitrary size, in *2016 Fourth International Symposium on Computing and Networking (CANDAR)* (2016), pp. 188–194
8. S. Minato, Zero-suppressed BDDs for set manipulation in combinatorial problems, in *Proceedings of the 30th ACM/IEEE Design Automation Conference* (1993), pp. 272–277
9. T. Ohashi, T. Tsuchiya, Generating high strength test suites for combinatorial interaction testing using ZDD-based graph algorithms, in *2017 IEEE 22nd Pacific Rim International Symposium on Dependable Computing (PRDC)* (2017), pp. 78–85

Interdisciplinary Discussions for Future Computer Science

Takeaki Uno

Abstract This paper explains the activities of the Kanda Lab in the AFSA project, the reasons for its establishment, its value, and its motivation. We analyze the current state of interdisciplinary integration obtained from the activities of the Kanda Lab. The AFSA project's activities in the art layer are presented as a new perspective on the power to create connections with other fields and to create new ideas from the discussions which are widely connected to academia and society that the field of computer science would implicitly share. This is then developed into the construction of a methodology for discussing and researching interdisciplinary integration, and for its efficient implementation. For this purpose, the Kanda Lab was designed and established as a place where researchers from different fields can easily discuss. We employed young researchers as full-time researchers who are interested in interdisciplinary integration from many fields including natural science, mathematics, and humanities. These researchers are required to be willing to construct one's own worldview. In the latter half of the paper, we will introduce the new perspective on the current state of interdisciplinary integration found in the discussions at the Kanda Lab, the new value of interdisciplinary integration that results from this, and an overview of the entire academic field.

1 Introduction

Many problems in computer science are linked to the analysis of real world, natural and social phenomena and support and contribute to human activities there, and solving these problems leads to value. The ART layer in the AFSA project is a conceptual or actual place where computer science theory and application intersect, created to focus on improving the quality of research results. This concept has been continuously upheld since the predecessor project of the AFSA project, and activities have been carried out based on this concept. As a result, theory and application are

T. Uno (✉)
National Institute of Informatics, Tokyo, Japan
e-mail: uno@nii.ac.jp

S. Minato et al. (eds.), *Algorithmic Foundations for Social Advancement*,
https://doi.org/10.1007/978-981-96-0668-9_5

organically connected, resulting in many high-quality research results, and accompanying this, many researchers are able to connect with others and discuss beyond their own research fields. If we think a little more broadly, this can also be seen as an example of interdisciplinary fusion actually producing results. Here, interdisciplinary fusion refers to the fusion of informatics or computer science with some other field including industry. Researchers and practitioners from different fields interact and discuss, which leads to new research and the next challenge. This cycle is going smoothly.

However, the activities carried out in the ART layer have not been always efficient. Many researchers have met new people, exchanged knowledge through many discussions, generated new ideas, formulated research questions, and actually conducted research. On the other hand, many researchers who visited the ART layer did not have good discussions, and did not produce any good ideas and research. Even if there are many encounters, only a few lead to new research or related discussions. Also, even if there are discussions, there are many cases where good ideas do not come out. Even if good ideas come out, they do not necessarily lead to further research. There are many cases where new knowledge is obtained and good ideas come out, but the ideas are left unexplored and forgotten because they are not in a position to research them. In other words, it is not always efficient, and the things produced have not always been put to good use.

Even though there are certainly people who are good at working in the ART layer. They smoothly build relationships by mutual understanding and exchanging interests from new encounters. In discussions, they come up with rational or innovative ideas from many perspectives and formulate research questions. Because research resources are limited, not all newly generated research questions are actually researched, but the quality of the questions themselves gives many researchers new perspectives, knowledge, and stimulation. This ability does not seem to be innate, and there are many cases where researchers who were not very good at it at first became better over time. In other words, this is a skill that can be acquired to some extent. Considering that good discussions and good research questions give good knowledge and stimulation to many researchers, it would be of great value if many researchers could possess this ability. The challenge is how to improve this ability, or how to create an environment in which such ability can be easily demonstrated and acquired.

When we consider the above issues, the question naturally arises as to why it is necessary to create new research questions in the art layer. If we only consider creating research questions, it seems much more efficient for each researcher to think of problems in their own field of expertise, where they have the most knowledge and experience of thinking. This is certainly true. However, if we think about it, we can also say that there are already plenty of research questions in the world that such experts think of and create in their own fields of expertise. Such questions would not provide researchers with new knowledge, ways of thinking, or inspiration. Research that suggests new ways of thinking and values to researchers would always be created by incorporating new ways of thinking and concerns outside of their field of expertise.

The need for people from various fields to discuss this issue can also be thought of as follows. Let us see a story as an example or metaphor that is originally given by a member of AFSA project, Prof. Kumiyo Nakakoji of Future University Hakodate. Imagine that there is a person who runs a business transporting good using horse-drawn carriages. This person considers using mechanical technology to make his business more efficient. However, if he does not clearly recognize the problems in his own business and reconstruct his current operations from multiple perspectives, there is a possibility that he will end up mechanizing things in a strange way. For example, mechanizing the horse and driver as a robot. Ideally, he should have developed a truck, but it would be difficult for a person who only has the concept of a horse-drawn carriage to come up with the idea of a new type of tool like a truck.

It is difficult for someone who is an expert on a particular problem or task to observe and analyze the problem they are facing, in the above case their work on the business, from multiple perspectives and describe only its essence in abstract terms. When it comes to applying technology, if only technicians and engineers think about it, they tend to fall into short-sighted solutions like mechanizing horses. This can also be inferred from the fact that many theoretical research results are not easily applied to society in a sufficiently reasonable and good way. This is inevitable that the quality of research and research questions that are created is higher when they are discussed from various perspectives. Discussions held in places where researchers and practitioners from many fields gather, such as the art layer, inevitably lead to efficient activities that produce high-quality research questions or research activities.

So why do these artistic activities need to be led by computer science researchers? People in academic and industrial fields, where technology is applied, are more likely to gain direct and significant benefits from such activities, and one might think that people in those fields are better suited and much motivated to running the artistic activities. However, on closer consideration, as we will explain below, it becomes clear that the activities of the art layer are closely connected to the essence of computer science.

In the field of computer science, especially in the research fields of algorithms and information mathematics to which the AFSA project belongs, there is a tendency to place a great deal of emphasis on the theoretical aspects, such as mathematics and computational complexity. However, theoretical research not connecting to the real world, or theoretical research connected to theoretical research itself, will not often receive high recognition in the field of computer science. Much of the research that computer science undertakes has its origins in the real world problems, and it often implicitly assumes that calculations and operations will actually be performed. In other words, research that asks questions that are linked to society, industry, science and technology, and has the potential and validity to be used in these areas is highly evaluated. This is a significant and major difference between computer science and mathematics. In addition, considering society and humans as sources of problems and addressing the methodology of giving value to them rather than just analyzing is a major difference from fields such as physics and other natural sciences. Even if the research is technically deep or mathematically sophisticated, it is often not of interest if it has no application or is not related to other technologies or natural sciences. Such research may not be accepted by academic journals. The application of theories and technologies in computer science is also of great value to the fields to which the theories and technologies are applied. Conversely, if it does not have much value, then the application of the technology, or even the technology itself, will be devalued in the context of computer science values.

There are few other academic disciplines that apply such diverse technologies and knowledge to such diverse fields. This is a major feature of computer science. Throughout its history, computer science has discussed with researchers in many fields, verbalized problems in those fields, and developed technologies to solve them. This means that the acquisition or creation of new concepts through discussion with other fields is essentially a characteristic of computer science that is not an essential characteristic in other fields. In other words, the activities carried out by the art layer can be said to be the explicit strengthening of the activities that computer science has been carrying out implicitly in its long history. Also, since one of the great values of computer science is the development of technologies to solve problems in other fields, this can be said to be one of the essences of computer science, and also connected to the activities in the art layer.

Since computer science has long developed problem-solving methods for other fields, it is thought that computer science has a lot of knowledge and implicit techniques for formulating or modeling problems in other fields. Various concepts exist and are dealt with in various fields, and each field has its own specialized knowledge. However, when it comes to mixing these concepts and techniques and creating possibilities that people can solve, problems with direction, or approaches to research questions, computer science is probably the field with the most knowledge to do this well. It seems that the activities of the art layer in the AFSA project are so effective because computer science is adjacent to them.

As part of the AFSA project, we planned to expand and develop the activities of the art layer, and create a place where researchers from various fields can gather. First, the participants in the discussions were changed from those involved in the theory and application of computer science to researchers from many research fields and practitioners in various industries. At the same time, we planned to go beyond the framework of simply applying theoretical research and to deal with a wide range of important issues related to computer science. This was designed to essentially utilize the strengths of the art layer, which is the discussions between researchers across fields and the resulting creation of high-quality research questions and ideas for research methods. By holding discussions that did not require actual research activities, we greatly expanded the reach of the researchers' thoughts without limiting them to what they themselves can implement.

In addition, we established a base called the Kanda Lab in Tokyo, Japan, where we placed several full-time young researchers with expertise in fields other than computer science, and created a system where discussions could be held at all times. To make it easy for active researchers at the forefront to visit the place, we selected a place that has good accessibility from all over Japan, including the Tokyo metropolitan area, so that they could stop by on business trips or while commuting, so that many new encounters of researchers and discussion would happen smoothly on a daily basis without holding large-scale events. We also held many discussion meetings and gatherings to increase interaction with AFSA project members and surrounding researchers, with aiming to make it become a physical symbol of the AFSA project and a central base of activity, connecting the project as a whole. In addition, we did not have fixed seats for each member inside the Kanda Lab, but instead used a free address system, allowing us to hold events of various sizes and reducing the psychological barrier of stepping into someone else's territory. The Kanda Lab's furniture was diverse, not too stylish or dirty, neat but slightly messy, and we also provided a kitchen and cooking utensils, making it as easy as possible for researchers to accept and be accepted their own values and lifestyles in the Kanda Lab, and to accept as many diverse people as possible in a relaxed state, including their daily lives and activities outside of research. The researchers assigned to the Kanda Lab are not people who have established a worldview in their own research area and are intensively devoting themselves to research in that area, but rather researchers who are trying to build their own worldview and who are also interested in interdisciplinary fusion. This is because the activities carried out at the Kanda Lab are also activities to create a worldview related to interdisciplinary fusion, and we select people who can think about, discuss, and create these activities as if they are their own, rather than engaging in these activities outside of themselves.

The objectives of the Kanda Lab are (1) to create research methods, research questions, and concepts for them that have been conducted in the art world through interdisciplinary discussions, and to compile and publish them as a problem catalog, (2) to construct a methodology that will enable such interdisciplinary discussions to be conducted efficiently, obtain high-quality results, and make the discussions more accessible and attractive to many researchers, and to describe it as a technology, and (3) to conceptualize abstract matters such as the current state of interdisciplinary fusion, the meaning and results of researchers interacting across fields, the structure of academic fields, and how to understand their differences from the perspective of interdisciplinary fusion through these activities. To this end, many researchers from various fields will be invited to hold discussions, and the perspectives and concepts gained from these discussions will be re-discussed by lab members to deepen and clarify them. Members of the Kanda Lab will put into practice some of the specific research plans that have emerged from these activities. Commonalities will be extracted from the activities, behavior, and thinking of diverse researchers in the discussions and exchanges held in the Kanda Lab, and their forms will be clarified by re-discussing them among members of the Kanda Lab. We also implemented some of these interdisciplinary technologies into practice outside the Kanda Lab, and observe and verify their effectiveness. As well as the problem catalog, we also document the findings and activities themselves, and make them widely available in some form of media.

This chapter, as well as Chaps. 5–12, were born out of the four-year activities of the Kanda Lab, which began in 2021. Below, we discuss the motivation, validity, and usefulness of the Kanda Lab's activities and goals.

We think that expanding the activities that have been carried out in the art layer and having discussions that involve people from fields other than computer science and its applications, especially humanities and social sciences, is not only about the project itself but also about the future of computer science itself. Of course, good results are produced by the activities of people in computer science and its applications. However, these results are limited to the overlap of computer science and its applications, and ideas rarely go beyond that. On the other hand, in activities in the art layer, even if people with seemingly unrelated expertise join the discussion, insights that were not thought of at the beginning of the discussion can be obtained, and new directions that are convincing and valuable can be obtained. In particular, many of these insights and values are related to humanities and social sciences. We think that this is natural, considering that the discussions that have been held in the art layer were not originally seeking value in a purely mathematical or business sense, but applications that have value and are useful to society and people. Also, from the perspective of considering issues related to humans and society, discussions held only by people with no expertise in humans or society can sometimes lead to a large deviation in direction. The reasons for this are explained below.

As an example, let us consider the toilet paper hoarding incident that occurred in Japan in February 2020, the beginning of COVID-19 era. This incident started when a person posted a fake rumor (maybe a joke, originally) on social media that there would be a shortage of toilet paper due to the COVID-19 pandemic. As a result, many people bought up toilet paper, making it difficult to obtain at supermarket. It is commonly believed that this was caused by many people feeling anxious about what to do if toilet paper became difficult to obtain, and so they bought more toilet paper than usual. However, some research and analysis suggest that this anxiety was not caused by the rumor, but rather by posts and media news warning people that the post was a fake rumor. It is also known that the number of people who actually came into contact with the fake rumor itself was overwhelmingly smaller than those who heard warnings about the fake rumor. In other words, it is highly likely that people bought more toilet paper as a result of receiving a lot of information that said it was a fake rumor and that there was no need to buy more.

This has a very big implication. In computer science, it is said that it is very important to develop technology to confirm that information is a fake, and technology to accurately inform people that fake information is a fake so that the spread of fake information does not cause chaos in society. However, in this case, both of these were achieved perfectly, and as a result, people hoarded toilet paper. In other words, it can be considered that this happened as a result of computer science perfectly achieving its goal. This means that there is no choice but to think that there was some fundamental discrepancy in the goal setting of computer science, which aims to contribute to society. In addition, this kind of phenomenon is called panic in social psychology. In this case, panic does not refer to an individual falling into a state of extreme confusion as is usually imagined, but rather to a state in which many people believe that "I am calm, but the people around me are surely unable to make calm decisions." From this perspective, the goal of computer science is not to accurately detect fake information and spread the results of that detection, but to create research questions, model them, and develop the methodologies to solve them to prevent people from falling into this state of panic, model them, and develop solutions.

Looking back, it seems that the problems that computer science deals with have not undergone any major updates since its inception. For example, the shortest path problem used in navigation systems was formulated more than 50 years ago as a problem of finding the path with the least cost, and its framework has not changed much to the present day. In the meantime, society and people's values have changed significantly, and there have been continuous and major changes in values and methodologies regarding what should be prioritized in various problems and how they should be solved. As a result, there are probably cases such as the toilet paper incident mentioned above, where the goals that computer science initially set are greatly distant from the values and systems of society. In order to bridge this gap and continue to accurately recognize the issues that computer science should tackle in the future, it is essential to continue to discuss issues from many perspectives, especially in places where specialized knowledge related to people and society gather, that are humanities and social science.

In many cases, diverse and rich ideas are presented in discussions at the art layer. The validity and feasibility of these ideas are then verified and improved. However, if none of the participants in the discussion can carry out research to which these ideas can be connected, the ideas are often left undeveloped and forgotten without being deepened or polished. This is somewhat reasonable, since the goal of discussions at the art layer was to conduct collaborative research or to achieve the unique goals of each participant. However, opportunities for researchers of theory and application to gather and discuss, such as those in the art layer, are valuable for many researchers, including those participating in the art layer themselves. Furthermore, the ideas that emerge from these discussions include not only concrete final deliverables such as research questions and plans, but also new perspectives, concepts, and approaches, which may not directly become results but may become the seeds of other research questions and plans. These perspectives, concepts, and approaches are very difficult for people who need them to research and obtain through seeking existing literature or having interviews, and in that sense, they are of great value. Considering these things, it would be a waste to leave the ideas that come out of discussions and the results of verification as they are. However, these ideas themselves are often elementary or ad-hoc, and if one were to record the ideas as they are, one would just end up with a messy pile of notes. In order for ideas to be revisited by others and for the knowledge to be utilized, the validity and feasibility of the ideas must be properly verified and improved, and their meaning, value, and effectiveness must be explained from many perspectives.

As mentioned above, the ideas that came up in the discussions, and the associated perspectives, values, and seeds of technology will be of great value if they are described and disclosed. Considering the general usefulness of such descriptions, they should be in a form that is easy to search and browse, specifically in the form of a database or catalog. In addition, such easy browsing will be of great value not only to people who simply need these concepts, but also to people who are simply looking for new ways of thinking, not based on one's own research needs, but simply by serendipitous encounters. In general, it is very difficult to consider whether one's current activities or current thoughts require consideration or verification from a certain perspective that one has not considered before. Even if one senses the possibility and necessity, it is also difficult to clarify which specific perspective is needed, or what the general perspective is applicable. In order to expand one's own thoughts, it is difficult to determine the direction in which to expand them, and one can only look for serendipitous opportunities in a somewhat comprehensive manner. To that end, the existence of a place where a wealth of high-quality perspectives, ways of thinking, and ideas are available and can be viewed all at once should be of great value. Even if you have a vague goal of exploring new research or adding a new direction to your own research, a place like this that is highly accessible and has a collection of good concepts will be of great value. It can provide hints for generating new research ideas and directions, as well as materials for thought, and support creativity.

When such new perspectives, thoughts and research questions given by art layer discussions are described in a problem catalog, it would be of great value to people who are not currently conducting computer science research or using computer science technology. Currently, many of the documents introducing computer science technology are about the results of research conducted to date, and they allow people to learn about the research conducted and what has been achieved until now. On the other hand, our problem catalog, which describes questions, ideas, and values that may be researched in the near future from many perspectives, allows people to get an overview of the scope and direction of computer science research results in the near future. Being able to imagine not only the current state of development but also future developments should be a great help in evaluating the value of computer science based on each person's situation and values. This applies equally to research, business, and ideas and activities in social activities.

Currently, there is not much of a culture that values or evaluates the act of writing and publishing such thoughts, perspectives, and ideas. Although there is certainly value in the act itself, the lack of putting value and motivation for doing so may hinder in-depth discussion of topics that one does not necessarily research. If researchers were given a certain amount of recognition and respect for simply asking research questions, creating perspectives, and developing concepts, they would do so more, and this would become an activity that benefits others and society.

There are certainly people in the art layer who are good at holding discussions and collaborative research, or at initiating these discussions and building relationships with people for this purpose. To generalize, there are certainly many researchers who are good at such advanced thinking activities as formulating research questions, thinking and coming up with ideas for them, debating, communicating their own ideas to others, and understanding the ideas of others. Furthermore, these people were by no means good at these things from the beginning, and people who were not good at them at first often become good at them later. This means that these abilities can be acquired. However, these are craftsman-like abilities that depend heavily on individual talent, and the means taken to acquire them are limited to merely taking inspiration by seeing and referring to the actions and ideas of others.

It is commonly recognized in many fields that the task of discussing, thinking, and formulating high-quality research questions is a very important part of conducting high-quality research. However, the situation is not such that many people can acquire the ability and methods to do so. It exists only as tacit knowledge of individuals, or as unverbalized shared knowledge of research fields, communities, or laboratories. In such a situation, only those with a favorable environment can master this ability, which is detrimental to the academic field. In addition, in such a situation, the task of creating concepts and formulating questions through discussion and thinking itself becomes ad hoc, and the same failures are repeated many times, and even when they do work, the reason for their success is not known. People would believe that such ability is really personal experiential knowledge. In addition, vague and unspecific advice is given to those who want to improve their research skills, such as "you have to meet many people and talk as much as possible, even they are selected randomly." In order to find new research questions and directions, fruitless discussions may be repeated, resulting in unnecessary costs.

When observing the activities of the art layer and hearing about know-how from those who are skilled in them, at least elementary commonalities can be found. If we assume that this is somewhat universal, then it is likely that there is a methodology that can be verbalized and practiced by many people. In other words, this kind of skilled way of working seems to be systematizable to some extent as a technique. It probably starts from something quite simple and elementary. Despite this, it seems that there are almost no descriptions of this methodology. If these skilled ways of working at the art layer were to be technicalized and described, it would become relatively easy for people to play an active role in interdisciplinary discussions. This would have a major impact on research and industry.

From this chapter onwards (Chaps. 5–12), we will describe the current state of interdisciplinary discussion and collaboration that the art layer wants to be, technologies for good and smooth interdisciplinary discussion and collaboration obtained from the activities of the Kanda Lab, and research questions and problems obtained from interdisciplinary discussions at the Kanda Lab. These are described from the perspective of the Kanda Lab, which is an interdisciplinary fusion lab that combines computer science, mathematics, natural science and humanities. It is very difficult to describe these matters from a universal and general standpoint, and it is unlikely that any reasonable and valid system for such description methodology can be created. Therefore, this time we will describe the perspectives and ideas gained from four years of activities at the Kanda Lab as our standpoint. Since the perspectives are constructed by selecting those that are highly common from the knowledge of many researchers, we believe that a certain degree of generality is guaranteed, and that they will be of good value at least to researchers and industrial people involved in interdisciplinary fusion. For the methodology of the following description, we will use a general method of logic and explanation developed and used in computer science to discuss the value and significance of new problems, the feasibility and validity of modeling, etc., which often appear at introduction and discussion of the articles in computer science. Specifically, it involves deriving hypotheses or seeing-as from observation and trials, and verifying and asserting their rationality, validity, generality and usefulness, etc. in a logical or conceptual sense.

In the following of this chapter, we will explain the current state and nature of interdisciplinary research from the perspective of the practice in the Kanda Lab. In Sect. 2, "Classifying Interdisciplinary Collaboration Research," we will observe at and classify interdisciplinary fusion research from the perspective of the researchers who are actually engaging interdisciplinary fusion research, and in Sect. 3, "Analyzing Difficulties on Interdisciplinary Discussions and Collaborations," we will explain the difficulties of interdisciplinary research from the perspective and standpoint of the practitioners who have actually attempted it. In Sect. 4, "Studying Interdisciplinarity by Interdisciplinary Discussions," we will explain the methodology of using interdisciplinary discussion to analyze the methodology of interdisciplinary fusion research itself. In Sect. 5, "New Overviews for Decomposing Research Areas," we will build a perspective from the concepts obtained from these interdisciplinary discussions, and describe a new way of characteristics of academic areas and classification method. In Sect. 6, "Independence of Concept Forming and Research Questioning Separating from Research Activity," we propose to make it independent that the parts of research questioning and creation of ideas from the research activities. We consider the value and feasibility of distributing many research questions as shared knowledge in the academic world. In Sect. 7, "Types for Various Understandings", we explain the categorization of individual ways of thinking that have emerged from these interdisciplinary activities, which might be heavily influenced by their field, in particular the ways in which people understand other people's concepts and concerns.

2 Classifying Interdisciplinary Collaboration Research

Currently, interdisciplinary collaborative research is strongly recommended by academic societies and also by governments. It can be considered that knowledge and thoughts from multiple disciplines, not just one, could contribute to breaking down the barriers of research, creating new values, and developing new fields of research. Even if not necessary, the gathering of individuals from various fields to collaboratively formulate research questions and engage in research activities is likely to uncover new values more readily.

However, when interdisciplinary collaborative research is encouraged, there seems to be little indication or evaluation of the content and methods of how the collaboration was done. When High-quality research results were obtained, then the works would receive high praise, but evaluations of the methods of collaborative research are seldom seen. If one wants to conduct effective interdisciplinary collaborative research, we have to look at, analyze, and evaluate interdisciplinary collaborative research. Further, it is necessary to analyze how individual researchers are engaging in collaborative research, to understand how the actual interdisciplinary collaborative research has been done widely. Here, based on the interdisciplinary interactions at the Kanda Laboratory, we would like to grasp the current situation of interdisciplinary collaborative research, by classifying the current forms of interdisciplinary collaborative research. Normally, such classifications would be based on the content of research or the fields being integrated, but here we will discuss the types of collaborative research based on activities of the researchers.

The first type involves using, say importing, technologies from other fields as tools in one's own field of research. For example, the use of AI technology in XX informatics, which has been prevalent recently, fits this category. Researchers in Field A adapt AI technology, data analysis techniques, and simulation technologies developed in informatics to suit the problems of Field A, using them to enhance the efficiency and quality of their research. In this case, the formulation of research questions and the values of the expected results are often based on the values and disciplines of Field A, and advances in informatics as an academic field often do not occur. This type also includes gaining efficiency and then new insights in physics or chemistry by introducing robotic or other experimental equipment improvement technologies from engineering. Changing the direction of research in engineering by using results from psychology is also included in this type.

The second type involves using and simultaneously developing technologies from other areas and making it a part of research activity of one's own research area. For example, creating databases in the humanities, developing experimental equipment in the natural sciences, and improving machine learning algorithms to get adapted in the domain data of the above-mentioned Field A, are cases in this type. Although constructing databases is a study in informatics, developing experimental equipment is a study in engineering, and improving the accuracy of machine learning algorithms is a study in informatics, these activities are carried out in the discipline of one's own research area in order to advance one's research area. In this scenario, the research questions and valuation are often based on the values and disciplines of the area adopting the technology, and the primary aim is seldom to develop the technology itself, such as theoretical understanding, constructing new methods, and seeking potential applications of technologies, which are important in the technology areas such as databases, engineering of experimental equipment, or machine learning.

The third type is the acquisition of topics from other areas. For instance, the areas of philosophy or law might take the topic of autonomous vehicles from engineering areas to consider its ethical implications and legal framework, or a researcher in informatics might take topics of building structures from architecture to consider issues of optimization. In informatics, this type of research is prevalent, and it is not an exaggeration to say that many new research questions are introduced in this manner. Also in this case, the research is conducted according to the values and disciplines of the area that adopts the topic, and the focus is rarely placed on the intrinsic usefulness or value of the topic itself.

When these types are considered, it appears that many interdisciplinary research efforts seen around the world fit into one of these categories. Moreover, these three types all involve importing technology, research activities, or topics from other areas. From the perspective of disciplines and values, this means that technologies, research activities, and topics belonging to one discipline or set of values are newly utilized or researched under other disciplines. On the other hand, interdisciplinary research often anticipates the creation of new fields and innovations, implying that updates of disciplines or establishments of new research disciplines is implicitly expected.

Observing the interdisciplinary discussion for creating new research questions at the Kanda Lab, many research ideas do not fit into the previously mentioned three categories. These ideas often involve introducing or creating new values and perspectives within one's own field. For instance, in literary studies, researchers may conduct a detailed analysis of a single article or articles of an author, with and for uncovering the historical context in which it was written, the psychology and characteristics of the author.

Due to the depth of analysis required, the texts often studied are lengthy and intricately constructed, and do not typically include contemporary, concise and short texts like those found on social media, which are demanded to be analyzed in recent era. Texts from social media, which often directly reflect the thoughts of the writers, could theoretically be easier for literary researchers to analyze the thoughts of the writers, but the brevity of SNS texts usually does not provide enough information to support thorough analysis. However, actually, the goal of analyzing social media is not to pinpoint the psychology of individual writers but rather to identify commonalities across many posts about a certain topic. From this kind of analysis, it is possible to derive thoughts and psychology that are common to many people regarding a certain social issue or incident, along with the basis that they appear in a large number of posts. This approach of identifying commonalities across many writers and texts does not traditionally exist in literature but is a fundamental concept in data science and informatics, where looking for primitive commonalities across many data points can lead to meaningful interpretations. If we are to incorporate data science's global view of data as a method of literary research and create a new way of reading texts for that purpose, we can say that this is a fusion of the discipline of literature and the discipline of informatics.

Here, we would like to introduce a fourth type of interdisciplinary integration that creates new research disciplines through the merging of disciplines. Bioinformatics might be an example of this type, where biology traditionally classified organisms based on observable characteristics. However, with genomic analysis, it is now possible to statistically determine genetic distances between species and then they reconstruct the way of classification of organisms based on distance of genomes. We can say that this represents a new discipline that emerged from the fusion of disciplines of biology and informatics.

While the first three types of interdisciplinary collaborative research might be more suitable for immediate research outcomes, the fourth type emerging at the Kanda Lab might be not so, but particularly intriguing and engaging. For instance, within the AFSA project, presentations of the fourth type of research attract significantly larger audiences and more heated discussions than other research presentations. It appears to spark curiosity and a desire among many researchers to learn about and engage with these studies. However, this new type of research discipline also entails significant challenges. Since the research methodologies of these researchers are usually not yet established, researchers often have to proceed by much trial and error. Additionally, finding appropriate venues to present such findings can be not easy, as many academic journals usually accept papers in the scope of their established disciplines, but tend to reject those not in the scope. Thus, creating a new discipline might mean that there are no direct academic journals available to accept the research.

3 Analyzing Difficulties on Interdisciplinary Discussions and Collaborations

Interdisciplinary collaborative research is frequently said to be challenging. We also faced various difficulties at the Kanda Lab in interdisciplinary collaboration. The essence of these difficulties at the Kanda Lab seems significantly different from what is commonly perceived. The commonly discussed challenges of interdisciplinary collaborative research would include lack of time for research and discussion, absence of opportunities to engage with researchers from other fields, and insufficient resources such as budget and staff. At the Kanda Lab, we started with sufficient time, opportunities, and resources. Nevertheless, despite these conditions being met, significant challenges in interdisciplinary collaboration were realized and unveiled. As we got understood what these difficulties were, the issues of time and budget seemed less fundamental. We discuss these challenges below.

Interdisciplinary collaborative research inherently involves transcending or even discarding existing disciplinary boundaries to create new disciplines, on which research is then conducted. Not all research does this, but the more innovative the research, the more likely it is to involve the creation of new disciplines. It is very much challenging all of these, to fuse several disciplines, to overcome one discipline and think in terms of other disciplines for which one has only beginner's knowledge, to find values in them, and to throw away even temporarily the disciplines of one's own field that might be one's identity. From the viewpoint of research of just exchanging technologies, aiming itself for the fusion of such difficult disciplines is even difficult. We have discussed this many times in other sections, so omit it here and explain other difficulties surrounding this difficulty.

Although this is not the case with all interdisciplinary research, the more innovative the research, the more likely it will involve the construction of a new discipline. On the other hand, if it is a new discipline, this means that it is difficult to pass peer review by academic journals that use existing disciplines as the standard for their values. Peer review typically makes validity and value judgments based on the journal's discipline. A new discipline often deviates from the existing journal's discipline, and its validity and value will not be recognized, especially if the methodology or values are updated. The more innovative interdisciplinary fusion is, the more difficult it is likely to find a place to submit the paper.

The claim above leads to the second difficulty, which one has to value the research fundamentally and independently. Creating value from scratch is difficult very much. It is not enough for the value to be recognized; it needs to be well-regarded by many. If one is working within an existing discipline, it is clear how to enhance the value under the discipline. In a new discipline, it is unclear what should be considered valuable, how to shape this value, and how it will be evaluated. It is challenging to construct good value under these circumstances.

The third challenge pertains to the practitioners of the research. Even after some value has been preliminarily established, subsequent steps involve conducting actual research activities, such as investigations, experiments, implementations, analyses, and system developments. However, interdisciplinary research often requires adopting novel methodologies, meaning researchers cannot use, or rely on, their familiar, specialized techniques. If all participants find research activities inefficient, they can hardly find the meaning of conducting the research. This inefficiency can compromise the quality of research outcomes, representing a substantial challenge.

We can show other challenges such as ensuring equal effort among researchers, and disparities in benefits derived from research outcomes across different fields. Some researchers may gain significantly while others benefit less, resulting in issues of fairness. These challenges stem from the heterogeneity of fields and researchers but are addressable through strategies such as negotiations and repeated collaborative efforts aimed at normalization. Although resolving these issues may incur higher costs, they are manageable problems. The abovementioned challenges are unique to interdisciplinary collaborative research, and clearly articulating and clarifying these difficulties can significantly enhance the efficiency of the methods used to facilitate interdisciplinary collaborative research.

4 Studying Interdisciplinarity by Interdisciplinary Discussions

Interdisciplinary discussions and research are generally considered to have many difficulties. Given their importance and difficulty, one might expect the existence of methodological studies or shared best practices. However, neither the members of the Kanda Laboratory nor the dozens of researchers who have visited have ever heard of such methodologies or know-how, even as rumors. It means that we should study and develop these methodologies ourselves. This exploration of methodologies is one of the missions of the Kanda Lab.

When we think about beginning actual research or investigation about these methodologies, the first consideration is which field this research belongs to. Focusing on the research subject, it may seem to fall within the humanities. While various research areas such as conversation analysis, discourse analysis, linguistics, and communication studies appear relevant, these disciplines primarily aim to analyze and understand real world phenomena rather than studying methods to achieve specific outcomes. For instance, literature studies examine literary works to identify distinctive features and merits but do not research techniques for creating excellent literature. Similar patterns exist in other research areas. Practical approaches for discussion, negotiation, or joint works that are parts of interdisciplinary discussions are more commonly found in general books sold in bookstores.

However, these tend to be how-to guides focusing on specific case solutions, often without attempting to grasp or convey underlying concepts. Moreover, for emerging practices like interdisciplinary discussions, even such books are scarce. When considering methodologies for interdisciplinary discussions, we must first determine which fields' insights to draw upon.

Another area that should be focused on is engineering. The engineering area partly studies mean to accomplish objectives, regardless of the domain to which these objectives belong. This approach seems suitable for studying methodologies as in our case. However, engineering typically relies on science and mathematics, constructing methods based on hypotheses that have been theoretically or experimentally proven with a degree of universality, and substantiating their effectiveness. Yet, it is unlikely to find scientific insights directly applicable to effective interdisciplinary fusion methods. Mathematics and statistics generally study only phenomena that can be reduced to numbers or treated symbolically. Sciences typically focus on subjects whose fundamental principles can be simply explained, rather than complex systems themselves. It seems improbable that these research areas could provide practically friendly insights into discussion methodologies, which likely involve intricately intertwined factors. Considering this, we might turn to the fields of design or art. While these areas might be able to address this issue, their outcomes may lack generalizability even if successful. To obtain observations, techniques, and insights with some degree of universality, it appears necessary to construct a new discipline.

We here do not want to aim to construct and propose a new discipline. Rather, we seek to explore potential components of such a discipline, drawing from various fields' approaches, research methodologies, and techniques, in other words, aspects of existing disciplines. Let us examine these components in the following. First, we consider the observational skills and perspective-taking abilities common in the humanities. In discussions at the Kanda Lab, humanities researchers frequently identified and articulated not only surface-level phenomena but also underlying factors and contextual elements within the overall flow of discussions. These are brought from any humanities researcher, not only from a certain person, thus we deduce that these skills are shared among humanities researchers. Other notable skills include effectively verbalizing concepts, discovering overlooked perspectives, metaphorically framing problems or concepts, and identifying discussion points or angles, which can be seen as techniques related to discovering and refining viewpoints and focal points. Such humanities-based methodologies and disciplines could be valuable for identifying and enhancing discussion points and perspectives.

Engineering or informatics research methods may be valuable in formulating problems based on these perspectives and observations, which might be solvable efficiently. In engineering and informatics, problems are generally formulated so that they could be solved efficiently. Thus, researchers in these areas decompose, or break down the original problem to extract some aspects that could be solvable. This approach differs significantly from the humanities, where researchers think more universal problems should be more important. Humanities often synthesize multiple issues to create more general, universal problem statements. As the main focus of the researchers is observing and analyzing these problems rather than devising solutions, less attention is paid to the difficulty or practicality of addressing the synthesized problems. Consequently, this thinking tends to move in the opposite direction of formulating actually solvable problems. Additionally, the concepts of structuring and modeling, common in engineering and informatics, could be valuable. These approaches of modeling and structuring involve not just describing problems as they appear but also transforming by projecting on other concepts, for seeking ways to solve the problems through observing isomorphisms or commonalities with other structures. Such modeling and structuring approaches could be highly beneficial in developing some methodologies for solving the actual problems.

The approach of deriving mechanisms and laws by building logical arguments from axioms and fundamental principles, as seen in mathematics and natural sciences, could be useful for verifying and constructing the validity and effectiveness of methods. Similarly, the inductive method of deriving hypotheses from data and real world observations, as used in statistics and data science, could be valuable for generating hypotheses from observed discussions and understanding the characteristics of constructed methods in real world scenarios. In general, the fusion of research fields and disciplines often refers to new research by combining research subjects and technologies, and there is a tacit expectation that some kind of research results will be produced. On contrary, the issue aforementioned is a collection and combination of research methodologies from various fields that are necessary and effective when someone wants to investigate, think about, or create something. Compared to the case just research results are interdisciplinary, our approach is assembling the most appropriate research methods from many research areas to tackle the problems, thus we think it has a good quality.

In this sense, it is very different from what is said interdisciplinary research recently. When one wants to create a method to do something well, the method one obtains does not necessarily produce any kind of research results. In other words, it does not necessarily take the form of research. On the other hand, the parts of the work to create the methods explained above are close to what researchers do as the core of their research activities, thus we think that it is effective to perform them in the same way as research activities. Research methodologies are highly effective not only in research, but also in industrial and administrative activities. We should look at research methodologies from the perspective of using them purely for their high effectiveness, rather than as a means to produce some kind of research results. This way, we could construct much more highly practical and effective methodologies for matters other than research.

We saw many discussions by researchers from the humanities and informatics fields at the Kanda Lab. From the discussions, we could recognize importance of the problems that the humanities research focuses on, and for the problems derived from a humanities perspective, there would be paid less attention from an engineering perspective or from a data science perspective, such as observing and inductively leading something by using big data. Even in the field of digital humanities, research that fully incorporates these approaches still seems scarce. Informatics are usually used as a tool for acquiring good research results efficiently. Combining these research methods and disciplines could potentially open up significant new research horizons in this important field. This endeavor at the Kanda Lab appears to be a kind of prototype for interdisciplinary fusion research in terms of synthesizing disciplines.

However, it would be considered that this interdisciplinary methodological research conducted at the Kanda Lab is unlikely to be highly evaluated in academic journals. While various insights are being gained, because it involves creating a new discipline, it is difficult to receive adequate evaluation under existing disciplinary frameworks. To achieve a high evaluation in existing research areas, the goal and methodology, and even discipline itself might need to be modified, changing the focus and the main argumentative approach of the research. Such modifications, however, may transform the outcome into something meaningless from the original purpose and perspectives. This situation seems to embody the dilemma of interdisciplinary research.

Fundamentally, gaining insights should be the primary goal, and having these insights evaluated by a specific community should be of secondary importance. At the Kanda Lab, researchers actively participate in interdisciplinary discussions and research, gaining experience and numerous insights. There is undoubtedly value in this process for the researchers. A part of these insights, after undergoing a form of generalization, are presented in writings like this, which are also made publicly available. While we believe this meets the minimum standards for research, how to add further value to this work remains a challenge for the future.

5 New Overviews for Decomposing Research Areas

When discussing the challenges of interdisciplinary discussion or collaboration, the difference in language is almost invariably mentioned. Although differences in values and research styles are also noted, it seems that most issues converge on the matter of language. However, observing interdisciplinary discussions at the Kanda Laboratory, it becomes clear that language difficulty is not such an obstacle. The meanings of words can be communicated well if just explained. In most discussions, unless delving deeply into someone's specialization, language differences do not pose a significant problem. When we mention this point to those who perceive language as a barrier, they often counter that "it's not just the words, but meanings, concepts, and thought processes that differ"; however, even these can be explained within a reasonable time. Indeed, observing discussions at the Kanda Lab, it is evident that not only language differences, but also conceptual differences are explained, understood, and discussions progress.

When asking members of the Kanda Lab about the difficulties of discussion, they often express the challenges of mutual understanding, such as not knowing why the other thinks in a certain way or why their values are shaped as they are. It seems that individuals recognize these deeper aspects of thinking and values as barriers. In general, each individual has one's own thoughts and values, so it is natural that thoughts and values differ a lot. It suggests that in this case, these aspects significantly vary from those they usually discuss with. From this point, we can deduce that there would be some typical, deeper attributes of thinking and values in each research area, and they are unique, and differ from that of other research areas.

Generally, differences between academic fields are often explained by their subjects of research or disciplinary distinctions. These differences are precisely what make interdisciplinary discussions meaningful. Looking at the discussions at the Kanda Lab, it appears that this difference can be easily resolved to some extent by explaining the difference, and it does not seem to be a barrier. In this case, when thinking about the difficulty of interdisciplinary collaborative research, it would not be good to think about the differences between research areas based on research subjects or disciplines. After all, interdisciplinary discussions are fundamentally about the interactions between individuals, and their inherent differences make these discussions challenging. Therefore, focusing on the individuals and the differences among individual researchers within those areas might reveal more about the essence of these challenges. We consider this point to provide deeper insights from the observations at discussions in the Kanda Lab from this essential perspective.

At the Kanda Lab, one often noted aspect of differences of individual researchers is what drives researchers to conduct their studies. For instance, researchers in mathematics or information mathematics often have a specific goal: by proving theorems, they aim to establish themselves as formidable scholars capable of such proofs. While some individuals are highly motivated by this objective, others are not. However, it is widely recognized in these areas that many researchers in these areas harbor these aspirations. From this perspective, even if a theorem is socially irrelevant and contributes nothing new to mathematics, the act of proving it—especially if it involves skillful techniques and innovative ideas—can be a source of joy and is often esteemed by peers. However, this benefit of increasing the skill or observing the power of proof is not shared by researchers in other fields such as chemistry or literature, thus one may find it baffling why someone would want to solve such seemingly pointless problems.

Natural scientists often harbor a desire to make significant discoveries that are connected to truth of the world. The ways and methods to achieve these discoveries are immaterial—whether it involves substantial funding or is found serendipitously, the intellectual satisfaction remains the same. Even if the discovery is made by someone else, the joy of learning about it is substantial. However, those with a mindset akin to mathematicians or information mathematicians may quickly lose interest in discoveries that do not require sophisticated techniques. This occurs even when collaborating with researchers from other academic disciplines or industries. For these collaborators, solving a problem efficiently, regardless of the method, is the primary concern. If a problem can be solved using simple, widely available methods, which is a very good solution. Conversely, researchers focused on optimization or algorithms find no interest in solutions that do not involve some degree of novelty or complexity, often leading to misunderstandings about why others do not share their enthusiasm.

In humanities research, there is a so called typically common motivation among researchers to resolve or confront significant internal conflicts or questions existing in one's heart. This sentiment is less prevalent among mathematicians or computer scientists, who might engage in problems that are completely external to one's own mind and being objectified. As a way to address this point, one might choose a topic, a certain literary work or its author in the case of literature, which no one else may pay attention to. However, in fields like computer science, where a high level of generality in research subjects is valued, such personal motivations can be difficult to comprehend. There is a tendency in these areas to focus on the technical aspects or the non-trivial nature of problems rather than personal engagement.

At the Kanda Lab, members frequently exchange ideas about each other's disciplinary traits, ways of thinking, or ideologies. While understanding these aspects does not fully reveal an individual's personality or the entirety of a discipline. However, repeating these exchanges many times enables members to predict and imagine each other's thoughts and ideas. They might do something to be like this like machine learning to anticipate, understanding the mechanisms of thinking within someone, or approximating through someone they know who shares similar thoughts.

Interestingly, when discussing researchers' traits, the focus is often not on the technical aspects of research or issues related to the content of discussions, but rather on more personal and character-driven aspects. For instance, questions such as whether researcher of philosophy have some researchers they aspire to be like, whether mathematicians are pleased if someone else solves a problem they are interested in, or whether chemists have problems they all wish to solve, dominate the discourse. While it might seem more direct to ask about research or discussion-related topics, these might not be helpful when the topic changes. Understanding someone's thought process on a topic unfamiliar to oneself can be hard. When we focus on understanding how people think, it might be seen as consuming time a lot, but actually it is efficient to ask about the issues common to many people, by this imaging similar persons from among your acquaintances, or how the other person think become easier. Once one understands the way of thinking about general and common issues, it will be relatively easy to infer the way of thinking about each discussion topic from there. The members of the Kanda Lab are not consciously adopting this method. No one was saying they were doing it in this way, and no one was able to verbalize it. It seems that they have found a method that has worked well from experience and are unconsciously using it.

Considering this perspective, when thinking about interdisciplinary collaborative research, there appears to be significant value in focusing on the nature, thought processes, and values of researchers from different areas rather than solely on research topics. Traditionally, when comparing two disciplines or contemplating their integration, the natural approach has been to compare the research subjects they deal with. However, merely comparing research subjects limits the understanding of interdisciplinary integration to changes in research topics alone. This way could not reach the potential for fundamental innovations such as generating new perspectives and ways of thinking by abandoning some aspects of existing disciplines.

We then consider which characteristics to focus on, in comparing researchers across research areas. If one wants to understand the researcher discussing with the person, and for the sake one is willing to compare oneself and the researcher, or researcher and some persons one and the researcher know, one should focus on the characteristics of the people that easily reflect a person's way of thinking and that make it easy to find differences from other people. In other words, it is better to focus on characteristics that vary greatly from person to person. However, if one seeks a more general comparison, such as comparing researchers in some research areas and those in the other areas, it would be prudent to focus on characteristics that are likely universally present in the areas, based on some solid reasoning. In this sense, asking whether a researcher admires certain other researchers may be inappropriate in this situation. Conversely, in computer science, the characteristic that researchers often have interests to the methodology of solving problems more than solving the problems themselves, is reasonable to be considered as somewhat valid, since computer science often includes the study of methods for solving problems taken from other disciplines. Researchers in literature might be more interested in deeply analyzing individual works or authors rather than adopting a big data approach that looks at average behaviors from large datasets, since researchers usually thoroughly analyze one article or an author, in literature. If these characteristics or hypotheses were purely derived from thought processes about disciplinary features and not grounded in reality, their validity remains questionable. The members of the Kanda Lab found out such traits of research areas through mutual observations during discussions, and each researcher recalled other researchers in one's own field that they knew, and came up with a certain degree of understanding, thus many members feel some level of validity in the traits. The examples of computer science and literature mentioned above are also some of the traits that emerged in this way at the Kanda Lab.

Generally speaking, it would be difficult to compare things using such highly abstract concepts or to discuss them in an unwavering and universal manner. It might be some issues that each researcher and each research community implicitly share. However, the method of thinking about this can be explicitly proposed. As with the varying definitions of AI, which exists as a solid concept despite differences, the variation in the nature of researchers across fields could become a universally considered and solid concept within academia, serving as a powerful force in advancing interdisciplinary integration. An instance is the above method of comparing academic fields from the above perspective and way of thinking, and it can be carried out generally.

When considering interdisciplinary research, it becomes apparent that focusing not only on research topics but also on the characteristics, thought processes, and values of researchers from various fields has considerable merit. Traditionally, the comparison between two disciplines, or their integration, has been focused on their respective research subjects. However, simply comparing research subjects constrains the perspective to mere changes in topics, overlooking the potential for significant innovations, such as breaking away from traditional disciplinary constraints or fostering new ways of thinking.

When assessing researchers across different fields, it is crucial to determine which characteristics should be emphasized. If the goal is to understand the researcher present, it may be more effective to focus on traits that reveal their thought processes and distinguish them from others, which are highly individualized. On the other hand, if a broader comparison is sought, it is advisable to concentrate on attributes that are widely regarded as inherent to the discipline. For instance, the inquiry into whether a researcher admires certain others may not be appropriate. Conversely, in computer science, where interest may lie more in the methods of solving problems than in the solutions themselves, this trait can be considered somewhat valid. Literature researchers might find themselves more engaged in in-depth analysis of specific works or authors, rather than a big data approach that seeks patterns in large datasets. While these characteristics or hypotheses might seem to stem merely from disciplinary features, their validity is questionable unless they are rooted in empirical observations. These traits have been identified through discussions among the Kanda Lab members, reflecting a reasonable consensus among peers within the same discipline.

Comparing such abstract concepts poses a challenge in achieving discussions with steadfast generality. These concepts are likely shared implicitly among researchers or within research communities. However, it is possible to explicitly propose methods of thinking about this. For example, similar to that the word AI exists as a solid concept despite its definition varies a lot according to the cases and persons, if the differences in researchers' traits across disciplines, while fluctuating among individuals and communities, become being recognized as a universally accepted and stable concept within academia, it becomes a significant driver for efficiently advancing interdisciplinary collaborations.

6 Independence of Concept Formaining and Questioning Separating from Research Results

Most researchers spend overwhelmingly more time on the research itself than on formulating questions. Moreover, the focus of their questioning tends to be limited to one's own research area or research topic. If one aims to achieve research outcomes within a limited time, naturally, the questions formulated are confined to one's own research area. The capacity to generate new perspectives, values, and ideas is, unfortunately, used only within a very limited scope.

Many researchers must possess strong capabilities in formulating questions. Creating new perspectives and questions is not an easy task, and requires high competence. Expertise and knowledge alone are not sufficient to generate new viewpoints and ideas, thus the ability to formulate questions and expertise are considered somewhat independent of each other. Formulating questions involves using one's knowledge, concepts, and values just to think. To nurture a good research question, it is necessary to validate and explore hypotheses through surveys or preliminary experiments, but initially, it only requires thinking, without the need for costly operations such as large experimental equipment. For example, in collaborative research between corporations and universities, university researchers often provide good perspectives and ideas for the problems faced by the corporations, while practical considerations may be lacking. Also in discussions at the Kanda Laboratory, participants of the discussions frequently present valuable opinions based on perspectives that the speaker never thought about. Structuring things, modeling, discovering overlooked points of interest, and forming perceptions are essential thinking activities common across many fields of research and can be considered a researcher's forte.

Formulating a good research question is often crucial for conducting successful research. No matter how diligently one engages in research activities, it is difficult to achieve good results without good research questions. The evaluation of research is primarily based on its outcomes. The formulation of the question itself is seldom the main focus of evaluation, except perhaps when grant applications are assessed. We might see a certain inefficiency in the fact that although formulating questions holds a vital role in research, it is rarely evaluated only as an item of good research outcome.

We could observe that research communities might have a lack of research questions. Recently, there is frequent mention of a scarcity of research resources, budgets, staff, and time, which is said to be contributing to the decline of Japan's research capabilities. However, there is little discussion on whether an adequate supply of research resources would lead to a dramatic improvement in research outcomes. To test this, we hypothetically asked several researchers if doubling all their resources, including budget, staff, time, and also your energy and passion, would double your research outcomes. Theoretically, an increase in resources should reduce opportunity losses and potentially double the research outcomes. Yet, while some said their outcomes would more than double, many estimated only a small increase, like a 1.3-fold increase. After further questioning about what is the reason not to be double, several researchers cited many kinds of practical constraints. After removing all such barriers to get the essential reason, finally, they often say that there is a lack of ideas, and research plans; they have less thought on what to do. If researchers had many research questions and research plans in mind, it would not take this long. Therefore, just as there is a shortage of resources, there seems to be a deficiency in research questions as well.

We think that this scarcity can be addressed by facilitating the circulation of research questions. In general, research questions are considered to be the property of the individual researcher. In other words, a research question belongs to the researcher who made the question, and if the question is much conceptual, the researcher oneself will be recognized as someone deeply concerning to the issues of the question. We propose to treat questions such that they exist independent from who made them or who study them that is not similar to general view of research questions as belonging to someone. In other words, the idea is that the person who studies a question does not have to be the same person who made the question, and the question does not belong to the person who made it. This kind of thinking is relatively common in mathematics, we want to accelerate this. Activate research activities that involve simply creating research questions, as well as research activities that involve studying research questions received from others. We want the research question itself to be distributed like a commodity, from the creator to the user.

Discussions at the Kanda Lab have generated a variety of interesting research questions, perspectives, and ideas, encompassing a unique worldview. These have not only stimulated the members of the Kanda Lab but also many researchers visited at the Kanda Lab. By collecting, publishing, and distributing these research questions and related concepts, many researchers could be inspired and acquire new challenges to tackle, and also significantly upgrading their own research concepts. The initiative to create a problem catalog in the AFSA project originated from such motivations.

This approach can be seen as a separation of questioning and research. Traditionally, research has been seen as starting with the formulation of research questions and proceeding by researching along these questions. The idea discussed here suggests a division of works between formulating questions and conducting the actual research. As researchers vary in their strengths, both in research and in formulating questions, it is beneficial for individuals to focus on what they excel at, enhancing the overall quality. Moreover, if questions are widely circulated, it will facilitate better matching between questions and researchers, potentially leading to more high-quality and efficient research.

Gathering such questions and publishing are likely to be cost-effective as it primarily involves researchers from various fields coming together to discuss and articulate their queries. Research questions are then formulated and then documented. The main resource required is the researchers' time, and efficient methods for interdisciplinary discussions have already been developed within this project. However, there are several difficulties. Many researchers formulate questions primarily for their own studies and may feel a strong sense of ownership over the questions they develop, even if they do not intend to research them themselves. This could lead to strong resistance to permit the others to research or modify their questions. There is also the issue of credit and authorship.

For instance, if a published question leads to significant research findings, should the originator of the question be credited in the resulting paper? Should they be mentioned only in references or acknowledged in the acknowledgements? In collaborative research, such issues would be already negotiated before the research commences, but if only the question is published beforehand, there might be no existing relationship between the researcher and the questioner, complicating negotiations. If the question has only been referenced, it could be cited in the bibliography, but it is unclear how similar a study must be to warrant authorship. Additionally, there is the potential for "question terrorism," where numerous questions are generated mechanically and preemptively claimed, blocking other research avenues. Currently, since questions are not typically subject to valuation or rights, such terrorism does not occur; however, if questions were to become a source of profit or rights, this could change.

Despite the challenges, the potential benefits of circulating research questions are significant. Similar to how software and web content are made available without predefined usage, effective rules have been established in these areas. For instance, free software often comes with predefined rights, which could be a model for public question sites. Such sites could define rules for referencing questions, and only those agreeing with these rules would publish their questions there. Another way is to prepare several templates of rules, allowing questioners to select the rules so that how their questions may be used. There is also a need of giving no rights to research questions to prevented rampant rights claims of submitted questions. The exact form of these regulations remains to be determined, but question circulation could potentially exist in some form.

In several research fields, the circulation of questions is already partially practiced. For example, in mathematics and computational sciences, open problem workshops are frequently held where at the beginning of the workshop, researchers present interesting questions that could potentially be solved with relatively short time, and the rest of the time is spent collaboratively addressing these questions. Various ideas and approaches are exchanged, and it is not uncommon for several questions to be solved during the workshop. Discussions and listings of unsolved problems or future challenges are also common in conferences and publications. However, these problems do not usually offer immediate solutions and may take decades to resolve or serve to direct the research area, thus not providing fascinating references for researchers starting their studies. Nonetheless, the value of spreading engaging questions to aid research is already recognized, and the circulation of questions might fit the desires of academic communities.

7 Types for Various Understandings

In this section, we would like to consider the types of understanding ways of researchers possibly due to the cultures of the research area, based on the observations of the members of the Kanda Lab. In discussions at the Kanda Laboratory, we sometimes observe that some participants struggle to grasp the topic being discussed. It would be sometimes solved by a simple one question, but sometimes even many questions could not lead to a satisfactory understanding, on the other hand. Discussions often progress before one has understood, resulting in difficulty catching up. Although one might eventually comprehend the point after several minutes, by then the discussion has moved significantly forward. However, these issues do not stem from an inability to understand someone's explanation or opinion per se. Understanding the context or meaning of the explanations or discussions is not sufficient to adequately follow the discussion.

What then is missing? When asked, participants offer various responses, such as "I can't grasp the feelings," "I don't understand why it is necessary," or "I can't think the topic from the other person's perspective." These could be rephrased as I did not become capable of "thinking" about the explanations and opinions presented. This phrasing seems to align with the sensations described by the participants who answered. Being able to think about a topic means that, for example, being able to construct an argument from the same facts, explain the matter from different perspectives, adding new values to it, or making decisions according to the values. It involves not merely acquiring knowledge, but also understanding the surrounding values, purposes, and connections to other concepts. To distinguish these two levels of understanding, the first is termed 'understanding of meaning,' and the second 'understanding for thinking.' Moreover, being in a state where one can think is referred to as "being able to think."

Participants in the discussion seem to implicitly recognize that there are two phases of understanding. They pose questions to facilitate their own thinking, and respondents offer answers to aid the questioner's cognitive process. Despite these efforts, it often takes time to reach getting sufficiently understood. It would be because the state of understanding the questioner is unconsciously aiming for is often significantly different from what the respondent assumes. Inquiring among the laboratory members about what it means to be in a state of understanding, or "being able to think" state, revealed that there are several patterns.

The first pattern is to look at and understand directly the issues and facts that are given by the speaker in the discussion, and think the issues by applying the background knowledge that the persons already knew, and the rules that are obtained by abduction with the speaker's words. This would be similar to thinking logically. They accept the facts and issues presented as they are, without getting why and how. The facts and issues are accepted as axioms or theorems, and the persons apply other laws to them for reasoning. The persons define that the issue is a problem in one's mind if the speaker says so, even though the person cannot understand why the issue is a problem, or how much the issue is important. For example, when university researchers and corporate personnel had a meeting to discuss a joint research project, researchers, who are unfamiliar with the corporate intricate disciplines, first accept the current corporate efforts as factual. The researchers then apply their knowledge of business activities, economics, and the marketing to speculate on how things might work in the corporate setting. Understanding with acquiring the rules from the speaker's words but without underlying speaker's thought is somewhat akin to machine learning or transfer learning, hence we refer to this pattern as the "Machine Learning Type."

The second method involves finding something in one's knowledge, which is often a typical example, and is similar to the issues given by the speaker. Then, they think the issues by approximating the something. For example, in a joint research project with university researchers and a company, if the company wants to analyze customer data, one might recall another company B that might have similar interests in data analysis, and so that one can think the issues surrounding of what are explained now, by referring and imagining the mindset and values in the company B. There might be inevitably differences, since it is only an approximation. One often identifies these potential differences by refining the approximation by additional information given by the speaker and also asking questions. We call this method "Example Approximation Type."

The third method involves recalling a different concept with the same structure in response to what is being explained. For instance, activity and evaluation of employees aim to increase the company's profits can be considered to partially isomorphic to university researcher's activity and evaluation by journal papers. They differ on persons, roles and objectives, but there is a partial structural isomorphism. This partial structural isomorphism is used to infer and understand the context of the current explanation given by the speaker. This method is called "Isomorphic Transcription Type." Similar to the Example Approximation, it involves asking about the differences, but since the structure is the same while the specifics greatly differ, one tends to use parables and rephrasing from different perspectives to convey isomorphism, leading to relatively advanced questions.

The fourth method digs down to the fundamental mechanisms underlying what the speaker explained, to reach a level of understanding necessary to form the speaker's thoughts. In any issues, values, interests, and decisions are given by humans. Thus we consider that the reasons, importance and other issues behind the explanation are common, at the deep level, whenever the topic comes from companies, governments, or academics. Since we are the same Homo sapiens, we should have the same or similar mechanisms of thoughts and emotions in the mind. Thus the reasons, importance and other issues should come from somewhat consistent in deep levels in the mind, and thus reasoning based on this mechanism can be useful. To understand the mechanism, they frequently ask the questions that are needed to be deeply explored, such as why you evaluate in that way, why they are conscious of particular issues or objectives, and other fundamental aspects. We call this method "Mechanism Construction Type."

When participants' understanding does not progress smoothly in the Kanda Lab, it often seems that the type of understanding of participants and that the speaker assumed for the participants is different. For example, if the questioner is trying to understand through Mechanism Construction Type, while the speaker assumes a Machine Learning Type, the speaker would be confused because it is difficult to understand why such questions are needed to be asked. This can lead to irrelevant and lengthy explanations or even completely off-target responses. Similarly, if the questioner is aiming for Example Approximation Type, but the speaker is assuming Mechanism Construction Type, the speaker might end up explaining the entire background at length.

Another aspect of these misunderstandings involves the starting point for thought processes. For someone in computer science, unraveling the structure of data holds significance and can easily become a starting point for thinking. However, for those from other disciplines, the significance of this might be hard to imagine. This is due to differences in expertise, but observing discussions at the Kanda Lab leads us to consider that such differences also exist in people's ways of thinking.

For example, while some people can easily accept the purpose and value of another's perspective, others find it difficult to engage unless they clarify the fundamental thoughts and emotions driving these issues. When faced with ambiguous terms or concepts, some are able to accept these without clarifying the meanings, and think along the explanations while listening, whereas some others must interpret them thoroughly to understand, which might lead to failing to catch up the discussion. For example, when a person proposes to think this issue from another viewpoint since the current discussion is ill-focused, someone may need to understand "what means ill-focused, why it is ill-focused", and thus the person cannot get how to think about the issues from new viewpoints.

Members of the Kanda Lab engage sometimes in Machine Learning Type, and sometimes in mechanism Construction Type, demonstrating flexibility in their approach to understanding and get enabled to think. They seem to adeptly combine and integrate these types to understand the explanations. On the other hand, there are noticeable individual differences in the starting points of their thoughts. Some persons consistently encounter difficulties with understanding objectives and values, while some others struggle with the ambiguity of words and terminologies. Additionally, there are those who cannot conceptualize without meticulously dissecting organizational or community structures, and some others who require an in-depth understanding of seemingly unconscious human behaviors. We could observe that Kanda Lab members select type of understanding such as Machine Learning Type and Example Approximation Type, according to their traits explained above, to engage in discussions.

In interdisciplinary discussions, the commonality of one's knowledge with another's are often large when it concerns with principal thoughts like motivations, objectives and importance. We have significant differences in expertise in interdisciplinary discussions, which may seem self-evident. Therefore, engaging in discussions on these aspects is the most direct way to be able to think the issues. Indeed, discussions at the Kanda Lab frequently start from this perspective, and even if they eventually delve into more technical and specialized topics, the initial focus often revolves around issues such as objectives, values, and thought processes.

For members of the Kanda Lab, to be able to think itself is a source of joy, and engaging in discussions about the explanations and opinions of others under the state of being able to think is an enjoyable activity, this is expressed by many members. Conversely, when one is not to be able to think, the joy and enthusiasm for participating in discussions diminish, making it difficult to foster a genuine interest in the discussion. When most participants find the discussion enjoyable, it of course tends to be more creative and progress as well.

On the other hand, even when one is able to think, whether good ideas emerge or one can engage with enthusiasm and enjoyment may depend on different factors, such as the ability to empathize with others or finding interest in the topic. In these four types of understanding, even with getting Machine Learning Type understanding, it can be hard to connect the current context of the explanations with one's own knowledge in a meaningful and valuable way, if the reasons for and the value of what is explained is not clear. This difficulty is similar in the case of Example Approximation Type. However, for Mechanism Construction Type understanding, it becomes easier to identify and assess new and interesting topics from the perspectives of value and interest, because the mechanisms of evaluation and interest are clear. Once understood in this type, we can robustly drive the discussion forward, generating many interesting ideas and opinions from important perspectives.

Observations and analyses of those discussed at the Kanda Lab underscore the importance of participants being in a state of being able to think about the current topics during discussions. If one seeks to replicate the dynamics of the Kanda Lab's discussions elsewhere, the presenters should design their presentations in a way that quickly brings participants to that state. Generally, when presenting research or similar topics, efforts are made to ensure the content is fully comprehended, aiming to clarify the most difficult and complicated parts, so that it maximizes understanding across all aspects of the discussion. However, when we aim to make them understand deeply to be able to think, optimal strategy should be maximizing each participant's deepest understanding or empathy, even though some parts are not clear. Moreover, the parts of the presentations that might be understood deeply by the participants should appear as early as possible in the presentation.

For many persons, comprehensible issues given by explanations are often those having similarities or resonating with the person's prior knowledge, making it easier to relate to. Since there are large differences in expertise in interdisciplinary discussions or public lectures to citizens, this similarity may involve sharing what researchers think about intriguing, interests, and challenges on the research. Therefore, ideally, presentations should first highlight these engaging aspects, or at least provide a minimal preamble before doing so. This strategy is totally different from traditional structured and storied presentation designs, and aligns naturally with the observations and hypotheses mentioned above. Indeed, when engaging in casual conversations, it is not uncommon to talk about what was enjoyable or surprising before delving into surrounding details, often making the conversation more engaging than a flawless but sequential explanation. Thus, this conversational style might make audiences of the presentations relaxed and enjoyable.

The observations and hypotheses discussed above guide a strategy of how participants should listen to presentations to understand well. If participants can quickly become able to think, they will find the presentation more engaging and their understanding of the remainder of the presentation will be enhanced. To achieve this, one should try to connect the presentation content with personal interests early on, or to understand and empathize with the presenter's perspective, to find intrigue and wonder in their thoughts, and so on. A simple way to do this is by asking questions during the presentation. Choosing topics of personal interest that seem relevant, and asking questions about connections, commonalities, the presenter's feelings, and what they find challenging or interesting can be effective.

This approach to questioning is aimed at connecting with one's interests rather than merely seeking clarification on unclear parts of the explanation. This means that even if some parts of the presenter's talk are semantically unclear, linking them to personal interests takes precedence over immediate semantic understandings. In interdisciplinary discussions, the content of explanations is often not fully comprehensible due to differences in expertise. Actually, in the Kanda Lab discussions, the initial focus is often on listening to the presenter's insights and connecting them to personal interests, rather than deepening logical or semantic understanding. Furthermore, even skipping a detailed understanding of meaning and logic can still lead to lively discussions and the emergence of new insights or concepts.

In presentations, understanding the meaning and logic to grasp the research content communicated by the presenter is traditionally prioritized. Questions are asked to aid this understanding, with queries about related or expanded content and connections to one's own research typically following. However, this common approach does not necessarily lead to fruitful discussions, at least not in the context of interdisciplinary practices like those at the Kanda Lab. Changing perspectives on how presentations are approached is crucial in developing effective discussion technique.

Acknowledgements We would like to thank the members of the Kanda Lab, Yuka Takedomi, Kouki Suetsugu, Tomoaki Abuku, Kazuhiro Kurita, Towa Suda, Tomohiro Matsuda, Kazuki Maeyama, Kanami Sugiyama, Ryuya Hora, Susumu Hashimoto, Giulia Punzi, Yuta Yamamoto, Shizuko Kuwata, and Aya Gotoda, who discussed many matters for the contexts of this article, and supported in writing this article. This project was partly supported by JSPS Grant-in-Aid for Transformative Research Areas (A) 20H05962.

Methodologies for Fruitful Interdisciplinary Discussions

Takeaki Uno

Abstract This chapter describes the methodology for conducting high-quality and effective interdisciplinary integration. It also describes the methodology for making interdisciplinary discussion forums and events attractive to researchers and practitioners with low barriers to participation. These techniques were developed by observing the actions and behaviors of AFSA project members and those around the project, when discussing and interacting in interdisciplinary settings, finding commonalities from them, and verbalizing them. These methods range from how to make good communication and ask questions, to how to understand the research of the other field, how to introduce yourself, and how to design and manage a discussion meeting. The reason why interdisciplinary integration is said to be difficult is probably because of the wide variety of techniques and know-how required to solve it. In addition, these techniques essentially overlap with the methodology of the research itself in each researcher's field of expertise, so developing interdisciplinary integration techniques will also lead to strengthening research capabilities in one's own research field.

1 Introduction

This chapter describes the technological methodology of human ways of thinking and behaving, based on observations of the activities of members at the Kanda Lab, with the aim of promoting interdisciplinary integration, mutual understanding between different fields, and high-quality active and smooth discussions.

It is generally said that conducting interdisciplinary research and formulating research questions are difficult. Many factors have been identified as the reasons for this, including differences in values and ways of thinking, and the lack of opportunities to meet researchers from different research areas. On the other hand, the research questions that arise from interdisciplinary fusion, or the disciplines of new research areas, are often not so complex or difficult to understand. It is difficult to create the

T. Uno (✉)
National Institute of Informatics, Tokyo, Japan
e-mail: uno@nii.ac.jp

S. Minato et al. (eds.), *Algorithmic Foundations for Social Advancement*,
https://doi.org/10.1007/978-981-96-0668-9_6

research questions themselves, and it is also difficult to realize them and to pursue research based on their value in the current situation, but the explanation itself is not so difficult. It is often relatively easy to understand what is behind the questions, such as where the ideas for the fusion come from, where the source of this fusion is, and how it came about. This often leads to the feeling that fusion research does not provide much value. However, in reality, if the research question is to pioneer a new field, the research questions that are first born or tackled should always be simple and elementary, since the field has never been studied before. They should not be technical or extend existing accumulated research results. In other words, perhaps the simplicity of the questions is the essence of interdisciplinary research in the first place, and the difficulty of interdisciplinary research does not come from the complexity of the research questions or the high level of skill. Difficulties in interdisciplinary research include environmental issues such as a lack of opportunities, but even in a situation where there are no major environmental problems, interdisciplinary research, discussion, and questioning remain difficult. Just as research activities that require a lot of thought and trial and error are difficult, conducting interdisciplinary research itself is difficult. Moreover, unlike research activities, we have more difficulty on interdisciplinary fusion research that we usually have no researchers engaging interdisciplinary fusion research, or the person's research activities that can be referred as good cases. This point is different from the difficulty of usual research activities.

We, the members of the Kanda Lab, also tried to raise research questions by interdisciplinary discussions, but at first it did not go so well. Even after long discussions, we often ended up in vain, and we felt a great sense of futility. However, as time passed, six months to a year, new things, values, and perspectives were increasingly found in the discussions. The researchers who visit the Kanda Lab are diverse, and thus it is probably not because they have gained knowledge of a specific field. It is true that they have become accustomed to discussing with researchers from different fields, but this accustomedness used here gives no detailed explanation. It is probably not just a matter of feelings. When observing the discussions at the Kanda Lab, one notices that the behavior, way of thinking in discussions, and the way they communicate and understand things of the members of the Kanda Lab have changed. In other words, it is thought that the members have realized and acquired that "it should be good to think in this way," and "I should behave in this way." In other words, it is thought that at least, one can become better at how to discuss in interdisciplinary fusion research, how to think about and communicate things, how to understand, and how to manage discussions.

The next issue would be how we can become good at it. There are many articles of such interdisciplinary discussions and exchange meetings, but they are mainly records such as the activities done by participants and organizers of interdisciplinary fusion research, and a strategy to make the interdisciplinary discussion and the observations. There are also descriptions of what purpose they had or what effect they were aiming for, but most of them are abstract and vague, such as "to create deep exchanges." There are few records that aim to have some effect on more specific and detailed problems that are faced when actually having interdisciplinary discussions. When planning and managing something based on some kind of problem awareness, there are a wide variety of barriers to make it successful. Also, when some kind of mechanism, or even just trick, is implemented for the plan, there are many factors that can be considered for the effect and cause of that mechanism. The more detailed the description of the plan, the more difficult it becomes for the reader to understand which specific barriers were solved by which parts of the mechanism, and how to deal with them. This is perhaps only natural, given that the more detailed the description of an individual, the less general it becomes.

In other words, each project is well thought out and run with a kind of art to make it a success. Similar problems seem to be solved in unique or sometimes ad-hoc ways based on the talents and the ways of thinking of the individuals who tackle them. Because it depends on the talents of the individuals, it is difficult to understand what the essential difficulties of the problem are, and what solutions have been given to them. The problem awareness and the solution are described in a complex and comprehensive manner. It is not clear which activities are effective for which part of the problem and why. People who read the description of the case can get inspiration, but it is difficult to understand what can be done to specifically improve which part of the problem they are facing. A more detailed explanation is needed, using simple and universal words and concepts, about what can be done to improve the results for each individual barrier. Even if only a part of the individual's problem awareness can be solved, it is important to extract from the problem awareness a part that is likely to be common to many people's problem awareness, create a concrete prescription for it, and approach it in such a way as to create a technology that can be done by many people.

Thinking about it, it seems that computer science has been continuously trying to understand other research fields and industry, and to make interdisciplinary fusion research. What makes computer science, especially information mathematics, different from mathematics is that it does not just deal with mathematics, but mathematics related to the world or society. For this reason, computer scientists have engaged in research activities by discussing with researchers and practitioners from many areas of academy and society, structuring and modeling their knowledge and concerns, incorporating them into the mathematical problems they are studying, developing techniques to handle them computationally, and deploying them to the world and society. To do this, it would have been necessary to understand the values and concepts of others and other areas, and to integrate them with the concepts of computer science. However, without a guidebook for such understanding and integration, and without an opportunity to learn it, individual researchers have no choice but to hone their techniques and know-how through trial and error. We believe that every time they confront people from the other fields, they have repeated similar trial and error to gain know-how, but the know-how they have gained has not been clearly passed on to their successors, and has been shared as a vague tacit knowledge that exists within the research area or research laboratory. However, if many people are performing similar actions in the same way, then we could build technology from the commonalities of actions by clarifying and verbalizing those commonalities so that many people can use them. Constructing technology allows people to acquire the same abilities without the trouble and time spent by their predecessors. Avoiding the same faults by verbalizing the past fails is one of the goals that academics aim for.

Articles about the skills related to linguistic and cognitive actions done in interdisciplinary discussions such as conversation, thinking, and building human relationships, are often written by a person with high these skills based on the person's experiences and thoughts, or by some writers who gave interviews to the persons having high skills. In other words, as with the above, it is likely that this is often personal. There are many technical guides and introductory books in this format, such as how to have a good conversation or know-how about running a company well. On the other hand, considering that such introductory books are not treated as a standard for improving skills, it can be seen that they are not a decisive factor in improving skills. Inefficiency of such books would come from the difficulty of verbalizing one's own actions and thoughts, and the difficulty of recognizing the difference in one's perspective and points of focus between oneself and others. It is easy to abstract one's own behavior and own thoughts because they are one's own actions, but on the other hand, because one can understand them in detail, there are many directions in which one can generalize and abstract them. What commonalities and hidden meanings one finds in each of one's own actions are therefore determined by one's subjectivity, or in other words, arbitrariness.

The meaning of what, why, how, and what to pay attention to when performing an action for a specific purpose changes greatly depending on how the action is perceived and valued, such as which part of the action is important and which part affects where. Since the way of perceiving and valuing differs greatly from person to person, the description of the same action will be very different from one individual to another, and even if one acts according to someone else's description, one will not necessarily get the same effect, and in fact, one will often lose it. Even with the same method, the practical aspects of the technique, such as what is ingenious, what to pay attention to, and when to use it, often differ greatly from one individual to another. It is often said that it is difficult to pass on tacit knowledge in the workplace or factory, but this is not only because tacit knowledge is difficult to put into words, but also because it relies heavily on the subjectivity of the individual, making it difficult to share the effects with others. This would also be true when one interviews a specific person to find out their skills and know-how. The same thing happens when one asks a factory worker or a manager about their tacit knowledge about their work. What one finds out is not necessarily useful to others. Unless it is very specific knowledge about a work process, what one thinks is important or amazing is unlikely to immediately become directly useful knowledge to others.

The techniques of the Kanda Lab described in this chapter were formed by observing the behavior of multiple Kanda Lab members and finding commonalities. The members of the Kanda Lab had trial and error using various methods for various matters related to thinking and language activities, such as conversation, thinking, interaction, understanding, and communication, with researchers and practitioners from different fields. Many of them are ineffective and fail, but they use the successful ones as a clue to create new methods that they consider to be effective and make them their own methodology. Then, after several months or even tens of months, each individual acquires a certain kind of technique. Perhaps because they communicate with each other in the same place, there are many commonalities and seem to be similar in such techniques. On the other hand, the techniques that each individual possesses are very unique.

Among the activities that are arrived at after a lot of trial and error, among those that are thought to be effective, we find actions and methods with high commonality, and verify them through discussion among members to clarify their form. The discussion techniques described in this chapter were obtained in this way. Therefore, there is no guarantee that they will be always effective when practiced in any places other than the Kanda Lab. By looking for commonalities among many cases, we have tried to make them as general as possible, but they are not completely universal, and we do not claim to be. Although it is merely a generalization of individual specific cases, we believe that the number of cases makes it possible to have concreteness that can be applied in situations other than the Kanda Lab.

The following sections explain these technical methodologies. In Sect. 2, "Open Discussion for Broad and Deep Thinking," we present the ideal of a discussion format that naturally encourages free and high-quality ideas without barriers for participants, and in Sect. 3, "Discussion with Bridging Partial Curiosity," we propose a method to allow participants to participate in a way that matches their level of motivation and to hold a high-quality discussion overall. In Sect. 4, "Curiosity Driven Designs for Interdisciplinary Discussion," we present the basic ideal that makes such discussions and seminars attractive and satisfying for a variety of researchers. In Sect. 5, "Setting Topics and Questions for Active Discussion," we explain how to create a topic when setting up a specific discussion meeting based on that ideal so that the participants could discuss smoothly, lively and deeply, and in Sect. 6, "Inner Side Self-introduction for Curiosity Connection," we introduce a methodology for self-introduction that allows participants to smoothly understand the each other's thought and values and become having interests in each other. In Sect. 7, "High-level Linguistic Activity; Paraphrasing, Metaphor and Seeing-as," we analyze the linguistic activities used for understanding and explaining used in discussions, and in Sect. 8, "Questioning for Deep Understanding Background," we explain how to ask questions to gain a deeper understanding of things in fields in which one is not familiar. In Sect. 9, "Salmon Interviewing for Deep Understanding," we explain a method of interviewing to understand the structure of the one's thoughts about research ideas. In Sect. 10, "Constructing and Reconstructing Research Concepts by Interviewing," we explain how to apply the interview method to clarify and verbalize one's own or someone else's research concept. Finally, in Sect. 11, "Description and Logic for New Discipline," we propose a method for describing the techniques extracted from such practice and also practice itself.

2 Open Discussion for Broad and Deep Thinking

When discussing topics interdisciplinary, it is often said that having an open discussion is crucial. What is the definition and meaning of an "open discussion" in precise terms may not be clear, but generally, it would imply that everyone feels that one can participate and express various opinions in the discussion. In workshops designed to facilitate such discussions with persons of diverse backgrounds, we often take care to ensure that no one's opinions are dismissed, everyone speaks equally, and as many views as possible are included in the summary of the discussion. In other words, this implies a level of safety where neither individuals nor their views are attacked, fairness in participation and engagement, and attention to ensuring that all opinions are considered without being ignored.

The Kanda Laboratory also has many discussions that could be considered being open. We could see discussions in other places that might be considered being open. However, it does not appear that norms or rules are consciously upheld as described above; instead, open discussions seem to be shaped by other reasons or mechanisms. For instance, the latter three aspects, refraining from negating others, everyone speaking, and including everyone's opinions in summaries, might not be practiced or emphasized at these discussions. Rather, these three requirements seem to be set to enhance the quality of the individual's experience during participation, since organizers may highly consider the experiences of the participants in the discussion. Meanwhile, the quality and experience of discussions at the Kanda Lab are perceived as high, with frequent feedback from participants stating that the discussions were fruitful, engaging, and beneficial. The quality of discussions at the Kanda Lab seems to be crafted through different reasons and mechanisms than those typically found in general workshops. We therefore, based on observations of discussions at the Kanda Lab, consider what may be leading to the quality of discussions, which may correspond to what people say about open discussion.

Observing discussions at the Kanda Lab, we often see negative comments on someone's ideas. However, those who receive such comments do not feel attacked. Considering that most participants are experts in their fields and have confidence in their thoughts, it might be concluded that they have much confidence in their thoughts, and so negative opinions are acceptable. However, this does not explain why they are not perceived as attacks. A closer observation of the content and motives of negative opinions reveals that these are often questions arising from a desire to understand the speaker's thoughts or opinions intended to refine the speaker's views, based on an understanding of their intentions and values.

Consider a discussion about finding ways to improve operations in a company. When a participant proposes an idea, a question like "I don't think that's good; why do you think so?" is not rejecting the idea but asking for its reason and rationale. More precisely, the questioner wants to understand the reasoning and potentially come to think about the merit in the opinion, and might want to be able to think in the same way. If another opinion states, "I think your idea is based on this focal point, but considering that point, I believe it won't work for this reason," it may be critical of the feasibility and interpretability of the idea itself, but it acknowledges and considers the proposer's perspective or values. Common to both is that the speaker's focal points and values are respected and not negated. In contrast, outright rejections like "Your opinion is trivial/There's no point in considering such things" can be seen as negating both the opinion itself and the speaker's presented perspective or values. In discussions at the Kanda Lab, respect and interests are paid to opinions that seem to diverge from the central point or those that one does not understand or that differ from one's own values. For incomprehensible points, various questions are asked to grasp the values, motivations, problem awareness, and aims in an understandable form. When values are understood, the validity and feasibility of the opinion are examined and commented upon. In both cases, attention is paid to the person's ideas and values who expressed the opinion, showing interest and consideration.

Another perspective on open discussions is whether the purpose or topic of the discussion is clearly defined or whether a conclusion is required. When the goal is clearly defined and there is a relatively strong demand to achieve it, the discussion naturally becomes directed, and opinions that do not align with this direction tend to receive less attention. Some participants may feel barriers for saying something, except for who are most likely to contribute to achieving the objective in the discussion. On the other hand, in brainstorming sessions aimed at generating ideas, the goal is to produce as many ideas as possible and create a list of ideas. In this case, one could say there is no specific direction and format at all. As a middle ground, there are discussion format where the first half of the discussion focuses on generating ideas and expanding the discussion, while the latter half moves towards convergence and summarization. The discussions observed at the Kanda Lab seem different from all of these. When an opinion is expressed, questions are asked to discuss and share the problem awareness and the values with all participants, with translating them into more general, essential explanations. Simultaneously, the value, feasibility, and validity of the opinion are discussed. Once sufficient discussion has taken place, they move on to the next idea. The depth to which each idea or opinion is explored depends on how much inspiration each participant receives from it and whether they feel there might be significant discoveries in related areas. They seem to move on to the next idea or opinion when everyone feels that further discussion is unlikely to yield much more.

If discussions with a concrete purpose and summary are seen as creating one large entity together, brainstorming can be viewed as arranging small, granular ideas side by side. When creating one thing together, it is difficult to deepen individual values due to efficiency concerns. On the other hand, brainstorming does not provide depth. In contrast, discussions at the Kanda Lab are like creating clusters of various sizes together, similar to the results of a cluster analysis in data science. While sufficient depth is achieved for each idea, it often takes a long time. This cluster-like structure of the Kanda Lab's discussions, where each topic born from the discussion achieves sufficient depth, is considered one factor that makes discussion feel open.

3 Discussion with Bridging Partial Curiosity

In the Kanda Laboratory, discussions often arise from casual conversations, seemingly without any pressure. This may be due to everyone being familiar with each other and often staying in the same room, which seems to lower psychological barriers. Indeed, it appears that more discussions occur when just colleagues who are already friends are simply in the same room together, indicating that they are fun to engage in such dialogues.

There is a belief that discussions initiated through casual conversations are highly beneficial, as seen in interactions during tea breaks at conferences or during social gatherings at banquets of conferences. Such casual interactions at poster sessions often yield deeper conversations than formal presentations. People gathering and engaging naturally in discussions tend to be more productive, and it is not uncommon for such interactions to lead to collaborative research projects.

On the other hand, it is extremely difficult to give researchers plenty of time to have conversations in the hope that this kind of fruitful discussions will occur. Since this kind of gain is obtained by chance, expecting luck is too much, which is a big problem in terms of efficiency. Researchers who participate in conversations will also have less motivation to participate if there is little chance of gaining fruit. They prefer to get results more reliably, and would rather pursue their own research than engage in such conversations.

Even if we gather people and hold a workshop just for this purpose, not so many people would join the workshop. Compared to general presentations such as keynote speeches, attending discussions seem to have a higher barrier to participation. Many people are hesitant, feeling obligated to contribute or behave as active participants, which can be pressuring or simply bothersome.

Observing how these discussions start, it typically begins with someone addressing a question or raising an issue to another person. The topic is then laid out for discussion and talked about among two or three individuals initially. As the conversation progresses, more people join in, while others listen in while continuing with their own work. This scenario differs from other workshops in general, in that the topics are smaller and more accessible, participants can join and leave as they like, and there are some participating and some do not.

Upon reflection, participants in general workshops seem to feel that they are always required to be on equal footing, constantly catching up with the discussion in real-time. They are also expected to position themselves as active contributors to the current topic and to have their own opinions ready. This can be a significant burden, and as the discussion progresses in directions that may not align with one's interests, it might become overwhelming and hard to keep up. When one is forced to behave dictated by the flow of the discussion, the person must feel being in uncomfortable place. This great burden is absent in the discussions at the Kanda Lab. We could not observe any other significant differences contributing to the ease of discussion. Hence, we would like to state a hypothesis that easy entry and no constant catch-up pressure would be keys to facilitating relaxed discussions.

Regarding easy entry, one aspect is the way to settle down the topics of discussion. This is described in another section, thus we omit the explanation here. Another aspect is that the discussion is typically advanced by someone who is knowledgeable about the question, answering or responding to it. In the discussions at the Kanda Lab, these persons are corresponding to the persons asking questions, the persons who can answer the questions, or simply the persons being asked the questions. As the conversation progresses between these people, issues are explained one by one, and the people listening around to them begin to understand what is being mentioned and what are the problems. Necessary explanations are provided sequentially, at the necessary time, allowing those listening persons to gradually understand the topic. The respondent becomes gradually able to understand or think about the content of the discussion and the issues in detail, from the respondent's perspective, and as the respondent explains one's understanding, the people around them also become able to think about it in detail. Concurrently, the focal points of the discussion shift to a place or a level of abstractness that everyone can engage with.

Another key point, "no constant catch-up pressure," is that such behaviors are allowed, such as just listening without participating in the discussion, doing one's own work, and dropping in and out of the discussion several times. In other words, one can freely decide one's own attitude toward participation in the discussion, and this is clearly stated to be allowed. One can participate in whatever part of the discussion one likes, as much as one likes, and from whatever distance one likes.

One does not have to concentrate all the time, and one is not forced to do anything. Without an atmosphere in which it is explicitly stated that they are allowed to vary their level of participation, people end up feeling like they are implicitly expected to always participate in the discussion with high concentration. The speakers who express their opinions often feel uncomfortable if there are people who are seeming not to listen to the persons speaking. However, if people are allowed to partially listen to and understand the context of the talk, then the speakers feel naturally drawn to talking to people who are currently actively participating in the discussion.

Furthermore, in general discussions, it is respected not to deny other people's opinions unnecessarily, and not to talk too long when expressing an opinion. In many cases at the Kanda Lab, opinions are not simply affirmed, but their value, motivations, and way of thinking are acknowledged. Comments have been made saying, like "This method may not be effective in terms of its value." In other words, opinions are not being rejected, but comments are given to rather improve the opinion or clarify some ambiguities. Taking a long time for one opinion or explanation is considered to be acceptable as long as they serve this purpose, and are not regarded as bad behaviors.

Furthermore, in general discussions, it is considered not good to have knowledge bias, i.e., some people have much knowledge about the topic of discussion and some quite less. However, in the Kanda Lab, this is rather the norm, and the discussions seem to be more exciting. In lively discussions like the above at the Kanda Lab, other than the time spent discussing highly specialized matters, there is often time spent for explaining someone's own opinion and responding to others. This is done for those who lack sufficient knowledge to acquire the knowledge by asking questions, which are needed for participating in the discussion efficiently. This exchange usually does not take much time and is a small part of the overall discussion. In that sense, it seems that dispersion in knowledge is not so much of a problem.

Furthermore, a lot of attention is paid to the fairness of the participants in general discussions. For example, choose a topic that is equally distant from all participants' professions. On the other hand, such topics are quite often far from everyone's expertise, and no one can provide detailed explanations or deep considerations. The seating arrangement is also fair, with everyone sitting at a similar distance from the center of the table and in the same position and posture. The facilitator often encourages people to speak their opinions, which is to control the discussions so that the opportunities, number of times, and time for speaking are equal.

In such a situation, everyone will feel or misunderstand that they are expected to participate and contribute equally to the discussion, even if they do not have such a purpose or awareness. Also, the person explaining their opinion may expect to be heard equally from everyone, and feel uncomfortable if someone is not listening. They may feel offended if their comments are ignored. In discussions at the Kanda Lab, this kind of fairness does not exist.

Instead of having people who do not seem to be listening to the discussion, there are always one or more people to whom each opinion is addressed. Opinions are being voiced to these people, so as long as these people are listening, understanding, and thinking, it does not matter what other participants are doing. Additionally, participants who are not the recipients of the message do not feel pressured to listen and understand the message since the voices are not directed at them. This is probably one of the reasons why discussions at the Kanda Lab are so lively even when they are not fair.

In fact, not all individual participants have the same level of enthusiasm and interest in the discussion, and each topic has different levels of need and interest. When an argument has a set purpose and achieving that goal is the most important thing, the argument itself becomes the most central entity, so to speak. In that case, participants are implicitly or explicitly expected to contribute to the discussion or purpose of the discussion. However, it is unlikely that participants in a discussion will share the same level of purpose and interest. There may be topics that one is not interested in or finds difficult to understand, and one may not have a strong desire to participate in the discussion in the first place.

In general, especially when participants from different fields gather, or when the relationships between participants are weak, such as when they meet each other for the first time, there is likely to be a great deal of diversity in their awareness of issues and interests. If we try to design discussions in a way that meets the different levels of individual motivations and interests of participants, the ways of participating in discussions will inevitably vary.

Based on observations of the discussions at the Kanda Lab, we would like to develop and propose a systematic method that embraces diverse participation consciousness. This method includes several issues such as the selection of the speaker who gives the topic at the discussion, and design of discussion environments. The details are as follows.

(1) Decide who will present the topic for discussion. A speaker should be a person who has an interest in a certain issue, is aware of a problem, or has some purpose, wants other participants to discuss, and to gain something from the discussion. The speaker can be considered as the originator of the discussion.
(2) The speaker sets the main topic of the discussion. Based on one's own awareness of issues and goals, choosing something that has room for discussion, which is, the topic seems to have much space for research and consideration, and is connected to adjacent issues and related matters, making it easy to think about.
(3) The speaker appoints at least two or more core participants.

    Core participants are chosen as persons who have a certain degree of understanding of the speaker's awareness of the issue, purpose, and expertise, and who can be deeply involved in the discussion.

    Core participants and the speaker serve as persons to be addressed, to which other participants can talk their opinions. Therefore, speakers and core participants should take part in the discussion from the beginning to the end, and try to always understand the content and situation of the discussion. When this becomes mandatory, this gives a big pressure to core participants, thus we ask multiple core participants so that there will be no problem even if there are times when some of them do not understand something or are not at the center of the discussion.
(4) The venue for the discussion consists of a central table, surrounded by desks or chairs. The participants lively participating in the discussion (in most cases the speaker and core participants) should be placed at the center table, and the remaining participants should sit around the periphery. Additionally, online remote participation may also be added, and this will be considered as the same position as the surrounding desks and chairs.
(5) Participants are free to choose styles of participation that suit their enthusiasm, interests, and time availability. Sit on the periphery and listen, move to focus only on what is interesting, or speak. While a topic you are not interested in is being discussed, you can spread out your laptop and do your own work, or you can quit or skip some parts of the discussion.
(6) The speaker or core participants make a break in the discussion once the topic changes or after a certain amount of time has passed, and briefly review and summarize the content of the discussion since the last break. The summary is not to accurately trace the discussion, but to summarize from a meta perspective, such as what was important, what new things were noticed, etc., the statements that moved the discussion to some extent, the trends in the participants' statements, and the flow of the discussion.

The aim of (1) to (3) of the above method is to ensure that there is always more than one person at the center of the discussion, and that the persons to whom participants are speaking are always existing in the discussion. (4) to (6) are to enable participants to smoothly change their level of participation depending on their level of enthusiasm and interest, and to not feel psychological resistance even if they behave this way.

We would like to introduce two examples of application of this discussion method. One is the ASFA colloquium, which was organized by the AFSA project for intra-project exchange. The speaker will give a one-hour presentation starting at 3:00 pm on the day of the event, and there will be time for participants to chat before and after. The speakers of the colloquium are asked not to present their research results deeply, but introduce more practical or basic issues related to one's research, so that many participants will be attracted and attend the colloquium without making it compulsory. However, the number of participants gradually decreased, and after a year of continuing to hold the meetings once a month, sometimes participants were the speaker, organizers, and members of the lab. Thinking that some kind of leverage was needed, we adjourned the meeting and resumed with a new format that applied the above method, except for (6). As a result, the number of participants almost doubled, and the events became very lively, often lasting more than an hour after the presentation. Observing the discussions, both online and on-site, some participants are enthusiastically expressing their opinions, while others are just listening or doing their own work. Persons giving opinions often change from time to time. Participants were able to behave freely as the organizers intended, and as a result, they were able to relax and participate in a way that satisfied their own interests.

Another example of an application is a discussion group for creating a problem catalog. Based on the presentations of the guests who visited the Kanda Lab, we held a meeting to discuss concretely structuring the problems to be solved in the future, starting from a somewhat abstract understanding of the problem. This applied all of the factors (1) to (6) above. As a result, many participants are able to participate, especially online, where participants come and go repeatedly, and when it comes to topics that are related to or of interest to their own specialty, they are able to contribute their own knowledge and ideas to the discussion. We believe that the benefits of allowing many participants to participate at their own pace have been demonstrated, as the quality of the discussion has been improved. At the center of the discussion, while the core participants are actively discussing various issues, from time to time, less active participants from the periphery or online participants often present high-quality viewpoints and knowledge based on their own expertise or ideas, and these opinions often cause discussions that have been somewhat blocked or off-topic to suddenly shift to the essentials.

It is very difficult to evaluate the quality of the discussions held. If we were to evaluate the quality based on the conclusions obtained from the discussions or the quality of the participants' experiences, we would not be able to think of the method described above. As a result, the kind of lively discussion that has been exemplified will not be possible. We consider that this method could have been developed by focusing on the inner fulfillment and motivations of the participants, rather than evaluating the discussion.

4 Curiosity Driven Designs for Interdisciplinary Discussion

One consistent challenge faced when organizing interdisciplinary discussions or workshops is attracting participants to attend the workshop. While having more attendees generally helps achieve the objectives of the meetings, it is important to consider the benefits to the participants themselves. Attendance should be voluntary, with individuals deciding to participate if they find it beneficial based on their personal circumstances. However, this approach often results in only a few participants. This is a big problem particularly in interdisciplinary settings like the AFSA Project, where researchers from various university departments gather. This is a significant issue in communities where individuals' circumstances widely differ. On the other hand, even those with limited initial interest in such workshops report high satisfaction levels, at least as observed in interdisciplinary sessions hosted by the Kanda Laboratory and the AFSA Project. This suggests that many who benefit from participating are not attending. On the other hand, researchers frequently express the importance of interdisciplinary fusion but lament the lack of opportunities to engage.

Despite available opportunities, the prevalent sentiment that these do not seem beneficial suggests a significant disconnect between pre-attendance perceptions and actual experiences. This could be due to the difficulty in envisioning the potential benefits given by participating in the workshops. To address this issue, it is crucial to analyze what actual participants deem as benefits and devise effective methods to communicate these advantages.

Observing the members of the Kanda Lab, it is evident that they enjoy participating in research meetings and discussions, regardless of the relevance to their specific research topics, and they gain some benefits from these engagements. Similar observations can be made about the members of the AFSA Project. Common among these enthusiastic participants is a preference for sessions where they can express their opinions and engage in discussions, rather than just listening passively. When asked about the benefits they derive, responses include gaining new perspectives, meeting new people, having the opportunity to think deeply, and could formulate new ideas through discussion. These benefits revolve around the ability to think, learn, and connect with others, but upon closer inspection, acquiring new knowledge involves more than just adding information to one's memory database. If acquiring knowledge were merely about gaining information, one could simply read documents as a substitute. The "knowing" mentioned here suggests that the participants enjoy and find value in thinking and expressing opinions, indicating that they are integrating new information into their existing knowledge frameworks, combining it with past insights to foster new thoughts. This is inferred from the observation that many people consider thinking and expressing opinions to be a gain and enjoyment.

This process of thinking and creating within oneself seems to be both enjoyable and perceived as beneficial, particularly in terms of enhancing one's cognitive abilities as a researcher. Meeting new people entails more than just forming casual acquaintances; it involves being influenced by their research methodologies, worldviews, and philosophies, thereby generating new ideas, sensations, and perspectives within oneself, which is significantly different from merely liking someone or appreciating their personality. In summary, the gains from such interactions often include new perspectives, ideas, or worldviews either formed or renewed within oneself, and the joy and benefits are derived from this process of intellectual engagement.

Hypothesizing that the joy comes from being able to create this way of thinking and perspective within oneself, we think good ways to organize and announce workshops. First, it is crucial that the participants are to be able to think, and to think with exchanging opinions among participants. To achieve this, creating an environment that is conducive to easy participation and open expression, as well as allotting ample time for discussion mentioned in another section, is vital. To aid in thoughtful engagement to topics discussing, it is important to encourage questions, especially allowing questions during the presentations, and also encourage participants to explain their values and thought processes to others, to achieve situations in that all participants understand those values and thought process well so that they can imagine and anticipate reactions and evaluations of the others when one proposes some topics or opinions. When promoting these meetings and inviting participants, it is important to communicate with these thoughts as the main focus. In other words, the announcements should be on what do participants expect to think or create in themselves, what do presenters and organizers expect to think and create in themselves. This approach helps potential attendees recall what gains others have enjoyed from the workshops and how they might similarly benefit.

We present some examples of this workshop designed in the manner discussed. The first one is a workshop gathered with researchers who are aided a Japanese young researcher fund PRESTO. PRESTO is a highly competitive research funding program in Japan, admitting only a few dozen applicants each year. Despite its focus on early-career researchers, the substantial funding amount has garnered high recognition and attracted many applicants, serving as a gateway for young academics. One distinctive feature of this funding is the mandatory for attending to biannual research meetings, which facilitate exchanges among those promising PRESTO researchers. Some applicants are drawn to the fund specifically for the opportunity to participate in these meetings, even more than the funding itself. However, since 2020, the COVID-19 pandemic has prohibited face-to-face gatherings, hindering active exchanges. When in-person meetings resumed in 2022, in order to recover the lost time, we made efforts to organize workshops using the method described above.

Specifically, we assumed to have workshops several times, the first session focuses on individuals giving self-introductions that delve into their inner thoughts, fostering an understanding of each other's perspectives and values. The subsequent sessions progress into discussions about the values and philosophies inherent in their fields of research, moving towards research topics. Given the diversity of the participants' fields, research presentations are structured not around technical details but rather on the challenges, objectives, and significance of the research, making it easier for participants to engage thoughtfully. Rather than technical explanations, presentations elucidate why certain methods were chosen, encouraging questions even during the presentations. Allow questioning during the presentation. Researchers participated are explained about the objectives and the format of the workshop carefully in advance, such that we pay much attention to carefully engagement with and understanding each other's thinking and values, rather than just knowledge of research content. The approach was highly praised by participants, marking a rare instance of such an event being continued successfully. Unlike typical voluntary gatherings, this meeting achieved an exceptionally high participation rate.

Another example is a research symposium exploring new computer architecture. The objective of this symposium is to construct computer architectures under newly developing devices by providing suitable algorithms enhancing the efficiency and hiding disadvantages. The attendances span many fields including devices, architecture, and algorithms. Although symposiums concerning with a kind of such dreams are much attractive, they seem to have little practical gain, making it difficult to ask for active participation. Therefore, this symposium was held with the same design as the above-mentioned funding research workshop. Rather than gathering participants via email or homepage, we used our personal connections to provide a somewhat detailed explanation to encourage their participation, using the same method of communication as above. This was also very well received by the participants, and although it is generally difficult to set the agenda and hold discussions without misunderstandings, the discussions were carried out very smoothly and lively.

The above examples are just two instances. They may not necessarily apply successfully elsewhere, and there might exist better methods. What we can get from these two examples is that, carefully analyzing what the participants have acquired and what brings them joy, describing the analysis for those who have never experienced such acquisitions can understand them, and design the connection to the benefits and values of participants, have potential to be very effective in improving the quality of research meetings, especially for interdisciplinary research meetings where direct benefits to researchers are not immediately apparent.

5 Setting Topics and Questions for Active Discussion

How to choose and set good topics is one of the difficulties of organizing a workshop for discussion, which always needs much time and thought. The subjects we wish to discuss are usually abstract, possibly leaving participants unclear on how to understand and engage in the topic. While a concrete topic can make the discussion easier to grasp and more approachable, it can also limit the depth and breadth of the conversation, and participants unfamiliar with specific examples may find it harder to contribute.

For instance, let us consider the topic of "reliability of AI." If we use this broad topic directly, participants may be unsure what they can think and say. Conversely, if a presenter suggests a more tangible prompt, such as "I want to create a chatbot that helps with tax procedures, and I need it to be trusted by users; what should I do?" participants can more easily understand what to consider and discuss. This clarity also facilitates more direct and relevant questions.

However, this discussion approach has its complexities. When actually engaging in the topic, participants need to consider aspects like tax regulations, internet services, and user psychology, areas they might not be familiar with. Without relevant expertise or experience, generating ideas can be difficult. Even when participants come up with various ideas based on general knowledge, they may not be able to judge feasibility, validity and quality of the idea, which needs frequent questions and explanations from the presenter. When there are many participants and discussion tables must be separated, tables without a presenter can struggle to maintain efficiency in their discussions. Thus, finding a good and appropriate level of abstraction, granularity, or generality in a topic is crucial for topics of fruitful discussions.

This difficulty in generating ideas has often been attributed to a lack of expertise, but it can also be seen differently. Even when discussions are based on familiar and common issues, barriers of expertise often seem to emerge, making thoughtful engagement challenging. More specifically, participants can think about the topic but may struggle to identify good ideas or understand what makes an idea valuable. When the objectives are clear, no matter how diligently considered, ideas that do not align with these objectives would be deemed worthless, at least we would feel so. This makes thinking and creating ideas difficult. When values or criteria are implicitly given and fixed, the participants' thinking is limited much, so that participants could not find some clues for getting new ideas.

Discussions that feel inaccessible or where it is difficult to share thoughts and opinions are not always inherently so, but discussions with fixed values can make it challenging to generate ideas and deepen the discussion. However, discussions without defined value axes are also problematic, as they can leave participants unclear about the objectives, making it difficult to think and speak effectively. Setting a topic involves choosing one that allows most participants to engage thoughtfully, which requires an appropriate level of granularity and abstraction, and also respecting and deepening new values that emerge during the discussion are essential.

Consider the previously mentioned example of "reliability of AI." When this title is said to be the topic of the discussion as it is, we feel that it is overly abstract and unclear in its objectives. Introducing a specific issue like the reliability of a tax-related chatbot could be too narrow and specific for some, so that many participants would not be able to think about it. We then broaden this to "a chatbot that teaches some based on expert knowledge", then it becomes easier for everyone to relate and project their experiences and expertise onto the problem. Moreover, we can additionally set different discussion goals that avoid fixed values. Those goals can be to get an overview or to be able to think about it. For these goals, we can give some questions to the participants such as "when people feel a chatbot is trustworthy," "in what cases a chatbot has to get trustworthy, and why there are not required to be trustworthy in some cases" and "what are done to get trustworthy in the community and society".

These questions surrounding the topic lead opinions from many perspectives given by participants, and synthesizing and verbalizing the opinions could give some insights and concepts. Another goal could be to consider ways in which chatbots can be trusted in different topics or scenarios. Since how trustworthiness is understood and discussed differs in the cases, we can examine many kinds of combinations of cases and concepts, this way we can drastically increase the variability of issues that we can think a lot about. This can lead to discussions about more fundamental issues, such as why we might not trust highly accurate chatbots or why we reject things even though they need not to be trusted but simply because they are untrustworthy. This way also gives a new topic "why resolving these issues is necessary" that could be thought smoothly. Such discussions require deep thinking but also often connect universally to many people's inherent values and ways of thinking, allowing everyone to introspect and find clues or insights, by looking and observing at one's mind carefully.

In addition to the event-design-type topic setting, at the Kanda Laboratory, we can observe another way where the initial topic is tailored to a specific individual, and then broad to other participants with abstracted. We refer to this as "addressed topic setting." In this way, we do not directly ask participants for their opinions on the abstract topic we originally have. Rather than that, we first ask specific participants for their opinions about the topic in relation to their expertise.

From the responses, we pick out several issues, then abstract the issues to topics that other participants can also participate in. It is difficult to think about and discuss abstract topics unless we have concrete points to discuss. This initial dialogue has the function of extracting viewpoints and points of contention, and showing concrete examples of abstract topics to all participants. Abstract topics are difficult to discuss as they are, but through this process, the topics are transformed into those with concepts and concrete topics that are common to the participants. This initial dialogue has the function of illustrating to all participants the viewpoints, issues, and concrete examples related abstract topics, as well as how the discussion would proceed if they were actually considered. In the context of the chatbot for tax-related matters of the aforementioned example, if there is a participant with legal expertise, one might ask, "I'm considering the reliability of tax-related chatbots. From a legal perspective, how do you think chatbots can gain trust?" Alternatively, one could ask someone who has previously sought advice on tax matters, "When you consult others about tax issues, how did you establish trust in the person or the information they provide?" If there are multiple participants to engage with, the same question can be posed across different fields, tailored to each person's area of expertise. If several participants have experience searching for information that requires reliability, their individual experiences can be explored. Through these processes, the discussion topic naturally becomes shared deeply among the participants in the forms that each participant can think and discuss easier.

This first question is created from the abstract theme behind it, so that the form and focus of the question are arranged and created according to the expertise and situation of the person to whom the question is asked. The person who planned the discussion, in this case the person asking the first question, changes what the person wants to discuss, the original topic, to suit the interests, expertise, and experience of the person he or she is speaking to, so that the other person is interested. This approach allows participants to naturally begin thinking about the topic, as questions are directed specifically at them, enabling them to contribute their opinions to the discussion. The second question is generated in a similar way. By asking questions to a person who has the experience that required them to gain specific tax-related knowledge about the feeling, points to be discussed, perspectives, the person asked question could become enable to think about the problem from the aspect that the person has much knowledge. As questions are posed to various participants, the topic and purpose of the discussion organically shift towards a common theme that all participants can engage with intellectually. When there is a specific objective for discussion, one can move the current discussion to that of the objective, by adding perspectives, introducing problem awareness, or revealing the underlying purpose. This method allows participants to transition to the intended topic while maintaining their individual thoughts and viewpoints, fostering an environment conducive to continued thinking and discussion.

At the Kanda Lab, discussions frequently begin with someone addressing another person in this manner. When guests visit the Kanda Lab for discussions, they often come with specific concerns and may present these through a presentation. In such cases, the curiosity and challenge for other participants lies in understanding and contemplating these concerns. Understanding becomes the primary task, leading to various questions being directed at the presenter from different angles. However, in discussions on topics like AI reliability among interested individuals, there may not be a highly specialized expert available to answer questions. In these situations, we usually prepare carefully designing the topics and issues in the discussion, while casual conversations often reveal an awareness of issues we think from the past, and lead to lively discussions, which actually follows the way of addressed topic setting. This approach is particularly common for small topics, such as asking others about fleeting doubts or everyday thoughts. Even when beginning with a minor topic, the discussion sometimes evolves to provide significant insights. It is speculated that the existence of small awareness often indicates the presence of larger, underlying concepts worthy of consideration and conceptualization.

6 Inner Side Self-Introduction for Curiosity Connection

Suppose that some researchers from different research areas gather to discuss and collaborate. If they have an interest in each other's fields or research, they may find it easier to create ideas and proceed with issues more smoothly and efficiently. Conversely, if they lack interest, their creativity may be somewhat limited. If the tasks in collaborative research are clearly defined and require no creative input, the work can be done in some sense mechanically. However, when formulating new research questions or developing research plans, creativity is often necessary, and the quality of the discussions and research can vary significantly depending on whether rich ideas can be generated. In general, it is very difficult for people to consciously foster interest in topics that they have no interest in. For instance, for someone who is not interested in mathematics, the prospect of engaging with research to prove a mathematical theorem can be daunting and difficult to become genuinely interested in.

Initially, the members of the Kanda Lab started with less interest in each other's research and research field. Philosophers did not have a deep interest in informatics. Mathematicians are not actively curious in literature to the extent that they want to have joint research. Even researchers who are interested in informatics tend to limit themselves to the general context of informatics, such as informatics is currently attracting a lot of attention in society, and that AI is changing the world. Nevertheless, once they gathered in the same place and joined the same project, they needed to learn about each other and their research to build relationships. Despite their initial lack of knowledge in each other's fields, the members of the Kanda Lab went through a lot of trial and error to know each other, and managed to establish good relationships relatively quickly. Observing at the process of trial and error, it seems that the key lies in the introduction of research and oneself, the approach of which is different from the styles of self-introductions and research introductions that are commonly carried out in interdisciplinary exchanges.

Self-Introductions at the Kanda Lab usually do not begin with conventional self-presentations but rather with specific questions. For example, conversations might start with questions like "How would a researcher of philosophy approach this issue?" or "Could computer science technology enable this?" These inquiries directly relate to the interlocutor's field, then it leads to introductions of their respective research domains, and then continues to personal backgrounds. This method likely serves to tie something currently being discussed, of mutual interest, to the one's research area, thereby facilitating an understanding tailored to personal engagement or providing cues for further comprehension. Moreover, the nature of responses to these questions often strays from typical explanations. For example, even for simply asked questions about technology in the research area, respondents avoid typical technical descriptions, such as "Contemporary AI is underpinned by deep learning, which fundamentally…." Instead of that, they focus on broader implications such as the significance of AI in informatics, its prominence, potential for future development, and how researchers engage with AI. Essentially, the dialogue shifts from mere technical details to an exploration of the technology's role and significance within the field, including how experts perceive and value it. Thus, questions tend not to probe the research directly but rather the researcher's perspective and the current state of the field, and the respondent answers under the same perspectives. This approach enables an empathetic connection, even if one does not initially have a personal interest in the specific research area, since we are the same "researcher" doing research that can be considered as same kind. By shifting the focus from the research topics of the researcher, they overcome barriers of disinterest. Additionally, by learning how another creates and organizes curiosities for research topics, they seem to indirectly fosters a personal interest in the same topic. By understanding the other person's interests and way of thinking, one will be able to think, "This kind of research might be interesting to the other person," or "This might be of some value to the other person." It means that one can think and come up with ideas on research topics of other researchers, and also can verify their values.

Following the initial responses and explanations, further inquiries and comments often continue at the Kanda Lab. Observations indicate that these subsequent discussions frequently involve comparisons, either between individuals themselves or their respective research areas. Such comparative analysis likely aims to identify commonalities, similarities, or distinctions to enhance understanding. By discovering what one shares with another, it deepens appreciation of their viewpoints, fostering empathy and interest. Once commonalities are established, differences are then explored. While it might be difficult to derive meaning from wholly disparate issues, by anchoring in shared aspects, meaningful distinctions can be articulated and appreciated.

Based on observations at the Kanda Lab, we would like to construct and propose a method for self-introduction aimed at rapidly enhancing mutual understanding and smoothly building good relationships when meeting new people or encountering new fields. We call this method the "Inner Side Self-introduction." It takes a relatively long time, and is designed to be generalized so that many people can use the method, regardless of profession or personal background. (1) Initially, the person making the self-introduction (speaker) briefly describes something about themselves, whether it be their job, hobby, or academic pursuits. For example, if there is a 30-min slot, they should spend about three minutes on this. If the introduction is longer, over 10 min, preparing presentation slides may be appropriate. (2) Instead of delving into detailed explanations of their work or research, the person should talk about how they view their work or study: what aspects are enjoyable, important, interesting, or challenging.

(3) The self-introduction should focus primarily on questions from the audience rather than the speaker's own narrative. Participants should ask questions that probe the reasons behind the speaker's thoughts, such as what prompted these thoughts, whether there are similar concepts in other fields, and so on. Questions for considering connections to the questioner's background knowledge and isomorphism to the questioner's expertise are also encouraged. The speaker should use metaphors and paraphrasing (in exact, describing in a different way) to explain isomorphisms and differences, making it easier for people from different fields to understand.

The aim of this method is to enable participants to understand the speaker's viewpoints and values regarding their work or research through (1) and (2), and to enable participants to recognize isomorphisms and differences between the speaker's and the participants' work or research through (3). Understanding these isomorphisms and differences not only provides new perspectives on the presenter and the questioner but also deepens the understanding among all participants. When more questions are asked and the discussion deepens, mutual understanding quickly develops, and mutual interest and respect are fostered among all participants. Furthermore, this self-introduction technique can be applied not only to self-introductions of persons, but also to presenting research fields, business sectors, schools, and tutoring services. Additionally, metaphors and paraphrasing to identify isomorphisms are frequently used in questions and comparisons. Isomorphism refers to the similarity in structure between different entities, such as having similar functions or roles, or in the relationships between organizations and individuals. For example, publishing a book in field A may be analogous to writing a paper in field B, or translating a book in field A may be equated with the same esteem as writing a textbook in field B. While the value and recognition of translations and textbooks can differ between fields A and B, often corresponding elements exist when considering functions or roles. More complex isomorphisms, such as those found in community structures, can also be often identified in the same way. Without recognizing these similarities and isomorphisms, others might be seen only as researchers just different from me. However, when isomorphism in research activities is identified, one can recognize that they are conducting research activities similar to one's activities in different forms. This realization allows for a deeper understanding of the other's research value and interest by projecting them onto the structure of one's own field. It also facilitates the development of ideas and thoughts in alignment with the other's values and interests.

Only after such recognitions of commonalities and isomorphisms are constructed can one perceive the essential differences between fields, such as finding aspects in one field that have no counterpart in another. For example, humanities research often involves the process of introspection by asking issues in the researcher's mind who is engaging in the research. This process of introspection might have no equivalent in the research activities in mathematics or natural sciences. Engineering may have an intrinsic desire to create and contribute to society, which may not have a rigid counterpart in literature. Only in such circumstances can one see and develop a deep interest in thoughts and concepts absent in one's own field, and wonder why such research activities, although similar in form, differ so much. Then, naturally, questions arise in one's mind, such as why the research activities are so different, even though they can be considered to be very similar? What are the origins of these differences? How do they affect and influence the philosophy and worldview in the research disciplines? How do they appear in which parts of research outcomes? One can not only recognize the differences but also cultivate interest and respect for the issues different from one's field.

As a result, building good relationships and friendships among members at the Kanda Lab was exceptionally rapid. Despite the limited face-to-face interaction due to the COVID-19 pandemic, within two to three months, members were as relaxed as old research colleagues, discussing with anticipating each other's thoughts. They even socialized as if they were friends from the past. Recognizing essential isomorphisms and differences, and holding interest and respect for them, likely contributed significantly to the development of good relationships.

Here we would like to show examples of applying this method of self-introduction. We first describe a practical example in a community of young researchers who are funded by "PRESTO" aided by Japanese funding agency JST. This fund is well-known for fostering active exchanges among funded researchers, often motivating their applications for funding. However, a group started in 2020 was unable to engage in any face-to-face exchanges due to the COVID-19 pandemic.

In 2022, when in-person meetings were permitted again, we were in need of catching up and rapidly deepening interactions to recover the lost quality of research activities and environments, thus we decided to use the Inner Side Self-introduction method. The meetings were held in two locations, Tokyo and Kyoto, with 20 young researchers gathering in Tokyo and 10 in Kyoto, each taking about 30 min to self-introduce themselves in the manner of Inner Side Self-introduction. The participation ratio was relatively higher than similar research meetings, partly because everyone was looking for interaction. In addition, there arose many questions that made it hard to believe that we were meeting for the first time, and a lively discussion that delved deeply into one's ideas took place. These meetings received very good reputations, and many people came to be seen as old friends after just two meetings. At later research meetings, those people lively discussed during breaks with only a few seconds without talking. Mutual understanding and good relationships were built efficiently.

Another application was done in a series of workshops initiated as part of the AFSA project. This workshop brought together researchers from diverse fields such as device engineering, computer architecture, quantum mechanics, quantum information, algorithms, and programming language. By sharing their insights, knowledge, and thoughts, the group aimed to design new computer architectures by accentuating strengths and concealing weaknesses of some architectures using new devices. Given the diversity of unrelated fields, the participants initially did not even know each other's names or faces. However, employing the Inner Side Self-introduction to share their research perspectives and field affiliations deepened their interactions. After two meetings, this led to profound discussions on individual research topics, enhancing mutual understanding and relationship building. Participants started feeling a sense of anticipation and interest in presenting their ideas at the workshop, finding meaning and value in making presentations. The expectation of being understood and generating interest serves as a strong motivation to present.

When we applied the method at the first meeting of newcomer students of a laboratory. By introducing themselves to each other and asking about their reasons and motivations for research, fun, and life in the manner of the method, the meeting became so exciting with many conversations. According to the researcher organizing the laboratory, it was the most active meeting in the past 10 years.

We would like to present another very different application of this method, used in a marriage-seminar in a certain region of Japan, where it was introduced as a way for men and women to enhance communication and foster connections. Unlike the original version designed for researcher interaction, this adapted version focused on sharing views about jobs, activities, and family perspectives, specifically tailored for understanding matrimonial purposes. Participants practiced Inner Side Self-introduction as explained, with each other in pairs. The feedback from participants was overwhelmingly positive. Surprisingly, one participant, who had been unsuccessful in finding a partner despite two years of attending matchmaking events, successfully formed a couple by using this method at another event the day after the seminar. The fact that a technique originally designed for academic networking could, with slight modifications, significantly contribute to building strong personal relationships in the broader society was a pure delight.

Reflecting on my own experiences attending conferences, I often find that meeting other researchers, rather than listening to research presentations, is my primary motive. Research information is readily accessible through papers and reviews, and unless it is a topic of deep personal interest, my motivation to attend diminishes. In general, the workshops and interdisciplinary meetings were usually predominantly focused on individual research presentations. We believe that centering around people and interests, and using techniques like Inner Side Self-introduction, could more effectively attract participants and create more satisfying events.

Traditionally, the exchange of ideas and values has been considered and examined as an informal, individual activity, often occurring during banquets and casual conversations at some academic conferences. If Inner Side Self-introduction were systematically applied, this exchange could be carried out on a larger scale and more systematically, potentially adding significant value to conferences and workshops by creating places with new dynamics.

7 High-Level Linguistic Activity; Paraphrasing, Metaphor and Seeing-as

Observing the discussions in the Kanda Laboratory, we quite frequently see sophisticated linguistic activities such as paraphrasing (explanations in the other words, in precise), metaphor, and "seeing-as" (here it means to construct a story, concept, or structure from some concepts by different perspectives, so that it would give clear understanding, new value, or similarity to some other concepts). While discussions are typically considered to involve arguing, persuading, and explaining one's theories, the dynamics at the Kanda Lab are quite different. The usage and purposes of paraphrasing, metaphor, and "seeing-as" also diverge significantly from what they are usually considered to be.

Generally, metaphors are recognized as seeking to enhance the quality of narrative or description, such as saying something is "white as snow." Paraphrasing is perceived to simplify matters or lead to conclusions, potentially summarizing statements like, "So, you agree with this opinion?" or "It means there is a low chance of a new discovery." Perspective-taking might be used to speculate about the underlying aspects of situations, as in considering motives and relationships in a case. For example, when thinking about the motives of the culprit in a certain case or the relationships between people behind. A parable can also mean an illustration. When presenting or explaining a certain thing or concept, exemplification is the act of specifically presenting what the thing or concept includes in its meaning, what it includes, its basis, what it is related to, etc. Analogies in the sense of illustration are also used in the discussion of the Kanda Lab, but since this is done almost in the same way as those observed commonly and generally, we will not consider them.

The paraphrasing used in the Kanda Lab involves describing the same matter from different viewpoints or meanings. Here, paraphrasing should mean "describing in a different way", or different description to pose new concepts, structures, questions or values. For instance, asking "Does conducting surveys with many people equate to collecting data and forming hypotheses?" generalizes specific research activities into more abstract terms. "Providing a theorem proof for a developed method means, in other words, assuring some quality to the users," describes research outputs from the perspective of the users. In this way, paraphrasing is employed to introduce new perspectives and meanings into discussions, deepen one's understanding, and achieve a more comprehensive understanding. This type of paraphrasing, distinct from the more general use, is referred to as "perspective paraphrasing."

Next, we explain the usage of metaphors. At the Kanda Lab, metaphors are often primarily used when conveying unfamiliar concepts to others or when attempting to understand concepts that are unclear to oneself. Unfamiliarity here does not pertain to a lack of logical comprehension, but rather to a grasp of concepts. For example, asking "Is publishing a book in humanities equivalent to having a journal paper accepted in our field?" reflects an attempt to understand the significance, purpose, and value of publishing in humanities by approximating it with a similar concept from one's own domain. In such cases, the response might simply be "Exactly," or it might mention details on the similarities and differences, such as "It is similar in terms of being an achievement, but publishing tends to involve more personal expression." Since there are many facets to any issue, by describing the similarities or differences, the respondent essentially selects certain aspects to focus on or ignore in future discussions. These aspects represent points of interest or potential focus for the respondent. If the questioner finds these aspects intriguing, they may comment further; if interested in other aspects, they might pose additional questions.

At this moment, the questioner, in trying to understand a concept that is unfamiliar, transcribes the meaning and structure articulated by the other into their own set of concepts, searching for issues having structural and semantic similarities that could present back to the respondent as candidates that could be similar to what the respondent wanted to say. The concepts and structures that the questioner shows to the respondent are chosen so that it might be familiar to the respondent. However, in the case of this particular question, there is a chance that the respondent may not fully grasp the significance of paper acceptance in their field. Often, the questioner will then explain the meaning of paper acceptance in their own field, focusing on aspects they consider important, such as "In our field, paper acceptance is seen both as an achievement and a kind of obligation, which can be both gratifying and pressuring." In summary, metaphors are used with the aim of understanding unfamiliar concepts or discourses on some unfamiliar concepts by considering their similarity to or commonality with one's own familiar concepts. This function is employed similarly when attempting to explain the concepts that are unfamiliar to the others. This metaphor usually transcribes on another concept, while paraphrasing (describing in a different way) usually just changes the viewpoints on the same concept. To distinguish this specific use of metaphor, we call metaphors of this usage "structure transcribing metaphors."

Next, we will explain the concept of "seeing-as". "Seeing-as" often occurs in discussions when a certain topic has been explored to a considerable depth. The seeing-as discussed here is similar to modeling in computer science and engineering, but it is not specialized in dealing with things symbolically like mathematical modeling. Instead, it seems to handle semantic and vague concepts as they are. Precisely, when one makes a "seeing-as" for a topic currently discussed, the person extracts certain aspects or points of focus from the topic, selects the parts of interest from them, and constructs a certain structure including the issues selected, based on their relationships, connections, forms, or qualities, so that it does not lose the original meaning and the structure to that the person is focusing on. This structure is then directly described, or compared with other concepts or structures in some concepts to discuss similarities, equivalences, or differences. In other words, making "seeing-as" is to extract specific aspects and parts from the current discussion and construct a new concept from them with keeping the isomorphism to the original discussion. For example, there is a seeing-as that "the field of mathematics is like a battle between all mathematicians against a giant monster called mathematics. Therefore, mathematicians cooperate with each other, and no one gets in the way of others." This explains the structure of researchers working on mathematics with their feelings, and their human relationships, using the structure of people fighting together to confront a giant monster. The distinctive feature of this seeing-as is that it transcribes it into a structure that includes feelings and relationships, while metaphors usually explain only correspondences between an object and another object, or an issue and another issue. In order to distinguish this seeing-as from the general meaning, we would like to call it "concept construction seeing-as."

The purpose of using "concept construction seeing-as" seems to be for organizing and summarizing a topic in discussions, proposing directions, and thinking about or influencing the ongoing discussion itself. For example, it is used to simplify when the discussion content becomes complex and difficult to grasp, to create a kind of landmark or lighthouse that everyone can see and understand by using only characteristic parts when there are many unclear aspects in the discussion content and it is difficult to establish a solid common understanding among participants. It is also used to structure (model) only the parts of interest within a specific concept to move from what has been discussed so far to formulating a new concrete problem. While it is a linguistic activity with a significantly important role in discussions, it often does not remain in the record or memo of the discussion since it is usually done to refine communications.

In summary, thinking and linguistic activities such as perspective rephrasing, structural transcribing metaphor, and "concept construction seeing-as" are considered to be tools used to enhance the quality of discussions when explaining to others, understanding others and their words, and organizing and controlling the discussion. In the Kanda Lab, where interdisciplinary discussions are conducted quite often, explaining issues unfamiliar to others, understanding others' explanations deeply, and organizing and controlling discussions are very important and frequently carried out. Therefore, these thinking and linguistic activities are observed very frequently. This allows discussions to proceed relatively smoothly; conversely, without them, discussions would not progress much.

Considering the opposite of the above, if discussion participants can skillfully perform these thinking and linguistic activities, discussions would proceed smoothly, and high-quality insights would likely be obtained. At present, there are not so many ways to become proficient in these skills; it would be done through try and error, and accumulating experience. Interdisciplinary discussions serve as an ideal practice ground in the sense that these thinking and linguistic activities frequently emerge. Young researchers who have graduated from the Kanda Lab seem to be relatively successful in subsequent discussions and communication with their surroundings in the new environments. Although it might be a small factor, this may serve as supporting evidence for the effectiveness of the Kanda Lab as a practice ground.

8 Questioning for Deep Understanding Background

In discussions at the Kanda Laboratory, there is an abundance of questions. Even during presentations, questions are frequently interjected. This mode of questioning is actually permitted, primarily because it seems to enhance participants' comprehension and the creativity of subsequent discussions. From the observations we see that being able to question during a presentation significantly correlates with more vibrant discussions and a higher quality of discussions in the Kanda Lab. We here aim to analyze and consider how, why and for what purpose these questions posed.

Generally, questions serve to clarify confusion. Three main types of confusion can be identified: misunderstanding the meaning of what is being said, failing to follow the logic or wanting to verify it, and questions regarding the nature, value, or potential of the topic discussed. Examples are the practicalities of the research to the utility of methods and the availability of data. These are simple clarification questions so the answer could be straightforward. Moreover, they rarely lead to further discussion. Such questions are quite common in academic and research conferences.

However, at the Kanda Lab, questions frequently transcend these categories. They are too diverse to classify but include inquiries about motivations or reasons, worldviews, trends within the research community, and changes in research methodologies or subjects. These questions probe the internal motivations of individuals, such as where their curiosity lies and what aspects of a subject, they find engaging. They differ a lot from usual questions in academic conferences.

Similar vigorous questioning occurs in our AFSA project seminars and other communities, especially those using our project's technology to foster interaction. By asking about the intent of questions, it can be considered that participants not only seek to understand the explanations and logic presented but also want to be able to think about the issues in the explanations. Being able to think entails reconstructing the story of the explanation from several material or sources, explaining its value or meaning from different perspectives, simulating potential scenarios under different conditions, and finding structural isomorphisms or similarities with other issues so that one can make a view according to these isomorphisms and similarities. While these questions vary widely in content, they all aim to achieve a deeper understanding or to grasp a kind of mechanism behind why things are studied or why they occur in certain ways, often through repeated questioning until satisfaction is reached. This process seems essential to the questioners, as evident from their enthusiastic engagement.

According to members of the Kanda Lab and their colleagues, when there are few questions during a discussion, participants often find it difficult to formulate questions. In academic conferences, we can often see that the chairperson encourages questions to participants, then participants had significant thought before asking. It suggests that the participants are not being able to think and generate questions as they would during lively discussing. Even if the presentation is understood, formulating questions remains a difficulty, indicating that understanding the content is a different issue from generating questions and facilitating discussion.

It would be sure that when participants are able to think about the presentation content, discussions become more vibrant. If the above questions are crucial to enabling this state, it might be better to continue one's questions until the person got understood even partially the content on their own, rather than receiving a variety of questions. If we have much time, extending the time for questions is beneficial; however, if time is limited, shortening the presentation and omitting details, encouraging participants to help clarify the context of the questions, and focusing deeply on a few questions rather than encouraging questions from everyone can be crucial. This necessitates a shift in values from organizers or discussion facilitators, from a belief in equal opportunity for all to ask questions to a focus on deeply exploring a few selected topics for greater participant benefit.

While it is possible to reflect on the content of a presentation after it has concluded, thoughts and queries that arise during the presentation often dissipate without being precisely articulated and are difficult to recall later. Therefore, questions concerning with these should be asked as they arise. Matters that are easily articulated or likely to be explained later should be verbalized and noted, and asked later or after conclusion. However, questions regarding vague and unclear issues should be prioritized, which is counterintuitive and the exact opposite of the typical prioritization of questions, but such an approach appears beneficial under the aforementioned hypothesis.

Questions are asked to understand, to gather information, or to seek opinions on assessments and judgments. By carefully considering the purpose behind each question, the nature of questioning can be redesigned to differ from traditional discussions. Furthermore, questions often provide benefits not only to the questioner but also to others, and simply pursuing equality and diversity in participant's questions seem less meaningful. These insights are derived from observations at the Kanda Lab, though different hypotheses and methods might emerge from further observations at other places.

9 Salmon Interviewing for Deep Understanding

In the Kanda Laboratory, whenever someone presents their research or introduces themselves, numerous questions arise. As mentioned in other sections, this questioning appears to be aimed at understanding until one can think deeply and creatively about the topic, and many members find great joy in achieving such comprehension. When they grasp this understanding, it feels like the final piece of a puzzle fitting perfectly into place, a sentiment expressed by many. Consequently, members ask a wealth of questions.

It is interesting that through repeatedly asking these questions, both the person explaining, and the person being questioned often realize things they were previously unaware of. Repeated questioning can reveal discrepancies between one's articulated understanding and their actual knowledge, highlighting that their understanding was superficial. This phenomenon, which is not rare but rather frequent. Such realizations often arise from one's own motivations and interests, but they also frequently arise from things outside of oneself, such as the way people in one's research area think, or the position of one's own research or technology in one's field. Both the questioner and the respondent make new discoveries and their understanding progresses. It seems like co-evolution, which is very interesting.

Questions like this are usually processes of trial and error, with both the person asking the question and the person being asked repeating it as hard as they can until they reach a breakthrough. Observing this over a long period reveals several commonalities. When a key question that leads to a breakthrough emerges amidst these repeated inquiries, addressing it can significantly accelerate understanding. This suggests that a kind of generalization or systematization is possible.

One major commonality is the direction of the questions. Questions about research can be broadly divided into two types: downstream questions about what the research leads to, its utility, and how it advances the goals of the field, and upstream questions about why the research is conducted, what its underlying interests and values are, and what assumptions it is based on. In trial and error of questioning, the latter type predominates. While downstream questions are also asked that are generally and frequently observed in academic conferences, it is mostly the upstream questions that activate vigorous discussion and exchange of knowledge. Interestingly, having many upstream questions often leads researchers to realize new aspects of their work and understand the structure of their research better.

Such backward-reaching questions seem to be commonly asked in many research areas, when a student joins a lab and presents something for the first time. When students join the lab, they are asked to read a paper, and then present it in front of the lab members. The paper may contain research questions or theorems to be proven, and after a student has explained these, questions such as "Why is it necessary to pose this question?" and "Why did they want to prove this theorem?" begin to emerge, moving backward in focus. When students struggle to answer, various related questions are posed, and sometimes the seminar concludes with just this type of inquiry. In this manner, students gradually acquire the essence of the research and their disciplines.

It was surprising that despite the commonality of this educational approach across disciplines, none of the members of the Kanda Lab and the project had recognized that it was being widely used or acknowledged the method and its effectiveness, despite not being explicitly articulated.

Furthermore, the questions posed in these seminars often come from instructors who know the answers and are designed to guide the students skillfully towards those answers. This type of backward-reaching questioning is also common in interviews with researchers conducted by science writers. Articles about researchers often follow this format. However, the questions asked there differ significantly from those in the Kanda Lab. Although the direction of the questioning is the same, the content varies greatly.

In the Kanda Lab, when a backward-reaching question is posed, it leads to a verification process of the answer. For example, if the reason given for studying A is to resolve B, the verification involves determining whether researching on A is a valid approach to solving B, checking the logic behind the connection. The questions involved first directly inquire whether researching A resolves B. Even if it does not resolve B entirely, the questions probe how the research on A relates to solving B. Indirectly, other potential research avenues like C are presented, asking why C was not chosen instead. This leads to discussions about the advantages of choosing A, such as lower costs, better quality, or greater generalizability, and also verifying the validity of these responses.

Additionally, questions that center 'A' to understand 'B' may explore whether 'B' is essential to 'A'. Specifically, whether resolving 'B' constitutes a valid reason for researching on 'A', and if the solution to 'B' is important enough to necessitate its resolution. These inquiries sometimes indirectly question whether addressing 'C' might be more valid. The responses usually explain the quality and value of resolving 'B' with 'A', clarifying why resolving 'B' is crucial and how it connects meaningfully with research on 'A'. In this way, the validity, value, and essence of the reasons are scrutinized, not just asked about. Consequently, the connection between the resolution of 'B' and the research on 'A' becomes clear and rigid. Such verification compels respondents to think deeply about issues they might typically dismiss in a few words, often leading them to discover weak points in their explanations or essential reasons and motives they had not realized or articulated before.

Once the connection between resolving 'B' and researching 'A' is well-established, questions then probe why 'B' is being resolved, exploring the motives, reasons, and appeal of this action. Similarly, the appeal and motives behind researching on 'A' are examined and verified. By continuing such inquiries, starting from the research of 'A', the exploration branches out like a river, unfolding various reasons, motives, interests, and appeals. These elements of interest sometimes converge and intertwine, forming a complex network of motives, interests, and reasons. This network construction becomes an effective method to fully understand the explanations of the research by listening and asking until one can deeply think about the research.

This questioning style has become a form of interviewing technique, which is technically derived from the questioning format used in the Kanda Lab. By repeating questions and tracing back the interviewee's explanations and thought processes like a branching river, this method is named the 'Salmon Interview'. Like salmon reliably navigating upstream, sometimes failing but eventually reaching their spawning grounds, this metaphor aptly describes the interview process.

When the author was invited by a researcher of optimization algorithms, the author conducted this interview with students in their optimization research lab. When asked why they chose to study optimization, motivations such as wanting to benefit society, the potential for earning money, and eliminating inefficiencies were mentioned. However, as we delved deeper with our questions, one student revealed that they had been affected by the disaster in Fukushima during his childhood. He felt unable to help people through their favorite sport, baseball, and wanted to contribute to local recovery. Another student recalled helping a friend for his study who could not attend high school, realizing that if he had taught more efficiently, without unnecessary long complicated explanations, it might have changed his friend's life. He so wanted to extinguish inefficiencies from the society not to lose one's happiness. Another expressed a desire to quickly become proficient to perform acts of filial piety and thus wanted to find employment as soon as possible. All these students were previously unaware that these motivations were driving their passions for optimization research. As you know, such very important unaware motivations, based on issues of one's life, would never be unveiled by just asking questions for research. This example strongly establishes the basis of the power of the Salmon Interview. At the same time, the author felt great joy in being able to witness the moment when these students discovered the depth of their own minds.

In the AFSA project as well, we broadcast these interviews in a manner similar to a radio show, creating events that introduce researchers' personalities. The goal was to enhance mutual understanding among project members, which had diminished during the COVID-19 pandemic, and to help individuals feel the presence of supportive colleagues. The response was overwhelmingly positive when the interviews were aired. While typical research seminars might attract fewer than ten participants, including administrative staff and secretaries, these events attracted about thirty persons. It seems that even if research topics are complicated and difficult, people naturally find interest in others as persons. The reasons behind research, its origins, and its appeal are understandable and relatable even without expertise or long explanations to resolve the difficulty. The casual setting, allowing attendees to listen while eating, working, or housekeeping, and able to easily catch up even if they missed something, also seemed to contribute to the favorable reception.

Salmon Interviewing has become a simple, concrete, and user-friendly technique developed at the Kanda Lab. As we describe in other sections, it has been applied to methods such as Inner Side Self-introduction that is easy to use and effective even for the general use. The development of the Salmon Interview has significantly reinforced our belief that the thinking and discussions researchers engage in daily have many commonalities and are amenable to form them as methodology.

10 Constructing and Reconstructing Research Concepts by Interviewing

Research questions or ideas often arise from discussions and typically represent only a small, or perhaps initial, part of a larger or clearer research plan. For instance, in discussions at the Kanda Lab, the original questions or ideas are merely a part of the broader research concept, serving only as clues or starting points. Most of the remaining parts of the research concept are developed through the thoughtful consideration of the researcher, based on the questions posed. Consequently, it is not uncommon for the research question and research plan finally obtained from the discussion to significantly deviate from the idea posed initially. It can be said that research questions and ideas merely serve as hints for the actual research plan.

On the other hand, looking at research in the Kanda Lab, the person who conducts the research obtained by the discussion is often the same one who originally posed the question or idea in the discussion. This may be due to a sense of responsibility or attachment to their own statements and ideas. However, the person who proposes an idea is often best positioned to think through the research plan derived from that idea. While questions and ideas may just be hints, they often contain at least some form of a research plan in the minds of those who proposed them. This is supported by that the originator of a question can often provide many insights, perspectives, and analyses as the discussion deepens. Deepening the questions can be seen as a process of using fragments of the initial research concept as clues to clarify the overall structure and simultaneously reconstruct it into a better form.

We want to uncover the underlying research concepts and plans from just simple questions and ideas not only when we discuss research topics and questions. For instance, when one wishes to start new research, the situations in which they want to define its direction, value, and connections or comparisons with other research are precisely these circumstances. In the researcher's mind, there might be some ideas or objectives for the new research, but many specifics are unclear or not thought. This is a common situation for researchers. These issues gradually become clearer as the research progresses, allowing the concept to be refined according to the results obtained. However, it is often necessary to initially clarify the value and plan of the research at the beginning. This is especially true when submitting project plans or applying for funding, where the research must be clearly structured with a high valuation before any real sense of the research can be gained.

Research questions or ideas often originate from discussions and usually form only a small part of a broader, more defined research plan. For instance, at the Kanda Lab, the initial questions or ideas are simply components of an overarching research concept, serving primarily as clues or starting points. The majority of the research concept is subsequently constructed by the researcher, who builds upon these initial questions through deliberate and reflective thought. As a result, it is common for the final research topic to diverge significantly from the original ideas, indicating that research questions and ideas are essentially just hints for framing the actual research plan.

Moreover, in the case of the Kanda Lab, the individual conducting the research often also originated the question or idea. This likely stems from a sense of responsibility or personal investment in their proposals. Although questions and ideas might only serve as preliminary hints, there often exists a more concrete research plan within the minds of those who proposed them. This capability is supported by the fact that as discussions deepen, the originator of a question can provide extensive insights, perspectives, and analyses. Enriching these questions involves using fragments from the initial research concept as clues to clarify and simultaneously refine the overall structure into a more effective form.

The need to clarify the underlying research plans from surfaced questions is not confined to discussions alone. For example, when initiating a new study, situations where one seeks to establish its direction, value, and relation to other studies align with these needs. Although the researcher might have preliminary ideas or objectives, many specifics may remain vague or unexplored. This scenario is frequently encountered by researchers. As the study progresses, these elements gradually become clearer, allowing for the reshaping of the research concept in response to emerging results. However, there are times when the value and planning of the research need to be somewhat clarified initially, particularly when submitting project proposals or applying for funding. In such cases, the research must be structured with a clear value proposition even before substantial insights into the study are gained.

The Salmon Interview technique is well-suited for such reconstruction of research ideas. By conducting interviews about a research concept, the interviewer clarifies and articulates the thoughts of the person holding that concept. By posing questions that trace back to the origin, the interviewer reaches the underlying values and motivations that form the basis of the research. At the same time, the path to reach the values and motivations are critically examined and formed so that it is logically connected. The network of insights gained through the Salmon Interview thus serves to clarify the research concept. Refer to the specifics of using the Salmon Interview for this purpose described in another section.

The objective of this method is to clarify or help construct the interviewee's research concept. (1) First, the interviewer listens to the research that the interviewee wants to conduct or the questions they have raised. (2) Next, the interviewer asks backward-reaching questions: Why is this research meaningful? What is intriguing, puzzling, and valuable about it? What inspired it, and what related research exists? (3) In response to the answers obtained, the interviewer, from various perspectives (primarily their own expertise or a general societal viewpoint), paraphrases (in exact, description in a different way) these answers, asking, "Is this what you mean?" or "Generally, this would be considered as such, but why do you find it interesting?" Researchers often consider certain aspects of their research as trivial when the research concept is not clear, not fully contemplating why it is necessary or valuable. Even if they have considered these aspects, they may not have articulated them in a way understandable to others. The purpose of this paraphrasing is to articulate and clarify these aspects. (4) After discussing the motivations and values, the interviewer explores alternative options that could arise from these motivations, asking questions like, "If that's your goal, might there be a reasonable approach to this research?" or "In that case, might this other approach be more valuable or feasible?" For example, if the reason is to contribute to society, the interviewer would ask why this particular method was chosen when there are many ways to contribute to society. This process continues until no other options seem viable, narrowing down the choices.

People are quite often unable to express their thoughts and themselves verbally. Since there is no inherent need to understand oneself in detail, individuals tend not to verbalize their inner experiences extensively. Consequently, they tend to use borrowed phrases or common expressions to superficially explain their deeper thoughts. This can lead to inaccuracies or misrepresentations. The process of explaining oneself thoroughly to others is, in essence, equivalent to confronting and verbalizing one's inner depths. During interviews at the Kanda Lab, we often observe that interviewees revise their initial statements, saying things like, "What I just said was not quite accurate; it's actually more like this," or "I didn't realize it before, but this is the correct reason." This process allows the interviewer to update their understanding of the interviewee's motivations and values. (5) Once the responses to a certain level of inquiry are clarified, the interviewer can probe further, asking questions such as, "Why are you motivated to conduct this research?" If there are multiple reasons or values, each can be explored and deepened separately. Sometimes, the elicited reasons or values converge at a deeper level. (6) Finally, the research concept is visualized as a network composed of the logical passes obtained from the consecutive questions. This is the goal of research concept clarification by interviewing. Using a similar method, members of the Kanda Lab have formed ten or more their research plans, which are accepted by the funding agencies in Japan, an acceptance rate far exceeding 70%, while the rate is around usually 30%. This suggests the effectiveness of research concept clarification through interdisciplinary collaboration.

This technique can also be effectively implemented as an event organized by university executives or University Research Administrators (URAs) to develop or practice research concepts. Participants may include early-career researchers, students, mid-career researchers with limited experience in fund applications, and any researchers aiming to enhance their research skills. The seminar typically begins with an explanation of the event's purpose and content, followed by an introduction to the salmon interview technique and practical exercises.

In the exercise, participants work in pairs (designated as A and B). Initially, A explains their research for 2–3 min, followed by B interviewing A about it. Rather than focusing on applications or developments, B inquires about the value, significance, reasons for conducting the research, and the process that led to the idea. B continues to probe deeper into the responses, asking for further reasons and meanings. For each motivation or reason, they clarify why other options were not chosen, elucidating the reasons behind unspoken or unchosen alternatives. Furthermore, they are asked to strive to rephrase the interviewee's words from different perspectives, use analogies with familiar concepts to explain complex ideas, and articulate thoughts as clearly and multi-dimensionally as possible. This process continues for 7–8 min, and then they switch the roles and do the same again.

This event format has already been implemented as a fund seminar organized by University Research Administrators (URAs) at Hiroshima University and Tokyo University of Science. Participating researchers had provided feedback such as, "It was an unprecedentedly fundamental experience" and "It provided a good opportunity to explain my research while also revealing aspects of my work I was unaware of." URA staff organizing the event had also commented that "it would be a workshop that URAs themselves should undergo," indicating both the high effectiveness of this method and how little known about such approaches for research concept construction.

Researchers' ability to conceptualize research and their conceptual skills is presumably somewhat developed, with considering that they could be professional researchers. However, these abilities seem to be perceived as innate talents possessed by individuals, but it can be actually trained. While research proposals and conceptual skills are evaluated, little attention is paid to the methods used to improve conceptualization or their outcomes. If more people were to focus on these aspects, it could lead to a society rich in innovative concepts and action plans, not only in research but also in industry and government sectors.

11 Description and Logic for New Discipline

The mission of the Kanda Laboratory is to construct a problem catalog through interdisciplinary discussions and to develop methodologies for effectively conducting such discussions. We undertook numerous activities and gained various insights to achieve this, and the achievements are described in the other chapters, and the other sections. It is not only challenging to establish these as methodologies but also difficult to find out how to describe these insights and methodologies, even more to construct arguments about them. For instance, it might be simple to describe a methodology, say A. It can be described only with what and how things should be done in certain situations. However, explaining what this technology is, and also how to explain it are difficult. Explaining something that is only applicable to the Kanda Lab might serve as a good case study, but it is hard to use as a reference in other contexts. To propose something as universally applicable, some evidence is required, but what to use as evidence remains unclear. At least, we surely did, observed, and thought something meaningful and got some insights, but how to argue about this and the content and manner of these arguments already pose significant difficulties.

As for addressing this difficulty, we first consider the scientific method of argumentation and description. Scientific claims and arguments must be unambiguous and interpreted the same way by any person. Furthermore, these claims require substantiation through experiments, observations, or mathematical analysis, and this substantiation must also be interpreted in a uniquely definitive way. The methodology we wish to propose lacks this objectivity and uniqueness, and its substantiation through scientific methods is challenging. If we attempt to use scientific means as in psychology, the claims inevitably pertain to micro-level phenomena, such as the frequency of utterances, direction of gazes, or the types and numbers of words used in statements. It would be difficult to argue the quality of discussions based on such facts.

Observing the nature of discussions, annotating them, and making data-driven claims could be considered. This method has the advantage of being able to symbolize qualitative aspects through annotations, but if it is to be analyzed in a data science manner, a certain amount of homogenous data is necessary. However, the discussions at the Kanda Lab can vary greatly depending on the participants and the topics. To achieve data homogeneity, it would be necessary to conduct similar discussions multiple times with members who have similar characteristics. To maintain participant homogeneity, we must focus only on traits that many people have in common, which do not suit interdisciplinary discussions involving highly specialized and diverse individuals. Moreover, on the annotation, attributes that can be universally judged must be given, which tends to lead to opposition, the emergence of new terms, and make it difficult to delve into deeper thoughts.

Furthermore, it is considered that participants in the discussions may feel resistant to record and analyze the comments in discussions. Each individual's opinion in a discussion is somewhat connected to their identity and capabilities, which are highly private matters. There would likely be significant resistance to annotating such data and making it public. Even merely recording audio and video could make participants wary, knowing that someone unfamiliar might observe them later, possibly causing them to hold back their opinions. This defensive stance could undermine the performance of the discussion itself. Considering methods to enhance the performance of fruitful discussions, this presents a significant obstacle.

Upon reflecting on these thoughts, we realize that our goal at the Kanda Lab is not to generalize and universalize the phenomena observed. What we seek is abstraction, and we desire the abstracted methods to manifest differently when applied in other contexts. This realization makes us question the value of thinking matters directly happened and observed in the discussions. An abstraction must first be handled by someone.

Such a descriptive approach might be referred by the humanities, where fields like anthropology, literature, and philosophy often engage in abstraction from observations. Thus, their methodologies could be highly instructive for considering how to abstract issues. However, there would be certain tendencies in how arguments are structured in the humanities. From discussions with humanities researchers at the Kanda Lab, several differences have been noted: First, humanities often argue for broad, universal themes that connect to the essence of people or societies, leading to a directed line of thought that can sometimes be persuasive. Second, there is a focus on detailed observation and description of individuals, treating them not as vague, indistinct parts of a group but as distinct entities. For instance, literary studies might involve detailed observation of specific aspects of an author's works, while anthropology might describe a community by closely observing and comparing individual actions and statements to articulate the community's unique characteristics. In other words, uniqueness and individual characteristics often play a major role in the description, which we want to avoid in our description. Third, descriptions in the humanities tend to follow a causal format, whereas fields like informatics often focus on correlations, not requiring clear distinctions between cause and effect. Fourth, each field in the humanities adheres to norms about what constitutes evidence and conclusions; for example, literary studies might derive psychological insights from detailed textual analysis, while philosophy starts with abstract concepts and concludes with them. None of these four styles align well with the Kanda Lab's approach, where we prefer not to detail individual discussions, and conclusions focus only on beneficial aspects of interdisciplinary discussions.

Furthermore, there appears to be differences in the methods of constructing arguments between the humanities and what is practiced at the Kanda Lab. According to interviews with humanities researchers at the Kanda Lab, when constructing a hypothesis and constructing an argument in the humanities, the scope of the hypothesis is determined to some extent in advance, or there are vague and unclear hypotheses. Then, from the observations and analyzes obtained, they often directly derive a hypothesis that synthesizes all them. In contrast, abstracting the nature of discussions at the Kanda Lab usually has no strong hypotheses, and involve gradually abstracting observations step-by-step and constructing interpretations. For example, after observing numerous statements in lab discussions, slightly more abstract concepts such as "using many parables" or "connecting to personal interests" are identified. These concepts are repeatedly refined, eventually forming hypotheses. The process of abstraction and hypothesis formation at the Kanda Lab often proceeds without knowing what will emerge from the observations and analysis, making it unsuitable for goals like achieving results significant to a specific discipline. However, since the direction of hypotheses and abstraction is not predetermined, we consider that each step of abstraction tends to be more valid.

Constructing arguments in such a way would not be easy to be described with following the traditional ways of descriptions of the humanities. For instance, the humanities often demand detailed descriptions of individuals and seek universality and generality through the claims. At the Kanda Lab, we prefer not to disclose individual statements explicitly, and generality is not in the claims. Thus, we need some new devised methods of making claims and descriptions. So, here we consider the following strategies:

1. Interpret and abstract the observed and heard details, identifying partial commonalities and isomorphisms with other concepts.
2. From obtained abstracted concepts, develop further abstraction or modeling the structures.
3. The concepts and hypotheses constructed are discussed among members to gain some agreement or assurance.
4. In descriptions, individual events are not detailed explicitly; instead, examples that embody the essence of the claims are mentioned, which need not be tied to specific facts and may well be hypothetical analogies similar to what was observed.
5. Do not claim that hypotheses and concepts are general and universal; they are those just derived from observations.

6. Consider deeply about validity of each abstraction and conceptualization, such as whether they could be more validly explained by other concepts, or whether the observations at the Kanda Lab could be a good and valid concrete example induced by the concepts.
7. When necessary to describe the flows and situations of discussions, construct a fictional narrative told with fictional persons, without disrupting the observed structure of the discussions. This is akin to not providing specific examples mentioned at item 4.

The practice of transforming observations into methodology or insights invariably faces barriers of requiring detailed descriptions and demands for generality. Essentially, publicizing the practice of observation is difficult, and such publicity itself can hinder the practice, and the hypotheses and concepts derived are only applicable within specific contexts. On the other hand, these hypotheses and concepts potentially hold significant meaning, necessitating effective and efficient methods of description and argumentation. The aforementioned methods are based on the presumption of honesty of the persons and lack measures to exclude fake observations and fake claims. Therefore, methods to verify the legitimacy of observations and the validity of hypothesis construction from other perspectives are necessary.

Acknowledgements We would like to thank the members of the Kanda Lab, Yuka Takedomi, Kouki Suetsugu, Tomoaki Abuku, Kazuhiro Kurita, Towa Suda, Tomohiro Matsuda, Kazuki Maeyama, Kanami Sugiyama, Ryuya Hora, Susumu Hashimoto, Giulia Punzi, Yuta Yamamoto, Shizuko Kuwata, and Aya Gotoda, who discussed many matters for the contexts of this article, and supported in writing this article. This project was partly supported by JSPS Grant-in-Aid for Transformative Research Areas (A) 20H05962.

Catalog of Problems for Future Computer Science

Takeaki Uno

Abstract This chapter introduces the problem catalog described in Chaps. 8 to 12. This problem catalog is a compilation of research questions and concepts that arise from discussions among researchers in different fields, a distinctive strength of the activity of the art layer in the AFSA project. The problems are shown in a form that does not necessarily involve research results. From among the many research questions that have arisen, we have selected those that have relatively significant innovations in existing research and much conceptual meaning, in order to avoid research questions that can be solved quickly and have a long-term and wide-ranging impact on people. In this chapter, we discuss the value and feasibility of creating research questions without research results, making those questions public, and sharing them widely as knowledge in the whole academic area. We also propose a free-format description method that allows for diversity of granularity, abstractness, and rigidity in describing such problems.

In the following chapters, we will present a catalog of problems that should be tackled in the future of computer science and have new concepts and value axes that might not be induced by extending the existing ones.

Generally, when considering future issues in a certain field in this way, one would take the approach of raising major topics and concerns that are likely to be relevant to the field in the future, and then composing a more specific set of problems by analyzing and discussing these topics in more detail. However, with this method, problems are considered based on the concepts and values currently shared by people in the field. Thus, problems will be constructed with a focus on solving current technological issues or developing them. This would be similar to the way many questions have been posed in computer science studies up in the past. In this problem catalog, we are attempting to compose a new set of problems by incorporating values and ways of thinking from a different viewpoint, and in that sense, we believe that the above method is inappropriate to our problem catalog.

T. Uno (✉)
National Institute of Informatics, Tokyo, Japan
e-mail: uno@nii.ac.jp

S. Minato et al. (eds.), *Algorithmic Foundations for Social Advancement*,
https://doi.org/10.1007/978-981-96-0668-9_7

The problems presented in the following chapters are a compilation and reconstruction of the perspectives, concepts, and values that emerged during discussions between researchers who visited the Kanda Lab and members of the Kanda Lab. As such, they are highly contingent and do not have the kind of inevitability or comprehensiveness that is necessary in light of the current technological trends described above. Instead, they contain new values and concepts that cannot be obtained by extending such technological trends. The perspectives and values that emerged in each discussion were later discussed and reconstructed by members of the Kanda Lab, sometimes changing their form, and were settled down to areas that were considered to be more general and abstract, conceptually independent and stable, and highly novel, reliable, and persuasive.

When discussing at the Kanda Lab, we try not to define the scope of the discussion, but rather let the discussion proceed freely in a direction that is likely to lead to new discoveries. Therefore, what is gained from the discussion has a great deal of diversity in terms of granularity, abstraction, direction, feasibility, and generality. Sometimes we obtain something close to a concrete research plan, sometimes we obtain some novel concept or value axis, and sometimes we simply obtain only realizations, possibilities, and perspectives. Therefore, there is no uniformity in meaning, value, abstraction, etc. for the knowledge and conditions assumed in each problem, and the topic itself. On the other hand, what is produced from the discussion is selected and deepened from the many possibilities explored in the discussion, so we believe that it is essential with high value and importance related to the topic. Also, in many discussions, the person who has a strong awareness of the central problem consciousness of the discussion, who wants to solve or tackle this problem, is often the one who provides the topic of the discussion or is the central figure, and one of the goals of the discussion is often to formulate research questions that will contribute to that person's research activities. Therefore, stated research questions are often within the scope of the central person's interests and concerns. This can be seen as a failure to make rational choices in the discussion that are in line with general or majority values or goals, but it can also be seen as a way of giving form to the deep, essential interests and concerns that the central figures likely have inside them, without being swayed by popular, superficial rationality.

Because the problems presented are diverse, the description of the problems in this chapter is not in a unified format. The format of each chapter is explored by the authors for the appropriate description method. Although the overall results may seem disjointed, we thought that exploring a description method that is appropriate for each problem would allow us to describe problems with diverse levels of abstraction and topics in an easy-to-understand manner. Creating a unified description method is so difficult if we want to describe the essence of each topic efficiently and concisely in a way that is easy to understand,

In each of the following Chaps. 8–12, the following problems will be presented.

Chapter 8, "Continuous Interval Hamming Distance-based Measures" by Giulia Punzi, is a problem constructed through discussions with bioinformatics researchers. It proposes a new distance having new type of efficiency that approaches the distance between genomes used in conventional bioinformatics from the perspective of computational efficiency.

Chapter 9, “Optimization Problem Formulations for Overcoming Difficulties in Real-world Projects” by Susumu Hashimoto, is a new concept and also new problems for optimization. We consider the surrounding circumstances of the given optimization problems when using the optimization function, and the factors of the people and organizations involved in the operation of the solution and decision-making, and consider how to model them, while the goal is to optimize a given objective function in conventional optimization.

Chapter 10, “Analysis of 20th French Philosophers Network” by Towa Suda, uses graph analysis techniques to analyze the relationships between eighteenth century French thinkers, discovering and interpreting new characteristics that differ from existing literary knowledge.

Chapter 11, “Social Media Analysis based on Humanities Reading Technique: Developing a Method for Measuring Slanderous Narratives Online” by Yuka Takedomi, is a study of abuse and slander on social media. We analyze the posts of abuse and slander by the research techniques of literature not only from the viewpoints of direct semantic abuses and slanders, but also those that indirectly pressure and attack the target persons involved by negatively touching on peripheral matters. We took a computer science approach to comprehensively analyze big data of abuse and slander, with detailed manual work by literary researchers, and obtained analytical results that support philosophical theorems in past research.

Chapter 12, “Reframing Problems: Analyzing the Design of Mixed Reality Tools Through the Lens of Fictionality” by Toshiro Kashiwagi, Yasuhiro Yamamoto, and Kumiyo Nakakoji, propose the concept of fictionality in mixed reality. Our new concept of fictionality is the fusion of concepts that are of fictionality that is given by the design of mixed reality system and is recognized and felt by the user of the system, and concept of fictionality that is addressed in literature in its long history.

Acknowledgements We would like to thank the members of the Kanda Lab, Yuka Takedomi, Kouki Suetsugu, Tomoaki Abuku, Kazuhiro Kurita, Towa Suda, Tomohiro Matsuda, Kazuki Maeyama, Kanami Sugiyama, Ryuya Hora, Susumu Hashimoto, Giulia Punzi, Yuta Yamamoto, Shizuko Kuwata, and Aya Gotoda, who discussed many matters for the contexts of this article, and supported in writing this article.

Continuous Interval Hamming Distance-Based Measures

Giulia Punzi

Abstract The Continuous Interval Hamming distance (CIH) was introduced in 2010 in the context of detecting similarity for huge string data, such as genome sequences. Given two input strings, this metric provides a guarantee on the number of errors between each pair of aligned substrings of a given length k (called k-mers), while retaining a good definition of maximality. Indeed, the set of CIH-maximal substrings of two strings can be used to define maximal areas of similarity within a limited error ratio, which is hard to do with other widespread measures. Still, CIH has a major drawback: it has a low tolerance for insertion and deletion errors, which arise quite commonly in practical applications. With the aim of overcoming this issue, in this chapter we go a step beyond, introducing several novel similarity measures based on CIH-maximal substrings.

1 Introduction

The majority of data that we modernly have at our disposal comes into textual form, and one of the most basic but essential operations in these contexts is determining the *similarity* of two bodies of text. Similarity notions are a central tool in a wide array of application areas, like plagiarism detection, detecting similarity between images, or finding similar structures from sequential data. One of the most notable application areas is *bioinformatics*, where comparing sequences that have undergone independent mutations [9] or structural variations [8] is crucial for producing genome sequence alignments [2], phylogenetic trees [19], and understanding genetic evolution [3]. Because of this variety of application areas, there are many models in the literature trying to formalize useful notions of string similarities (or analogously, distances), each with its pros and cons.

G. Punzi (✉)
University of Pisa, Pisa, Italy
e-mail: giulia.punzi@unipi.it

National Institute of Informatics, Tokyo, Japan

S. Minato et al. (eds.), *Algorithmic Foundations for Social Advancement*,
https://doi.org/10.1007/978-981-96-0668-9_8

The most basic type of distance expresses the number of local changes necessary to transform one string into the other. The oldest and most immediate one is the Hamming distance, counting the number of positions at which the two strings differ. For example, the Hamming distance of AATCAG and ACTCAT is two (mismatches underlined). While this measure is the fastest, running in linear time in the length of the strings, it is also the least expressive. Indeed, any character insertion or deletion causes this measure to explode, providing little information about this often frequent type of change: AATCAG and ACATCA have Hamming distance 5. The most notable distance based on local changes is the edit distance (or Levenshtein distance), which counts the number of insertions, deletions, and substitutions of letters necessary to transform a string into another. For instance, AATCAG and ACATCA from before have an edit distance of two. Unfortunately, there is a conditional lower bound showing that several variants of this measure cannot be computed in strongly sub-quadratic time (in the length of the strings) unless the popular Strong Exponential Time Hypothesis fails [4]. Similar conditional quadratic lower bounds hold for other related measures, like the famous Longest Common Subsequence [1]. Despite this, they are still the most widely employed type of measure for general purposes, since they have a reasonable tradeoff between efficiency and simplicity.

Still, measures based on local information cannot often capture global transformations, and as such they are not fit to express more complex models. This is why there is a class of statistics-based similarity notions: they estimate global similarity based on the number of occurrences of certain common patterns. An example of such a measure is the Jaccard index of the k-mers. The k-mers of a string are its substrings of a given length k. For two strings X and Y, consider the sets X_k and Y_k of their k-mers; the Jaccard index is then given by $\frac{|X_k \cap Y_k|}{|X_k \cup Y_k|}$ [15]. In other words, it is an estimate of the number of k-mers that the two strings have in common. Computing this index exactly still requires quadratic time, and thus approximations or estimates are sometimes employed [12]. The main downside of the measures of this type is their non-positionality: when changing the order of the patterns the measure often doesn't change. For instance, AATACCGAC and GACCCAATA would be considered very similar for $k = 2$. Because of this, such measures are not fit for our purposes.

Not only is real data voluminous, but it is also prone to errors, which are often introduced during data collection. A notable example of this is the problem of genome sequencing [6], where we want to align sequenced data to a reference genome, with the challenge being that the data may contain some sequencing errors. Still, in many cases, the error ratio is limited: for instance, when employing some sequencing technologies the rate of sequencing errors is known to be typically below 5% [16]. Thus, similarity measures allowing for a bounded error ratio between sequences are an important tool in this field and in similar error-prone applications. A measure that takes error ratios into account is the *Continuous Interval Hamming distance* (CIH), introduced by Uno [17]. Given an input parameter k, if the CIH equals a specific value d, then we cannot have more than d errors being less than k positions apart. Still, it retains a good definition of maximality, which is uncommon for other measures when taking into account the error ratio. We wish to exploit the distributed-error property of the CIH distance, extending it to define several new measures aimed at approximating the similarity of two input strings X and Y.

Preliminaries and Notation

A *string* S is a sequence of characters from an alphabet Σ of size σ. In the examples of this section, we employ the DNA alphabet $\Sigma = \{\texttt{A}, \texttt{C}, \texttt{G}, \texttt{T}\}$, since bioinformatics is the most notable application area. Let $S = c_1, \ldots, c_n$ be a string of length n (denoted $|S| = n$); we denote with $S[i] = c_i$ the character occurring at the i-th position of S. A *substring* $T = S[i, j] = c_i, \ldots, c_j$ is a sequence of contiguous characters of S, denoted $T \subseteq S$. A k-*mer* of S is a substring of length k. The k-mer starting at the i-th position of S is called the i-th k-mer, and we denote it by $S_k(i)$. There are three main operations on strings, called *edit operations*. An *insertion* of character $c \in \Sigma$ in string X is the operation $X = \alpha\beta \rightarrow \alpha c\beta$. A *deletion* is the opposite operation: $X = \alpha c\beta \rightarrow \alpha\beta$. Lastly, a *substitution* of character $c \in \Sigma$ with $d \in \Sigma$ is the operation $X = \alpha c\beta \rightarrow \alpha d\beta$. For instance, given $X = \texttt{ACGTGGAC}$, an insertion of $\texttt{C}$ after the second position yields $\texttt{AC}\underline{\texttt{C}}\texttt{GTGGAC}$, a deletion of the first $\texttt{G}$ yields string $\texttt{ACTGGAC}$, and the substitution of the last $\texttt{C}$ with a $\texttt{T}$ yields $\texttt{ACGTGGA}\underline{\texttt{T}}$.

The two most common distances between strings are the Hamming distance and the edit (or Levenshtein) distance. Given $X = x_1 \ldots x_n$ and $Y = y_1 \ldots y_n$ of the same length, their *Hamming distance*, denoted by $d_H(X, Y)$, is the number of positions at which they differ, called *mismatches*: $|\{1 \leq i \leq n \mid x_i \neq y_i\}|$. It is equivalent to the minimum number of substitutions required to transform X into Y. The more general *edit distance*, denoted by $d_e(X, Y)$, is the minimum number of edit operations (insertions, deletions, substitutions) necessary to transform string X into string Y.

2 The Continuous Interval Hamming Distance

The definition of *Continuous Interval Hamming distance* (CIH) was first given in [17]. Its aim was to speed up an algorithm for computing all pairs of k-mers from a given set that are at a small distance with respect to each other. Given two strings of the same length, CIH is the maximum Hamming distance of pairs of k-mers starting at the same positions:

Definition 1 Let X and Y of length n; we define $CIH(X, Y, k) = \max_{1 \leq i \leq n-k} d_H(X_k(i), Y_k(i))$

As an example, consider strings $X = \texttt{GACAGTCAT}$ and $Y = \texttt{GCCATTCAG}$. Then, $CIH(X, Y, 3) = 1$ and $CIH(X, Y, 4) = 2$. Indeed, we can see that all aligned 3-mers have Hamming distance 1, while we have the shaded pairs of 4-mers achieving distance 2 (mismatches are underlined):

$X = \texttt{G}\ \underline{\texttt{A}}\ \texttt{C}\ \texttt{A}\ \underline{\texttt{G}}\ \texttt{T}\ \texttt{C}\ \texttt{A}\ \underline{\texttt{T}}$
$Y = \texttt{G}\ \underline{\texttt{C}}\ \texttt{C}\ \texttt{A}\ \underline{\texttt{T}}\ \texttt{T}\ \texttt{C}\ \texttt{A}\ \underline{\texttt{G}}$

Remark 1 Given a fixed k, CIH is a distance:

- $CIH(X, X, k) = 0$, and if X differs from Y at position i, then $d_H(X_k(i), Y_k(i)) > 0$, and thus also $CIH(X, Y, k) > 0$;
- Symmetry follows from the symmetry of Hamming distance;
- Let X, Y, Z be three strings of the same length. Since the Hamming distance is a distance, for every i it holds that $d_H(X_k(i), Z_k(i)) \leq d_H(X_k(i), Y_k(i)) + d_H(Y_k(i), Z_k(i))$. In particular, it holds for the $\hat{i}$ realizing the maximum:

$$CIH(X, Z, k) = d_H(X_k(\hat{i}), Z_k(\hat{i})) \leq d_H(X_k(\hat{i}), Y_k(\hat{i})) + d_H(Y_k(\hat{i}), Z_k(\hat{i})) \\ \leq CIH(X, Y, k) + CIH(Y, Z, k).$$

Remark 2 A similar definition of Continuous Interval Edit distance can be given by considering d_e instead of d_H between k-mers. Here we start with the Hamming distance as it is the most fundamental, leaving edit distance for future work.

Computation. Let X and Y be two strings of length n. Given one value of k, the distance $CIH(X, Y, k)$ can be computed in $O(k + (n - k)) = O(n)$, thanks to the following observation: if we have $d_H(X_k(i), Y_k(i))$, we can compute $d_H(X_k(i + 1), Y_k(i + 1))$ in constant time. Indeed, it is sufficient to subtract one if $X_k(i)[1] \neq Y_k(i)[1]$ and add one if $X_k(i + 1)[k] \neq Y_k(i + 1)[k]$. We thus only need to fully compute $d_H(X_k(1), Y_k(1))$ in $O(k)$ time, and then we can update it in $O(1)$ for every one of the other $n - k$ pairs of k-mers, while retaining the maximum.

The natural next step is to build a data structure that can compute $CIH(X, Y, k)$ for any queried k. Given $d^* = d_H(X, Y)$, we here show how to build such a data structure in $O(n + (d^*)^2)$ time, which can answer each query in $O(\log(d^*))$ time. First, let $M_i \in \{1, ..., n\}$ for $i \in \{1, d^*\}$ be the indices of the mismatches between X and Y; computing this set requires $O(n)$ time. For any $d \in \{1, ..., d^*\}$, we define the "jumping point" of the continuous Hamming distance as the minimum k which achieves this value: $k_d = \min\{k \in \{1, ..., n\} \mid CIH(X, Y, k) = d\}$. It is clear that, if $X \neq Y$, we have $k_1 = 1$; for the other values of d we use the following:

Lemma 1 *For* $d \geq 2$, *we have* $k_d = \min_{j-i=d-1} (M_j - M_i + 1)$.

Proof By definition of CIH and k_d, we have that $CIH(X, Y, k_d) = d$ but $CIH(X, Y, k_d - 1) < d$ if and only if (i) we have at most d mismatches separated by k_d positions, where d is reached by at least one pair of positions, but (ii) we never have d mismatches being less than k_d positions apart. The first condition is equivalent to having $M_{i+d-1} - M_i + 1 \leq k_d$ for all i, together with the existence of $\hat{i}$ such that $M_{\hat{j}} - M_{\hat{i}} + 1 = k_d$, where $\hat{j} = \hat{i} + d - 1$ (note that $\hat{j} - \hat{i} = d - 1$). Instead, (ii) happens if and only if for any choice of i, j such that $j - i = d - 1$, we have $M_j - M_i + 1 > k_d - 1$. That is, it ensures the minimality of k_d for reaching d as distance. As such, (i) and (ii) together are equivalent to $k_d = \min_{j-i=d-1}(M_j - M_i + 1)$. □

By using Lemma 1, computing k_d requires $O(d^*)$ time; as such, all values of k_d can be computed in $O(d^{*2})$ time. Once we have all such values stored in a sorted data structure D, we can find the greatest value of d such that $k_d \leq k$ for any queried $k \in \{1, ..., n\}$. This directly gives $CIH(X, Y, k) = d$, by binary search on D, in $O(\log(d^*))$.

CIH-maximal substrings

The strength of CIH, with respect to Hamming or edit distances, is that it has a good definition of maximality within an error ratio r. Maximality is a useful property, as it allows us to choose a single representative for a class of items. Given two strings X, Y and a distance D, we say that a pair of substrings $S_1 \subseteq X$, $S_2 \subseteq Y$ having the same length ($|S_1| = |S_2|$) *satisfies error ratio* r if $\frac{D(S_1,S_2)}{|S_1|} \leq r$. Furthermore, S_1 and S_2 are *maximal within error ratio* r if they cannot be extended: there are no $S_1' \subseteq X$, $S_2' \subseteq Y$ that satisfy error ratio r such that $S_1 \subsetneq S_1'$, $S_2 \subsetneq S_2'$. Measures like the Hamming or edit distance are not practical for this purpose for two main reasons:

1. *Error ratio is not monotone when extending strings by one character.* We may have a pair of substrings that satisfy the error ratio r, and when extending them just by one symbol at the end or beginning we do not satisfy r anymore. Still, this pair could be non-maximal, as if we add enough symbols we can decrease the error ratio, and satisfy r again. This happens for instance when we have a certain number of mismatches, which increase the error ratio, followed by a longer streak of matching parts, which overall lowers the error ratio enough. This is an undesirable property in the maximality context, as it makes it hard to maximalize a given pair of substrings. For example, let $X = \texttt{C}\overline{\texttt{ACG}\underline{\texttt{TAC}}}\texttt{C}$ and $Y = \overline{\texttt{ACT}\underline{\texttt{TAG}}}\texttt{A}$, for $r = \frac{1}{3}$ under either Hamming or edit distance: both the underlined and overlined pairs satisfy error ratio r, but the intermediate strings GTAC and TTAG do not.
2. *There may be many maximal pairs, all representing the same similar substring.* Let $r = \frac{1}{2}$ for $X = \texttt{AAACGTTT}$ and $Y = \texttt{TTTCGAAA}$: pairs (AACG, TTCG), (ACGT, TCGA), and (CGTT, CGAA) would be considered maximal under Hamming or edit distance, even if they are redundant: they all represent similarity for the same common substring CG, to which we are adding the maximum amount of errors on either side which still allows us to satisfy r.

The Continuous Interval Hamming distance provides a maximality notion which overcomes these issues: given two strings X and Y of any length, a parameter k, and a threshold parameter τ, we say that a pair of substrings $X' = X[i, i + \ell]$ and $Y' = Y[j, j + \ell]$ is *CIH-maximal* if $CIH(X', Y', k) \leq \tau$, and X' and Y' cannot be further extended, neither to the left nor to the right, while retaining CIH bounded by τ: $CIH(X[i - 1, i + \ell], Y[j - 1, j + \ell], k) > \tau$ and $CIH(X[i, i + \ell + 1], Y[j, j + \ell + 1], k) > \tau$. The author of [17] provided an algorithm to find all CIH-maximal substrings of two given input strings. The algorithm runs in $O(\sigma + 2^k(|X| + |Y| + \tau N))$ time and $O(|X| + |Y| + \sigma)$ space, where $N = O(|X||Y|)$ is the number of pairs of k-mers of X and Y at distance smaller than τ.

Advantages. When adopting CIH, we have a good definition of maximality within error ratio r, by choosing τ, k such that $r \approx \frac{\tau}{k}$ appropriately,[1] in the sense that the two issues described before do not apply:

1. (ACGTAC, ACTTAG) would be CIH-maximal for $k = 3$ and $\tau = 1$, having $r = \frac{1}{3}$.
2. The CIH-maximal pair would be unique, depending on k and τ. For instance, when $k = 2$ and $\tau = 1$ the only CIH-maximal pair would be (ACGT, TCGA).

We note that CIH-maximal substrings are more restrictive than the given error ratio. In fact, they enforce a certain *distribution of the errors* as well: since all k-mers have distance smaller than τ, we are guaranteed to have no more than τ errors every k positions. For example, $X = \texttt{AC}\underline{\texttt{GAT}}\texttt{CGAT}$ and $Y = \texttt{AC}\underline{\texttt{CTC}}\texttt{CGAT}$ would be considered distant for $k = 3$ and $\tau = 1$, since there is a pair of k-mers at distance 3 (mismatches are underlined). On the other hand, $X = \texttt{AC}\underline{\texttt{G}}\texttt{AT}\underline{\texttt{C}}\texttt{GA}\underline{\texttt{T}}$ and $Y = \texttt{AC}\underline{\texttt{C}}\texttt{AT}\underline{\texttt{A}}\texttt{GA}\underline{\texttt{G}}$, which have the same Hamming distance, would be considered similar: here the errors are distributed every $k = 3$ positions.

Drawbacks. If we introduce even one insertion/deletion, we can see how this measure is not so robust: let $X = \texttt{ACGATCGAT}$ and $Y = \texttt{ACGA}\underline{\texttt{C}}\texttt{TCGA}$; here an insertion for the underlined C occurred, together with a deletion of the last T. The CIH for $k = 3$ now reaches the maximum value of 3: indeed, the k-mers starting at position 5 are TCG and CTC, respectively. This is because the alignment of the synchronously sliding k-mers is disrupted by insertions or deletions. To address this problem, we will introduce our first measures in Sect. 3, where k-mers can slide asynchronously, and, as such, we have more tolerance for sparse insertions/deletions.

3 Sliding CIH-Based Measures

We now introduce several new measures, which can be seen as generalizations of CIH, aimed at circumventing some of its drawbacks. These measures can be easily defined through paths on a special matrix: the k-mer distance matrix $\mathcal{M}_k$. Given two given strings X and Y of lengths $|X|$, $|Y|$, we define an $(|X| - k + 1) \times (|Y| - k + 1)$ matrix where each entry contains the corresponding distance between k-mers (see Fig. 1):

$$\mathcal{M}_k(i, j) = d_H(X_k(i), Y_k(j)).$$

We note how $\mathcal{M}_1$ is a 0/1 matrix, having $\mathcal{M}_1 = 1$ if and only if $X[i] \neq Y[j]$: this is similar to *dot plots*, a representation used since the 1970s to visualize string

[1] To be more precise, by choosing τ, k s.t. $r = \frac{\tau}{k}$, the output CIH-maximal substrings might be slightly over error ratio r according to CIH. Indeed, the worst case is realized when the CIH-maximal strings both start and end with τ mismatches: e.g. $X = \texttt{AAT}$ and $Y = \texttt{GAC}$ for $r = \frac{1}{2}$ when we choose $k = 2, \tau = 1$. In this case, choosing k, τ such that $r = \frac{\tau+\tau}{k+\tau}$ takes care of this worst case.

	A	C	G	A	C	T	C	G	A	T
A	0	4	4	2	4	1	4			
C	4	1	3	4	3	4	0			
G	4	4	2	2	4	4	4			
A	3	4	3	3	1	4	4			
T	1	4	4	3	4	0	4			
C	4	1	3	4	3	4	0			
G										
A										
T										

	A	C	G	A	C	C	C	T	C	G	A	T
A	0	4	4	2	3	3	4	1	4			
C	4	1	4	4	2	3	3	4	0			
G	4	4	1	3	4	2	4	4	4			
A	3	4	3	2	3	4	1	4	4			
T	1	4	4	3	3	3	4	0	4			
C	4	1	4	4	2	3	3	4	0			
G												
A												
T												

Fig. 1 Left: matrix $\mathcal{M}_4$ for $X = \text{ACGATCGAT}$ and $Y = \text{ACGA}\underline{\text{C}}\text{TCGAT}$, with one insertion. Shaded in gray is the valid path achieving optimal $SIH(X, Y, 4)$. Right: barrier of k-mers at a high distance when $Y = \text{ACGA}\underline{\text{CCC}}\text{TCGA}$ has multiple insertions

similarity [7]. Furthermore, a similar matrix is used to compute several variations of the edit distance via usual dynamic programming (edit distance, Hamming distance, LCS length, to name a few) [10, 11, 13, 14, 18].

We can fill $\mathcal{M}_k$ in $O((|X| + |Y|)k + |X||Y|)$ time. Indeed, given (i, j), we can derive the content of $(i + 1, j + 1)$ in $O(1)$ time, as described before for CIH computation. Thus, we compute the $O(|X| + |Y|)$ entries of the first row and column, each requiring $O(k)$ time, and then fill other entries diagonal-wise in $O(1)$ time per entry.

On this matrix, we define a *valid path* P as a sequence of cells $(i_1, j_1), \ldots, (i_p, j_p)$ that starts at the upper left corner $(i_1, j_1) = (1, 1)$, ends at the lower right corner $(i_p, j_p) = (|X| - k + 1, |Y| - k + 1)$ and such that either $i_{h+1} = i_h + 1$ or $j_{h+1} = j_h + 1$, or both. We use the notation $(i, j) \in P$ for the cells that P traverses. An example of valid path is shown shaded in the left of Fig. 1. We denote the set of all valid paths as $\mathcal{P}(\mathcal{M}_k)$.

3.1 Sliding Interval Hamming Dissimilarity Measure

We are now ready to introduce our first novel measure, the *Sliding Interval Hamming measure* $SIH(X, Y, k)$. The core idea is as follows: consider CIH where instead of comparing $X_k(i)$ only with $Y_k(i)$, we wish to compare it also with $Y_k(j)$ for $j \neq i$. More specifically, we want to find the minimum value of Hamming distance achievable when the k-mers that we compare can slide *asynchronously*, but still move forward in the strings. We can formally define the measure using valid paths in the k-mer matrix $\mathcal{M}_k$:

Definition 2 Let $\mathcal{M}_k$ be the k-mer matrix for strings X, Y. Then,

$$SIH(X, Y, k) = \min_{P \in \mathcal{P}(\mathcal{M}_k)} \max_{(i,j) \in P} \mathcal{M}_k(i, j)$$

In other words, $SIH(X, Y, k) \leq d$ if and only if there exists P valid path such that each cell traversed $(i, j) \in P$ contains a value $\mathcal{M}_k(i, j) \leq d$. Hence, we want to minimize the maximum distance between any pair of k-mers chosen along the path.

Remark 3 Note that $SIH(X, Y, k)$ is **not** a distance. Indeed, $SIH(\texttt{AA}, \texttt{AAAAA}, 2) = 0$, even if the two strings are different.

Computation. We can find such an optimal path through dynamic programming, by computing for each (i, j) the minimum d such that there is a path from $(1, 1)$ to (i, j), with all entries bounded by d. Given the values for $(i-1, j)$, $(i, j-1)$, and $(i-1, j-1)$, we can compute the value for (i, j) as the minimum of these three and of the entry $\mathcal{M}_k(i, j)$. Thus, $SIH(X, Y, k)$ can be computed in $O(|X||Y|)$ time and space. We can reduce the space to $O(\min(|X|, |Y|))$ by computing both $\mathcal{M}_k$ and the dynamic programming values on the fly, proceeding *antidiagonal-wise*, i.e., for each $l = 1, ..., \min(|X|, |Y|)$ considering cells such that $i + j = l$ for increasing i. Indeed, after computing the first row and column of $\mathcal{M}_k$, given (i, j) with $i + j = l$, its value in $\mathcal{M}_k$ as well as its dynamic programming value can both be computed in $O(1)$, solely based on $(i-1, j)$, $(i, j-1)$, and $(i-1, j-1)$, which belong to antidiagonals $l-1$ and $l-2$. Thus, we only need to keep information about the dynamic programming values and about the $\mathcal{M}_k$ entries for at most three antidiagonals at a time, each requiring $O(\min(|X|, |Y|))$ space. Thus, we can perform on-the-fly computation in $O(k(|X| + |Y|) + |X||Y|)$ total time, but only $O(\min(|X|, |Y|))$ space.

Advantages. This measure can tolerate some insertions and deletions, as long as they are distributed. Let $X = \texttt{ACGATCGAT}$ and $Y = \texttt{ACGA}\underline{\texttt{C}}\texttt{TCGA}$, where the underlined insertion took place. We have seen in the previous section that $CIH(X, Y, 3) = 3$. Instead, we have $SIH(X, Y, 3) = 2 < 3$. If we increase k, we see this even more dramatically: the CIH still achieves the maximum value $CIH(X, Y, 4) = 4$, realized by 4-mers TCGA and CTCG, while we still have $SIH(X, Y, 4) = 2$, realized by the shaded path in the left of Fig. 1. Note that there is a horizontal step in the path, at the insertion position. This is in line with *edit paths*, used to compute edit distance on a similar matrix, where horizontal steps correspond to insertions and vertical ones to deletions (with respect to X) [11, 18].

Drawbacks. The main drawback of this measure is that it reaches the maximum value of k as soon as the two strings have a single k-mer where they do not match well, even if they are identical in the rest. Thus, it is not suitable for poorly-distributed errors. For instance, consider the following modification of the previous strings, where three insertions occurred instead of one: $X = \texttt{ACGATCGAT}$, $Y = \texttt{ACGA}\underline{\texttt{CCC}}\texttt{TCGAT}$. We can see that, due to the high number of consecutive insertions, there is a barrier of 4s in the matrix in the right of Fig. 1 (shaded in red), which needs to be crossed by any valid path. Thus, the sliding Hamming distance reaches the maximum value of four. This is deeply unfair, as we have $SIH(X, Y, 4) = 4$, the same as $SIH(\texttt{AAAAAAAA}, \texttt{TTTTTTTT}, 4) = 4$, which are way less similar than the previous pair.

Thus, this measure is better than CIH, but still not very good at discerning different strings. This issue will be addressed and improved through the next step.

3.2 *Sum-Sliding Hamming Dissimilarity Measure*

The next measure we introduce, called the *Sum-Sliding Hamming measure* $SSIH(X, Y, k)$, tries to give a global picture of the k-mer distances, instead of a local one like the sliding Hamming measure, by considering valid paths in the k-mer matrix with normalized *minimum sum*:

Definition 3 Let $\mathcal{M}_k$ be the k-mer matrix for strings X, Y. Then,

$$SSIH(X, Y, k) = \min_{P \text{ valid path in } \mathcal{M}_k} \frac{1}{|P|} \sum_{(i,j)\in P} \mathcal{M}_k(i, j),$$

where $|P|$ denotes the length of the path. Note that the values of which we take the minimum (the sum along the path divided by its length) represent the minimum average distance between k-mers on the given path.

Remark 4 Again, the SSIH measure is **not** a distance: $SSIH(\texttt{AA}, \texttt{AAAAA}, 2) = 0$.

Computation. The computation of $SSIH(X, Y, k)$ can be performed similarly to the computation of $SIH(X, Y, k)$, where we consider as dynamic programming value the normalized sum of the path up to (i, j) instead of the maximum along the path. Thus, we have two possibilities: if we are given $\mathcal{M}_k$, we can compute $SSIH(X, Y, k)$ in further $O(|X||Y|)$ time; otherwise we can compute the measure on the fly in $O(k(|X| + |Y|) + |X||Y|)$ time and $O(\min(|X|, |Y|))$ space.

Advantages. Contrarily to SIH, the SSIH measure can remain small if the strings are very similar almost everywhere, with just one k-mer where they do not match

	A	C	G	A	C	C	C	T	C	G A T
A	0	4	4	2	3	3	4	1	4	
C	4	1	4	4	2	3	3	4	0	
G	4	4	1	3	4	2	4	4	4	
A	3	4	3	2	3	4	1	4	4	
T	1	4	4	3	3	3	4	0	4	
C	4	1	4	4	2	3	3	4	0	
G										
A										
T										

	A	C	G	A	C	C	C	T	C	G A T
A	0	∞	∞	∞	∞	∞	∞	1	∞	
C	∞	1	∞	∞	∞	∞	∞	∞	0	
G	∞	∞	1	∞	∞	∞	∞	∞	∞	
A	∞	∞	∞	∞	∞	∞	1	∞	∞	
T	1	∞	∞	∞	∞	∞	∞	0	∞	
C	∞	1	∞	∞	∞	∞	∞	∞	0	
G										
A										
T										

Fig. 2 Left: Matrix $\mathcal{M}_4$ for $X = \texttt{ACGATCGAT}$ and $Y = \texttt{ACGA}\underline{\texttt{CCC}}\texttt{TCGAT}$; the shaded path is optimal for $SSIH(X, Y, 4)$. Right: Matrix $\mathcal{M}_4(1)$ for the same strings. There are four diagonals in this matrix, starting at position $(1, 1)$, $(1, 8)$, $(5, 1)$, and $(4, 7)$. The two compatible diagonals contributing to LCMS are shaded, with coverage of $12/15$

well. Indeed, consider the example from the previous section: let $X = \texttt{ACGATCGAT}$ and $Y = \texttt{ACGA\underline{CCC}TCGAT}$, with $SIH(X, Y, 4) = 4$. For the Sum-Sliding measure, we obtain the optimal shaded path P from the left of Fig. 2, with sum 12.

Thus, when normalizing by $|P| = 9$, we obtain $SIH(X, Y, 4) = 12/9 \approx 1.33$. Furthermore, SSIH can correctly distinguish completely dissimilar strings from strings with just one set of modifications. Indeed, the distance between $X' = \texttt{AAAAAAAA}$ and $Y' = \texttt{TTTTTTTT}$ is the maximum value of 4, correctly expressing the difference between the two pairs X, Y and X', Y' that was not captured by SIH.

Drawbacks. While this measure allows for understanding the minimum possible average amount of errors, it is not quite fit for identifying sections of the strings having a given error distribution, since the path must cover all the strings' positions. The next and final measure we provide will overcome this issue.

4 LCMS Similarity Measure

We have seen a couple of measures based on the number of errors one might find through a "continuous" path from $(1, 1)$ to $(|X| - k + 1, |Y| - k + 1)$ in the k-mer matrix. We wish to overcome the final disadvantage, given by the necessity of covering all k-mers of the strings. To this end, we perform the *dual operation* with respect to previous measures: instead of using k-mer distances while covering all positions of the strings, we wish to maximize the number of string positions we can cover while remaining under a certain fixed k-mer distance threshold τ. More formally:

Definition 4 Let τ be a threshold and let the *τ-bounded k-mer matrix* $\mathcal{M}_k(\tau)$ be

$$\mathcal{M}_k(\tau) = \begin{cases} \mathcal{M}_k(i, j) & \text{if } \mathcal{M}_k(i, j) \leq \tau; \\ \infty & \text{otherwise.} \end{cases}$$

A *diagonal* of length h starting at (i, j), denoted $d(i, j, h)$, is a sequence (i, j), $(i + 1, j + 1)$, ..., $(i + h - 1, j + h - 1)$ of finite entries of $\mathcal{M}_k(\tau)$. We say that $d(i, j, h)$ *covers* k-mers $X_k(i)$, ..., $X_k(i + h - 1)$ and $Y_k(j)$, ..., $Y_k(j + h - 1)$. Two diagonals $d(i, j, h)$, $d(i', j', h')$ are *compatible* if they do not cover any common k-mers: $i + h - 1 < i'$ and $j + h - 1 < j'$ (or vice-versa). See the right of Fig. 2.

The *Longest CIH-Maximal Substrings Sequence* (LCMS) is the maximum amount of k-mers of X and Y that can be covered by non-overlapping diagonals, normalized by the total number of k-mers $|X| - k + 1 + |Y| - k + 1$.

The LCMS is a special case of the *LCS from fragments problem* [5]. In this problem, we are given a set of fragments, which are common substrings of the two strings that are considered to be "matching" according to some definition (in our case the diagonals), and we are asked for the longest possible arrangement of non-overlapping fragments. The authors solve this problem as a min-cost path in a specific grid graph, by using sparse dynamic programming.

Computation. To compute LCMS, we need to first compute the τ-bounded k-mer matrix $\mathcal{M}_k(\tau)$. To this end, we define a diagonal to be *maximal* if it cannot be extended in either direction with finite entries. We note that maximal diagonals correspond to CIH-maximal substrings. As such, we could directly compute the matrix using the $O(\sigma + 2^k(|X| + |Y| + \tau N))$ time and $O(|X| + |Y| + \sigma)$ space algorithm to compute CIH-maximal substrings from [17], where N is the number of finite entries of $\mathcal{M}_k(\tau)$. If this exceeds the $O((|X| + |Y|)k + |X||Y|)$ time required to compute the whole $\mathcal{M}_k$, we can instead fill the latter and then discard entries bigger than τ. Once we have the matrix, we can then use Baker and Giancarlo's algorithm for LCS from fragments [5], which requires further $O(M \log\log(\min(M, |X||Y|/M)))$ time, where M is the number of fragments, that is, the number of maximal diagonals. Since we have $N = O(M^2)$ in the worst case, we have a total time of $O(\min(\sigma + 2^k(|X| + |Y| + \tau M^2), (|X| + |Y|)k + |X||Y|) + M \log\log(\min(M, |X||Y|/M)))$ for computing LCMS similarity.

Advantages. This measure can tolerate any number of insertions or deletions. Indeed, it identifies the parts of the strings that have few distributed errors and considers them to be "matching" the ones that have few distributed errors, like in the sliding Hamming distance. For the previous example, with $k = 4$ and $\tau = 1$, we have LCMS given by two diagonals (shaded in the right of Fig. 2) with a similarity score of $12/15 = 0.8$. Each matching pair of substrings identified by the diagonals, `(ACGATC, ACGACC)` and `(ATCGAT,CTCGAT)`, has CIH bounded by $\tau = 1$.

Drawbacks and future work. The main drawback of this measure, which is also common to all the previous ones, is its computational requirement. Indeed, for large-scale applications like bioinformatics, quadratic time is often too slow for practical purposes. Therefore, the next step is to develop provably efficient heuristics to approximate and test our measures in real-world scenarios.

Acknowledgements This work was carried out while the author was a postdoctoral researcher at the National Institute of Informatics. The author is grateful for the fruitful discussions with Takeaki Uno, Kazuhiro Kurita, and Sasha Darmon on the topics of this chapter, which helped shape the presented results. The author would also like to particularly thank Takeaki Uno for fostering the interdisciplinary environment at Kanda lab. This work was supported by MEXT KAKENHI Grant Number 20H05962.

References

1. A. Abboud, A. Backurs, V.V. Williams, Tight hardness results for lcs and other sequence similarity measures, in *2015 IEEE 56th Annual Symposium on Foundations of Computer Science* (IEEE, 2015), pp. 59–78
2. S.F. Altschul, W. Gish, W. Miller, E.W. Myers, D.J. Lipman, Basic local alignment search tool. J. Mol. Biol. **215**(3), 403–410 (1990)

3. A.F. Auch, S.R. Henz, B.R. Holland, M. Göker, Genome blast distance phylogenies inferred from whole plastid and whole mitochondrion genome sequences. BMC Bioinform. **7**, 1–16 (2006)
4. A. Backurs, P. Indyk, Edit distance cannot be computed in strongly subquadratic time (unless seth is false), in *Proceedings of the forty-seventh annual ACM symposium on Theory of computing* (2015), pp. 51–58
5. B.S. Baker, R. Giancarlo, Sparse dynamic programming for longest common subsequence from fragments. J. Algorithms **42**(2), 231–254 (2002)
6. R.D. Fleischmann, M.D. Adams, O. White, R.A. Clayton, E.F. Kirkness, A.R. Kerlavage, C.J. Bult, J.-F. Tomb, B.A. Dougherty, J.M. Merrick et al., Whole-genome random sequencing and assembly of haemophilus influenzae rd. Science **269**(5223), 496–512 (1995)
7. A.J. Gibbs, G.A. McIntyre, The diagram, a method for comparing sequences: its use with amino acid and nucleotide sequences. Eur. J. Biochem. **16**(1), 1–11 (1970)
8. S.S. Ho, A.E. Urban, R.E. Mills. Structural variation in the sequencing era. Nat. Rev. Genet. **21**(3), 171–189 (2020)
9. M. Lynch, M.S. Ackerman, J.-F. Gout, H. Long, W. Sung, W. Kelley Thomas, P.L. Foster, Genetic drift, selection and the evolution of the mutation rate. Nat. Rev. Genet. **17**(11), 704–714 (2016)
10. G. Navarro, A guided tour to approximate string matching. ACM Comput. Surv. (CSUR) **33**(1), 31–88 (2001)
11. S.B. Needleman, C.D. Wunsch, A general method applicable to the search for similarities in the amino acid sequence of two proteins. J. Mol. Biol. **48**(3), 443–453 (1970)
12. B.D. Ondov, T.J. Treangen, P. Melsted, A.B. Mallonee, N.H. Bergman, S. Koren, A.M. Phillippy, Fast genome and metagenome distance estimation using Minhash. Mash. Genome Biol. **17**, 1–14 (2016)
13. D. Sankoff, Matching sequences under deletion/insertion constraints. Proc. Natl. Acad. Sci. **69**(1), 4–6 (1972)
14. P.H. Sellers, On the theory and computation of evolutionary distances. SIAM J. Appl. Math. **26**(4), 787–793 (1974)
15. S. Seth, N. Välimäki, S. Kaski, A. Honkela, Exploration and retrieval of whole-metagenome sequencing samples. Bioinformatics **30**(17), 2471–2479 (2014)
16. N. Stoler, A. Nekrutenko (2021) Sequencing error profiles of illumina sequencing instruments. NAR Genomics Bioinform. **3**(1), lqab019 (2021)
17. T. Uno, Multi-sorting algorithm for finding pairs of similar short substrings from large-scale string data. Knowl. Inf. Syst. **25**, 229–251 (2010)
18. R.A. Wagner, M.J. Fischer, The string-to-string correction problem. J. ACM (JACM) **21**(1), 168–173 (1974)
19. A. Zielezinski, H.Z. Girgis, G. Bernard, C.-A. Leimeister, K. Tang, T. Dencker, A.K. Lau, S. Röhling, J.J. Choi, M.S. Waterman et al., Benchmarking of alignment-free sequence comparison methods. Genome Biol. **20**(1), 1–18 (2019)

Optimization Problem Formulations for Overcoming Difficulties in Real-World Projects

Susumu Hashimoto

Abstract This chapter explores the challenges in applying optimization techniques to real-world decision-making projects. While many such challenges can be modeled as mathematical problems, practical implementation often faces obstacles due to the complexity of real-world scenarios. We propose three novel optimization problems that address practical issues: high-performance but opaque algorithms, practitioner's tacit knowledge, and consensus among practitioners. These aim to bridge the gap between theoretical research and real-world applications. For each proposed problem, we discuss potential algorithmic strategies.

1 Introduction

Many real-world decision-making challenges can be formulated as optimization problems, and research has been conducted on modeling these and developing algorithms to solve them for various cases. However, real-world issues may not be solved using the same procedures as in research. For instance, even if a real-world problem can be carefully modeled through discussions with practitioners, it is generally difficult to construct a formulation that truly captures reality. Moreover, it is necessary to persuade each practitioner to adopt mathematical models or algorithms. In this way, simply formulating an idealized situation and solving it may not be sufficient for practical applications.

This chapter introduces new optimization (related) problems that address various practical situations, bridging the gap between research and real-world issues. In the rest of the chapter, we assume that the problems are solved in collaboration with practitioners to address real-world decision-making issues. First, let us define an optimization model (P) as follows:

$$\begin{aligned} (P) \quad & \text{minimize} && f(x) \\ & \text{subject to} && x = (x_1, \ldots, x_n) \in D \subseteq \mathbb{V}^n, \end{aligned}$$

S. Hashimoto (✉)
National Institute of Informatics, Chiyoda, Japan
e-mail: hashimoto_s@nii.ac.jp

S. Minato et al. (eds.), *Algorithmic Foundations for Social Advancement*,
https://doi.org/10.1007/978-981-96-0668-9_9

where x is an n-dimensional decision variable vector, D is the feasible region, and $\mathbb{V}$ is the set of values that each decision variable can be assigned, such as $\{0, 1\}$ or $\mathbb{R}$. We consider (P) to be the optimization problem that truly represents a real-world projects, and we propose three new problems that consider practical situations.

2 Enumerating Insights for Optimization Problems

Discrete optimization has a high degree of expressive power, enabling them to formulate various real-world scenarios. However, even for fundamental models such as the traveling salesman problem and set covering problem, many problems belong to the NP-hard class. Consequently, numerous heuristics have been explored to tackle these problems. For particularly complex instances, employing high-performance metaheuristics, such as genetic algorithms, is common practice to obtain approximate solutions swiftly. For a comprehensive treatment of genetic algorithms, see Eiben and Smith [2]. On the other hand, a significant drawback of these high-performance metaheuristics is that their procedures become black-box operations, obscuring their internal mechanisms. As a result, minor alterations to the input data or inaccuracies of the model may render the obtained solution unusable, necessitating a complete recalculation from scratch. One intuitive strategy to mitigate this issue is to prepare diverse solutions. Relevant existing research in this field includes employing evolutionary algorithms to enumerate optimal solutions [3] and solving the problem of maximizing the entropy of a set of approximate solutions [4]. Nevertheless, this strategy merely provides multiple high-quality solutions, making it challenging to derive their inherent properties. If such properties could be obtained, it would enable analyzing the reasons behind generating undesirable solutions or distinguishing crucial decision variables and assignments. Consequently, even if this strategy is adopted, it may impede meta-level process improvements, as it does not contribute to discovering constraints necessary to bring the mathematical model closer to reality or efficiently investing efforts to refine the model inputs for obtaining better solutions.

For optimization problems encountered in engineering applications, it is known that a law called the proximate optimality principle (POP) holds empirically. POP asserts that good solutions tend to share similar structures, where a structure refers to the partial assignment of values to decision variables. Conversely, under POP, there exist specific structures that good solutions are likely to have, and identifying these structures can provide insights for obtaining good solutions. Therefore, in this part, we propose the problem of mining insights, such as what structures can lead solutions to be high-quality for discrete optimization problem (P) where POP holds. First, we define the good structures as follows:

Definition 1 Let $s : \{1, \ldots, n\} \to \mathbb{V}$ be a partial function and $x = (x_1, \ldots, x_n) \in \mathbb{V}^n$ be an n-dimensional vector. Define a function $h : \{1, \ldots, n\} \to \mathbb{V}$ such that $h(i) = x_i$ for $i \in \{1, \ldots, n\}$. Then, we say that x has a *structure* s if and only if s is a restriction of h. We denote this by $x \rhd s$ or $s \lhd x$.

Definition 2 Let $\alpha \gg 1$ be a constant, $x \in D$ be a solution of (P), $s \lhd x$ be a structure, and $G(D) \subseteq D$ be a given set of good solutions. s is said to be an $\alpha-$good structure of (P) if the following conditions (a), (b) and (c) hold:

(a) $\left|\{x' \in G(D) \mid x' \rhd s\}\right| > 0$,

(b) $\alpha \dfrac{|G(D)|}{|D|} \leq \dfrac{\left|\{x' \in G(D) \mid x' \rhd s\}\right|}{|\{x' \in D \mid x' \rhd s\}|}$,

(c) s is maximal among the structures satisfying (a) and (b) for inclusion of partial maps, i.e., any structure $s' \lhd x$ with $s' \neq s$ and $s'(i) = s(i)$ for all $i \in dom(s)$ does not satisfy (a) and/or (b).

Note that a partial function $f : X \rightarrow Y$ is a function from a subset of X to Y, where f may not be defined for all elements of X. The set $G(D)$ refers to a specific set of solutions that are deemed to be of good quality. In this context, we are considering the use of the set of approximate solutions or local optima. Additionally, α denotes the degree to which a good structure is likely to appear in a good solution. Using the definition of good structures, we provide the following problem:

Problem 1 Given an optimization problem model (P), a good solution set $G(D) \subseteq D$, and a constant $\alpha \gg 1$, enumerate all $\alpha-$good structures of (P).

By solving Problem 1 and enumerating good structures, the practitioners can obtain insights that the structure leads solutions to be good. However, since the number of solutions in (P) is generally exponential, determining whether a structure satisfies Definition 2 is difficult in practice. Hence, directly solving Problem 1 is computationally intractable. Therefore, it may be necessary to relax the problem, such as approximating D and $G(D)$ through random sampling, or instead of Definition 2, employing techniques such as clustering to gather similar good solutions, and regarding the structures extracted from them as good structures.

3 Optimization Problems Reflecting Practitioners' Tacit Knowledge

Explaining tacit knowledge, such as practitioners' preferences and rules of thumb, presents a challenge in constructing models that accurately reflect reality. For instance, when commuting by bicycle from home to the workplace, the decision-making process regarding the route may involve various factors beyond the common-sense criterion of favoring shorter routes. While one can formulate and solve the problem as a shortest-path problem, in the real world, considerations such as the presence of a supermarket along the route being preferable or hills being less desirable may influence the choice. Thus, enumerating all such factors in advance is necessary to formulate a truly accurate optimization problem, but it is virtually impossible.

To tackle optimization problems where the true objective function is unknown, there is a field of study known as black-box optimization (BBO). BBO is a framework for finding optimal solutions using an oracle instead of the objective function itself, thereby eliminating the need for an explicit functional representation of the objective. For more detail, see Audet and Hare [1]. However, applying BBO to the optimization problems described above is challenging due to the difficulty of quantifying implicit preferences. In this part, we present an optimization problem that reflects practitioners' tacit knowledge by extending BBO under the following assumption:

Assumption 1 The true optimization problem (P) is unknown.

Assumption 2 The following optimization problem (P') is given:

$$\begin{array}{lll} (P') & \text{minimize} & g(x) \\ & \text{subject to} & x = (x_1, \ldots, x_n) \in D \subseteq \mathbb{V}^n. \end{array}$$

Assumption 3 There exists a positive correlation between the function values of f and g.

Assumption 4 There exists an oracle that can determine whether $f(x) < f(y)$, $f(x) > f(y)$ or $f(x) = f(y)$ for any two solutions $x, y \in D$.

These assumptions are based on the premise that we solve problems with practitioners. Assumption 1 represents a scenario where the true objective function involves tacit knowledge, making it difficult to explicitly describe the functional form and obtain accurate objective values for solutions. Assumption 2 assumes a situation where an optimization problem has been modeled through discussions with the practitioners. This assumption includes the premise that the feasible regions of the two optimization problems (P) and (P') are identical. This premise does not lose generality because even if a solution, denoted by $\bar{x}$, is deemed unacceptable by the practitioners, this can be expressed by assigning a sufficiently large value to $f(\bar{x})$. Assumption 3 postulates that the model (P') partially represents the real-world problem and that the goodness defined by the model cannot be ignored. Assumption 4 assumes that practitioners can be regarded as an oracle capable of evaluating the quality of solutions. This assumption is reasonably realistic since practitioners select solutions to carry out their work in reality.

Using the assumptions above, this part proposes the following problem:

Problem 2 Under Assumptions 1–4, solve (P).

In contrast to the BBO, while the objective values of solutions cannot be obtained in this problem, unguaranteed approximate values can be obtained through the given function g. Therefore, the basic strategy for solving Problem 2 is to enumerate good solutions for (P') as candidates and then explore desirable solutions for (P) among the candidates by comparing solutions through the oracle (i.e., the practitioners). This strategy is analogous to the practical workflow: solving the formulated model, having the practitioners evaluate the solutions, and providing feedback.

In order to find the optimal solution of Problem 2, it is necessary to enumerate all the elements of D. Therefore, no exact polynomial-time algorithm exists since optimization problems typically have an exponential or infinite number of feasible solutions. Consequently, developing heuristics is essential for solving this problem. As a promising direction for heuristics, if we consider discrete optimization and assume POP, the following methods may be applied to the problem, utilizing the techniques introduced in Sect. 2:

1. Enumerating relaxed good structures for (P') and solution(s) containing each structure.
2. Identify the best structures by comparing the best solutions or the average ranks of the solutions for each structure using Assumption 4.
3. Fix the best structure in (P').
4. Repeat 1-3 until no relaxed good structure is found in (P').
5. Fix the remaining variables by applying a normal heuristic or an exact algorithm to (P').

This technique allows us to establish an algorithm to construct a solution by repeating the process of finding and fixing a good structure.

4 Optimization Problems to Reach Consensus Among Multiple Practitioners on the Objective Function

Widely important objectives in practice, such as cost or efficiency, are often difficult to compute exactly. Furthermore, the computational time of optimization solvers or heuristics depends on the computational time of the objective function. Therefore, simpler and more tractable proxy indicators are often employed instead of the exact objective function. Practitioners from various backgrounds may be involved in the actual decision-making process, and they may hold different beliefs regarding the objectives. Consequently, when the exact objective function is computationally intractable, a consensus must be reached among them on what proxy indicators should be employed.

Some research exists on methods for reaching consensus based on individual preferences and studies on mathematical modeling of group decision-making. Zha et al. [5] provide a detailed review of this subject. These studies can be applied to our scenario if each practitioner can evaluate the objective functions. In order to achieve this, it is necessary to investigate the characteristics of the solutions obtained by using each objective function. One of the most straightforward approaches is to solve test cases for each objective function and compare the obtained (sub)optimal solutions. However, since the optimal solutions conform to their respective objective functions, even slight improvements may cause various decision variables to change. Consequently, it is difficult to discern the characteristics of the objective functions by merely comparing the optimal solutions.

In this part, we present a problem that facilitates the comparison of different objective functions in order to reach a consensus among multiple practitioners who hold differing beliefs as follows:

Problem 3 Let $D \subseteq \mathbb{V}^n$ be a set, $x_1^*, x_2^*, \ldots, x_m^* \in D$ be elements of the set, $g_1, g_2, \ldots, g_m : D \to \mathbb{R}$ be functions, and $\beta \geq 1$ be a constant. Suppose that $x_1^*, x_2^*, \ldots, x_m^*$ are (sub)optimal solutions of optimization problems whose feasible regions are D and objectives are minimizing $g_1, g_2, \ldots, g_m$, respectively. Then, solve the following optimization problem (P_2):

$$
\begin{array}{lll}
(P_2) \quad \text{minimize} & \displaystyle\sum_{i=1}^{n} \|x_i - x'\|_1 & \\
\text{subject to} & g_i(x_i) \leq \beta g_i(x_i^*) & \text{for all} \quad 1 \leq i \leq m \\
& x_i \in D & \text{for all} \quad 1 \leq i \leq m \\
& x' \in \mathbb{V}^n, &
\end{array}
$$

where $\|\cdot\|_1$ represents the L1 norm or the sum of the absolute values of the vector's components.

The optimization problem (P_2) aims to minimize the deviation of each objective function's solution from a reference solution denoted by x'. The first constraint allows for a compromise of up to a factor of β in the search relative to each given (sub)optimal solution. Intuitively, the solutions $x_1, \ldots, x_m$ obtained from this problem are expected to be more comparable, with many variables being fixed and only the crucial ones differing at the expense of optimality. Note that this problem involves m optimization problems, and thus, finding the optimal solution in (P_2) is a computationally hard task. On the other hand, if $x_1, \ldots, x_m$ are fixed, the optimal x' can be easily calculated. Exploiting this, we provide an effective algorithmic framework as following steps:

1. Set a terminate condition.
2. Find an initial solution.
3. Select an integer $i \in \{1, \ldots, m\}$.
4. Fix all variables except x_i and solve (P_2).
5. Update the solution and recompute the optimal x'.
6. Repeat steps 3–5 until the terminate condition is satisfied.

Acknowledgements This work was partly supported by MEXT KAKENHI Grant Number 20H05962.

References

1. C. Audet, W. Hare, *Derivative-Free and Blackbox Optimization*. Springer Series in Operations Research and Financial Engineering. (Springer International Publishing, 2018)
2. A.E. Eiben, J.E. Smith, *Introduction to Evolutionary Computing*, 2nd edn. (Springer Publishing Company, Incorporated, 2015)

3. T. Huang, Y.J. Gong, S. Kwong, H. Wang, J. Zhang, A niching memetic algorithm for multi-solution traveling salesman problem. IEEE Trans. Evol. Comput. **24**(3), 508–522 (2019)
4. T. Ulrich, L. Thiele, Maximizing population diversity in single-objective optimization, in *Proceedings of the 13th Annual Conference on Genetic and Evolutionary Computation, GECCO'11*. (Association for Computing Machinery, New York, NY, USA, 2011), pp. 641–648. https://doi.org/10.1145/2001576.2001665
5. Q. Zha, Y. Dong, F. Chiclana, E. Herrera-Viedma, Consensus reaching in multiple attribute group decision making: a multi-stage optimization feedback mechanism with individual bounded confidences. IEEE Trans. Fuzzy Syst. **30**(8), 3333–3346 (2022). https://doi.org/10.1109/TFUZZ.2021.3113571

Analysis of the 20th-Century French Philosophers' Network

Towa Suda

Abstract This study, conducted as part of Group A01 of the KAKENHI Transformative Research Areas, applies network analysis to 20th-century French philosophers by drawing on Wikipedia's "Influences/Influenced by" data. By calculating metrics such as degree, betweenness, closeness, and eigenvector centrality, it illuminates the relationships and influences among these philosophers, thereby complementing the traditional intellectual history approach, which has largely centered on textual interpretation. In doing so, the study highlights the potential of interdisciplinary research between informatics and the humanities, demonstrating how large-scale data and mathematical methods can provide new insights.

1 Introduction

This section provides an overview of the network analysis of 20th century French philosophers conducted by the author [1] through research within Group A01 of the KAKENHI Transformative Research Areas (A) "Creation and Organization of Innovative Algorithmic Foundations for Social Advancement". Group A01 fosters interdisciplinary collaboration, offering a platform for researchers from diverse fields to identify new challenges and develop innovative solutions.

The present study aims to comprehensively capture the relationships and influences among philosophers, contrasting with traditional intellectual history, which has primarily focused on individual philosophers and their texts. By mathematically analyzing networks derived from Wikipedia's "Influences/Influenced by" data, this study seeks to elucidate the overall structure and characteristics of 20th-century French intellectual circles. This approach exemplifies the interdisciplinary research pursued by Group A01, demonstrating how informatics methods can unlock new possibilities for the humanities.

T. Suda (✉)
National Institute of Informatics, Tokyo, Japan
e-mail: sudatowa@nii.ac.jp

S. Minato et al. (eds.), *Algorithmic Foundations for Social Advancement*,
https://doi.org/10.1007/978-981-96-0668-9_10

2 From "Humanistic Reading" to "Mathematical Reading" in Intellectual History

Traditional research in intellectual history has primarily adopted a "humanistic reading" approach. This method involves closely interpreting individual philosophers' works and analyzing their content and influence on other thinkers. For example, it might include a detailed reading of Pierre Klossowski's *Sade, My Neighbor* and examining the influence of theology and Georges Bataille within it. This approach is essential for focusing on textual details and deepening qualitative understanding of ideas.

However, "humanistic reading" has its limitations. First, because it focuses on specific texts or philosophers based on researchers' interests and expertise, it can be difficult to grasp the broader structure of the intellectual landscape. Additionally, there is a risk that researchers' subjectivity and preconceptions may affect their interpretations.

In contrast, the analysis of philosophers' networks adopts a "mathematical reading" approach. This method seeks to obtain objective insights by converting relationships between philosophers into data and analyzing it using network analysis, a mathematical technique. For instance, the influential relationship between Michel Foucault and Martin Heidegger can be represented as part of a network and quantitatively analyzed based on its structure.

It is important to note that "humanistic reading" and "mathematical reading" are not opposing methods; rather, they are complementary. Insights gained from "mathematical reading" can be interpreted and validated through "humanistic reading," while findings from "humanistic reading" can be substantiated by "mathematical reading."

3 Network Analysis in the Humanities

Network analysis has been increasingly applied in the humanities, particularly in historical studies. Recently, a dedicated journal focused on network analysis in historical research [2] was launched and continues to be published. In contrast, the use of network analysis in philosophy and literature remains relatively limited. While there have been studies such as the analysis and visualization of Socrates' social network [3] and the examination of relationships between characters in novels and plays [4], this field still holds significant potential for further development.

Similar to this study, there have been attempts to create and visualize networks from Wikipedia's influence data [5]. However, these efforts primarily aimed to create graphical user interfaces (GUIs) and did not engage in in-depth analysis or interpretation of the networks.

Franco Moretti and his colleagues, pioneers in applying informatics methods to literary studies, introduced the concept of "distant reading" [6] to offer a broader perspective on literary research, which has traditionally focused on individual works. While Moretti's team uses big data to map "World Literature" across regions and time periods, this study focuses on creating networks, performing mathematical calculations, and examining the results in the context of existing research in philosophy and literature. Additionally, this study is unique in its goal to develop new mathematical methods for analyzing these networks.

4 Methods and Results of the Analysis of the 20th-Century French Philosophers' Network

To implement this "mathematical reading," a network of 20th-century French philosophers was first constructed based on their influence relationships. The study began by selecting 131 prominent 20th-century French philosophers and writers listed in a dictionary of French philosophy and thought [7]. Information on their influences and those they influenced was then scraped from the "Influences/Influenced" sections of the Wikipedia entries (English, French, and Japanese versions) for these 131 philosophers. Based on this data, 651 additional names that appeared in the influence relationships were added to the original 131, creating a directed graph of 782 individuals using Python's NetworkX library [8].

Four centrality measures were applied to this network: degree, betweenness, closeness, and eigenvector centrality. The definitions and interpretations of each measure are as follows:

Degree Centrality: Indicates the number of connections a node has. Philosophers with high degree centrality have influenced or been influenced by many others. Maurice Merleau-Ponty had the highest degree centrality, reflecting his broad impact on diverse philosophical movements. Of the 47 individuals he influenced, 23 were Anglophone researchers (from the US, Canada, UK, and Australia), and their areas of expertise extended beyond phenomenology to include experimental psychology, philosophy of mind, cognitive philosophy, and feminism. This high degree centrality not only reflects the richness of information in his English Wikipedia entry but also suggests that Merleau-Ponty's writings, such as his engagement with Gestalt psychology in *Phenomenology of Perception*, offered insights with broad appeal and influence across various fields.

Degree Centrality (for individuals not in the initial 131): German-language thinkers such as Karl Marx, Friedrich Nietzsche, Immanuel Kant, Sigmund Freud, and G.W.F. Hegel showed high degree centrality. This finding provides quantitative support for the widely accepted view that 20th-century French thought was profoundly influenced by German philosophy.

Betweenness Centrality: Measures how often a node appears on the shortest paths between other nodes. Philosophers with high betweenness centrality can be seen as "mediators" connecting different groups. Seven of the top 10 individuals with high betweenness centrality (Maurice Merleau-Ponty, Jean-Paul Sartre, Gilles Deleuze, Jacques Lacan, Jacques Derrida, Michel Foucault, and Simone Weil) are also among the top 10 in degree centrality, suggesting a strong correlation between high degree and betweenness centrality. Interestingly, Roland Barthes (29th in degree centrality), Henri Lefebvre, and Jean-François Lyotard (both 32nd in degree centrality) rank high in betweenness centrality.

Closeness Centrality: Represents the average shortest path length from a node to all other nodes. Nodes with high closeness centrality are efficiently positioned to reach any other node in the network. However, this concept is difficult to fully apply in the context of human interactions within intellectual history, and further examination is needed to assess its relevance in this area of research.

Eigenvector Centrality: Measures the influence of a node based on the centrality of its connections. Philosophers with high eigenvector centrality are strongly connected to other influential philosophers. Interestingly, Maurice Merleau-Ponty, who ranked first in degree centrality, does not appear in the top 10 for eigenvector centrality. This suggests that many of the nodes connected to Merleau-Ponty have low degree centrality themselves, indicating connections with relatively isolated individuals in the network. In contrast, Jacques Derrida, Gilles Deleuze, and Michel Foucault, who are all in the top 10 for degree centrality, also rank highly in eigenvector centrality.

5 Future Directions and Challenges

This study has demonstrated the potential of network analysis to offer new insights into intellectual history. However, addressing potential biases in Wikipedia data remains a significant challenge. Future research should incorporate alternative methods, such as citation network analysis using scholarly literature databases, to provide a more robust and academically grounded perspective on philosophical influences.

One promising direction for future research is the application of community mining techniques to the network. By comparing computationally identified communities with established groupings from existing research (e.g., journals, schools of thought), this approach can shed light on the underlying relationships within intellectual communities. This analysis facilitates a deeper understanding of how accurately established communities reflect actual relationships, and provides an opportunity to interpret computationally discovered communities through the lens of philosophical and literary research.

Further research will also expand the analysis to include networks based on citation relationships, alumni connections, and data extracted from dictionaries and philosophy texts. Overlaying these networks with the existing Wikipedia-based network will enable comparisons and enhance the interpretive process. This future research will not be limited to individuals; it will also include concepts, locations, and other relevant entities as nodes, allowing for a broader exploration of 20th-century French intellectual history.

6 By Way of Conclusion: The Necessity of Interdisciplinary Research

Informatics is a discipline of "methods," and its progress relies on collaboration with other fields [9]. For example, natural language processing technology cannot advance without insights from linguistics and psychology. Similarly, big data analysis can only address real-world problems through cooperation with disciplines such as sociology and economics. The challenges that informatics addresses span various areas of society, and solving them requires specialized knowledge and techniques from each relevant field.

Building on these characteristics of informatics, Group A01 aims to explore new possibilities by fostering collaboration among researchers from diverse disciplines, drawing on their collective expertise. The research on philosophers' networks exemplifies this need for interdisciplinary collaboration. By applying mathematical methods such as network analysis to large-scale data from Wikipedia, it becomes possible to reveal relationships and structures among philosophers that traditional intellectual history may overlook. This achievement underscores the potential of combining informatics with the humanities, opening new avenues for research and understanding.

Acknowledgements My sincere thanks to Kanami Sugiyama, Kazuki Maeyama, Yuka Takedomi, and Kazuhiro Kurita for their invaluable contributions to the Analysis of 20th French Philosophers Network project. I am deeply indebted to Takeaki Uno for inspiring this interdisciplinary research and providing the environment for this collaboration. This research was supported by "Strategic Research Projects" grant from ROIS (Research Organization of Information and Systems).

References

1. T. Suda, et al. Analysis of 20th French Philosophers Network using Wikipedia Data. In *Proceedings of Humanities and Computer (Jinmoncom) 2022* (2022), pp. 193–198 (In Japanese)
2. *Journal of Historical Network Research (JHNR).* Available at: https://jhnr.net/. Accessed Jan 2025
3. D.H. Cline, The Social Network of Socrates, *CHS Research Bulletin*, 7 (2019). Available at: http://nrs.harvard.edu/urn-3:hlnc.essay:ClineD.The_Social_Network_of_Socrates.2019. Accessed Jan 2025
4. F. Moretti, Network Theory, Plot Analysis. *Literary Lab Pamphlet* 2 (2011). Available at: https://litlab.stanford.edu/LiteraryLabPamphlet2.pdf. Accessed Jan 2025
5. L.R.G. Oliveira, Philosopher's Web. Available at: https://kumu.io/GOliveira/philosophers-web#map-b9Ts7W5r. Accessed Jan 2025
6. F. Moretti, *Distant Reading* (Verso, London, UK, 2013)

7. M. Kobayashi, Y. Kobayashi, M. Sakabe, S. Matsunaga (eds.), *Dictionary of French Philosophy and Thought* (Kôbundo, Tokyo, Japan, 1999) (In Japanese)
8. NetworkX. Available at: https://networkx.org/. Accessed Jan 2025
9. T. Suda, Far from Intuitions: a French Literature Scholar's Perspective on Algorithm Research. IPSJ Mag. **65**(2) (2024) (In Japanese)

Social Media Analysis Based on Literary Reading Techniques: Developing a Method for Measuring Derogatory Narratives Online

Yuka Takedomi

Abstract This chapter combines literary theory with informatics in order to explore derogatory narratives on social media. It begins with a study aimed at understanding online slander and derogatory narratives quantitatively and qualitatively. Two approaches are introduced: the analysis of derogatory narratives related to sexual violence and the examination of broader derogatory comments across various social media topics. A typology is developed to categorize these comments, revealing recurring patterns and common logical distortions. Despite their diverse expressions, many of these narratives rely on clichés and stereotypes. The chapter also reflects on insights gained from this interdisciplinary collaboration, noting the challenges that arise when integrating distinct fields. While traditional humanities research often integrates informatics technologies to support humanities values, this study takes the reverse approach by applying literary reading techniques to the analysis of data typically handled within informatics. The tacit knowledge of the humanities and the reading techniques used in literary studies, made explicit through exposure to other disciplines, are examined. Finally, the discussion notes the results of this author's own reflections on shifts in values and mindset when it comes to interdisciplinary endeavors. By outlining the research process and the insights gained, this chapter provides a new perspective of the challenges posed by interdisciplinary collaboration.

1 Introduction

This chapter presents research conducted by the author, an expert in literary theory with limited expertise in informatics, in collaboration with informatics researchers. It begins by outlining a quantitative and qualitative feasibility study aimed at understanding derogatory narratives on social media, a subject long studied in the humanities. This research aims to conduct an in-depth qualitative analysis of social media

Y. Takedomi (✉)
National Institute of Informatics, Tokyo, Japan
e-mail: yuka_takedomi@nii.ac.jp

S. Minato et al. (eds.), *Algorithmic Foundations for Social Advancement*,
https://doi.org/10.1007/978-981-96-0668-9_11

data using literary reading techniques, ultimately seeking to facilitate the semi-automated processing of such deep analysis using large language models. While many studies at the intersection of the humanities and informatics—such as those in Digital Humanities—focus on integrating informatics technologies into the frameworks of humanities' values, this research takes the reverse approach. Instead of applying informatics techniques to existing frameworks in the humanities, it exports and applies literary reading techniques to the analysis of text data, traditionally handled within informatics.

In the subsequent section, the author reflects on insights gained from this interdisciplinary collaboration, which is often singled-out for the various challenges it entails. The chapter goes on to examine the tacit knowledge of the humanities, and the reading techniques of literary studies—as made explicit through contact with other disciplines. Finally, the discussion explores the results of the author's own reflection, including personal experiences, on shifts in values and mindset. By outlining the research process, the direct and indirect insights gained, and the author's own personal transformation through practical experience, this chapter aims to provide a new perspective of the challenges created through interdisciplinary collaboration.

2 The Challenge of "Measuring" Derogatory Narratives Online

In this section, we explore the complexities involved in quantitatively and qualitatively analyzing derogatory narratives on social media. After reviewing the background and objectives of the problem and outlining the procedure for establishing the research question itself, two practical studies will be introduced. The first, analyzes derogatory narratives related to sexual violence, and the second, addresses derogatory narratives across broader topics.

2.1 The Rise of Slander and Derogatory Remarks on Social Media

Every day, we encounter countless words on social media. These words, as narratives with nuances and contexts, affect our emotions [1]. With the ubiquitous nature of social media, we are in an unprecedented era where countless personal narratives are written, shared and read by strangers. Over the past decade, the rise of social media has empowered diverse individual voices, which differ significantly from the "objective" and "impartial" discourses of traditional mass media that were previously inaccessible to us [2]. Individual posts can create unexpected waves, spreading widely and rapidly, significantly impacting individuals and society. One of the darkest issues within this play of light and shadow is the problem of slander and derogatory remarks.

Although derogatory remarks, in a sense, are part of human nature and have existed unchanged since ancient times, several modern issues are at play here. Words, now visible as text, are accessible to anyone at any time online, and once targeted, individuals can feel as though an overwhelming barrage of words is directed solely at them. Moreover, others in that same online space, are forced to witness what seems like an act of bullying. Even without being a direct target, the outcome for these onlookers may be hurt or a retreat from the online space fearing they could be next. While the gravity of this issue, which has driven people to suicide, has become widely recognized, there is still ambiguity surrounding what kind of comments, in what situations, could lead to such levels of despair. Approaches to solving this issue include establishing laws and regulations, as well as implementing technological controls, but all of these measures are currently insufficient, as they fail to fully address the complexity and pervasiveness of online slander and derogatory remarks. Using a linguistic analysis approach, "offensive language" or "abusive words" can be detected to some extent through natural language processing technology. After a dataset on English hate speech was released in 2016 [3], Google's Jigsaw launched Perspective API in 2017 and organized the Comment Classification Challenge to help flag and classify toxic speech. However, it is essential to note that not only overt slander hurts people. Harmful expressions can take many forms, such as sarcasm, irony, accusatory phrases, or logical arguments designed to evoke guilt in the target. Even seemingly innocuous expressions, such as confirming facts about an incident, pointing out alternative possibilities, or expressing personal opinions, can be hurtful. Determining whether a narrative is hurtful depends on various factors, including context, topics, nuance, style, and the perspective of the reader. It is imperative, therefore, to consider how the meaning of a narrative, encompassing not only the literal meaning of words but also the context, influences the reader.

In Japanese, words or actions that harm a person are referred to as *誹謗中傷* (*Hibo-chusho*). In English, terms like *defamation* or *slander* refer to acts that damage a person's reputation and, in some cases, may be considered legal offenses. *Hibo-chusho* encompasses the meanings of defamation and slander but is broader and less clearly defined. It also includes words or actions that have the potential to hurt someone. It reflects that we are not only harmed by baseless lies or explicit insults but also by the malice we perceive in others' words and the subtle nuances in their expressions. Given this, grasping the full scope of what *Hibo-chusho* signifies becomes crucial. However, because the definition of the term itself is unclear, it is difficult to understand precisely what it refers to or to grasp its underlying mechanisms. This lack of clarity hinders people's ability to think and understand the phenomenon accurately. To illuminate the term's exact meaning we decided to articulate the full scope of *Hibo-chusho* (in following sections referred to as "derogatory narrative") through a thorough analysis of Japanese social media data.

2.2 The Overall Landscape of Derogatory Narratives

In order to gain access to the nuance of this problem, we first manually read and observed numerous derogatory narratives posted on various social media platforms. At first glance, the language used to harm others appears to be expressed in many ways, with few phrases exactly matching, making them seem diverse. However, upon closer examination, it became clear that these expressions often rely on clichés and stereotypical patterns, displaying similar leaps in logic and the use of diversionary tactics. Even where the expressions used differed, by extracting the meta-structure of those narratives—that is, by considering the intent and function of the narratives rather than their surface-level meanings—certain common patterns could be uncovered. For example, narratives that begin with the phrase "I don't mean to discriminate, but..." and then proceed with discriminatory remarks, or narratives that cast doubt on the validity of someone's behavior or statements by saying, "Normally, this would never happen". Thus, we set out to extract the patterns rather than the exact wording from derogatory narratives. By identifying and interpreting these patterns to create a typology, we could label individual narratives at a deeper level, beyond the surface meaning of the words or the meanings of individual terms. This allowed us to conduct a quantitative analysis, analyzing the types of narratives which exist and in what proportions. Therefore, by conducting an in-depth qualitative analysis in a data-driven manner to create a typology, and then by annotating the data based on these typologies, a clearer picture of the vast and ambiguous world of derogatory narratives in social media posts becomes accessible.

2.3 Typology and Analysis of Comments on Sexual Violence—Test Case on Yahoo! Japan News

As a test case, we focused on analyzing a corpus of social media comments related to news about sexual violence posted on Yahoo! Japan News and developed a typology for classification. These comments related to various sexual violence cases, including those committed by celebrities, in the film industry, and against children. A key advantage of drawing on Yahoo! Japan News comments is their placement directly below the articles, which clarifies the context and topic users are responding to. Additionally, these comments tend to be longer than those on platforms like Twitter, enabling examination of their logical structure and argumentative flow in greater detail. To create the typology, we manually analyzed around 8,500 comments, identifying recurring phrases, common logical patterns, and similar leaps in reasoning. We also compiled a list of frequently observed narrative structures. Based on these observations, we grouped the comments by narrative style and any reasoning used to deny the victims' claims. This categorization process is central to our research and requires significant reliance on judgement. It reflects the chosen analytical approach and ensures the data is organized in a way that allows for meaningful, practical analysis based on the narratives in the dataset.

The typology was constructed by grouping narratives based on their format and the reasoning behind their denial. Examples include "acknowledging the occurrence of sexual violence but criticizing the victim for benefiting from it" and "questioning whether the sexual violence occurred, while undermining the credibility of the victim's statements." By listing these narrative features and categorizing them according to their structure and the rationale for denial, we ultimately organized the negative narratives into five categories with 14 subcategories. For example, in the category "acknowledging the occurrence of sexual violence but questioning the victim's responsibility" (N1), we created the subcategory "acknowledging the occurrence of sexual violence but criticizing the victim for benefiting from it" (N1a). Similarly, in the category "questioning whether sexual violence occurred" (N2), we included the subcategory "questioning whether sexual violence occurred while undermining the credibility of the victim's statements" (N2a). Supportive narratives and other types of responses were also categorized based on their narrative characteristics. Using this typology, we annotated the comments accordingly. As a result, we found that, consistent with previous sociological studies, adult female victims were blamed more often than child victims [4]. We also identified narratives corresponding to philosophical theories distinguishing sexism (discrimination based on attributes) from misogyny (moral blaming for not fulfilling gender roles) [5]. Moreover, the data revealed that explicitly sexist comments were relatively few, while misogynistic comments involving moral blaming were much more common. Other hypotheses drawn from the data include that minors with a profession were slandered similarly to adult women, and that celebrities were often targeted with slander related to their appearance or nationality. To ensure the typology's validity, we randomly sampled comments and asked two co-authors, researchers in philosophy and literature, to annotate them. Annotations matched between two of the three annotators in 88% of cases, showing a higher-than-expected agreement on the categorization. [6, 7].

2.4 *Typology and Clustering of Cross-Topic Derogatory Narratives*

A comprehensive observation of social media narratives revealed that comments fitting our typology appeared across various topics, such as celebrity scandals, political mockery, royal family news, and crime reports. To address this, we developed an original typology applicable to a broader range of subjects using a data-driven approach, listing narrative features while considering contextual word usage and nuances. To handle cross-topic narratives, the typology needed to be more comprehensive than the one used for comments on sexual violence. This is because it required the flexibility to be applicable across various topics, rather than being specialized for a single one, and the universality to be consistently applied across various contexts and backgrounds. To develop this typology, we manually read tens of thousands of comments to identify the ideal level of granularity (e.g., "criticizing for failing to prove the unprovable, thereby questioning the testimony's credibility," or "criticizing for not taking unnecessary responsibility"). We then selected news topics with around 10,000 comments and applied micro-clustering to group comments with similar vocabulary into clusters.

The advantage of clustering is not only that it makes large volumes of comments easier to navigate, but it also provides an alternative perspective on biases in manual reading. Additionally, clustering can uncover similarities that might be missed by human analysis. The micro-clustering method used allows us to obtain clusters of similar comments by intuitively defining their similarity, without needing to predefine the number of clusters [8]. Moreover, since no random numbers are used, the results are reproducible. In data preprocessing, we experimented with adding particles typically omitted in clustering and extracting comments containing only high-frequency nouns to achieve results that were easy for humans to interpret. As a result, we identified several clusters corresponding to the manually created typology and were able to assign meanings to these clusters.

While this research is a feasibility study, our ultimate goal is to develop a semi-automated method for classifying comments using large language models, with clustering assisting in the labeling process.

3 Tacit Knowledge in the Humanities

This research aims to combine the core values of the humanities (qualitative, detailed reading) and informatics (quantitative understanding and mechanization). It sought to quantify elements like language nuances and context, traditionally seen as qualitative and unquantifiable, by classifying them in a way that is highly interpretable and convincing. This approach makes it possible to analyze subjects both qualitatively and quantitatively. Once conceived, this idea may seem obvious and logical, but in reality, it emerged from sustained, boundary-crossing collaboration of humanities and informatics researchers, successfully integrating their disciplinary values. This section will reflect on the implicit values of the humanities that emerged through interdisciplinary research, using our analytical approach as an example.

Humanities disciplinary techniques require the comprehensive observation of subject matter to identify broad questions and hypotheses. Data aligned with research objectives is then collected, hypotheses developed (based on the researcher's knowledge and goals), and data analyzed accordingly. Using textual analysis in literature as an example, the process typically involves the deep reading of primary sources and comprehensive reading of secondary sources and related materials. After constructing hypotheses about the text or author, their validity is verified by quoting and analyzing relevant parts of the text and supporting them with related works. This sequence of steps can be compared to the hypothetico-deductive model. Here, it is also implicitly assumed that the quotes or descriptions used to support claims must fit like puzzle pieces—precise and in relation to the research purpose. Additionally, in the humanities, there is a strong emphasis on preserving subtle nuances by handling complex concepts or expressions in as close to their original form as possible. As a result, operations commonly used in informatics—such as abstracting part of a concept or breaking it down into simpler elements to solve incrementally—are often avoided in the humanities, as the complexity and subtle nuances of the original material are prioritized first and foremost. This reflects a value system different from that of informatics. In this study, awareness of this tacit value system arose during the annotation of comments on sexual violence. While attempting to assign a single label to each comment, a collaborator from informatics asked, "Why not assign multiple labels?" However, for the humanities researchers of the team, accustomed to applying one detailed and accurate description to each item, the suggestion was difficult to understand at the time. Through continued collaboration, it became clear why this point was one of divergence—that is, assigning to a single category is a characteristic of the humanities. In the humanities, if the correct, singular label cannot be assigned, it is often seen as a sign that the classification itself may be flawed.

To elaborate further on literary studies analytical approaches, researchers start with the premise that the work being analyzed holds inherent value. The focus is on situating the individuality of the author within a historical context through the aesthetic aspects of the work or on identifying excellence and attributing value to the piece. Many scholars in this field develop a strong attachment to the works and authors they study, with little inclination to generalize the unique qualities of individual authors through theoretical frameworks. Literary theory is employed to enhance the understanding of specific authors and works, aiming for greater precision in their representation. Consequently, quantitative analysis and objective verification are of lesser importance, and the number of subjects analyzed does not inherently increase the study's value. In literary research, there is less motivation to construct theories that derive generalizations across a wide range of subjects because such generalizations detract from the unique nature of the subject at hand.

The value systems of different fields differ significantly. Even when there are seemingly shared words and concepts, their meanings and associations often vary across disciplines. Although communication in collaborative research may appear straightforward, there are times when the meaning or intent behind a comment from a researcher in another field becomes unclear, or disagreements arise over the research direction. The use of the same words or concepts with different meanings or nuances is likely one of the fundamental reasons interdisciplinary research projects often encounter challenges [9].

4 What Are Literary Reading Techniques?

In literary studies, especially in author-focused research that aims to deepen understanding of a specific author in relation to their works, a broad range of texts can serve as the research corpus. These include not only the author's complete works, but also their diaries, letters, chronologies, personal relationships, studies of the historical context of the texts, and classical works of literary criticism. Researchers must continuously decide which aspects to focus on, which theory to apply, and which methods to follow in analyzing the work, making the process of literary research difficult to generalize. These reading techniques are neither explicitly verbalized nor systematically taught within a methodological framework. Instead, they are regarded as a form of craftsmanship, learned through experience and intuition, often referred to as *sense*. However, collaborative research with informatics has made it necessary to explicitly explain the processes literary scholars use for interpretation.

As previously mentioned, literary research constructs hypotheses through comprehensive textual analysis, testing these with further verification to add layers of persuasiveness to the argument. Two key literary reading techniques are central in this complex process of interpretation and validation. The first is the ability to extract deeper meanings from a text beyond its surface level, and to persuasively demonstrate why these interpretations are valid. The second involves gathering these deeper meanings from multiple texts, reinterpreting them at a meta-level, and synthesizing them into broader concepts.

In the study mentioned above, the texts were first comprehensively read manually, following the same method used in literary research. Deeper meanings, including the writer's hidden intentions and emotions behind various expressions, were interpreted and documented. Next, narratives with similar deep meanings were reexamined to understand the reasons for their resemblance, focusing on the meta-level meanings underlying narratives. A typology was then constructed based on the structure of the statements and the reasoning behind their denial. In other words, scattered expressions were reorganized based on shared deeper meanings and reinterpreted within a new conceptual framework. In this way, literary reading techniques were applied to social media analysis.

In interpreting literary texts, scholars closely examine various aspects of the text and its author. For example, they analyze the order in which the story is presented, the focalization of the narrative, the significance of recurring (or absence of) images or words, and the connection between specific words and the author's emotions. Such advanced techniques could be widely applied beyond the field, yet scholars use them exclusively for literary analysis. This study was based on the idea that, since these methods clearly have technical aspects, they could also be applied in an engineering context to analyze non-literary texts. Before collaborating with researchers in informatics, considering these methods as technical skills which could be applied beyond literary studies had not occurred to the literary scholars on the team. To informatics researchers, who constantly seek new applications for their techniques, it must have seemed odd that these skills weren't being applied more broadly. For literary scholars, interpreting social media texts is relatively straightforward compared to literary ones. However, assigning meaning to large datasets required a different approach to the close reading of a specific author or work. For example, the appropriate level of granularity had to be considered, and interpretations had to be made at that level. Thus, analyzing social media required capturing a coarser level of meaning compared to reading literature.

5 Personal Motivations and Shifts in Perspective Through This Research

This research stemmed from personal motivation. In 2017, when survivors of sexual violence began sharing their experiences after long periods of silence, relentless slander spread across social media. Witnessing this provoked a deep sense of anger and sadness that was hard to express. Along with the desire to understand why such cruelty occurs, I felt a growing need to find a way to describe and confront this unjust and inexplicable phenomenon outside the realm of the humanities. I realized that the writing style of the humanities can be difficult for those unfamiliar with its discipline. At the same time, I began to feel that methods relying primarily on appealing to individual experiences, emotions, or ethics would only resonate with those who were already concerned about the issue.

Conducting this research brought about a significant shift in perspective. Previously, social media seemed to be filled with malice, buried like landmines, and every instance of slander caused emotional harm. However, after reading numerous comments for analysis, it became clear that what once seemed like an endless stream of unknowable slander was largely a collection of clichés and flawed reasoning. There appeared to be little variation in the emotions behind the harmful words or the motivations for using them. If words can act as weapons that hurt others, understanding their nature allows for more effective countermeasures. The process of breaking down, analyzing, and quantifying what once appeared to be an unfathomable threat had a clearly positive impact on mental well-being. Another interesting aspect of this research was that comprehensive reading not only deepened understanding of the subject but also altered the shape of the problem. While we tend to believe we understand slander conceptually, the data reveals concrete ways in which our assumptions are mistaken. Many borderline narratives exist that cannot be easily labeled as slander or derogatory remarks. When we feel wounded by narratives that simply state facts or use a forceful tone, is it truly because they are "slander"? Perhaps the focus should be on how words act performatively, rather than the words themselves. As more data is examined, more questions like these emerge. This shift in focus led to a broader interest in understanding the mechanisms of human narratives and relationships, beyond these limited topics.

6 Conclusion

This chapter has discussed research on social media narratives while reflecting on interdisciplinary experiences that were part of conducting that research and are often obscured in academic papers. Interdisciplinary research offers many advantages, such as revealing insights overlooked by conventional approaches and creating connections with new fields. While the humanities often focus on deep, individualized analysis, they lack a shared foundation for cross-disciplinary study. However, quantifying qualitative data can help establish a common ground for interdisciplinary research, enabling researchers from different fields to engage without shared disciplinary knowledge. Yet, as disciplines are integrated, dilemmas arise—what seems new in one field may not be as novel in another, and certain subjects may not be easily assessed by those outside the field.

This collaborative research has explored how the humanities can contribute to both its own discipline and informatics. By challenging the notion that literary research must focus solely on literary works and applying nuanced literary techniques—such as attention to language and context—to social media, this approach can broaden the humanities' scope and enrich informatics. These literary reading techniques have already been applied to research on identifying major shifts in public opinion from large-scale social media data and are beginning to yield promising results [10].

Acknowledgements I would like to thank Tomohiro Matsuda, Towa Suda, Kanami Sugiyama, Susumu Hashimoto, and Kazuki Maeyama for their valuable discussions and helpful feedback on this project. I would also like to thank Jill Mowbray-Tsutsumi for the thoughtful comments and feedback on this manuscript. I am deeply grateful to Takeaki Uno for the years of stimulating discussions, collaborative efforts, and insightful advice. This project was partly supported by JSPS Grant-in-Aid for Transformative Research Areas (A) 20H05962 and Grant-in-Aid for Scientific Research (C) 24K15204.

References

1. K. Wahl-Jorgensen, *Emotions, Media and Politics* (Polity Press, Cambridge, 2019)
2. R. Coward, *Speaking Personally: The Rise of Subjective and Confessional Journalism* (Palgrave Macmillan, Houndmills, Basingstoke, 2013)
3. Z. Waseem, D. Hovy, Hateful symbols or hateful people? Predictive features for hate speech detection on Twitter, in *Proceedings of the NAACL Student Research Workshop* (2016), pp. 88–93
4. R. A. DiBennardo, Ideal victims and monstrous offenders: how the news media represent sexual predators. Socius: Sociol. Res. Dyn. World **4** (2018)
5. K. Manne, *Down Girl: The Logic of Misogyny* (Oxford University Press, New York, 2018)
6. Y. Takedomi, T. Matsuda, T. Suda, T. Uno, Categorization and annotation of misogynic narrative against #metoo, in *IPSJ Symposium Series: Jinmoncom* (2022), pp. 213–220 [In Japanese]
7. Y. Takedomi, T. Suda, K. Kurita, R. Kobayashi, T. Matsuda, T. Uno, Extracting clichés: typify slanderous expressions against the confessions in the #MeToo movement, in *Digital Humanities Conference 2022 Conference Abstracts* (2022), pp. 695–696
8. T. Uno, H. Maegawa, T. Nakahara, Y. Hamuro, R. Yoshinaka, M. Tatsuta, Micro-clustering by data polishing. IEEE BigData **2017**, 1012–1018 (2017)
9. A. Rapoport, Various meanings of "Theory". Am. Polit. Sci. Rev. **52**(4), 972–988 (1958)
10. R. Kobayashi, Y. Takedomi, Y. Nakayama, T. Suda, T. Uno, T. Hashimoto, M. Toyoda, N. Yoshinaga, M. Kitsuregawa, L. E. C. Rocha, Evolution of public opinion on COVID-19 vaccination in Japan: large-scale Twitter data analysis. J. Med. Internet Res. **24**(12), e41928 (2022)

Reframing Problems: Analyzing the Design of Mixed Reality Tools Through the Lens of Fictionality

Toshiro Kashiwagi, Yasuhiro Yamamoto, and Kumiyo Nakakoji

Abstract Designing computational technologies for people and society is often viewed as an ill-defined problem-solving task, where the identification of problems and the development of solutions evolve simultaneously. This chapter presents a case study on designing two novel interactive MR (Mixed-Reality) tools, examining how people accept physically and digitally blended phenomena in ways similar to how they engage with fiction in novels and films. We demonstrate how the concept of fictionality, drawn from the humanities, helps us analyze the design of these MR tools by understanding the intertwined relationship between users and technologies.

1 Introduction

Human-Computer Interaction (HCI) research studies argue that people change by reacting to or adapting to tools and environments [13]. While computational technologies address a variety of societal and cognitive problems, they sometimes serve as opportunities to identify unprecedented behaviors or phenomena about people and society.

The human-centered system design approach is, in its essence, not about designing computational technologies for the status quo of people and society. It is about envisioning a desirable situation in the future [11], composed of computational solutions and people and society co-existing with such unseen solutions. It is a design task, fundamentally demonstrating an ill-structured problem-solving task [10]. Finding a problem and constructing a solution depend on each other [9], forming a hermeneutic circle [2], making the conventional divide-and-conquer problem-solving approach unfeasible.

T. Kashiwagi · Y. Yamamoto · K. Nakakoji (✉)
Future University Hakodate, 116-2 Kamedanakano, Hakodate, Hokkaido 041-8655, Japan
e-mail: kumiyo@acm.org

T. Kashiwagi
e-mail: g3120001@fun.ac.jp

Y. Yamamoto
e-mail: yxy@acm.org

S. Minato et al. (eds.), *Algorithmic Foundations for Social Advancement*,
https://doi.org/10.1007/978-981-96-0668-9_12

In addition to developing new computational algorithms and tools, we must strive to better understand how people and society would adapt and change when co-existing with emerging technologies. This chapter presents our MR (Mixed Reality)-based DITTO (Digital Instruments and Tangibles Theater Orchestrated) project as a case study to illustrate how we should approach designing an innovative computational artifact by simultaneously taking human traits and cognitions into account.

The particular type of MR environments we present here uses an optical see-through head-mounted display (HoloLens2), where a user can directly see the physical environment through the transparent glass, together with digital objects displayed on the glass, thereby seemingly overlaid on existing objects in the physical surroundings. We also implement some physical computing mechanisms so that the user's manipulation of a digital object in the MR environment would change the physical surroundings. While most VR and MR studies have aimed at making digital representations as *realistic* as possible to make the user experience more natural and immersed, we have found through our preliminary user studies that the distinction between physical (real) and digital (virtual) may not as quintessential as it initially seems for people to interact with the MR environment naturally.

This chapter presents DITTO-Mirror and DITTO-Spotlight to illustrate how a user interacts with digital and physical objects and perceives emerging phenomena in such MR environments. We analyzed the design and implementations of these tools by instantiating actual user experience by taking the perspective of how we produced the *fictionality* of the MR engagement. The goal of this chapter is to illustrate how taking such a concept from the humanities helps us understand the intertwined relationship between people and technologies; it is not about arguing that fictionality is the optimum concept for this matter.

In what follows, we first describe how we reframe conventional problems in MR research and argue for the approach that focuses on fictionality. We then explain DITTO-Mirror and DITTO-Spotlight as concrete instantiations, discuss the design and implementations of two DITTO tools from the perspective of fictionality, and conclude the chapter.

2 Problem Reframing: Reality as Fiction in Mixed Reality Environments

Mixed Reality (MR) is a technical concept with over thirty years of history. In 1994, Milgram and Kishino [8] illustrated MR as the gradational combination of (physical) reality and (digital) virtuality. A user wearing HoloLens2, for instance, perceives the surrounding environment by viewing the rendered images displayed on its head-mounted see-through display; thereby, the user sees the digital objects as if they exist in the physical world.

The primary technological problems that VR or MR research has been dealing with include how to faithfully reproduce digital objects as if they exist in the real world. Examples include shading processing, making virtual objects appear exposed to natural lighting, and occlusion processing, such as hiding virtual objects behind the user's hands [3, 5–7].

Some other systems use MR technology to produce situations in which people can experience interactions between physical and digital objects. These systems have primarily been presented as artworks and installations. Kobito -Virtual Brownies- [1], for instance, was an MR installation that allowed a user to interact with a virtual character of Kobito (i.e., dwarf) and a physical tea can placed on a table. Meta Flowers [12] is a more recent MR installation in which the shadows of an actual vase, flowers, and virtual flowers appear compositely on the table.

In these works, the viewer perceives physical and digital objects as naturally integrated, as if they coexist and interact. Is this the result of successfully making digital objects look as realistic (physical) as possible? The answer is probably *no.*

Our previous work [4] on analyzing users' behavior in using one of our MR tools has found that users are likely to naturally engage in a mixed reality world composed of physical and digital objects even if the digital objects are distinctively "not real." We have also found that, unlike our initial hypothesis in which physical laws override digitally generated principles, once people get used to interactions among blended (i.e., physical and digital) objects, they may find physical laws slightly unnatural.

These findings indicate that people naturally accept and interpret such blended reality in the same way as they accept fiction in books and movies. Whether they know whether the story or narrative is true or false, as long as there is a *consistent* world that a user can experience, they can accept it as fiction. A new research question for MR technologies, then, is how to design good fiction for an interactive mixed-reality environment.

3 Illustrative Technology: DITTO Tools

Our DITTO (Digital Instruments and Tangibles Theater Orchestrated) research project has been building an exploratorium with dozens of prototyped MR tools. Each of these produces an MR experience in which physical and digital objects coexist and interact in the user's perceived world. Manipulating a physical object dynamically changes the appearance of digital objects, and manipulating digital objects affects physical ones. This section briefly explains two DITTO tools, DITTO-Mirror and DITTO-Spotlight, to illustrate the particular type of fictionality of the MR experience.

3.1 *DITTO-Mirror*

DITTO-Mirror creates an MR experience where a digital (virtual) object appears reflected in a real (physical) mirror.

3.1.1 A User's Interaction

A user wearing HoloLens2, seated at a table with a mirror, sees a small virtual object (a monkey face, referred to as virtual object A) floating in the physical world. The user may freely move virtual object A around through a pinching gesture while its mirror image, another virtual object (referred to as virtual object A'), appears reflected in the physical mirror on the table. Figure 1 shows a user wearing HoloLens2 manipulating virtual object A in front of the mirror. When the user attempts to grasp virtual object A, the user's reflected image in the mirror also appears to be trying to grasp virtual object A. When the user manipulates virtual object A, virtual object A' follows the hand's reflection in the mirror. When virtual object A is brought closer to the edge of the mirror, virtual object A' gradually disappears in the same way that the user's hand ceases to be reflected in the mirror.

3.1.2 Implementation

DITTO-Mirror produces the reflection of the virtual object (virtual object A) to manipulate by providing another virtual object (virtual object A') that moves symmetrically with virtual object A relative to the mirror. A marker is attached to the physical mirror, allowing HoloLens2 to recognize its position, orientation, and surface. HoloLens2 also recognizes the user's hand gesture to display virtual object A as if the user is holding the virtual object. The tool then dynamically determines where

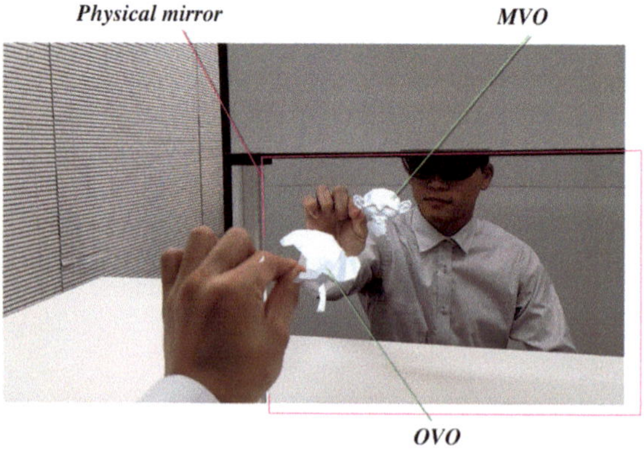

Fig. 1 The first-person view of the user wearing HoloLens2 playing with DITTO-Mirror

to display virtual object A' to mirror the manipulation of virtual object A from the user's viewpoint (Fig. 2).

3.2 *DITTO-Spotlight*

DITTO-Spotlight creates an MR experience in which the actual cube and table seem to be illuminated by a virtual spotlight object that the user manipulates.

3.2.1 A User's Interaction

A user wearing HoloLens2 and standing in front of the table with a wooden cube sees a small virtual object (a red cylinder, referred to as a virtual spotlight) floating in the physical world. The virtual spotlight has a bright, lamp-like sphere at one end of a cylinder, showing the light's direction. The user can move it around by pointing it from some distance (i.e., with a pinching gesture while aiming a ray from the fingertips). The cube and table are shaded as if illuminated by the virtual spotlight. Figure 3 shows a user with HoloLens2 manipulating the virtual spotlight above the cube. When the user directs the virtual spotlight toward the cube, it appears as if the cube's shadow is cast onto the table by the lighting effect. When the virtual spotlight is moved, it seems as if the shadow enlarges, elongates, or disappears. Shadings also appear on the surface of the cube.

3.2.2 Implementation

DITTO-Spotlight produces the shading created by the virtual spotlight by projecting a generated image onto the surface of the physical cube and table using two projectors. The two projectors are installed diagonally opposite each other above the desk and

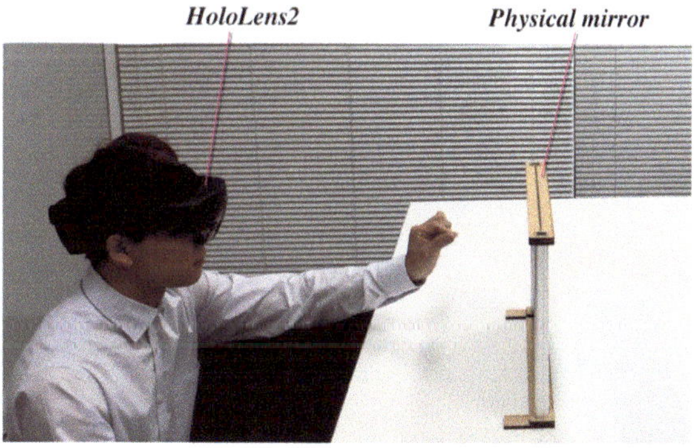

Fig. 2 A spectator's view of the user wearing HoloLens2 playing with DITTO-Mirror

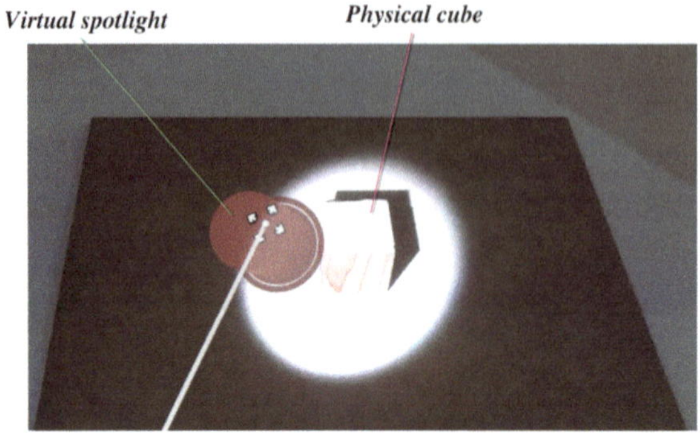

Fig. 3 The first-person view of the user wearing HoloLens2 playing with DITTO-Spotlight

are connected to a program that communicates with HoloLens2 via TCP (Fig. 4). The cube, table, two projectors, and the virtual spotlight are pre-aligned. The program generates two images (for each of the two projectors) to draw the cube's shadow based on the virtual spotlight's position and direction.

4 An Anatomy of the DITTO Tools' Design

The DITTO-Mirror and DITTO-Spotlight allow users to imagine fictitious phenomena using both physical and digital objects as components. The actual part the user sees through the see-through display is the world as it physically exists, and every object in the real world has substance and obeys the laws of physics. In contrast, the virtual part of the world is generated by a computer, and digitally computed objects displayed in the virtual world are controlled by programs developed a priori. DITTO-Mirror produces the virtual phenomenon corresponding to the function of reality

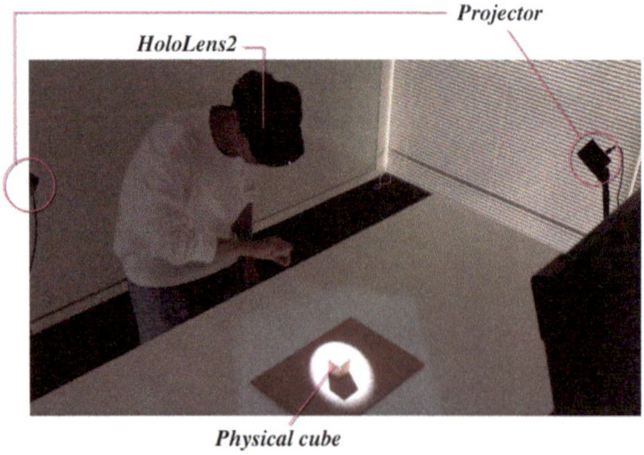

Fig. 4 A spectator's view of the user wearing HoloLens2 and playing DITTO-Mirror (note: figure captions are added after capturing the image)

Table 1 Perceived phenomena in DITTO tools

	(1) Physically observable phenomena	(2) Virtually represented objects	(3) Blended interactivity
DITTO-Mirror	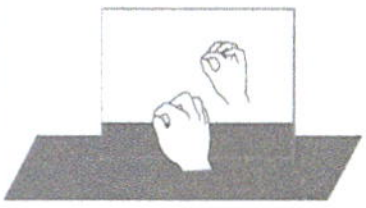		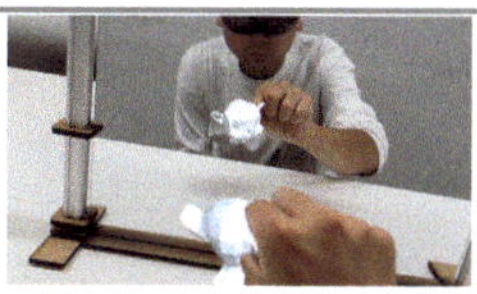
DITTO-Spotlight			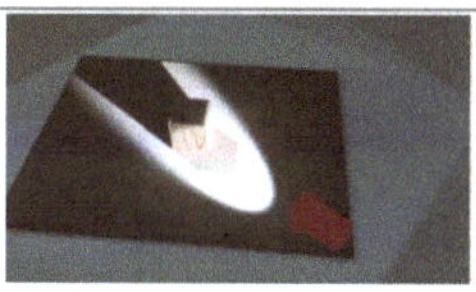

(i.e., reflection by a mirror). DITTO-Spotlight produces the physical phenomenon corresponding to the function of virtuality (i.e., illumination by a spotlight).

4.1 Perceived Phenomena in DITTO Tools

Table 1 organizes the phenomena for each DITTO tool along three axes: (1) Physically observable, (2) Virtual presented, and (3) Blending the real and the virtual.

(1) ***Physically observable***. This is what is actually happening in the physical world and is directly perceivable by a user. In DITTO-Mirror, the user's hands, body, and surrounding objects are reflected in the physical mirror. In DITTO-Spotlight, varying gradients of light appear across the surfaces of the cube and table, which are generated by two projectors located above the table.

(2) ***Virtually presented***. This is what is digitally visualized and is observable by the user only through the HoloLens2 see-through display. In DITTO-Mirror, one virtual object moves symmetrically across the mirror to the other virtual object manipulated by the user's hand. In DITTO-Spotlight, a red cylinder with a bright sphere placed on one of its bases is the virtual object to be manipulated by the user.

(3) ***Blending the real and the virtual***. This is an MR experience that blends what is happening in the real (physical) world with the virtual (digital) world. Manipulating a virtual object results in changes in the physical environment, which users naturally accept as part of the fiction. In DITTO-Mirror, two symmetrically moving virtual objects lead the user to assume the fictitious phenomenon: *the virtual object is reflected in the real mirror*. In DITTO-Spotlight, varying the gradation of light on the surfaces of the cube and table in response to moving and orienting the virtual object leads the user to assume a fictitious phenomenon: *the virtual object is illuminating the physical world*.

DITTO tools seem to lead users to believe in or accept fictitious phenomena, thereby allowing them to interact naturally with the MR environments. When trying to understand a new phenomenon, people often unconsciously draw parallels and analogies with phenomena they are already familiar with. We produce a mental model and adjust it in our minds so that we can consistently accept the new phenomenon.

Unlike VR (virtual reality), which reproduces or reconstructs the real world, MR (mixed reality) mixes virtual objects with the physical world as the user sees them simultaneously. VR generally aims to mimic real-world situations and environments; 3D models and gravity simulations represent natural objects and physical phenomena. Users accept the representations (virtual objects and events) as actual happening based on the mental model and are wholly immersed in the virtual world. In contrast, MR users are not wholly immersed in the virtual world. Instead, they are situated in the physical world alongside digital objects, creating a blended reality.

With DITTO-Mirror, the behavior of two virtual objects represents the effect of the physical mirror's reflection. The user sees that both the user's physical hand and a virtual object are reflected in the physical mirror, which seems to strengthen the fictionality that the virtual object is reflected in the physical mirror. With DITTO-Spotlight, the user perceives that the gradation of light on the cube and the table surfaces is the effect of lighting by the virtual spotlight object. The physical lighting and shading effects dynamically change as the user moves and turns the spotlight virtual object. Although it is the result of projected images by the two projectors above the table, this experience seems to strengthen the fictionality that the virtual spotlight is illuminating the actual cube and table.

4.2 Producing MR Fictionality

The problem then becomes how to design and produce such fictionality for an interactive MR environment.

DITTO Tools are implemented by *replicating* and *mimicking* certain physical phenomena. By *replicating*, we mean modeling or simulating a phenomenon. By *mimicking*, we mean pretending a phenomenon happens. We argue that incorporating the concept of fictionality helps us better understand how to design innovative MR experiences, such as those offered by the DITTO tools. The replication can be seen as the plot in fiction, while the mimicry can be viewed as the mechanism that depicts this plot.

In Table 2, we organized the design and implementation along three axes for each ditto tool: (a) Plot in Fiction, (b) Plot Mechanism, and (c) Worldbuilding.

(a) *Plot in Fiction*: Physical phenomena that are replicated in DITTO tools and are perceived by the user can be extracted as plots in fiction. A plot represents what the fiction is about. In DITTO-Mirror, the user accepts a mirror image of a virtual object

Table 2 Design and implementation toward producing fictitious MR experience

	(a) Plot in fiction	(b) Plot mechanism	(c) World-building
DITTO-Mirror	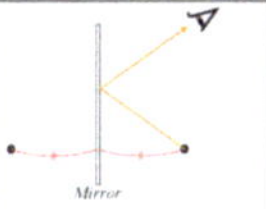		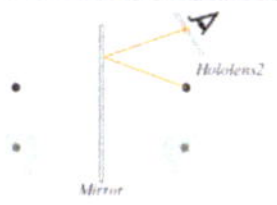
DITTO-Spotlight	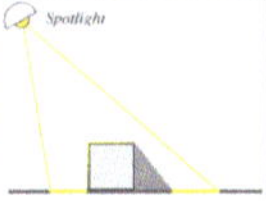	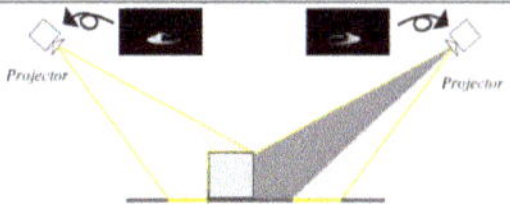	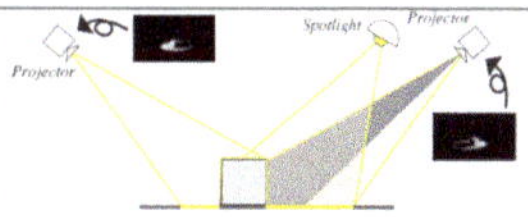

as reflected by a physical mirror. In DITTO-Spotlight, the user accepts physical shadow and illumination as cast by a virtual spotlight.

(b) ***Plot Mechanism***: A plot mechanism is something that actually makes it possible for a user to experience the plot naturally and is often hidden from the user (i.e., users are not expected to pay attention to this mechanism). The mechanism should not be entirely mechanically driven but should be implemented so that the naturally occurring effects and the effects generated by the mechanism influence each other. In the case of DITTO-Mirror, a symmetric copy of the virtual object is used as a plot mechanism, which produces the seeming mirror image by moving in sync. In DITTO-Spotlight, two projectors are used as plot mechanisms. They produce the lighting effect seemingly by the virtual spotlight by mapping computed cast images on the cube and table.

(c) ***Worldbuilding***: The fictional experience is created when the user interacts with the MR environment. In DITTO-Mirror, when the user manipulates a virtual object, the set of the user's hand and the virtual object, and the set of the reflected image of the user's hand and the copy of the virtual object, move symmetrically almost in a real-time manner. In the case of DITTO-Spotlight, the casted image, superimposed as ambient light on the surfaces of the physical cube and table through the two projectors, dynamically changes by following the position of the virtual spotlight manipulated by the user.

5 Discussions

This chapter introduced a case story about reframing the VR (virtual reality) research problems, which essentially aim to increase the reality of virtual objects, into novel interactive MR problems, which study how people accept physically and digitally blended phenomena in a way similar to how people accept fiction in novels and films. We presented DITTO-Mirror and DITTO-Spotlight, two interactive MR tools we implemented in the DITTO project, to illustrate how users interact with digital and physical objects and perceive emerging phenomena in such MR environments. By examining actual user experiences, we analyzed the design and implementation of the tools from the perspective of how we produced the fictionality of the MR engagement.

The approach presented here demonstrated a design process in contrast to a conventional engineering problem-solving approach. We first built computational tools, and then we analyzed how users interact with and perceive the tools while also modeling and developing a theoretical framework to understand the emerging phenomena and the relationship between people and technologies. We have brought in the notion of fictionality, which has long been cultivated in the study of creative literature and films, as a way for us to understand the problem better. Note that our goal here is not to argue that fictionality is the best concept for understanding this issue. Rather, it is one of many possible ways to address the problem, and there could be numerous concepts to help us understand emerging technologies and phenomena.

We illustrated how adopting a core concept from the humanities may help us understand the intertwined relationship between people and technologies. Ultimately, this approach could pave the way for more human-centered design methods that integrate creative insights into the development of emerging technologies, fostering a deeper connection between technology and its societal implications.

Acknowledgements We are very grateful to Ellen Yi-Luen Do, Mark D. Gross, Andrea van der Hoek, Takeaki Uno, Tomohiro Matsuda, Yuka Takedomi, and Towa Suda for their valuable discussions, comments and feedback in anatomizing and contextualizing this work. This project was partly supported by JSPS Grant-in-Aid for Transformative Research Areas (A) 20H05962.

References

1. T. Aoki, T. Matsushita, Y. Iio, H. Mitake, T. Toyama, S. Hasegawa, R. Ayukawa, H. Ichikawa, M. Sato, T. Kuriyama, K. Asano, T. Kawase, I. Matumura, Kobito: virtual brownies, in *ACM SIGGRAPH 2005 Emerging Technologies*, SIGGRAPH'05, New York, NY, USA (2005), pp. 11–es. (Association for Computing Machinery)
2. R. Coyne, A. Snodgrass, Is designing mysterious? Challenging the dual knowledge thesis. Des. Stud. **12**(3), 124–131 (1991)
3. Y. Feng, Estimation of light source environment for illumination consistency of augmented reality, in *2008 Congress on Image and Signal Processing*, vol. 3 (2008), pp. 771–775
4. T. Kashiwagi, Y. Yamamoto, K. Nakakoji, The interfering virtual world and the unnatural real world (in Japanese), in *IPSJ SIG Technical Report*, 2023-EC-69, no. 18 (2023), pp. 1–8. (Oct 2023)
5. S. lketani, M. Sato, M. lmura, Augmented reality image generation with optical consistency using generative adversarial networks, in *2020 IEEE Conference on Virtual Reality and 3D User Interfaces Abstracts and Workshops (VRW)* (2020), pp. 614–615

6. T. Luo, Z. Liu, Z. Pan, M. Zhang, A virtual-real occlusion method based on gpu acceleration for mr, in *2019 IEEE Conference on Virtual Reality and 3D User Interfaces (VR)* (2019), pp. 1068–1069
7. D. Mandl, K.M. Yi, P. Mohr, P.M. Roth, P. Fua, V. Lepetit, D. Schmalstieg, D. Kalkofen, Learning lightprobes for mixed reality illumination, in *2017 IEEE International Symposium on Mixed and Augmented Reality (ISMAR)* (2017), pp. 82–89
8. P. Milgram, F. Kishino, A taxonomy of mixed reality visual displays. IEICE Trans. Inf. Syst. **77**, 1321–1329 (1994)
9. K. Nakakoji, G. Fischer, Intertwining knowledge delivery and elicitation: a process model for human-computer collaboration in design. Knowl. Based Syst. **8**(2), 94–104 (1995). (Human-computer collaboration)
10. H. Rittel. Planning problems are wicked problems, in *Developments in Design Methodology* (1984), pp. 135–144
11. H.A. Simon, *The Sciences of the Artificial*, 3rd edn. (MIT Press, Cambridge, MA, 1996)
12. K. Sonobe, M. Furukawa, A. Yamanaka, H. Ohmura, T. Shibayama, R. Nakagawa, Meta flowers: an analogy of life in the xr era, in ACM SIGGRAPH 2022 Immersive Pavilion, SIGGRAPH'22, New York, NY, USA (2022). (Association for Computing Machinery)
13. Y. Yamamoto, K. Nakakoji, Interaction design of tools for fostering creativity in the early stages of information design. Int. J. Hum Comput Stud. **63**(4), 513–535 (2005)

Part III
Selected Topics on Algorithmic Foundations

The last part, spanning the Chapters "Solving Rep-tile by Computers: Performance of Solvers and Analyses of Solutions" to "Perpetual Scheduling under Frequency Constraints", highlights selected topics on the innovative algorithmic foundations developed through the project, focusing on intriguing subjects and the latest ongoing research.

Solving Rep-Tile by Computers: Performance of Solvers and Analyses of Solutions

Mutsunori Banbara, Kenji Hashimoto, Takashi Horiyama, Kosuke Oguri, Shin-ichi Minato, Masaaki Nishino, Masahiko Sakai, Ryuhei Uehara, Yushi Uno, and Norihito Yasuda

Abstract A *rep-tile* is a polygon that can be dissected into smaller copies (of the same size) of the original polygon. A *polyomino* is a polygon that is formed by joining one or more unit squares edge to edge. These two notions were first introduced and investigated by Solomon W. Golomb in the 1950s and popularized by Martin Gardner in the 1960s. Since then, dozens of studies have been made in communities

---

M. Banbara · K. Oguri · M. Sakai
Nagoya University, Nagoya, Japan
e-mail: banbara@i.nagoya-u.ac.jp

K. Oguri
e-mail: oguri@trs.css.i.nagoya-u.ac.jp

M. Sakai
e-mail: sakai@i.nagoya-u.ac.jp

K. Hashimoto
Kagawa University, Takamatsu, Japan
e-mail: hashimoto.kenji@kagawa-u.ac.jp

T. Horiyama
Hokkaido University, Sapporo, Japan
e-mail: horiyama@ist.hokudai.ac.jp

S. Minato
Kyoto University, Kyoto, Japan
e-mail: minato@i.kyoto-u.ac.jp

M. Nishino · N. Yasuda
NTT Corporation, Tokyo, Japan
e-mail: masaaki.nishino.uh@hco.ntt.co.jp

N. Yasuda
e-mail: norihito.yasuda.hn@hco.ntt.co.jp

R. Uehara (✉)
JAIST, Nomi, Ishikawa, Japan
e-mail: uehara@jaist.ac.jp

Y. Uno
Osaka Metropolitan University, Osaka, Japan
e-mail: yushi.uno@omu.ac.jp

S. Minato et al. (eds.), *Algorithmic Foundations for Social Advancement*,
https://doi.org/10.1007/978-981-96-0668-9_13

of recreational mathematics and puzzles. We first focus on the specific rep-tiles that have been investigated in these communities. Since the notion of rep-tiles is so simple that can be formulated mathematically in a natural way, we can apply a representative puzzle solver, a MIP solver, and SAT-based solvers for solving the rep-tile problem in common. In comparing their performance, we can conclude that the SAT-based solvers are the strongest in the context of simple puzzle solving. We then turn to analyses of the specific rep-tiles. Using some properties of the rep-tile patterns found by solvers, we can complete analyses of specific rep-tiles up to certain sizes, and find new series of solutions for the rep-tiles which have never been found.

1 Introduction

In some games like Tetris, polygons obtained by joining unit squares edge to edge are used as their pieces. These polygons are called polyominoes, and they have been used in popular puzzles since at least 1907. Solomon W. Golomb introduced the name polyomino in 1953 and was widely investigated [3]. It was popularized in the 1960s by the famous column in *Scientific American* written by Martin Gardner [4].

Golomb is also known as an inventor of the notion of rep-tile. A polygon P is called rep-tile if it can be dissected into smaller copies of P. Especially, if P can be dissected into n copies, it is said to be rep-n. An example of a rep-tile of rep-4 is given in Fig. 1. We can observe that each of 4 copies can be dissected into 4 smaller copies, which give us rep-16. That is, a rep-tile of rep-n is also rep-n^i for any positive integer $i = 1, 2, \ldots$. We also extend the rep-tile of rep-n by tiling n copies to make a larger pattern. That is, we can tile the plane by repeating this process. It is known that some rep-tile can be used to generate acyclic tiling (i.e., the tiling pattern cannot be identical by shifting and rotation). Both cyclic and acyclic tilings have been well investigated since they have applications to chemistry, especially, crystallography [5]. From the viewpoints of mathematics and art, the notion of rep-tile is popular as we can obtain tiling of the plane with the same shapes of different sizes by replacing a part of the rep-tiles by their copies recursively.

Gardner introduced the polyomino rep-tiles in [5]. Precisely, he introduced three 6-ominoes (polyominoes formed by 6 unit squares) in Fig. 2 as rep-tiles of rep-144. When the article [5] was written, the minimum number of dissections for these three rep-tiles was conjectured as 144. Namely, they are the rep-tiles of rep-144, and not rep-k for any $1 < k < 144$. However, they have been found out that the left *stair-*

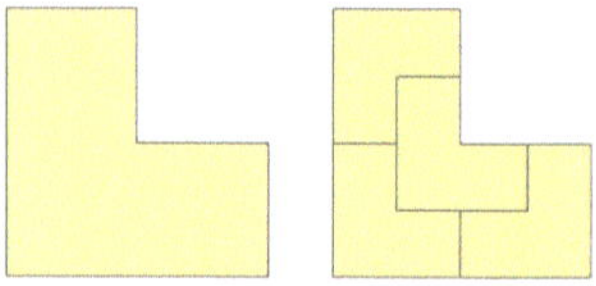

Fig. 1 An example of a rep-tile of rep-4

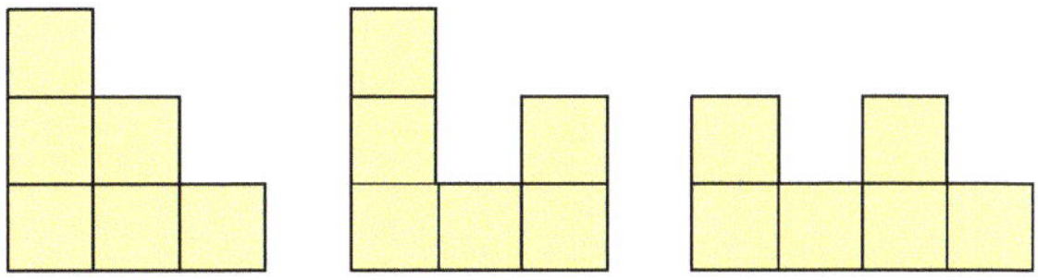

Fig. 2 The 6-ominoes of *stair-shape*, *J-shape*, and *F-shape*

shape is a rep-tile of rep-121, the central *J-shape* is a rep-tile of rep-36, and the right *F-shape* is a rep-tile of rep-64 [2, 5].

Polyomino rep-tiles have a long history mainly in the contexts of puzzles and recreational mathematics. They have been investigated since the 1950s, however, they have relied on discoveries by hand. In fact, there are many constructive solutions for these puzzles on the web page [2] However, these puzzles have not yet "solved" in the strict sense since any nonexistent results for these cases have not yet be given.

In this research, we first experiment on these three polyominoes in Fig. 2 and check if they are rep-n for each n by the representative approaches by a computer. Since the notion of a rep-tile is a quite simple puzzle, we can represent the conditions of a rep-tile in several different natural ways in the terms of representative problem solvers. Therefore, we can compare the performance of the different problem solvers using such a simple puzzle as a common problem. We use the following three different approaches to solving the rep-tiles by a computer.

Puzzle solver and implementation based on dancing links: Nowadays, most puzzle designers use a free puzzle solver. It is based on a data structure called dancing links proposed by Knuth. It is said that dancing links is the data structure that allows us to perform backtracking efficiently, and hence it is suitable to analyze puzzles. Although we do not know the details of the implementation of the free puzzle solver, we also independently implemented two algorithms; one uses dancing links, and the other uses dancing links with ZDD to make it faster.

MIP solver: When we formalize the solutions of a rep-tile by constraint integer programming, we can solve it by mixed integer programming (MIP) solvers. The conditions of a rep-tile can be formalized in a relatively simple integer programming (IP), and we can decide if the rep-tile has a solution if and only if the corresponding instance in the form of the IP is feasible. Since each feasible solution corresponds to a solution, the number of feasible solutions also gives the number of solutions of the rep-tile. In this formulation, the feasibility is the issue and hence the optimization term in the MIP solver is redundant.

SAT-based solver: Most instances of the integer programming can be solved by SAT-based solvers with some modifications of constraints. It is the case for the conditions of a rep-tile, and hence the IP formulation can be translated to the constraints of the SAT-based solvers.

In summary, the puzzle solver and programs based on dancing links, even if we use ZDD, cannot solve rep-tiles of rep-n for large n. However, this fact does not mean the limit of using a computer. The MIP solver can solve rep-tiles of rep-n for larger n than the puzzle solvers. Moreover, we found out that the SAT-based solvers

Table 1 The number of distinct dissections of k^2-omino rep-tiles, where each number indicates the number of solutions, where 0 means no solution, > 0 means at least one solution, and ? means unknown

k	1	2	3	4	5	6	7	8	9	10	11
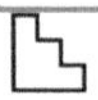	1	0	0	0	0	0	0	0	0	0	3285826288129513816
	1	0	0	0	0	262144	0	0	0	0	0
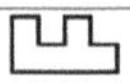	1	0	0	0	0	0	0	1358954496	51539607552	0	0

k	12	13	14	15	16
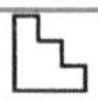	7513742553498633531870412820	421105971327597731222250323968	0	0	0
	545409716939029673955819520	0	0	0	0
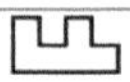	693242756013012824879005696	3658830332096120778961977344	0	> 0	> 0

k	17	18
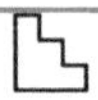	0	0
	0	770949096601587852647246241922618979582218649016246741657190 4
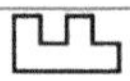	> 0	?

k	19	20	21	22	23	24	25
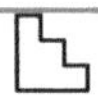	?	?	?	?	> 0	> 0	> 0
	0	0	0	0	0	> 0	0
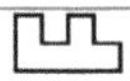	> 0	> 0	> 0	?	> 0	> 0	> 0

can solve much larger sizes than the MIP solver. These results were contrary to our expectations.

By using a model counting method with a SAT-based solver, we succeeded to count the number of solutions of rep-tiles of certain sizes, which are bigger than the previously known results. Our results are summarized in Table 1. (As we will describe later, there exist n-omino rep-tiles only when $n = k^2$ for some positive integer k. Therefore, we will consider k^2-omino rep-tiles for $k = 1, 2, \ldots$.)

By examining in detail the number of solutions and the specific individual solutions, we obtain two major new results regarding rep-tiles.

Each 0 in Table 1 indicates that there is no rep-tile of rep-k^2 for the corresponding 6-omino. Since the previously known results of rep-tiles only indicate the existence of a solution constructively, it remains open whether there is a solution for other sizes. In this paper, we show for the first time that there is no solution up to a certain size. It was conjectured that these three rep-tiles of rep-144 were the minimum size in [5], and then gradually, smaller solutions were shown constructively. However, it has never been proved that they are the minimum number. Our results in Table 1 reveal for the first time that they are all the minimum rep-tiles. They put an end to the history of exploration of these rep-tiles for more than 50 years.

As for the size in which solutions exist, we succeed in completely characterizing some of the solutions by analyzing the number of solutions and patterns of these solutions. They contain whole new types of solutions that are not included in previously known constructive solutions. We also succeed in constructing solutions with completely different characteristics from the known solutions by combining a constructive method and a search using these new types of solutions as clues. By developing these new types of solutions, it may be possible to find completely new solutions even for sizes that are previously expected to have no solution.

2 Preliminaries

A *polyomino* is a simple polygon that can be obtained by joining unit squares edge by edge. All polygons in this paper are polyominoes. For an integer s, a polyomino of area s is called an *s-omino*. A simple polygon P is a *rep-tile* of *rep-n* if P can be dissected into n congruent polygons similar to P.

In this paper, we focus on polyomino rep-tiles. Then the following theorem is important.

Theorem 1 *When a polyomino P is a rep-tile of rep-n, n is a square number. That is, there exists a natural number k such that $n = k^2$.*

Proof Let P be a t-omino. That is, P consists of t unit squares. By assumption, P can be dissected to n copies of P', where P' is similar to P. Then, since a unit square has an edge of length 1, the corresponding square of P' has an edge of length $1/\sqrt{n}$. Let ℓ be the length of a shortest edge e of the polyomino P. Then, ℓ is an integer and ℓ should be a multiple of $1/\sqrt{n}$ since this edge e is formed by tiling P'. Therefore, $\sqrt{n}$ should be an integer, and hence n is a square number. □

By Theorem 1, a polyomino P cannot be a rep-tile of rep-n when n is not a square number. Therefore, we assume that $n = k^2$ for some positive integer k without loss of generality. In order to compare to the previous results, we focus on the three 6-ominoes shown in Fig. 2 in this paper. We call each of them *stair-shape*, *J-shape*, and *F-shape*, respectively.

Among these three 6-ominoes, the J-shape and the F-shape are concave, and hence the concave part should be filled by the other piece to construct a rep-tile. Precisely, a polyomino P is *concave* if there exists a unit square not belonging to P but it shares three edges with P. We call this square *concave square* of P.

In this research, we solve the polyomino rep-tile problem for the three 6-ominoes by some problem solvers. When we use MIP solver or SAT-based solvers, we have to describe the constraints of the rep-tile problem. Here we give the common way for the representation.

As a simple example, we consider a domino (or 2-omino) P of rep-4. In this case, since $4 = 2^2$ is the square number of $k = 2$, we consider P as an 8-omino of size 4×2 by scaling 2 and fill P by 4 dominoes of size 2×1. We first assign a unique number to each unit square of P. We let $\begin{array}{|c|c|c|c|}\hline 0&1&2&3\\\hline 4&5&6&7\\\hline\end{array}$ for example. When we tile 4 dominoes on the 8-omino P, a binary variable $A(i, j)$ using the numbers of unit squares indicates a way of each domino. To make the representation unique, we assume that $i < j$. For example, when $A(0, 1) = 1$, it means that a domino covers the unit squares 0 and 1. For this P, we use 10 binary variables ($A(0, 1)$, $A(1, 2)$, $A(2, 3)$, $A(4, 5)$, $A(5, 6)$, $A(6, 7)$, $A(0, 4)$, $A(1, 5)$, $A(2, 6)$, $A(3, 7)$) to represent if a domino covers the corresponding unit squares.

Next, we introduce constraints for each unit square. Precisely, since each unit square i should be covered by just one domino, we have the following constraints.

$$\begin{aligned}
&\text{Constraint for the square 0}: && A(0,1) + A(0,4) = 1\\
&\text{Constraint for the square 1}: && A(0,1) + A(1,2) + A(1,5) = 1\\
&\text{Constraint for the square 2}: && A(1,2) + A(2,3) + A(2,6) = 1\\
&\text{Constraint for the square 3}: && A(2,3) + A(3,7) = 1\\
&\text{Constraint for the square 4}: && A(4,5) + A(0,4) = 1\\
&\text{Constraint for the square 5}: && A(4,5) + A(5,6) + A(1,5) = 1\\
&\text{Constraint for the square 6}: && A(5,6) + A(6,7) + A(2,6) = 1\\
&\text{Constraint for the square 7}: && A(6,7) + A(3,7) = 1
\end{aligned}$$

It is clear that P is a rep-tile of rep-4 if and only if there is a solution that satisfies these eight constraints.

In this paper, we wrote programs that generate the declarations of the binary variables and the corresponding constraints for each combination of 6-ominoes stair-shape, J-shape, or F-shape, and a square number $n = k^2$.

3 Comparisons of Solvers

As representative problem solvers, we chose BurrTools as a puzzle solver, SCIP as a MIP solver, and clingo and NaPS as SAT-based solvers. For each of the three rep-tiles, we list their running time for solving the rep-tile. The details and resources of the solvers follow them. Tables 2, 3, 4 summarize the running times of solvers for

Table 2 Time (sec.) for deciding if  is a rep-tile of rep-k^2 (NaPS finishes its computation after the time limit when $k = 16$)

k (Solution?)	6(×)	7(×)	8(×)	9(×)	10(×)	11(✓)	12(✓)	13(✓)	14(×)	15(×)
BurrTools 0.6.3	< 1	2	5760	?	?	?	?	?	?	?
DLX(1st solution)	< 1	15	?	?	?	?	< 1	?	?	?
DLX(all solutions)	?	?	?	?	?	?	?	?	?	?
DLZ(1st solution)	< 1	< 1	< 1	391	OF	OF	< 1	OF	OF	OF
DLZ(all solutions)	?	?	?	?	?	?	OF	OF	?	?
SCIP 7.0.2	1	1	1	1	56	42	7	120	?	?
clingo 5.4.0	< 1	< 1	< 1	< 1	< 1	1	2	2	8	?
NaPS 1.02b2	< 1	< 1	< 1	< 1	< 1	< 1	< 1	1	17	6388
k (Solution?)	16(×)	17(×)	18(×)	19(?)	20(?)	21(?)	22(?)	23(✓)	24(✓)	25(✓)
clingo 5.4.0	?	2946	?	?	?	?	?	8911	26973	?
NaPS 1.02b2	(421700)	1163	12530	?	?	?	?	529	1415	1744

Table 3 Time (sec.) for deciding if  is a rep-tile of rep-k^2

k (Solution?)	6(✓)	7(×)	8(×)	9(×)	10(×)	11(×)	12(✓)	13(×)	14(×)	15(×)
BurrTools 0.6.3	6	< 1	< 1	?	?	?	?	?	?	?
DLX(1st solution)	< 1	< 1	?	?	?	?	< 1	?	?	?
DLX(all solutions)	< 1	?	?	?	?	?	?	?	?	?
DLZ(1st solution)	< 1	< 1	< 1	< 1	< 1	241	< 1	146	OF	OF
DLZ(all solutions)	< 1	?	?	?	?	?	6	?	?	?
SCIP 7.0.2	1	1	1	5	9	14	69	4	6	19800
clingo 5.4.0	< 1	< 1	< 1	1	2	5	4	2	4	5
NaPS 1.02b2	< 1	< 1	< 1	< 1	1	2	2	7	52	116
k (Solution?)	16(×)	17(×)	18(✓)	19(×)	20(×)	21(×)	22(×)	23(×)	24(✓)	25(×)
clingo 5.4.0	6	11	9	5336	41489	?	?	?	1454	?
NaPS 1.02b2	208	282	113	1531	116400	?	?	?	1675	?

each rep-tile. In the tables, DLX indicates the algorithm based on dancing links, DLZ indicates the algorithm based on dancing links with ZDD, which are implemented by ourselves to compare with BurrTools. We omit the cases $k < 6$ since they are too short, and each number represents seconds. The symbol ? means timeout in this case. We set the time limit for each solver as 10 minutes (600 seconds) in DLX/DLZ, 12 hours (43200 seconds) in clingo, and 2 days (172800 seconds) in NaPS. The entry OF in DLZ means "overflow of cache". After each k, we put ✓, ×, and ? which mean "there exists a solution", "there exists no solution", and "we do not know if there is a solution or not," respectively.

Comparing to the DLX based on just dancing links, BurrTools implements some more tricks. The DLZ, which uses not only dancing links but also ZDD, performs

Table 4 Time (sec.) for deciding if 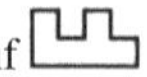 is a rep-tile of rep-k^2

k (Solution?)	6(×)	7(×)	8(✓)	9(✓)	10(×)	11(×)	12(✓)	13(✓)	14(×)	15(✓)
BurrTools 0.6.3	< 1	960	172800	?	?	?	?	?	?	?
DLX(1st solution)	< 1	< 1	< 1	< 1	?	?	< 1	?	?	?
DLX(all solutions)	?	?	?	?	?	?	?	?	?	?
DLZ(1st solution)	< 1	< 1	< 1	< 1	< 1	102	< 1	20	?	?
DLZ(all solutions)	?	?	< 1	< 1	?	?	OF	OF	?	?
SCIP 7.0.2	1	2	43	13	11	259200	?	?	?	?
clingo 5.4.0	< 1	< 1	< 1	1	3	4	11	37	97	372
NaPS 1.02b2	< 1	< 1	< 1	< 1	2	3	10	14	671	688
k (Solution?)	16(✓)	17(✓)	18(?)	19(✓)	20(✓)	21(✓)	22(?)	23(✓)	24(✓)	25(✓)
clingo 5.4.0	244	134	?	18022	6498	?	?	?	?	?
NaPS 1.02b2	316	505	?	7455	6249	8485	?	47550	131900	146200

more efficiently than DLX, however, it causes memory overflow when the search space becomes larger. Comparing to the algorithms based on dancing links, the MIP solver SCIP can deal with a larger scale. We note that we do not need the optimization function of the MIP solver in rep-tile. When we use SAT-based solvers clingo and NaPS, the range that can handle is much wider than the other problem solvers.

The details of each experiment are described below, however, there are differences in resources depending on problem solvers. This is because the authors split up to perform experiments that was good at each tool. The difference in computation results due to the difference in resources is considered to be tens to hundreds of times, however, considering the scale of the problem that increases exponentially and the actual computation results in Tables 2, 3, and 4, it can be seen that the differences of these constant factors do not affect our conclusion. The following are the details for each experimental environment.

3.1 *Puzzle Solvers*

BurrTools 0.6.3[1] is widely recognized as the standard puzzle solver in the puzzle society. It supports a variety of grids and also supports 2D and 3D for puzzles that ask to pack a given set of pieces into a given frame (without overlapping or gaps). According to the web page of BurrTools, it is based on the data structure dancing links proposed by Knuth, who wrote a 270-page textbook [6]. Dancing links is a data structure for efficiently performing backtracking in a tree search by depth-first search. In the literature [6], many examples are taken from famous puzzles as applications of backtracking in search trees. In fact, the polyomino packing puzzle, which is essentially the same as the rep-tile, is also taken up in detail as an example. In our

[1] http://burrtools.sourceforge.net/.

experiments, the machine used has an Intel Core i5-7300U (2.60 GHz) CPU and 8 GB of RAM. It is the limit of analysis for $k = 8$, namely, the rep-tile of rep-64 in each pattern.

BurrTools does various tunings internally, however, the details are not public. For comparison, we first implemented using dancing links as they are. The machine used has a CPU of Ryzen 7 5800X (3.8 GHz) and 64 GB of RAM. The C program for the experiment used DLX1[2] developed by Knuth. When using DLX1, it turns out that $k = 12$ is the limit in terms of finding a solution, and $k = 6$ is difficult in terms of finding all solutions. Next, we tried to speed up the search by combining dancing links with ZDD. The C program for the experiment used DLX6[3] developed by Knuth. The word ZDD is an abbreviation for Zero-suppressed Binary Decision Diagram, and it is a data structure that shares subtree structures that appear in common in the binary decision tree. In particular, the memory efficiency is further improved compared to the normal BDD by not maintaining the path when the result becomes 0 (see [8] for details). If ZDD is used in a tree search like our problem, since it is not necessary to repeatedly search the already searched subtree, a significant speedup can be expected. On the other hand, it is necessary to store all the subtrees once searched in the cache, and hence the memory efficiency is worse than the depth-first search tree. By speeding up using ZDD, it is possible to achieve up to $k = 13$ in the sense of finding a solution, and $k = 9$ for the F-shape and $k = 12$ for the J-shape in the sense of finding all the solutions. However, when the scale was larger than that, the search could not be completed due to lack of memory.

3.2 *MIP Solver*

As the MIP solver, SCIP 7.0.2[4] was used in this research. The way of modeling is as introduced in Sect. 2. SCIP requires a term for optimization, however, it is redundant in our model. Hence, we minimize the sum of binary variables as a dummy. Whenever it is feasible, the result comes to $n = k^2$, so it acts as a double check for the feasible solution.

The machine used in the experiment has an Intel Core i5-7300U (2.60GHz) CPU and 8GB of RAM. Although the results a bit vary, it can be seen that the solvable range is wider than when BurrTools is used.

---

[2] See https://www-cs-faculty.stanford.edu/~knuth/programs.html and https://www-cs-faculty.stanford.edu/~knuth/programs/dlx1.w for the details.

[3] https://www-cs-faculty.stanford.edu/~knuth/programs/dlx6.w.

[4] https://www.scipopt.org/.

3.3 SAT-Based Solvers

Some SAT-based solvers support Pseudo Boolean Constraints (PBs) (see [7] for details). All the constraints used in the above MIP solver are within the range of PB except for the optimization term. Here, the optimization term in the MIP solver was redundant information when finding solutions of the rep tile. Therefore, when the optimization term is deleted from the constraint descriptions used in the above MIP solver, it can be solved by the SAT-based solvers that can handle PBs as they are.

In this research, we used two typical SAT-based solvers for deciding satisfiability; clingo 5.4.0[5] and NaPS 1.02b2.[6] The machine used to run clingo has an Intel Core i7 (3.2GHz) CPU and 64GB of memory, and the machine used to run NaPS has a Core i3 (3.8GHz) CPU and 64GB of memory. Each computation time corresponds to the time for finding the first solution in the other solvers. Even considering the differences among the execution environments, it can be concluded that the range that can be solved by the SAT-based solvers is dramatically expanded compared to the puzzle solver and the MIP solver.

3.4 How to Count the Number of Solutions

From the experiments, it was found that the best method for determining the existence of the solution is to use the SAT-based solvers. The SAT-based solvers used in Sect. 3.3 have the function of finding all solutions in addition to determining whether or not it is satisfiable. However, it is not practical since it will take time due to the large number of solutions. On the other hand, the projected model counting solver GPMC[7] cannot find a solution for given constraints in CNF, however, the number of solutions can be found at high speed.

Therefore, in order to compute the number of solutions, we first determine the satisfiability using NaPS, next convert the constraints described in PB to the CNF using the conversion function of NaPS if it is satisfiable. Then the number of models was counted by GPMC. (To be more precise, when PBs are converted to CNF, variables other than the binary variable of interest are also generated. Therefore, the GPMC projection model counting function is used to count only the number of satisfiable assignments to the variable of interest. We can count the number of satisfiable solutions by this way.)

Table 1 summarizes the number of solutions obtained by combining NaPS and GPMC in this way. The entry written as > 0 in the table is the entry confirmed that the solution exists using NaPS, and the entry that specifically describes the number of solutions is the entry that was successfully counted by GPMC. The ? mark indicates

---

[5] https://potassco.org/clingo/.

[6] https://www.trs.cm.is.nagoya-u.ac.jp/projects/NaPS/.

[7] https://www.trs.cm.is.nagoya-u.ac.jp/projects/PMC/.

that any solution could not be found after running NaPS for 2 days. Here, for the $k = 16$ in stair-shape, a solution was found when the time limit was exceeded.

4 Analysis and New Solutions

As shown in Sect. 3, through this research, we were able to compute the number of solutions of rep-tile solutions up to a previously unknown size. Specifically, in each case, the existence of solutions was determined by NaPS, and the number of solutions was counted by GPMC. However, although the total number of solutions can be found with this method, the details of the solutions are not clear. In this section, we observe the solutions by NaPS and the number of solutions by GPMC, referring to the known results, and clarify the details of solutions for some k. As a result, we find new solutions that were not included in the known results at all. We will look at this in detail for each 6-omino.

4.1 J-Shape 6-Omino

The following property is useful for analysis of J-shape 6-omino (hereafter, we assume $k > 1$ to simplify):

Lemma 1 *Let k be an integer such that J-shape 6-omino is a rep-tile of rep-k^2. Then k^2 is an even number and any tiling by k^2 copies of J-shape can be dissected into $k^2/2$ 12-ominoes such that they consist of*  *and*  *(or their mirror images).*

Proof A J-shape piece P is concave. That is, it has a unit square not belonging to P but sharing three edges of P. To cover this unit square by the other J-shape, we have only two ways shown above. This implies the lemma. □

We obtain a corollary by Lemma 1.

Corrollary 1 *For any odd number $n > 1$, a J-shape 6-omino is not a rep-tile of rep-n. Therefore, for any odd number $k > 1$, a J-shape 6-omino is not a rep-tile of rep-k^2.*

By Theorem 1 and Corollary 1, it is sufficient to check whether a J-shape 6-omino is a rep-tile of rep-k^2 only for even k. Moreover, by Lemma 1, we can decide if a J-shape 6-omino is a rep-tile by checking of tiling using only two 12-omino pieces 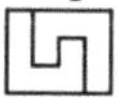 and . Using this method, we can complete the computation for k larger than the experiments in Sect. 3. By combining the arguments with the results in Sect. 3, we obtain the following theorem for the J-shape 6-omino:

Theorem 2 *For a rep-tile of the J-shape 6-omino of rep-k^2, we have the following:*
(0) There exists no rep-tile of rep-k^2 for an odd number k (except $k = 1$). There exists no rep-tile of rep-k^2 for $k = 2, 4, 8, 10, 14, 16, 20, 22$.
(1) Case $k = 6$: All solutions can be obtained by the following way: We first dissect the 216-omino P into 18 rectangles of size 3×4 as shown in Fig. 3 and then replace each rectangle by  *or its mirror image.*
(2) Case $k = 12$: All solutions can be obtained by the following way: We first dissect the 864-omino P into 72 rectangles of size 3×4 and then replace each rectangle by  *or its mirror image.*
(3) Case $k = 18$: All solutions can be obtained by using a method known as weighted projected model counting. *There are some solutions that contain both*  *and* .
(4) Case $k = 24$: There are some solutions that contain both  *and* .

Proof (0) We can obtain the results for odd k by Corollary 1. The search results by SAT-based solvers in Table 3 give us the results for $k \leq 20$. By Lemma 1, we perform the search of tiling by copies of two 12-ominoes for larger k. Using NaPS, we confirmed that there is no rep-tile of rep-k^2 for $k = 22$.
(1) Case $k = 6$: The known solutions for the J-shape 6-omino on the web page [2] are based on the arrangement of the rectangle . In fact, when $k = 6$, the pattern in which 18 rectangles are arranged (Fig. 3) is shown on the web page. There are two ways to dissect each rectangle to a pair of two copies of the J-shape 6-omino;  or its mirror image. When $k = 6$, the number 262144 of solutions matches $2^{18} = 262144$. That is, in the case of $k = 6$, there are at least 2^{18} solutions based on the dissection into the rectangles in Fig. 3, which is equal to the number of solutions actually counted by GPMC. Since they match, we can guarantee that no other solution exists.
(2) When $k = 12$, the number of solutions is 5454097169390296739558l9520. This number is much larger than 2^{72}, which is obtained by the same dissection of the

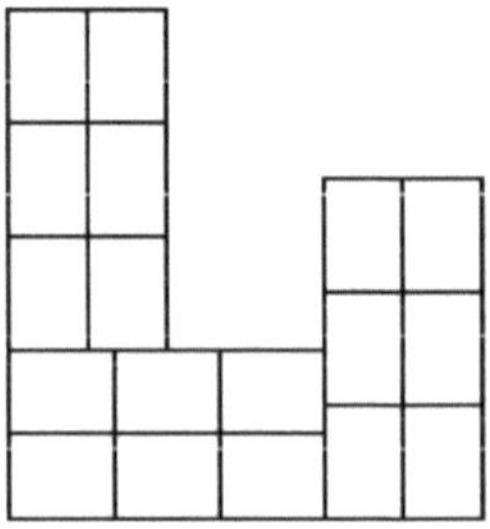

Fig. 3 Construction of tiling based on rectangles of size 3×4 for $k = 6$

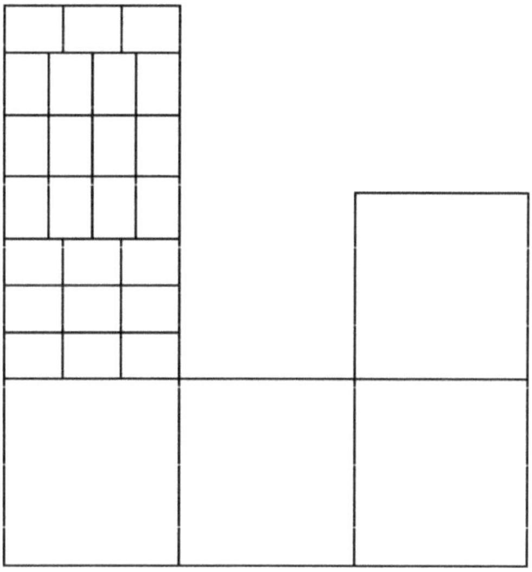

Fig. 4 Part of construction of tiling based on rectangles of size 3×4 for $k = 12$

case $k = 6$. The reason can be expressed as follows. We first consider a square corresponding to the unit square of the J-shape polyomino P. In the rep-tile for $k = 12$, the square is of size 12×12. Then we can tile this square by tiling 12 rectangles of size 3×4 in vertical or horizontal. (We note that we have no such a choice in Fig. 3, and the dissection is uniquely determined.) Therefore, we have to consider the number of ways of tiling of rectangles in vertical or horizontal. Moreover, when we consider a large rectangle obtained by joining these squares of size 12×12, there are variants of tiling of rectangles of size 3×4. A concrete example is shown in Fig. 4. In this example, the rectangle of size 12×24 in P is dissected into rectangles of size 12×3, 12×12, and 12×9. It is not easy to count the number of distinct dissections of P into rectangles of size 3×4. Therefore, we first count the number of dissections of P for $k = 12$ into rectangles of size 3×4 (and 4×3) by GPMC, which finishes soon. As a result, the number of ways of dissections is 115495. Here, we can confirm that $545409716939029673955819520 = 115495 \times 2^{72}$. Therefore, every rep-tile for $k = 12$ can be obtained by two steps; first, dissect P into rectangles of size 3×4 and 4×3, and then replace each of them by  or its mirror image.

(4) We here consider the case $k = 24$ before the case $k = 18$. By Lemma 1, we can decide if there is a solution that uses  in a tiling by J-shape 6-omino by searching using two types of 12-ominoes. Moreover, when we specify the range of the number of copies of each of two 12-ominoes, we can decide if there is a solution that contains both  and 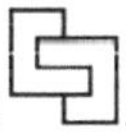. As a result, we found that there were such solutions for ($k = 18$ and) $k = 24$; see Figs. 5 and 6.

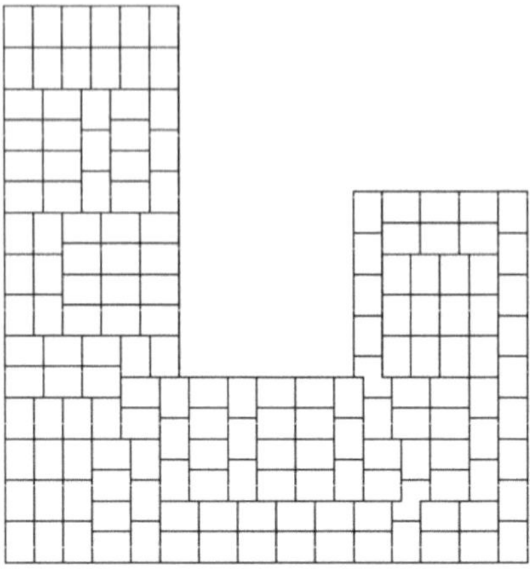

Fig. 5 A rep-tile of rep-18^2 of J-shape 6-omino that contains 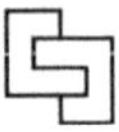

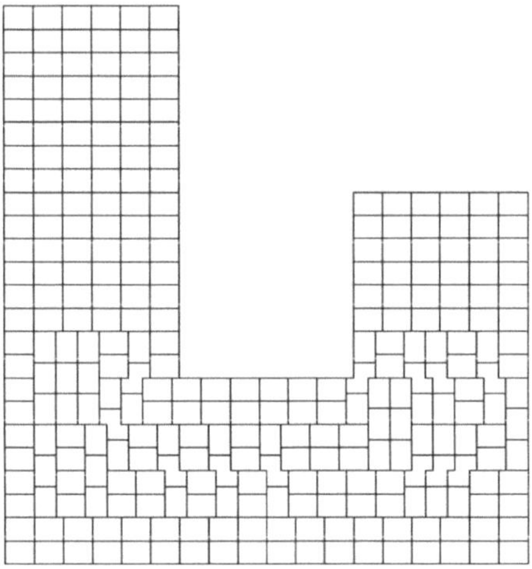

Fig. 6 A rep-tile of rep-24^2 of J-shape 6-omino that contains 

(3) We here note that this chapter is based on the results obtained in 2021 [1] except the case $k = 18$ for this J-shape 6-omino, which is obtained in 2023 by Kosuke Oguri, Kenji Hashimoto, and Masahiko Sakai. In this case, the number of solution is 7709490966015878526472462419226189795822186490162467416571904. We here briefly give the method, which is known as *weighted projected model counting*: We used an extended GPMC so that each variable can have its weight. In the tiling of a big  by small copies of it, we can observe that we have to fill it by using copies of one of  and . However, each  has two ways of filling (by its mirror), while 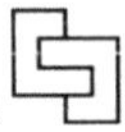 has one way. Therefore, we gave weight 2 to , and 1 to

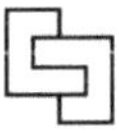 and count up the ways of filling by them with the weights. That is, we count the ways of packing by copies of 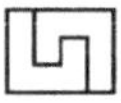 of weight 2 and 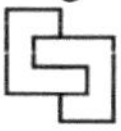 of weight 1, which gives us the number of solutions by copies of the J-shape 6-omino. We note that, in the same way of the case $k = 24$, we found solutions that contain both 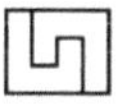 and  in the case $k = 18$, which is the smallest size by the results in the cases (1) and (2). □

We note that the solutions that contain  are new solutions not included in previously known results. So far, in the case $k = 18$, there are solutions that contain x copies of  for every even number x from 2 to 46. There is no such solution when $x \geq 47$. That is, all solutions containing 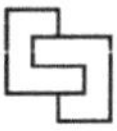 we found have even number of pairs of this form. We conjecture that there are solutions that contain  for $k > 24$.

4.2 F-Shape 6-Omino

The known rep-tiles of the F-shape 6-omino are a bit complicated, however, the solutions posted on the web page [2] are explained as follows: We first combine two copies of the F-shape 6-omino to form 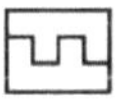, 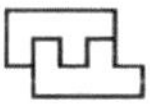, and 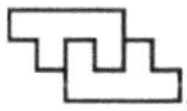, then next arrange them appropriately, and finally place one copy of the F-shape 6-omino if necessary. In this placement, 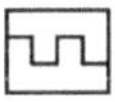 is a rectangle, hence replacing it with its mirror image gives us many distinct solutions.

We summarize our results in the following theorem. Among them, we found new types of solutions that cannot be explained in the way of previously known results for $k = 8, 15, 16, 17$.

Theorem 3 *For a rep-tile of the F-shape 6-omino of rep-k^2, we have the following:*
(0) There exists no rep-tile of rep-k^2 for $k = 2, 3, 4, 5, 6, 7, 10, 11, 14$.
(1) Case $k = 8$: All solutions can be obtained by the following way: We first dissect the 384-omino P in one of the ways shown in Fig. 7, and then replace each rectangle by 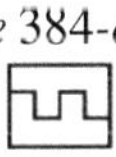 *or its mirror image.*

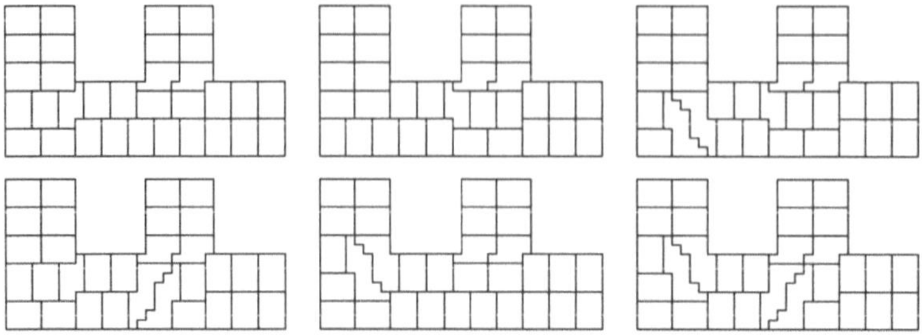

Fig. 7 All solutions of rep-tiles of rep-8^2 for the F-shape 6-omino (we can obtain many variants when we fill each rectangle 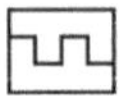 or its mirror image)

(2) Case $k = 9$*: All solutions can be obtained by the following way: We first dissect the* 486*-omino* P *in one of the ways shown in Figs. 8 and 9 and then replace each rectangle by* 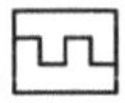 *or its mirror image.*
(3) Case $k = 12, 13, 19, 20, 21, 23, 24, 25$*: There exist rep-tiles of rep-*k^2*. The number of solutions in the case* $k = 12, 13$ *can be found in Table 1.*
(4) Case $k = 15, 16, 17$*: There exist rep-tiles of rep-*k^2 *that include the pattern given in Fig. 10.*

Proof (0), (3) We can determine the (non)existence of rep-tiles up to $k = 25$ by SAT-based solvers. By using GPMC, we can count the number of solutions (in the existence case) for each k up to 13.
(1), (2) By using NaPS and GPMC, we obtain that the numbers of solutions for $k = 8$ and $k = 9$ are 1358954496 and 51539607552, respectively. We then enumerate all non-concave polyominoes that can be obtained by combining two or three copies of the F-shape 6-omino, and find all tilings using them. After that, we count the number of ways of tilings that can be obtained by filling each rectangle of size 3×4 by 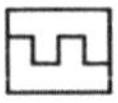 or its mirror image. The numbers of tilings should be at most 1358954496 and 51539607552 for $k = 8$ and $k = 9$, respectively. In fact, we found that we have already listed all tilings since they are equal in both cases. The patterns of solutions are listed in Figs. 7, 8, and 9. We use the all non-concave 18-polyominoes obtained by combining three copies of the F-shape 6-omino, however, in fact, only 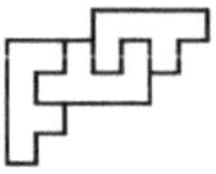 and 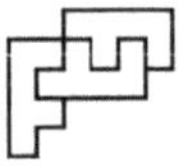 are required to enumerate all solutions for $k = 8$ and $k = 9$.

Precisely, when $k = 8$, there exist six essentially different dissections. When we consider replacing each rectangle by 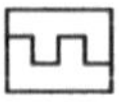 or its mirror image, we obtain the number of solutions given by Fig. 7 is equal to $2^{24} + 2 \times 2^{26} + 2^{27} + 2 \times 2^{29} = 1358954496$ that coincident with the number of solutions obtained by running NaPS and GPMC.

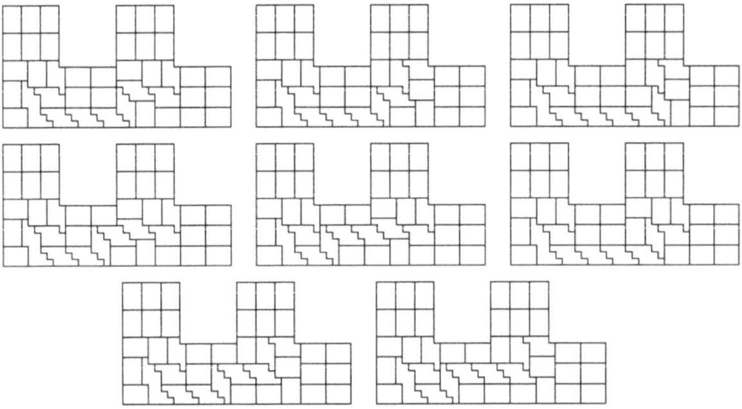

Fig. 8 All solutions of rep-tiles of rep-9^2 for the F-shape 6-omino (1/2)

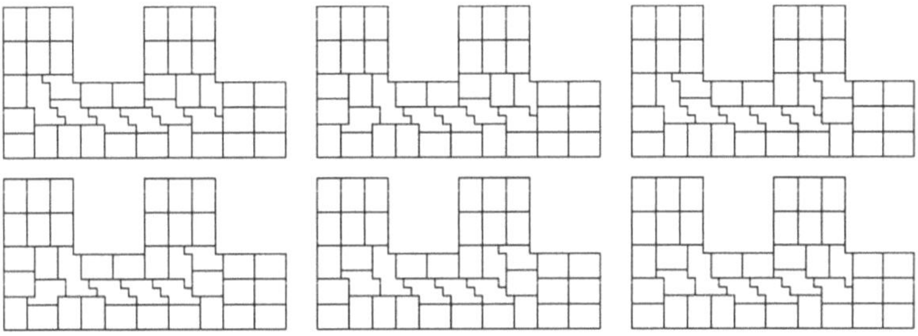

Fig. 9 All solutions of rep-tiles of rep-9^2 for the F-shape 6-omino (2/2)

When $k = 9$, we have fourteen essentially different dissections. By considering the numbers of rectangles in these dissections, the total number of solutions given by Figs. 8 and 9 is $8 \times 2^{30} + 2 \times 2^{32} + 4 \times 2^{33} = 51539607552$ that contains all solutions obtained by NaPS and GPMC.

Checking all of these solutions, we can confirm that we can construct any rep-tile for $k = 9$ by combining 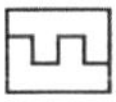, 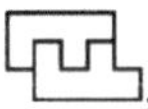, and 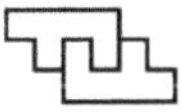 and add one copy of the F-shape 6-omino if necessary. Moreover, the last one copy is added to form 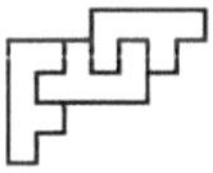 or 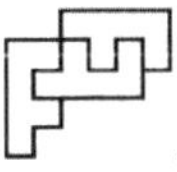. Concretely, 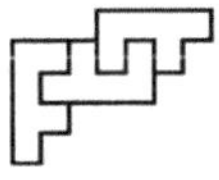 is used in the eight patterns in Fig. 8, and 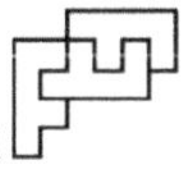 is used in the six patterns in Fig. 9. That is, when $k = 9$, we can construct any solution by tiling some copies of 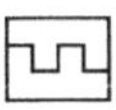, 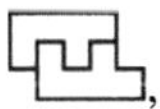, and 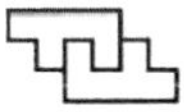 with one copy of 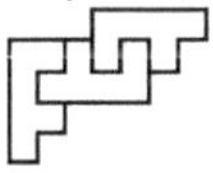 or

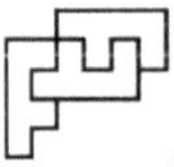. In other words, these solutions can be represented in the same way of the previously known results.

However, when $k = 8$, we cannot construct all solutions in the way of the previously known results. More precisely, the first two patterns among six patterns in Fig. 7 can be represented in this way, however, the next three patterns require to add two copies of the F-shape 6-omino. Moreover, the last pattern requires to add four copies of the F-shape 6-omino. That is, among six patterns in Fig. 7, there are only two patterns that can be represented in the way of the previously known results and the other four patterns give us new solutions. Especially, in the last two patterns in Fig. 7, we have to place both copies of 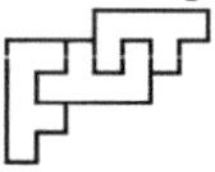 and 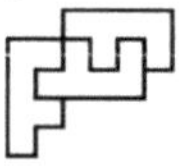 after placements of copies of 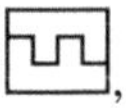, 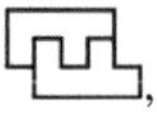, and 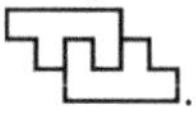.

□

(4) In the case of $k = 8$ or $k = 9$, we can construct all rep-tiles by tiling non-concave polyominoes obtained by combining two or three copies of the F-shape 6-omino. Then, is this common in all the rep-tiles by the F-shape 6-omino? It is not the case. We first note that there exist patterns that require four or more copies of the F-shape 6-omino. A concrete example is given in Fig. 10. (There are no rep-tile containing such a pattern in the previously known results.) We searched rep-tiles that require copies of the pattern in Fig. 10 with non-concave polyominoes obtained by combining two or three copies of the F-shape 6-omino. Then there are some solutions (Fig. 11) containing the pattern in Fig. 10 for $k = 15, 16, 17$. They are completely different rep-tiles from the previously known solutions.

4.3 Stair-Shape 6-Omino

Since the stair-shape 6-omino is not concave (in our definition) contrast with the J-shape and F-shape 6-ominoes, it is difficult to search its rep-tile pattern systematically. However, by generating the unit patterns obtained by combining a few copies of the stair-shape to cancel the zig-zag part of it and tiling the copies of these unit patterns,

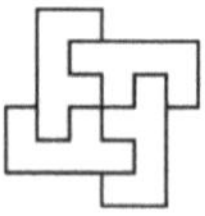

Fig. 10 A non-concave 24-omino that requires four copies of the F-shape 6-omino (any removal of one or two copies makes concave)

Fig. 11 Examples of rep-tiles that contain the pattern in Fig. 10 for $k = 15, 16, 17$

we succeeded to generate all patterns of solutions for $k = 11$. The results can be summarized as follows:

Theorem 4 *For a rep-tile of the stair-shape 6-omino of rep-k^2, we have the following:*
(0) There exists no rep-tile of rep-k^2 for $k = 2, 3, 4, 5, 6, 7, 8, 9, 10, 14, 15, 16, 17, 18$.
(1) Case $k = 11$: All solutions can be obtained by the following way: We first dissect the 726-omino P into one of three patterns in Fig. 12. Then replace each polygon by , 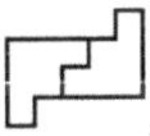, *or* 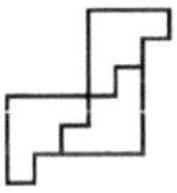 *(or their mirror images). We note that the previously known results are included in Fig. 12a, and the patterns in Fig. 12b and c are new solutions that we found in this research.*
(2) Case $k = 12, 13, 23, 24, 25$: There exist rep-tiles of rep-k^2. The number of solutions in the case $k = 12, 13$ can be found in Table 1.

Proof We omit all the cases except $k = 11$ since they were obtained by NaPS and GPMC. (Here we note that $k = 16$ is an exception: the solution in this case could not be obtained by the time limit, however, we could obtain it when we extend the time

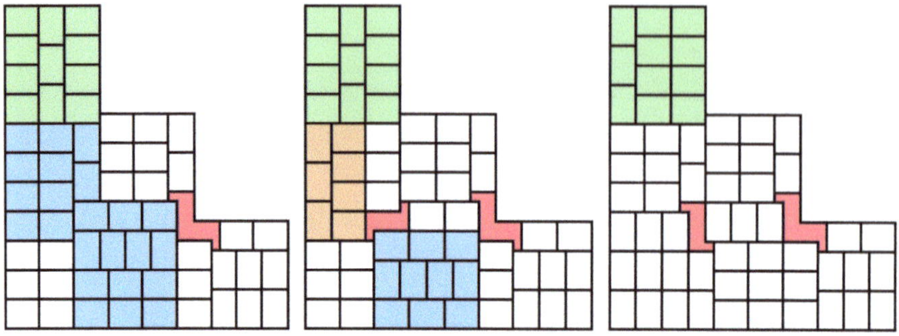

(a) (b) (c)

Fig. 12 Three solutions of the stair-shape 6-omino for $k = 11$

limit.) When $k = 11$, we perform the search by using three 12-ominoes obtained by 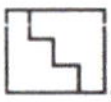, 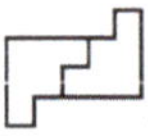, and 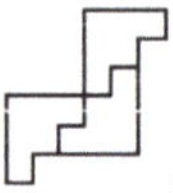. We have three groups by the search.

The first pattern is given in Fig. 12a: It uses 59 copies of 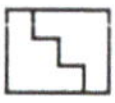 and one copy of 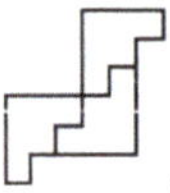. There are three ways of tiling the left upper green rectangle by 11 rectangles of size 3×4, and six ways of tiling the blue polygon by 23 rectangles of size 3×4. (For the latter blue polygon, there are three ways of tiling of the left upper blue rectangle of size 11×12, four ways of tiling of the right lower blue rectangle of size 12×13, and one in common, which implies six ways in total.) Since we can make a mirror image with respect to the line of 45°, the total number of solutions in the pattern in Fig. 12a is $2 \times 18 \times 2^{59} = 20752587082923245568$.

The next pattern is given in Fig. 12b, which uses 58 copies of 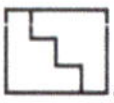, one copy of 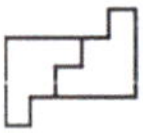, and one copy of 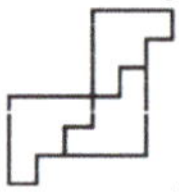. In this case, there are three ways to tile the left upper green rectangle, two ways to tile the central brown rectangle, and three ways to tile the lower blue rectangle. The last pattern in Fig. 12c also uses 58 copies of 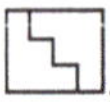, one copy of 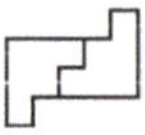, and one copy of 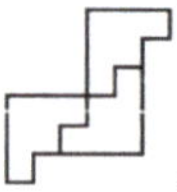. It has three ways to tile the green rectangle. In total, the number of solutions in patterns in Fig. 12b and c is $2 \times (18 + 3) \times 2^{58} = 12105675798371893248$.

Therefore, when we add all solutions in the patterns in Fig. 12a, b and c, it makes $42 \times 2^{58} + 36 \times 2^{59} = 32858262881295138816$, which is equal to the number of solutions in Table 1. Therefore, we cover all rep-tiles for $k = 11$. □

Acknowledgements This research is partially supported by Kakenhi (17K00017, 18H04091, 20H05964, 21K11757).

References

1. M. Banbara, K. Hashimoto, T. Horiyama, S. Minato, K. Nakamura, M. Nishino, M. Sakai, R. Uehara, Y. Uno, N. Yasuda, Solving rep-tile by computers: performance of solvers and analyses of solutions (Oct 2021). arXiv:2110.05184
2. A.L. Clarke, Polyomino Reptiles. http://www.recmath.org/PolyPages/PolyPages/index.htm?RepO6.htm. Accessed Aug 2021
3. S.W. Golomb. *Polyominoes: The Fascinating New Recreation in Mathematics* (Charles Scribner's Sons, 1965)
4. M Gardner, *Hexaflexagons, Probability Paradoxes, and the Tower of Hanoi: Martin Gardner's First Book of Mathematical Puzzles and Games* (Cambridge University Press, 2008)
5. M Gardner, *Knots and Borromean Rings, Rep-Tiles, and Eight Queens: Martin Gardner's Unexpected Hanging* (Cambridge University Press, 2014)
6. D.E. Knuth, in *The Art of Computer Programming: Dancing Liniks*, vol. 4, pre-fascicle 5c, (Sept 2019)
7. D.E. Knuth, in*The Art of Computer Programming: Satisfiability*, vol. 4, Fascicle 6, (2015)
8. D.E. Knuth, in *The Art of Computer Programming: Bitwise Tricks & Techniques; Binary Decision Diagrams*, vol. 4, Fascicle 1 (2009)

Parallel Redundancy Removal in *lrslib* with Application to Projections

David Avis and Charles Jordan

Abstract We describe a parallel implementation in *lrslib* for removing redundant halfspaces and finding a minimum representation for an H-representation of a convex polyhedron. By a standard transformation, the same code works for V-representations. We use this approach to speed up the redundancy removal step in Fourier-Motzkin elimination. Computational results are given including a comparison with Clarkson's algorithm, which is particularly fast on highly redundant inputs.

Keywords Redundancy removal · Convex hulls · Minimum representations · Fourier-Motzkin elimination · Parallel processing

1 Introduction

In this section we give a general overview of the topics to be discussed, leaving formal definitions for the next section. In this paper we deal with convex polyhedra which we assume, to avoid trivialities, are non-empty. The computational problems of (1) removing redundancy, (2) finding a minimum representation and (3) projecting a system of m linear inequalities in $\mathbb{R}^n$ (an H-representation) are fundamental in many areas of mathematics and science. The first two problems are usually solved using linear programming (LP), and the third via Fourier-Motzkin (F-M) elimination. Linear programming is solvable in polynomial time and so are the first two problems. Projection is more difficult and was shown to be NP-hard by Tiwary [7]. Similar

Partially supported by JSPS Kakenhi Grants 20H00579, 20H00595, 20H05965, 22H05001 and 23K11043.

D. Avis (✉)
School of Informatics, Kyoto University, Kyoto, Japan
e-mail: avis@cs.mcgill.ca

School of Computer Science, McGill University, Montréal, Québec, Canada

C. Jordan
Department of Information and Management Science, Otaru University of Commerce, Otaru, Japan
e-mail: skip@res.otaru-uc.ac.jp

S. Minato et al. (eds.), *Algorithmic Foundations for Social Advancement*,
https://doi.org/10.1007/978-981-96-0668-9_14

problems arise when the input is given by a set of vertices and extreme rays (a V-representation). In this case, the first two problems are computationally equivalent to the inequality setting whereas the projection problem is easier and can be solved in polynomial time.

For the redundancy problem, the *classic method* is to consider each inequality in turn. Checking redundancy of a given inequality (ie, whether it can be removed without changing the solution set) can be done by solving one LP and each redundant inequality is deleted once it is found. This simple approach requires m LPs to be solved, with the number of constraints equal to m minus the number of redundancies already encountered. Clarkson [3] introduced an output-sensitive improvement. Again m LPs are solved but the number of constraints is bounded by the number of non-redundant inequalities, see Sect. 3 for details. Fukuda et al. [6] also presented an output-sensitive approach to redundancy removal based on the sign structure of all associated LP dictionaries. The complexity contains an exponential term in the dimension and it does not appear to have been implemented.

In general, certain inequalities may be satisfied as equations by the solution set for the entire system and these are known as linearities. In the minimum representation problem, all linearities must be identified and all redundancy removed. Redundant inequalities cannot be linearities. For a given non-redundant inequality, a second LP can be used to determine if it is a linearity. Alternatively this can be done by solving a single large LP as shown by Freund et al. [4], although the practicality of that method is unclear.

The projection problem is to project the polyhedron into a subspace. For the easier problem (projecting a V-representation), we simply select the the coordinates of the input vectors that remain after the projection and then find a minimum representation. The output polyhedron has fewer dimensions and at most as many vertices and rays, so is smaller than the input. For projecting an H-representation, the F-M method eliminates one variable at a time but the number of inequalities can increase by a quadratic factor at each step. Many of these may be redundant, so an efficient implementation includes repeated redundancy removal.

The methods outlined above for redundancy removal are sequential, however they seem good candidates for parallelization. The classic method is particularly simple and is what we chose to implement. The subtleties involved are a main topic of this paper. The paper is organized as follows. The next section contains formal definitions. Section 3 explains how we parallelize redundancy removal and minimum representation algorithms, and also contains a brief description of Clarkson's algorithm. Section 4 shows how parallelization is used to speed up F-M elimination and computational results are given in Sect. 5. Finally we give some conclusions and directions for future research.

2 Basic Definitions

We begin by giving some basic definitions related to polyhedra and linear programming. For more information, see the books by Chvátal [2], Fukuda [5] and Ziegler [8]. Given an $m \times n$ matrix $A = (a_{ij})$, an m dimensional vector b and a possibly empty subset $J \subseteq \{1, \ldots, m\}$ we let A_J and b_J denote the submatrix of A and subvector of b with rows indexed by J. We denote by A_{-J} and b_{-J} the submatrix and subvector where the rows corresponding to the indices J have been deleted. In the case where $J = \{i\}$ is a singleton we write A_i, b_i, A_{-i}, b_{-i} respectively.

Let L and I be a partition of $\{1, \ldots, m\}$. A *convex polyhedron*, or simply *polyhedron*, P is defined as:

$$P = \{x \in \mathbb{R}^n : b_L + A_L x = 0,\ b_I + A_I x \geq 0\}. \tag{1}$$

This description of a polyhedron is known as an *H-representation* and the rows indexed by L are called linearities. To avoid trivialities we will assume that all polyhedra discussed in this paper are non-empty; this can be tested by a linear program (LP). We may also assume that the system of equations defined by L is linearly independent, using Gaussian elimination if necessary to delete dependencies.

Another way to describe P is by a *V-representation*. In this case we have finite sets of vectors V, R, S in $\mathbb{R}^n$ of vertices, rays and linearities. The fundamental Minkowski-Weyl theorem states that for every P defined by (1)

$$P = \text{conv}(V) + \text{conic}(R) + \text{lin}(S). \tag{2}$$

In words, every $x \in P$ can be expressed as the sum of a convex combination of vertices, a nonnegative combination of rays and a linear combination of linearities. The most fundamental problem in polyhedral computation is the conversion of an H-representation to a V-representation and vice versa. The former problem is often called the *vertex enumeration problem* and the latter problem the *facet enumeration problem*. This computation forms the core of *lrslib*, see [1] for a discussion of how it is solved in parallel.

For $i \in I$, we let P_{-i} denote the polyhedron defined by A_{-i} and b_{-i}. If $P = P_{-i}$ we say that row i is *redundant*. This is equivalent to saying that each $x \in P_{-i}$ satisfies $b_i + A_i x \geq 0$. If each such x actually satisfies $b_i + A_i x > 0$ we say row i is *strongly redundant* otherwise it is *weakly redundant*. Finally if for each $x \in P$ we have $b_i + A_i x = 0$, we say that row i is a *hidden linearity* and index i can be moved to the set L if the rows indexed by L remain linearly independent. Otherwise row i is deleted.

The H-representation (1) of P is *non-redundant* if there are no redundant indices i. It is a *minimum representation* if it is non-redundant and contains no hidden linearities. In this case the dimension of P is $n - |L|$ and P is *full dimensional* if L is empty. The first part of this paper describes a parallel method for removing redundancies and computing a minimum description of a polyhedron based on linear programming. We also describe Clarkson's algorithm [3] which gives a much more efficient LP approach when the input polyhedron is highly redundant. However, this method seems more challenging to parallelize.

Section 4 concerns projections of polyhedra. Let A and B partition the column indices $\{1, \ldots, n\}$. For $x \in P$ we write $x = (x_A, x_B)$ to represent the corresponding decomposition of x into subspaces $\mathbb{R}^A$ and $\mathbb{R}^B$ that partition $\mathbb{R}^n$. The *projection* of P onto the subspace $\mathbb{R}^A$ is given by

$$P_A = \{x_A \in \mathbb{R}^A : \exists x = (x_A, x_B) \in P\}. \tag{3}$$

We will show how the parallel redundancy method described in Sect. 3 can be used to speed up the operation of the F-M method of computing projections.

3 Parallel Redundancy Removal and Finding a Minimum Representation

Assume we are given an H-representation (1) of a non-empty polyhedron P where L defines a linearly independent set of equations. Choose $i \in I$ and consider the two LPs:

$$z_{\min} = \min b_i + A_i x \quad \text{s.t.} \quad b_{-i} + A_{-i} x \geq 0 \tag{4}$$

$$z_{\max} = \max b_i + A_i x \quad \text{s.t.} \quad b_{-i} + A_{-i} x \geq 0. \tag{5}$$

The status of the i-th inequality is determined by the following well known proposition based on the definitions. For completeness we give a short proof.

Proposition 1 *The inequality $b_i + A_i x \geq 0$ is a linearity if $z_{\max} = 0$ otherwise it is*

(a) weakly redundant if $z_{\min} = 0$
(b) strongly redundant if $z_{\min} > 0$
(c) non-redundant if $z_{\min} < 0$ or unbounded

Proof In the LP dictionary (see Chvátal [2]) the i-th inequality is represented using the non-negative slack variable x_{n+i} as

$$x_{n+i} = b_i + A_i x. \tag{6}$$

LP (5) seeks to find a feasible point in P_{-i} that satisfies the inequality strictly. If $z_{\max} = x_{n+i} = 0$ this is not possible so the inequality is in fact a linearity. Otherwise LP (4) seeks to find a point in P_{-i} that violates the constraint. If $z_{\min} = x_{n+i} \geq 0$ then the inequality cannot be violated so it is redundant, and if $z_{\min} > 0$ it is strongly redundant. Finally if $z_{\min} < 0$ then there is some feasible point in P_{-i} that violates the constraint and hence it is non-redundant. □

It might seem that the proposition leads immediately to a parallel algorithm for redundancy removal: check and classify each row index independently. However this fails due to the possibility of duplicated rows, and in the presence of linearities these may be hard to discover. For example, consider the system:

$$
\begin{aligned}
3 + x_1 - 2x_2 &= 0 \\
x_1 &\geq 0 \\
-6 - x_1 + 4x_2 &\geq 0.
\end{aligned}
$$

Both rows 2 and 3 considered independently are redundant since if we add twice row 1 to row 3 we obtain row 2. They are both weakly redundant: we can eliminate either one but not both. But if each of these rows is considered by a different processor both will be marked redundant, which is an error as one of them must remain as non-redundant. This problem becomes more acute when the system contains hidden linearities which can easily mask duplication. Nevertheless, inequalities classified as linearities, strongly redundant or non-redundant will all be correctly classified. Only weakly redundant inequalities are problematic.

To solve this problem we recall that for full dimensional polyhedra, ie, when there are no linearities, the H-representation is unique up to multiplication of rows by positive scalars. In this case we can reduce each row by its greatest common divisor (GCD) and then sort the rows to reveal and remove duplication. Now each remaining inequality can be tested independently and in parallel to see if it is redundant. Our general strategy will be to first find any hidden linearities in P. Then we will use the linearities to eliminate variables until the resulting system is full dimensional.

As a first step, we can check whether the H-representation (1) has any hidden linearities by the single LP:

$$
\max x_{n+1} \quad \text{s.t.} \quad b_L + A_L x = 0, \;\; b_I + A_I x \geq \mathbb{1}_{|I|}\, x_{n+1} \tag{7}
$$

where $\mathbb{1}_t$ denotes a column of t ones. The LP terminates with $x_{n+1} > 0$ if and only if there is a point in P that does not lie on the boundary of any inequality and so there are no hidden linearities. If there are any hidden linearities then they can be identified via Proposition 1 and this can be done in parallel. If there are no hidden linearities then LP (5) does not need to be solved when classifying the inequality set I. The complete procedure is described below for a polyhedron P given as (1).

Parallel algorithm for finding a minimum representation

(a) Solve LP (7) to determine if there are any hidden linearities. If there are none, set $W = I$ and go to step (c).

(b) (parallel) For each $i \in I$ determine the status of $b_i + A_i x \geq 0$ according to Proposition 1. Place i into the corresponding subset S (strongly redundant), W (weakly redundant), N (non-redundant) or otherwise add it to L and remove it from I.

(c) Remove any index $i \in L$ from L for which $b_i + A_i x = 0$ is linearly dependent.

(d) For each remaining index $i \in L$, use equation $b_i + A_i x = 0$ to remove one variable from $b_I + A_I x \geq 0$ by substitution.
(e) Reduce each inequality by its GCD and eliminate any duplicate rows from I obtaining an index set J and the reduced system $\overline{b_J} + \overline{A_J} x \geq 0$. Note there is no linearity in this system as it is full dimensional.
(f) (parallel) For each $i \in W \cap J$ determine the status of inequality i by solving LP (4) for the reduced system, classifying them as in step (b).

Observe that if there are no hidden linearities then only one LP needs to be solved for each index in I. When there are hidden linearities, the number of LPs to solve depends on the order of solving LPs (4) and (5) in step (b). If we solve them in the order described, then the second LP only needs to be solved when a weak redundant inequality is found. This is the order used in *lrslib*. In the reverse order, the second LP needs to be solved whenever a linearity is not found. In either case a further LP is required for each weakly redundant inequality in step (f).

A modified procedure requires at most 2 LPs to be solved per inequality when there are hidden linearities. In step (b) we could just solve (5) and hence determine all linearities in I. We define W to be all remaining inequalities and proceed as given. This approach will be faster if most inequalities are weakly redundant, since these require only 2 LPs rather than 3. However, if most inequalities are not weakly redundant or hidden linearities then it will be slower as most of the time only the LP (4) needs to be solved.

The size of the LPs to be solved can be greatly reduced in cases where most of the input is redundant using a method introduced by Clarkson [3]. He states his method in terms of identifying the extreme points of a given set of input points in $\mathbb{R}^d$. The equivalent algorithm stated in terms of detecting redundant inequalities in an H-representation is given in Sect. 7.1 of [5]. Quoting from [3] (emphasis ours):

Clarkson's algorithm [3]

The algorithm here is as follows: process the points of S in turn, maintaining a set $E \subset S$ of extreme points. Given $p \in S$, it is possible in $O(|E|) = O(A)$ time, using linear programming, to either show that p is a convex combination of points of E, or find a witness vector n for p, so that $n \cdot p > n \cdot q$ for all $q \in E$. If the former, p is not extremal and can be disregarded for further consideration. If the latter, although p is not necessarily an extreme point of S, one can easily in $O(n)$ time find the point $p' \in S$ that maximizes $n \cdot p'$. Such a **point is extremal**, and can be added to E; note that it cannot already be in E.

Suppose the number of extreme points is k which is much smaller than the input size m. Then the LP to be solved can never have more than k constraints compared with m constraints in the classic method. We note one point that is not mentioned in [3]. In the description above it is assumed that p' is unique. But there may be many points of S on the hyperplane $n \cdot x = n \cdot p'$. If these points are not in convex position a non-extreme point of S on the maximizing hyperplane may be selected and marked as extremal in the output. To resolve these degenerate cases a further recursive search may be needed on this hyperplane, increasing the worst-case computational complexity somewhat.

We will see in Sect. 5 that Clarkson's method is considerably faster than the classical method for inputs with high redundancy. It is usually somewhat faster even on inputs with low redundancy since the LPs it solves start out small, gradually increasing to the full set of non-redundant constraints at the end of the run. In the classical method, all LPs contain all constraints at the beginning and redundant constraints are deleted. To our knowledge there is no publicly available parallel implementation of Clarkson's method and it looks like an interesting challenge.

Finally an alternative, but usually much slower, method of computing a minimum representation is via the H/V transformation. Starting with any H-representation, a minimum representation of its V-representation will be produced. This can then be re-input to produce a minimum representation of the original H-representation. Although this is often impractical, it is a good way to independently verify results on relatively small instances when testing codes.

Conversely, for many problems it is faster to first compute a minimum representation before doing an H/V conversion. This is because the minimum representation computation is usually easier and the potential reduction in problem size and degeneracy speeds up the H/V conversion. However, in Sect. 5 we will see instances where this is not the case.

4 Projection by the Fourier-Motzkin Method

Projection of a polyhedron P along coordinate axes to a lower dimension is an important problem in many areas. For this problem the complexity is very different for H-representations and V-representations. We start with the latter because it is very straightforward: simply delete the coordinates of the vertices/rays/linearities that are to be projected out. This will normally generate a redundant V-representation and the methods of the last section can be used to remove any redundancies.

The F-M method can be used to project an H-representation. See [5] or [8] for details. We give a sketch here to describe how parallel redundancy removal can be used. The basic idea is to project out one variable at a time. We start with an H-representation (1) of P and for simplicity describe how to project out x_n. A minor modification allows the elimination of any arbitrary variable.

Fourier-Motzkin elimination of $\mathbf{x_n}$

(a) If there is an $i \in L$ with coefficient $a_{in} \neq 0$, use the equation of row i to eliminate x_n getting a new H-representation. Go to step (d).
(b) Define index sets

$$R = \{i \in I : a_{in} > 0\} \quad S = \{i \in I : a_{in} < 0\} \quad Z = \{i \in I : a_{in} = 0\}$$

Since $b_L + A_L x = 0$ and $b_Z + A_Z x \geq 0$ do not contain x_n they remain unchanged after projecting out x_n.
(c) For each $r \in R$ and $s \in S$ combine the inequalities

$$-b_r - \sum_{j=1}^{n-1} a_{rj}x_j \le a_{rn}x_n \qquad -a_{sn}x_n \le b_s + \sum_{j=1}^{n-1} a_{sj}x_j \tag{8}$$

obtaining

$$\frac{-b_r - \sum_{j=1}^{n-1} a_{rj}x_j}{a_{rn}} \le x_n \le \frac{b_s + \sum_{j=1}^{n-1} a_{sj}x_j}{-a_{sn}}. \tag{9}$$

Deleting x_n we get a new inequality in the remaining variables. The new H-representation has $|L|$ equations and $|Z| + |R||S|$ inequalities.

(d) Compute a minimum representation of the new H-representation.

The correctness of this procedure is not difficult to establish, see either of the two earlier references for details. By repeating the procedure a projection onto any subset of coordinate axes can be found.

It is clear that virtually all the computational time will be taken in step (d) since in the worst case there may be roughly $n^2/4$ inequalities in the system. Various methods have been proposed to do this computation (see e.g. [5]) but in *lrslib* we use the parallel algorithm described in the previous section for finding a minimum representation of the new H-representation. A key observation is that checking for hidden linearities only needs to be done initially for the input polyhedron P.

Proposition 2 *If the input H-representation of P for Fourier-Motzkin elimination is a minimum representation then the H-representation produced in either step (a) or (c) of the procedure will not contain hidden linearities.*

Proof By assumption, P has dimension $n - |L|$. If step (a) is executed one equation is eliminated from L and the number of variables becomes $n - 1$. The dimension is unchanged and there can be no hidden linearities introduced.

If step (c) is executed, suppose (9) becomes a linearity for a certain pair r, s. The inequalities become equations and we can equate coefficients obtaining $b_r/a_{rn} = b_s/a_{sn}$ and $a_{rj}/a_{rn} = a_{sj}/a_{sn}$, $j = 1, \dots, n$. Therefore (8) defines a hidden linearity, a contradiction. □

As pointed out in the introduction, it is generally much easier to project a V-representation than to project an H-representation. We can make use of this fact to produce a projection of an H-representation without using F-M elimination. Let P_H be the H-representation of a polyhedron P as in (1). Suppose a projection map π projects P onto Q. F-M elimination directly computes $Q_H = \pi(P_H)$. However, as shown in Figure 1 one can first convert P_H into its V-representation P_V, compute $Q_V = \pi(P_V)$ and finally compute Q_H from Q_V. The first and third operations are H/V transformations. The success of this method depends on doing these more efficiently than the F-M elimination computation. We will see this in Sect. 5.

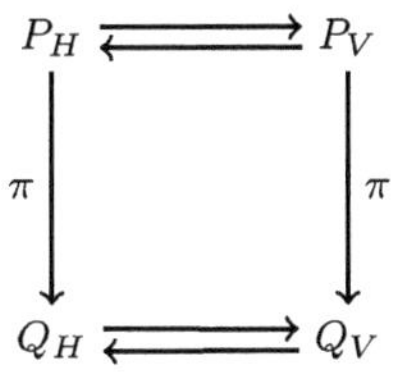

Fig. 1 Golden square

5 Computational Results

In this section we give computational results using two parallel clusters of computers at Kyoto University. For most results we used the *mi* cluster of three similar machines containing Ryzen Threadripper CPUs with a total of 160 cores and average clock speed of 2.8GHz. We made timings for 8 cores (typical laptop), 32 cores (high performance desktop) and 160 cores (small cluster). Some results are given using the *mai* cluster with AMD Opteron CPUs with somewhat slower 2.3 GHz clock speed. Our implementation is included in *lrslib* v.7.3.[1] All programs used do computations in exact arithmetic.

5.1 Redundancy Removal and Minimum Representation

In this section we present some computational results to illustrate the speedup obtained by using parallel processing for redundancy removal and computing a minimum representation. The single processor version is executed by *lrs* with options `testlin` and `redund`, aliased as *minrep*, and the parallel version is executed by *mplrs* with the `minrep` option. Our intention is not to do a comparison with other methods. However, we include results using Clarkson's algorithm *clark*, as implemented in *cddlib* v.0.94 m[2] by Komei Fukuda, to show the remarkable speedups it achieves for highly redundant problems. The results are shown in Table 1 and the problems are described in the Appendix. They range from problems with no redundancy, at the top of the table, to problems for which almost all input is redundant, at the bottom. As expected *clark* gives best performance for the highly redundant problems. Parallel processing gives good speedups for the classical method.

[1] https://cgm.cs.mcgill.ca/~avis/C/lrs.html

[2] https://github.com/cddlib/cddlib

Table 1 Redundancy removal (time in seconds, *mi* cluster)

Name	H/V	m_{in}	d_{in}	m_{out}	Redundancy %	*clark*	*minrep*	*mplrs*		
								8 cores	32 cores	160 cores
sphere	V	20001	3	20000	0.01	1899	4833	830	197	51
r500	V	500	100	500	0	6747	15067	2682	672	203
lambda	V	2001	63	2000	0.1	16270	27042	6137	2018	668
tsp7	H	3447	21	3444	0.1	165	203	18	4	3
ucube	H	40000	6	3551	91	729	8515	2085	645	289
ctype	V	9075	35	36	99	194	9518	5656	721	203
ducube	H	40000	6	261	99	83	2814	636	296	145

Table 2 One round of F-M elimination (time in seconds, *mi* cluster)

Name (H-reps)	m_{in}	d_{in}	m_{FM}	m_{out}	Redundancy %	*clark*	*fel*	*mplrs*		
								8 cores	32 cores	160 cores
lambda2	1080	63	4560	4320	5	>300000‡	6981	1327	521	236
ducube2	261	6	16897	1686	90	202	1310	329	87	29
hec	755	30	20029	949	95	455	237	76	53	29
cp6	368	15	18592	224	99	59	273	55	15	9
ucube2	3551	6	3134438	17947	99	732814†	–	–	–	–
sphere2	500	3	62436	61	100	89	935	421	148	149

† *mai*, also see Table 3
‡ suspected bug

5.2 Fourier-Motzkin Elimination

For these experiments, the input for each problem is an H-representation and we do one round of F-M elimination eliminating the last column. As explained in Sect. 4, almost all of the work consists of redundancy elimination in step (d) of the procedure. We extracted the inequality system created in step (c) so that we could test parallelization and Clarkson's algorithm on problems of this sort. The problems tested are basically the same as before, with a few exceptions, and we use the non-redundant version. The non-redundant description of *ctype* is a 36-dimensional simplex so projection is trivial. For *sphere* we first computed an H-representation to use as an input file. Since the result is too big, we use the first 500 rows of the H-representation renaming the result *sphere2*. Similarly, *lambda2* is part of the H-representation corresponding to *lambda*. *ucube2* is the non-redundant H-representation of *ucube*. We add two additional combinatorial polytopes. The results are given in Table 2.

In Table 2, m_{FM} is the number of new inequalities produced in step (c) of F-M elimination and m_{out} the number of those remaining after redundancy removal. Redundancy increases as we go down the table and so does the efficiency of *clark*. Parallel processing again gives substantial speedups up to 32 cores but with limited improvement after that.

The problem *ucube2* demonstrates the use of the golden square from Fig. 1. An immediate application of F-M generates 396,193,328 inequalities for redun-

Table 3 Projections of *ucube2* by golden square (times in days:hours:minutes), *mi* cluster

ucube2	$H \rightarrow V$						$V \xrightarrow{\pi} H_{nr}$				
m_H	m_V	*lcdd*	*lrs*	8 procs	32 procs	160 procs	d_{out}	*lrs*	8 procs	32 procs	160 procs
3551	303965	14:07	:01	:01	:00	:00	5	>7:00:00	>7:00:00	2:20:21	1:07:55
							4	16:43	11:21	5:29	3:20
							3	2:25	:50	:31	:25
							2	:02	:09	:06	:10
ucube2	$V \xrightarrow{\pi} V_{nr}$						$V_{nr} \rightarrow H_{nr}$				
d_{out}	$m_{V_{nr}}$	*clark*	*minrep*	8 cores	32 cores	160 cores	$m_{H_{nr}}$	*lrs*	8 cores	32 cores	160 cores
5	121735	4:22:35	>7:00:00	>7:00:00	2:21:43	23:13	17947	>7:00:00	3:03:44	19:25	6:39
4	24405	2:04:23†	19:12:20†	4:11:17†	2:04:09†	13:45†	11817	1:30	:25	:07	:03
3	1875	:58	1:23:28	17:55	5:24	3:18	1604	:00	:00	:00	:00
2	40	:01	21:55	7:07	4:37	2:14	40	:00	:00	:00	:00

† *mai* cluster

dancy removal, a formidable computation. Starting with the non-redundant H-representation of *ucube2* F-M generates 3,134,438 inequalities for redundancy removal which is still a very challenging computation. Using *clark* on *mai32ef* this took over eight days even though it is 99% redundant. This direct approach to the problem is out of reach for *minrep*/*mplrs*,however we can solve the problem via vertex enumeration. Doing so we obtain only 303,965 vertices which we can project to lower dimension and then convert to an H-representation. The results are given in Table 3.

The top left part of the table shows the computation time of the non-redundant V-representation V of *ucube2* from its H-representation H. We use *lcdd* from *cddlib* to verify the results using the double description method. V is then projected to $d = 5, 4, 3, 2$, which introduces redundancy, and is essentially instantaneous. For each projection the top right of the table shows a direct computation of its H-representation, which will be non-redundant and is denoted H_{nr}. For $d = 5$, only the 32-core and 160-core runs could be completed within one week. Running times for the other dimensions are much faster, decreasing as the dimension diminishes. Note that with F-M elimination the opposite occurs: due to its iterative approach running times increase as the dimension diminishes.

The bottom parts of the table give the results of first removing redundancy from V getting V_{nr} and then using it to compute H_{nr}. Most of the time is taken in the first step, shown in the bottom left part. Again running times decrease dramatically as the dimension decreases. Redundancy is high in the lower dimensions, and so *clark* does very well there. For $d = 5$ it is interesting the running times using 32 and 160 cores are very close to those obtained by the direct H_{nr} computation.

6 Conclusions and Future Directions

We have introduced a parallelization of the classical approach to redundancy removal which gives substantial speedups with modest hardware up to about 32 cores. The return on increasing the number of cores is modest, possibly due to the relatively high fixed startup computations which each processor must make. This begins to dominate the solution time as the number of input rows to process decreases with the number of cores. So one future direction is to improve the scaling to a large number of cores.

As an application we used the codes for redundancy removal in F-M elimination, obtaining similar results. For highly redundant problems Clarkson's algorithm, as implemented by Fukuda, gives extremely good performance without any parallelization. As F-M elimination can produce extremely high redundancy it is particularly well suited for this purpose. An interesting challenge is to find an efficient method to parallelize Clarkson's algorithm.

The number of new inequalities produced by F-M elimination is highly dependent on the input problem, as we see in Table 2. As we saw in the case of *ucube2*, it can be considerably faster to first compute a V-representation, project it, and recompute an H-representation. This is increasingly competitive for problems where it is required to project into a relatively low dimension. A final future direction would be to produce a hybrid code for F-M elimination that combines both methods automatically selecting the more appropriate method for each instance.

Acknowledgements The authors would like to thank William Cook for pointing out the paper of Freund et al. and Komei Fukuda for discussions on Clarkson's algorithm. This research was supported by JSPS Kakenhi Grants 20H00579, 20H00595, 20H05965, 22H05001 and 23K11043.

Appendix

We briefly describe the test problems used in Sect. 5.

- *sphere* is a random set of 20000 rational points on the unit sphere. We added a redundant vertex at line 13451 of the input.
- *r500* is a random set of 500 points in the 100-dimensional cube with coordinates between 1 and 9.
- *lambda* derives from the Lambda polytope in quantum physics and was contributed by Selman Ipek. For Table 1 we added a redundant constraint at line 1393 of the input.
- *tsp7* is the seven city travelling salesman polytope. We added 3 hidden linearities.
- *cp6* is the 6 point cut polytope.
- *ucube*, *ctype* and *ducube* were downloaded from Komei Fukuda's webpage: https://people.inf.ethz.ch/fukudak/ClarksonExp/ExperimentCtype.html (*ctype* was contributed by Mathieu Dutour).

- *hec* is the holographic cone, again from quantum physics, developed with Sergio Hernández-Cuenca.

To get the intermediate polyhedra for input to *clark* for Table 2 one can *fel* with the `verbose` option added.

References

1. D. Avis, C. Jordan, mplrs: A scalable parallel vertex/facet enumeration code. Math. Program. Comput. **10**(2), 267–302 (2018)
2. V. Chvátal, *Linear Programming* (W.H. Freeman, 1983)
3. K. L. Clarkson, More output-sensitive geometric algorithms, in *35th Annual Symposium on Foundations of Computer Science (FOCS 1994)* (IEEE Computer Society, 1994), pp. 695–702
4. R. M. Freund, R. Roundy, M.J. Todd, Identifying the set of always-active constraints in a system of linear inequalities by a single linear program, in *Working papers 1674-85* (Massachusetts Institute of Technology (MIT), Sloan School of Management, 1985)
5. K. Fukuda. *Polyhedral Computation* (ETH, Zurich, 2020). https://doi.org/10.3929/ethz-b-000426218
6. K. Fukuda, B. Gärtner, M. Szedlák, Combinatorial redundancy detection, in *31st International Symposium on Computational Geometry (SoCG 2015), Leibniz International Proceedings in Informatics (LIPIcs)*, vol. 34. (Schloss Dagstuhl–Leibniz-Zentrum für Informatik, 2015), pp. 315–328
7. H.R. Tiwary, On computing the shadows and slices of polytopes (2008). arXiv:0804.4150
8. G.M. Ziegler, *Lectures on Polytopes, Graduate Texts in Mathematics*, vol. 152. (Springer, 1995)

Bridging Algorithmic Foundations with Information Security and Privacy: Set-k-Multicover Problem and Homomorphic Secret Sharing

Alexandre Auzel and Vorapong Suppakitpaisarn

Abstract We explore the connections between two fields of study—the algorithmic foundations and the domains of information security and privacy. The principles of algorithmic foundations are instrumental in enhancing the efficiency of cryptographic systems. This is particularly relevant for post-quantum cryptography systems like isogeny-based cryptography, which benefit from efficient implementations. Conversely, methods from information privacy can be applied to ensure the trustability of several combinatorial algorithms, including linear integer programming and triangle counting. In this chapter, we delve into the role of algorithms capable of determining a lower bound for the set-k-multicover problem in ensuring the security of homomorphic secret sharing systems. Homomorphic secret sharing is a scheme that enables the delegation of computational tasks to servers while maintaining the confidentiality of our data. Within this framework, servers are tasked with producing a computational outcome based on the secrets of clients, without gaining any knowledge about the clients themselves. We posit that the maximum number of clients that this system can accommodate is directly linked to the optimal value of the set-k-multicover problem. Consequently, to calculate the upper limit of clients that the system can feasibly support, we introduce an algorithm aimed at identifying a lower bound for the optimal solution of this problem.

1 Algorithmic Foundations for Efficient Information Security System

In this chapter, we explore the connections between two fields of study—the algorithmic foundations and the domains of information security and privacy. It is known

This work is supported by KAKENHI Grant 21H05845 and 23H04377.

A. Auzel
CentraleSupelec 3 rue Joliot-Curie, 91192 Gif-sur-Yvette, Cedex, France
e-mail: alexandre.auzel@student-cs.fr

V. Suppakitpaisarn (✉)
The University of Tokyo, 7-3-1 Hongo, Bunkyo-ku, Tokyo 113-0033, Japan
e-mail: vorapong@is.s.u-tokyo.ac.jp

S. Minato et al. (eds.), *Algorithmic Foundations for Social Advancement*,
https://doi.org/10.1007/978-981-96-0668-9_15

that the connections between those areas are particularly strong. Through various examples, we will demonstrate how advancements and research in one field can significantly bolster and inform developments in the other.

The first focus is how algorithmic foundations can give efficient information security system. There are many works which devise to give an efficient cryptographic system, a bottleneck of several systems. Those include algorithms for classical cryptography such as RSA [53] or elliptic curve cryptography [40, 44]. Most of the algorithms proposed for RSA are numeric algorithms for prime field arithmetic such as algorithms based on the Chinese remainder theorem [54], modular multiplication [6], or modular reduction [27, 52]. On the other hand, as the calculation of elliptic curve cryptography is more complicated than RSA, one can employ combinatorial optimization techniques such as genetic algorithm [42] or dynamic programming algorithm [58, 59].

In addition to the development of efficient algorithms, researchers are also interested in finding the lower bound of the computation time needed for each cryptographic system or each implementation [1, 9, 41, 57]. To achieve this, foundational algorithmic concepts, including information theory, have been employed to identify these minimum computation times.

Developing an efficient cryptographic system is crucial, but equally important is the analysis of its security. Cryptanalysis is a fundamental approach in this analysis, where algorithms are developed to break cryptographic systems. For this purpose, specific algorithms employ techniques such as Pollard's rho method [11, 49] and the baby step-giant step method [3, 21, 55].

1.1 Efficient Algorithms for Post-Quantum Cryptography

Ongoing research is trying to improve traditional encryption methods like RSA and elliptic curve cryptography. However, it is already known that these methods will not stand up to quantum computers, as pointed out by [56]. This situation makes it crucial to work on new types of encryption that quantum computers cannot break. This new branch of encryption is known as post-quantum cryptography. The most notable types within this field are lattice-based cryptography [4, 31] and isogeny-based cryptography [2, 7, 8].

The computational demands of post-quantum cryptography generally surpass those of traditional cryptographic systems, necessitating the development of efficient implementations for these advanced systems [10]. This chapter delves into a particular combinatorial optimization challenge encountered while enhancing the efficiency of isogeny-based cryptographic computations.

Given that this article targets researchers specializing in algorithmic foundations, we omit detailed discussions of isogeny-based cryptography. The cryptographic system's computations are illustrated as a graph in Fig. 1, where each node symbolizes a specific state within the calculation process. The starting point is denoted by the node $v_{1,1}$, and the endpoint by $v_{n,1}$. Connections between nodes, or edges, represent individual computational steps in the system, each consuming a nearly equal amount of computational resources.

Hence, the most efficient computation corresponds to the shortest path from node $v_{1,1}$ to node $v_{n,1}$. Nonetheless, there is a constraint that, for any given i, j, to perform the computation signified by the edge $(v_{i,j}, v_{i+1,j})$, one must first reach the state $v_{i,n-i+1}$. Given this constraint, finding the shortest path becomes a complex task. To address this challenge, a dynamic programming algorithm has been suggested as a solution [39].

Identifying the most effective computation strategy becomes significantly more difficult in the context of parallel computing [35], where it is possible to execute multiple computational steps simultaneously. We approach this challenge as a scheduling problem with precedence constraints [47, 48]. Although finding optimal solutions is beyond reach with our current methods, we explore two traditional algorithms. The Coffman-Graham algorithm [12] delivers an optimal solution when limited to two processors, and the Hu algorithm [32] achieves optimality for precedence graphs that are trees. While neither algorithm guarantees optimal outcomes for our specific scenario, our experiments demonstrate they considerably enhance the solutions presented in [35].

Our goal remains to create an algorithm that can determine the optimal scheduling for this scenario. At present, we are formulating the problem as a scheduling problem with and/or precedence constraints [23]. To proceed to node $v_{i,j}$, it is necessary to complete either node $v_{i-1,j}$ *or* node $v_{i,j}$, *and* also ensure the completion of node $v_{i-1,n-i}$.

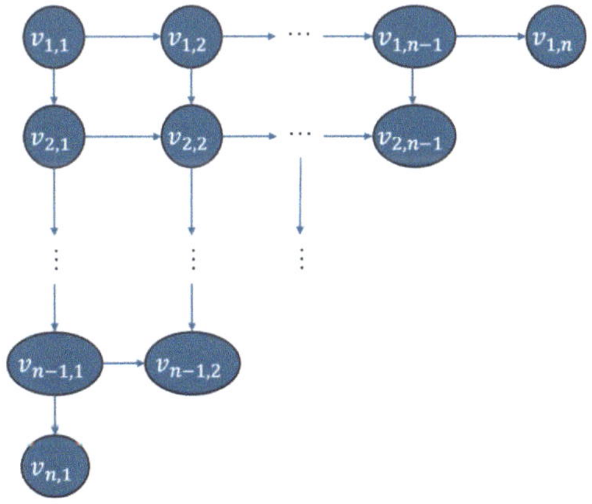

Fig. 1 Calculation in an isogeny-based cryptographic system

2 Graph Algorithms Under Local Differential Privacy

While algorithmic foundations help in speeding up the calculation of cryptographic systems, information privacy can make algorithms more trustworthy. Often, these algorithms handle sensitive user data as input. If users lack trust in the algorithms' handling of their information, they might withhold accurate data or refuse to share their sensitive information altogether. The absence of accurate user information compromises the reliability of the algorithm's output.

Local differential privacy stands out as a widely adopted method for ensuring the confidentiality of user data [13, 20], and is utilized by tech giants like Apple, Microsoft, and Google [15, 16, 19]. This approach requires users to obscure their data prior to transmitting it to the server. Consequently, it necessitates the development of algorithms that can reliably interpret and work with this obscured information.

In this chapter, we focus on graph algorithms based on the local differential privacy. The setting for those graph algorithms is illustrated in Fig. 2. We assume that each user knows the list of their friends, and they consider the list as a sensitive information. This perspective is rational, as people typically prefer to keep their associations, especially with those of dubious standing, from becoming public knowledge.

Suppose that our user group is numbered from 1 to n. The friendship status between user i and others can be represented by a vector $v_i \in \{0, 1\}^n$, where $v_i[j] = 1$ indicates user i is friends with user j, and $v_i[j] = 0$ indicates they are not. The collection of these vectors, $[v_1, \ldots, v_n]$, serves as the adjacency matrix for a graph or social network. Consider a scenario where we aim to analyze certain aspects of

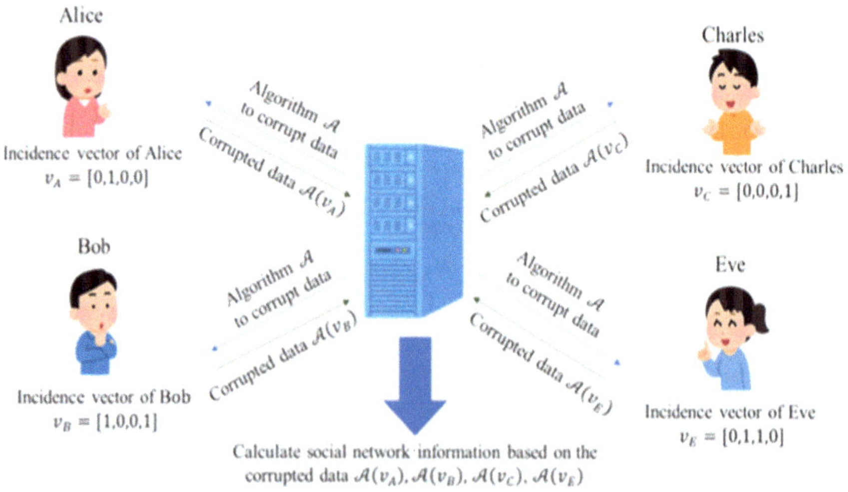

Fig. 2 Settings for graph algorithms under local differential privacy

this network, under the condition that each user i wishes to keep their friendship vector v_i confidential. Within this structure, we distribute a randomized algorithm $\mathcal{A}$ to all users, who then apply it to obscure their data before sending this altered information back to us. Consequently, our task is to create an algorithm which is robust against this distorted information.

We are now ready to introduce the concept of local differential privacy in the context of graphs, often referred to as *ϵ-edge local differential privacy* [50]. Informally, we desire an algorithm $\mathcal{A}$ such that, upon observing the modified output $\mathcal{A}(v_i)$, no individual (other than user i) can accurately deduce whether $v_i[j] = 0$ or $v_i[j] = 1$ for any pair of indices $i, j \in \{1, \ldots, n\}$. Specifically, for any two vectors v_i and v_i' that differ in just a single element, the outcomes $\mathcal{A}(v_i)$ and $\mathcal{A}(v_i')$ should be nearly indistinguishable. Let $\mathcal{S}$ denote the range of $\mathcal{A}$. We ensure that for any element of $\mathcal{S}$, the probability ratio $\Pr[\mathcal{A}(v_i) \in S] / \Pr[\mathcal{A}(v_i') \in S]$ is bounded between $e^{-\epsilon}$ and e^{ϵ}. When ϵ is small, the probabilities $\Pr[\mathcal{A}(v_i) \in S]$ and $\Pr[\mathcal{A}(v_i') \in S]$ are approximately equal, indicating minimal leakage of information from v_i. Conversely, a larger ϵ value implies a greater degree of information leakage.

One of the randomized algorithms $\mathcal{A}$ which can protect users' information is the Laplacian mechanism [17]. It is employed when there is a need to obtain a piece of information $R(v_i) \in \mathbb{R}$ from each user. For any user data vector v and a set of vectors $n(v)$ that differ from v by one element, the sensitivity of the function R, denoted as $s(R)$, is defined as $s(R) := \max_{v \in \{0,1\}^n, v' \in n(v)} |R(v) - R(v')|$. To ensure ϵ-edge local differential privacy, the Laplacian mechanism introduces noise derived from the Laplace distribution, parameterized by $s(R)/\epsilon$, to $R(v_i)$. Specifically, when $Lap(s(R)/\epsilon)$ represents a value sampled from this distribution with parameter $s(R)/\epsilon$, the algorithm's output is given by $\mathcal{A}(v_i) = R(v_i) + Lap(s(R)/\epsilon)$.

Imagine we aim to determine the total number of connections within a social network. For this purpose, let $d(v_i)$ represent the count of connections linked to each user, meaning $d(v_i)$ equals the number of entries valued at one within v_i. By aggregating the exact counts of $d(v_i)$ from all users, the total connection count can be derived using $\frac{1}{2} \sum_{i=1}^{n} d(v_i)$. However, directly sharing $d(v_i)$ poses a risk of revealing sensitive user information. To protect privacy, we employ the Laplacian mechanism. With the sensitivity $s(d)$ established as one, the adjusted value received from each user, i, is expressed as $\mathcal{A}(v_i) = d(v_i) + Lap(1/\epsilon)$. Consequently, an estimate of the network's total connections is given by $\frac{1}{2} \sum_{i=1}^{n} \mathcal{A}(v_i)$. This approach has been proven to yield accurate estimations, both theoretically and empirically.

While assessing the total number of connections within a social network can be straightforward under local differential privacy protocols, computing other statistics of the network with privacy considerations poses a greater challenge. For instance, when aiming to disclose the count of k-stars in the network, which is defined as $\sum_i \binom{d(v_i)}{k}$, where $d(v_i)$ denotes the degree of node i, a direct approach might involve each node revealing $R(v_i) = \binom{d(v_i)}{k}$, safeguarded by the Laplacian mechanism. Yet, this method introduces a significant complication: the sensitivity of the R function could escalate to as much as n^{k-1}. Such a high sensitivity results in a substantially increased error margin in the reported counts, undermining the accuracy of the publication.

As mentioned earlier, the general approach provided by algorithms like the Laplacian mechanism does not suffice for the publication of numerous graph statistics. This shortfall has led to the creation of specialized algorithms aimed at specific graph statistical measures. These dedicated algorithms facilitate tasks such as the enumeration of k-stars [30, 36], the counting of triangles [18, 37, 38, 43], core decomposition [14, 29], clustering [28, 45], and measuring centrality [5]. Each algorithm is tailored to efficiently and accurately compute these statistics while adhering to privacy constraints, overcoming the limitations inherent in more generalized approaches.

3 Case Study: Set k-Multicover Problem and Homomorphic Secret Sharing

In the first two sections, we have discussed connections between two fields of study - the algorithmic foundations and the domains of information security and privacy. In this section, we delve into a particular case study when we use a solution of the set k-multicover problem to guarantee the security of the homomorphic secret sharing.

In the context of distributed computing, one or more clients wish to delegate a costly calculation to several servers in order to have access to more powerful resources and to be able to parallelize calculations. Cryptography plays an important role in these processes. The calculation servers often do not belong to the clients, and the input data may be confidential. We therefore need to find a way of ensuring that the servers can carry out the calculations, but cannot have access to all the input data in clear text, even if a number of servers can communicate with each other and collaborate.

One of the technologies used is Homomorphic Secret Sharing (HSS) [46]. Its concept is to divide the input data x into S random parts so that $x = x_1 + \cdots + x_S$. Then an encryption and distribution strategy is applied so that

- each server can calculate a part of the calculation,
- servers that can collude cannot find the input data,
- clients can calculate the final result by summing the results of each server.

Let us take an example: we have 2 clients with 2 input data and 3 servers. We suppose that we know which servers can collude

- collusion 1: servers 1 and 2
- collusion 2: servers 1 and 3
- collusion 3: servers 2 and 3

Let us assume that the number of shares is equal to the number of collisions. Each client partitions its input data in $S = 3$ shares: $x = x_1 + x_2 + x_3$ and $y = y_1 + y_2 +$

y_3. We want to compute $xy = x_1y_1 + x_1y_2 + x_1y_3 + x_2y_1 + x_2y_2 + x_2y_3 + x_3y_1 + x_3y_2 + x_3y_3$. The encryption and distribution strategy follows:

- The server i receives x_j and y_j if i is not in collusion j. Otherwise it receives $Enc(x_j)$ and $Enc(y_j)$ where Enc is the encryption function.
- The homomorphic and linear encryption function has good properties so that a server can compute $Enc(x_iy_j)$ if it has $(x_i, Enc(y_j))$, $(Enc(x_i), y_j)$ or (x_i, y_j) (At most $k = 1$ share can be encrypted in order to compute the product $Enc(x_iy_j)$).

In this example, any monomial $Enc(x_iy_j)$ can be computed by at least one server. For instance, $Enc(x_1y_3)$ can be computed by server 1 because server 1 is in collusion 1 but not in collusion 3 so it has the shares $Enc(x_1)$ and y_3. Therefore, the computation is possible thanks to Enc's good properties. Once every monomial has been computed, a central server can sum up the partial result: $Enc(xy) = \sum Enc(x_iy_j)$ and send it back to the clients which can decrypt and obtain xy (Fig. 3).

3.1 Problem—Maximum Number of Clients Supported

One question we can ask ourselves is how many clients can be supported with the following setting:

- collusion sets
- the number maximum of encrypted shares to compute a monomial, denoted by k
- the number of servers

In the example mentioned earlier, we saw that 2 clients can be supported. Let us add a third client, and let us suppose that the input of the client is $z = z_1 + z_2 + z_3$. Now we want to compute $Enc(xyz)$ by computing every monomial $Enc(x_iy_jz_l)$ for $1 \leq i, j, l \leq 3$. Looking at the monomial $(i = 2, j = 3, l = 1)$ we see that

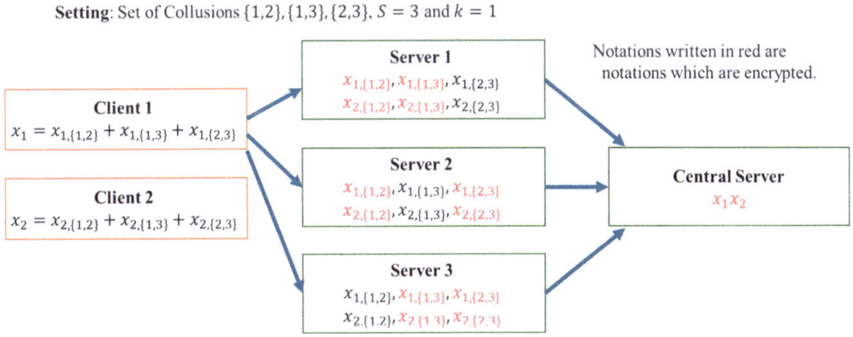

Fig. 3 The homomorphic secret sharing scheme for the case that, when x_i is the secret of user i, we want to calculate $x_1 \cdot x_2$ using three servers

- server 1 cannot compute $Enc(x_2y_3z_1)$ because server 1 has 2 encrypted shares: $Enc(x_2)$ and $Enc(z_1)$
- server 2 cannot compute $Enc(x_2y_3z_1)$ because server 2 has 2 encrypted shares: $Enc(y_3)$ and $Enc(z_1)$
- server 3 cannot compute $Enc(x_2y_3z_1)$ because server 3 has 2 encrypted shares: $Enc(x_2)$ and $Enc(y_3)$

Therefore, some monomials cannot be computed so 3 clients are not supported by this instance. To support 3 clients we must increase the number of servers or the power of computation by increasing k. Therefore, we will try to answer to the following question:

> Given a number of servers, a set of collusions, and the maximum number of encrypted shares supported in monomial computation, what is the maximum of clients that can be supported?

Suppose that the input of client i is a_i, the shares of a_i are $a_{i,j}$ for $1 \leq j \leq S$, the collection of collusions are $s_1, \ldots, s_d \in \{1, \ldots, S\}$. The problem can be reformulated as follows:

> What is the maximum d such that for any monomial $a_{1,s_1} \times \ldots \times a_{d,s_d}$ ($a_{i,j}$ is the share of client i corresponding to the collusion j) of size d, there is at least one server m such that m is in at most k collusions among the collusions $s_1, \ldots, s_d \in \{1, \ldots, S\}$?

Indeed, if it is the case, then m has at most k encrypted shares among $a_{1,s_1}, \ldots, a_{d,s_d}$ so it can compute the monomial. Since all monomials can be computed, d clients is supported. Since any monomial can just be described by the d collusions its shares correspond to, we will use the following form:

> **What is the maximum d such that for any combination of d collusions $s_1, \ldots, s_d$, there is at least one server m such that m is in at most k collusions among those d collusions?**

3.2 *Relationship with the Minimum k-Multicover Problem*

To tackle this problem, we will need to formulate our instances. Let $k \in \mathbb{N}$ be the maximum number of encrypted shares in the computation of a monomial, let $n \in \mathbb{N}$ be the number of servers, and let C be a collection of collusions. We assume that each collusion has size larger than 1. Also, let $t = max(|S_i|)$ be the maximum set size in C. An instance can therefore be defined by 3 values: (k, n, C). Mathematically, we search:

> **The maximum d such that** $\forall (S_1, \ldots S_d) \in C^d, \exists m \in [1, n], |\{S \in \{S_1, \ldots, S_d\}, m \in S\}| \leq k$

Example 1 ([46]) In this example, let us suppose that C contains every possible sets of size t: $C = \{S \subseteq [1, n], |S| = t\}$. To solve our problem is equivalent to find the maximum d such that for all $S_1, \ldots, S_d \in C^d$ (any monomial), there exists $m \in [1, n]$ (at least one server) such that $|\{S \in \{S_1, \ldots, S_d\} : m \in S\}| \leq k$ (in at most k collusions).
In this case, $d \geq \frac{(k+1)n-1}{t}$.

Proof Consider d sets $S_1, ..., S_d$ within a collection C. Assume that no server appears in k or fewer of these sets. Under this condition, the total number of occurrences is not smaller than $(k+1)n$. Conversely, if the total number of occurrences is less than $(k+1)n$, then there exists at least one server that is included in k or fewer sets. Given that the total number of occurrences equals dt, it follows that $d \geq \frac{(k+1)n-1}{t}$. □

Here, the proof is based on the fact that all the collusion sets have the same size. The purpose of this chapter is to find the value of d in the general case.

A graph is defined as a pair $G = (V, E)$, where V is a set consisting of n elements, and E is a collection of pairs of elements from V. An hypergraph extends this concept by allowing E to include subsets of any size from V, referred to as hyperedges. A set k-multicover is a subset Cov of E such that for every vertex $v \in V$, there are at least k edges in Cov that contain v. The minimum set k-multicover problem aims to find the smallest such subset Cov that satisfies this condition. We denote an optimal solution of the minimum set k-multicover problem by Cov_k.

In order to solve our problem in the general case, we are going to use the following theorem.

Theorem 1 *If (k, n, C) is one instance of our problem and d is the maximum number of clients that can be supported by our instance, then $d = |Cov_{k+1}| - 1$ where Cov_{k+1} is a minimum set-$(k+1)$-cover of the hypergraph $G = ([1, n], C)$.*

Proof In the first part of our proof, we will demonstrate that $d \geq |Cov_{k+1}| - 1$. Following that, in the second step, we will argue that $d < |Cov_{k+1}|$.

1. Let $a = |Cov_{k+1}| - 1$ and consider a elements $S_1, ..., S_a$ from a set C. There must exist an element m within the range $[1, n]$ such that m appears in no more than k of these sets S_i. This must be the case, otherwise, these a sets would constitute a $(k+1)$-cover of $[1, n]$ that is smaller than Cov_{k+1}, which would contradict the definition of Cov_{k+1} as the minimum size of a set-$(k+1)$-cover of $[1, n]$. Therefore, the number of sets S_i containing m satisfies $|\{S \in \{S_1, ..., S_a\} : m \in S\}| \leq k$. Consequently, we establish that $d \geq |Cov_{k+1}| - 1$.
2. Assuming $a \geq |Cov_{k+1}|$, consider a set $\mathcal{S}$ of size a that includes all elements of Cov_{k+1}. By definition, Cov_{k+1} ensures that each element m from the set $[1, n]$ is included in at least $k+1$ subsets within $\mathcal{S}$. This scenario implies that $\mathcal{S}$ cannot be computed on any single server. Consequently, it follows that $d < |Cov_{k+1}|$. □

Here is an illustration of the theorem's result using an example:

Example 2 Consider the case discussed in the previous section with $V = \{1, 2, 3\}$ and $C = \{\{1, 2\}, \{1, 3\}, \{2, 3\}\}$, where $k = 1$. The size of $|Cov_2|$ is 3. Consequently, we find that $d = |Cov_2| - 1 = 2$, as shown previously. Note that supporting 3 clients is not possible in this scenario.

Based on Theorem 1, we can conclude that solving our problem is feasible using algorithms designed for the set k-multicover problem. If the set k-multicover problem can be solved exactly, our problem can also be addressed effectively. However, the set

k-multicover problem is recognized as NP-hard, a complexity attributed to its base case, the set cover problem when $k = 1$, which is known to be NP-hard [22]. There exist studies on exact algorithms for the set k-multicover problem (such as [33, 34]). However, we believe that these algorithms do not scale practically for our applications.

There is substantial research on approximation algorithms for the set k-multicover problem, as seen in studies such as [24, 26, 51]. These algorithms aim to produce a feasible set k-multicover, denoted as Cov'_{k+1}, which is not guaranteed to be minimal. Consequently, the size of Cov'_{k+1} is likely to exceed that of the optimal cover Cov_{k+1}. If we were to use $|Cov'_{k+1}| - 1$ as our service capacity, it could lead to an overestimation of the number of clients we can serve. In our context, such an overestimation might result in information leakage. Therefore, these approximation algorithms cannot be directly applied in our setting. In this chapter, we will focus on developing an algorithm to calculate a lower bound for $|Cov'_{k+1}|$. We aim to give a large lower bound as possible, as that would lead to a better utility of our system.

To conclude, our problem is

> To calculate a large value of C such that $C \leq |Cov_{k+1}|$. We aim to give an approximation algorithm of which the outcome is $\alpha \cdot |Cov_{k+1}| \leq C \leq |Cov_{k+1}|$ for some α close to 1.

We have not found any existing literature that directly addresses this problem. This scenario illustrates how applications in information security can inspire novel challenges in combinatorial optimization, thereby contributing to the advancement of the field.

3.3 LP Integrality Gap

A widely used method to calculate the lower bound in combinatorial optimization involves the relaxation of integer linear programming problems.

We first explore the integer linear programming (ILP) of the minimum set k-multicover problem. The ILP is as follows:

- **Input**: $k, n, C = \{S_1, ..., S_m\}$
- **Output**: $(x_1, ..., x_m) \in \{0, 1\}$
- **Constraint**: $\forall i \in [1, n], \sum_{j, i \in S_j} x_j \geq k$
- **Objective**: Minimize $\sum x_i$

Let $OptCov_k$ be its optimal solution and $|OptCov_k| = OPT$:

Since ILP is not solvable in polynomial time we cannot compute the optimal solution $OptCov_k$ and its objective value OPT in a scalable way.

On the other hand, the relaxation of this ILP is solvable. It can be stated as follows:

- **Input**: $k, n, C = \{s_1, ..., s_m\}$
- **Output**: $(x_1, ..., x_m) \in [0, 1]$
- **Constraint**: $\forall i \in [1, n], \sum_{j, i \in S_j} x_j \geq k$
- **Objective**: Minimize $\sum x_i$.

Let OPT_f represent the optimal value of the relaxed problem. Given that this relaxation of the ILP is linear programming, which can be solved in polynomial time, we can efficiently and scalably compute the value of OPT_f.

Since the solution set of the relaxed problem includes the solution set of the integer linear programming (ILP) instance, we have

$$OPT_f \leq OPT$$

Consequently, OPT_f can be used as the lower bound for $|OptCov_k|$, and we can define d' as:

$$d' = OPT_f - 1 \leq OPT - 1 = |OptCov_k| - 1 = d$$

This implies that d' clients can be supported by our instance $(k - 1, n, C)$. To evaluate how close d' is to d, we will explore the integrality gap (IG), defined as:

$$IG = \max_{\text{instance } I} \frac{OPT(I)}{OPT_f(I)}$$

The integrality gap helps in understanding the extent of approximation when comparing the optimal solutions of the ILP and its relaxed counterpart for the minimum set-k-cover problem.

At the time of writing this article, the exact value of the integrality gap (IG) remains undetermined. To our knowledge, the research conducted by Gorgi, Ouali, Srivastav, and Hachimi explores the integrality gap for the set k-multicover problem, providing a lower bound for this value [25]. Our goal is to establish a more precise lower bound and additionally propose an upper bound in the subsequent sections.

3.3.1 Upper Bound of IG

To find an upper bound of the integrality gap (IG), we are going to give a solution to the set k-multicover problem based on a randomized rounding algorithm. Suppose that the objective value of that solution for instance I is $SOL_{algo}(I)$, and, for all instance I, let RR be a number such that

$$RR \geq \frac{OPT_f(I)}{SOL_{algo}(I)}.$$

Since, $SOL_{algo}(I) \geq OPT(I)$, we obtain that

$$RR \geq \max_{\text{instance } I} \frac{OPT_f(I)}{SOL_{algo}(I)} \geq \max_{\text{instance } I} \frac{OPT_f(I)}{OPT(I)} = IG.$$

Hence, RR is an upper bound of IG.

Our randomized rounding algorithm

Let us consider that the solution to the relaxed linear program is represented by the fractional vector $X_f = (x_1, ..., x_m)$. To construct an integer solution, we define the values of x_i^* using the following probabilistic approach:

$$x_i^* = 0 \text{ with probability } (1 - x_i)^f \text{ and } 1 \text{ with probability } 1 - (1 - x_i)^f$$

Let l represent the maximum number of sets to which an element belongs, which is equivalent to the maximum number of collusions a server can participate in. Here, f is defined as a function of n:

$$f(n) = \frac{l(k-1)}{k(l+1-k)} \log_2(l) + \frac{l}{kl - k^2 + k} \log_2(4n).$$

This formulation allows us to transition from a fractional to an integer solution while managing the distribution of probabilities according to the given function f.

The expected value of SOL_{algo} can be calculated as follows:

$$\begin{aligned}\mathbb{E}(SOL_{algo}) &= \sum_i \left(P(x_i^* = 1) \times 1 + P(x_i^* = 0) \times 0\right)\\ &= \sum_i \left(1 - (1 - x_i)^f\right) \leq f \sum_i x_i.\end{aligned}$$

This implies that $\mathbb{E}(SOL_{algo}) \leq f \times OPT_f$.

Feasibility of the randomized rounding algorithm

Next, we calculate the probability that the solution obtained by the randomized rounding algorithm is feasible. We begin our proof by the following lemma:

Lemma 1 *For all $e \in [1, n]$, $\mathbb{P}$(e is not k covered) $\leq \frac{1}{4n}$.*

Proof Suppose that element e is included in sets $S_1, \ldots, S_l$, where $k \leq l \leq m$. According to the feasibility of the fractional solution, the sum of the fractional values assigned to these sets satisfies $\sum_{i=1}^{l} x_i \geq k$. If e is not covered by at least k sets in the rounded solution, it indicates that fewer than k of the x_i^* values have been rounded up to 1.

$$\mathbb{P}(e \text{ is not } k \text{ covered}) \leq \sum_{\{t_1, \ldots, t_{l-k+1}\} \subseteq [1,l]} (1 - x_{t_1})^f \times \ldots \times (1 - x_{t_{l-k+1}})^f$$

Let $P(x_1, \ldots, x_l) = \sum_{\{t_1, \ldots, t_{l-k+1}\} \subseteq [1,l]} (1 - x_{t_1})^f \times \cdots \times (1 - x_{t_{l-k+1}})^f$. In the remaining part of this proof, we aim to calculate the upper bound of $P(x_1, \ldots, x_l)$. We find the maximum value of $P(x_1, \ldots, x_l)$ when $\sum_{i=1}^{l} x_i \geq k$ and $x_i \in [0, 1]$. We can notice that, for all i and for all $\epsilon > 0$,

$$P(x_1, \ldots, x_i + \epsilon, \ldots, x_l) \leq P(x_1, \ldots, x_i, \ldots, x_l)$$

Hence, to find the upper bound, we can assume $\sum_{i=1}^{l} x_i = k$. As a result, we have that $x_l = k - \sum_{i=1}^{l-1} x_i$.

Let us define $g(x_1, \ldots, x_{l-1}) = P(x_1, \ldots, x_{l-1}, k - \sum_{i=1}^{l-1} x_i)$. If $k = l$, $x_i = 1$ for all x_i and $P(x_1, \ldots, x_l) = 0$. Hence, it is enough to assume that $k < l$.

To determine the maximum of P, we will calculate the partial derivatives of g and identify where the summation of them are zero. We have that

$$\frac{\partial g}{\partial x_i} = \sum_{\{t_1,\ldots,t_{l-k+1}\}\subseteq[1,l]} \frac{\partial}{\partial x_i}(1 - x_{t_1})^f \times \ldots \times (1 - x_{t_{l-k+1}})^f.$$

We consider the derivative of each term in the summation. Each term corresponds to the set $\{t_1, \ldots, t_{l-k+1}\} \subset [1, l]$. There are four cases based on the set corresponding to the term:

1. if $i \notin \{t_1, \ldots, t_{l-k+1}\}, l \notin \{t_1, \ldots, t_{l-k+1}\}$: In this case, the partial derivative is zero.
2. if $i \in \{t_1, \ldots, t_{l-k+1}\}, l \notin \{t_1, \ldots, t_{l-k+1}\}$: In this case, the partial derivative is the following:
$$-f(1 - x_i)^{f-1} \prod_{t\in\{t_1,\ldots,t_{l-k+1}\}\setminus\{i\}} (1 - x_t)^f.$$
3. if $i \notin \{t_1, \ldots, t_{l-k+1}\}, l \in \{t_1, \ldots, t_{l-k+1}\}$: In this case, the partial derivative is the following:
$$f(1 - x_l)^{f-1} \prod_{t\in\{t_1,\ldots,t_{l-k+1}\}\setminus\{l\}} (1 - x_t)^f.$$
4. if $i, l \in \{t_1, \ldots, t_{l-k+1}\}$: In this case, the partial derivative is the following:

$$f\left((1 - x_i)^f(1 - x_l)^{f-1} - (1 - x_l)^f(1 - x_i)^{f-1}\right) \prod_{t\in\{t_1,\ldots,t_{l-k+1}\}\setminus\{i,l\}} (1 - x_t)^f.$$

By summing the partial derivatives of all the terms, we obtain:

$$\frac{\partial g}{\partial x_i} = f\left((1 - x_i)^{f-1}(1 - x_l)^{f-1} \sum_{i,l-k-1} - \left((1 - x_i)^{f-1} - (1 - x_l)^{f-1}\right) \sum_{i,l-k}\right)$$

where $\sum_{i,N} = \sum_{\{t_1,\ldots,t_N\}\subseteq[1,l-1]\setminus\{i\}} (1 - x_{t_1})^f \times \ldots \times (1 - x_{t_N})^f.$

Without loss of generality, we can suppose that $x_1 \leq \cdots \leq x_l$ so that, for all i, $(1 - x_i)^{f-1} - (1 - x_l)^{f-1} \geq 0$.

Next, let us analyze cases which can make the partial derivatives equal zero.

1. $\sum\limits_{i,l-k-1} = \sum\limits_{i,l-k} = 0$: This implies that $P(x_1, \ldots, x_l)$ is zero.
2. $x_i = 1$: The partial derivative is then equal to zero when $x_i = x_l$ or $\sum_{i,l-k} = 0$. However, as $\sum_{i,l-k} = 0$ implies that $P(x_1, \ldots, x_l) = 0$, we reach the maximum value of $P(x_1, \ldots, x_l)$ only when $x_l = x_i$.
3. $x_l = 1$: Similar to the previous case, we reach the maximum value only when $x_l = x_i$.
4. $(1 - x_i)^{f-1}(1 - x_l)^{f-1} \sum\limits_{i,l-k-1} = ((1 - x_i)^{f-1} - (1 - x_l)^{f-1}) \sum\limits_{i,l-k}$: Define $r = \frac{\sum_{i,l-k-1}}{\sum_{i,l-k}} \geq 1$, and define a as $(1 - x_i)$ and b as $(1 - x_l)$. The equation becomes $\frac{1}{a^{f-1}} + ar = \frac{1}{b^{f-1}} + br$, which holds true if either $a = b$ or if a and b assume two particular values dependent on f. As we have the flexibility to select f after obtaining the x_i, we can ensure this condition never occurs by wisely choosing f.

By the case analysis, we can conclude that $P(x_1, \ldots, x_l)$ only when $x_i = x_l$ for all i. Hence, we conclude that the function is maximized when $x_i = \frac{k}{l}$ for all $1 \leq i \leq l$. Therefore,

$$P(x_1, \ldots, x_n) \leq \binom{l}{k-1}\left(1 - \frac{k}{l}\right)^{f(l-k+1)} \leq \binom{l}{k-1} \exp\left(-\frac{kf(l-k+1)}{l}\right).$$

Let us take $f = \frac{l(k-1)}{k(l+1-k)} \log_2(l) + \frac{l}{kl-k^2+k} \log_2(4n)$. Thus,

$$\begin{aligned}
\log_2(P) &\leq \log_2\left(\binom{l}{k-1}\right) - \frac{kf(l-k+1)}{l} \\
&\leq (k-1)\log_2(l) - \frac{k}{l}(l-k+1)\left(\frac{l}{l-k}\log_2(l) + \frac{l}{kl-k^2}\log_2(4n)\right) \\
&\leq \left((k-1) - \frac{kl(l-k+1)(k-1)}{lk(l-k+1)}\right)\log_2(l) - \frac{lk(l-k+1)}{lk(l-k+1)}\log_2(4n) \\
&\leq \log_2(1/4n).
\end{aligned}$$

We then can obtain the lemma statement. □

We are now ready to prove the main theorem of this section.

Theorem 2 *Let* $\alpha = 4\left(\frac{l(k-1)}{k(l+1-k)} \log_2(l) + \frac{l}{kl-k^2+k} \log_2(4n)\right)$. *There is a solution of the set k-multicover problem, denoted by* SOL_{algo}, *such that* $SOL_{algo} \leq \alpha \cdot OPT$. *1*

Proof By Lemma 1, we obtain that

$$\begin{aligned}\mathbb{P}(X^* \text{ is not a set-}k\text{-multicover}) &\leq n \times \mathbb{P}(\text{an element } e \text{ is not } k\text{-covered})\\ &\leq n \times \frac{1}{4n} \leq \frac{1}{4}.\end{aligned}$$

Moreover, with Markov's inequality, we get

$$\mathbb{P}\left(SOL_{algo} > 4\mathbb{E}\left(SOL_{algo}\right)\right) \leq \frac{1}{4}.$$

By using these two inequalities, we finally obtain that

$$\mathbb{P}\left(X^* \text{ is a set-}k\text{-cover and } SOL_{algo} \leq \alpha \cdot OPT_f\right) \geq \frac{1}{2}$$

Therefore, by iterating the algorithm several times, it is highly probable to achieve a solution stated in this theorem statement. □

When we assume that $k \ll l \ll n$, the approximation ratio α obtained in the previous theorem is closed to $\log_2(n)/k$. This implies that the integrality gap tends to be smaller when k is larger.

3.3.2 Lower Bound of IG

To establish a lower bound for the integrality gap, we will select a specific instance and determine its OTP and OTP_f values. Consequently, we can derive that $IG \geq \frac{OTP}{OTP_f}$.

Let us define $U = \{0, 1\}^q \setminus \{0\}$ and

$$C = \left\{S_\beta = \{e \in U : \langle e, \beta \rangle = 1 \bmod 2\}_{\beta \in \{0,1\}^q}\right\}.$$

We will consider the set C as an instance of the set k-multicover problem. In the following lemma, we determine both the optimal value and the objective value of the relaxed solution.

Lemma 2 *Let OPT be the optimal value of the minimum set k-multicover problem for the instance given above. We have that $OPT \geq \log_2(n+1)$.*

Proof We use the same instance as in Theorem 4.1 of [60]. In the lecture note, it is proved that the optimal value of the minimum set cover of this instance is $\log_2(n+1)$. We therefore derive from there that, for any $k \geq 1$, the optimal value of the minimum set k-multicover problem is not smaller than $\log_2(n+1)$. □

Lemma 3 *Let OPT_f be the optimal value of relaxation of the minimum set k-multicover problem for the instance given above. We have that $OPT_f \leq 2k$.*

Proof Let the output variable x_S be $2k/|C|$ for all $S \in C$. Since for any $z \in U$, we have z being in half of the set in C, we obtain that

$$\sum_{S:z\in S} x_S = \frac{|C|}{2} \times \frac{2k}{|C|} = k,$$

and verify that this $(x_S)_{S\in C}$ is a solution of the instance.

Because the objective value of this solution is $\sum_S x_S = |C| \cdot 2k/|C| = 2k$, we have that $OPT_f \leq 2k$. □

We then can obtain the following theorem.

Theorem 3 *The integrality gap for the minimum set k-multicover problem, denoted by IG, is not smaller than* $\log_2(n+1)/2k$.

Proof Recall that $IG := \max_{\text{instance } I} OPT(I)/OPT_f(I)$. We therefore obtain from the previous lemmas that $IG \geq OPT/OPT_f \geq \log_2(n+1)/2k$. □

One might think that the lower bound derived from the previous theorem, $\log_2(n+1)/2k$, asymptotically aligns with the upper bound from Theorem 1, $\log_2(n)/k$. However, that is not true. The approximation ratio of $\log_2(n)/k$ is achieved only under the conditions $k \ll l \ll n$. In the context of this section, where $l = n/2$, such conditions do not hold. Consequently, a gap persists between the upper and lower bounds, which we acknowledge as a topic for future investigation.

4 Conclusion

Information Privacy and Security represent research domains that offer the potential to introduce novel and compelling problems to algorithmic studies. In this chapter, we delve into the correlation between homomorphic secret sharing and the minimum set k-multicover problem. The optimal value in the minimum set k-multicover problem delineates the maximum number of clients feasible within homomorphic secret sharing. However, for this specific application, an approximation solution is insufficient—we require a precise lower bound for the optimal value. Thus, we advocate for employing the relaxed problem solution as a lower bound and demonstrate the resulting integrality gap. Consequently, under the conditions where $k \ll l \ll n$, we establish that the integrality gap does not exceed $\log_2(n)/k$. Conversely, we identify an instance where the integrality gap amounts to $\log_2(n+1)/2k$.

We hold the belief that narrowing the gap between the lower and upper bounds is achievable. Our experimental findings suggest that enhancing the lower bound to $\log_2(n)$ is feasible. Additionally, we anticipate the development of algorithms capable of more accurately approximating the lower bound of the optimal value. These issues remain as areas for future investigation.

Acknowledgements This work is supported by KAKENHI Grant 21H05845 and 23H04377. Alexandre Auzel carried out this research during his exchange at The University of Tokyo. The authors express their gratitude to Prof. Hiroshi Imai for hosting him.

References

1. R. Avanzi, F. Sica, Scalar multiplication on Koblitz curves using double bases, in *VietCrypt'06* (Springer, 2006), pp. 131–146
2. G. Banegas, D.J. Bernstein, F. Campos, T. Chou, T. Lange, M. Meyer, B. Smith, J. Sotáková, CTIDH: faster constant-time CSIDH. IACR Trans Cryptogr Hardw Embed Syst **2021**(4), 351–387 (2021)
3. D. Bernstein, T. Lange, Two grumpy giants and a baby. Open Book Ser. **1**(1), 87–111 (2013)
4. D.J. Bernstein, C. Chuengsatiansup, T. Lange, C. Van Vredendaal, NTRU prime. IACR Cryptol. ePrint Arch. **2016**, 461 (2016)
5. L. Betzer, V. Suppakitpaisarn, Q. Hillebrand, Local differential privacy for number of paths and katz centrality (2023). arXiv:2310.14000
6. T. Blum, C. Paar, Montgomery modular exponentiation on reconfigurable hardware. In: ARITH'99 (IEEE, 1999), pp. 70–77
7. M. Campagna, C. Costello, B. Hess, A. Jalali, B. Koziel, B. LaMacchia, P. Longa, M. Naehrig, J. Renes, D. Urbanik et al., Supersingular isogeny key encapsulation (2019)
8. W. Castryck, T. Lange, C. Martindale, L. Panny, J. Renes, CSIDH: an efficient post-quantum commutative group action, in *ASIACRYPT'18* (Springer, 2018), pp. 395–427
9. P. Chalermsook, H. Imai, V. Suppakitpaisarn, Two lower bounds for shortest double-base number system. IEICE Trans Fundam Electron Commun Comput Sci **98**(6), 1310–1312 (2015)
10. D.D. Chen, N. Mentens, F. Vercauteren, S.S. Roy, R.C. Cheung, D. Pao, I. Verbauwhede, High-speed polynomial multiplication architecture for ring-LWE and SHE cryptosystems. IEEE Trans Circuits Syst I: Regul Pap **62**(1), 157–166 (2014)
11. J.H. Cheon, J. Hong, M. Kim, Speeding up the Pollard rho method on prime fields, in *ASIACRYPT'08* (Springer, 2008), pp. 471–488
12. E.G. Coffman, R.L. Graham, Optimal scheduling for two-processor systems. Acta informatica **1**, 200–213 (1972)
13. G. Cormode, S. Jha, T. Kulkarni, N. Li, D. Srivastava, T. Wang, Privacy at scale: local differential privacy in practice, in *ICDM'18*, pp. 1655–1658 (2018)
14. L. Dhulipala, Q.C. Liu, S. Raskhodnikova, J. Shi, J. Shun, S. Yu, Differential privacy from locally adjustable graph algorithms: k-core decomposition, low out-degree ordering, and densest subgraphs, in *FOCS'22* (IEEE, 2022), pp. 754–765
15. Differential Privacy Team, Apple: Learning with privacy at scale (2017)
16. B. Ding, J. Kulkarni, S. Yekhanin, Collecting telemetry data privately. Adv. Neural Inf. Process. Syst. **30** (2017)
17. C. Dwork, F. McSherry, K. Nissim, A. Smith, Calibrating noise to sensitivity in private data analysis, in *TCC'06* (Springer, 2006), pp. 265–284
18. T. Eden, Q.C. Liu, S. Raskhodnikova, A. Smith, Triangle counting with local edge differential privacy, in *ICALP'23* (2023)
19. Ú. Erlingsson, V. Pihur, A. Korolova, Rappor: randomized aggregatable privacy preserving ordinal response, in *CCS'14*, pp. 1054–1067 (2014)
20. A. Evfimievski, J. Gehrke, R. Srikant, Limiting privacy breaches in privacy preserving data mining, in *PODS'03*, pp. 211–222 (2003)

21. S.D. Galbraith, P. Wang, F. Zhang, Computing elliptic curve discrete logarithms with improved baby-step giant-step algorithm. Adv. Math. Commun. **11**(3), 453–469 (2017)
22. M.R. Garey, D.S. Johnson, *Computers and intractability*, vol. 174 (Freeman San Francisco, 1979)
23. D.W. Gillies, J.W.S. Liu, Scheduling tasks with and/or precedence constraints. SIAM J. Comput. **24**(4), 797–810 (1995)
24. A. Gorgi, M. El Ouali, A. Srivastav, M. Hachimi, Approximation algorithm for the multicovering problem. J. Comb. Optim. **41**, 433–450 (2021)
25. A. Gorgi, M.E. Ouali, A. Srivastav, M. Hachimi, Repeated randomized algorithm for the multicovering problem (2021). arXiv:2101.09080
26. N.G. Hall, D.S. Hochbaum, A fast approximation algorithm for the multicovering problem. Disc. Appl. Math. **15**(1), 35–40 (1986)
27. W. Hasenplaugh, G. Gaubatz, V. Gopal, Fast modular reduction, in *ARITH'07* (IEEE, 2007), pp. 225–229
28. J. Hehir, A. Slavković, X. Niu, Consistent spectral clustering of network block models under local differential privacy. J. Priv. Confidity. **12**(2) (2022)
29. M. Henzinger, A. Sricharan, L. Zhu, Tighter bounds for local differentially private core decomposition and densest subgraph (2024). arXiv:2402.18020
30. Q. Hillebrand, V. Suppakitpaisarn, T. Shibuya, Unbiased locally private estimator for polynomials of laplacian variables, in *KDD'23*, pp. 741–751 (2023)
31. J. Hoffstein, J. Pipher, J.H. Silverman, NTRU: a ring-based public key cryptosystem, in *International algorithmic number theory symposium* (Springer, 1998), pp. 267–288
32. T.C. Hu, Parallel sequencing and assembly line problems. Oper. Res. **9**(6), 841–848 (1961)
33. Q.S. Hua, Y. Wang, D. Yu, F.C. Lau, Set multi-covering via inclusion-exclusion. Theor. Comput. Sci. **410**(38–40), 3882–3892 (2009)
34. Q.S. Hua, D. Yu, F.C. Lau, Y. Wang, Exact algorithms for set multicover and multiset multicover problems, in *ISAAC'09* (Springer, 2009), pp. 34–44
35. A. Hutchinson, K. Karabina, Constructing canonical strategies for parallel implementation of isogeny based cryptography, in *Indocrypt'18* (Springer, 2018), pp. 169–189
36. J. Imola, T. Murakami, K. Chaudhuri, Locally differentially private analysis of graph statistics, in *USENIX'21*, pp. 983–1000 (2021)
37. J. Imola, T. Murakami, K. Chaudhuri, Communication-efficient triangle counting under local differential privacy, in *USENIX'22* pp. 537–554 (2022)
38. J. Imola, T. Murakami, K. Chaudhuri, Differentially private triangle and 4-cycle counting in the shuffle model, in *CCS'22*, pp. 1505–1519 (2022)
39. D. Jao, L. De Feo, Towards quantum-resistant cryptosystems from supersingular elliptic curve isogenies, in *PQCrypto'11* (Springer, 2011), pp. 19–34
40. N. Koblitz, Elliptic curve cryptosystems. Math. Comput. **48**(177), 203–209 (1987)
41. D. Krenn, V. Suppakitpaisarn, S. Wagner, On the minimal hamming weight of a multi-base representation. Journal of Number Theory **208**, 168–179 (2020)
42. J. Kuepper, A. Erbsen, J. Gross, O. Conoly, C. Sun, S. Tian, D. Wu, A. Chlipala, C. Chuengsatiansup, D. Genkin et al., CryptOpt: verified compilation with randomized program search for cryptographic primitives. PLDI'23 **7**, 1268–1292 (2023)
43. Y. Liu, T. Wang, Y. Liu, H. Chen, C. Li, Edge-protected triangle count estimation under relationship local differential privacy. IEEE Trans. Knowl. Data Eng.
44. V.S. Miller, Use of elliptic curves in cryptography, in *CRYPTO'85* (Springer, 1985), pp. 417–426
45. S. Mukherjee, V. Suppakitpaisarn, Robustness for spectral clustering of general graphs under local differential privacy (2023). arXiv:2309.06867
46. K. Phalakarn, V. Suppakitpaisarn, N. Attrapadung, K. Matsuura, Constructive t-secure homomorphic secret sharing for low degree polynomials, in *INDOCRYPT'21* (Springer, 2021), pp. 763–785
47. K. Phalakarn, V. Suppakitpaisarn, M.A. Hasan, Speeding-up parallel computation of large smooth-degree isogeny using precedence-constrained scheduling, in *ACIST'22* (Springer, 2022), pp. 309–331

48. K. Phalakarn, V. Suppakitpaisarn, F. Rodríguez-Henríquez, M.A. Hasan, Vectorized and parallel computation of large smooth-degree isogenies using precedence-constrained scheduling. IACR Trans. Cryptogr. Hardw. Embed. Syst. **2023**(3), 246–269 (2023)
49. J.M. Pollard, A monte carlo method for factorization. Nordisk Tidsskrift Informationsbehandling (BIT) Numer. Math. **15**(3), 331–334 (1975). https://doi.org/10.1007/bf01933667
50. Z. Qin, T. Yu, Y. Yang, I. Khalil, X. Xiao, K. Ren, Generating synthetic decentralized social graphs with local differential privacy, in *CCS'17*, pp. 425–438 (2017)
51. R. Raman, S. Ray, Improved approximation algorithm for set multicover with non-piercing regions, in *SEA'20. Schloss-Dagstuhl-Leibniz Zentrum f*ür *Informatik* (2020)
52. P. Ren, R. Suda, V. Suppakitpaisarn, Efficient additions and montgomery reductions of large integers for simd, in *ARITH'23* (IEEE, 2024)
53. R.L. Rivest, A. Shamir, L. Adleman, A method for obtaining digital signatures and public-key cryptosystems. Commun. ACM **21**(2), 120–126 (1978)
54. M. Shand, J. Vuillemin, Fast implementations of RSA cryptography, in *ARITH'93* (IEEE, 1993), pp. 252–259
55. D. Shanks, Class number, a theory of factorization, and genera. Proc. Symp. Math. Soc. **20**, 415–440 (1971)
56. P.W. Shor, Polynomial-time algorithms for prime factorization and discrete logarithms on a quantum computer. SIAM Rev. **41**(2), 303–332 (1999)
57. V. Suppakitpaisarn, Tight lower bound for average number of terms in optimal double-base number system using information-theoretic tools. Inf. Process. Lett. **175**, 106226 (2022)
58. V. Suppakitpaisarn, M. Edahiro, H. Imai, Calculating average joint hamming weight for minimal weight conversion of d integers, in *WALCOM'12* (Springer, 2012), pp. 229–240
59. V. Suppakitpaisarn, M. Edahiro, H. Imai, Fast elliptic curve cryptography using minimal weight conversion of d integers, in *AISC'12*, pp. 15–26 (2012)
60. K. Zhang, J. Nelson, *CS 224: advanced algorithms lecture* vol. 12 (2017). https://people.seas.harvard.edu/~cs224/spring17/lec/lec12.pdf

A Survey: SWAP Test and Its Applications to Quantum Complexity Theory

Harumichi Nishimura

Abstract The SWAP test is a fundamental tool commonly used in the theory of quantum information and computation while its understanding and applications have been investigated in the literature. This survey focuses on the SWAP test in the studies of quantum complexity theory. We review the basics of the SWAP test, some tests related to it, and their properties, and report their applications in quantum complexity theory.

1 Introduction

More than 30 years have passed since Shor's integer factoring algorithm [75], and many quantum algorithms have been developed in the literature [25]. However, some of them are not for solving any problem that is handled by classical computers, but a subroutine for other quantum algorithms or protocols. Such a representative one is quantum phase estimation [51], which approximates the phase corresponding to an eigenvalue of a unitary operator given as input. It has been frequently used as a subroutine of many quantum algorithms such as Kitaev's integer factoring algorithm [51] and the Harrow–Hassidim–Lloyd algorithm for linear equations [42]. Now you may imagine that it would be nice to estimate how close two given quantum states are. The best tool in quantum computation for this task is the SWAP test (or controlled-SWAP test). The SWAP test was first introduced by Barenco, Berthiaume, Deutsch, Ekert, Jozsa, and Macchiavello [10].[1] It implements the projection to the symmetric subspace of a bipartite system. In Ref. [10], it was utilized as a quantum error correction technique. Nowadays, it has been utilized in quantum machine learning and

[1] Reference [10] appeared before the Nielsen-Chuang book [66] but the book did not cover the SWAP test. This seems to be one of the few exceptions to what is now a commonplace concept in quantum information science.

H. Nishimura (✉)
Nagoya University, Nagoya, Japan
e-mail: hnishimura@i.nagoya-u.ac.jp

S. Minato et al. (eds.), *Algorithmic Foundations for Social Advancement*,
https://doi.org/10.1007/978-981-96-0668-9_16

NISQ algorithms, for instance, by embedding two classical huge data into quantum states, and measuring the closeness using the SWAP test.

Quantum complexity theory is also one of the topics that would benefit from the SWAP test. The first appealing use of the SWAP test in quantum complexity theory was given by Buhrman et al. [16]. Since then, the SWAP test has been utilized always to develop quantum complexity theory in the literature.

In this survey, we review the basics of the SWAP test and its related concepts. We then overview its applications to quantum complexity theory. Although the overview is not exhaustive, it does include recent developments in its use.

2 SWAP Test and Its Related Concepts

This survey assumes a familiarity with basic concepts of quantum information and computation such as states, measurements, and quantum circuits [66, 79, 80]. A quantum system in a quantum algorithm (or protocol) is called a (quantum) register. A composite system $\mathcal{A} \otimes \mathcal{B}$ of two registers $\mathcal{A}$ and $\mathcal{B}$ is sometimes denoted as $(\mathcal{A}, \mathcal{B})$. For any square matrix A, $\mathrm{tr}(A)$ denotes the trace of A. Let $[n] := \{1, 2, \ldots, n\}$ for any positive integer n.

We start by recalling the SWAP operator. It is the unitary operator on a bipartite system $\mathcal{H} = \mathcal{A} \otimes \mathcal{B}$ defined by

$$\mathrm{SWAP}|i\rangle|j\rangle = |j\rangle|i\rangle,$$

where $|i\rangle$ (resp., $|j\rangle$) denotes a basis state on $\mathcal{A}$ (resp. $\mathcal{B}$). Following the name, it represents the operation that swaps the contents of the two systems.

The symmetric subspace of $\mathcal{H}$, denoted by Sym (or rigorously $\mathrm{Sym}_{\mathcal{H}}$), is the subspace that is invariant by the SWAP operator. That is, it is defined as

$$\mathrm{Sym} := \{|\psi\rangle \in \mathcal{H} \mid \mathrm{SWAP}|\psi\rangle = |\psi\rangle\}. \tag{1}$$

An element of the symmetric subspace is called a symmetric state. Moreover, its orthogonal complement $\mathrm{Sym}^{\perp}$ is represented as

$$\mathrm{Sym}^{\perp} = \{|\psi\rangle \in \mathcal{H} \mid \mathrm{SWAP}|\psi\rangle = -|\psi\rangle\}, \tag{2}$$

and is called the anti-symmetric subspace. An element of $\mathrm{Sym}^{\perp}$ is called anti-symmetric. The projection to the symmetric subspace, Π_{Sym}, and that of the anti-symmetric subspace, $\Pi_{\mathrm{Sym}^{\perp}}$, can be written as

$$\Pi_{\mathrm{Sym}} = \frac{I + \mathrm{SWAP}}{2}, \quad \Pi_{\mathrm{Sym}^{\perp}} = \frac{I - \mathrm{SWAP}}{2}.$$

As the simplest example, let us consider the case that the two systems $\mathcal{A}$ and $\mathcal{B}$ are both one-qubit ones. The symmetric subspace is the subspace spanned by the three symmetric states $|00\rangle$, $|11\rangle$, and $|\Psi^+\rangle := \frac{1}{\sqrt{2}}(|01\rangle + |10\rangle)$. The anti-symmetric subspace is the one-dimensional subspace spanned by $|\Psi^-\rangle := \frac{1}{\sqrt{2}}(|01\rangle - |10\rangle)$. We refer to, for instance, Refs. [23, 41, 79] for more details on symmetric subspaces.

The SWAP test is the quantum algorithm described as follows:

SWAP test
Input registers: two n-qubit registers $\mathcal{I}_1$ and $\mathcal{I}_2$

1. Prepare $|+\rangle := \frac{1}{\sqrt{2}}(|0\rangle + |1\rangle)$ in a one-qubit register called ancilla, $\mathcal{A}$; or equivalently, prepare $|0\rangle$ and apply the Hadamard gate $\mathsf{H} = \frac{1}{\sqrt{2}}\begin{pmatrix} 1 & 1 \\ 1 & -1 \end{pmatrix}$ on $\mathcal{A}$.
2. Perform the controlled-SWAP operation on $(\mathcal{I}_1, \mathcal{I}_2)$ with control register $\mathcal{A}$, that is, swap the two registers $\mathcal{I}_1$ and $\mathcal{I}_2$ iff the content of $\mathcal{A}$ is 1.
3. Apply the Hadamard gate H on ancilla $\mathcal{A}$, measure $\mathcal{A}$ in the computational basis, and accept iff the measurement outcome is 0; or equivalently, measure $\mathcal{A}$ in the Hadamard basis, and accept iff the outcome corresponds to $|+\rangle$.

When two pure states $|\psi\rangle$ and $|\varphi\rangle$ are given as input (i.e., $|\psi\rangle \otimes |\varphi\rangle$ is given to $\mathcal{I}_1 \otimes \mathcal{I}_2$), the acceptance probability of the SWAP test is represented by

$$\Pr[\text{accept}] = \frac{1}{2} + \frac{1}{2}|\langle\psi|\varphi\rangle|^2. \tag{3}$$

This implies that the SWAP test may be useful for approximating the fidelity between two pure states $|\psi\rangle$ and $|\varphi\rangle$ $(= |\langle\psi|\varphi\rangle|)$.

The SWAP test implements the projection to the symmetric subspace on the registers $\mathcal{I}_1$ and $\mathcal{I}_2$ when the test accepts. The post-state when the test accepts becomes a symmetric state while the post-state when the test rejects (i.e., does not accept) becomes an anti-symmetric state. For example, when both $\mathcal{I}_1$ and $\mathcal{I}_2$ are one-qubit registers and the input to $\mathcal{I} := \mathcal{I}_1 \otimes \mathcal{I}_2$ is

$$\alpha|00\rangle + \beta|11\rangle + \gamma|\Psi^-\rangle,$$

the state after step 2 is

$$|+\rangle_{\mathcal{A}}(\alpha|00\rangle + \beta|11\rangle)_{\mathcal{I}} + \gamma|-\rangle_{\mathcal{A}}|\Psi^-\rangle_{\mathcal{I}}$$

by Eq. (1) and Eq. (2), where $|-\rangle = \frac{1}{\sqrt{2}}(|0\rangle - |1\rangle)$. Thus, by step 3 (measurement in the Hadamard basis $\{|+\rangle, |-\rangle\}$), we have the post-state $\frac{\alpha|00\rangle+\beta|11\rangle}{\sqrt{|\alpha|^2+|\beta|^2}}$ when the test accepts, and $|\Psi^-\rangle$ when it rejects. This exactly implements the projection to the symmetric subspace when the test accepts (and also the projection to its orthogonal complement, the anti-symmetric subspace when the test rejects).

When two mixed states (represented by density operators) ρ and σ are given as input, the acceptance probability of the SWAP test is represented by

$$\Pr[\text{accept}] = \frac{1}{2} + \frac{1}{2}\text{tr}(\rho\sigma). \tag{4}$$

In particular, when $\rho = \sigma$,

$$\Pr[\text{accept}] = \frac{1}{2} + \frac{1}{2}\text{tr}(\rho^2). \tag{5}$$

(The proof can be found in Ref. [55].) Since ρ is a pure state iff $\text{tr}(\rho^2) = 1$ ([66, Exercise 2.71]), the SWAP test can be used for testing the purity of a given state [2, 30, 54, 55, 72, 73]. For instance, the following fact is given in Ref. [2].

Lemma 1 (Proposition 2.10 in Ref. [2]) *Suppose $\langle\psi|\rho|\psi\rangle \leq 1 - \varepsilon$ for all pure states $|\psi\rangle$ (that is, the purity of ρ is low). Then, the SWAP test between ρ and any mixed state σ accepts with probability at most $1 - \frac{\varepsilon}{2}$.*

Next, we present some rigidity on a quantum state input to the SWAP test, which follows from the fact that the SWAP test implements the projection on the symmetric subspace when it accepts. Henceforth, for any mixed state ρ on the composite system $\mathcal{A} \otimes \mathcal{B}$, $\text{tr}_{\mathcal{A}}(\rho)$ (resp., $\text{tr}_{\mathcal{B}}(\rho)$) denotes the reduced state on $\mathcal{B}$ (resp., $\mathcal{A}$) obtained by tracing out $\mathcal{A}$ (resp., $\mathcal{B}$). The following lemma says that if the SWAP test accepts with high probability, the two reduced states obtained from the input must be close.

Lemma 2 (Informal statement of Lemma 5 in Ref. [33] or Lemma 5.1 in Ref. [71]) *If a $2n$-qubit state ρ is given to $\mathcal{I}_1 \otimes \mathcal{I}_2$ (the two input registers), the SWAP test accepts with high probability if and only if $\text{tr}_{\mathcal{I}_1}(\rho)$ is close to $\text{tr}_{\mathcal{I}_2}(\rho)$, that is,*

$$\text{tr}_{\mathcal{I}_1}(\rho) \approx \text{tr}_{\mathcal{I}_2}(\rho).$$

Destructive SWAP test

The so-called *destructive SWAP test* [34] simulates the acceptance probability of the SWAP test (Eq. (3) as well as Eq. (4)) without using any ancilla qubit (see Ref. [34] or Appendix C in Ref. [31] for the proofs). Its description is as follows.

Destructive SWAP test
Input registers: two n-qubit registers $\mathcal{I}_1$ and $\mathcal{I}_2$.

1. Do the following for all $j \in [n]$.

1. Apply the CNOT operation where the control qubit is the jth qubit of $\mathcal{I}_1$ and the target qubit is the jth qubit of $\mathcal{I}_2$.
2. Apply the Hadamard gate H on the jth qubit of $\mathcal{I}_1$.
3. Measure the jth qubits of $\mathcal{I}_1$ and $\mathcal{I}_2$ in the computational basis, and let $o_{j,1}$ and $o_{j,2}$ denote the measurement outcomes.

2. Accept iff the number of indices j satisfying $o_{j,1}o_{j,2} = 1$ is odd.

Actually, when we consider the $n = 1$ case as the simplest example, the unitary part of the destructive SWAP test transforms the Bell states $|\Phi^+\rangle, |\Phi^-\rangle, |\Psi^+\rangle$, and $|\Psi^-\rangle$, where $|\Phi^\pm\rangle = \frac{1}{\sqrt{2}}(|00\rangle \pm |11\rangle)$ and $|\Psi^\pm\rangle = \frac{1}{\sqrt{2}}(|01\rangle + |10\rangle)$, into $|00\rangle, |01\rangle, |10\rangle$, and $|11\rangle$, respectively. Thus, the final measurement of the destructive SWAP test can distinguish perfectly the symmetric states from the anti-symmetric state similarly to the SWAP test. However, it does not implement the projection to the symmetric subspace since given $|\Psi^+\rangle$ as input, the post-state when the test accepts is not $|\Psi^+\rangle$ but $\frac{1}{2}(|01\rangle\langle 01| + |10\rangle\langle 10|)$.

Permutation test

The *permutation test* (which was also first introduced in Ref. [10]) is a natural multipartite generalization of the SWAP test. Namely, it implements the projection to the symmetric subspace of a k-partite system $\mathcal{A} = \mathcal{A}_1 \otimes \mathcal{A}_2 \otimes \cdots \otimes \mathcal{A}_k$ $(k \geq 2)$,

$$\mathrm{Sym}^k := \{|\psi\rangle \in \mathcal{A} \mid W_\sigma |\psi\rangle = |\psi\rangle \text{ for all } \sigma \in S_k\}.$$

Here, S_k denotes the symmetric group on $[k]$, and W_σ is the unitary operator defined by

$$W_\sigma |i_1\rangle|i_2\rangle \cdots |i_k\rangle := |i_{\sigma(1)}\rangle|i_{\sigma(2)}\rangle \cdots |i_{\sigma(k)}\rangle,$$

where $|i_\mu\rangle$ is a basis vector of $\mathcal{A}_\mu$. That is, W_σ implements the permutation of the k subsystems $\mathcal{A}_1, \ldots, \mathcal{A}_k$ by σ.

The permutation test is the quantum algorithm performed as follows:

Permutation test
Input registers: k n-qubit registers $\mathcal{I}_1, \mathcal{I}_2, \ldots, \mathcal{I}_k$.

1. Prepare $|0\rangle$ in a $(k!)$-dimensional register (ancilla) $\mathcal{A}$.
2. Apply the quantum Fourier transformation

$$F_{k!} := \frac{1}{\sqrt{k!}} \sum_{\nu,\mu} e^{\frac{2\pi i \nu\mu}{k!}} |\nu\rangle\langle\mu|$$

on $\mathcal{A}$ to generate the state $\frac{1}{\sqrt{k!}}\sum_{j=0}^{k!-1}|j\rangle$.
3. Perform the controlled-permutation operation on $(\mathcal{I}_1, \mathcal{I}_2, \ldots, \mathcal{I}_k)$ with control register $\mathcal{A}$; that is, if the content of $\mathcal{A}$ is j, then apply W_{σ_j} to $\mathcal{I}_1 \otimes \cdots \otimes \mathcal{I}_k$, where σ_j is the jth permutation on S_k.
4. Apply the inverse of F_m on ancilla $\mathcal{A}$, measure $\mathcal{A}$ in the computational basis, and accept iff the measurement outcome is 0.

The acceptance probability of the permutation test is described by

$$\Pr[\text{accept}] = \frac{1}{\sqrt{k!}}\sum_{i=0}^{k!-1}\prod_{m=1}^{k}\langle\psi_m|\psi_{\sigma_i(m)}\rangle.$$

(The proof is easy but seen in Ref. [49] for instance.) A good point is that the acceptance probability when there are (at least) two orthogonal pure states in the input registers is $\frac{1}{k}$ which is lower than the SWAP test ($=\frac{1}{2}$). This point is sometimes used for applications ([7, 12, 48] for instance).

Recently, an analogue of Lemma 2 for the permutation test was given in Ref. [44]. A destructive version of the permutation test seems not to appear in the literature to our best knowledge.

Symmetrization-by-permutation

The following procedure, called *symmetrization-by-permutation* in this survey,[2] is simple but useful (we see an example in the next section).

Symmetrization-by-permutation
Input registers: k n-qubit registers $\mathcal{I}_1, \mathcal{I}_2, \ldots, \mathcal{I}_k$.

1. Permute k registers uniformly at random.
2. Output the k registers in order.

By definition of the symmetric subspace, the output after symmetrization-by-permutation is a symmetric state.

Product test

The *product test* is a subroutine obtained by using SWAP tests to verify whether a given state is a product state or not. This test was first introduced in quantum

[2] Note that the projection to the symmetric subspace is called symmetrization in Ref. [10], and thus we add the term "by permutation".

complexity theory by Harrow and Montanaro [43]. The algorithm is performed as follows.

Product test
Input registers: two kn-qubit registers I_1 and I_2 that consist of k n-qubit registers $I_{1,j}$ and $I_{2,j}$ ($j = 1, 2, \ldots, k$), respectively.
1. Do the following for each $j \in [k]$.
a. Perform the SWAP test on $I_{1,j}$ and $I_{2,j}$.
2. Accept iff all the k SWAP tests accept.

A very useful property of the product test is described as follows.

Theorem 1 (Informal statement of Theorem 1 in Ref. [43]) *Given two copies of kn-qubit state $|\psi\rangle$ as input, the product test accepts with high probability only if $|\psi\rangle$ is close to a product state, that is,*

$$|\psi\rangle \approx |\psi_1\rangle \otimes |\psi_2\rangle \otimes \cdots \otimes |\psi_k\rangle$$

for some n-qubit states $|\psi_1\rangle, |\psi_2\rangle, \ldots, |\psi_k\rangle$.

Recently, the proof of Theorem 1 in Ref. [43] was simplified, and also the quality was improved by Soleimanifer and Wright [76]. Moreover, Ref. [3] constructed some asymmetric version of the product test in a study of a quantum version of the polynomial-time hierarchy.

Distillation by SWAP tests

Recently, distillation procedures obtained by applying SWAP tests sequentially have been explored in the literature [22, 45].

In Ref. [22], focusing on one of the two registers (I_1 and I_2) of the SWAP test, for instance, I_1, it was observed that the post-state in I_1 when the input is $\rho \otimes \sigma$ and the measurement outcome of the ancilla register is b is represented as

$$\frac{1}{2} \cdot \frac{\rho + \sigma + (-1)^b(\rho\sigma + \sigma\rho)}{1 + (-1)^b \mathrm{tr}(\rho\sigma)}. \tag{6}$$

Using Eq. (6) as a stepping stone, Ref. [22] gave a method that distills a depolarized state with high quality (i.e., far from the completely mixed state) from many copies of depolarized states with low qualities.

In Ref. [45], a distillation procedure under other conditions was discovered. Assume that the n-qubit target state to be distilled is $|\tau\rangle$, and each of given samples $|\psi_1\rangle, \ldots, |\psi_m\rangle$ is reasonably close to $|\tau\rangle$, that is, it has a constant (independent of n) fidelity with $|\tau\rangle$. Moreover, any two of the samples $|\psi_i\rangle$ and $|\psi_j\rangle$ are orthogonal when they are restricted to the orthogonal complement of span($|\tau\rangle$), i.e., $\langle\psi_i|(I - |\tau\rangle\langle\tau|)|\psi_j\rangle = 0$. Then, Ref. [45] proved that $m = \mathrm{poly}(n)$ is sufficient to distill τ with high probability and high fidelity (see Theorem 5.7 in Ref. [45] for the actual statement and Theorem 5.10 under the case where the conditions are relaxed).

More general distillation procedures that unify the above conditions would be nice for future work.

Quantum fingerprinting

A good partner of the SWAP test is *quantum fingerprinting*; it was first introduced by Buhrman, Cleve, Watrous, and de Wolf [16] to check whether two strings are equal or not by short quantum messages. Here, a quantum fingerprint of a bit string x of length n, $|\psi_x\rangle$, satisfies the following properties:

1. $|\psi\rangle$ is an m-qubit state where $m = O(\log n)$.
2. For any $x \neq y$, $|\langle\psi_x|\psi_y\rangle|$ is close to 0 (almost orthogonal).

For instance, it can be constructed as

$$|\psi_x\rangle := \frac{1}{\sqrt{m}}\sum_{j=1}^{m}|j\rangle|E(x)_j\rangle,$$

where $E : \{0,1\}^n \to \{0,1\}^m$ with $m = O(n)$ is an error-correcting code such that for $x \neq y$,

$$\frac{|\{j \in [m] \mid E(x)_j \neq E(y)_j\}|}{m} \geq c$$

for some constant $c > 0$ (e.g., Justesen code [39, 62]), and $E(x)_j$ is the jth bit of $E(x)$. Other quantum fingerprinting can be constructed using a polynomial [28], a random linear code [27, 29], and more.

In the next section, we fix such a set of quantum fingerprints $\{|\psi_x\rangle \mid x \in \{0,1\}^n\}$.

3 Applications

3.1 SMP Setting in Communication Complexity

The first application of the SWAP test in quantum complexity theory was given by Buhrman, Cleve, Watrous, and de Wolf [16] as an exponential separation between quantum and classical communication complexity.

The SMP setting is the simplest and weakest one in communication complexity [57, 67, 81].

Definition 1 (*SMP*) In the SMP (simultaneous message passing) setting, there are three parties, Alice, Bob, and the referee. Alice has her input x, and Bob has his input y while the referee has no input. Each of Alice and Bob sends a message to the referee. The goal is that the referee outputs $f(x, y)$ for a designated function f. Its communication complexity is measured by the sum of lengths of messages sent by Alice and Bob.

One of the most well-studied functions in communication complexity is the equality function $\mathrm{EQ}_n : \{0,1\}^n \times \{0,1\}^n \to \{0,1\}$ defined by $\mathrm{EQ}_n(x, y) = 1$ if $x = y$, and 0 otherwise. It was known that the classical (randomized) communication complexity of EQ_n in the SMP setting is $\Theta(\sqrt{n})$ [5, 9, 65]. On the contrary, Ref. [16] proved that the quantum communication complexity in the SMP setting is $O(\log n)$. Their quantum SMP protocol is as follows.

Quantum SMP protocol for EQ
Input: $x \in \{0,1\}^n$ for Alice; $y \in \{0,1\}^n$ for Bob.

1. Alice sends the referee a quantum register $\mathcal{A}$ that contains the fingerprint of x, $|\psi_x\rangle$. Bob sends the referee a quantum register $\mathcal{B}$ that contains the fingerprint of y, $|\psi_y\rangle$.
2. The referee performs the SWAP test on $\mathcal{A}$ and $\mathcal{B}$. Accept iff it accepts.

In fact, when $x = y$, the acceptance probability is 1 by Eq. (3) while when $x \neq y$, the acceptance probability is $\frac{1}{2} + \frac{1}{2}|\langle\psi_x|\psi_y\rangle|^2 \approx \frac{1}{2}$ thanks to the second property of quantum fingerprinting.

Yao [82] extended the result of Ref. [16] from the equality function to the functions that have $O(1)$ randomized communication complexity in the SMP setting where Alice and Bob have shared randomness[3] such as a Hamming distance function (that asks whether two strings have a Hamming distance smaller than a constant). He used the SWAP test in his protocol to estimate the fidelity between Alice's state and Bob's state that encode messages in a classical protocol as quantum superposition.

References [8, 37] are examples of recent usages for the SWAP test in quantum communication complexity.

3.2 *Distributed Quantum Certification*

The distributed NP systems (or Merlin–Arthur systems) have been a well-studied topic in distributed computing since the seminal work in Ref. [56] (see Ref. [32] for a survey). Remarkable points different from a standard NP system are (i) the verification is done by one-turn (or $O(1)$-turn) communication among multiple parties who are some nodes in a network; (ii) for any no-instance, it suffices that some node rejects (while all nodes must accept for any yes-instance).

[3] This condition was further expanded in Ref. [35].

As its quantum analogue (or a distributed analogue of quantum Merlin–Arthur systems (QMA)), the concept of distributed quantum Merlin–Arthur (dQMA) protocols on a network was introduced by Fraigniaud, Le Gall, Nishimura, and Paz [33]. Here, we give a definition of it on a line network.

Definition 2 (*dQMA on a line*) In a dQMA protocol on a line of length n, the verifier (Arthur) consists of $k+1$ nodes, $v_0, v_1, \ldots, v_k$, where v_i and v_{i+1} are neighbors for each $i \in \{0, 1, \ldots, k-1\}$. The prover (Merlin) sends a quantum register (or a set of registers) to each node, and then each node communicates with its neighbors by one-turn quantum communication. Finally, each node performs local quantum computation, and outputs accept or reject. The dQMA protocol has completeness a and soundness error b when the following holds:

- (completeness) For any yes-instance, the probability that all the nodes accept is at least a.
- (soundness) For any no-instance, the probability that all the nodes accept is at most b.

Now we consider the equality problem (EQ) on a line defined as follows: an input $x \in \{0, 1\}^n$ is given to v_0 and another input $y \in \{0, 1\}^n$ is given to v_k. The input pair (x, y) is a yes-instance iff $x = y$. In Ref. [33], it was shown that there is a dQMA protocol with completeness 1 and soundness error $\frac{1}{3}$ and with $O(k^2 \log n)$-qubit proof for each node while in the classical case, $\Omega(n)$-bit length proof to some node is necessary. Thus, there is an exponential gap between quantum and classical proof lengths as long as $k = O(\log n)$.

Instead of the original dQMA protocol in Ref. [33], we present a dQMA protocol given in Ref. [44] for the simplicity of the sketchy analysis given below. It is performed as follows.

Distributed quantum Merlin–Arthur protocol for EQ on the line network
Input: $x \in \{0, 1\}^n$ for the left-end node v_0; $y \in \{0, 1\}^n$ for the right-end node v_k.

1. The prover sends two registers $\mathcal{R}_{j,1}$ and $\mathcal{R}_{j,2}$ to each intermediate node v_j $(j = 1, 2, \ldots, k-1)$.
2. Each intermediate node v_j applies symmetrization-by-permutation for $\mathcal{R}_{j,1}$ and $\mathcal{R}_{j,2}$ (that is, swaps them with probability $\frac{1}{2}$).
3. The left-end node v_0 prepares the fingerprint $|\psi_x\rangle$ in a register $\mathcal{R}_{0,2}$, and the right-end node v_k prepares $|\psi_y\rangle$ in a register $\mathcal{R}_{k,1}$.
4. The left-end node v_0 sends $\mathcal{R}_{0,2}$ to the neighbor v_1, and each intermediate node v_j sends $\mathcal{R}_{j,2}$ to the right neighbor v_{j+1}.
5. Each intermediate node v_j performs the SWAP test on $\mathcal{R}_{j-1,2}$ and $\mathcal{R}_{j,1}$, and v_k performs the SWAP test on $\mathcal{R}_{k-1,2}$ and $\mathcal{R}_{k,1}$.
6. Each node accepts if the SWAP test accepts, and rejects otherwise.

By the following theorem, running the above dQMA protocol $O(k^2)$ times in parallel leads to the desired result.

Theorem 2 *The above dQMA protocol has perfect completeness (i.e., completeness* 1*) and soundness error* $1 - \Omega(\frac{1}{k^2})$.

Proof (Sketch) When $x = y$, the prover can send $|\psi_x\rangle \otimes |\psi_x\rangle$ to each intermediate node, and then all the nodes accept.

When $x \neq y$, assuming that the probability that all nodes accept is close to 1, we can lead to a contradiction. Due to symmetrization-by-permutation, the reduced state $\rho_{j,1}$ of $\mathcal{R}_{j,1}$ is the same as the reduced state $\rho_{j,2}$ of $\mathcal{R}_{j,2}$, that is, $\rho_{j,1} = \rho_{j,2}$. By Lemma 2, for every $j \in \{0, 1, \ldots, k-1\}$, $\rho_{j,2}$ must be close to $\rho_{j+1,1}$ for all nodes to accept, which implies

$$\rho_{0,2} \approx \rho_{1,1} = \rho_{1,2} \approx \rho_{2,1} = \rho_{2,2} \approx \cdots \approx \rho_{k,1}.$$

However, this contradicts the fact that $\rho_{0,2} = |\psi_x\rangle\langle\psi_x|$ and $\rho_{k,1} = |\psi_y\rangle\langle\psi_y|$ are almost orthogonal (thanks to the second property of quantum fingerprinting). □

3.3 Quantum Interactive Proofs

The third example of applications picked up is from a (single-prover) quantum interactive proof system (introduced by Watrous [78]). It is a communication game between an unlimitedly powerful quantum party called the prover and a quantum polynomial-time party called the verifier. The game is represented by a quantum circuit on quantum registers $\mathcal{P}, \mathcal{M}, \mathcal{V}$ on the initial state $|0\rangle$ (all-0 state) where the prover and the verifier apply their unitary operations alternately:

- The prover applies some unitary operation P_j which acts nontrivially only on $\mathcal{P} \otimes \mathcal{M}$.
- The verifier applies some unitary operation V_j which acts nontrivially only on $\mathcal{M} \otimes \mathcal{V}$, and is represented by a uniformly generated polynomial-size quantum circuit.

When the number of turns is odd (resp., even), the prover (resp., verifier) first applies a unitary operation. For instance, when the number of turns is 3, the final state (before the measurement) is $V_2 P_2 V_1 P_1 |0\rangle$. Finally, the verifier measures the first qubit of $\mathcal{V}$ in the computational basis, and accepts iff the outcome is 1. Thus, a quantum interactive proof system is represented by $(\{P_i\}_i, \{V_j\}_j)$, where the operations $\{P_i\}$ by the prover are for the case where the prover acts honestly for the verifier.

Now, a promise problem $A = (A_{\text{yes}}, A_{\text{no}})$ is in the complexity class QIP(k, a, b) iff there is a k-turn quantum interactive proof system $(\{P_i\}_i, \{V_j\}_j)$ such that:

- (completeness) If $x \in A_{\text{yes}}$, then the verifier accepts with probability at least a under the prover's honest operations $\{P_i\}$.

- (soundness) If $x \in A_{\mathrm{no}}$, then the verifier accepts with probability at most b under any prover's (possibly malicious) operations $\{\widetilde{P}_i\}$.

Let $\mathrm{QIP}(k) := \mathrm{QIP}(k, \frac{2}{3}, \frac{1}{3})$ and $\mathrm{QIP} := \bigcup_{k \in \mathrm{poly}} \mathrm{QIP}(k, \frac{2}{3}, \frac{1}{3})$.

Kitaev and Watrous [52] showed a surprising result QIP = QIP(3), which means that any quantum interactive proof systems can be parallelized into only 3 turns (this situation is completely different from the classical interactive proof systems which are considered to be not parallelizable into $O(1)$ turns). A core protocol for the result is to prove that $\mathrm{QIP}(2k-1, 1, 1-\varepsilon)$ is contained in $\mathrm{QIP}(3, 1, 1-\Omega(\frac{\varepsilon^2}{k^2}))$. The procedure by the verifier in the protocol is as follows:

Parallelization of quantum proof systems with perfect completeness
Let $\{V_1, \ldots, V_k\}$ be the unitary operations of the verifier in the original $(2k-1)$-turn quantum interactive proof system for a promise problem in $\mathrm{QIP}(2k-1, 1, 1-\varepsilon)$.

1. The verifier receives registers $\mathcal{M}_1, \ldots, \mathcal{M}_k$ and $\mathcal{V}_1, \ldots, \mathcal{V}_k$ from the prover. Reject if $\mathcal{V}_1$ does not contain the all-0 state.
2. Apply V_k on $(\mathcal{M}_k, \mathcal{V}_k)$, and measure the first qubit of $\mathcal{V}_k$ in the computational basis. Reject if the outcome is 0 (reject). Apply the inverse of V_k on $(\mathcal{M}_k, \mathcal{V}_k)$.
3. Prepare two one-qubit ancilla registers $\mathcal{B}$ and $\mathcal{B}'$ in state $|\Phi^+\rangle = \frac{1}{\sqrt{2}}(|00\rangle + |11\rangle)$.
4. Choose $r \in [k-1]$ uniformly at random.
5. Apply V_r to $(\mathcal{M}_r, \mathcal{V}_r)$, perform a controlled-SWAP on $\mathcal{V}_r$ and $\mathcal{V}_{r+1}$ with control register $\mathcal{B}$.
6. Send $\mathcal{M}_r, \mathcal{M}_{r+1}, \mathcal{B}'$ and r to the prover.
7. The verifier receives $\mathcal{B}'$ from the prover, performs a CNOT operation on $(\mathcal{B}, \mathcal{B}')$, performs the Hadamard gate H on $\mathcal{B}$, and measures $\mathcal{B}$ in the computational basis. Accept iff the outcome is 0.

The protocol uses a variant of the SWAP test from step 5 to step 7. The verifier expects that $(\mathcal{M}_j, \mathcal{V}_j)$ contains the message-verifier registers part of the state after $2j-1$ turns in the original quantum interactive proof system,

$$P_j V_{j-1} P_{j-1} \cdots V_1 P_1 |0\rangle,$$

where $\{P_j\}$ is the set of the prover's honest operations. Thus, the state after step 5 is expected as

$$\frac{1}{\sqrt{2}} |00\rangle_{\mathcal{B},\mathcal{B}'} (V_r P_r \cdots V_1 P_1 |0\rangle)_{\mathcal{Q}_r} (P_{r+1} V_r P_r \cdots V_1 P_1 |0\rangle)_{\mathcal{Q}_{r+1}}$$

$$+\frac{1}{\sqrt{2}}|11\rangle_{\mathcal{B},\mathcal{B}'}(P_{r+1}V_rP_r\cdots V_1P_1|0\rangle)_{Q_r}(V_rP_r\cdots V_1P_1|0\rangle)_{Q_{r+1}},$$

where $Q_j = \mathcal{P}_j \otimes \mathcal{M}_j \otimes \mathcal{V}_j$ and $\mathcal{P}_j$ is expected to be the prover's register after $2j-1$ turns in the original quantum interactive proof system. Then the honest prover can change this into

$$\frac{1}{\sqrt{2}}|00\rangle_{\mathcal{B},\mathcal{B}'}(P_{r+1}V_rP_r\cdots V_1P_1|0\rangle)_{Q_r}(P_{r+1}V_rP_r\cdots V_1P_1|0\rangle)_{Q_{r+1}}$$
$$+\frac{1}{\sqrt{2}}|11\rangle_{\mathcal{B},\mathcal{B}'}(P_{r+1}V_rP_r\cdots V_1P_1|0\rangle)_{Q_r}(P_{r+1}V_rP_r\cdots V_1P_1|0\rangle)_{Q_{r+1}},$$

which disentangles $(\mathcal{B},\mathcal{B}')$ with the other registers. The expected content of $(\mathcal{B},\mathcal{B}')$ is $|\Phi^+\rangle$, and then it becomes $|00\rangle$ at step 7.

On the contrary, any malicious prover cannot disentangle $(\mathcal{B},\mathcal{B}')$ with the others since the verifier keeps $\mathcal{B}$ (see Ref. [52] for the detailed analysis). This is a key point why the soundness proof works well. Similar techniques for enforcing the prover(s) to act honestly are used in other quantum interactive proof systems (for instance, [50, 53, 68]).

Note that the SWAP test can be replaced with the destructive SWAP test for the two examples in the previous subsections since those utilize only the acceptance probability of the SWAP test and the rigidity obtained from it. Such a replacement seems to be not possible in the example of this subsection since it uses a procedure itself of the SWAP test essentially.

3.4 *Other Applications*

Quantum Proof Systems

The complexity class QMA(k) (introduced by Kobayashi et al. [55]) is the class of promise problems that have a quantum Merlin–Arthur system with k disentangled proofs (QMA(k) system), that is, the verifier (Arthur) can verify whether a given instance (input) is a yes-instance or not in quantum polynomial time with the help of k disentangled quantum messages. In Ref. [55], the SWAP test was used to show that any QMA(3) system can be converted into a QMA(2) system while the completeness-soundness gap becomes worse, and its recovery was a notorious open problem (until Ref. [43]). Aaronson et al. [2] showed that NP-complete problems can be verified by a QMA($O(\sqrt{n})$) system with the total proof length $O(\sqrt{n}\log n)$ (where each prover sends only a $O(\log n)$-qubit message).[4] After that, as a breakthrough result, Harrow and Montanaro [43] showed that QMA(k) = QMA(2) for any $k \geq 2$, which enabled us to recover the completeness-soundness gap, and NP-complete problems can be verified by a QMA(2) system with the total proof length $O(\sqrt{n}\log n)$ (where

[4] Later, it was shown that the same result can be obtained without using the SWAP test [19].

each prover sends a $O(\sqrt{n}\log n)$-qubit message). To show this result, they used the product test (mentioned in Sect. 2) so that the verifier can force two provers to send k disentangled proofs.

Blier and Tapp [14] showed that a 3-coloring problem can be verified in quantum polynomial time with the help of two disentangled quantum messages whose length is only logarithmic in the input length while the completeness-soundness gap is 1/poly. To check whether a graph has a 3-coloring map c, the verifier expects that two copies of the uniform superposition $\sum_v |v\rangle|c(v)\rangle$ (which omits the normalized factor) would be sent from the two provers, and applies the SWAP test on the two copies together with the other two tests for checking the validity of the copies. There are many follow-up works based on the Blier–Tapp protocol ([13, 18, 21, 47, 60] for instance). In particular, Jeronimo and Wu [47] showed that $\mathrm{QMA}^+(2) = \mathrm{NEXP}$, where $\mathrm{QMA}^+(2)$ is a variant of QMA(2) such that quantum proofs have only nonnegative amplitudes.[5]

The complexity class QCMA is the class of promise problems that can be verified in quantum polynomial time with the help of a *classical* proof. There are some problems such that SWAP tests are used for showing that they are in QCMA [20, 36]; in those cases, one state $|\psi\rangle$ is easy to construct but it is not easy to construct the POVM measurement $\{|\psi\rangle\langle\psi|, I - |\psi\rangle\langle\psi|\}$, and the other state compared with $|\psi\rangle$ is difficult to construct efficiently.

As other examples of applications, Rosgen [71–73] used the SWAP test to show the QIP-completeness or QMA-completeness of some problems on quantum circuits. In Ref. [54], the SWAP test was used with several tools such as the quantum de Finetti theorem to show that any problem in QMA has a QIP(2) system with perfect completeness and constant soundness error, where the verifier has only to send a constant number of halves of EPR pairs. We can refer to Refs. [24, 48, 74] for other recent usages of the SWAP test in QMA(2) proof systems.

Quantum state synthesis

Quantum state synthesis (generating a target quantum state) has been a recent hot topic in quantum complexity theory (for instance, [1, 26, 45, 59, 63, 69, 70]), and state synthesis analogues of quantum complexity classes such as stateQMA [26] and stateQIP [70] have been investigated in the literature. Rosenthal and Yuen [70] used thoughtful sequential SWAP tests to show a quantum interactive protocol for generating quantum states in polynomial space (state synthesis version of $\mathrm{PSPACE} \subseteq \mathrm{QIP}$).[6] In Ref. [45], the distillation procedure mentioned in Sect. 2 was utilized to show that there is a quantum algorithm that can generate a target state by only one query to its elaborated classical description.

---

[5] It is still open whether the result leads to QMA(2) = NEXP or not. See Refs. [11, 48].

[6] Later, the state synthesis versions of PSPACE = QIP [46] and PSPACE = QIP(6) [78] were proved [63, 69].

Quantum cryptography

The first application to quantum cryptography was given by Gottesman and Chuang [38]. They proposed a quantum digital signature based on a (information-theoretic) quantum one-way function $x \mapsto |\psi_x\rangle$ (where $|\psi_x\rangle$ is a quantum fingerprint of x) under the following simple idea:

1. A signer S chooses a secret key k_b to sign a bit b.
2. S prepares $(|\psi_{k_0}\rangle, |\psi_{k_1}\rangle)$ as the public key.
3. S sends a certifier C a message $(b, |k_b\rangle)$ to sign b.
4. C checks its validity by the SWAP test using the second part of the message and the state that corresponds to b in the pair of the public key.

Since the work of Ref. [38], many quantum cryptographic protocols use the SWAP (or permutation) test such as zero knowledge [53], commitment [17, 64], message authentication code (MAC) [7], quantum money [12], and position verification [4].

Property testing and estimation on quantum states

There are algorithmic and complexity results on testing some properties of quantum states or estimating distance measures between quantum states using the SWAP test ([6, 40, 58, 61, 68, 77] for instance). In Ref. [77], it was shown that if two pure quantum states are given as black-box unitaries (or quantum circuit descriptions) that generate them, the trace distance between them can be estimated within additive error ε by $O(\frac{1}{\varepsilon^2})$ queries to the black boxes by combining the SWAP test with amplitude estimation [15]. In Ref. [68], a promise problem asking whether two pure states given as quantum circuit descriptions are close was shown to be BQP-complete. In Ref. [6], the SWAP test was shown to be optimal for estimating inner product $\mathrm{tr}(\rho\sigma)$ in that any test needs $\Omega(\frac{1}{\varepsilon^2})$ copies of mixed states ρ and σ to estimate it within additive error ε (the SWAP test needs $O(\frac{1}{\varepsilon^2})$ copies via Eq. (4)).

Acknowledgements This work is dedicated to the memory of Takeshi Koshiba who first showed me a glimpse into the competitive world of theory of cryptography. This work was partly supported by the JSPS KAKENHI grants JP20H05966, JP21H04879, JP22H00522, JP24H00071, and by the MEXT Q-LEAP grants JPMXS0120319794.

References

1. A. Aaronson, The complexity of quantum states and transformations: from quantum money to black holes (2016). arXiv:1607.05256
2. S. Aaronson, S. Beigi, A. Drucker, B. Fefferman, P. Shor, The power of unentanglement. Theory Comput. **5**, 1–42 (2009)
3. A. Agarwal, S. Gharibian, V. Koppula, D. Rudolph, Quantum polynomial hierarchies: Karp-Lipton, error reduction, and lower bounds (2024). arXiv:2401.01633
4. R. Allerstorfer, H. Buhrman, F. Speelman, P. Verduyn Lunel, Towards practical and error-robust quantum position verification (2021). arXiv:2106.12911
5. A. Ambainis, Communication complexity in a 3-computer model. Algorithmica **16**(3), 298–301 (1996)

6. A. Anshu, Z. Landau, Y. Liu, Distributed quantum inner product estimation, in *Proceedings of the 54th ACM Symposium on Theory of Computing (STOC2022)*, pp. 44–51 (2022)
7. P. Ananth, A. Gulati, F. Kaleogu, Y.T. Lin, Pseudorandom isometries, in *Proceedings of the 43rd Annual International Conference on the Theory and Applications of Cryptographic Techniques (EUROCRYPT2024)*, pp. 226–254 (2024)
8. S. Arunachalam, U. Grish, N. Lifshitz, One clean qubit suffices for quantum communication complexity (2023). arXiv:2310.02406
9. L. Babai, P.G. Kimmel, Randomized simultaneous messages: solution of a problem of Yao in communication complexity, in *Proceedings of the 12th Annual IEEE Conference on Computational Complexity (CCC1997)*, pp. 239–246 (1997)
10. A. Barenco, A. Berthiaume, D. Deutsch, A. Ekert, R. Jozsa, C. Macchiavello, Stabilization of quantum computations by symmetrization. SIAM J. Comput. **26**(5), 1541–1557 (1997)
11. R. Bassirian, B. Fefferman, K. Marwaha, Quantum Merlin-Arthur and proofs without relative phase, in *Proceedings of the 15th Innovations in Theoretical Computer Science Conference (ITCS2024)*, pp. 9:1–9:19 (2024)
12. A. Behera, O. Sattath, Almost public quantum coins (2020). arXiv:2002.12438
13. S. Beigi, NP versus $\mathrm{QMA}_{\log}(2)$. Quantum Inf. Comput. **10**(1–2), 141–151 (2010)
14. H. Blier, A. Tapp, A quantum characterization of NP. Comput. Complex. **21**(3):499–510 (2012). An early version is arXiv:0709.0738
15. G. Brassard, P. Høyer, M. Mosca, A. Tapp, Quantum amplitude amplification and estimation. AMS Contemp. Math. **305**, 53–74 (2002)
16. H. Buhrman, R. Cleve, J. Watrous, R. de Wolf, Quantum fingerprinting. Phys. Rev. Lett. **87**(16), 167902 (2001)
17. A. Chailloux, I. Kerenidis, B. Rosgen, Quantum commitments from complexity assumptions. Comput. Complex. **25**, 103–151 (2016)
18. A. Chailloux, O. Sattath (2012) The complexity of the separable Hamiltonian problem, in *Proceedings of the 27th annual IEEE Conference on Computational Complexity (CCC2012)*, pp. 32–41 (2012)
19. J. Chen, A. Drucker, Short multi-prover quantum proofs for SAT without entangled measurements (2010). arXiv:1011.0716
20. N.-H. Chia, C.-N. Chou, J. Zhang, R. Zhang, Quantum meets the minimum circuit size problem, in *Proceedings of the 13th Innovations in Theoretical Computer Science Conference (ITCS2022)*, pp. 47:1–47:16 (2022)
21. A. Chiesa, M. Forbes, Improved soundness for QMA with multiple provers. Chicago J. Theor. Comput. Sci. 1:1–1:23 (2013)
22. A.M. Childs, H. Fu, D. Leung, Z. Li, M., Ozols, V. Vyas, Streaming quantum state purification (2023). arXiv:2309.16387
23. M. Christandl, *The Structure of Bipartite Quantum States—Insights from Group Theory and Cryptography*, Ph.D. thesis, University of Cambridge (2006). arXiv:quant-ph/0604183
24. E. Culf, A. Mehta, New approaches to complexity via quantum graphs (2023). arXiv:2309.12887
25. A.M. Dalzell, S. McArdle, M. Berta, P. Bienias, C.-F. Chen, A. Gilyén, C.T. Hann, M.J. Kastoryano, E.T. Khabiboulline, A. Kubica, G. Salton, S. Wang, F.G.S.L. Brandão, Quantum algorithms: a survey of applications and end-to-end complexities (2023). arXiv:2310.03011
26. H. Delavenne, F. Le Gall, Y. Liu, M. Miyamoto, Quantum Merlin-Arthur proof systems for synthesizing quantum states (2023). arXiv:2303.01877
27. R. de Wolf, *Quantum Computing: Lecture Notes* (2019). arXiv:1907.09415
28. R. de Wolf, *Quantum Computing and Communication Complexity*, Ph.D. thesis, University of Amsterdam (2001)
29. J.F. Doriguello, A. Montanaro, Quantum sketching protocols for Hamming distance and beyond. Phys. Rev. A **99**, 062331 (2019)
30. A.K. Ekert, C.M. Alves, D.K.L. Oi, M. Horodecki, P. Horodecki, L.C. Kwek, Direct estimations of linear and nonlinear functionals of a quantum state. Phys. Rev. Lett. **88**(21), 217901 (2002)

31. S. Endo, Z. Cai, S.C. Benjamin, X. Yuan, Hybrid quantum-classical algorithms and quantum error mitigation. J. Phys. Soc. Jpn. **90**, 032001 (2021)
32. L. Feuilloley, Introduction to local certification. Disc. Math. Theor. Comput. Sci. **23**(3), 9:1–9:23 (2021)
33. P. Fraigniaud, F. Le Gall, H. Nishimura, A. Paz, Distributed quantum proofs for replicated data, in *Proceedings of the 12th Innovations in Theoretical Computer Science Conference (ITCS2021)*, pp. 28:1–28:20 (2021)
34. J.C. Garcia-Escartin, P. Chamorro-Posada, SWAP test and Hong-Ou-Mandel effect are equivalent. Phys. Rev. A **87**, 052330 (2013)
35. D. Gavinsky, J. Kempe, R. de Wolf, Strengths and weaknesses of quantum fingerprinting, in *Proceedings of the 21st Annual IEEE Conference on Computational Complexity (CCC2006)*, pp 288–298 (2006)
36. S. Gharibian, J. Sikora, Ground state connectivity of local Hamiltonians. ACM Trans. Comput. Theory **10**(2), 8:1–8:28 (2018)
37. U. Girish, R. Raz, W. Zhan, Quantum versus randomized communication complexity, with efficient players. Comput. Complex. **31**(2), 17:1–17:44 (2022)
38. D. Gottesman, I. Chuang, Quantum digital signatures (2001). arXiv:quant-ph/0105032
39. V. Gruswami, A. Rudra, M. Sudan, Essential Coding Theory, (Draft of the book). https://cse.buffalo.edu/faculty/atri/courses/coding-theory/book/
40. G. Gutoski, P. Hayden, K. Milner, M.M. Wilde, Quantum interactive proofs and the complexity of separability testing. Theory Comput. **11**(3), 59–103 (2015)
41. A.W. Harrow, The church of the symmetric subspace (2013). arXiv:1308.6595
42. A.W. Harrow, A. Hassidim, S. Lloyd, Quantum algorithm for linear systems and equations. Phys. Rev. Lett. **103**, 150502 (2009)
43. A.W. Harrow, A. Montanaro, Testing product states, quantum Merlin-Arthur games and tensor optimization. J. ACM **60**(1), 3:1–3:43 (2013). An early version appeared in FOCS2010
44. A. Hasegawa, S. Kundu, H. Nishimura, On the power of quantum distributed proofs, in *Proceedings of the 43rd ACM Symposium on Principles of Distributed Computing (PODC2024)*, pp. 220–230 (2024)
45. S. Irani, A. Natarajan, C. Nirkhe, S. Rao, H. Yuen, H., Quantum search-to-decision reductions and the state synthesis problem, in *Proceedings of the 37th Conference on Computational Complexity (CCC2022)*, pp. 5:1–5:19 (2022)
46. R. Jain, Z. Ji, S. Upadhyay, J. Watrous, QIP= PSPACE. J. ACM **58**(6), 30:1–30:27 (2011)
47. F.G. Jeronimo, P. Wu, The power of unentangled quantum proofs with non-negative amplitudes, in *Proceedings of the 55th ACM Symposium on Theory of Computing (STOC2023)*, pp. 1629–1642 (2023)
48. F.G. Jeronimo, P. Wu, Dimension independent distinguishers from unentanglement and applications, in *Proceedings of the 39th Computational Complexity Conference (CCC2024)*, pp. 26:1–26:28 (2024)
49. M. Kada, H. Nishimura, T. Yamakami, The efficiency of quantum identity testing of multiple states. J. Phys.: Math. Theor. **41**, 395309 (2008)
50. J. Kempe, H. Kobayashi, K. Matsumoto, B. Toner, T. Vidick, Entangled games are hard to approximate. SIAM J. Comput. **40**(3), 848–877 (2011)
51. A. Kitaev, Quantum computations: algorithms and error correction. Russian Math. Surv. **52**(6), 1191–1249 (1997)
52. A. Kitaev, J. Watrous, Parallelization, amplification, and exponential time simulation of quantum interactive proof systems, in *Proceedings of the 32nd ACM Symposium on Theory of Computing (STOC2000)*, pp. 608–617 (2000)
53. H. Kobayashi, General properties of quantum zero-knowledge proofs, in *Proceedings of the 5th Theory of Cryptography Conference (TCC2008)*, pp. 107–124 (2008)
54. H. Kobayashi, F. Le Gall, H. Nishimura, Stronger methods of making quantum interactive proofs perfectly complete. SIAM J. Comput. **44**(2), 243–289 (2015)
55. H. Kobayashi, K. Matsumoto, T. Yamakami, Quantum Merlin-Arthur proof systems: are multiple Merlins more helpful to Arthur? Chicago J. Theor. Comput. Sci. 3:1–3:19 (2009). An early version is arXiv:quant-ph/0110006

56. A. Korman, S. Kutten, D. Peleg, Proof labeling schemes. Distrib. Comput. **22**(4), 215–233 (2010)
57. E. Kushilevitz, N. Nisan, *Communication Complexity* (Cambridge University Press, 1997)
58. F. Le Gall, Y. Liu, Q., Wang, Space-bounded quantum state testing via space-efficient quantum singular value transformation (2023). arXiv:2308.05079
59. F. Le Gall, M. Miyamoto, H. Nishimura, Distributed Merlin-Arthur synthesis of quantum states and its applications, in *Proceedings of the 48th Symposium on Mathematical Foundations of Computer Science (MFCS2023)*, pp. 63:1–63:15 (2023)
60. F. Le Gall, S. Nakagawa, H. Nishimura, On QMA protocols with two short quantum proofs. Quantum Inf. Comput. **12**(7–8), 589–600 (2012)
61. Y. Liu, Quantum state testing beyond the polarizing regime and quantum triangular decomposition (2023). arXiv:2303.01952
62. F.J. MacWilliams, N.J.A. Sloane, *The Theory of Error-Correcting Codes*, North-Holland (1977)
63. T. Metger, H. Yuen, stateQIP= statePSPACE, in *Proceedings of the 64th IEEE Symposium on Foundations of Computer Science (FOCS2023)*, pp. 1349–1356 (2023)
64. T. Morimae, B. Nehoran, T. Yamakawa, Unconditionally secure commitments with quantum auxiliary inputs (2023). arXiv:2311.18566
65. I. Newman, M. Szegedy, Public versus private coin flips in one round communication games, in *Proceedings of the 28th ACM Symposium on Theory of Computing (STOC1996)*, pp. 561–570 (1996)
66. M.A. Nielsen, I.L. Chuang, *Quantum Computation and Quantum Information* (Cambridge University Press, 2000)
67. A. Rao, A. Yehudayoff, *Communication Complexity and Applications* (Cambridge University Press, 2020)
68. S. Rethinasamy, R. Agarwal, K. Sharma, M.M. Wilde, Estimating distinguishability measures on quantum computers. Phys. Rev. A **108**, 012409 (2023)
69. G. Rosenthal, Efficient quantum state synthesis with one query, in *Proceedings of the 35th ACM-SIAM Symposium on Discrete Algorithms (SODA2024)*, pp. 2508–2534 (2024)
70. G. Rosenthal, H. Yuen, Interactive proofs for synthesizing quantum states and unitaries, in *Proceedings of the 13th Innovations in Theoretical Computer Science Conference (ITCS2022)*, pp. 112:1–112:4 (2022)
71. B. Rosgen, Distinguishing short quantum computations, in *Proceedings of the 25th International Symposium on Theoretical Aspects of Computer Science (STACS2008)*, pp. 597–608 (2008)
72. B. Rosgen, Testing non-isometry is QMA-complete, in *Proceedings of the 5th Theory of Quantum Computation, Communication and Cryptography (TQC2010)*, pp. 63–76 (2010)
73. B. Rosgen, Testing quantum circuits and detecting insecure encryption, in *Proceedings of the 7th Theory of Quantum Computation, Communication and Cryptography (TQC2012)*, pp. 74–86 (2012)
74. A. She, H. Yuen, Unitary property testing lower bounds by polynomials, in *Proceedings of the 14th Innovations in Theoretical Computer Science Conference (ITCS2023)*, pp. 96:1–96:17 (2023)
75. P.W. Shor, Polynomial-time algorithms for prime factorization and discrete logarithms on a quantum computer. SIAM J. Comput. **26**(5), 1484–1509 (1997). An early version appeared in FOCS1994
76. M. Soleimanifar, J. Wright, Testing matrix product states, in *Proceedings of the 33rd ACM-SIAM Symposium on Discrete Algorithms (SODA2022)*, pp. 1679–1701 (2022)
77. Q. Wang, Z. Zhang, Fast quantum algorithms for trace distance estimation. IEEE Trans. Inf. Theory **70**(4), 2720–2733 (2024)
78. J. Watrous, PSPACE has constant-round quantum interactive proof systems. Theor. Comput. Sci. **292**, 575–588 (2003). An early version appeared in FOCS1999
79. J. Watrous, *The Theory of Quantum Information* (Cambridge University Press, 2018)
80. M.M. Wilde, *Quantum Information Theory* (Cambridge University Press, 2017)

81. A.C.-C. Yao, Some complexity questions related to distributive computing, in *Proceedings of the 11th ACM Symposium on Theory of Computing (STOC1979)*, pp. 209–213 (1979)
82. A.C.-C. Yao, On the power of quantum fingerprinting, in *Proceedings of the 35th ACM Symposium on Theory of Computing (STOC2003)*, pp. 77–81 (2003)

Recent Developments in Quantum Distributed Algorithms

François Le Gall

Abstract This article surveys recent developments in the field of quantum distributed algorithms. We first explain the results by Le Gall and Magniez (PODC 2018) and Le Gall, Nishimura and Rosmanis (STACS 2019), which introduced quantum distributed algorithms faster than classical distributed algorithms in two central models of distributed computing. We then describe other recent developments in quantum distributed computing.

1 Introduction

The central question investigated in quantum distributed computing is: does quantum communication (i.e., sending quantum bits instead of classical bits) make distributed algorithms more powerful. While early works by Tani, Kobayashi and Matsumoto on quantum leader election [34] and by Ben-Or and Hassidim on Byzantine agreement [6] showed the potential of quantum distributed computing, investigating quantum advantage in other fundamental settings (such as the LOCAL model and CONGEST model described below) was left as open problems in early surveys on quantum distributed computing [4, 14].

Until recently, answers were indeed mostly negative: Gavoille, Kosowski and Markiewicz [20] investigated quantum versions of the LOCAL model but did not find any significant quantum advantage. Elkin et al. [16] showed that for many important graph-theoretic problems, there is no quantum advantage in the CONGEST model.

In 2018 and 2019, however, Le Gall and Magniez [29] and Le Gall, Nishimura and Rosmanis [31] showed significant quantum advantages in those models. In the CONGEST model, Ref. [29] showed how to compute the diameter of a network quadratically faster than any classical algorithm, while Ref. [31] showed that in the LOCAL model there is an even larger quantum advantage. These results lead to a surge of research in quantum distributed computing that has lead to many results in the past five years.

F. Le Gall (✉)
Nagoya University, Nagoya, Japan
e-mail: legall@math.nagoya-u.ac.jp

S. Minato et al. (eds.), *Algorithmic Foundations for Social Advancement*,
https://doi.org/10.1007/978-981-96-0668-9_17

In this survey we first describe the main result of Ref. [29] in Sect. 2, then explain the main result of Ref. [31] in Sect. 3 and finally present those recent developments in Sect. 4.

2 Quantum Computation of the Diameter

In this section, we present the result from Le Gall and Magniez [29] that gives an efficient quantum distributed algorithm for computing the diameter in the CONGEST model.

The CONGEST model. The network is represented by an unweighted and undirected graph $G = (V, E)$, where nodes represent processors and edges represent communication channels. Each node is given a unique identifier. We typically write $|V| = n$ and assume for simplicity that each node knows n.[1] In the classical (i.e., non-quantum) CONGEST model, communication occurs between nodes with round-based synchrony and each channel has only $O(\log n)$-bit bandwidth, i.e., at each round each node can send a $O(\log n)$-bit message to each of its neighbors. In the quantum CONGEST model, the only difference is that nodes represent quantum computers, edges represent quantum channels, and each message now becomes a quantum message of $O(\log n)$ quantum bits (qubits). Since quantum computers can simulate classical computers, and qubits can encode classical bits, the quantum CONGEST model is clearly as least as powerful as the classical CONGEST model.

In both the classical and quantum CONGEST models, we are mainly interested in the round complexity (sometimes simply called the time complexity), i.e., the number of rounds needed to solve a computational task.

Classical algorithms for the diameter. The diameter D of the network is defined as the largest distance between two nodes of the graph:

$$D = \max_{u,v \in V} \{d(u, v)\},$$

where $d(u, v)$ denotes the distance (i.e., minimum number of hops) between nodes u and v. In this section, we consider the problem of computing the exact value of the diameter in the CONGEST model. This task can be solved in $O(n)$ rounds by classical algorithms [24, 33]. In the classical setting, a matching lower bound $\tilde{\Omega}(n)$ has been first shown by Frischknecht et al. [19],[2] and then extended to sparse networks [1] and even to deciding whether the network has diameter 2 or diameter 3 [24].

---

[1] If unknown, the value of n can be computed in $O(D)$ rounds, which has no impact on the complexity of the algorithms discussed in this section. (Here D represents the diameter of the graph, which is defined later in this section.).

[2] In this paper the notation $\tilde{O}(\cdot)$ suppresses poly$(\log n)$ factors, and the notation $\tilde{\Omega}(\cdot)$ suppresses $\frac{1}{\mathrm{poly}(\log n)}$ factors.

Table 1 Upper and lower bounds on the quantum and classical round complexities of computing the diameter in the CONGEST model. Here n denotes the number of nodes in the network and D denotes the diameter

Classical	Quantum
$O(n)$ [24, 33]	$\tilde{O}(\sqrt{nD})$ [29]
$\tilde{\Omega}(n)$ [1, 19, 24]	$\tilde{\Omega}(\sqrt{n}+D)$ [29]
	$\tilde{\Omega}(n^{1/3}D^{2/3}+\sqrt{n})$ [32]

Quantum algorithms for the diameter. The main contribution of Ref. [29] is the following theorem.

Theorem 1 ([29]) *There exists a $\tilde{O}(\sqrt{nD})$-round quantum distributed algorithm that computes with high probability the diameter of the network in the CONGEST model.*

In particular, when $D = O(1)$, the quantum algorithm from Ref. [29] works in $\tilde{O}(\sqrt{n})$ rounds, which gives a quadratic improvement over classical distributed algorithms.

Concerning lower bounds, Ref. [29] showed the lower bound $\tilde{\Omega}(\sqrt{n}+D)$ by a reduction from the 2-party communication complexity of the disjointness function. Interestingly, the lower bound for the *bounded-round* quantum communication complexity of the disjointness function by Braverman et al. [8] was needed (as discussed in [29], applying the standard lower bound for arbitrary protocols leads to a significantly weaker lower bound). This bound has later been improved to $\tilde{\Omega}(n^{1/3}D^{2/3}+\sqrt{n})$ by Magniez and Nayak [32]. All these complexities are represented in Table 1.

Overview of the quantum algorithm. At a high level, the approach leading to Theorem 1 can be described as a distributed implementation of quantum search [21] and its generalizations (quantum amplitude amplification [7] or minimum/maximum finding [15]).

Let us first explain a natural approach to compute the diameter. The eccentricity of a vertex $u \in V$ is defined as

$$\mathrm{ecc}(u) = \max_{v \in V}\{d(u, v)\}.$$

The trivial—but crucial—observation is that

$$D = \max_{u \in V}\{\mathrm{ecc}(u)\}.$$

In order to compute the diameter, it is thus enough to compute the maximum eccentricity over all vertices of the graph. Using the quantum maximum finding algorithm [15] this can be done in the centralized (i.e., non-distributed) setting in $\tilde{O}(\sqrt{n} \cdot r)$ time, where r represents the time complexity of computing the eccentricity of one vertex.

The idea is to implement the quantum maximum finding algorithm in the distributed setting by electing a leader in the network who will coordinate the implementation of the quantum algorithm. Such a leader can be elected in $O(D)$ rounds since the nodes have distinct identifiers (for instance the node with the largest identifier can be chosen as the leader). The complexity of the implementation will be $\tilde{O}(\sqrt{n} \cdot r' + D)$ rounds, where r' denotes the *round complexity* of computing the eccentricity of one vertex. Since the eccentricity of one vertex can be computed in $O(D)$ rounds using a standard technique called "breadth-first search," we obtain round complexity

$$\tilde{O}(\sqrt{n} \cdot D),$$

which already matches the upper bound of Theorem 1 for small D.

To obtain the upper bound of Theorem 1 for larger values of D, more work is needed. The key observation is that the breadth-first search technique can be adapted to compute simultaneously the eccentricity of $\Theta(D)$ vertices (instead of the eccentricity of only one vertex) in $O(D)$ rounds. We can reduce the search space by dividing the n vertices into (roughly) n/D blocks of (roughly) D vertices and use quantum search to find one block that contains a vertex of maximum eccentricity. The overall complexity becomes

$$\tilde{O}(\sqrt{n/D} \cdot D) = \tilde{O}(\sqrt{nD}),$$

which gives the complexity of Theorem 1.

3 Advantage in the LOCAL Model

In this section we present the result from Le Gall, Nishimura and Rosmanis [31] that exhibited a significant quantum advantage in the other central model of distributed computing, the LOCAL model.

Statement of the result. The LOCAL model is defined similarly to the CONGEST model. The only difference is that in the LOCAL model, each message can be arbitrarily large (remember that in the CONGEST model, each message can only be of length $O(\log n)$).

For each integer $t \geq 1$, Ref. [20] exhibited a computational problem that can be solved in t rounds in the quantum setting but requires $2t$ rounds in the classical setting. The main result from Ref. [31] shows a significantly larger advantage as follows.

Theorem 2 ([31]) *There exists a computational problem over a network of n nodes that can be solved with 2 rounds in the quantum LOCAL model, but requires $\Omega(n)$ rounds in the classical LOCAL model.*

The computational problem. The computational problem used to prove Theorem 2 is inspired by a construction from Ref. [5], which was also used in Refs. [9, 28] to prove separations between quantum and classical constant-depth circuit complexities.

Consider a ring of n nodes $v_0, v_1, \ldots, v_{n-1}$, where n is a power of 3, and interpret it as a triangle (see Fig. 1 for an illustration). We denote by V_R, V_L and V_B the node sets of the right side, the left side and the bottom side of the triangle, respectively.

Each of the three corners receives as input a bit (the top corner receives b_0, the right corner receives b_1 and the left corner receives b_2). The other nodes do not receive any input. As output, each node v_i should output one bit, which we denote by m_i, such that all the m_i's together satisfy the following two global conditions:

$$m_R \oplus m_B \oplus m_L = 0 \tag{1}$$

and

$$\begin{cases} m_E = 0 & \text{if } (b_0, b_1, b_2) = (0,0,0), \\ m_E \oplus m_R \oplus m_L = 1 & \text{if } (b_0, b_1, b_2) = (0,1,1), \\ m_E \oplus m_R \oplus m_B = 1 & \text{if } (b_0, b_1, b_2) = (1,0,1), \\ m_E \oplus m_B \oplus m_L = 1 & \text{if } (b_0, b_1, b_2) = (1,1,0), \end{cases} \tag{2}$$

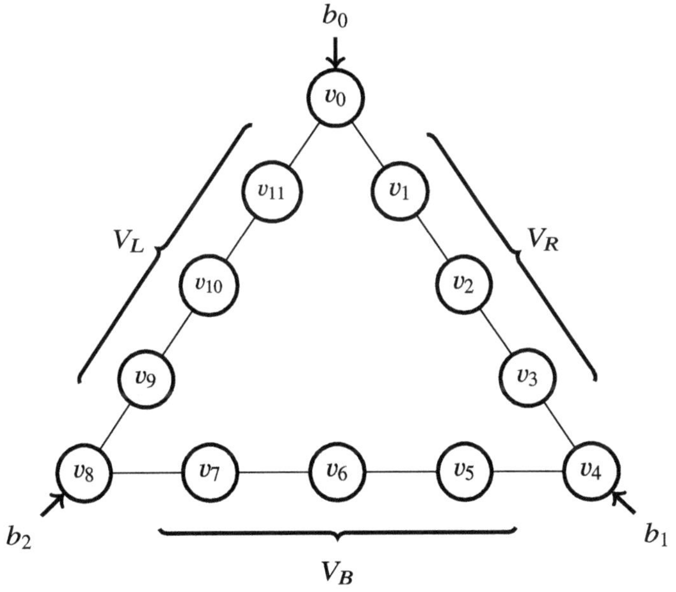

Fig. 1 The construction with $n = 12$. Each corner (nodes v_0, v_4 and v_8) receives a bit as input. Each node v_i, for $i \in \{0, \ldots, 11\}$, outputs a bit m_i. For this example we have $m_E = m_0 \oplus m_2 \oplus m_4 \oplus m_6 \oplus m_8 \oplus m_{10}$, $m_R = m_1 \oplus m_3$, $m_B = m_5 \oplus m_7$ and $m_L = m_9 \oplus m_{11}$

where the four bits m_E, m_R, m_B and m_L are are defined as follows:

$$m_E = \bigoplus_{\substack{i\in\{0,\ldots,n-1\}\\ i \text{ even}}} m_i \quad \text{(the parity of the output of all nodes with even index)}$$

$$m_R = \bigoplus_{\substack{i\in\{0,\ldots,n-1\}\\ i \text{ odd},\ v_i\in V_R}} m_i \quad \text{(the parity of the output of all nodes in } V_R \text{ with odd index)}$$

$$m_B = \bigoplus_{\substack{i\in\{0,\ldots,n-1\}\\ i \text{ odd},\ v_i\in V_B}} m_i \quad \text{(the parity of the output of all nodes in } V_B \text{ with odd index)}$$

$$m_L = \bigoplus_{\substack{i\in\{0,\ldots,n-1\}\\ i \text{ odd},\ v_i\in V_L}} m_i \quad \text{(the parity of the output of all nodes in } V_L \text{ with odd index)}$$

The quantum algorithm. The quantum algorithm solving this problem is fairly easy. Consider the graph state associated with the whole triangle.[3]. Ref. [31] showed that this graph state can be constructed in 2 rounds in the LOCAL model. The idea is as follows: each node creates a node initialized to $|0\rangle$, locally applies a Hadamard gate on it and then communicates with its neighbors to implement the CZ gate. The output of the quantum algorithm is then obtained as follows. Each non-corner node measures its qubit in an appropriate basis (the "X basis") and outputs the measurement outcome. Each of the three corner nodes also measures its qubit, but in a basis depending on their input bit (the "X basis" when the input is 0 or the "Y basis" when the input is 1). The measurement outcomes are easy to analyze using standard techniques. Here is their main property as follows.

Proposition 1 ([5, 9, 31]) *For any bits b_0, b_1, b_2 and any measurement outcome, Conditions (1) and (2) are satisfied.*

It is easy to show that any classical algorithm that outputs an output satisfying with high probability both Conditions (1) and (2) requires $\Omega(n)$ rounds in the LOCAL model. The intuition is as follows: if a classical algorithm uses less that $n/6$ rounds, it is impossible to gather at the same node information about two distinct input bits (since the input bits are at distance $n/3$). Additionally, no node in V_B can get any information about b_0, no node in V_L can get any information about b_1, and no node in V_R can get any information about b_2. Consequently, if a classical algorithm uses less that $n/6$ rounds, then each m_i can be specified by a fairly elementary function of the inputs. It is easy to check that no such elementary functions can satisfy simultaneously Conditions (1) and (2).

[3] Graph states are a special type of quantum states that are associated with graphs [23]. Let $G = (V, E)$ be any undirected graph on n nodes. The graph state associated with G is the quantum state on n qubits (1 qubit associated with each node of G) constructed in the following way: first initialize each of these n qubits to the $|0\rangle$ state; then apply a Hadamard gate on each qubit; finally, for each edge $\{u, v\} \in E$, apply a Controlled-Z gate (CZ) on the two qubits corresponding to u and v

Remark 1 In the quantum algorithm described above, each message actually consists of a constant number of qubits. In consequence, this quantum algorithm can be implemented in 2 rounds not only in the quantum LOCAL model but also in the quantum CONGEST model. We thus actually obtain a similar separation between the quantum CONGEST model and the classical LOCAL model.

4 Recent Developments

After the results presented in Sects. 2 and 3 were published, there has been a surge of research on quantum distributed algorithms. In this section we give a short overview of these recent developments.

Recent results about the quantum CONGEST model. Wu and Yao [35] have first extended the result of Ref. [29] to weighted graphs: they have designed a quantum algorithm faster than the best classical algorithms for the computation of the diameter in weighted graphs (i.e., the maximum shortest distance between any two nodes) as well.

Next, van Aperdoorn and de Vos [3] have shown how to generalize the framework from Ref. [29] in order to implement in the distributed setting *any* quantum query complexity (e.g., quantum walks) by selecting a leader, asking the leader to implement the algorithm, and communicating with the other nodes of the network to implement each query. Crucially, Ref. [3] analyzed the complexity of the resulting distributed algorithm and showed that it can be characterized in terms of the *parallel* query complexity of the original problem.

Finally, Izumi, Le Gall and Magniez [26] have shown how to apply the techniques from Ref. [29] to design a quantum algorithm that checks if a graph contains a triangle as a subgraph in $\tilde{O}(n^{1/4})$ rounds, which outperforms the best known classical algorithm (from Ref. [12]) that has complexity $\tilde{O}(n^{1/3})$. This result was soon improved by Censor-Hillel et al. [10], who obtained a $\tilde{O}(n^{1/5})$-round quantum algorithm for triangle finding in the CONGEST model. More generally, Censor-Hillel et al. [10] showed how to use these techniques to design quantum distributed algorithms checking if a graph contains small cliques (note that a triangle is a clique of size 3). Very recently, Fraigniaud et al. [18] have designed quantum algorithms checking if a graph contains small cycles based on this approach as well.

Recent results about the quantum CONGEST-CLIQUE model. The CONGEST-CLIQUE model is a variant of the CONGEST model in which at each round a message can be transmitted between *any* two nodes of the network (remember that in the original CONGEST model messages can be sent only between *adjacent* nodes). In the CONGEST-CLIQUE model, a quantum algorithm faster than the best known classical algorithms has been constructed for the All-Pair Shortest Path (APSP) problem over weighted directed graphs [25].

Theorem 3 ([25]) *There is a quantum algorithm that solves with high probability the All-Pairs Shortest Path problem over weighted directed graphs in* $\tilde{O}(n^{1/4})$ *rounds in the CONGEST-CLIQUE model.*

The best known upper bound for the APSP in the classical CONGEST-CLIQUE is the $\tilde{O}(n^{1/3})$ upper bound due to Censor-Hillel et al. [11]. While no non-trivial lower bound is known on the classical complexity of APSP in the CONGEST-CLIQUE model (proving non-trivial lower bounds for *any* explicit problem in this model is notoriously hard!), this gives strong evidence of the superiority of quantum distributed computing over classical distributed computing in the CONGEST-CLIQUE model as well.

The approach of Ref. [25] consists in reducing the APSP problem to the problem of detecting all edges involved in at least one negative triangle (a negative triangle is a triangle in which the sum of the weights of the three edges is negative). Solving the APSP problem requires solving a quadratic number of instances of the triangle finding problem simultaneously, which can be done by a very careful implementation.

Recent results about the quantum LOCAL model. As described in Sect. 3, there already exists a huge separation between the power of classical and quantum algorithms in the LOCAL model [31]. The problem used to achieve this goal, however, cannot be *checked* locally: checking if the output satisfies Conditions (1) and (2) requires $\Omega(n)$ rounds.

Most problems studied in the literature on the LOCAL model, however, have the property that checking if the output is valid can be done in a constant number of rounds. Problems satisfying this property are called *locally checkable problems (LCPs)*. A central example is graph coloring, for which the output can be checked locally by having each node send its color to its neighbors. A fundamental question is thus to understand whether there exists a quantum advantage in the LOCAL model for an LCP. This question was also considered in Ref. [4] when discussing the quantum complexity of graph coloring in the LOCAL model.[4] Very recently Akbari et al. [2] and Coiteux-Roy et al. [13] have investigated this question and obtained partial results. Unfortunately, these results are currently mainly negative: for many problems (e.g., coloring in networks of arbitrary topology), there is no quantum advantage. Finding a quantum advantage for an LCP (or proving that no such advantage exists!) is still one of the most important open problems in distributed quantum computing.

Recent results on quantum verification. Fraigniaud, Le Gall, Nishimura and Paz [17] have investigated the power of distributed quantum proofs in distributed computing: each node of the network receives, additionally to its input, a quantum state (the *quantum proof*) from an all-powerful but untrusted party. The main result in Ref. [17] shows that there exist problems that can be solved by quantum protocols using quantum proofs exponentially shorter than in the classical setting. Hasegawa, Kundu and Nishimura further investigated the power (and limitations) of quantum

---

[4] Reference [4] asks in particular whether computing a 3-coloring in a ring can be done faster in the quantum setting than in the classical setting.

distributed proofs [22]. Other works include Ref. [27], which considered the problem of generating quantum states using provers, and Ref. [30], which investigated the power of interactive quantum distributed proofs.

Acknowledgements The author was supported by the Grants-in-Aid for Transformative Research Areas (A) KAKENHI 20H05966.

References

1. A. Abboud, K. Censor-Hillel, S. Khoury, Near-linear lower bounds for distributed distance computations, even in sparse networks, in *Proceedings of the 30th International Symposium on Distributed Computing (DISC 2016)*, pp. 29–42 (2016)
2. A. Akbari, X. Coiteux-Roy, F. d'Amore, F. Le Gall, H. Lievonen, D. Melnyk, A. Modanese, S. Pai, M.-O. Renou, V. Rozhoň, J. Suomela, Online locality meets distributed quantum computing (2024). ArXiv:2403.01903
3. J. van Apeldoorn, T. de Vos, A framework for distributed quantum queries in the CONGEST model, in *Proceedings of the 2022 ACM Symposium on Principles of Distributed Computing (PODC 2022)*, pp. 109–119 (2022)
4. H. Arfaoui, P. Fraigniaud, What can be computed without communications? SIGACT News **45**(3), 82–104 (2014)
5. J. Barrett, C.M. Caves, B. Eastin, M.B. Elliott, S. Pironio, Modeling Pauli measurements on graph states with nearest-neighbor classical communication. Phys. Rev. A **75**, 012103 (2007)
6. M. Ben-Or, A. Hassidim, Fast quantum Byzantine agreement, in *Proceedings of the 37th Annual ACM Symposium on Theory of Computing (STOC 2005)*, pp. 481–485 (2005)
7. G. Brassard, P. Høyer, A. Tapp, Quantum counting, in *Proceedings of the 25th International Colloquium on Automata, Languages and Programming (ICALP 1998)*, pp. 820–831 (1998)
8. M. Braverman, A. Garg, Y. Kun-Ko, J. Mao, D. Touchette, Near-optimal bounds on bounded-round quantum communication complexity of disjointness, in *Proceedings of the 56th Annual IEEE Symposium on Foundations of Computer Science (FOCS 2015)*, pp. 773–791 (2015)
9. S. Bravyi, D. Gosset, R. König, Quantum advantage with shallow circuits. Science **362**(6412), 308–311 (2018)
10. K. Censor-Hillel, O. Fischer, F. Le Gall, D. Leitersdorf, R. Oshman, Quantum distributed algorithms for detection of cliques, in *Proceedings of the 13th Innovations in Theoretical Computer Science Conference (ITCS 2022)*, pp. 35:1–35:25 (2022)
11. K. Censor-Hillel, P. Kaski, J.H. Korhonen, C. Lenzen, A. Paz, J. Suomela, Algebraic methods in the congested clique. Distrib. Comput. (2016)
12. Y.-J. Chang, T. Saranurak, Improved distributed expander decomposition and nearly optimal triangle enumeration, in *Proceedings of the 2019 ACM Symposium on Principles of Distributed Computing (PODC 2019)*, pp. 66–73 (2019)
13. X. Coiteux-Roy, F. d'Amore, R. Gajjala, F. Kuhn, F. Le Gall, H. Lievonen, A. Modanese, M.-O. Renou, G. Schmid, J. Suomela, No distributed quantum advantage for approximate graph coloring, in *Proceedings of the 56th ACM Symposium on Theory of Computing (STOC 2024)*, pp. 1901–1910 (2024)
14. V.S. Denchev, G. Pandurangan, Distributed quantum computing: a new frontier in distributed systems or science fiction? SIGACT News **39**(3), 77–95 (2008)
15. C. Dürr, P. Høyer, A quantum algorithm for finding the minimum (1996). ArXiv: quant-ph/9607014
16. M. Elkin, H. Klauck, D. Nanongkai, G. Pandurangan, Can quantum communication speed up distributed computation? in *Proceedings of the 33rd ACM Symposium on Principles of Distributed Computing (PODC 2014)*, pp. 166–175 (2014)

17. P. Fraigniaud, F. Le Gall, H. Nishimura, A. Paz, Distributed quantum proofs for replicated data. In *Proceedings of the 12th Innovations in Theoretical Computer Science Conference (ITCS 2021)*, pp. 28:1–28:20 (2021)
18. P. Fraigniaud, M. Luce, F. Magniez, I. Todinca, Even-cycle detection in the randomized and quantum CONGEST model, in *Proceedings of the 43rd ACM Symposium on Principles of Distributed Computing (PODC 2024)*, pp. 209–219 (2024)
19. S. Frischknecht, S. Holzer, R. Wattenhofer, Networks cannot compute their diameter in sublinear time, in *Proceedings of the 23rd Annual ACM-SIAM Symposium on Discrete Algorithms (SODA 2012)*, pp. 1150–1162 (2012)
20. C. Gavoille, A. Kosowski, M. Markiewicz, What can be observed locally? in *Proceedings of the 23rd International Symposium on Distributed Computing (DISC 2009)*, volume 5805 of *LNCS* (Springer, 2009), pp. 243–257
21. L.K. Grover, A fast quantum mechanical algorithm for database search, in *Proceedings of the 28th Annual ACM Symposium on the Theory of Computing (STOC 1996)*, ed. by G.L. Miller (ACM, 1996), pp. 212–219
22. A. Hasegawa, S. Kundu, H. Nishimura, On the power of quantum distributed proofs, in *Proceedings of the 43rd ACM Symposium on Principles of Distributed Computing (PODC 2024)*, pp. 220–230 (2024)
23. M. Hein, J. Eisert, H.J. Briegel, Multiparty entanglement in graph states. Phys. Rev. A **69**, 062311 (2004)
24. S. Holzer, R. Wattenhofer, Optimal distributed all pairs shortest paths and applications, in *Proceedings of the 2012 ACM Symposium on Principles of Distributed Computing (PODC 2012)*, pp. 355–364 (2012)
25. T. Izumi, F. Le Gall, Quantum distributed algorithm for the All-Pairs Shortest Path problem in the CONGEST-CLIQUE model, in *Proceedings of the 38th ACM Symposium on Principles of Distributed Computing (PODC 2019)*, pp. 84–93 (2019)
26. T. Izumi, F. Le Gall, F. Magniez, Quantum distributed algorithm for triangle finding in the CONGEST model, in *Proceedings of the 37th International Symposium on Theoretical Aspects of Computer Science (STACS 2020)*, pp. 23:1–23:13 (2020)
27. F. Le Gall, M. Miyamoto, H. Nishimura, Distributed merlin-arthur synthesis of quantum states and its applications, in *Proceedings of the 48th International Symposium on Mathematical Foundations of Computer Science (MFCS 2023)*, pp. 63:1–63:15 (2023)
28. F. Le Gall, Average-case quantum advantage with shallow circuits, in *Proceedings of the 34th Computational Complexity Conference (CCC 2019)*, pp. 21:1–21:20 (2019)
29. F. Le Gall, F. Magniez, Sublinear-time quantum computation of the diameter in CONGEST networks, in *Proceedings of the 37th ACM Symposium on Principles of Distributed Computing (PODC 2018)*, pp. 337–346 (2018)
30. F. Le Gall, M. Miyamoto, H. Nishimura, Distributed quantum interactive proofs, in *Proceedings of the 40th International Symposium on Theoretical Aspects of Computer Science (STACS 2023)*, pp. 63:1–63:15 (2023)
31. F. Le Gall, H. Nishimura, A. Rosmanis, Quantum advantage for the LOCAL model in distributed computing, in *Proceedings of the 36th International Symposium on Theoretical Aspects of Computer Science (STACS 2019)*, pp. 49:1–49:14 (2019)
32. F. Magniez, A. Nayak, Quantum distributed complexity of set disjointness on a line. ACM Trans. Comput. Theory **14**(1):5:1–5:22 (2022)
33. D. Peleg, L. Roditty, E. Tal, Distributed algorithms for network diameter and girth, in *Proceedings of the 39th International Colloquium on Automata, Languages, and Programming (ICALP 2012)*, pp. 660–672 (2012)
34. S. Tani, H. Kobayashi, K. Matsumoto, Exact quantum algorithms for the leader election problem. ACM Trans. Comput. Theory **4**(1):1:1–1:24 (2012)
35. X. Wu, P. Yao, Quantum complexity of weighted diameter and radius in CONGEST networks, in *Proceedings of the 42nd ACM Symposium on Principles of Distributed Computing (PODC 2022)*, pp. 120–130 (2022)

On the Simulation and Verification of Noisy Quantum Circuits

Seiichiro Tani

Abstract Noise is the most serious obstacle to developing quantum computers. This article reviews two recently published results that answer the essential questions on noisy quantum circuits in particular meaningful situations expected in the near future. The purpose of the article is not to provide comprehensive surveys but to introduce how to apply some essential state-of-the-art techniques to the simulation and verification of noisy quantum circuits. The first part reveals that even slight noise at the end of computation spoils the quantum advantage under a particular noise model. This raises the question of verifying that a given quantum circuit is not significantly affected by noise. The second part shows an efficient verification method of a given quantum circuit with the help of a smaller verified quantum circuit when the circuit to be verified is sparse and shallow.

1 Introduction

Quantum computers are expected to have the potential for computational advantages over classical computers. The most famous evidence for exponential quantum speed-up over classical computing is Shor's polynomial-time quantum algorithm for factoring [16]. Subsequently, many quantum algorithms for particular problems have been found as evidence of exponential speed-ups. These results, if they provably achieve such speed-ups, imply that the extended (strong form of) Church-Turing Thesis [1] is false; in terms of complexity theory, they imply that the class of problems solvable by efficient classical algorithms is a *proper* subset of the class of those solvable by efficient quantum algorithms. Moreover, Grover [10] showed that quantum advantages exist for a much broader class of problems by providing a quantum search algorithm, although the speed-up is only quadratic in this case.

Recognizing the potential of quantum computing, numerous national and enterprise projects are underway worldwide to develop quantum computers. These efforts reflect the global interest and investment in this promising field. Since there are still

S. Tani (✉)
Waseda University, Shinjuku, Tokyo 169-8050, Japan
e-mail: tani@waseda.jp

S. Minato et al. (eds.), *Algorithmic Foundations for Social Advancement*,
https://doi.org/10.1007/978-981-96-0668-9_18

many engineering issues to resolve, quantum computers developed in the near future are expected to have restricted functionality and limited computational resources. Thus, what has recently gathered the attention of many experts and non-experts has been to clarify the computational power of so-called sub-universal quantum computing models [11], which are supposed to model near-future quantum computers, by investigating the hardness of exactly or approximately simulating on classical computers the output distributions of quantum circuits in the quantum computing models. Although most of this kind of research deals with noise-free circuits (except for, e.g., [8]), it is very difficult or almost impossible to remove noise, which affects more or less the functionality, from fabricated quantum circuits. Without quantum error-correcting technologies, such quantum circuits could not have the computational power expected in the ideal noise-free model. This poses several problems regarding noise-affected quantum circuits. Two essential ones are listed below.

1. What is the impact of noise on the quantum computational power? More specifically, when does noise begin to degrade or spoil the quantum advantage?
2. How can one know whether noise affects the computation of physically implemented quantum circuits? Alternatively, how can one tell whether the effect of noise on the circuits is sufficiently small?

Each of these questions is still too abstract to answer with a single statement. This article introduces the approaches and essential ideas used in Refs. [6, 17] to answer the above questions in particular meaningful situations using state-of-the-art techniques.

To (partially) answer the first question, a possible approach to knowing the impact of noise on computational power is to examine the classical simulatability of a target class of quantum circuits affected by noise in specific noise models. Bremner, Montanaro, and Shepherd [6] found that the effect of depolarizing noise, one of the major noise models, is closely related to the *noise operator*, which has been heavily studied in the context of Fourier analysis of Boolean functions [13], to obtain a classical simulator for Instantaneous Quantum Polynomial (IQP) circuits. Takahashi, Takeuchi, and Tani [17] generalized this result to a broader class of quantum circuits, including IQP circuits, with less prior knowledge of noise rate. Interestingly, that class of quantum circuits includes those proved to have computational supremacy in the noise-free setting (under plausible complexity-theoretic assumptions) [2, 5, 21]. Thus, the results [6, 17] imply that (even a tiny) noise can spoil the quantum advantage. Section 3 outlines how to efficiently simulate on classical computers the output distribution of the class of quantum circuits when the depolarizing noise with constant rates affects the circuits at the end of computation [17].

The research field related to the second question is known as quantum circuit verification. There are many aspects of research in this field, such as gate-by-gate verification, verification of the output distribution, output state tomography, and proof-system-based verification (see [9, 18] and the references therein). However, answering the second question is very challenging in general from an engineering point of view. This is because it may require a tremendous amount of classical resources (e.g., computation time or memory); otherwise, it may require a quantum circuit that has already been verified of size comparable to that of the target circuit to be verified. A typical goal among many formulations of verification is to decide with high probability whether the output state ρ of the target circuit on input $|0^n\rangle$ is close to the corresponding output state $|\psi\rangle$ of the ideal circuit. To make the goal modest and feasible, let us assume that a smaller quantum circuit with verified functionality is available. Even with these relaxed requirements, it is still inevitable and challenging to divide the target circuit into smaller pieces without losing too much information and derive sufficient information for the final decision from the partial information extracted from the pieces. Section 4 outlines the algorithm given in [18] for estimating $\langle\psi|\rho|\psi\rangle$ by using polynomially many copies of ρ when the target circuit is implemented on a sparse quantum computing chip (defined later) and has logarithmic depth as the current and near-future quantum circuits known as Noisy Intermediate-Scale Quantum (NISQ) [15] circuits.

2 Terminology

For a complex number $\gamma = \alpha + \beta i$ for some $\alpha, \beta \in \mathbb{R}$, we write $\Re\gamma$ to mean the real part of γ, i.e., $\Re\gamma = \alpha$.

We often use E to mean the average of the value of a function over its argument drawn uniformly at random from a domain. For instance, $\mathsf{E}_{x\in\{0,1\}^n}[f(x)]$ represents the average of function value $f(x)$ over x drawn from $\{0, 1\}^n$ uniformly at random.

For a bit-string $x \in \{0, 1\}^n$, the Hamming weight of x (the number of 1's in x) is denoted by $|x|$.

We assume readers' basic knowledge of quantum computing (see standard textbooks, e.g., [12]). In this article, we use the following standard notations: For elementary single-qubit states, $|0\rangle := \left(\begin{smallmatrix}1\\0\end{smallmatrix}\right)$, $|1\rangle := \left(\begin{smallmatrix}0\\1\end{smallmatrix}\right)$, $|+\rangle := (|0\rangle + |1\rangle)/\sqrt{2}$, $|-\rangle := (|0\rangle - |1\rangle)/\sqrt{2}$. $|+_i\rangle := (|0\rangle + i|1\rangle)/\sqrt{2}$, $|-_i\rangle := (|0\rangle - i|1\rangle)/\sqrt{2}$. For multi-qubit states, we may use $|0^n\rangle$ instead of $|0\rangle^{\otimes n}$. We also use the following elementary unitary on a single qubit:

$$\mathrm{X} := \left(\begin{smallmatrix}0&1\\1&0\end{smallmatrix}\right), \mathrm{Y} := \left(\begin{smallmatrix}0&-i\\i&0\end{smallmatrix}\right), \mathrm{Z} := \left(\begin{smallmatrix}1&0\\0&-1\end{smallmatrix}\right), \mathrm{H} := \tfrac{1}{\sqrt{2}}\left(\begin{smallmatrix}1&1\\1&-1\end{smallmatrix}\right), \mathrm{T} := \left(\begin{smallmatrix}1&1\\1&e^{\pi i/8}\end{smallmatrix}\right),$$

and $\mathrm{S} := \mathrm{T}^2$. The four operators, X, Y, Z, and the identity I, are called Pauli operators and form an orthogonal basis of the linear space of linear operators on $\mathbb{C}^2$. For $(n+1)$-qubit operators, let $\Lambda(U) := |0\rangle\langle 0| \otimes I_{2^n} + |1\rangle\langle 1| \otimes U$ for any n-qubit unitary operator U, where we mean by I_D the identity operator in the D-dimensional space. For instance, $\Lambda(\mathrm{Z}) = |0\rangle\langle 0| \otimes I_2 + |1\rangle\langle 1| \otimes \mathrm{Z}$ and $\Lambda(\Lambda(\mathrm{Z})) = |0\rangle\langle 0| \otimes I_4 + |1\rangle\langle 1| \otimes \Lambda(\mathrm{Z})$. We also mean $\Lambda(\mathrm{Z})$ and $\Lambda(\Lambda(\mathrm{Z}))$ by CZ and CCZ, respectively.

3 Simulation of Quantum Circuits with Depolarizing Noise

3.1 CT States and CT-ECS Circuits

For a pure quantum state $|\phi\rangle$ on n qubits, we say that $|\phi\rangle$ is a computationally tractable (CT) state if the distribution p such that $p(x) = |\langle x|\phi\rangle|^2$ for each $x \in \{0, 1\}^n$ is classically samplable in polynomial time in n and $\langle x|\phi\rangle$ is classically computable in polynomial time for each x. For instance, any product state is a CT state.

For a unitary Hermitian operator U on n qubits, we say that U is an efficiently computable sparse (ECS) operation if the matrix representation of U in the computational basis has at most polynomially many nonzero entries in each column, and the jth nonzero entries in any specified column and its associated row index are classically computable in polynomial time. We say that a quantum circuit C on n qubits is CT-ECS if C is of the form of VU for polynomial-size circuits U, V such that (1) $U|0^n\rangle$ is CT, (2) $V^\dagger \mathrm{Z}_j V$ is ECS for every $1 \leq j \leq n$, where Z_j is a Pauli Z operator on the jth qubit. The class of CT-ECS circuits contains several interesting classes.

Lemma 1 ([17]) *Let C be one of the following quantum circuits on n qubits: an IQP, a Clifford Magic, a conjugated Clifford, or a constant-depth quantum circuit. Then, C is CT-ECS.*

- *An IQP circuit is of the form* $H^{\otimes n} D H^{\otimes n}$*, where D is a polynomial-size quantum circuit consisting of* Z, CZ, *and* CCZ *gates [4, 5].*
- *A Clifford Magic circuit is of the form* $ET^{\otimes n} H^{\otimes n}$*, where E is a polynomial-size Clifford circuit, i.e., a circuit consisting of H, S, and* CZ *gates [21].*
- *A conjugated Clifford circuit is of the form* $R_x(-\theta)^{\otimes n} R_z(-\phi)^{\otimes n} E R_z(\phi)^{\otimes n} R_x(\theta)^{\otimes n}$ *for arbitrary real numbers* ϕ, θ*, where E is a polynomial-size Clifford circuit, and* R_x *and* R_z *are the rotations around x and z axes, respectively, on the Block sphere [2].*
- *A constant-depth quantum circuit is a polynomial-size quantum circuit with constant depth [7, 19].*

This lemma implies that the class of CT-ECS circuits contains those whose output probability distributions are not classically simulatable (under plausible complexity theoretic assumptions) [2, 5, 21].

3.2 Depolarizing Noise and Fourier Expansion

Let C be a quantum circuit over n qubits, and let $p(x) = |\langle x|C|0^n\rangle|^2$ be the probability that n-bit outcome x is obtained when $C|0^n\rangle$ is measured in the computational basis. We can write $p(x)$ in the Fourier basis as follows:

$$p(x) = \sum_{S \in \{0,1\}^n} \hat{p}(S)(-1)^{x \cdot S},$$

where $\hat{p}(S)$ is a Fourier coefficient defined as $\hat{p}(S) = \mathsf{E}_{x \in \{0,1\}^n}[p(x)(-1)^{x \cdot S}]$ for each $S \in \{0, 1\}^n$.

If we assume the depolarizing noise operator

$$D_\varepsilon(\rho) = (1 - \varepsilon)\rho + \varepsilon \frac{\mathrm{I}}{2}$$

acts on each output qubit of C just before the measurement, then the resulting output probability $\tilde{p}$ is

$$\tilde{p}(x) = \sum_{S \in \{0,1\}^n} (1 - \varepsilon)^{|S|} \hat{p}(S)(-1)^{x \cdot S}, \tag{1}$$

since the effect of $D_\varepsilon(\rho)$ is essentially the same as the noise operator well-studied in the literature on the Fourier analysis of Boolean functions [13].

We want to sample distribution $\tilde{p}$. First, observe that, if $\hat{p}$ is not too large everywhere (i.e., anti-concentrated, which will be defined rigorously in the next subsection), then the high order terms (with respect to $|S|$) in $\tilde{p}(x)$ are small enough to be cut off to get a good approximation. More concretely, it turns out that keeping only the terms with $|S|$ being constant is enough to get a good approximation. This means that $\tilde{p}(x)$ can be approximated with only polynomially many terms. Thus, if each $\hat{p}(S)$ can be computed (approximately) in classical polynomial time, then $\tilde{p}$ can be approximated in classical polynomial time. However, the obtained approximate function q of $\tilde{p}$ is not necessarily a probability distribution in general, since q may be negative at some point or the sum of $q(x)$ over all x may not be equal to one. Thus, sampling a distribution close to $\tilde{p}$ is not straightforward even when q is given. Fortunately, it turns out to be possible as discussed later.

3.3 Computing Approximate Function of $\tilde{p}$

To make sure that $\hat{p}$ is anti-concentrated, we assume the output probability p of the (noise-free) circuit C is anti-concentrated, i.e.,

$$\sum_{x \in \{0,1\}^n} p(x)^2 \leq \frac{\alpha}{2^n},$$

for a *known* constant α. This implies that $\hat{p}$ is also anti-concentrated by Parseval's equality $\|p\|_2^2 = 2^n \|\hat{p}\|_2^2$:

$$\sum_{S \in \{0,1\}^n} \hat{p}(S)^2 \leq \frac{\alpha}{4^n}.$$

As for computing Fourier coefficients, it can be shown that each Fourier coefficient can be approximated in classical polynomial time with high probability for CT-ECT circuits, as in the following lemma (the proof will be sketched in Sect. 3.5).

Lemma 2 ([17]) *Let C be an arbitrary CT-ECS circuit on n qubits. For each $x \in \{0,1\}^n$, let $p(x) = |\langle x|C|0^n\rangle|^2$ be the probability that x is obtained when $C|0^n\rangle$ is measured in the computational basis. For an arbitrary polynomial f in n, there exists a polynomial-time randomized algorithm that, for given $S \in \{0,1\}^n$ with $|S| = O(1)$, outputs a real number $\hat{p}'(S)$ such that*

$$\Pr\left[|\hat{p}(S) - \hat{p}'(S)| \le \frac{1}{2^n f(n)}\right] \ge 1 - \frac{1}{\exp(n)},$$

where the probability is taken over the random coins used by the algorithm.

In addition, we relax the requirement of exactly knowing the value of the parameter ε appearing in D_ε to that of knowing only approximate value λ of ε such that

$$\lambda \le \varepsilon \le \lambda(1 + O(1)).$$

By putting these fact together, we approximate $\tilde{p}(x)$ in eq. (1) as

$$q(x) = \sum_{S \in \{0,1\}^n :\, |S| \le c} (1-\lambda)^{|S|} \hat{p}'(S)(-1)^{x \cdot S},$$

where c is a constant depending on α, λ and the simulation accuracy, and $\hat{p}'(S)$ is an approximate value of $\hat{p}(S)$, computed by the polynomial-time randomized algorithm given in Lemma 2. The formal statement is as follows.

Theorem 1 ([17]) *Let C be an arbitrary CT-ECS circuit on n qubits and let $p\colon \{0,1\}^n \to [0,1]$ be the probability distribution of the n-bit outcomes obtained when $C|0^n\rangle$ is measured in the computational basis. Let $\tilde{p}\colon \{0,1\}^n \to [0,1]$ be the probability distribution of the n-bit outcomes obtained when $(D_\varepsilon)^{\otimes n}(C|0^n\rangle\langle 0^n|C^\dagger)$ is measured in the computational basis, where $D_\varepsilon(\rho)$ is the depolarizing noise operator on a single qubit defined as*

$$D_\varepsilon(\rho) = (1-\varepsilon)\rho + \varepsilon\frac{\mathrm{I}}{2}.$$

Assuming that

1. *p is anti-concentrated, i.e., $\sum_{x \in \{0,1\}^n} p(x)^2 \le \alpha/2^n$ with a known constant α,*
2. *an approximate value λ of $0 < \varepsilon < 1$ is known such that*

$$\lambda \le \varepsilon \le \lambda(1 + O(1)),$$

there exists a polynomial-time randomized algorithm that, for a given description of C *and constants* $\lambda, \alpha(\geq 1), 0 < \delta < 1$, *outputs every Fourier coefficient of a function* $q\colon \{0,1\}^n \to \mathbb{R}$ *that is within* $\delta/3$ *from* $\tilde{p}$ *with exponentially small error probability:*

$$\Pr\left[\|\tilde{p} - q\|_1 \leq \frac{\delta}{3}\right] \geq 1 - \frac{1}{\exp(n)}.$$

3.4 Approximate Sampling of $\tilde{p}$

Although q approximates $\tilde{p}$, the function q is not necessarily a probability distribution in general in the sense that $\sum_x q(x)$ may not be equal to one or $q(x)$ may be negative for some x. Thus, sampling a distribution close to $\tilde{p}$ is not straightforward even when q is given.

Fortunately, we can do such sampling by using the classical algorithm provided by Bremner-Montanaro-Shepherd [6]. To describe the algorithm, we define $S_\epsilon = 1$ and $S_y = \sum_{x\in\{0,1\}^n, x_1\cdots x_k = y} q(x)$ for every $1 \leq k \leq n$ and $y \in \{0,1\}^k$, where ϵ denotes the empty string. The sampling algorithm is described as follows:

1. Set $y \leftarrow \epsilon$.
2. Perform the following procedure n times:
   a. If $S_{yz} < 0$ for some $z \in \{0,1\}$, set $y \leftarrow y\bar{z}$, where $\bar{z} = 1 - z$.
   b. Otherwise, set $y \leftarrow y0$ with probability S_{y0}/S_y and $y \leftarrow y1$ with probability $1 - S_{y0}/S_y$.
3. Output $y \in \{0,1\}^n$.

Let $\mathrm{Alg}(q)$ be the output distribution of this algorithm. If q is close to $\tilde{p}$, then $\mathrm{Alg}(q)$ is also close to $\tilde{p}$ as stated by the following lemma.[1]

Lemma 3 ([6]) *Let* $\tilde{p}$ *be a probability distribution on* $\{0,1\}^n$. *Assuming that* $q\colon \{0,1\}^n \to \mathbb{R}$ *and* $\|q - \tilde{p}\|_1 \leq \delta$, *it holds* $\|\mathrm{Alg}(q) - \tilde{p}\|_1 \leq 4\delta$.

Remark 1 Assuming that $\sum_x q(x) = 1$, the bound in the statement can be improved to $\|\mathrm{Alg}(q) - \tilde{p}\|_1 \leq 3\delta$. This assumption is satisfied by the algorithm in Theorem 1, which uses the following observation: First, note that

$$\begin{aligned}\sum_x q(x) &= \sum_x \sum_{S\in\{0,1\}^n:\,|S|\leq c} (1-\lambda)^{|S|}\hat{p}'(S)(-1)^{x\cdot S}\\ &= \sum_{S\in\{0,1\}^n:\,|S|\leq c} (1-\lambda)^{|S|}\hat{p}'(S)\sum_x(-1)^{x\cdot S} = 2^n \cdot \hat{p}'(0^n).\end{aligned}$$

[1] This is a slightly improved version of the statement in [6].

Also note that $\hat{p}(0^n) = \mathsf{E}_x[p(x)(-1)^{0^n \cdot x}] = 1/2^n$ for *any* probability distribution p. If the algorithm uses $1/2^n$ as the value of $\hat{p}'(0^n)$, the approximation error does not increase and $\sum_x q(x) = 1$ holds. □

Thus, Theorem 1 and Lemma 3 imply that we can approximately sample $\tilde{p}$ with additive error δ with respect to the l_1 norm.

Theorem 2 ([17]) *Define CT-ECS circuit C, probability distributions $p, \tilde{p}$, and depolarizing error parameter ε as in Theorem 1. Assuming that*

1. *p is anti-concentrated, i.e., $\sum_{x \in \{0,1\}^n} p(x)^2 \leq \alpha/2^n$ with a known constant α,*
2. *an approximate value λ of $0 < \varepsilon < 1$ is known such that $\lambda \leq \varepsilon \leq \lambda(1 + O(1))$,*

there exists a polynomial-time randomized algorithm that samples the distribution $\tilde{p}$ with accuracy δ in l_1 norm and with exponentially small error probability for given description of C and constants $\lambda, \alpha(\geq 1), 0 < \delta < 1$.

3.5 Approximating Fourier Coefficients

We close this section by providing the key idea used in the proof of Lemma 2. The starting point is the following fact, proved by Van den Nest.

Theorem 3 (Theorem 3 [20]) *Let U be an arbitrary quantum operator on n qubits such that $U|0^n\rangle$ is CT, and O be an arbitrary observable with $||O|| \leq 1$, where $||O||$ is the largest eigenvalue of O in the absolute sense. Let V be an arbitrary quantum operator on n qubits such that $V^\dagger O V$ is ECS, and f be an arbitrary polynomial in n. Then, there exists a polynomial-time randomized algorithm which outputs a real number r such that*

$$\Pr\left[\left|\langle 0^n|U^\dagger V^\dagger O V U|0^n\rangle - r\right| \leq \frac{1}{f(n)}\right] \geq 1 - \frac{1}{\exp(n)}.$$

The following lemma relates $\langle 0^n|U^\dagger V^\dagger O V U|0^n\rangle$ to a Fourier coefficient.

Lemma 4 ([17]) *Let C be an arbitrary quantum circuit on n qubits, and let p be its output probability distribution over $\{0, 1\}^n$ such that $p(x) = |\langle x|C|0^n\rangle|^2$ are the probability that x is obtained when $C|0^n\rangle$ is measured in the computational basis. Then,*

$$\widehat{p}(S) = \frac{1}{2^n}\langle 0^n|C^\dagger Z^S C|0^n\rangle$$

for any $S = S_1 \cdots S_n \in \{0, 1\}^n$, where $Z^S = \bigotimes_{j=1}^n Z_j^{S_j}$, i.e., the tensor product of a Pauli-Z operator on the j-th qubit with $S_j = 1$ for any $1 \leq j \leq n$.

Proof Since $p(x) = |\langle x|C|0^n\rangle|^2$, we have

$$\begin{aligned}\widehat{p}(S) &= \frac{1}{2^n}\sum_{x\in\{0,1\}^n} p(x)(-1)^{S\cdot x} = \frac{1}{2^n}\sum_{x\in\{0,1\}^n} \langle 0^n|C^\dagger|x\rangle\langle x|C|0^n\rangle(-1)^{S\cdot x}\\ &= \frac{1}{2^n}\sum_{x\in\{0,1\}^n} \langle 0^n|C^\dagger X^x|0^n\rangle\langle 0^n|X^x C|0^n\rangle(-1)^{S\cdot x},\end{aligned}$$

where X^x denotes $H^{\otimes n}Z^x H^{\otimes n}$ for any $x \in \{0,1\}^n$. Since it holds that $|0^n\rangle\langle 0^n| = \frac{1}{2^n}\sum_{t\in\{0,1\}^n} Z^t$, we have

$$\begin{aligned}\widehat{p}(S) &= \frac{1}{2^{2n}}\sum_{x\in\{0,1\}^n}\sum_{t\in\{0,1\}^n} \langle 0^n|C^\dagger X^x Z^t X^x C|0^n\rangle(-1)^{S\cdot x}\\ &= \frac{1}{2^{2n}}\sum_{t\in\{0,1\}^n} \langle 0^n|C^\dagger Z^t C|0^n\rangle \sum_{x\in\{0,1\}^n}(-1)^{(S\oplus t)\cdot x} = \frac{1}{2^n}\langle 0^n|C^\dagger Z^S C|0^n\rangle,\end{aligned}$$

where $S \oplus t$ is the bit-wise EXOR of S and t.

If C is a CT-ECS circuit, C is the form of VU such that $U|0^n\rangle$ is CT and $V^\dagger Z_j V$ is ECS for any $1 \le j \le n$. Thus,

$$C^\dagger Z^S C = U^\dagger V^\dagger Z^S V U.$$

If S satisfies $|S| = O(1)$, $V^\dagger Z^S V$ can be shown to be ECS. Since $U|0^n\rangle$ is CT and $||Z^S|| \le 1$, $C^\dagger Z^S C$ satisfies the conditions of $U^\dagger V^\dagger O V U$ in Theorem 3. Thus, Lemma 4 and Theorem 3 together imply the existence of a polynomial time randomized algorithm that computes a Fourier coefficient of the output distribution of any CT-ECS circuit. This proves Lemma 2.

4 Verification with Smaller Quantum Circuits

This section considers only unitary circuits. For simplicity, we may use the same symbol to represent both a unitary operator and a circuit realizing the unitary operator. Although such a circuit is not unique, we always consider a fixed circuit, which is arbitrary or clear from the context. For instance, we write "circuit U" to mean a fixed circuit realizing a unitary operator U.

4.1 Verification of Quantum Circuits

When we consider a quantum circuit with a fixed gate set consisting of single-qubit gates and the controlled-Z (CZ) gate, we can naturally represent the circuit as a graph (called a *circuit graph*) as in the case of Boolean circuits. For a quantum circuit C with the underlying gate set, we define the *denseness* of C as the minimum size of a cut of the circuit graph of C induced by partitioning the set of qubits C acting on into two subsets of $\Omega(n)$ qubits. The denseness of C is thus the number of CZ gates across the cut.

Let $\tilde{U}$ be a physically implemented quantum circuit that is supposed to realize a target unitary circuit U on n qubits.[2] We want to verify that the output state ρ of $\tilde{U}$ is close to $U|0^n\rangle\langle 0^n|U^\dagger$ in fidelity, by using another physically implemented quantum circuit smaller than U that has already been verified (called a "trusted" circuit). More specifically, assuming that U consists of one-qubit gates and CZ gates, and that a classical description of U is known, the goal is to estimate the fidelity $\langle\psi|\rho|\psi\rangle$ with as few copies of ρ as possible, where $|\psi\rangle := U|0^n\rangle$.

To achieve this goal using the smaller trusted quantum circuit, the basic idea is to partition the n qubits into two disjoint sets and consider the sub-circuit acting on each set separately. A straightforward partition does not work since there are at least D CZ gates across the partition for the denseness D of U. We instead represent $\langle\psi|\rho|\psi\rangle$ as a convex combination of simpler terms.

Since $|0^n\rangle\langle 0^n| = \frac{1}{2^n}\sum_{\mathbf{k}\in\{0,1\}^n} \mathrm{Z}^{\mathbf{k}}$, where $\mathrm{Z}^{\mathbf{k}} = \prod_{i=1}^n \mathrm{Z}_i^{k_i}$ for $\mathbf{k} := (k_1, \ldots, k_n)$ with $k_i \in \{0, 1\}$ and Z_i is the Pauli Z operator acting on the ith qubit, we have $U|0^n\rangle\langle 0^n|U^\dagger = \frac{1}{2^n}\sum_{\mathbf{k}\in\{0,1\}^n} U\mathrm{Z}^{\mathbf{k}}U^\dagger$. This implies

$$\begin{aligned}\langle\psi|\rho|\psi\rangle &= \mathrm{Tr}\left(\rho|\psi\rangle\langle\psi|\right) = \mathrm{Tr}\left(\rho U|0^n\rangle\langle 0^n|U^\dagger\right)\\ &= \frac{1}{2^n}\sum_{\mathbf{k}\in\{0,1\}^n} \mathrm{Tr}\left(\rho U\mathrm{Z}^{\mathbf{k}}U^\dagger\right)\\ &= \mathsf{E}_{\mathbf{k}\in\{0,1\}^n}\left[\mathrm{Tr}\left(\rho U\mathrm{Z}^{\mathbf{k}}U^\dagger\right)\right]. \end{aligned} \tag{2}$$

Note that $\mathrm{Tr}\left(\rho U\mathrm{Z}^{\mathbf{k}}U^\dagger\right)$ is real, since $U\mathrm{Z}^{\mathbf{k}}U^\dagger$ is Hermitian.

4.2 Partitioning the Set of Qubits

Suppose that we partition the set of the n qubits into disjoint sets S and T of qubits to achieve the denseness D of U. Then, there are D CZ gates across the associated cut. We can thus write

[2] Since $\tilde{U}$ is a physical implementation of U, it may be natural to assume that $\tilde{U}$ acts on n qubits. However, we can consider the case where $\tilde{U}$ acts on m qubits for some $m > n$ and has a specified n-qubit subset of m qubits as the output qubits. The following discussion also holds in this case.

$$U = (v^{(D+1)} \otimes w^{(D+1)}) \cdot \mathrm{CZ}^{(D)} \cdot (v^{(D)} \otimes w^{(D)}) \cdot \mathrm{CZ}^{(D-1)} \cdots \mathrm{CZ}^{(1)}(v^{(1)} \otimes w^{(1)}),$$

where $v^{(i)}$ and $w^{(i)}$ are unitary operators not across the cut, and $\mathrm{CZ}^{(i)}$ is the ith CZ gate across the cut. Further, we replace each CZ gate across the cut with a linear combination of product operators [3], $\mathrm{CZ} = \frac{1}{2}\sum_{i,j\in\{0,1\}}(-1)^{ij}\sigma_i \otimes \sigma_j$, where $\sigma_0 = I_2$ and $\sigma_1 = Z$, to obtain

$$\begin{aligned} U &= \frac{1}{2^D}\sum_{\mathbf{i},\mathbf{j}\in\{0,1\}^D}(-1)^{\mathbf{i}\cdot\mathbf{j}}\left[v^{(D+1)}\sigma_{i_D}\cdots\sigma_{i_1}v^{(1)}\right]\otimes\left[w^{(D+1)}\sigma_{j_D}\cdots\sigma_{j_1}w^{(1)}\right] \\ &= \frac{1}{2^D}\sum_{\mathbf{i},\mathbf{j}\in\{0,1\}^D}(-1)^{\mathbf{i}\cdot\mathbf{j}}V_{\mathbf{i}}\otimes W_{\mathbf{j}}, \end{aligned}$$

where $\mathbf{i} := (i_1, \ldots, i_D)$ and $\mathbf{j} := (j_1, \ldots, j_D)$, and $V_{\mathbf{i}} := v^{(D+1)}\sigma_{i_D}\cdots\sigma_{i_1}v^{(1)}$ and $W_{\mathbf{j}} := w^{(D+1)}\sigma_{j_D}\cdots\sigma_{j_1}w^{(1)}$. This means that U can be represented as the expectation over $\mathbf{i}, \mathbf{j}$ of the tensor product of unitary operators acting only on S and T, respectively.

Recall that we want to estimate $\langle\psi|\rho|\psi\rangle = \mathsf{E}_{\mathbf{k}\in\{0,1\}^n}\left[\mathrm{Tr}\left(\rho U \mathrm{Z}^{\mathbf{k}} U^\dagger\right)\right]$. By using the above representation of U, we have

$$\begin{aligned} \mathrm{Tr}\left(\rho U \mathrm{Z}^{\mathbf{k}} U^\dagger\right) &= \Re\,\mathrm{Tr}\left(\rho U \mathrm{Z}^{\mathbf{k}} U^\dagger\right) \\ &= \frac{1}{4^D}\sum_{\mathbf{i},\mathbf{j},\mathbf{i}',\mathbf{j}'\in\{0,1\}^D}(-1)^{\mathbf{i}\cdot\mathbf{j}+\mathbf{i}'\cdot\mathbf{j}'}\Re\,\mathrm{Tr}\left(\rho(V_{\mathbf{i}}\otimes W_{\mathbf{j}})\mathrm{Z}^{\mathbf{k}}(V_{\mathbf{i}'}\otimes W_{\mathbf{j}'})^\dagger\right) \\ &= 4^D\mu(\mathbf{k}), \end{aligned} \tag{3}$$

where

$$\mu(\mathbf{k}) := \mathsf{E}_{\mathbf{i},\mathbf{j},\mathbf{i}',\mathbf{j}'\in\{0,1\}^D}\left[(-1)^{\mathbf{i}\cdot\mathbf{j}+\mathbf{i}'\cdot\mathbf{j}'}\Re\,\mathrm{Tr}\left(\rho(V_{\mathbf{i}}\otimes W_{\mathbf{j}})\mathrm{Z}^{\mathbf{k}}(V_{\mathbf{i}'}\otimes W_{\mathbf{j}'})^\dagger\right)\right].$$

Thus, estimating $\mu(\mathbf{k})$ suffices. Note that $(V_{\mathbf{i}}\otimes W_{\mathbf{j}})\mathrm{Z}^{\mathbf{k}}(V_{\mathbf{i}'}\otimes W_{\mathbf{j}'})^\dagger$ is a tensor product of unitary operators acting on S and T, respectively. However, since it is not necessarily Hermitian, we cannot estimate $\mu(\mathbf{k})$ straightforwardly. Fortunately, we can use the trick shown in Lemma 5 to estimate $\mu(\mathbf{k})$.

Lemma 5 ([3]) *As shown in Fig. 1, define*

$$Q := (H \otimes I_{2^n})(\Lambda(V_{\mathbf{i}'}^\dagger \otimes W_{\mathbf{j}'}^\dagger))(\mathrm{X} \otimes I_{2^n})(\Lambda(V_{\mathbf{i}}^\dagger \otimes W_{\mathbf{j}}^\dagger))(\mathrm{X}H \otimes I_{2^n})$$

and $\Phi(\rho) := Q(|0\rangle\langle 0| \otimes \rho)Q^\dagger$ *for any n-qubit state ρ. Let $b \in \{0, 1\}$ and $z \in \{0, 1\}^n$ be the classical outcomes of the measurement in the computational basis on the first and the remaining qubits of $\Phi(\rho)$, respectively. For every $\mathbf{k} \in \{0, 1\}^n$ and $\mathbf{i}, \mathbf{j}, \mathbf{i}', \mathbf{j}' \in \{0, 1\}^D$, define a random variable $\alpha_{\mathbf{kiji'j'}} \in \{1, -1\}$ such that $\alpha_{\mathbf{kiji'j'}}(b, \mathbf{z}) = 1$ if $\mathbf{z} \cdot \mathbf{k} = \mathbf{i} \cdot \mathbf{j} \oplus \mathbf{i}' \cdot \mathbf{j}' \oplus b$ and $\alpha_{\mathbf{kiji'j'}}(b, \mathbf{z}) = -1$ otherwise. Then,*

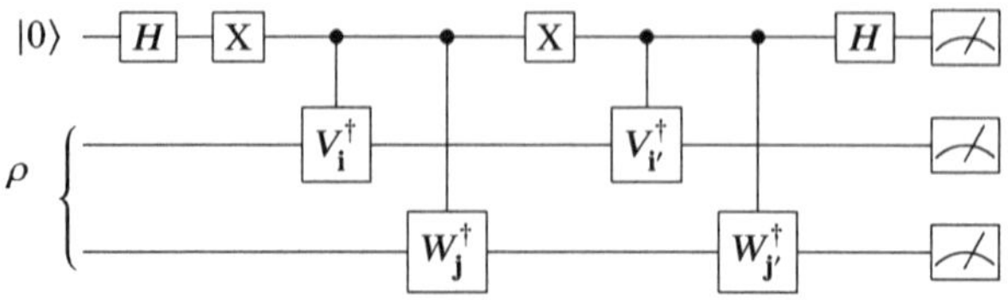

Fig. 1 Quantum Circuit Q on $n+1$ qubits given in Lemma 5

$$\mathsf{E}_{b,\mathbf{z}}[\alpha_{\mathbf{kiji'j'}}(b,\mathbf{z})] = (-1)^{\mathbf{i}\cdot\mathbf{j}+\mathbf{i'}\cdot\mathbf{j'}} \Re \operatorname{Tr}\left(\rho(V_{\mathbf{i}} \otimes W_{\mathbf{j}})\mathsf{Z}^{\mathbf{k}}(V_{\mathbf{i'}} \otimes W_{\mathbf{j'}})^{\dagger}\right),$$

where the expectation is over the probability distribution of the measurement outcomes.

The circuit shown in Lemma 5 essentially applies the following operator to ρ:

$$\frac{1}{\sqrt{2}}\left[|+\rangle(V_{\mathbf{i}}^{\dagger} \otimes W_{\mathbf{j}}^{\dagger}) + |-\rangle(V_{\mathbf{i'}}^{\dagger} \otimes W_{\mathbf{j'}}^{\dagger})\right].$$

A downside of this circuit is to have multi-qubit gates across the newly introduced single qubit and S, and those across the single qubit and T, reconnecting the two sets S and T via the single qubit. We thus need the second trick to make these gates have no intersecting qubits.

4.3 Dividing the Evolution of States

Before applying the second trick, we rearrange the gates in the circuit in Fig. 1 to get another circuit shown in Fig. 2. Then, we apply Lemma 6 to obtain yet another circuit shown in Fig. 3, which acts on four quantum registers ($\mathsf{S}_1, \mathsf{S}_2, \mathsf{T}_1, \mathsf{T}_2$), where S_1 and T_1 consist of the first and the last qubits, respectively, and S_2 and T_2 consist of the qubits in sets S and T, respectively.

Lemma 6 ([14]) *Let σ be an $(n+1)$-qubit state on qubits $q_0, \ldots, q_n$. Let M be an observable on the $n+1$ qubits. Then, $\operatorname{Tr}[M\sigma]$ is the expected value of the output of the following procedure, where $P_1 = P_2 = \mathrm{I}$, $P_3 = P_4 = \mathrm{X}$, $P_5 = P_6 = \mathrm{Y}$, and $P_7 = P_8 = \mathrm{Z}$; $|\phi_1\rangle = |\phi_7\rangle = |0\rangle$, $|\phi_2\rangle = |\phi_8\rangle = |1\rangle$, $|\phi_3\rangle = |+\rangle$, $|\phi_4\rangle = |-\rangle$, $|\phi_5\rangle = |+_i\rangle$, $|\phi_6\rangle = |-_i\rangle$, $c_1 = c_2 = c_3 = c_5 = c_7 = 0$, and $c_4 = c_6 = c_8 = 1$:*

(I) For every $i = 1, \ldots, 8$, do the following:

1. *Measure q_0 with observable P_i and let $o_i \in \{1, -1\}$ be the outcome corresponding to the eigenvalues of P_i.*
2. *Prepare $|\phi_i\rangle$ on q_0.*
3. *Measure $q_0, \ldots, q_n$ with observable M and let m_i be the outcome corresponding to the eigenvalues of M.*

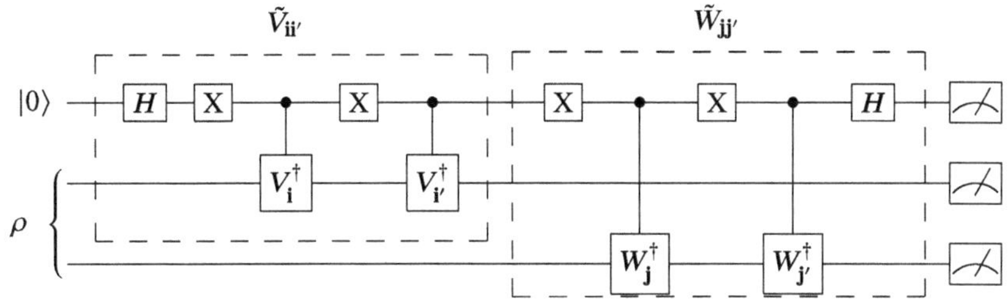

Fig. 2 Quantum circuit obtained from the circuit in Fig. 1 by rearranging gates

Fig. 3 Quantum circuit obtained from the circuit in Fig. 2 by applying Lemma 6

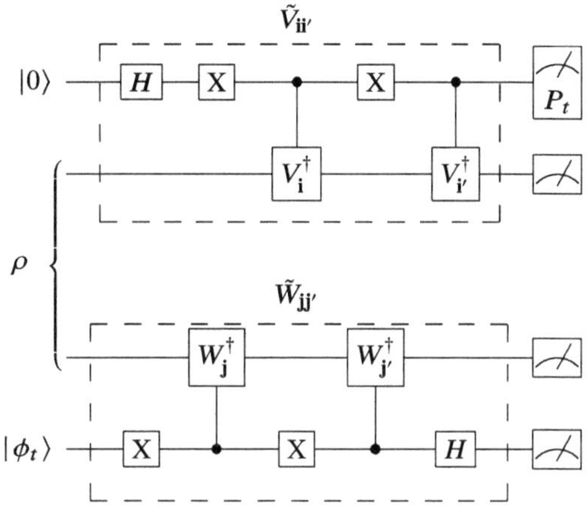

(II) Output $\frac{1}{2}\sum_{i=1}^{8}(-1)^{c_i} o_i m_i$.

In other words, $\mathrm{Tr}[M\sigma] = \frac{1}{2}\sum_{i=1}^{8}(-1)^{c_i}\,\mathrm{Tr}\left[(P_i \otimes M)(\sigma \otimes |\phi_i\rangle\langle\phi_i|)\right]$.

Let $\tilde{V}_{\mathbf{ii}'}$ and $\tilde{W}_{\mathbf{jj}'}$ be unitary operators on registers $(\mathsf{S}_1, \mathsf{S}_2)$ and $(\mathsf{T}_1, \mathsf{T}_2)$, respectively, such that

$$\tilde{V}_{\mathbf{ii}'} := \Lambda(V_{\mathbf{i}'}^{\dagger})(\mathrm{X} \otimes \mathrm{I})\Lambda(V_{\mathbf{i}}^{\dagger})(\mathrm{X}H \otimes \mathrm{I}),$$

$$\tilde{W}_{\mathbf{jj}'} := (H \otimes \mathrm{I})\Lambda(W_{\mathbf{j}'}^{\dagger})(\mathrm{X} \otimes \mathrm{I})\Lambda(W_{\mathbf{j}}^{\dagger})(\mathrm{X} \otimes \mathrm{I}),$$

as shown in Fig. 2. Then, Lemma 6 with $\sigma := \tilde{V}_{\mathbf{ii}'}(|0\rangle\langle 0| \otimes \rho)\tilde{V}_{\mathbf{ii}'}^{\dagger}$ and

$$M := \sum_{b\in\{0,1\},\mathbf{z}\in\{0,1\}^n} \alpha_{\mathbf{kiji}'\mathbf{j}'}(b,\mathbf{z}) \cdot \tilde{W}_{\mathbf{jj}'}^{\dagger}\left(|b\rangle\langle b| \otimes |\mathbf{z}\rangle\langle\mathbf{z}|\right)\tilde{W}_{\mathbf{jj}'},$$

yields the subroutine used to estimate $\mathsf{E}_{b,\mathbf{z}}[\alpha_{\mathbf{kiji}'\mathbf{j}'}(b,\mathbf{z})]$ given in Table 1.

Table 1 Subroutine for estimating $\mathsf{E}_{b,\mathbf{z}}[\alpha_{\mathbf{kiji'j'}}(b,\mathbf{z})]$

Subroutine EstAlpha$(\mathbf{k}, \mathbf{i}, \mathbf{j}, \mathbf{i}', \mathbf{j}')$
(I) For every $t = 1, \ldots, 8$, do the following:
1. Initialize registers $(\mathsf{S}_2, \mathsf{T}_2)$ to state ρ.
2. Do the following:
a. Initialize S_1 to $\|0\rangle$.
b. Apply $\tilde{V}_{\mathbf{ii'}}$ to $(\mathsf{S}_1, \mathsf{S}_2)$.
c. Measure S_1 with P_t to get $o_t \in \{1, -1\}$.
d. Measure S_2 in the computational basis to get $\mathbf{z}_t^{(\mathsf{S})} \in \{0,1\}^{\|\mathsf{S}\|}$.
3. Do the following:
a. Initialize T_1 to $\|\phi_t\rangle$.
b. Apply $\tilde{W}_{\mathbf{jj'}}$ to $(\mathsf{T}_1, \mathsf{T}_2)$.
c. Measure T_1 in the computational basis to get $b_t \in \{0, 1\}$.
d. Measure T_2 in the computational basis to get $\mathbf{z}_t^{(\mathsf{T})} \in \{0,1\}^{\|\mathsf{T}\|}$.
(II) Set $\mathbf{z}_t := \mathbf{z}_t^{(\mathsf{S})} \circ \mathbf{z}_t^{(\mathsf{T})}$ ($\circ$ means concatenation) and output $\frac{1}{2}\sum_{t=1}^{8}(-1)^{c_t} o_t \cdot \alpha_{\mathbf{kiji'j'}}(b_t, \mathbf{z}_t)$.

We should note that only stage (I) requires quantum circuits, and that steps 2 and 3 in stage (I) act on disjoint registers.

We claim that the expected value of the output $\frac{1}{2}\sum_{i=1}^{8}(-1)^{c_i} o_i \cdot \alpha_{\mathbf{kiji'j'}}(b_t, \mathbf{z}_t)$ is equal to $\mathsf{E}_{b,\mathbf{z}}[\alpha_{\mathbf{kiji'j'}}(b,\mathbf{z})]$: For fixed $\alpha_{\mathbf{kiji'j'}}$, let $\alpha(b,\mathbf{z}) := \alpha_{\mathbf{kiji'j'}}(b,\mathbf{z})$ for simplicity. By definition, $\mathsf{E}_{b,\mathbf{z}}[\alpha(b,\mathbf{z})]$ is

$$\sum_{b\in\{0,1\},\mathbf{z}\in\{0,1\}^n} \mathrm{Tr}\left[(|b\rangle\langle b| \otimes |\mathbf{z}\rangle\langle\mathbf{z}|)\, \tilde{W}_{\mathbf{jj'}} \tilde{V}_{\mathbf{ii'}} (|0\rangle\langle 0| \otimes \rho) \tilde{V}_{\mathbf{ii'}}^{\dagger} \tilde{W}_{\mathbf{jj'}}^{\dagger}\right] \alpha(b,\mathbf{z})$$
$$= \mathrm{Tr}\left[M_{\mathbf{jj'}} \tilde{V}_{\mathbf{ii'}} (|0\rangle\langle 0| \otimes \rho) \tilde{V}_{\mathbf{ii'}}^{\dagger}\right], \quad (4)$$

where $M_{\mathbf{jj'}} := \sum_{b\in\{0,1\},\mathbf{z}\in\{0,1\}^n} \alpha(b,\mathbf{z}) \cdot \tilde{W}_{\mathbf{jj'}}^{\dagger} (|b\rangle\langle b| \otimes |\mathbf{z}\rangle\langle\mathbf{z}|)\, \tilde{W}_{\mathbf{jj'}}$ is an observable. It follows from Lemma 6 with $M := M_{\mathbf{jj'}}$ and $\sigma := \tilde{V}_{\mathbf{ii'}} (|0\rangle\langle 0| \otimes \rho) \tilde{V}_{\mathbf{ii'}}^{\dagger}$ that the expected value of the output of EstAlpha in Table 1 is equal to $\mathsf{E}_{b,\mathbf{z}}[\alpha(b,\mathbf{z})]$.

Table 2 Description of the entire algorithm

1. Take $\mathbf{k} \in \{0,1\}^n$ uniformly at random T times and output the average, over the T samples of $\mathbf{k}$'s, of the output of the next step.
2. Take $(\mathbf{i}, \mathbf{j}, \mathbf{i}', \mathbf{j}') \in (\{0,1\}^D)^4$ uniformly at random T times and output the average, over the T samples of $(\mathbf{i}, \mathbf{j}, \mathbf{i}', \mathbf{j}')$'s, of the output of the next step.
3. Run EstAlpha$(\mathbf{k}, \mathbf{i}, \mathbf{j}, \mathbf{i}', \mathbf{j}')$ T times and output the average of the T output values of EstAlpha.

4.4 The Final Algorithm and Its Consequence

The previous subsections are summarized as follows:

$$\begin{aligned}
\langle\psi|\rho|\psi\rangle &= \mathsf{E}_{\mathbf{k}\in\{0,1\}^n}\left[\mathrm{Tr}\left(\rho U Z^{\mathbf{k}} U^{\dagger}\right)\right] \\
&= \mathsf{E}_{\mathbf{k}\in\{0,1\}^n}\left[4^D \mathsf{E}_{\mathbf{i},\mathbf{j},\mathbf{i}',\mathbf{j}'\in\{0,1\}^D}\left[(-1)^{\mathbf{i}\cdot\mathbf{j}+\mathbf{i}'\cdot\mathbf{j}'}\Re\,\mathrm{Tr}\left(\rho(V_{\mathbf{i}}\otimes W_{\mathbf{j}})Z^{\mathbf{k}}(V_{\mathbf{i}'}\otimes W_{\mathbf{j}'})^{\dagger}\right)\right]\right] \\
&= \mathsf{E}_{\mathbf{k}\in\{0,1\}^n}\left[4^D \mathsf{E}_{\mathbf{i},\mathbf{j},\mathbf{i}',\mathbf{j}'\in\{0,1\}^D}\left[\mathsf{E}_{b,\mathbf{z}}[\alpha_{\mathbf{kiji'j'}}(b,\mathbf{z})]\right]\right] \\
&= \mathsf{E}_{\mathbf{k}\in\{0,1\}^n}\left[4^D \mathsf{E}_{\mathbf{i},\mathbf{j},\mathbf{i}',\mathbf{j}'\in\{0,1\}^D}\,\mathrm{Tr}\left[M_{\mathbf{jj}'}\tilde{V}_{\mathbf{ii}'}(|0\rangle\langle 0|\otimes\rho)\tilde{V}_{\mathbf{ii}'}^{\dagger}\right]\right] \\
&= \mathsf{E}_{\mathbf{k}\in\{0,1\}^n} 4^D \mathsf{E}_{\mathbf{i},\mathbf{j},\mathbf{i}',\mathbf{j}'\in\{0,1\}^D} \\
&\quad \frac{1}{2}\sum_{t=1}^{8}(-1)^{c_t}\,\mathrm{Tr}\left[(P_t\otimes M)((\tilde{V}_{\mathbf{ii}'}(|0\rangle\langle 0|\otimes\rho)\tilde{V}_{\mathbf{ii}'}^{\dagger})\otimes|\phi_t\rangle\langle\phi_t|)\right],
\end{aligned}$$

where the first equality follows from Eq. (2), the second follows from Eq. (3), the third follows from Lemma 5, the fourth follows from Eq. (4), and the last follows from Lemma 6.

Therefore, $\langle\psi|\rho|\psi\rangle$ can be estimated with high precision for a sufficiently large T by performing the algorithm described in Table 2.

In particular, low-dense circuits can be verified with a polynomial number of copies of the target state.

Theorem 4 (Theorem 1[18]) *Let U be an n-qubit quantum circuit with denseness $D = O(\log n)$ with respect to a partition of the n qubits into two disjoint sets of m and $n-m$ qubits, respectively, for $m \geq n/2$, consisting of* CZ *gates and single-qubit gates. For any n qubit state ρ and $|\psi\rangle := U|0^n\rangle$, their fidelity $\langle\psi|\rho|\psi\rangle$ can be estimated with accuracy ϵ with probability at least $1-\delta$ by performing an $(m+1)$-qubit trusted quantum circuit on $2^{O(D)}\mathrm{p}(1/\epsilon, \log(1/\delta))$ copies of ρ for a certain polynomial* p, *if the trusted quantum circuit is within $O(\epsilon/4^D)$ in the diamond norm from the ideal circuit.*

Most real quantum circuits support the applicability of two-qubit gates not on every pair of qubits but only on neighboring pairs. This applicability is represented as a graph (called a *connectivity graph*), where each node represents a qubit, and two nodes are connected with an edge if and only if two-qubit gates are applicable to the corresponding qubit pair.

We say an n-qubit quantum computing chip is *sparse* if its associated connectivity graph can be divided into two disjoint subgraphs with $\Theta(n)$ nodes by removing a constant number of edges. This means the case where the minimum cut size of a balanced partition of the connectivity graph is at most some constant. Suppose we implement a quantum circuit on a sparse computing chip. The denseness D is then closely related to the depth d of the circuit: Consider a partition of the underlying qubit set into two disjoint subsets witnessing the sparseness of the chip. Then, there are at most a constant number of CZ gates across the two subsets of qubits that can be performed in parallel. Thus, the denseness D is bounded by $O(d)$. For instance, if such a circuit is shallow (i.e., it has depth $O(\log n)$), then Theorem 4 implies that the output state of such a circuit can be verified with polynomially many samples of the output states.

4.5 Intuitions Behind Lemmas 5 and 6

Lemma 5 can be proved with a straightforward calculation, but it is more understandable to regard it as a corollary of the following lemma.

Lemma 7 *For unitary operators U_+, U_- acting on n qubits, let $\Phi = \Phi(U_+, U_-)$ be the quantum circuit on $n+1$ qubits such that $\Phi|0\rangle|\tau\rangle = \frac{1}{\sqrt{2}}|+\rangle U_+|\tau\rangle + \frac{1}{\sqrt{2}}|-\rangle U_-|\tau\rangle$. For any positive semidefinite operator M acting on n qubits such that $0 \le \|M\| \le 1$, let $M' = |0\rangle\langle 0| \otimes M + |1\rangle\langle 1| \otimes (I - M)$.*

Then, for any n-qubit state ρ, the probability of measuring M' on $\Phi(|0\rangle\langle 0| \otimes \rho)$ is

$$p = \frac{1}{2}\left[1 + \Re\,\mathrm{Tr}[\rho U_+^\dagger (2M - I) U_-]\right].$$

Moreover, define a random variable $\alpha \in \{1, -1\}$ such that $\alpha = 1$ if M' is measured on $\Phi(|0\rangle\langle 0| \otimes \rho)$ and $\alpha = -1$ if $I - M'$ is measured. Then, it holds that

$$\mathsf{E}[\alpha] = \Re\,\mathrm{Tr}[\rho U_+^\dagger (2M - I) U_-],$$

where the expectation is over the probability distribution of the measurement outcomes.

Lemma 7 can be regarded as a (non-trivial) modification of the so-called Hadamard Test. To apply Lemma 7 to our case, set $U_+ = (V_{\mathbf{i}} \otimes W_{\mathbf{j}})^\dagger$ and $U_- = (V_{\mathbf{i}'} \otimes W_{\mathbf{j}'})^\dagger$. Moreover, let

$$M = \frac{1}{2}\left(I + (-1)^{\mathbf{i}\cdot\mathbf{j}+\mathbf{i}'\cdot\mathbf{j}'} \mathsf{Z}^{\mathbf{k}}\right).$$

Then, we have $2M - I = (-1)^{\mathbf{i}\cdot\mathbf{j}+\mathbf{i}'\cdot\mathbf{j}'} \mathsf{Z}^{\mathbf{k}}$. Therefore, Lemma 7 implies that

$$\mathsf{E}[\alpha] = (-1)^{\mathbf{i}\cdot\mathbf{j}+\mathbf{i}'\cdot\mathbf{j}'} \Re\,\mathrm{Tr}\left(\rho (V_{\mathbf{i}} \otimes W_{\mathbf{j}}) \mathsf{Z}^{\mathbf{k}} (V_{\mathbf{i}'} \otimes W_{\mathbf{j}'})^\dagger\right).$$

Finally, it can be shown that M' is measured if and only if the outcomes $b, \mathbf{z}$ satisfy $b \oplus \mathbf{z} \cdot \mathbf{k} \oplus \mathbf{i} \cdot \mathbf{j} \oplus \mathbf{i}' \cdot \mathbf{j}' = 0$. This gives Lemma 5.

Lemma 6 is based on the following intuition. Let A be any 2×2 matrix. Since

$$\left\{ \frac{1}{\sqrt{2}}\mathrm{I}, \frac{1}{\sqrt{2}}\mathrm{X}, \frac{1}{\sqrt{2}}\mathrm{Y}, \frac{1}{\sqrt{2}}\mathrm{Z} \right\}$$

forms an orthonormal basis of the space $L(\mathbb{C}^2)$ of linear operators on $\mathbb{C}^2$ (with respect to Hilbert-Schmidt inner-product), we can write

$$A = \frac{1}{2}\operatorname{Tr}(A\mathrm{I})\mathrm{I} + \frac{1}{2}\operatorname{Tr}(A\mathrm{X})\mathrm{X} + \frac{1}{2}\operatorname{Tr}(A\mathrm{Y})\mathrm{Y} + \frac{1}{2}\operatorname{Tr}(A\mathrm{Z})\mathrm{Z}.$$

We regard this as the output of the identity channel Φ over $L(\mathbb{C}^2)$:

$$\Phi(A) = \frac{1}{2}\operatorname{Tr}(A\mathrm{I})\mathrm{I} + \frac{1}{2}\operatorname{Tr}(A\mathrm{X})\mathrm{X} + \frac{1}{2}\operatorname{Tr}(A\mathrm{Y})\mathrm{Y} + \frac{1}{2}\operatorname{Tr}(A\mathrm{Z})\mathrm{Z}.$$

By using the spectral decomposition of the four Pauli matrices, we have

$$\begin{aligned}\Phi(A) = &\frac{1}{2}\operatorname{Tr}(A\mathrm{I})\left(|0\rangle\langle 0| + |1\rangle\langle 1|\right) + \frac{1}{2}\operatorname{Tr}(A\mathrm{X})\left(|+\rangle\langle +| - |-\rangle\langle -|\right)\\ &+ \frac{1}{2}\operatorname{Tr}(A\mathrm{Y})\left(|+_i\rangle\langle +_i| - |-_i\rangle\langle -_i|\right) + \frac{1}{2}\operatorname{Tr}(A\mathrm{Z})\left(|0\rangle\langle 0| - |1\rangle\langle 1|\right).\end{aligned}$$

By using c_i, P_i, and $|\phi_i\rangle$ defined in Lemma 6, this can be rewritten as

$$\Phi(A) = \frac{1}{2}\sum_{i=1}^{8}(-1)^{c_i}\operatorname{Tr}(AP_i)|\phi_i\rangle\langle\phi_i|.$$

Recall that we want to compute $\operatorname{Tr}[M\sigma]$ in the lemma. For simplicity, let us assume that σ is a single-qubit state. By using the identity map Φ, we have

$$\begin{aligned}\operatorname{Tr}[M\sigma] = \operatorname{Tr}[M\Phi(\sigma)] &= \operatorname{Tr}\left[M\left(\frac{1}{2}\sum_{i=1}^{8}(-1)^{c_i}\operatorname{Tr}(\sigma P_i)|\phi_i\rangle\langle\phi_i|\right)\right]\\ &= \frac{1}{2}\sum_{i=1}^{8}(-1)^{c_i}\operatorname{Tr}(\sigma P_i)\operatorname{Tr}[M|\phi_i\rangle\langle\phi_i|].\end{aligned}$$

Lemma 6 is proved by generalizing this idea to the case of multi-qubit state σ.

5 Conclusion

We have outlined the techniques used in the two recently published results concerning noisy quantum circuits so as to convey the idea of state-of-the-art techniques in an intuitive but not too abstract way. We hope this article deepens readers' understanding of those techniques and helps them resolve open problems. Due to the purpose of this article, we have omitted some extensions of the results, which include the classical simulation of quantum circuits when the noise rate on each output qubit may be different, and the verification of nearly sparse quantum computing chips such as those whose connectivity graphs are planar. We recommend interested readers refer to the original papers [17, 18].

Acknowledgements I would like to express my sincere gratitude to Yasuhiro Takahashi and Yuki Takeuchi for their valuable comments on an early draft of this article. This work was partially supported by JSPS KAKENHI Grant Numbers 20H05966.

References

1. S. Arora, B. Barak. *Computational Complexity: A Modern Approach* (Cambridge University Press, 2009)
2. A. Bouland, J.F. Fitzsimons, D.E. Koh, Complexity classification of conjugated Clifford circuits. In *Proceedings of the 33rd Computational Complexity Conference (CCC)*, volume 102 of *Leibniz International Proceedings in Informatics*, pp. 21:1–21:25 (2018)
3. S. Bravyi, G. Smith, J.A. Smolin, Trading classical and quantum computational resources. Phys. Rev. X **6**(2), 021043 (2016)
4. M.J. Bremner, R. Jozsa, D.J. Shepherd, Classical simulation of commuting quantum computations implies collapse of the polynomial hierarchy. Proc. R. Soc. A **467**(2126), 459–472 (2011)
5. M.J. Bremner, A. Montanaro, D.J. Shepherd, Average-case complexity versus approximate simulation of commuting quantum computations. Phys. Rev. Lett. **117**(8), 080501 (2016)
6. M.J. Bremner, A. Montanaro, D.J. Shepherd, Achieving quantum supremacy with sparse and noisy commuting quantum computations. Quantum **1**, 8 (2017)
7. S. Fenner, F. Green, S. Homer, and Y. Zhang, Bounds on the power of constant-depth quantum circuits, in *Proceedings of Fundamentals of Computation Theory (FCT)*, volume 3623 of *Lecture Notes in Computer Science*, pp. 44–55 (2005)
8. K. Fujii, S. Tamate, Computational quantum-classical boundary of noisy commuting quantum circuits. Sci. Rep. **6**, 25598 (2016)
9. A. Gheorghiu, T. Kapourniotis, E. Kashefi, Verification of quantum computation: an overview of existing approaches. Theory Comput. Syst. **63**(4), 715–808 (2019)
10. L.K. Grover, A fast quantum mechanical algorithm for database search, in *Proceedings of the Twenty-Eighth Annual ACM Symposium on Theory of Computing*, pp. 212–219 (1996)
11. A.W. Harrow, A. Montanaro, Quantum computational supremacy. Nature **549**, 203–209 (2017)
12. M.A. Nielsen, I.L. Chuang, *Quantum Computation and Quantum Information* (Cambridge University Press, 2000)
13. R. O'Donnell, *Analysis of Boolean Functions* (Cambridge University Press, 2014)
14. T. Peng, A.W. Harrow, M. Ozols, X. Wu, Simulating large quantum circuits on a small quantum computer. Phys. Rev. Lett. **125**(15) (2020)

15. J. Preskill, Quantum computing and the entanglement frontier, in *25th Solvay Conference on Physics "The Theory of the Quantum World"* (2011)
16. P.W. Shor, Polynomial-time algorithms for prime factorization and discrete logarithms on a quantum computer. SIAM J. Comput. **26**(5), 1484–1509 (1997)
17. Y. Takahashi, Y. Takeuchi, S. Tani, Classically simulating quantum circuits with local depolarizing noise. Theor. Comput. Sci. **893**, 117–132 (2021)
18. Y. Takeuchi, Y. Takahashi, T. Morimae, S. Tani, Divide-and-conquer verification method for noisy intermediate-scale quantum computation. Quantum **6**, 758 (2022)
19. B.M. Terhal, D.P. DiVincenzo, Adaptive quantum computation, constant-depth quantum circuits and Arthur-Merlin games. Quantum Inf. Comput. **4**(2), 134–145 (2004)
20. M. van den Nest, Simulating quantum computers with probabilistic methods. Quantum Inf. Comput. **11**(9&10), 784–812 (2011)
21. M. Yoganathan, R. Jozsa, S. Strelchuk, Quantum advantage of unitary Clifford circuits with magic state inputs. Proc. R. Soc. A **475**(2225) (2019)

Succinct Representations of Graphs

Sankardeep Chakraborty and Kunihiko Sadakane

Abstract As the size of data we obtain increases, the importance of algorithms and data structures for efficiently handling big data also increases. Succinct representations are representations of objects which are compressed as much as possible, while keeping the ability of accessing them quickly. Such representations have been proposed in the past two decades for strings and trees, but those for graphs were not well studied. In this article, we survey recent progress in succinct representations for some graph classes.

1 Introduction

Succinct representations are representations of objects which use the minimum number of bits to represent them. This number of bits are called the *information-theoretic lower bound*. In this article, we focus on succinct representations of undirected graphs. A naive representation of a graph is the adjacency matrix that uses $n(n-1)/2$ bits for a graph with n vertices. This representation is succinct for general graphs, but may not be succinct for some classes of graphs. For example, an ordered tree with n nodes can be represented in $2n$ bits. Therefore we need to design a succinct representation for each graph class.

In this article, we focus on unlabeled graphs because of the following reasons. Let $U(n)$ and $L(n)$ be the set of non-isomorphic unlabeled and node-labeled graphs with n vertices in some graph class respectively. Then it holds that

$$|U(n)| \leq |L(n)| \leq |U(n)| \cdot n!$$

S. Chakraborty · K. Sadakane (✉)
Graduate School of Information Science and Technology, The University of Tokyo, Hongo 7-3-1, Bunkyo-ku, Tokyo 113-8656, Japan
e-mail: sada@mist.i.u-toyo.ac.jp

S. Chakraborty
e-mail: sankardeep.chakraborty@gmail.com

S. Minato et al. (eds.), *Algorithmic Foundations for Social Advancement*,
https://doi.org/10.1007/978-981-96-0668-9_19

because any unlabeled graph can be obtained from a labeled graph, and any node-labeled graph can be obtained by giving distinct integers from 1 to n to the vertices of an unlabeled graph. Let $\mathrm{ITLB}(C)$ denote the information-theoretic lower bound for graph class C. Then it holds[1]

$$\mathrm{ITLB}(L(n)) \geq \mathrm{ITLB}(U(n)) \geq \mathrm{ITLB}(L(n)) - n \log n.$$

Definition 1 Let $Z(n)$ be the information-theoretic lower bound for set $S(n)$, and let $f(n)$ be the number of bits to encode an element in $S(n)$ using some representation. Then this representation is said to be

- compact if $f(n) = \mathrm{O}(Z(n))$, and
- succinct if $f(n) = Z(n) + \mathrm{o}(Z(n))$.

It is enough to consider only labeled graphs if $U(n) = \omega(n \log n)$ because if $\mathrm{ITLB}(U(n)) = \mathrm{ITLB}(L(n)) - \mathrm{o}(\mathrm{ITLB}(L(n)))$, a succinct representation for labeled graphs is also succinct for unlabeled graphs. We mainly consider graph classes with $\mathrm{ITLB}(U(n)) = \mathrm{O}(n \log n)$.

Figure 1 shows a hierarchy of graph classes. Boxes show graph classes and lines between boxes show that upper classes contain lower classes. Black curve lines show boundaries between classes. Green, orange, and red boxes show graph classes whose information-theoretic lower bounds are $\Theta(n)$, $\Theta(n \log n)$, and $\Theta(n^2)$ bits, and they are called *linear classes, factorial classes*, and *quadratic classes*, respectively. Between the factorial class and the quadratic class, there is another class called *super-factorial class*.

We want to support basic operations on a graph $G = (V, E)$:

- $\mathrm{adjacent}(v, u)$: returns yes if $u, v \in V$ are adjacent, and no otherwise.
- $\mathrm{neighbor}(v)$: returns the set of vertices w which are adjacent to v.
- $\mathrm{degree}(v)$: returns the number of adjacent vertices to v. That is, $\mathrm{degree}(v) = |\mathrm{neighbor}(v)|$.

We add some data structures to a succinct/compact representation for supporting these operations quickly. For quadratic and super-factorial classes, $\mathrm{degree}(v)$ is easy because we can store the answer for each vertex using $\log n$ bits. Then the query is done in constant time and the additional space is $n \log n = \mathrm{o}(\mathrm{ITLB}(U(n)))$. Therefore the representation still remains succinct. On the other hand, for factorial classes we cannot use this approach because adding $n \log n$ bits violates the succinctness.

[1] Throughout the paper we assume the base of logarithm is two. Furthermore, as in previous works, our model of computation is a RAM machine, with $\mathrm{O}(1)$ time access on words of size $\Theta(\lg n)$.

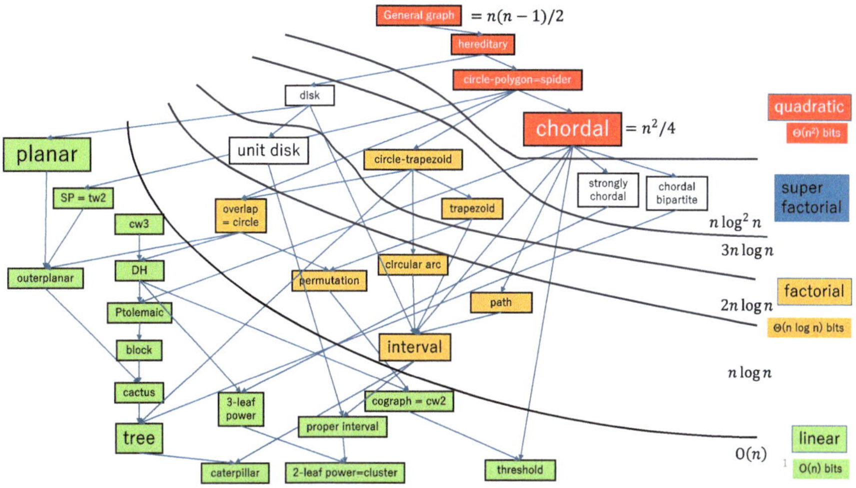

Fig. 1 Hierarchy of graph classes

2 Quadratic Classes

We begin by considering quadratic graph classes, defined as those where ITLB$(U(n))$ and ITLB$(L(n)) \in \Theta(n^2)$. For these classes, a naive representation via adjacency matrices is already compact. However, the primary challenge lies in designing succinct data structures that permit optimal query performance. To date, only a limited number of such data structures have been developed, leaving numerous graph classes without succinct representations. In the following, we briefly survey known results and identify open problems.

- A graph class S is termed *hereditary* if and only if, for any graph $G \in S$, the removal of any vertex v results in a graph $G - v \in S$. For hereditary graph classes where $U(n) = \Omega(n^2)$, Alekseev [4] provided a succinct representation, although this structure does not support any queries.
- Farzan and Munro [20] proved that there exists a constant $\delta > 0$ such that for a graph with $n^\delta < m < n^{2-\delta}$ where m is the number of edges in the graph, the succinct matrix representation of the graph does not support constant access and successor queries. They also introduced a succinct data structure for arbitrary graphs on n vertices and m edges with $m < n^\delta$ or $m > n^2/\log^{1-\delta} n$ that enables constant-time adjacency, neighbor, and degree queries. Starting from an adjacency matrix of size n^2 bits containing m ones (corresponding to the edges of the graph G), they designed data structures based on the matrix's edge density. They distinguished five different density regimes, offering constant-time query structures for each via appropriate matrix decompositions. For graphs with $n^\delta < m < n^2/\log^{1-\delta}$, they gave a compact representation.

- Munro and Wu [36] presented a succinct data structure for *chordal graphs* using $n^2/4 + o(n^2)$ bits, achieving information-theoretic optimality. This work was later extended by He et al. [23], who improved the query times for adjacency, neighbor, and degree queries to constant time. Their approach constructs a clique tree of the input chordal graph based on its maximal cliques, followed by a decomposition of the tree to produce the requisite data structures. Balakrishnan et al. [6] subsequently enhanced both the upper and lower bounds for chordal graphs with *bounded vertex leafage*. However, the question of whether constant-time query data structures for these graphs can be achieved remains open.
- Munro and Nicholson [31] developed a succinct data structure using $n^2/4 + o(n^2)$ bits to represent a *partially ordered set (poset)*, supporting constant-time precedence queries between elements. This structure can succinctly encode both the transitive closure and transitive reduction graph of the poset. They also demonstrated that reachability queries in arbitrary directed graphs can be supported in constant time. Their method involves preprocessing the poset by removing edges from its transitive closure to reduce its height, which facilitates space-efficient encoding through either balanced biclique subgraphs or sparse connections. Efficient data structures for specific classes of posets have also been proposed [18, 34, 35, 45].

Despite these advances, many graph classes still lack succinct data structures. Examples include *string graphs* [37] and *C_4-free graphs* [37]. Another significant open challenge is the formulation of time-space trade-off lower bounds for the aforementioned results.

3 Super-Factorial Classes

We now turn our attention to *super-factorial* graph classes. To the best of our current understanding, only two graph classes have been definitively shown to belong to this category: *strongly chordal graphs and chordal bipartite graphs*. Despite this, the design of succinct data structures for these graphs remains a formidable challenge and has been identified as an open problem in the pioneering work of Spinrad [40, 41]. These graph classes represent a highly significant subclass of chordal graphs, given their wide-ranging applications across multiple disciplines. For instance, in relational database theory, strongly chordal graphs play a critical role and are referred to as β-acyclic hypergraphs (see Fagin [17] for a detailed examination of their significance). In the realm of parallel and distributed computing, these graphs are valuable for modeling and analyzing communication patterns and dependencies in parallel algorithms and data structures [25]. Additionally, in matrix computations and numerical linear algebra, strongly chordal graphs are intimately connected with the notion of totally balanced matrices [30]. Another intriguing research direction involves identifying new graph classes that belong to the super-factorial category by establishing explicit lower bounds on their counting complexity.

4 Factorial Classes

In contrast to the preceding two categories, the factorial class encompasses a wider array of graph data structures, accompanied by a greater diversity in the techniques underlying these structures. It is important to observe that, unlike the quadratic and super-factorial classes, a straightforward approach to storing the degree of vertices does not yield succinct representations in the factorial class. As a result, all succinct data structures for this class must treat degree queries as a separate task. Below, we provide a brief overview of several succinct data structures developed for graphs within this class.

- Beginning with the work of Acan et al. [2] on the succinct representation of *interval graphs* and their subclasses, significant advancements have been made in this area. Specifically, they demonstrated that an arbitrary interval graph with n vertices can be stored using an information-theoretic minimal space of $n \log n + O(n)$ bits, while supporting constant-time degree, adjacency, and neighborhood queries. It has also been established that this upper bound is tight, due to the explicit lower bounds for unlabeled interval graphs due to Acan et al. [2] and for labeled interval graphs due to Gavoille and Paul [21]. Extending their work, Acan et al. [2] also provided succinct representations for special cases such as *unit/proper interval graphs* and *circular-arc graphs*. However, for circular-arc graphs, the query times are not constant, and whether one can design succinct data structures with constant-time degree, adjacency, and neighborhood queries for circular-arc graphs remains an open question.
- Chakraborty and Jo [11] investigated succinct data structures within bounded parameter regimes, showing that by assuming bounded degree or bounded chromatic number, it is possible to surpass the information-theoretic space bounds for interval graphs while maintaining efficient query times. Subsequently, He et al. [22] improved both the space bounds and query times. Studying parameterized succinct data structures under such bounded assumptions presents an intriguing avenue for further exploration, particularly to determine whether the information-theoretic lower bounds can be further reduced while supporting efficient queries.
- Balakrishnan et al. [7] addressed the problem of designing succinct data structures for *path graphs*—a proper subclass of chordal graphs and a proper superclass of interval graphs—on n vertices, with efficient support for degree, adjacency, and neighborhood queries. Their succinct data structure occupies $n \log n + o(n \log n)$ bits of space, while supporting adjacency queries in $O(\log n)$ time, neighborhood queries in $O(d \log n)$ time (where d is the degree of the queried vertex), and degree queries in $\min\{O(\log^2 n), O(d \log n)\}$ time. Recently, He et al. [23] improved these query times to $O(\log n / \log \log n)$ while maintaining succinct space usage.
- Tsakalidis et al. [42] presented succinct data structures for *permutation graphs*, their *bipartite permutation* subgraphs, and *circular permutation* supergraphs. Notably, they provided two implementations for representing permutation graphs: one based on points on a two-dimensional grid and another based on arrays,

with each method yielding distinct query times. Additionally, their data structures support not only standard degree, adjacency, and neighborhood queries but also distance and shortest-path queries optimally.

- Acan et al. [1] developed succinct data structures for intersection graphs on a circle, encompassing classes such as *circle graphs, k polygon circle graphs*, and *trapezoid graphs*. They first established a general lower bound for these graph classes and then provided matching upper and lower bounds for succinct representations of each class. Acan et al. [2] also introduced the method of *partial coloring* for counting interval graphs, a technique that has since been widely adopted in the study of various graph classes [1, 5–7, 42]. Sauermann [39] later provided a unified framework for deriving tight lower bounds on the number of labeled graphs in any *semi-algebraic graph class*, which includes many of the aforementioned classes.
- Chakraborty et al. [10] introduced succinct data structures for *deterministic finite automata (DFA)* on n vertices with an alphabet size Σ, allowing for optimal time verification of whether a string is accepted by the DFA. Such automata can be viewed as directed regular graphs where each vertex has degree Σ. Cotumaccio et al. [16] provided related data structures for non-deterministic automata, using a parameter known as the *co-lex width*.

The methodologies behind succinct data structures for factorial-class graphs are remarkably diverse. While many of these data structures directly represent the input graph without decomposing it, some decompose the graphs into smaller subgraphs or find tree-like equivalents that are recursively decomposed into succinct representations. However, the query times for many of these structures remain suboptimal, and improving them to constant or near-constant times remains an open challenge. Another significant area for further investigation involves establishing concrete lower bounds for the trade-off between query times and space usage. Moreover, there are numerous important graph classes, such as *unit disk* and *disk graphs*, for which we have yet to develop succinct or even compact data structures.

5 Linear Classes

The most extensively studied graphs within the linear class are *trees* and *planar graphs*. Both of these graph classes hold significant theoretical interest and have numerous practical applications. Extensive research has been conducted in this domain, and the overarching strategy behind the development of these succinct data structures can be summarized as follows. The structure of interest is decomposed into small fragments of size $O(\log n)$, which are small enough to be processed in $o(n)$ time and space, with each fragment represented by an index. The relationships between these fragments are encoded in a graph G, composed of $O\left(\frac{n}{\log n}\right)$ such fragments, while the storage overhead remains $O(n)$ using classical pointer techniques. By grouping $\log n$ fragments into larger components of size $O(\log^2 n)$, connections between these larger and smaller fragments are managed with pointers of size $O(\log n)$ and $O(\log \log n)$, respectively. This multi-level approach ensures sublinear overheads of $O\left(\frac{n \log n}{\log^2 n}\right)$ and $O\left(\frac{n \log \log n}{\log n}\right)$, while maintaining the succinctness of the data structure. What follows is a brief survey of several data structures based on this template.

- For a comprehensive discussion on succinct data structures for *binary trees, cardinal trees, ordinal trees*, and *dynamic binary trees*, we direct readers to the excellent surveys by Munro and Rao [33] and Raman and Rao [38], which cover a wealth of developments in this area.
- Since the foundational work by Turán [43], *planar graphs* have been the focus of extensive research [3, 14, 15, 24, 26, 29, 32], culminating in the optimal data structures developed by Blelloch and Farzan [9]. Notably, they introduced a succinct data structure supporting constant-time adjacency, degree, and neighborhood queries for separable graphs—a broad class that includes *planar graphs, planar maps, bounded-genus graphs*, and others. These graphs are characterized by admitting separators of size $O(n^c)$, where $c < 1$.
- Another line of inquiry has focused on graph representations with bounded width parameters. Farzan and Kamali [19] developed compact data structures for graphs with *bounded treewidth*, while Kamali [27] extended this to *bounded clique-width graphs*, later made succinct with improved query times by Chakraborty et al. [13]. Kamali [28] also produced compact representations for graphs with *small bandwidth* and *small treedepth*. However, efficient data structures for graphs with parameters such as bounded twin-width or bounded rank-width remain unknown, presenting an intriguing challenge for future research.
- Building on the work of Uno et al. [44] and Blelloch and Farzan [9], Chakraborty et al. [12] introduced succinct data structures for a variety of graph classes, including *series-parallel, block-cactus, Ptolemaic, distance-hereditary, cographs*, and 3-*leaf power graphs*. These structures support optimal degree, adjacency, and neighborhood queries. Notably, their method achieves optimal space usage even in cases where the exact space lower bounds for these graph classes are not fully understood.
- Berg et al. [8] developed compact data structures for *polyominoes*, efficiently supporting both neighborhood queries, which report adjacent cells, and visibility queries, which determine whether a straight line can be drawn within the polyomino between two specified cells.

In conclusion, we have provided a brief overview of succinct and compact data structures for linear-class graphs. Several open questions remain for future exploration. Designing succinct or compact data structures for many important graph width parameters continues to be a significant challenge. Although Blelloch and Farzan [9] introduced a unified approach for designing succinct data structures for separable graphs, it is unclear whether this approach can be generalized to prove the existence of succinct data structures for all graphs within the linear class. While their method applies to some graphs in this class, it fails to extend to others. Despite decades of research into data structures for trees and planar graphs, the trade-offs between space redundancy and query time are still not fully understood, posing a significant open problem. Finally, it would be valuable to identify other important graph classes belonging to the linear class by establishing explicit counting lower bounds and designing optimal encodings for such graphs.

6 Conclusion

We have examined succinct and compact data structures for various graph classes that support efficient navigational query times. Beyond their theoretical significance, such data structures hold considerable practical value, particularly in light of the exponential increase in the volume of data requiring structured storage. Notably, the majority of these data structures can be constructed in linear time from their standard representations. However, for a few cases, it remains an open problem whether a linear-time construction can be achieved. Another significant challenge lies in optimizing the space required for preprocessing. Moreover, a wide array of graphs emerges from fields such as computational biology and computational geometry, yet there has been relatively little research dedicated to their succinct representation. Finally, establishing lower bounds for the time-space trade-offs for these graph classes presents a formidable open problem in the domain of data structures.

References

1. H. Acan, S. Chakraborty, S. Jo, K. Nakashima, K. Sadakane, S.R. Satti, Succinct navigational oracles for families of intersection graphs on a circle. Theor. Comput. Sci. 928:151–166 (2022)
2. H. Acan, S. Chakraborty, S. Jo, S.R. Satti, Succinct encodings for families of interval graphs. Algorithmica **83**(3), 776–794 (2021)
3. L.C. Aleardi, O. Devillers, G. Schaeffer, Optimal succinct representations of planar maps. In Nina Amenta and Otfried Cheong, editors, *Proceedings of the 22nd ACM Symposium on Computational Geometry, Sedona, Arizona, USA*, 5–7 June 2006 (ACM, 2006), pp. 309–318
4. V.E. Alekseev, Hereditary classes and coding of graphs. Problemy Kibernet **39**, 151–164 (1982)
5. G. Balakrishnan, S. Chakraborty, S. Jo, N.S. Narayanaswamy, K. Sadakane, Succinct data structure for graphs with d-dimensional t-representation, in *Data Compression Conference, DCC 2024, Snowbird, UT, USA*, 19–22 Mar. 2024, ed. by A. Bilgin, J.E. Fowler, J. Serra-Sagristà, Y. Ye, J.A. Storerpage (IEEE, 2024), p. 546
6. G. Balakrishnan, S. Chakraborty, N.S. Narayanaswamy, K. Sadakane, Succinct data structure for chordal graphs with bounded vertex leafage in *19th Scandinavian Symposium and Workshops on Algorithm Theory, SWAT 2024, June 12-14, 2024, Helsinki, Finland*, volume 294 of *LIPIcs*, ed. by H.L. Bodlaender (Schloss Dagstuhl - Leibniz-Zentrum für Informatik, 2024), pp. 4:1–4:16
7. G. Balakrishnan, S. Chakraborty, N.S. Narayanaswamy, K. Sadakane, Succinct data structure for path graphs. Inf. Comput. **296**, 105124 (2024)

8. M. Berg, S. Kamali, K. Ling, C. Sigrist, Space-efficient data structures for polyominoes and bar graphs, in *Data Compression Conference, DCC 2024, Snowbird, UT, USA*, 19–22 Mar 2024, ed. by A. Bilgin, J.E. Fowler, J. Serra-Sagristà, Y. Ye, J.A. Storer (IEEE, 2024), pp. 253–262
9. G.E. Blelloch, A. Farzan, Succinct representations of separable graphs, in *Combinatorial Pattern Matching, 21st Annual Symposium, CPM 2010, New York, NY, USA, June 21-23, 2010. Proceedings*, volume 6129 of *Lecture Notes in Computer Science*, ed. by A. Amir, L. Parida (Springer, 2010), pp. 138–150
10. S. Chakraborty, R. Grossi, K. Sadakane, S.R. Satti, Succinct representation for (non)deterministic finite automata. J. Comput. Syst. Sci. **131**, 1–12 (2023)
11. S. Chakraborty, S. Jo, Compact representation of interval graphs and circular-arc graphs of bounded degree and chromatic number. Theor. Comput. Sci. **941**, 156–166 (2023)
12. S. Chakraborty, S. Jo, K. Sadakane, S.R. Satti, Succinct data structures for series-parallel, block-cactus and 3-leaf power graphs, in *Combinatorial Optimization and Applications—15th International Conference, COCOA 2021, Tianjin, China, 17–19 Dec. 2021, Proceedings*, volume 13135 of *Lecture Notes in Computer Science*, ed. by D.-Z. Du, D. Du, C. Wu, D. Xu (Springer, 2021), pp. 416–430
13. S. Chakraborty, S. Jo, K. Sadakane, S.R. Satti, Succinct data structures for bounded clique-width graphs. Discret. Appl. Math. **352**, 55–68 (2024)
14. Y.-T. Chiang, C.-C. Lin, H.-I. Lu, Orderly spanning trees with applications to graph encoding and graph drawing, in *Proceedings of the Twelfth Annual Symposium on Discrete Algorithms, January 7-9, 2001, Washington, DC, USA*, ed. by S.R. Kosaraju (ACM/SIAM, 2001), pp. 506–515
15. R. Chih-Nan Chuang, A. Garg, X. He, M.-Y. Kao, H.-I. Lu, Compact encodings of planar graphs via canonical orderings and multiple parentheses, in *Automata, Languages and Programming, 25th International Colloquium, ICALP'98, Aalborg, Denmark, July 13–17, 1998, Proceedings*, volume 1443 of *Lecture Notes in Computer Science*, ed. by K. Guldstrand Larsen, S. Skyum, G. Winskel (Springer, 1998), pp. 118–129
16. N. Cotumaccio, N. Prezza, On indexing and compressing finite automata, in *Proceedings of the 2021 ACM-SIAM Symposium on Discrete Algorithms, SODA 2021, Virtual Conference*, 10–13 Jan. 2021, ed. by D. Marx (SIAM, 2021), pp. 2585–2599
17. R. Fagin, Degrees of acyclicity for hypergraphs and relational database schemes. J. ACM **30**(3), 514–550 (1983)
18. A. Farzan, J. Fischer, Compact representation of posets, in *Algorithms and Computation—22nd International Symposium, ISAAC 2011, Yokohama, Japan, 5–8 Dec. 2011. Proceedings*, volume 7074 of *Lecture Notes in Computer Science*, ed. by T. Asano, S.-I. Nakano, Y. Okamoto, O. Watanabe (Springer, 2011), pp. 302–311
19. A. Farzan, S. Kamali, Compact navigation and distance oracles for graphs with small treewidth, in *Automata, Languages and Programming—38th International Colloquium, ICALP 2011, Zurich, Switzerland, 4–8 July 2011, Proceedings, Part I*, volume 6755 of *Lecture Notes in Computer Science*, ed. by L. Aceto, M. Henzinger, J. Sgall (Springer, 2011), pp. 268–280
20. A. Farzan, J. Ian Munro, Succinct encoding of arbitrary graphs. Theor. Comput. Sci. **513**, 38–52 (2013)
21. C. Gavoille, C. Paul, Optimal distance labeling for interval graphs and related graph families. SIAM J. Discret. Math. **22**(3), 1239–1258 (2008)
22. M. He, J. Ian Munro, K. Wu, Succinct data structures for bounded degree/chromatic number interval graphs, in *Data Compression Conference, DCC 2024, Snowbird, UT, USA, March 19-22, 2024*, ed. by A. Bilgin, J.E. Fowler, J. Serra-Sagristà, Y. Ye, J.A. Storer (IEEE, 2024), pp. 502–511
23. M. He, J. Ian Munro, K. Wu, Succinct data structures for path graphs and chordal graphs revisited, in *Data Compression Conference, DCC 2024, Snowbird, UT, USA, 19–22 Mar. 2024* (IEEE, 2024), pp. 492–501
24. X. He, M.-Y. Kao, H.-I Lu, A fast general methodology for information—theoretically optimal encodings of graphs, in *Algorithms—ESA '99, 7th Annual European Symposium, Prague, Czech Republic, July 16-18, 1999, Proceedings*, volume 1643 of *Lecture Notes in Computer Science*, ed. by J. Nesetril (Springer, 1999), pp. 540–549

25. B. Hendrickson, T.G. Kolda, Graph partitioning models for parallel computing. Parallel Comput. **26**(12), 1519–1534 (2000)
26. G. Jacobson, Space-efficient static trees and graphs, in *30th Annual Symposium on Foundations of Computer Science, Research Triangle Park, North Carolina, USA*, 30 Oct.–1 Nov. 1989 (IEEE Computer Society, 1989), pp. 549–554
27. S. Kamali, Compact representation of graphs of small clique-width. Algorithmica **80**(7), 2106–2131 (2018)
28. S. Kamali, Compact representation of graphs with bounded bandwidth or treedepth. Inf. Comput. **285**(Part), 104867 (2022)
29. H.-I. Lu, Linear-time compression of bounded-genus graphs into information-theoretically optimal number of bits, in *Proceedings of the Thirteenth Annual ACM-SIAM Symposium on Discrete Algorithms, 6–8 Jan. 2002, San Francisco, CA, USA*, ed. by D. Eppstein (ACM/SIAM, 2002), pp. 223–224
30. A. Lubiw, Doubly lexical orderings of matrices. SIAM J. Comput. **16**(5), 854–879 (1987)
31. J. Ian Munro, P.K. Nicholson, Succinct posets. Algorithmica **76**(2), 445–473 (2016)
32. J. Ian Munro, V. Raman, Succinct representation of balanced parentheses and static trees. SIAM J. Comput. **31**(3), 762–776 (2001)
33. J. Ian Munro, S. Srinivasa Rao, Succinct representation of data structures, in *Handbook of Data Structures and Applications*, ed. by D.P. Mehta, S. Sahni (Chapman and Hall/CRC, 2004)
34. J. Ian Munro, B. Sandlund, C. Sinnamon, Space-efficient data structures for lattices, in *17th Scandinavian Symposium and Workshops on Algorithm Theory, SWAT 2020, 22–24 June 2020, Tórshavn, Faroe Islands*, volume 162 of *LIPIcs*, ed. by S. Albers (Schloss Dagstuhl-Leibniz-Zentrum für Informatik, 2020), pp. 31:1–31:22
35. J. Ian Munro, C. Sinnamon, Time and space efficient representations of distributive lattices, in *Proceedings of the Twenty-Ninth Annual ACM-SIAM Symposium on Discrete Algorithms, SODA 2018, New Orleans, LA, USA, 7–10 Jan. 2018*, ed. by A. Czumaj (SIAM, 2018), pp. 550–567
36. J. Ian Munro, K. Wu, Succinct data structures for chordal graphs, in *29th International Symposium on Algorithms and Computation, ISAAC 2018, 16–19 Dec. 2018, Jiaoxi, Yilan, Taiwan*, volume 123 of *LIPIcs* (Schloss Dagstuhl - Leibniz-Zentrum für Informatik, 2018), pp. 67:1–67:12
37. J. Pach, B.A. Reed, Y. Yuditsky, Almost all string graphs are intersection graphs of plane convex sets. Discret. Comput. Geom. **63**(4), 888–917 (2020)
38. R. Raman, S. Srinivasa Rao, Succinct representations of ordinal trees, in *Space-Efficient Data Structures, Streams, and Algorithms—Papers in Honor of J. Ian Munro on the Occasion of His 66th Birthday*, volume 8066 of *Lecture Notes in Computer Science*, ed. by A. Brodnik, A. López-Ortiz, V. Raman, A. Viola (Springer, 2013), pp. 319–332
39. L. Sauermann, On the speed of algebraically defined graph classes. Adv. Math. **380**, 107593 (2021)
40. J.P. Spinrad, Nonredundant 1's in gamma-free matrices. SIAM J. Discret. Math. **8**(2), 251–257 (1995)
41. J.P. Spinrad, *Efficient Graph Representations*, volume 19 of *Fields Institute Monographs* (American Mathematical Society, 2003)
42. K. Tsakalidis, S. Wild, V. Zamaraev, Succinct permutation graphs. Algorithmica **85**(2), 509–543 (2023)
43. G. Turán, On the succinct representation of graphs. Discret. Appl. Math. **8**(3), 289–294 (1984)
44. T. Uno, R. Uehara, S.-I. Nakano, Bounding the number of reduced trees, cographs, and series-parallel graphs by compression. Discret. Math. Alg. Appl. **5**(2) (2013)
45. T. Yanagita, S. Chakraborty, K. Sadakane, S.R. Satti, Space-efficient data structure for posets with applications, in *18th Scandinavian Symposium and Workshops on Algorithm Theory, SWAT 2022, 27–29 June 2022, Tórshavn, Faroe Islands*, volume 227 of *LIPIcs* (Schloss Dagstuhl - Leibniz-Zentrum für Informatik, 2022), pp. 33:1–33:16

A Satisfiability Algorithm for Depth Two Circuits with a Sub-Quadratic Number of Symmetric and Threshold Gates

Suguru Tamaki

Abstract We consider depth 2 unbounded fan-in circuits with symmetric and linear threshold gates. We present a deterministic algorithm that, given such a circuit with n variables and m gates, counts the number of satisfying assignments in time $2^{n-\Omega\left(\left(\frac{n}{\sqrt{m}\cdot\mathrm{poly}(\log n)}\right)^a\right)}$ for some constant $a > 0$. Our algorithm runs in time super-polynomially faster than 2^n if $m = O(n^2/\log^b n)$ for some constant $b > 0$. Previously, such algorithms were only known for bounded depth circuits with linear threshold gates and a slightly super-linear number of *wires* [Impagliazzo-Paturi-Schneider, FOCS 2013 and Chen-Santhanam-Srinivasan, CCC 2016]. We also show that depth 2 circuits with $O(n^2/\log^b n)$ symmetric and linear threshold gates in total cannot compute an explicit function computable by a deterministic $2^{O(n)}$-time Turing machine with an NP oracle. Previously, even slightly super-linear lower bounds on the number of gates were not known until recently Kane and Williams [STOC 2016] showed that depth 2 linear threshold circuits with $o(n^{3/2}/\log^3 n)$ gates cannot compute an explicit function computable in linear time.

1 Introduction

We are concerned with circuits that consist of unbounded fan-in symmetric and linear threshold gates. Let $x_1, x_2, \ldots, x_n$ be Boolean variables and $f : \{0,1\}^n \to \{0,1\}$ be a Boolean function. We say f is *symmetric* if there exists a function $g : \mathbb{Z} \to \{0,1\}$ such that $f(x) = g(\sum_{i=1}^n x_i)$ holds. We say f is a *linear threshold* function (LTF) if there exist $w_0, w_1, \ldots, w_n \in \mathbb{Z}$ such that $f(x) = \mathrm{sgn}(w_0 + \sum_{i=1}^n w_i x_i)$ holds, where $\mathrm{sgn} : \mathbb{Z} \to \{0,1\}$ is the sign function defined as $\mathrm{sgn}(y) = 1$ if and only if $y \geq 0$.

In this paper, we present satisfiability algorithms and circuit size lower bounds for depth 2 circuits with symmetric and linear threshold gates as described in

S. Tamaki (✉)
University of Hyogo, 8-2-1 Gakuennishi-machi, Nishi-ku, Kobe, Hyogo 651-2197, Japan
e-mail: tamak@sis.u-hyogo.ac.jp

S. Minato et al. (eds.), *Algorithmic Foundations for Social Advancement*,
https://doi.org/10.1007/978-981-96-0668-9_20

the next section. Note that each gate of such a circuit may be of a different type, e.g., $g_1(\sum_{i=1}^n x_i)$, $g_2(\sum_{i=1}^n x_i)$, ..., $\mathrm{sgn}(w_{1,0} + \sum_{i=1}^n w_{1,i}x_i)$, $\mathrm{sgn}(w_{2,0} + \sum_{i=1}^n w_{2,i}x_i)$, ...

1.1 Our Contribution

Satisfiability Algorithms

In this paper, we present the following satisfiability algorithms.

Theorem 1 (Main 1) *There exist a constant $c > 0$ and a deterministic algorithm that, given a depth 2 circuit C with n variables and m gates, where each gate is either symmetric or linear threshold, runs in time $2^{n-\Omega\left(\left(\frac{n}{\sqrt{m}\cdot\mathrm{poly}(\log n)}\right)^c\right)}$ and counts the number of satisfying assignments for C.*

Previously, Impagliazzo, Paturi and Schneider [53] showed that the satisfiability of a depth 2 linear threshold circuit with n variables and m *wires* can be solved in randomized time $2^{n-\mu(m/n)n}$, where $\mu(c) = 1/c^{O(c^2)}$. Chen and Santhanam [27] improved the running time as $\mu(c) = 1/c^{O(c)}$. Chen, Santhanam and Srinivasan [28] showed that the satisfiability of a depth d linear threshold circuit with n variables and $n^{1+\varepsilon_d}$ wires can be solved in randomized time $2^{n-n^{\varepsilon_d}}$, where $\varepsilon_d = 1/2^{O(d)}$.

Note that a depth 2 linear threshold circuit with m gates may have $O(mn)$ wires. We are not aware of satisfiability algorithms that beat brute force search for depth 2 circuits with symmetric and linear threshold gates as Theorem 1 or even for depth 2 circuits with only symmetric gates. To summarize, our algorithm is deterministic, can solve a counting version of the satisfiability problem and handle larger size circuits (of depth 2) with additional gate types. Our algorithm can be generalized to handle bounded depth layered circuits, where each layer consists of either AND/OR/XOR gates or symmetric and linear threshold gates and the fan-in of symmetric and linear threshold gates satisfies some condition.

1.1.1 Circuit Lower Bounds

As a byproduct of Theorem 1, we obtain the following circuit lower bounds.

Theorem 2 (Main 2) *There exist a language $L \in \mathrm{E}^{\mathrm{NP}}$ and a constant $c > 0$ such that any family of depth 2 circuits with $O(n^2/\log^c n)$ gates, where each gate is either symmetric or linear threshold, cannot compute L.*

Here E^{NP} is the class of languages computable by deterministic $2^{O(n)}$-time NP-oracle Turing machines. It has been a longstanding open question whether E^{NP} can be computed by depth 2 circuits with $n^{1.01}$ threshold gates until very recently Kane and Williams [62] showed that depth 2 circuits with $o(n^{3/2}/\log^3 n)$ linear threshold gates cannot compute an explicit function computable in linear time.

Again we are not aware of non-trivial lower bounds for depth 2 circuits with symmetric and linear threshold gates as Theorem 2 or even for depth 2 circuits with only symmetric gates. To summarize, we show lower bounds for larger size circuits with additional gate types computing a less explicit function.

1.2 Background and Related Work

The motivation for studying the satisfiability problem of depth 2 linear threshold circuits is twofold: First, the problem contains as special cases both of the maximum satisfiability problem and 0-1 integer linear programming, which have been well studied in the area of exponential time algorithms, e.g., [27, 34, 50, 89, 90, 99] and implementations of practical solvers. Second, proving super-polynomial lower bounds against depth 2 linear threshold circuits is one of the major open questions in Boolean circuit complexity. Below we elaborate on the second point.

Bounded depth linear threshold circuits have been studied extensively as a model of neural network. Such circuits are powerful enough to implement arithmetic operations such as iterated multiplication, division and powering; see, e.g., [71] and even candidate pseudorandom function generators [57, 73, 76]. The latter fact explains the difficulty of proving lower bounds for bounded depth linear threshold circuits by the "Natural Proof" barrier due to Razborov and Rudich [20, 83, 107] although it is believed that such circuits cannot compute some functions in NP or even in P. There has been much effort to reveal the expressive power of linear threshold circuits; see, e.g., [32, 33, 35, 38, 40–42, 45, 48, 52, 59–61, 66, 75, 81, 82, 84], to name a few.

The connection between satisfiability algorithms and circuit lower bounds, developed by Williams and subsequent authors [16, 54, 102, 103, 105, 107, 109], is a promising approach to avoid such barriers; see also [80, 86, 104, 108] for surveys. Since the success of using the connection to actually prove new circuit lower bounds, i.e., super-polynomial lower bounds for $\mathbf{ACC}^0$ circuits computing a language in NEXP [105], many satisfiability algorithms that beat brute force search have been designed for various circuit classes [4, 5, 24, 77, 79, 94, 109]. Interestingly, some papers showed average-case circuit lower bounds directly from the analyses of their satisfiability algorithms [11, 18, 22, 23, 37, 51, 85, 91, 92].

The results of this paper were first announced as [95]. Alman, Chan and Williams [2] independently obtained similar and more general results around the same time. Since then, we have seen progress on circuit satisfiability algorithms [3, 12, 13, 31, 56, 58, 64, 65, 69, 70, 78, 93], circuit lower bounds [1, 21, 26, 43, 44, 49, 55, 63, 67, 68, 97, 100, 101, 110] and the connection between them [17, 19, 25, 29, 39, 87, 111, 112]. However, improving Theorems 1, 2 to those with "super"-quadratic number of gates still remains an open problem.

1.3 Techniques

The polynomial method is a powerful technique in Boolean circuit complexity [8]. In his remarkable result, Williams [105] used the polynomial method to design satisfiability algorithms beating brute force search for $\mathbf{ACC}^0$ circuits. Since then, Williams and his coauthors have developed algorithms for many interesting problems such as the circuit satisfiability problem for restricted classes of circuits [109], all-pairs shortest paths [30], Hamming nearest neighbors [6] and related problems [7]; see also [106].

We follow the approach of [109] that gives satisfiability algorithms beating brute force search for $\mathbf{ACC}^0 \circ \mathbf{THR}$ and $\mathbf{ACC}^0 \circ \mathbf{SYM}$ circuits. The approach is summarized as follows: (1) Given an n-variate circuit $C \in \mathbf{ACC}^0 \circ \mathbf{THR}$, consider a circuit $C'(y) := \bigvee_{a\in\{0,1\}^{n'}} C(y, a)$ for some $n' < n$. (2) Represent C' as a circuit in $\mathbf{SYM} \circ \mathbf{SYM}$ using simulation techniques, in particular, the simulation of Beigel and Tarui [15] that transforms a circuit in $\mathbf{ACC}^0$ to a circuit in $\mathbf{SYM} \circ \mathbf{AND}$. (3) Apply the "fast evaluation algorithm" for $\mathbf{SYM} \circ \mathbf{SYM}$ to obtain the truth table of C'.

We implement the above approach, focusing on Item (2), for $\mathbf{THR} \circ \mathbf{THR}$ circuits. If we use the construction of "probabilistic polynomials" for symmetric and linear threshold functions due to Srinivasan [88], we can represent C' as a "probabilistic circuit" in $\mathbf{SYM} \circ \mathbf{SYM}$. This implementation of Item (2) is sufficient to obtain randomized algorithms.

In order to design deterministic algorithms, we derandomize probabilistic polynomials of [88]. It turns out that *pseudorandom generators for space-bounded computation* due to Nisan [74] are sufficient for our purpose. We also use *modulus-amplifying polynomials* [98, 113] to complete a deterministic implementation of Item (2) in a similar way to [15, 30].

Our circuit lower bounds follow from the connection between satisfiability algorithms and circuit lower bounds, in particular, the one due to Ben-Sasson and Viola [16].

2 Preliminaries

We use the following notations: $\mathbb{Z}$ is the set of integers, $\mathbb{N}$ is the set of natural numbers, i.e., non-negative integers, $\mathbb{Z}_m$ is the quotient ring of integers modulo m, identified with $\{0, 1, \ldots, m-1\}$, and $\mathbb{F}_2$ is the finite field of order 2, identified with $\{0, 1\}$.

For a positive integer n, $[n] := \{1, 2, \ldots, n\}$. For real numbers $a < b$, (a, b) is the open interval between a and b. For $y \in \mathbb{Z}$, $|y|$ is the absolute value of y. For a finite set S, $|S|$ is the cardinality of S. For $x \in \{0, 1\}^n$, $|x|$ is the *Hamming weight* of x, i.e., $|x| = \sum_{i=1}^{n} x_i$.

The logarithm of x to base 2 is $\lg x$ and that to base e is $\ln x$. We use random access machines as our computation model.

2.1 Probability and Derandomization

We use the following results in Sect. 3.1.

Lemma 1 (The Chernoff-Hoeffding bound [46]) *Let $X_1, \ldots, X_n$ be independent and identically distributed Bernoulli random variables with $\mathbf{Pr}[X_i = 1] = 1 - \mathbf{Pr}[X_i = 0] = 1/m$. Then, it holds that*

$$\mathbf{Pr}[|n/m - \sum_{i=1}^{n} X_i| > t] \leq 2e^{-2t^2/n}.$$

Lemma 2 (Nisan [74]) *Let $f : \mathbb{Z}_m^n \to \{0, 1\}$ be a function computable in space $O(\lg(n \lg m))$. Then, there exists a function $G : \{0, 1\}^\ell \to \mathbb{Z}_m^n$ with $\ell = O(\lg^2((n \lg m)/\varepsilon))$ such that*

- $|\mathbf{Pr}[f(x) = 1] - \mathbf{Pr}[f(G(y)) = 1]| \leq \varepsilon$*, where x and y are respectively sampled from $\mathbb{Z}_m^n$ and $\{0, 1\}^\ell$ uniformly at random, and*
- *G is computable in time* $\text{poly}(n \lg m)$.

2.2 Boolean Circuits

Let $x_1, x_2, \ldots, x_n$ be Boolean variables and $f : \{0, 1\}^n \to \{0, 1\}$ be a Boolean function. We say f is W-*sum* if there exists a function $g : \mathbb{Z} \to \{0, 1\}$ and $w_1, \ldots, w_n \in \mathbb{N}$ with $\sum_{i=1}^n w_i \leq W$ such that $f(x) = g(\sum_{i=1}^n w_i x_i)$ holds. Note that we can realize a W-sum function as a W-variate symmetric function by regarding $w_i x_i$ as a sum of w_i variables. In what follows, we identify Boolean functions and logic gates.

We denote by **AND**, **OR**, **XOR**, **SYM**, $\mathbf{SUM}_W$, **THR** the set of AND gates, the set of OR gates, the set of XOR gates, the set of symmetric gates, the set of W-sum gates and the set of linear threshold gates, respectively. Let $\mathcal{G}_0, \mathcal{G}_1, \ldots, \mathcal{G}_{d-1} \in \{\mathbf{AND}, \mathbf{OR}, \mathbf{XOR}, \mathbf{SYM}, \mathbf{SUM}_W, \mathbf{THR}\}$ be sets of logic gates. We denote by $\mathcal{G}_0 \circ \mathcal{G}_1 \circ \cdots \circ \mathcal{G}_{d-1}$ the set of depth d unbounded-fan-in layered Boolean circuits such that layer i contains gates from $\mathcal{G}_i$ and all the gates at layer i are only fed by gates at layer $i + 1$. Layer 0 corresponds to the output gate and layer d consists of input variables and constants 0, 1. We allow inputs and outputs of gates to be negated unless otherwise specified.

We need the following upper bounds on the weights of linear threshold functions in Sect. 3.3.

Lemma 3 (Muroga [72]) *For all $w_0, w_1, \ldots, w_n \in \mathbb{Z}$, there exist $w'_0, w'_1, \ldots, w'_n \in \mathbb{Z}$ with $|w'_i| = 2^{O(n \lg n)}$ such that* $\text{sgn}(w_0 + \sum_{i=1}^n w_i x_i) = \text{sgn}(w'_0 + \sum_{i=1}^n w'_i x_i)$ *holds. In addition, $w'_0, w'_1, \ldots, w'_n$ can be efficiently obtained.*

We use the following results in Sect. 4.

Lemma 4 (Maciel-Thérien [71]; see also Sect. 2.2 in Williams [109]) *There exists a positive integer* $c_{\mathbf{mt}}$ *such that for all* n*-variate* $f \in \mathbf{THR}$*, there exists a circuit*

$$C \in \mathbf{OR} \circ \mathbf{AND} \circ \mathbf{XOR} \circ \mathbf{OR} \circ \mathbf{AND} \circ \mathbf{SYM}$$

that is equivalent to f *and consists of at most* $n^{c_{\mathrm{mt}}}$ *wires.*

Lemma 5 (Beigel [9]) *For all circuit* $C \in \mathbf{AND} \circ \mathbf{SYM}$ *whose AND gate at layer* 0 *has fan-in* t_1 *and symmetric gates at layer* 1 *have fan-in at most* t_2*, there exists a circuit* $C' \in \mathbf{SYM}$ *that is equivalent to* C *and whose fan-in is at most* $(t_2 + 1)^{t_1}$.

Lemma 6 (Williams [109]) *There exists a positive constant* $c_{\mathbf{w}}$ *and an algorithm that, given an* n*-variate circuit* $C \in \mathbf{SYM} \circ \mathbf{SYM}$ *whose symmetric gate at layer* 0 *has fan-in at most* t_1 *and symmetric gates at layer* 1 *have fan-in at most* t_2 *such that* $t_1 t_2 \leq 2^{c_{\mathrm{w}} n}$*, prints the truth table of* C *in time* $\mathrm{poly}(n)2^n$.

2.3 Polynomials

Let $x_1, x_2, \ldots, x_n$ be formal variables and $K \in \{\mathbb{F}_2, \mathbb{Z}\}$. In this paper, each variable always takes the values 0 or 1, hence the identity $x_i^2 = x_i$ holds. A *monomial* is a product of variables, i.e., $\prod_{i \in S} x_i$ for some $S \subseteq [n]$. For $S = \emptyset$, we regard $\prod_{i \in S} x_i$ as 1. We can represent a K*-polynomial* P as a sum of terms, of the form $P(x) = \sum_{S \subseteq [n]} a_S \prod_{i \in S} x_i$, where $a_S \in K$. Whenever we consider a $\mathbb{Z}$-polynomial, $|a_S| = 2^{O(n)}$ is assumed unless otherwise stated. The *degree* of P, denoted by $\deg(P)$, is defined as

$$\deg(P) := \max\{|S| \mid S \subseteq [n], a_S \neq 0\}.$$

Note that we can regard an $\mathbb{F}_2$-polynomial P as a Boolean circuit in $\mathbf{XOR} \circ \mathbf{AND}$ as

$$P(x) = \bigoplus_{S \subseteq [n]} \left(a_S \bigwedge_{i \in S} x_i \right).$$

We need the following combinatorial facts in Sects. 3 and 4.

Lemma 7 *The number of monomials of degree at most* k *is* $M(n,k) = \sum_{i=0}^{k} \binom{n}{i}$*. If* $k \leq n/2$, $M(n,k) \leq k\binom{n}{k}$.

Lemma 8 (Powering) *Given an* n*-variate degree* k *polynomial* P *represented as a sum of terms, and a positive integer* d*, we can represent* P^d*, the* d*th power of* P*, as a sum of terms in time*

$$\mathrm{poly}(n) \sum_{i=1}^{d-1} M(n,k) M(n,ik) \leq \mathrm{poly}(n) M(n,dk).$$

Lemma 9 (Composition) *Let p be a degree d_1 polynomial in n_1 variables and $p_1, p_2, \ldots, p_{n_1}$ be degree d_2 polynomials in the same n_2 variables. Then, $p(p_1, p_2, \ldots, p_{n_1})$ can be represented as a sum of terms in time* $\mathrm{poly}(n_1, n_2)M(n_1, d_1)M(n_2, d_1 d_2)$.

We use the following construction of polynomials approximating symmetric functions in Sect. 3.1.

Lemma 10 (Corollary 2.7 in Bhatnagar-Gopalan-Lipton [10], Lemma 3.1 in Alman-Williams [6]) *For all n-variate function $f \in$ **SYM** and integers $s \geq 0, t \geq 1$ with $s + t \leq n$, there exists an $\mathbb{F}_2$-polynomial p of degree at most $O(t)$ such that $f(x) = p(x)$ holds if $s \leq |x| \leq s + t$. In addition, p can be constructed in time* $\mathrm{poly}(n)\binom{n}{O(t)}$.

We need the following construction of *modulus-amplifying polynomials* [98, 113] in Sect. 4.

Lemma 11 (Beigel-Tarui [15]) *For every positive integer ℓ, the degree $(2\ell - 1)$ univariate $\mathbb{Z}$-polynomial*

$$F_\ell(y) := 1 - (1 - y)^\ell \sum_{j=0}^{\ell-1} \binom{\ell + j - 1}{j} y^j$$

satisfies

- *if $y = 0 \bmod 2$, then $F_\ell(y) = 0 \bmod 2^\ell$,*
- *if $y = 1 \bmod 2$, then $F_\ell(y) = 1 \bmod 2^\ell$.*

In addition, for $0 \leq i \leq 2\ell - 1$, the coefficient of y^i in the polynomial F_ℓ has magnitude at most $2^{O(\ell)}$.

2.4 Probabilistic Polynomials

For a Boolean function $f : \{0, 1\}^n \to \{0, 1\}$, a probability distribution $\mathcal{P}$ over polynomials is an *ε-error probabilistic polynomial* for f if for all $x \in \{0, 1\}^n$, $\mathbf{Pr}_{p \sim \mathcal{P}}[f(x) \neq p(x)] \leq \varepsilon$ holds [96]. The *degree* of a probabilistic polynomial $\mathcal{P}$ is the maximum degree of polynomials in the support of $\mathcal{P}$, i.e., $\max\{\deg(p) \mid \mathbf{Pr}_{q \sim \mathcal{P}}[p = q] > 0\}$. A probabilistic polynomial $\mathcal{P}$ has *r-randomness* if we can sample a polynomial from $\mathcal{P}$ with r uniformly random bits.

We need the following construction of time and randomness efficient probabilistic polynomials for AND/OR functions in Sect. 4.

Lemma 12 (Beigel-Reingold-Spielman and Tarui [14, 96]) *For every $\varepsilon \in (0, 1/2)$, there exists an ε-error probabilistic $O(\lg^2 n \cdot \lg(1/\varepsilon))$-randomness probabilistic $\mathbb{F}_2$-polynomial $\mathcal{P}$ of degree $d = O(\lg n \cdot \lg(1/\varepsilon))$ for n-variate AND/OR functions. Furthermore, we can sample a polynomial from $\mathcal{P}$ in time $O(\mathrm{poly}(n)\binom{n}{d})$.*

3 Randomness Efficient Probabilistic Polynomials

In this section, we present the main technical ingredients of our satisfiability algorithms, that is, a time and randomness efficient version of probabilistic polynomials for weighted symmetric and linear threshold functions due to Srinivasan [88].

Lemma 13 (Randomness efficient version of Theorem 11 in [88]) *For every* $\varepsilon \in (0, 1/2)$, $W \in \mathbb{N}$ *and an* n*-variate* $f \in \mathbf{SUM}_W$, f *has an* ε*-error* $O(\lg^2((n \lg\lg W)/\varepsilon))$*-randomness probabilistic* $\mathbb{F}_2$*-polynomial* $\mathcal{P}$ *of degree* $d = O(\lg^4 W \sqrt{n} \lg(1/\varepsilon))$. *Furthermore, we can sample a polynomial from* $\mathcal{P}$ *in time* $O(\mathrm{poly}(n)\binom{n}{d})$.

Lemma 14 (Randomness efficient version of Theorem 12 in [88]) *For every* $\varepsilon \in (0, 1/2)$ *and an* n*-variate* $f \in \mathbf{THR}$, f *has an* ε*-error* $O(\lg^2(n/\varepsilon))$*-randomness probabilistic* $\mathbb{F}_2$*-polynomial* $\mathcal{P}$ *of degree* $d = O(\lg^5 n \sqrt{n} \lg(1/\varepsilon))$. *Furthermore, we can sample a polynomial from* $\mathcal{P}$ *in time* $O(\mathrm{poly}(n)\binom{n}{d})$.

Lemma 15 below is the key result of this section. First we need some definitions. For $m \in \mathbb{N}$, $r \in \mathbb{Z}_m$, $w \in \mathbb{Z}_m^n$, we define functions $\mathrm{mod}_{m,r}^n : \{0,1\}^n \to \{0,1\}$, $\mathrm{mod}_{m,r,w}^n : \{0,1\}^n \to \{0,1\}$, as follows:

- $\mathrm{mod}_{m,r}^n(x) = 1$ if and only if $\sum_{i=1}^n x_i \equiv r \bmod m$,
- $\mathrm{mod}_{m,r,w}^n(x) = 1$ if and only if $\sum_{i=1}^n w_i x_i \equiv r \bmod m$.

Lemma 15 (Randomness efficient version of Lemma 13 in [88]) *For every* $\varepsilon \in (0, 1/2)$, $\mathrm{mod}_{m,r,w}^n$ *has an* ε*-error* $O(\lg^2((n \lg m)/\varepsilon))$*-randomness probabilistic* $\mathbb{F}_2$*-polynomial* $\mathcal{P}$ *of degree* $d = O(m\sqrt{n} \lg(1/\varepsilon))$. *Furthermore, we can sample a polynomial from* $\mathcal{P}$ *in time* $O(\mathrm{poly}(n)\binom{n}{d})$.

We prove the above lemma in the next section. The proof is based on the observation that uniformly random bits in the construction of [88] can be replaced by the outputs of the pseudorandom generators for space-bounded computation due to Lemma 2.

Once we establish Lemma 15, we can prove Lemmas 13 and 14 following the lead of [88] with careful calculation of parameters. The proofs are given in Sects. 3.2 and 3.3 respectively.

3.1 Weighted Modulo Functions

In this section, we prove Lemma 15.

Fix integers $m \geq 2$ and $r \in \mathbb{Z}_m$ and an integer vector $w \in \mathbb{Z}_m^n$. Let $v \in \mathbb{Z}_m^n$. We define functions $M_{m,r} : \mathbb{Z}_m \to \{0,1\}$, $M_{m,r,w,v}^n : \{0,1\}^n \to \{0,1\}^n$ and a set $R_{m,r,v}^n \subseteq \mathbb{Z}_m^{m-1}$ as follows:

- $M_{m,r}(y) = 1$ if and only if $y \equiv r \bmod m$,
- $(M^n_{m,r,w,v}(x))_i := M_{m,r}(w_i x_i + v_i)$,
- $R^n_{m,r,v} := \{(r_1, r_2, \ldots, r_{m-1}) \in \mathbb{Z}_m^{m-1} \mid \sum_{i=1}^{m-1} i r_i \equiv r + \sum_{i=1}^{n} v_i \bmod m\}$.

Note that $M_{m,r}(w_i x_i + v_i) \in \{0, 1, x_i, 1 - x_i\}$ holds for fixed m, r, w_i, v_i. The following lemma shows how to reduce the evaluation of $\mathrm{mod}^n_{m,r,w}(x)$ to the evaluation of $\mathrm{mod}^n_{m,r'}(x')$ for many pairs (r', x').

Lemma 16 (Sect. 3.1 in [88]) *For all $v \in \mathbb{Z}_m^n$ and $x \in \{0,1\}^n$, it holds that*

$$\mathrm{mod}^n_{m,r,w}(x) = \sum_{u \in R_{m,r,v}} \bigwedge_{i=1}^{m-1} \mathrm{mod}^n_{m,u_i}(M^n_{m,r,w,v}(x)).$$

Let $P^n_{m,r} : \{0,1\}^n \to \{0,1\}$ be an $\mathbb{F}_2$-polynomial of degree $O(t)$ such that $P^n_{m,r}(x) = \mathrm{mod}^n_{m,r}(x)$ if $|x| \in \{\lfloor n/m \rfloor - t, \ldots, \lfloor n/m \rfloor + t\}$. By Lemma 10, the existence of $P^n_{m,r}$ is guaranteed. In addition, $P^n_{m,r}$ can be constructed in time $\mathrm{poly}(n)\binom{n}{O(t)}$. Let us define an $\mathbb{F}_2$-polynomial $Q^n_{m,r,w,v} : \{0,1\}^n \to \{0,1\}$ as follows:

$$Q^n_{m,r,w,v}(x) := \sum_{u \in R_{m,r,v}} \prod_{i=1}^{m-1} P^n_{m,u_i}(M^n_{m,r,w,v}(x)).$$

The following lemma is immediate from the property of $P^n_{m,r}$ and the definition of $Q^n_{m,r,w,v}$.

Lemma 17 *If $|M^n_{m,r,w,v}(x)| \in \{\lfloor n/m \rfloor - t, \ldots, \lfloor n/m \rfloor + t\}$, then $Q^n_{m,r,w,v}(x) = \mathrm{mod}^n_{m,r,w}(x)$ holds.*

We are ready to prove Lemma 15.

Proof of Lemma 15 If we select $v_i \in \mathbb{Z}_m$ uniformly at random, then we have $\mathbf{Pr}_{v_i}[M_{m,r}(w_i x_i + v_i) = 1] = 1/m$. Hence, if we select $v \in \mathbb{Z}_m^n$ uniformly at random, then by Lemma 1, we have

$$\mathop{\mathbf{Pr}}_{v}[|M^n_{m,r,w,v}(x)| \notin \{\lfloor n/m \rfloor - t, \ldots, \lfloor n/m \rfloor + t\}] \le 2e^{-2t^2/n}.$$

Let $\ell = O(\lg^2((n \lg m)/\delta))$ and $G : \{0,1\}^\ell \to \mathbb{Z}_m^n$ be the pseudorandom generator due to Lemma 2. Since $|M^n_{m,r,w,v}(x)|$ as a function of v can be computed in space $O(\lg(n \lg m))$, if we select $s \in \{0,1\}^\ell$ uniformly at random, then we have

$$\mathop{\mathbf{Pr}}_{s}[|M^n_{m,r,w,G(s)}(x)| \notin \{\lfloor n/m \rfloor - t, \ldots, \lfloor n/m \rfloor + t\}] \le 2e^{-2t^2/n} + \delta.$$

This implies

$$\mathop{\mathbf{Pr}}_{s}[Q^n_{m,r,w,G(s)}(x) \neq \mathrm{mod}^n_{m,r,w}(x)] \le 2e^{-2t^2/n} + \delta.$$

If we set $t = \sqrt{(n/2)\ln(4/\varepsilon)}$ and $\delta = \varepsilon/2$, then the right-hand side is at most ε and the degree of $Q^n_{m,r,w,G(s)}(x)$ is $O(tm)$. This completes the proof.

3.2 Weighted Sum Functions

In this section, we prove Lemma 13.

Fix a function $g : \mathbb{Z} \to \{0, 1\}$ and natural numbers $w_1, \ldots, w_n$ with $\sum_{i=1}^n w_i = W$. Let $f(x) = g(\sum_{i=1}^n w_i x_i)$, $\ell := \lceil \lg W \rceil + 2$, $p_1 < \cdots < p_\ell$ be first ℓ primes and $s := \sum_{i=1}^{\ell} p_i$.

Note that $\prod_{i=1}^{\ell} p_i > 2^\ell > 2W$. By the prime number theorem, $p_\ell = O(\lg W \cdot \lg\lg W)$ holds and this implies $s = O(\lg^2 W \cdot \lg\lg W)$.

We define functions $M^n_{m,w} : \{0, 1\}^n \to \{0, 1\}^m$ for $m \in \mathbb{N}$ and $M^n_w : \{0, 1\}^n \to \{0, 1\}^s$ as follows:

- $M^n_{m,w}(x) := (\mathrm{mod}^n_{m,0,w}(x), \ldots, \mathrm{mod}^n_{m,m-1,w}(x))$,
- $M^n_w(x) := (M^n_{p_1,w}(x), \ldots, M^n_{p_\ell,w}(x))$.

Since we can reconstruct $\sum_{i=1}^n w_i x_i$ from $M^n_w(x)$ by the Chinese remainder theorem, we have the following.

Lemma 18 (Sect. 3.2 in [88]) *There exists a function $h : \{0, 1\}^s \to \{0, 1\}$ such that $f(x) = h(M^n_w(x))$ holds.*

Note that h can be written as an $\mathbb{F}_2$-polynomial of degree at most s and is determined by the values $g(0), g(1), \ldots, g(W)$. We are ready to prove Lemma 13.
Proof of Lemma 13 For each p_i and $r \in \mathbb{Z}_{p_i}$, there exists a δ-error $O(\lg^2((n \lg p_i)/\delta))$-randomness probabilistic $\mathbb{F}_2$-polynomial $\mathcal{P}_{p_i,r}$ of degree $O(p_i\sqrt{n \lg(1/\delta)})$ by Lemma 15. We sample an $\mathbb{F}_2$-polynomial $P_{p_i,r}$ from $\mathcal{P}_{p_i,r}$, replace $\mathrm{mod}^n_{p_i,r,w}$ by it in M^n_w and then obtain a polynomial Q for f by composing h. Note that we use same random bits of length at most $O(\lg^2((n \lg p_\ell)/\delta))$ to sample every $P_{p_i,r}$.

By the union bound, we have $\mathbf{Pr}[Q(x) \neq f(x)] \leq s\delta$. If we set $\delta = \varepsilon/s$, the degree of Q is $O(sp_\ell\sqrt{n \lg(1/\delta)}) = O(\lg^4 W\sqrt{n \lg(1/\varepsilon)})$ and the length of random bits is $O(\lg^2((n \lg\lg W)/\varepsilon))$. This completes the proof.

3.3 Linear Threshold Functions

In this section, we prove Lemma 14.

Fix integers $w_0, w_1, \ldots, w_n \in \mathbb{Z}$, let $F(x) = w_0 + \sum_{i=1}^n w_i x_i$ and consider $\mathrm{sgn}(F(x)) \in \mathbf{THR}$. Without loss of generality, $|w_i| \leq 2^{O(n \lg n)}$ holds due to Lemma 3. We assume that $|F(x)| \geq n + 2$. Otherwise, we consider $(n + 2)(2F(x) + 1)$ instead since for all $x \in \{0, 1\}^n$, it holds that $\mathrm{sgn}(F(x)) = \mathrm{sgn}((n + 2)(2F(x) + 1))$ and $|(n + 2)(2F(x) + 1)| \geq n + 2$.

Let $\ell := \lceil \lg((n+1)\max_i |w_i|) \rceil$. We need the following definitions for $1 \le l \le \ell$:

- $w_i^{(l)} := \begin{cases} \lfloor w_i/2^l \rfloor & \text{if } w_i \ge 0, \\ w_i^{(l)} = \lceil w_i/2^l \rceil & \text{if } w_i < 0, \end{cases}$
- $F^{(l)}(x) := w_0^{(l)} + \sum_{i=1}^n w_i^{(l)} x_i$,
- $\mathrm{ins}^{(l)}(x) = 1$ if and only if $w_0^{(l)} + \sum_{i=1}^n w_i^{(l)} x_i \in \{-n-1, -n, \ldots, n, n+1\}$,
- $\mathrm{pos}^{(l)}(x) = 1$ if and only if $w_0^{(l)} + \sum_{i=1}^n w_i^{(l)} x_i \in \{0, 1, \ldots, n, n+1\}$,
- $\mathrm{ins}_p^{(l)}(x) = 1$ if and only if $w_0^{(l)} + \sum_{i=1}^n w_i^{(l)} x_i \equiv k \bmod p$ for some $k \in \{-n-1, -n, \ldots, n, n+1\}$,
- $\mathrm{pos}_p^{(l)}(x) = 1$ if and only if $w_0^{(l)} + \sum_{i=1}^n w_i^{(l)} x_i \equiv k \bmod p$ for some $k \in \{0, 1, \ldots, n, n+1\}$.

Hofmeister gives the following characterization of linear threshold functions.

Lemma 19 (page 139, [47])
If $F(x) \ge 0$, then there exists a unique l such that $\neg\mathrm{ins}^{(l-1)}(x) \wedge \mathrm{pos}^{(l)}(x) = 1$ holds. If $F(x) < 0$, then for all l, $\neg\mathrm{ins}^{(l-1)}(x) \wedge \mathrm{pos}^{(l)}(x) = 0$ holds.

The following lemma implies Lemma 14 almost immediately.

Lemma 20 *For every $\varepsilon \in (0, 1/2)$ and l, $f \in \{\mathrm{ins}^{(l)}, \mathrm{pos}^{(l)}\}$ has an ε-error $O(\lg^2(n/\varepsilon))$-randomness probabilistic $\mathbb{F}_2$-polynomial $\mathcal{P}$ of degree $d = O(\lg^4 n\sqrt{n \lg(1/\varepsilon)})$. Furthermore, we can sample a polynomial from $\mathcal{P}$ in time $O(\mathrm{poly}(n)\binom{n}{d})$.*

First we prove Lemma 14 assuming Lemma 20 and then prove Lemma 20.
Proof of Lemma 14 For each l, there exist δ-error $O(\lg^2(n/\delta))$-randomness probabilistic $\mathbb{F}_2$-polynomials $\mathcal{P}_{\mathrm{ins}}^{(l)}$ and $\mathcal{P}_{\mathrm{pos}}^{(l)}$ of degree $O(\lg^4 n\sqrt{n \lg(1/\delta)})$ for $\mathrm{ins}^{(l)}$ and $\mathrm{pos}^{(l)}$ respectively by Lemma 20. We sample an $\mathbb{F}_2$-polynomial $P_{\mathrm{ins}}^{(l)}$ from $\mathcal{P}_{\mathrm{ins}}^{(l)}$ and an $\mathbb{F}_2$-polynomial $P_{\mathrm{pos}}^{(l)}$ from $\mathcal{P}_{\mathrm{pos}}^{(l)}$ and construct an $\mathbb{F}_2$-polynomial $P(x) := \sum_{l=1}^{\ell}(1 - P_{\mathrm{ins}}^{(l-1)(x)})P_{\mathrm{pos}}^{(l)}(x)$. Note that we use same random bits of length at most $O(\lg^2(n/\delta))$ to sample every $P_{\mathrm{ins}}^{(l)}, P_{\mathrm{pos}}^{(l)}$.
By the union bound, we have $\mathbf{Pr}[P(x) \ne f(x)] \le 2\ell\delta$. If we set $\varepsilon = 2\ell\delta$, the degree of Q is $O(\lg^5 n\sqrt{n \lg(1/\varepsilon)})$ and the length of random bits is $O(\lg^2(n/\varepsilon))$.
This completes the proof of Lemma 14.
Proof of Lemma 20 We show a proof for $\mathrm{ins}^{(l)}$. The proof for $\mathrm{pos}^{(l)}$ is almost identical. The main idea is that we compute $\mathrm{ins}_p^{(l)}$ instead of $\mathrm{ins}^{(l)}$ for a random prime p. Note that $\mathrm{ins}_p^{(l)} \in \mathbf{SUM}_W$ for $W \le pn$. There exists an ε-error $O(\lg^2((n \lg\lg W)/\delta))$-randomness probabilistic $\mathbb{F}_2$-polynomial $\mathcal{P}_p^{(l)}$ of degree $O(\lg^4 W\sqrt{n \lg(1/\delta)})$ for $\mathrm{ins}_p^{(l)}$ by Lemma 13.
Let $t := \lceil Cn^2 \lg n/\delta \rceil$ for a sufficiently large constant $C > 0$ and $p_1 < \cdots < p_t$ be first t primes. Note that $p_i = O(t \lg t)$ by the prime number theorem. We rely on the following lemma.

Lemma 21 (Sect. 3.3 in [88]) *If $\mathrm{ins}^{(l)}(x) = 1$, then $\mathrm{ins}_p^{(l)}(x) = 1$. If $\mathrm{ins}^{(l)}(x) = 0$ and i is selected from $\{1, 2, \ldots, t\}$ uniformly at random, then $\mathbf{Pr}_i[\mathrm{ins}_{p_i}^{(l)}(x) = 1] \le \delta$.*

We construct an $\mathbb{F}_2$-polynomial Q for $\text{ins}^{(l)}$ as follows. First, select $i \in \{1, 2, \ldots, t\}$ uniformly at random. Then, sample a polynomial P from $\mathcal{P}^{(l)}_{p_i}$ and let $Q(x) := P(x)$.

By the union bound, we have

$$\mathbf{Pr}[Q(x) \neq \text{ins}^{(l)}(x)] \leq \mathbf{Pr}[\text{ins}^{(l)}_{p_i}(x) \neq \text{ins}^{(l)}(x)] + \mathbf{Pr}[P(x) \neq \text{ins}^{(l)}_{p_i}(x)] \leq 2\delta.$$

If we set $\varepsilon = 2\delta$, the degree of Q is $O(\lg^4 n\sqrt{n \lg(1/\varepsilon)})$ and the length of random bits is $O(\lg^2(n/\varepsilon))$.

This completes the proof of Lemma 20.

4 Satisfiability Algorithms

In this section, we prove the following theorem.

Theorem 3 *There exist a constant $c > 0$ and a deterministic algorithm that, given a depth 2 linear threshold circuit C with n variables and m gates, runs in time $2^{n-\Omega\left(\left(\frac{n}{\sqrt{m}\cdot\text{poly}(\lg n)}\right)^c\right)}$ and counts the number of satisfying assignments for C.*

Remark 1 The proof of Theorem 1 is essentially the same or even simpler and omitted, i.e., (1) we use Lemma 13 instead of 14 if necessary and (2) we do not have to apply Lemma 4 if a gate at the bottom layer is symmetric.

Let $C \in \mathbf{THR} \circ \mathbf{THR}$ be an n-variate circuit whose gate at layer 0 has fan-in at most m. For a positive integer n', we define a function $K : \{0, 1\}^{n-n'} \to \{0, 1, \ldots, 2^{n'}\}$ as $K(y) := \sum_{a\in\{0,1\}^{n'}} C(y, a)$. Our goal is to construct an expression $K' = \sum_i a_i G_i$, where $a_i \in \mathbb{Z}, G_i \in \mathbf{SYM}$, such that $K \equiv K'$. Then ith bit of the binary representation of $K'(y) \in \{0, 1\}^{n'+1}$ can be regarded as a function in $\mathbf{SYM} \circ \mathbf{SYM}$. We can apply Lemma 6 to obtain all the values of $K(y)$ if we select the underlying parameters appropriately.

Proof of Theorem 3 By Lemma 4, there exists $C' \in \mathbf{THR} \circ \mathbf{OR} \circ \mathbf{AND} \circ \mathbf{XOR} \circ \mathbf{OR} \circ \mathbf{AND} \circ \mathbf{SYM}$ that is equivalent to C and has at most $t = mn^{c_{\text{mt}}}$ wires. Let $g_1, g_2, \ldots, g_s$ be symmetric gates at the bottom layer in C'. Let $C'' \in \mathbf{THR} \circ \mathbf{OR} \circ \mathbf{AND} \circ \mathbf{XOR} \circ \mathbf{OR} \circ \mathbf{AND}$ be an s-variate circuit with at most t wires such that $C''(g_1, \ldots, g_s) \equiv C'$.

Lemma 22 *Let $D \in \mathbf{THR} \circ \mathbf{OR} \circ \mathbf{AND} \circ \mathbf{XOR} \circ \mathbf{OR} \circ \mathbf{AND}$ be an n-variate circuit with $t = \text{poly}(n)$ wires, where the threshold gate at layer 0 has fan-in at most $m = O(n^2)$. There exists an ε-error $O(\lg n \lg^2(n/\varepsilon))$-randomness probabilistic $\mathbb{F}_2$-polynomial $\mathcal{P}$ of degree $d = O(\lg^9 n \lg^5(1/\varepsilon)\sqrt{m})$ for D. Furthermore, we can sample from $\mathcal{P}$ in time $O(\text{poly}(n)\binom{n}{d})$.*

Proof We replace the threshold gate at layer 0 by a δ-error probabilistic $\mathbb{F}_2$-polynomial from Lemma 14 and replace each AND/OR gate by a δ-error probabilistic $\mathbb{F}_2$-polynomial from Lemma 12, where we set $\delta = \varepsilon/(t+1)$, and obtain a circuit

$$D' \in (\mathbf{XOR} \circ \mathbf{AND}) \circ (\mathbf{XOR} \circ \mathbf{AND}) \circ (\mathbf{XOR} \circ \mathbf{AND}) \circ \mathbf{XOR} \circ (\mathbf{XOR} \circ \mathbf{AND}) \circ (\mathbf{XOR} \circ \mathbf{AND}).$$

Note that we use the same random bits to sample each probabilistic polynomial. By repeatedly using Lemma 9, we obtain a circuit $D'' \in \mathbf{XOR} \circ \mathbf{AND}$ that is equivalent to D'. By the union bound, D' is an ε-error probabilistic $\mathbb{F}_2$-polynomial for D. The degree of D'' is $d = O(\lg^9 n \lg^5(1/\varepsilon)\sqrt{m})$ and the randomness of D' is $O(\lg n \lg^2(n/\varepsilon))$ by the choice of δ. In addition, the construction of D'' takes time $O(\text{poly}(n)\binom{n}{d})$ since we apply Lemma 9 at most

1. t times with $d_1 = d_2 = O(\lg n \lg(1/\varepsilon)), n_1 = t, n_2 = n$,
2. t times with $d_1 = O(\lg n \lg(1/\varepsilon)), d_2 = O(\lg^2 n \lg^2(1/\varepsilon)), n_1 = t, n_2 = n$,
3. m times with $d_1 = O(\lg n \lg(1/\varepsilon)), d_2 = O(\lg^3 n \lg^3(1/\varepsilon)), n_1 = t, n_2 = n$,
4. once with with $d_1 = O(\lg^5 n\sqrt{m} \lg(1/\varepsilon)), d_2 = O(\lg^4 n \lg^4(1/\varepsilon)), n_1 = m, n_2 = n$.

This completes the proof.

Let $l = O(\lg n \lg^2(n/\varepsilon)$ and select $r \in \{0,1\}^l$ to sample a polynomial P_r for C'' due to Lemma 22 in time $\text{poly}(n)\binom{s}{d_1}$, where $d_1 = O(\lg^9 n \lg^5(1/\varepsilon)\sqrt{m})$. Then we construct a $\mathbb{Z}$-polynomial $Q_r := F_\ell(P_r)$, where F_ℓ is the degree $(2\ell - 1)$ $\mathbb{Z}$-polynomial from Lemma 11 and we regard P_r as a $\mathbb{Z}$-polynomial in the natural way. We can represent Q_r as

$$Q_r = \sum_{S \subseteq [s]:|S| \le d_2} a_S \prod_{i \in S} g_i$$

in time $\text{poly}(n)\binom{s}{d_2}$, where $d_2 = O(\ell \lg^9 n \lg^5(1/\varepsilon)\sqrt{m})$ and $a_S = n^{O(d_2)}$. For each $\prod_{i \in S} g_i \in \mathbf{AND} \circ \mathbf{SYM}$, we apply Lemma 5 and obtain a circuit $g_S \in \mathbf{SYM}$ with $n^{O(d_2)}$ wires. Let $Q'_r := \sum_{S \subseteq [s]:|S| \le d} a_S g_S$. Finally we define $R : \{0,1\}^{n-n'} \to \mathbb{Z}$ as

$$R(y) := \sum_{a \in \{0,1\}^{n'}, r \in \{0,1\}^l} Q'_r(y, a) \bmod 2^\ell.$$

Note that if $2^\ell > 2^l$, then by Lemma 11 and the error probability of Q'_r, we have

$$C(x', a) = 1 \Rightarrow (1-\varepsilon)2^l \le \left(\sum_{r \in \{0,1\}^l} Q'_r(y, a) \bmod 2^\ell\right) \le 2^l,$$
$$C(x', a) = 0 \quad \Rightarrow 0 \le \left(\sum_{r \in \{0,1\}^l} Q'_r(y, a) \bmod 2^\ell\right) \le \varepsilon 2^l.$$

In addition, if $2^\ell > 2^{n'} 2^l$, then we have

$$R(y) \in (2^l(1-\varepsilon)K(y), 2^l\{(1-\varepsilon)K(y)+\varepsilon 2^{n'}\}).$$

If we set $\varepsilon < 1/2^{n'+1}$ and define $\tilde{R}(y)$ as the nearest integer of $R(y)/2^l$, then $\tilde{R}(y) = K(y)$ holds.

We set $n' = (n/(\sqrt{m}\lg^{c_1} n))^{c_2}$ for sufficiently large $c_1 > 0$ and small $c_2 > 0$, $\varepsilon = 1/2^{n'+2}$ and $\ell = n' + l + 1$. Then, we see that the construction of R takes time at most $2^{n-n'}$. Furthermore, for each i, the ith bit of the binary representation of $R(y)$ can be represented as a circuit in **SYM** $\circ$ **SYM** so that the condition of Lemma 6 is satisfied as an $n - n'$-variate circuit.

This completes the proof.

5 Circuit Lower Bounds

In this section, we give a proof sketch of Theorem 2.

We use the connection between satisfiability algorithms and circuit lower bounds due to Ben-Sasson and Viola [16]. Let C_n be a set of functions from $\{0, 1\}^n$ to $\{0, 1\}$. C_n is *closed under projections* if for all $f \in C_n$, indices $i, j \le n$ and a bit b, it holds that

$$\neg f,\ f(x_1, \ldots, x_{i-1}, x_j \oplus b, x_{i+1}, \ldots, x_n),\ f(x_1, \ldots, x_{i-1}, b, x_{i+1}, \ldots, x_n) \in C_n.$$

C_n is *efficiently closed under projections* if it is closed under projections and gives a description of $f \in C_n$; we can compute in poly($|f|$), descriptions of

$$\neg f,\ f(x_1, \ldots, x_{i-1}, x_j \oplus b, x_{i+1}, \ldots, x_n),\ f(x_1, \ldots, x_{i-1}, b, x_{i+1}, \ldots, x_n) \in C_n.$$

Theorem 4 ([16]) *Let C_n be efficiently closed under projections. If the satisfiability problem of the form $f_1 \wedge f_2 \wedge f_3$ for $f_1, f_2, f_3 \in C_{n+O(\lg n)}$ can be deterministically solved in time $2^{n-\omega(\lg n)}$, then there exists a language $L \in \mathrm{E}^{\mathrm{NP}}$ such that $L_n \notin C_n$ holds for infinitely many n. Here L_n denotes the indicator function of $L \cap \{0, 1\}^n$.*

It is easy to see that we can modify the proof of Theorem 3 to handle a circuit of the form $C_1 \wedge C_2 \wedge C_3$, where $C_1, C_2, C_3 \in$ (**SYM** $\cup$ **THR**) $\circ$ (**SYM** $\cup$ **THR**), because the degree of the "final polynomial" is larger by a factor of at most 3. The class of depth 2 circuits with m symmetric and linear threshold gates is clearly efficiently closed under projections. This completes the proof of Theorem 2.

Acknowledgements We are deeply grateful to Srikanth Srinivasan who explained us why pseudorandom generators due to [36, 74] are sufficient to obtain randomness efficient versions of his constructions from [88] and kindly allowed us to use the idea in this paper. We would like to thank Ruiwen Chen, Ramamohan Paturi, Rahul Santhanam and Stefan Schneider for useful discussion and valuable comments. This work was supported in part by MEXT KAKENHI (24106003, 20H05961,

20H05967); JSPS KAKENHI (26330011, 16H02782, 22K11909); the John Mung Advanced Program of Kyoto University. Part of the work was performed while the author was at Department of Computer Science and Engineering, University of California, San Diego, and the Simons Institute for the Theory of Computing, Berkeley.

References

1. J. Alman, L. Chen, Efficient construction of rigid matrices using an NP oracle. SIAM J. Comput. (2022). (published electronically)
2. J. Alman, T.M. Chan, R. Williams, Polynomial representations of threshold functions and algorithmic applications, in *Proceedings of the IEEE 57th Annual Symposium on Foundations of Computer Science (FOCS)*, pp. 467–476 (2016)
3. J. Alman, T.M. Chan, R. Ryan Williams, Faster deterministic and Las Vegas algorithms for offline approximate nearest neighbors in high dimensions, in *Proceedings of the 31st ACM-SIAM Symposium on Discrete Algorithms (SODA)*, pp. 637–649 (2020)
4. K. Amano, A. Saito, A nonuniform circuit class with multilayer of threshold gates having super quasi polynomial size lower bounds against NEXP, in *Proceedings of the 9th International Conference on Language and Automata Theory and Applications (LATA)*, pp. 461–472 (2015)
5. K. Amano, A. Saito, A satisfiability algorithm for some class of dense depth two threshold circuits. IEICE Trans. **98**-D(1), 108–118 (2015)
6. J. Alman, R. Williams, Probabilistic polynomials and Hamming nearest neighbors, in *Proceedings of the IEEE 56th Annual Symposium on Foundations of Computer Science (FOCS)*, pp. 136–150 (2015)
7. A. Abboud, R. Williams, H. Yu, More applications of the polynomial method to algorithm design, in *Proceedings of the Twenty-Sixth Annual ACM-SIAM Symposium on Discrete Algorithms (SODA)*, pp. 218–230 (2015)
8. R. Beigel, The polynomial method in circuit complexity, in *Proceedings of the 8th Annual Structure in Complexity Theory Conference*, pp. 82–95 (1993)
9. R. Beigel, When do extra majority gates help? Polylog(n) majority gates are equivalent to one. Comput Complex **4**, 314–324 (1994)
10. N. Bhatnagar, P. Gopalan, R.J. Lipton, Symmetric polynomials over Z_m and simultaneous communication protocols. J. Comput. Syst. Sci. **72**(2), 252–285 (2006)
11. P. Beame, R. Impagliazzo, S. Srinivasan, Approximating AC^0 by small height decision trees and a deterministic algorithm for $\#AC^0$ SAT, in *Proceedings of the 27th Conference on Computational Complexity (CCC)*, pp. 117–125 (2012)
12. S. Bajpai, V. Krishan, D. Kush, N. Limaye, S. Srinivasan, A #SAT algorithm for small constant-depth circuits with PTF gates. Algorithmica **84**(4), 1132–1162 (2022)
13. A. Björklund, P. Kaski, R. Williams, Solving systems of polynomial equations over GF(2) by a parity-counting self-reduction, in *Proceedings of the 46th International Colloquium on Automata, Languages, and Programming (ICALP)*, pp. 26:1–26:13 (2019)
14. R. Beigel, N. Reingold, D.A. Spielman, The perceptron strikes back, in *Proceedings of the Sixth Annual Structure in Complexity Theory Conference*, pp. 286–291 (1991)
15. R. Beigel, J. Tarui, On ACC. Comput. Complex. **4**, 350–366 (1994)
16. E. Ben-Sasson, E. Viola, Short PCPs with projection queries, in *Proceedings of the 41st International Colloquium on Automata, Languages, and Programming (ICALP), Part I*, pp. 163–173 (2014)
17. G. Bathie, R. Ryan Williams, Towards stronger depth lower bounds, in *Proceedings of the 15th Innovations in Theoretical Computer Science Conference (ITCS)*, pp. 10:1–10:24 (2024)

18. R. Chen, Satisfiability algorithms and lower bounds for Boolean formulas over finite bases, in *Proceedings of the 40th International Symposium on Mathematical Foundations of Computer Science (MFCS), Part II*, pp. 223–234 (2015)
19. Y. Chen, Y. Huang, J. Li, H. Ren, Range avoidance, remote point, and hard partial truth table via satisfying-pairs algorithms, in *Proceedings of the 55th Annual ACM Symposium on Theory of Computing (STOC)*, pp. 1058–1066 (2023)
20. T.Y. Chow, Almost-natural proofs. J. Comput. Syst. Sci. **77**(4), 728–737 (2011)
21. L. Chen, S. Hirahara, H. Ren, Symmetric exponential time requires near-maximum circuit size, in *Proceedings of the 56th Annual ACM SIGACT Symposium on Theory of Computing (STOC)* (2024)
22. R. Chen, V. Kabanets, Correlation bounds and #SAT algorithms for small linear-size circuits. Theor. Comput. Sci. **654**, 2–10 (2016)
23. R. Chen, V. Kabanets, A. Kolokolova, R. Shaltiel, D. Zuckerman, Mining circuit lower bound proofs for meta-algorithms. Computat. Complex. **24**(2), 333–392 (2015)
24. R. Chen, V. Kabanets, N. Saurabh, An improved deterministic #SAT algorithm for small De Morgan formulas. Algorithmica **76**(1), 68–87 (2016)
25. L. Chen, Z. Lu, X. Lyu, I.C. Oliveira, Majority versus approximate linear sum and average-case complexity below NC^1, in *Proceedings of the 48th International Colloquium on Automata, Languages, and Programming (ICALP)*, pp. 51:1–51:20 (2021)
26. S. Chen, P.A. Papakonstantinou, Depth reduction for composites. SIAM J. Comput. **48**(2), 668–686 (2019)
27. R. Chen, R. Santhanam, Improved algorithms for sparse MAX-SAT and MAX-k-CSP, in *Proceedings of the 18th International Conference on Theory and Applications of Satisfiability Testing (SAT)*, pp. 33–45 (2015)
28. R. Chen, R. Santhanam, S. Srinivasan, Average-case lower bounds and satisfiability algorithms for small threshold circuits. Theory Comput. **14**(1), 1–55 (2018)
29. L. Chen, R. Ryan Williams, Stronger connections between circuit analysis and circuit lower bounds, via PCPs of proximity, in *Proceedings of the 34th Computational Complexity Conference (CCC)*, pp. 19:1–19:43 (2019)
30. T.M. Chan, R. Ryan Williams, Deterministic APSP, orthogonal vectors, and more: quickly derandomizing Razborov-Smolensky. ACM Trans. Algorithms **17**(1), 2:1–2:14 (2021)
31. I. Dinur, Improved algorithms for solving polynomial systems over GF(2) by multiple parity-counting, in *Proceedings of the 2021 ACM-SIAM Symposium on Discrete Algorithms, SODA 2021, Virtual Conference*, 10–13 Jan. 2021, pp. 2550–2564 (2021)
32. J. Forster, M. Krause, S.V. Lokam, R. Mubarakzjanov, N. Schmitt, H.-U. Simon, Relations between communication complexity, linear arrangements, and computational complexity, in *Proceedings of the 21st Conference on Foundations of Software Technology and Theoretical Computer Science (FSTTCS)*, pp. 171–182 (2001)
33. J. Forster, A linear lower bound on the unbounded error probabilistic communication complexity. J. Comput. Syst. Sci. **65**(4), 612–625 (2002)
34. A. Frank, É. Tardos, An application of simultaneous diophantine approximation in combinatorial optimization. Comb. **7**(1), 49–65 (1987)
35. M. Goldmann, J. Håstad, A.A. Razborov, Majority gates versus general weighted threshold gates. Comput. Complex. **2**, 277–300 (1992)
36. P. Gopalan, D.M. Kane, R. Meka, Pseudorandomness via the discrete Fourier transform. SIAM J. Comput. **47**(6), 2451–2487 (2018)
37. A. Golovnev, A.S. Kulikov, A.V. Smal, S. Tamaki, Gate elimination: circuit size lower bounds and #SAT upper bounds. Theor. Comput. Sci. **719**, 46–63 (2018)
38. M. Goldmann, On the power of a threshold gate at the top. Inf. Process. Lett. **63**(6), 287–293 (1997)
39. M. Gurumukhani, R. Paturi, P. Pudlák, M.E. Saks, N. Talebanfard, Local enumeration and majority lower bounds, in *Proceedings of the 39th Conference on Computational Complexity (CCC)*, pp. 17:1–17:25 (2024)

40. P. Gopalan, R.A. Servedio, Learning and lower bounds for AC^0 with threshold gates, in *Proceedings of the 13th APPROX and the 14th RANDOM*, pp. 588–601 (2010)
41. H.D. Gröger, G. Turán, On linear decision trees computing Boolean functions, in *Proceedings of the 18th International Colloquium on Automata, Languages and Programming (ICALP)*, pp. 707–718 (1991)
42. J. Håstad, M. Goldmann, On the power of small-depth threshold circuits. Comput.Complex. **1**, 113–129 (1991)
43. P. Hatami, W.M. Hoza, A. Tal, R. Tell, Fooling constant-depth threshold circuits (extended abstract), in *Proceedings of the 62nd IEEE Annual Symposium on Foundations of Computer Science (FOCS)*, pp. 104–115 (2021)
44. P. Hatami, W.M. Hoza, A. Tal, R. Tell, Depth-d threshold circuits versus depth-$(d+1)$ AND-OR trees, in *Proceedings of the 55th Annual ACM Symposium on Theory of Computing (STOC)*, pp. 895–904 (2023)
45. A. Hajnal, W. Maass, P. Pudlák, M. Szegedy, G. Turán, Threshold circuits of bounded depth. J. Comput. Syst. Sci. **46**(2), 129–154 (1993)
46. W. Hoeffding, Probability inequalities for sums of bounded random variables. J. Am. Stat. Assoc. **58**(301), 13–30 (1963)
47. T. Hofmeister, A note on the simulation of exponential threshold weights, in *Proceedings of the Second Annual International Conference on Computing and Combinatorics (COCOON)*, pp. 136–141 (1996)
48. K.A. Hansen, V.V. Podolskii, Exact threshold circuits, in *Proceedings of the 25th Annual IEEE Conference on Computational Complexity (CCC)*, pp. 270–279 (2010)
49. X. Huang, E. Viola, Average-case rigidity lower bounds, in *Proceedings of the 16th International Computer Science Symposium in Russia (CSR)*, pp. 186–205 (2021)
50. R. Impagliazzo, S. Lovett, R. Paturi, S. Schneider, 0-1 integer linear programming with a linear number of constraints, in *Electronic Colloquium on Computational Complexity (ECCC)*, TR14-24 (2014)
51. R. Impagliazzo, W. Matthews, R. Paturi, A satisfiability algorithm for AC^0, in *Proceedings of the 23rd Annual ACM-SIAM Symposium on Discrete Algorithms (SODA)*, pp. 961–972 (2012)
52. R. Impagliazzo, R. Paturi, M.E. Saks, Size-depth tradeoffs for threshold circuits. SIAM J. Comput. **26**(3), 693–707 (1997)
53. R. Impagliazzo, R. Paturi, S. Schneider, A satisfiability algorithm for sparse depth two threshold circuits, in *Proceedings of the 54th Annual IEEE Symposium on Foundations of Computer Science (FOCS)*, pp. 479–488 (2013)
54. H. Jahanjou, E. Miles, E. Viola, Local reduction. Inf. Comput. **261**, 281–295 (2018)
55. V. Kabanets, D.M. Kane, Z. Lu, A polynomial restriction lemma with applications, in *Proceedings of the 49th Annual ACM SIGACT Symposium on Theory of Computing (STOC)*, pp. 615–628 (2017)
56. V. Kabanets, S. Koroth, Z. Lu, D. Myrisiotis, I.C. Oliveira, Algorithms and lower bounds for De Morgan formulas of low-communication leaf gates. ACM Trans. Comput. Theory **13**(4), 23:1–23:37 (2021)
57. M. Krause, S. Lucks, Pseudorandom functions in TC^0 and cryptographic limitations to proving lower bounds. Comput. Complex. **10**(4), 297–313 (2001)
58. V. Kabanets, Z. Lu, Satisfiability and derandomization for small polynomial threshold circuits, in *Approximation, Randomization, and Combinatorial Optimization. Algorithms and Techniques (APPROX/RANDOM)*, pp. 46:1–46:19 (2018)
59. M. Krause, P. Pudlák, On the computational power of depth-2 circuits with threshold and modulo gates. Theor. Comput. Sci. **174**(1–2), 137–156 (1997)
60. M. Krause, Geometric arguments yield better bounds for threshold circuits and distributed computing. Theor. Comput. Sci. **156**(1&2), 99–117 (1996)
61. M. Krause, S. Waack, Variation ranks of communication matrices and lower bounds for depth-two circuits having nearly symmetric gates with unbounded fan-in. Math. Syst.Theory **28**(6), 553–564 (1995)

62. D.M. Kane, R. Williams, Super-linear gate and super-quadratic wire lower bounds for depth-two and depth-three threshold circuits, in *Proceedings of the 48th ACM Symposium on Theory of Computing Conference (STOC)*, pp. 633–643 (2016)
63. Z. Li, Symmetric exponential time requires near-maximum circuit size: simplified, truly uniform, in *Proceedings of the 56th Annual ACM SIGACT Symposium on Theory of Computing (STOC)* (2024)
64. D. Lokshtanov, I. Mikhailin, R. Paturi, P. Pudlák, Beating brute force for (quantified) satisfiability of circuits of bounded treewidth, in *Proceedings of the 29th Annual ACM-SIAM Symposium on Discrete Algorithms (SODA)*, pp. 247–261 (2018)
65. D. Lokshtanov, R. Paturi, S. Tamaki, R. Ryan Williams, H. Yu, Beating brute force for systems of polynomial equations over finite fields, in *Proceedings of the Twenty-Eighth Annual ACM-SIAM Symposium on Discrete Algorithms (SODA)*, pp. 2190–2202 (2017)
66. S. Lovett, S. Srinivasan, Correlation bounds for poly-size AC^0 circuits with $n^{1-o(1)}$ symmetric gates, in *Proceedings of the 14th APPROX 2011 and the 15th RANDOM*, pp. 640–651 (2011)
67. J. Li, T. Yang, $3.1n - o(n)$ circuit lower bounds for explicit functions, in *Proceedings of the 54th Annual ACM SIGACT Symposium on Theory of Computing (STOC)*, pp. 1180–1193 (2022)
68. A. Mukherjee, A. Basu, Lower bounds over boolean inputs for deep neural networks with ReLU gates, in *Electronic Colloquium on Computational Complexity (ECCC)*, TR17-190 (2017)
69. T. Makita, A. Nagao, T. Okada, K. Seto, J. Teruyama, A satisfiability algorithm for deterministic width-2 branching programs. IEICE Trans. Fundam. Electron. Commun. Comput. Sci. **105**-A(9), 1298–1308 (2022)
70. H. Morizumi, A satisfiability algorithm for synchronous boolean circuits. IEICE Trans. Inf. Syst. **104**-D(3), 392–393 (2021)
71. A. Maciel, D. Thérien, Threshold circuits of small majority-depth. Inf. Comput. **146**(1), 55–83 (1998)
72. S. Muroga, *Threshold Logic and Its Applications* (Wiley, 1971)
73. E. Miles, E. Viola, Substitution-permutation networks, pseudorandom functions, and natural proofs. J. ACM **62**(6), 46 (2015)
74. N. Nisan, Pseudorandom generators for space-bounded computation. Combinatorica **12**(4), 449–461 (1992)
75. N. Nisan, The communication complexity of threshold gates, in *Proceedings of Combinatorics, Paul Erdős is Eighty*, pp. 301–315 (1993)
76. M. Naor, O. Reingold, Number-theoretic constructions of efficient pseudo-random functions. J. ACM **51**(2), 231–262 (2004)
77. A. Nagao, K. Seto, J. Teruyama, A moderately exponential time algorithm for k-IBDD satisfiability. Algorithmica **80**(10), 2725–2741 (2018)
78. A. Nagao, K. Seto, J. Teruyama, Satisfiability algorithm for syntactic read-k-times branching programs. Theory Comput. Syst. **64**(8), 1392–1407 (2020)
79. S. Nurk, An $O(2^{0.4058m})$ upper bound for circuit SAT (2009)
80. I.C. Oliveira, Algorithms versus circuit lower bounds, in *Electronic Colloquium on Computational Complexity (ECCC)*, TR13-117 (2013)
81. V.V. Podolskii, Exponential lower bound for bounded depth circuits with few threshold gates. Inf. Process. Lett. **112**(7), 267–271 (2012)
82. R. Paturi, M.E. Saks, Approximating threshold circuits by rational functions. Inf. Comput. **112**(2), 257–272 (1994)
83. A.A. Razborov, S. Rudich, Natural proofs. J. Comput. Syst. Sci. **55**(1), 24–35 (1997)
84. A.A. Razborov, A. Wigderson, $n^{\Omega(\log n)}$ lower bounds on the size of depth-3 threshold circuits with AND gates at the bottom. Inf. Process. Lett. **45**(6), 303–307 (1993)
85. R. Santhanam, Fighting perebor: New and improved algorithms for formula and QBF satisfiability, in *Proceedings of the 51th Annual IEEE Symposium on Foundations of Computer Science (FOCS)*, pp. 183–192 (2010)
86. R. Santhanam, Ironic complicity: satisfiability algorithms and circuit lower bounds. Bull. EATCS **106**, 31–52 (2012)

87. R. Santhanam, An algorithmic approach to uniform lower bounds, in *Proceedings of the 38th Computational Complexity Conference (CCC)*, pp. 35:1–35:26 (2023)
88. S. Srinivasan, On improved degree lower bounds for polynomial approximation, in *Proceedings of the 33rd IARCS Annual Conference on Foundations of Software Technology and Theoretical Computer Science (FSTTCS)*, pp. 201–212 (2013)
89. T. Sakai, K. Seto, S. Tamaki, Solving sparse instances of max SAT via width reduction and greedy restriction. Theory Comput. Syst. **57**(2), 426–443 (2015)
90. T. Sakai, K. Seto, S. Tamaki, J. Teruyama, Improved exact algorithms for mildly sparse instances of max SAT. Theor. Comput. Sci. **697**, 58–68 (2017)
91. T. Sakai, K. Seto, S. Tamaki, J. Teruyama, Bounded depth circuits with weighted symmetric gates: satisfiability, lower bounds and compression. J. Comput. Syst. Sci. **105**, 87–103 (2019)
92. K. Seto, S. Tamaki, A satisfiability algorithm and average-case hardness for formulas over the full binary basis. Comput. Complex. **22**(2), 245–274 (2013)
93. K. Seto, J. Teruyama, An exact algorithm for oblivious read-twice branching program satisfiability. IEICE Trans. Fundam. Electron. Commun. Comput. Sci. **99**-A(6):1019–1024 (2016)
94. A. Tal, #SAT algorithms from shrinkage, in *Electronic Colloquium on Computational Complexity (ECCC)*, TR15-114 (2015)
95. S. Tamaki, A satisfiability algorithm for depth two circuits with a sub-quadratic number of symmetric and threshold gates, in *Electronic Colloquium on Computational Complexity (ECCC)*, TR16-100 (2016)
96. J. Tarui, Probablistic polynomials, AC^0 functions, and the polynomial-time hierarchy. Theor. Comput. Sci. **113**(1), 167–183 (1993)
97. R. Tell, Quantified derandomization of linear threshold circuits, in *Proceedings of the 50th Annual ACM SIGACT Symposium on Theory of Computing (STOC)*, pp. 855–865 (2018)
98. S. Toda, PP is as hard as the polynomial-time hierarchy. SIAM J. Comput. **20**(5), 865–877 (1991)
99. K. Ueno, Exact algorithms for 0-1 integer programs with linear equality constraints (2014). arXiv:1405.6851 [cs.DS]
100. E. Viola, New lower bounds for probabilistic degree and AC^0 with parity gates. Theory Comput. (2024). (to appear)
101. N. Vyas, R. Ryan Williams, Lower bounds against sparse symmetric functions of ACC circuits: expanding the reach of #SAT algorithms. Theory Comput. Syst. **67**(1), 149–177 (2023)
102. F. Wang, NEXP does not have non-uniform quasipolynomial-size ACC circuits of $o(\log \log n)$ depth, in *Proceedings of the 8th Annual Conference on Theory and Applications of Models of Computation (TAMC)*, pp. 164–170 (2011)
103. R. Williams, Improving exhaustive search implies superpolynomial lower bounds. SIAM J. Comput. **42**(3), 1218–1244 (2013)
104. R. Williams, Algorithms for circuits and circuits for algorithms, in *Proceedings of the 29th Annual IEEE Conference on Computational Complexity (CCC)*, pp. 248–261 (2014)
105. R. Williams, Nonuniform ACC circuit lower bounds. J. ACM **61**(1), 2 (2014)
106. R. Williams, The polynomial method in circuit complexity applied to algorithm design (invited talk), in *Proceedings of the 34th International Conference on Foundation of Software Technology and Theoretical Computer Science (FSTTCS)*, pp. 47–60 (2014)
107. R.R. Williams, Natural proofs versus derandomization. SIAM J. Comput. **45**(2), 497–529 (2016)
108. R.R. Williams, Some ways of thinking algorithmically about impossibility. ACM SIGLOG News **4**(3), 28–40 (2017)
109. R.R. Williams, New algorithms and lower bounds for circuits with linear threshold gates. Theory Comput. **14**(1), 1–25 (2018)
110. R.R. Williams, Limits on representing Boolean functions by linear combinations of simple functions: thresholds, ReLUs, and low-degree polynomials, in *Proceedings of the 33rd Computational Complexity Conference (CCC)*, pp. 6:1–6:24 (2018)

111. R.R. Williams, The orthogonal vectors conjecture and non-uniform circuit lower bounds, in *Proceedings of the 65th IEEE Annual Symposium on Foundations of Computer Science (FOCS)*, pp. 1372–1387 (2024)
112. R.R. Williams, Self-improvement for circuit-analysis problems, in *Proceedings of the 56th Annual ACM SIGACT Symposium on Theory of Computing (STOC)*, pp. 1374–1385 (2024)
113. A.C.-C. Yao, On ACC and threshold circuits, in *Proceedings of the 31st Annual Symposium on Foundations of Computer Science (FOCS)*, pp. 619–627 (1990)

Soft Margin Boosting as Frank-Wolfe Algorithms

Ryotaro Mitsuboshi, Kohei Hatano, and Eiji Takimoto

Abstract We consider the LPBoost family of boosting algorithms for the ℓ_1-norm regularized soft margin optimization, where the problem instance is implicitly given as a huge scale LP problem and the goal is to efficiently find an optimal solution with the aid of a certain oracle. Although the optimal solution yields a linear classifier with good generalization ability, the LPBoost family is less popular, since all existing algorithms in the family are either very slow on real data or have no theoretical convergence guarantees. In this chapter, we first show that each algorithm in the LPBoost family can be viewed as an instance of a general scheme for solving convex optimization known as the Frank-Wolfe method, and thus its convergence guarantee can be immediately applied. The Frank-Wolfe method has the feature that the convergence guarantee remains to hold even when arbitrary update rules including the standard one are greedily applied in each iteration. Taking advantage of the feature, we propose an algorithm that performs efficiently on real data while maintaining the same convergence guarantees as the existing methods.

1 Introduction

This chapter introduces the relationship between some boosting algorithms for soft margin optimization and the Frank-Wolfe algorithms. After that, we propose a boosting algorithm that optimizes the soft margin while maintaining a convergence guarantee.

Theory and algorithms for large-margin classifiers have been studied extensively since those classifiers guarantee low generalization errors when they have large margins over training examples (e.g., [24, 28]). In particular, the ℓ_1-norm regularized

R. Mitsuboshi (✉) · K. Hatano · E. Takimoto
Address of Institute, Kyushu University/Riken AIP, Fukuoka, Japan
e-mail: ryotaro.mitsuboshi@inf.kyushu-u.ac.jp

K. Hatano
e-mail: hatano@inf.kyushu-u.ac.jp

E. Takimoto
e-mail: eiji@inf.kyushu-u.ac.jp

S. Minato et al. (eds.), *Algorithmic Foundations for Social Advancement*,
https://doi.org/10.1007/978-981-96-0668-9_21

soft margin optimization problem, defined later, is a formulation of finding sparse large-margin classifiers based on the linear program (LP). This problem aims to optimize the ℓ_1-margin by combining multiple hypotheses from some hypothesis class $\mathcal{H}$. The resulting classifier tends to be sparse, so ℓ_1-margin optimization is helpful for feature selection tasks. Off-the-shelf LP solvers can solve the problem, but they are still not efficient enough for a huge class $\mathcal{H}$.

Boosting is a framework for solving the ℓ_1-norm regularized margin optimization even though $\mathcal{H}$ is infinitely large. Various boosting algorithms have been invented. LPBoost [8] is a practical algorithm that often works effectively. Although LPBoost terminates rapidly, it is shown that it takes $\Omega(m)$ iterations in the worst case, where m is the number of training examples [35]. Shalev-Shwartz et al. [32] invented an algorithm called Corrective ERLPBoost (we call this algorithm Corr. ERLPBoost for shorthand). Corr. ERLPBoost and ERLPBoost find ϵ-approximate solutions in $O(\ln(m/\nu)/\epsilon^2)$ iterations, where $\nu \in [1, m]$ is the soft margin parameter. The difference is the time complexity per iteration; ERLPBoost solves a convex program (CP) for each iteration, while Corr. ERLPBoost solves a sorting-like problem. Although ERLPBoost takes much time per iteration, it takes fewer iterations than Corr. ERLPBoost in practical applications. For this reason, ERLPBoost is faster than Corr. ERLPBoost. Our primary motivation is to investigate boosting algorithms with provable iteration bounds, which perform as fast as LPBoost.

This paper has two contributions. Our first contribution is to give a unified view of boosting for soft margin optimization. We show that LPBoost, ERLPBoost, and Corr. ERLPBoost are instances of the Frank-Wolfe algorithm.

Our second contribution is to propose a generic scheme for boosting based on the unified view. Our scheme combines a standard Frank-Wolfe algorithm and *any* algorithm and switches one to the other at each iteration in a non-trivial way. We show that this scheme guarantees the same convergence rate, $O(\ln(m/\nu)/\epsilon^2)$, as ERLPBoost and Corr. ERLPBoost. One can incorporate any update rule to this scheme without losing the convergence guarantee so that it takes advantage of better updates of the second algorithm in practice. In particular, we propose to choose LPBoost as the secondary algorithm, and we call the resulting algorithm Modified LPBoost (MLPBoost).

In experiments on real datasets, MLPBoost works comparably with LPBoost, and MLPBoost is the fastest among theoretically guaranteed algorithms, as expected.

2 Preliminary

Let $S := ((\boldsymbol{x}_i, y_i))_{i=1}^m \in (\mathcal{X} \times \mathcal{Y})^m$ be a sequence of m examples, where $\mathcal{X}$ is some set and $\mathcal{Y} = \{\pm 1\}$. Let $\mathcal{H} \subset [-1, +1]^{\mathcal{X}}$ be a set of hypotheses. Throughout this chapter, we assume that $\mathcal{H}$ is a finite set. It is convenient to regard each $h \in \mathcal{H}$ as the canonical basis vector $\boldsymbol{e}_h \in \{0, 1\}^{\mathcal{H}}$ that has 1 only on the h-th coordinate. We denote m-dimensional capped probability simplex as $\Delta_{m,\nu} := \{\boldsymbol{d} \in [0, 1/\nu]^m \mid \|\boldsymbol{d}\|_1 = 1\}$, where $\nu \in [1, m]$. We write $\Delta_m = \Delta_{m,1}$ for shorthand. For a set $C \subset \mathbb{R}^{\mathcal{H}}$, we denote the convex hull of C as $\mathrm{ConvHull}(C) := \left\{\sum_{s \in C} w_s s \mid \boldsymbol{w} \in \Delta_{\mathcal{H}}\right\}$.

Definition 1 (*strongly convex function*) A function $f : \mathbb{R}^m \to \mathbb{R}$ is said to be η-strongly convex over a convex set $C \subset \mathbb{R}^m$ w.r.t. a norm $\|\cdot\|$ if

$$\forall \boldsymbol{x}, \boldsymbol{y} \in C, \quad f(\alpha \boldsymbol{x} + (1-\alpha)\boldsymbol{y}) \le \alpha f(\boldsymbol{x}) + (1-\alpha) f(\boldsymbol{y}) - \frac{\eta}{2}\|\boldsymbol{y} - \boldsymbol{x}\|^2.$$

If an α-strongly convex function is differentiable, the above definition is equivalent to the following one.

$$\forall \boldsymbol{x}, \boldsymbol{y} \in C, \quad f(\boldsymbol{y}) \ge f(\boldsymbol{x}) + (\boldsymbol{y} - \boldsymbol{x})^\top \nabla f(\boldsymbol{x}) + \frac{\eta}{2}\|\boldsymbol{y} - \boldsymbol{x}\|^2.$$

For example, the relative entropy function $\boldsymbol{d} \mapsto \sum_{i=1}^m \frac{d_i}{1/m}$ from the uniform distribution is 1-strongly convex w.r.t. the ℓ_1-norm.

Similarly, we define smooth functions.

Definition 2 (*smooth function*) A function $f : \mathbb{R}^m \to \mathbb{R}$ is said to be η-smooth over a convex set $C \subset \mathbb{R}^m$ w.r.t. a norm $\|\cdot\|$ if

$$\forall \boldsymbol{x}, \boldsymbol{y} \in C, \quad f(\boldsymbol{y}) \le f(\boldsymbol{x}) + (\boldsymbol{y} - \boldsymbol{x})^\top \nabla f(\boldsymbol{x}) + \frac{\eta}{2}\|\boldsymbol{y} - \boldsymbol{x}\|^2.$$

We also define Fenchel conjugate.

Definition 3 (*Fenchel conjugate*) The Fenchel conjugate $f^\star : \mathbb{R}^n \to [-\infty, +\infty]$ of a function $f : \mathbb{R}^n \to [-\infty, +\infty]$ is defined as

$$f^\star(\boldsymbol{y}) = \sup_{\boldsymbol{x} \in \mathbb{R}^n} \boldsymbol{y} \cdot \boldsymbol{x} - f(\boldsymbol{x}).$$

For example, let $\mathbb{I}_{\Delta_m} : \mathbb{R}^m \to \{0, +\infty\}$ be the indicator function such that $\mathbb{I}_{\Delta_m}(\boldsymbol{d}) = 0$ iff $\boldsymbol{d} \in \Delta_m$. Then, the Fenchel conjugate of $\mathbb{I}_{\Delta_m}$ is $\mathbb{I}^\star_{\Delta_m}(\boldsymbol{\theta}) = \max_{i \in [m]} \theta_i$. Furthermore, it is well known that if f is a $1/\eta$-strongly convex function w.r.t. a norm $\|\cdot\|$ for some $\eta > 0$, $f^\star$ is an η-smooth function w.r.t. the dual norm $\|\cdot\|_\star$. Further, if f is a strongly convex function, the gradient vector of $f^\star$ is written as $\nabla f^\star(\boldsymbol{\theta}) = \arg\sup_{\boldsymbol{d} \in \mathbb{R}^m} \left(\boldsymbol{d}^\top \boldsymbol{\theta} - f(\boldsymbol{d})\right)$. One can find the proof of these properties here [3, 32].

Lemma 1 *Let $f, g : \mathbb{R}^m \to (-\infty, +\infty]$ be functions such that*

$$\exists c > 0, \quad \forall \boldsymbol{\theta}, \quad f(\boldsymbol{\theta}) \le g(\boldsymbol{\theta}) \le f(\boldsymbol{\theta}) + c.$$

Then, $f^\star(\boldsymbol{\mu}) - c \le g^\star(\boldsymbol{\mu}) \le f^\star(\boldsymbol{\mu})$ holds for all $\boldsymbol{\mu}$.

The following theorem is a main tool for this chapter.

Input: A set of training examples $S = \{(\boldsymbol{x}_1, y_1), (\boldsymbol{x}_2, y_2), \ldots, (\boldsymbol{x}_m, y_m)\} \subset \mathcal{X} \times \mathcal{Y}$.
For $t = 1, 2, \ldots, T$:

1. Booster chooses a distribution $\boldsymbol{d}_t \in \Delta_m$ over S.
2. Weak Learner returns a hypothesis $h_t \in \mathcal{H}$.

Booster chooses a weight vector $\boldsymbol{w} \in \Delta_T$ over $\{h_1, h_2, \ldots, h_T\} \subset \mathcal{H}$.
Output: The convex combination $\sum_{t=1}^T w_t h_t$.

Fig. 1 The boosting protocol

Theorem 1 (Fenchel duality theorem *[3]*) *Let* $f : \mathbb{R}^m \to (-\infty, +\infty]$ *and* $g : \mathbb{R}^{\mathcal{H}} \to (-\infty, +\infty]$ *be convex functions, and a linear map* $A : \mathbb{R}^m \to \mathbb{R}^{\mathcal{H}}$. *Define the Fenchel problems*

$$\gamma = \inf_{\boldsymbol{d}} f(\boldsymbol{d}) + g(\boldsymbol{d}^\top A), \qquad \rho = \sup_{\boldsymbol{w}} -f^\star(-A\boldsymbol{w}) - g^\star(\boldsymbol{w}). \tag{1}$$

Then, $\gamma \geq \rho$ *holds. Further,* $\gamma = \rho$ *holds if*[1] $\mathbf{0} \in \mathrm{core}\left(\mathrm{dom}\, g - A^\top \mathrm{dom}\, f\right)$. *Furthermore, points* $\bar{\boldsymbol{d}}$ *and* $\bar{\boldsymbol{w}}$ *are optimal solutions for problems in Eq. (1), respectively, if and only if* $-A\bar{\boldsymbol{w}} \in \partial f\left(\bar{\boldsymbol{d}}\right)$ *and* $\bar{\boldsymbol{w}} \in \partial g\left(\bar{\boldsymbol{d}}^\top A\right)$.

2.1 Boosting

Boosting is known as a class of algorithms for supervised learning. Boosting is a protocol between two algorithms: the booster and the weak learner. For each iteration $t = 1, 2, \ldots, T$, the booster chooses a distribution $\boldsymbol{d}_t \in \Delta_m$ over the training examples S. Then, the weak learner returns a hypothesis $h_t \in \mathcal{H}$ to the booster from some pre-defined finite set $\mathcal{H} \subset [-1, +1]^{\mathcal{X}}$. The boosting algorithm aims to produce a convex combination $H_T = \sum_{t=1}^T w_t h_t$ of the hypotheses $\{h_1, h_2, \ldots, h_T\} \subset \mathcal{H}$ that achieves a goal. Figure 1 summarizes the boosting protocol. Here, we note that some boosting algorithms, such as Graph Separation Boosting [1], consider other compositions $H_T = f(h_1, h_2, \ldots, h_T)$ with an aggregation rule f rather than a convex combination of functions. But this setting is beyond the scope of this section, so we left readers to check them if you are interested.

This section focuses on boosting algorithms that optimize the soft margin. Soft margin optimization is defined as

[1] For a set $C \subset \mathbb{R}^{\mathcal{H}}$, $\mathrm{core}\,(C) = \{\boldsymbol{w} \in C \mid \forall \boldsymbol{v} \in \mathbb{R}^{\mathcal{H}}, \exists t > 0, \forall \tau \in [0, t], \boldsymbol{w} + \tau \boldsymbol{v} \in C\}$ and $\mathrm{dom}\, g - A^\top \mathrm{dom}\, f = \{\boldsymbol{w} - A^\top \boldsymbol{d} \mid \boldsymbol{w} \in \mathrm{dom}\, g, \boldsymbol{d} \in \mathrm{dom}\, f\}$.

$$\max_{\rho, \boldsymbol{w}, \boldsymbol{\xi}} \quad \rho - \frac{1}{\nu} \sum_{i=1}^{m} \xi_i \quad \text{subject to} \quad y_i \sum_{h \in \mathcal{H}} w_h h(\boldsymbol{x}_i) \geq \rho - \xi_i, \quad \forall i \in [m],$$
$$\boldsymbol{w} \in \Delta_{\mathcal{H}}, \quad \boldsymbol{\xi} \geq \mathbf{0}.$$

Intuitively, the soft margin optimization aims to find a convex combination of hypotheses that maximizes the margin for most points. The rest points are regarded as outliers. In this sense, soft margin optimization is robust for outliers. The parameter $\nu \in [1, m]$ controls the ratio of outliers. That is, the optimal $\boldsymbol{w}$ regards at most ν points as outliers. Similar formulation is found in Support Vector Machines [29]. Therefore, an algorithm that optimizes the soft margin is applicable even though a convex combination of hypotheses that perfectly classifies the training points does not exist.

The main advantage of the margin optimization is its generalization error bound. Let $\rho > 0$ be a margin parameter and let $H : \mathcal{X} \to [-1, +1]$ be a hypothesis. Assume that all the training instances in S are drawn i.i.d. from a fixed but unknown distribution $\mathcal{D}$ over $\mathcal{X} \times \mathcal{Y}$. Then, the following holds with high probability [28].

$$\Pr_{(\boldsymbol{x}, y) \sim \mathcal{D}} \mathbf{1}[y \neq H(\boldsymbol{x})] \leq \frac{1}{m} \sum_{i=1}^{m} \mathbf{1}[y_i H(\boldsymbol{x}_i) \leq \rho] + O\left(\frac{\ln |\mathcal{H}|}{\sqrt{\rho^2 m}}\right).$$

Here, $\mathbf{1}[P]$ is the function such that $\mathbf{1}[P] = 1$ if P is true and 0 otherwise. As the inequality indicates, a large-margin classifier guarantees a better generalization error. Following the work by [28], many margin-based error bounds have been developed [12, 13]. Some of them focus on deriving a error bound based on the kth smallest margin, which also holds for $k = 1$. All the works suggest that a large-margin classifier guarantees a small generalization error. Thus, finding a large-margin hypothesis $H = \sum_{h \in \mathcal{H}} w_h h$ is a reasonable goal.

In order to analyze the soft margin boosting algorithms, we need to define the weak learnability. To define the weak learnability for margin optimization, we consider the dual problem of the soft margin optimization. For notational simplicity, let $A \in [-1, +1]^{m \times \mathcal{H}}$ be the matrix such that $A_{i,h} = y_i h(\boldsymbol{x}_i)$. Then, the soft margin optimization can be written as

$$\max_{\rho, \boldsymbol{w}, \boldsymbol{\xi}} \quad \rho - \frac{1}{\nu} \sum_{i=1}^{m} \xi_i \quad \text{subject to} \quad (A\boldsymbol{w})_i \geq \rho - \xi_i, \quad \forall i \in [m], \tag{2}$$
$$\boldsymbol{w} \in \Delta_{\mathcal{H}}, \quad \boldsymbol{\xi} \geq \mathbf{0}.$$

The edge minimization problem, the Lagrange dual problem of (2), is

$$\min_{\boldsymbol{d}} \max_{h \in \mathcal{H}} (\boldsymbol{d}^\top A)_h + \mathbb{I}_{\Delta_{m,\nu}}(\boldsymbol{d}).$$

The quantity $(\boldsymbol{d}^\top A)_h = \sum_{i=1}^m d_i y_i h(\boldsymbol{x}_i)$ is often called the *edge* of the hypothesis h w.r.t. the distribution $\boldsymbol{d} \in \Delta_{m,\nu}$. Shalev-Shwartz et al. [32] showed that by letting $g(\boldsymbol{d}) \triangleq \max_{h \in \mathcal{H}} (\boldsymbol{d}^\top A)_h$ and $f(\boldsymbol{d}) \triangleq \mathbb{I}_{\Delta_{m,\nu}}(\boldsymbol{d})$, one can rewrite the soft margin optimization problem in a much simpler form via Theorem 1.

$$\max_{\boldsymbol{w} \in \Delta_{\mathcal{H}}} -\mathbb{I}^\star_{\Delta_{m,\nu}}(-A\boldsymbol{w}) = \max_{\boldsymbol{w} \in \Delta_{\mathcal{H}}} \min_{\boldsymbol{d} \in \Delta_{m,\nu}} \boldsymbol{d}^\top A \boldsymbol{w}. \tag{3}$$

Here, we note that the duality gap is zero since the core of $\operatorname{dom} g - A^\top \operatorname{dom} f = \mathbb{R}^{\mathcal{H}}$ is $\mathbb{R}^{\mathcal{H}}$, which satisfies $\boldsymbol{0} \in \operatorname{core}\left(\operatorname{dom} g - A^\top \operatorname{dom} f\right)$. The soft margin optimization aims to find an optimal combined hypothesis $\sum_{h \in \mathcal{H}} \bar{w}_h h$, where $\bar{\boldsymbol{w}} \in \Delta_{\mathcal{H}}$ is an optimal solution of Eq. (3). Although the edge minimization and soft margin optimization problems are formulated as a linear program, solving the problem for a huge class $\mathcal{H}$ is hard. Boosting is a standard approach to dealing with the problem.

To analyze a boosting algorithm, one needs to assume the performance of the weak learner.

Assumption 1 (*The γ-weak learnability for margin optimization*) A γ-weak learner takes a distribution $\boldsymbol{d} \in \Delta_{m,\nu}$ over training examples and returns a hypothesis $h \in \mathcal{H}$ such that $(\boldsymbol{d}^\top A)_h = \sum_{i=1}^m d_i y_i h(\boldsymbol{x}_i) \geq \gamma$.

Here, we emphasize that the parameter γ is unknown to the boosting algorithm. With this assumption, the goal of booster is to find a weight vector $\boldsymbol{w} \in \Delta_{\mathcal{H}}$ such that

$$\min_{\boldsymbol{d} \in \Delta_{m,\nu}} \boldsymbol{d}^\top A \boldsymbol{w} \geq \gamma - \epsilon \tag{4}$$

for arbitrarily small $\epsilon > 0$. Note that if the weak learner returns a hypothesis $h \in \mathcal{H}$ that maximizes the edge $(\boldsymbol{d}^\top A)_h$, the above goal becomes to find an ϵ-approximate solution of Eq. (3).

Find $\bar{\boldsymbol{w}} \in \Delta_{\mathcal{H}}$ such that

$$-\mathbb{I}^\star_{\Delta_{m,\nu}}(-A\bar{\boldsymbol{w}}) = \min_{\boldsymbol{d} \in \Delta_{m,\nu}} \boldsymbol{d}^\top A \bar{\boldsymbol{w}} \geq \max_{\boldsymbol{w} \in \Delta_{\mathcal{H}}} \min_{\boldsymbol{d} \in \Delta_{m,\nu}} \boldsymbol{d}^\top A \boldsymbol{w} - \epsilon = \max_{\boldsymbol{w} \in \Delta_{\mathcal{H}}} -\mathbb{I}^\star_{\Delta_{m,\nu}}(-A\boldsymbol{w}) - \epsilon.$$

Therefore, this chapter aims to find a convex combination $\sum_{h \in \mathcal{H}} w_h h$ of hypotheses in $\mathcal{H}$ satisfying Eq. (4).

2.2 The Frank-Wolfe Algorithms

Frank-Wolfe (FW) is a class of optimization algorithms that only uses first-order information of the objective and a linear optimization oracle over the feasible region. The original FW algorithm is a first-order iterative algorithm invented by Marguerite and Philip [10]. The FW algorithm solves the problems of the form: $\min_{\boldsymbol{x} \in C} f(\boldsymbol{x})$, where $C \subset \mathbb{R}^m$ is a closed convex set and $f : C \to \mathbb{R}^m$ is an η-smooth and convex

Input: Initial point $x_1 \in C$ and an accuracy parameter $\epsilon > 0$.
For $t = 1, 2, \ldots, T$:

1. Observe a gradient $\nabla f(x_t)$ at $x_t \in C$.
2. Find an extreme point $s_t \in \arg\min_{s \in C} s \cdot \nabla f(x_t)$.
3. If $(x_t - s_{t+1})^\top \nabla f(x_t) \leq \epsilon$ then set $T = t - 1$ and **break**.
4. Choose a next iterate $x_{t+1} \in C$.

Output: $x_{T+1} \in C$ such that $f(x_{T+1}) - \min_{x \in C} f(x) \leq \epsilon$.

Fig. 2 The Frank-Wolfe protocol.

function. The best advantage of the FW algorithm is the projection-free property; there is no projection onto C, so the running time per iteration is faster than the projected gradient methods.

In each iteration $t = 1, 2, \ldots,$ the FW algorithm seeks an extreme point $s_{t+1} \in C$ that minimizes the inner product $s_{t+1}^\top \nabla f(x_t)$. Then, it updates the iterate as $x_{t+1} = x_t + \lambda_t (s_{t+1} - x_t)$ for some $\lambda_t \in [0, 1]$. Although the classical result [10, 18] suggests $\lambda_t = 2/(t+1)$, one can choose other step size like $\lambda_t := \text{clip}\, \frac{(x_t - s_{t+1})^\top \nabla f(x_t)}{\eta \|s_{t+1} - x_t\|^2}$, where $\text{clip}\, x = \max\{0, \min\{1, x\}\}$. This λ_t minimizes the right-hand side of the smoothness relation $f(x_{t+1}) = f(x_t + \lambda_t(s_{t+1} - x_t)) \leq f(x_t) + \lambda_t \nabla f(x_t) \cdot (s_{t+1} - x_t) + \frac{\eta}{2}\lambda_t^2 \|s_{t+1} - x_t\|^2$, and is often called the *short-step* strategy. Alternatively, one can choose

$$\lambda_t \in \arg\min_{\lambda \in [0,1]} f(x_t + \lambda(s_{t+1} - x_t))$$

by line search. This step size improves the objective more than the short-step strategy. Since the FW algorithm aims to find an optimal solution, one can choose $x_{t+1} \in \arg\min_{x \in \text{ConvHull}(\{s_1, \ldots, s_{t+1}\})} f(x)$. This rule is called the *Fully Corrective* update (e.g., [18]). Although the fully corrective update yields x_{t+1} that most decreases the objective over the convex hull, it loses the fast computational advantage per iteration. One can find other updated rules developed so far, such as Away-step, Pairwise, and Blended Pairwise rules, but this topic is outside the scope of our thesis, so please check the papers [7, 17, 22, 26, 34]. Figure 2 summarizes the Frank-Wolfe protocol. Line 3 measures the optimality gap. By the optimality of s_{t+1} and the convexity of f, the following holds for all $x^\star \in C$.

$$(x_t - s_{t+1})^\top \nabla f(x_t) \geq (x_t - x^\star)^\top \nabla f(x_t) \geq f(x_t) - f(x^\star).$$

Therefore, $(x_t - s_{t+1})^\top \nabla f(x_t) \leq \epsilon$ implies $f(x_t) - \min_{x^\star \in C} f(x^\star) \leq \epsilon$.

Let $\text{diam}(C) \triangleq \max_{a, b \in C} \|a - c\|$ be the diameter of C. FW algorithms converge to an ϵ-approximate solution in $O(\eta\, \text{diam}(C)^2/\epsilon)$ iterations if the objective function is η-smooth[2] w.r.t. a norm $\|\cdot\|$ over C [10, 18]. This bound is optimal for non-strongly

[2] Some papers, such as Ravi et al. [27] and Hazan et al. [14, 15], suggest techniques for general convex functions.

convex but smooth objective since some paper showed $\Omega(1/t^{1+\delta})$ for arbitrarily small $\delta > 0$ [4, 38]. On the other hand, some FW-type algorithms converge linearly when the objective function is not only smooth but also strongly convex [22, 26, 34].

3 Related Work

Many boosting algorithms that maximize the soft margin have been invented [9, 31], but here we introduce three important algorithms, LPBoost [8], ERLPBoost [36], and Corrective ERLPBoost [32].

LPBoost [8] is a practical boosting algorithm for solving problem in Eq. (3). In each iteration t, LPBoost updates its distribution as an optimal solution to problem

$$\boldsymbol{d}_t \leftarrow \arg\min_{\boldsymbol{d}} \max_{k\in[t]} (\boldsymbol{d}^\top A)_{h_k} + \mathbb{I}_{\Delta_{m,\nu}}(\boldsymbol{d}).$$

That is, LPBoost uses an optimal solution to the edge minimization problem over the hypothesis set $\{h_1, h_2, \ldots, h_t\} \subset \mathcal{H}$. LPBoost converges to an ϵ-accurate solution rapidly in practice. However, Warmuth et al. [35] proved that LPBoost converges in $\Omega(m)$ iterations for the worst case. In the same paper, SoftBoost [35], the soft margin version of TotalBoost [37], is invented. SoftBoost converges in $O(\ln(m/\nu)/\epsilon^2)$ iterations, but it tends to be too conservative. Thus, SoftBoost is not practical because it takes time. After that, the stabilized version of LPBoost, ERLPBoost, was invented by Warmuth et al. [36]. The main idea behind ERLPBoost comes from the bundle method [33]. Bundle methods [21, 23, 30] are stabilized versions of the cutting-plane method [20]. The cutting-plane method is known to cause a zig-zag phenomenon, and thus, it converges very slowly in some situations [2, 23]. The cutting-plane method corresponds to LPBoost in this case. Therefore, ERLPBoost can be seen as a stabilized version of LPBoost, i.e., an instance of the bundle method. ERLPBoost updates the distribution as the solution of

$$\boldsymbol{d}_t \leftarrow \arg\min_{\boldsymbol{d}} \max_{k\in[t]} (\boldsymbol{d}^\top A)_{h_k} + \mathbb{I}_{\Delta_{m,\nu}}(\boldsymbol{d}) + \frac{1}{\eta} D_{\mathrm{KL}}(\boldsymbol{d}).$$

Here, $D_{\mathrm{KL}}(\boldsymbol{d}) = \sum_{i=1}^m d_i \ln \frac{d_i}{1/m}$ is the relative entropy from the uniform distribution $\frac{1}{m}\mathbf{1} \in \Delta_{m,\nu}$. They proved that ERLPBoost finds a solution that achieves Eq. (4) in $O(\ln(m/\nu)/\epsilon^2)$ iterations. They also demonstrate that ERLPBoost tends to terminate in fewer iterations than LPBoost. The disadvantage of ERLPBoost is its computational complexity; ERLPBoost solves convex programs in each iteration. This disadvantage leads to much more computation time than LPBoost. The Corrective ERLPBoost (Corr. ERLPBoost, for short) [32] is the corrective version of ERLPBoost. This algorithm achieves the same iteration bound with much faster computation per iteration than LPBoost. Unlike LPBoost and ERLPBoost, Corr. ERLPBoost

Table 1 Soft margin boosting algorithms their upper and lower bound of the number of weak learner calls. The column Sub-problem per round shows the problem that the boosting algorithms solve. m is the number of training examples, ϵ is the accuracy parameter for Eq. (4), and $\nu \in [1, m]$ is the capping parameter

Algorithm	Upper bound	Lower bound	Sub-problem per round
LPBoost [8]	–	$\Omega(m)$	Linear program (LP)
Corr. ERLPBoost [32]	$O(\ln(m/\nu)/\epsilon^2)$	–	Sorting
SoftBoost [35]	$O(\ln(m/\nu)/\epsilon^2)$	–	Convex program (CP)
ERLPBoost [36]	$O(\ln(m/\nu)/\epsilon^2)$	–	Convex program (CP)

maintains the weight $\boldsymbol{w}_t \in \Delta_{\mathcal{H}}$ that only has non-zero values on the entries corresponding to the past hypotheses $\{h_1, h_2, \dots, h_t\} \subset \mathcal{H}$. Corr. ERLPBoost updates its distribution over the training instances as

$$\boldsymbol{d}_t \leftarrow \arg\min_{\boldsymbol{d}} \boldsymbol{d}^\top A \boldsymbol{w}_t + \mathbb{I}_{\Delta_{m,\nu}}(\boldsymbol{d}) + \frac{1}{\eta} D_{\mathrm{KL}}(\boldsymbol{d}). \tag{5}$$

After receiving a hypothesis $h_{t+1} \in \mathcal{H}$ with the corresponding basis $\boldsymbol{e}_{h_{t+1}} \in \Delta_{\mathcal{H}}$, Corr. ERLPBoost updates the weights on hypotheses as $\boldsymbol{w}_{t+1} = \boldsymbol{w}_t + \lambda_t(\boldsymbol{e}_{h_{t+1}} - \boldsymbol{w}_t)$, where $\lambda_t \in [0, 1]$ is some proper value. Although this update rule seems to be a convex program, Shalev-Shwartz et al. [32] showed an algorithm that solves Eq. (5) in $O(m \ln m)$ time. This algorithm seems better than LPBoost and ERLPBoost. However, Warmuth et al. [36] demonstrated that Corr. ERLPBoost takes much more iterations than LPBoost and ERLPBoost. Therefore, the overall computation time is worse than LPBoost. Table 1 summarizes the boosting algorithms for soft margin optimization.

To the best of our knowledge, there is only one previous work that suggests a relation between a boosting algorithm and the Frank-Wolfe algorithm [6]. Their paper shows that AdaBoost [11] is an instance of the Frank-Wolfe algorithm. However, their interpretation is only for the primal problem, while ours comes from the primal-dual problems.

4 The Relation Between Soft Margin Boosting and FW Algorithms

We first show a unified view of the boosting algorithms via Fenchel duality. From this view, LPBoost, ERLPBoost, and Corr. ERLPBoost can be seen as instances of the Frank-Wolfe algorithm with different step sizes and objectives. Using this knowledge, we derive a new boosting scheme.

4.1 A Unified View of Boosting for the Soft Margin Optimization

This section assumes that the weak learner always returns a hypothesis $h \in \mathcal{H}$ that maximizes the edge w.r.t. the given distribution. We start by revisiting Corr. ERLPBoost. Recall that Corr. ERLPBoost (and ERLPBoost) aim to solve the convex program

$$\min_{\boldsymbol{d}} \max_{h \in \mathcal{H}} (\boldsymbol{d}^\top A)_h + f(\boldsymbol{d}),$$

where $f \triangleq \mathbb{I}_{\Delta_{m,\nu}} + \frac{1}{\eta} D_{\mathrm{KL}}$. Since $\frac{1}{\eta} D_{\mathrm{KL}}$ is a $\frac{1}{\eta}$-strongly convex function w.r.t. ℓ_1-norm, so is f. Denoting $g(\boldsymbol{\theta}) = \max_{h \in \mathcal{H}} \theta_h$, one can obtain the Fenchel dual problem

$$\max_{\boldsymbol{w} \in \Delta_{\mathcal{H}}} -f^\star(-A\boldsymbol{w}) = -\min_{\boldsymbol{w} \in \Delta_{\mathcal{H}}} f^\star(-A\boldsymbol{w}) = -\min_{\boldsymbol{\theta} \in -A\Delta_{\mathcal{H}}} f^\star(\boldsymbol{\theta}),$$

where $-A\Delta_{\mathcal{H}} \triangleq \{-A\boldsymbol{w} \mid \boldsymbol{w} \in \Delta_{\mathcal{H}}\}$. By definition, $\operatorname{core}\left(\operatorname{dom} g - A^\top \operatorname{dom} f\right) = \mathbb{R}^{\mathcal{H}}$, which implies $\boldsymbol{0} \in \operatorname{core}\left(\operatorname{dom} g - A^\top \operatorname{dom} f\right)$ so the duality gap is zero. Further, $f^\star$ is an η-smooth function w.r.t. ℓ_∞-norm. Thus, the soft margin optimization problem becomes a minimization problem of a smooth function.

In each iteration t, Corr. ERLPBoost updates the distribution $\boldsymbol{d}_t \in \Delta_{m,\nu}$ over examples as the optimal solution of Eq. (5). This computation corresponds to the gradient computation $\nabla f^\star(\theta_t)$, where $\theta_t = -A\boldsymbol{w}_t$. Then, obtain a basis vector $\boldsymbol{e}_{h_{t+1}} \in \Delta_{\mathcal{H}}$ corresponding to hypothesis $h_{h_{t+1}} \in \mathcal{H}$ that maximizes the edge; $h_{t+1} \in \arg\max_{h \in \mathcal{H}} (\boldsymbol{d}_t^\top A)_h$. We can write this calculation regarding the gradient of $f^\star$;

$$\arg\max_{\boldsymbol{e}_h : h \in \mathcal{H}} \boldsymbol{d}_t^\top A\boldsymbol{e}_h = \arg\min_{\boldsymbol{e}_h : h \in \mathcal{H}} (-A\boldsymbol{e}_h)^\top \nabla f^\star(\boldsymbol{\theta}_t) = \arg\min_{\boldsymbol{\theta} \in -A\Delta_{\mathcal{H}}} \boldsymbol{\theta}^\top \nabla f^\star(\boldsymbol{\theta}_t).$$

Thus, finding a hypothesis that maximizes edge corresponds to solving linear programming in the Frank-Wolfe algorithm. Further, Corr. ERLPBoost updates the weights as $\boldsymbol{w}_{t+1} = \boldsymbol{w}_t + \lambda_t(\boldsymbol{e}_{h_{t+1}} - \boldsymbol{w}_t)$, where λ_t is the short-step.[3] From these observations, we can say that the Corr. ERLPBoost is an instance of the Frank-Wolfe algorithm. Since $f^\star$ is η-smooth, we can say that this algorithm converges in $O(\eta/\epsilon)$ iterations for a max-edge weak learner.

Similarly, we can say that LPBoost and ERLPBoost are instances of the Frank-Wolfe algorithm. Let $\mathcal{E}_t := \{\boldsymbol{e}_h \mid h \in \{h_1, h_2, \ldots, h_t\}\}$ be the set of basis vectors corresponding to the hypotheses up to round t. LPBoost and ERLPBoost update the distribution as the optimal solutions $\boldsymbol{d}_t^{\mathrm{L}} \in \partial \mathbb{I}^\star_{\Delta_{m,\nu}}(-A\boldsymbol{w}_t^{\mathrm{L}})$ and $\boldsymbol{d}_t^{\mathrm{E}} = \nabla f^\star(-A\boldsymbol{w}_t^{\mathrm{E}})$, where

[3] They also suggest the line search update. This case yields a better progress than short-step, so the same iteration bound holds.

Algorithm 1: A theoretically guaranteed boosting scheme

Input: Training examples $S = ((\boldsymbol{x}_i, y_i))_{i=1}^m \in (\mathcal{X} \times \{\pm 1\})^m$, a g-weak learner $\mathcal{W} : \Delta_m \to \mathcal{H}$, a FW algorithm $\mathcal{F}$, a secondary algorithm $\mathcal{B}$, and parameters $\nu \in [1, m]$ and $\epsilon > 0$.

Set $A = (y_i h(\boldsymbol{x}_i)) \in [-1, +1]^{m \times \mathcal{H}}$.

Obtain a hypothesis $h_1 = \mathcal{W}(\boldsymbol{d}_0) \in \mathcal{H}$, where $\boldsymbol{d}_0 = \frac{1}{m}\mathbf{1}$.

Set $\boldsymbol{w}_1 = \boldsymbol{e}_1$.

for $t = 1, 2, \ldots, T$ **do**

  Compute the distribution $\boldsymbol{d}_t = \nabla f^\star(-A\boldsymbol{w}_t) = \arg\min_{\boldsymbol{d} \in \Delta_{m,\nu}} \left[\boldsymbol{d}^\top A \boldsymbol{w}_t + \frac{1}{\eta} D_{\mathrm{KL}}(\boldsymbol{d}) \right]$.

  Obtain a hypothesis $h_{t+1} = \mathcal{W}(\boldsymbol{d}_t) \in \mathcal{H}$.

  Set $\epsilon_t := \min_{0 \le \tau \le t} (\boldsymbol{d}_\tau^\top A)_{h_{\tau+1}} + f^\star(-A\boldsymbol{w}_t)$ and let $\mathcal{E}_{t+1} := \{\boldsymbol{e}_{h_\tau}\}_{\tau=1}^{t+1}$.

  if $\epsilon_t \le \epsilon/2$ **then** Set $T = t$, **break**

  Compute the FW weight $\boldsymbol{w}_{t+1}^{\mathcal{F}} = \mathcal{F}(A, \boldsymbol{w}_t, \boldsymbol{e}_{h_{t+1}}, \mathcal{E}_t, \boldsymbol{d}_t)$.

  Compute the secondary weight $\boldsymbol{w}_{t+1}^{\mathcal{B}} = \mathcal{B}(A, \mathcal{E}_{t+1})$.

  Update the weight $\boldsymbol{w}_{t+1} \leftarrow \arg\min_{\boldsymbol{w} \in \{\boldsymbol{w}_{t+1}^{\mathcal{F}}, \boldsymbol{w}_{t+1}^{\mathcal{B}}\}} f^\star(-A\boldsymbol{w})$.

end

Output: Combined classifier $H_T = \sum_{t=1}^T w_{T,t} h_t$.

Algorithm 2: The short-step rule $\mathcal{F}\,(A, \boldsymbol{w}, \boldsymbol{e}, \mathcal{E}, \boldsymbol{d})$

Input: A matrix $A \in [-1, +1]^{m \times \mathcal{H}}$, vectors $\boldsymbol{w}, \boldsymbol{e} \in \mathbb{R}^{\mathcal{H}}$ and $\boldsymbol{d} \in \mathbb{R}^m$, and a set $\mathcal{E} \subset \mathbb{R}^{\mathcal{H}}$.

Output: $\boldsymbol{w} \leftarrow \boldsymbol{w} + \lambda(\boldsymbol{e} - \boldsymbol{w})$, where $\lambda = \operatorname{clip} \frac{\boldsymbol{d}^\top A(\boldsymbol{e}-\boldsymbol{w})}{\eta \|A(\boldsymbol{e}-\boldsymbol{w})\|_\infty^2}$.

$$
\begin{aligned}
\text{LPBoost:} \quad & \boldsymbol{w}_t^{\mathrm{L}} \leftarrow \arg \max_{\boldsymbol{w} \in \mathrm{ConvHull}(\mathcal{E}_t)} -\mathbb{I}^\star_{\Delta_{m,\nu}}(-A\boldsymbol{w}), \\
\text{ERLPBoost:} \quad & \boldsymbol{w}_t^{\mathrm{E}} \leftarrow \arg \max_{\boldsymbol{w} \in \mathrm{ConvHull}(\mathcal{E}_t)} -f^\star(-A\boldsymbol{w}).
\end{aligned} \tag{6}
$$

Therefore, we can say that LPBoost and ERLPBoost are instances of the fully corrective FW algorithm for objectives $\mathbb{I}^\star_{\Delta_{m,\nu}}$ and $f^\star$, respectively. Under the max-edge weak learner assumption, one can derive the same iteration bound for ERLPBoost and Corr. ERLPBoost since $f^\star$ is η-smooth w.r.t. ℓ_∞-norm and $\operatorname{diam}(-A\Delta_{\mathcal{H}}) = \max_{\boldsymbol{w}_1, \boldsymbol{w}_2 \in \Delta_{\mathcal{H}}} \|A(\boldsymbol{w}_1 - \boldsymbol{w}_2)\|_\infty \le 2$. We summarize these connections to the following theorem.

Theorem 2 *LPBoost, ERLPBoost, and Corr. ERLPBoost are instances of the FW algorithm.*

Algorithm 3: LPBoost rule $\mathcal{B}(A, \mathcal{E})$

Input: A matrix $A \in [-1, +1]^{m \times \mathcal{H}}$ and a set $\mathcal{E} \subset \mathbb{R}^{\mathcal{H}}$.
Output: $\boldsymbol{w} \leftarrow \arg\max_{\boldsymbol{w} \in \mathrm{ConvHull}(\mathcal{E})} \min_{\boldsymbol{d} \in \Delta_{m,\nu}} \boldsymbol{d}^\top A \boldsymbol{w}$.

4.2 A General Boosting Scheme for Soft Margin Optimization

We propose a FW-like boosting scheme from the previous observations, shown in Algorithm 1. Algorithm 1 takes two update rules, a FW update rule $\mathcal{F}$ and a secondary update rule $\mathcal{B}$. Both algorithms return a weight $\boldsymbol{w} \in \Delta_{\mathcal{H}}$. Intuitively, the FW update rule $\boldsymbol{w}_t^{\mathcal{F}}$ is a safety net for the convergence guarantee, and the secondary update is for better performance in practice. Further, the convergence analysis only depends on the FW update $\boldsymbol{w}_{t+1}^{\mathcal{F}}$, so that one can incorporate any update rule to $\mathcal{B}$. For example, one can use the update rule stated in Eq. (6) as $\mathcal{B}(A, \mathcal{E}_{t+1})$. Algorithm 1 becomes ERLPBoost in this case since $\boldsymbol{w}_{t+1} = \boldsymbol{w}_{t+1}^{\mathcal{B}}$ holds for any t. Even through this setting, the convergence guarantee holds so that we can prove the same convergence rate for ERLPBoost by our general analysis.

Recall that our primary objective is to find a weight vector $\boldsymbol{w}$ that optimizes Eq. (3). The most practical algorithm, LPBoost, solves Eq. (3) over past hypotheses, so using the solution as $\mathcal{B}$ is a natural choice. Algorithm 3 summarizes this update. Note that the LPBoost update differs from the fully corrective FW algorithm since the objective function is $f^\star$, not $\mathbb{I}^\star_{\Delta_{m,\nu}}$.

Furthermore, as described by Shalev-Shwartz et al. [32], one can compute the distribution $\boldsymbol{d}_t = \nabla f^\star(-A\boldsymbol{w}_t)$ by a sorting-based algorithm, which takes $O(m \ln m)$ iterations.[4] Thus, the time complexity per iteration depends on the secondary algorithm $\mathcal{B}$.

Before getting into the convergence analysis, we first justify the stopping criterion in Algorithm 1. This criterion is similar to the one in FW but strictly better than it. Therefore, our algorithms tend to converge in early iterations.

Lemma 2 *Let* $\epsilon_t := \min_{0 \le \tau \le t} (\boldsymbol{d}_\tau^\top A)_{h_{\tau+1}} + f^\star(-A\boldsymbol{w}_t)$ *be the optimality gap and let* $\eta = \frac{2}{\epsilon} \ln \frac{m}{\nu}$. *Then,* $\epsilon_t \le \frac{\epsilon}{2}$ *implies* $-\mathbb{I}^\star_{\Delta_{m,\nu}}(-A\boldsymbol{w}_t) \ge \gamma - \epsilon$.

Proof By the weak-learnability assumption, $\epsilon_t \ge \gamma + f^\star(-A\boldsymbol{w}_t)$. The statement follows from Lemma 1.

Now, we prove the convergence rate for our scheme. This theorem also covers the convergence rate for ERLPBoost and Corr. ERLPBoost.

Theorem 3 (A convergence rate for Algorithm 1) *Under Assumption 1, let* $\mathcal{F}$ *be the FW update with classic step* $\lambda_t = \frac{2}{t+2}$, *or short-step as in Algorithm 2. Then, for any secondary algorithm* $\mathcal{B}$, *Algorithm 1 finds a solution satisfying Eq. (4) in* $O\left(\frac{1}{\epsilon^2} \ln \frac{m}{\nu}\right)$ *iterations.*

[4] They also suggest a linear time algorithm, see [16].

Proof First of all, we prove the bound for the classic step size. We start by showing the recursion

$$\epsilon_{t+1} \leq (1 - \lambda_t)\epsilon_t + 2\eta\lambda_t^2. \tag{7}$$

By using the definition of $\boldsymbol{w}_{t+1}$ and the η-smoothness of $f^\star$,

$$\begin{aligned}\epsilon_t - \epsilon_{t+1} &\geq f^\star(-A\boldsymbol{w}_t) - f^\star(-A\boldsymbol{w}_t^{\mathcal{F}}) \\ &= f^\star(-A\boldsymbol{w}_t) - f^\star(-A\boldsymbol{w}_t + \lambda_t A(\boldsymbol{w}_t - \boldsymbol{e}_{h_{t+1}})) \\ &\geq \lambda_t (A(\boldsymbol{e}_{h_{t+1}} - \boldsymbol{w}_t))^\top \nabla f^\star(-A\boldsymbol{w}_t) - 2\eta\lambda_t^2, \end{aligned} \tag{8}$$

where the last inequality holds since $A \in [-1, +1]^{m \times \mathcal{H}}$ and $\boldsymbol{e}_{h_{t+1}}, \boldsymbol{w}_t \in \Delta_{\mathcal{H}}$. By the non-negativity of the entropy function and the definition of $\boldsymbol{d}_t$, we get

$$\begin{aligned}(A(\boldsymbol{e}_{h_{t+1}} - \boldsymbol{w}_t))^\top \nabla f^\star(-A\boldsymbol{w}_t) &= \boldsymbol{d}_t^\top A(\boldsymbol{e}_{h_{t+1}} - \boldsymbol{w}_t) \\ &\geq \left[\min_{0\leq\tau\leq t} (\boldsymbol{d}_\tau^\top A)_{h_{\tau+1}} - \boldsymbol{d}_t^\top A\boldsymbol{w}_t - \frac{1}{\eta} D_{\mathrm{KL}}(\boldsymbol{d}_t)\right] \\ &= \left[\min_{0\leq\tau\leq t} (\boldsymbol{d}_\tau^\top A)_{h_{\tau+1}} + f^\star(-A\boldsymbol{w}_t)\right] = \epsilon_t. \end{aligned} \tag{9}$$

Combining Eq. (8) and Eq. (9), we obtain Eq. (7).

Now, we have Eq. (7). We will show that $\epsilon_t \leq \frac{8\eta}{t+2}$ by induction on $t \geq 1$. For the base case $t = 1$, $\epsilon_1 \leq 2\eta\lambda_t^2 \leq \frac{8\eta}{3}$, so the inequality holds. Assume that the inequality holds for t. Using Eq. (7) and the induction hypothesis, $\epsilon_{t+1} \leq \frac{t}{t+2}\frac{8\eta}{t+2} + \frac{8\eta}{(t+2)^2} \leq \frac{8\eta}{t+3}$. Therefore, the inequality holds for all $t \geq 1$. By the definition of η, $\epsilon_T \leq \frac{\epsilon}{2}$ holds in $T = \frac{32}{\epsilon^2}\ln\frac{m}{\nu} - 2$ iterations. Combining with Lemma 2 yields the convergence rate.

For the short-step case, that is, the case where we employ Algorithm 2 as $\mathcal{F}$, we get a similar recursion:

$$\begin{aligned}\epsilon_t - \epsilon_{t+1} &\geq f^\star(-A\boldsymbol{w}_t) - f^\star(-A\boldsymbol{w}_t^{\mathcal{F}}) \\ &\geq \lambda_t (A(\boldsymbol{e}_{h_{t+1}} - \boldsymbol{w}_t))^\top \nabla f^\star(-A\boldsymbol{w}_t) - \frac{\eta}{2}\lambda_t^2 \|A(\boldsymbol{w}_t - \boldsymbol{e}_{h_{t+1}})\|_\infty^2 \quad (10) \\ &\geq \lambda (A(\boldsymbol{e}_{h_{t+1}} - \boldsymbol{w}_t))^\top \nabla f^\star(-A\boldsymbol{w}_t) - 2\eta\lambda^2, \qquad \forall\lambda \in [0, 1]. \end{aligned}$$

Since the short-step is the maximizer of Eq. (10), the last inequality holds for all $\lambda \in [0, 1]$. Optimizing λ in RHS and applying Inequality (9), we get $\epsilon_t - \epsilon_{t+1} \geq \frac{\epsilon_t^2}{8\eta}$. Using Lemma 20 in [32], we obtain the same iteration bound.

Theorem 3 shows a convergence guarantee for the *classic step* and the *short-step*. The line search $\arg\min_{\lambda\in[0,1]} f^\star\left(-A(\boldsymbol{w}_t + \lambda(\boldsymbol{e}_{h_{t+1}} - \boldsymbol{w}_t))\right)$ always yields better progress than the *short-step*, so the same iteration bound holds.

Other variants of the boosting scheme

The FW update rule $\boldsymbol{w}_{t+1}^{\mathcal{F}} \leftarrow \mathcal{F}\left(A, \boldsymbol{w}_t, \boldsymbol{e}_{h_{t+1}}, \mathcal{E}_t, \boldsymbol{d}_t\right)$ of Algorithm 2 comes from the FW algorithm with short-step sizes. One can apply other update rules, such as Pairwise Frank-Wolfe Algorithm [22] and Blended Pairwise Frank-Wolfe Algorithm [34], as $\mathcal{F}$. These algorithms converge to an ϵ-approximate solution in $O(\eta/\epsilon)$ rounds for our objective function $f^\star$. Though the convergence rate is the same, some experiments showed that these algorithms are fast in practice. So, developing FW algorithms also improves Algorithm 1.

5 Experiment

First of all, we note that the gradient boosting algorithms, like XGBoost [5] or LightGBM [19], solve different problems, so we do not compare ours to them. We compared LPBoost, ERLPBoost, Corr. ERLPBoost, and our scheme on Gunnar Rätsch's benchmark datasets.[5] We used a computer with Intel Xeon Gold 6124 CPU 2.60GHz processors. We call Algorithm 1 with the secondary algorithm shown in Algorithm 3 as MLPBoost. In MLPBoost, we adopt the short-step strategy as the Frank-Wolfe step size. Since the parameter η is a huge value, we expect the secondary algorithm, the LPBoost sub-routine, to be adopted much more frequently. One can try other step strategies, but it is enough for this experiment to show the performance of our algorithm. As in the original Corrective ERLPBoost, we also used the short-step strategy. We used the Gurobi optimizer 9.0.1[6] to solve the sub-problems of these boosting algorithms. The sub-problem of ERLPBoost cannot be a solvable directory, so we use the sequential quadratic programming technique [25].
Computation time
We used the tolerance parameter $\epsilon = 0.01$ and the capping parameter $\nu = 0.05m$, where m is the number of training examples. We measured the running time for each round. As discussed in the previous sections, the soft margin optimization regards at most ν examples as outliers. We used the weak learner that returns a decision tree of depth 2. The splitting rule for the decision tree is based on the entropic impurity. The algorithms may take long to converge, so we abort the computations after an hour. Figure 3 shows the comparison for the benchmark datasets. Here, we note that the curves show the soft margin objective defined in Eq. (3), which is not the objective function for ERLPBoost, CERLPBoost, and MLPBoost. Therefore, the curves for these algorithms do not increase monotonically. As we expected, MLPBoost performs like LPBoost for some datasets. Although the results highly depend on the datasets, MLPBoost performs well compared to ERLPBoost and Corr. ERLPBoost.
The worst case for LPBoost
Fig. 3 shows that LPBoost outperforms other algorithms. Although LPBoost has no non-trivial iteration bound, it has the worst-case lower bound. For the worst case,

[5] https://github.com/tdiethe/gunnar_raetsch_benchmark_datasets.
[6] https://www.gurobi.com/.

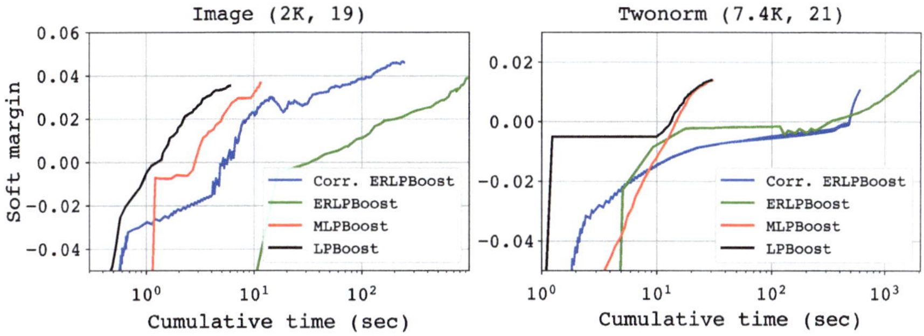

Fig. 3 Comparison of the algorithm for the benchmark datasets with parameters $\epsilon = 0.01$ and $\nu = 0.05m$. The vertical axis shows the soft margin objective values and the horizontal one shows the cumulative time (seconds). The tuple on each title shows (# of examples, # of features).

Table 2 The worst-case behavior of LPBoost when given m training examples with capping parameter $\nu = 1$. As suggested by Warmuth et al. [35], one can extend to the soft margin setting $\nu \in (1, m]$. Even for such cases, similar phenomena happen

	LPBoost	ERLPBoost	Corr. ERLPBoost	MLPBoost
# of iterations	$m/2$	2	2	2

it takes $m/2$ iterations [35]. The paper suggests a weak learner for the worst case, which picks one from $O(m)$ hypotheses. The hypothesis set has two good hypotheses that construct a margin-maximizing combined hypothesis, and the rest are the bad ones. One of the good hypotheses can be attained at the first iteration, which gives uniform distribution to the weak learner. Since LPBoost assigns zero weight to some examples, the weak learner chooses bad hypotheses repeatedly. Even in this case, MLPBoost and ERLPBoost terminate in 2 iterations.[7] These algorithms put a non-zero weight for all examples so the weak learner can produce the good hypothesis in the second iteration. We summarize this fact in Table 2 since the experiment figure has no information due to the behavior.

6 Conclusion

This chapter explores the relation between soft margin boosting algorithms and Frank-Wolfe algorithms. The unified view allows us to easily prove a convergence rate for boosting algorithms. Furthermore, introducing heuristic algorithms into the scheme can achieve a better convergence rate for practical situations without losing the convergence guarantee.

Acknowledgment This work was partly supported by JSPS KAKENHI Grant Number JP20H05967.

[7] The code is available at https://github.com/rmitsuboshi/miniboosts.

References

1. N. Alon, A. Gonen, E. Hazan, S. Moran, Boosting simple learners. *TheoretiCS* **2** (2023)
2. A. Belloni, *Introduction to bundle methods*. Technical report, Technical report, Operation Research Center, MIT (2005)
3. J.M. Borwein, A.S. Lewis, *Convex Analysis* (Springer, New York, 2006), pp. 65–96
4. M.D. Canon, C.D. Cullum, A tight upper bound on the rate of convergence of Frank-Wolfe Algorithm. SIAM J. Control **6**(4), 509–516 (1968)
5. T. Chen, C. Guestrin. XGBoost: a scalable tree boosting system, in *Proceedings of the 22nd ACM SIGKDD International Conference on Knowledge Discovery and Data Mining, (KDD 2016)* (Association for Computing Machinery, 2016), pp. 785–794
6. K.L. Clarkson, Coresets, sparse greedy approximation, and the Frank-Wolfe algorithm. ACM Trans. Algorithms **6**(4), 63:1–63:30 (2010)
7. C.W. Combettes, S. Pokutta, Boosting Frank-Wolfe by chasing gradients, in *Proceedings of the 37th International Conference on Machine Learning, (ICML 2020)*, volume 119 of *Proceedings of Machine Learning Research* (PMLR, 2020), pp. 2111–2121
8. A. Demiriz, K.P. Bennett, J. Shawe-Taylor, Linear programming boosting via column generation. Mach. Learn. **46**(1–3), 225–254 (2002)
9. C. Domingo, O. Watanabe, MadaBoost: a Modification of AdaBoost, in N. Cesa-Bianchi, S.A. Goldman, (eds.), *Proceedings of the Thirteenth Annual Conference on Computational Learning Theory (COLT 2000)* (Morgan Kaufmann, 2000), pp. 180–189
10. M. Frank, P. Wolfe, An algorithm for quadratic programming. Naval Res. Log. Q. **3**(1–2), 95–110 (1956)
11. Y. Freund, R.E. Schapire, A decision-theoretic generalization of on-line learning and an application to boosting. J. Comput. Syst. Sci. **55**(1), 119–139 (1997)
12. W. Gao, Z. Zhou, On the doubt about margin explanation of boosting. Artif. Intell. **203**, 1–18 (2013)
13. A. Grønlund, L. Kamma, K.G. Larsen, A. Mathiasen, J. Nelson, Margin-Based generalization lower bounds for boosted classifiers, in H.M. Wallach, H. Larochelle, A. Beygelzimer, F. d'Alché-Buc, E.B. Fox, R. Garnett (eds.), *Advances in Neural Information Processing Systems 32: Annual Conference on Neural Information Processing Systems 2019, (NeurIPS 2019)*, pp. 11940–11949 (2019)
14. E. Hazan, S. Kale, Projection-free online learning, in *Proceedings of the 29th International Conference on Machine Learning, (ICML 2012)* (2012). icml.cc/Omnipress
15. E. Hazan, E. Minasyan, Faster projection-free online learning, in J.D. Abernethy, S. Agarwal (eds.), *Conference on Learning Theory, (COLT 2020)*, volume 125 of *Proceedings of Machine Learning Research*, PMLR, pp. 1877–1893 (2020)
16. M. Herbster, M.K. Warmuth, Tracking the best linear predictor. J. Mach. Learn. Res. **1**, 281-309 (2001)
17. J. Guélat, P. Marcotte, Some comments on Wolfe's 'away step.' Math. Program. **35**, 110–119 (1986)
18. M. Jaggi, Revisiting Frank-Wolfe: projection-free sparse convex optimization, in *Proceedings of the 30th International Conference on Machine Learning, ICML 2013*, volume 28 of *JMLR Workshop and Conference Proceedings*, pp. 427–435 (2013). JMLR.org
19. G. Ke, Q. Meng, T. Finley, T. Wang, W. Chen, W. Ma, Q. Ye, T. Liu, LightGBM: a highly efficient gradient boosting decision tree, in *Advances in Neural Information Processing Systems 30: Annual Conference on Neural Information Processing Systems 2017, (NIPS 2017)*, pp. 3146–3154 (2017)
20. J.E. Kelley Jr., The cutting-plane method for solving convex programs. J. Soc. Ind. Appl. Math. **8**(4), 703–712 (1960)
21. K.C. Kiwiel, Proximity Control in Bundle Methods for Convex Nondifferentiable Minimization. Math. Program. **46**, 105–122 (1990)

22. S. Lacoste-Julien, M. Jaggi, On the global linear convergence of Frank-Wolfe optimization variants, in *Advances in Neural Information Processing Systems 28: Annual Conference on Neural Information Processing Systems 2015, (NIPS 2015)*, pp. 496–504 (2015)
23. C. Lemaréchal, A. Nemirovskii, Y.E. Nesterov, New variants of bundle methods. Math. Program. **69**, 111–147 (1995)
24. M. Mohri, A. Rostamizadeh, A. Talwalker, *Foundation of Machine Learning*, 2nd ed. (The MIT Press, 2018)
25. J. Nocedal, S.J. Wright. *Numerical Optimization* (Springer, 1999)
26. F. Pedregosa, G. Négiar, A. Askari, M. Jaggi, Linearly Convergent Frank-Wolfe without Line-Search, in *The 23rd International Conference on Artificial Intelligence and Statistics, (AISTATS 2020)*, Proceedings of Machine Learning Research, PMLR (2020)
27. S.N. Ravi, M.D. Collins, V. Singh, A Deterministic Nonsmooth Frank Wolfe Algorithm with coreset guarantees. INFORMS J. Optim. **1**(2), 120–142 (2019)
28. R.E. Schapire, Y. Freund, P. Bartlett, W.S. Lee, Boosting the margin: a new explanation for the effectiveness of voting methods. Ann. Stat. **26**(5), 1651–1686 (1998)
29. B. Schölkopf, A.J. Smola, R.C. Williamson, P.L. Bartlett, New support vector algorithms. Neural Comput. **12**(5), 1207–1245 (2000)
30. H. Schramm, J. Zowe, A version of the bundle idea for minimizing a nonsmooth function: conceptual idea, convergence analysis, numerical results. SIAM J. Optim. **2**(1), 121–152 (1992)
31. R.A. Servedio, Smooth boosting and learning with malicious noise. J. Mach. Learn. Res. **4**, 633–648 (2003)
32. S. Shalev-Shwartz, Y. Singer, On the equivalence of weak learnability and linear separability: new relaxations and efficient boosting algorithms. Mach. Learn. **80**(2–3) (2010)
33. C.H. Teo, S.V.N. Vishwanathan, A.J. Smola, Q.V. Le, Bundle methods for regularized risk minimization. J. Mach. Learn. Res. **11**, 311–365 (2010)
34. K. Tsuji, K. Tanaka, S. Pokutta, Pairwise conditional gradients without swap steps and Sparser Kernel Herding, in *International Conference on Machine Learning, (ICML 2022)*, volume 162 of *Proceedings of Machine Learning Research* (2022)
35. M. Warmuth, K. Glocer, G. Rätsch, Boosting algorithms for maximizing the soft margin, in *Advances in Neural Information Processing Systems 20 (NIPS 2007)*, pp. 1585–1592 (2007)
36. M.K. Warmuth, K.A. Glocer, S.V.N. Vishwanathan, Entropy regularized LPBoost, in *Proceedings of the 19th International Conference on Algorithmic Learning Theory, (ALT 2008)*, volume 5254 (Springer, 2008), pp. 256–271
37. M.K. Warmuth, J. Liao, G. Rätsch, Totally corrective boosting algorithms that maximize the margin, in *Proceedings of the 23rd international conference on Machine learning (ICML 2006)*, pp. 1001–1008 (2006)
38. P. Wolfe, Convergence theory in nonlinear programming. *Integer and nonlinear programming*, pp. 1–36 (1970)

Cost Graph Colorings

Yasuko Matsui and Shin-Ichi Nakano

Abstract Graph colorings are ubiquitous in the modeling of real-world problems. There are many applications and conjectures, which are still open and studied by various mathematicians and computer scientists. In this paper, we deal with cost graph colorings as an important subfield of graph colorings. In cost graph coloring, each color has a distinct cost, and we need to pay the cost each time to color each vertex or edge. Our task is to find a coloring with the minimum total cost. The cost coloring problems are NP-hard in general; however, polynomial time algorithms are known for certain classes of graphs.

1 Introduction

Graph coloring is a very active field of research in graph theory [4] and has numerous applications including scheduling.

For instance, we consider some scheduling problems in schools. Assume that we have a set V of classes and a set E of conflict pairs of classes. Because a conflict pair of classes share a student, the two classes cannot be held at the same time slot. Then our task is to assign each class to one of time slots so that each time slot has no conflict pair of classes. One can solve the problem by coloring each vertex of graph $G = (V, E)$ so that any two vertices connected by an edge are different colors. We assign the vertices with color i to time slot i. We typically strive for coloring with the minimum number of colors.

Assume that each time slot has a different cost because you need to pay more to the instructor late at night, or an electricity company with summer afternoons extra charge. Now our task is to assign each class to one of time slots with no conflict and

Y. Matsui (✉)
Department of Mathematical Sciences, School of Science, Tokai University, 4-1-1 Kita-kaname, Hiratsuka, Kanagawa 259-1292, Japan
e-mail: yasuko@tokai.ac.jp

S.-I. Nakano
Faculty of Informatics, Gunma University, 4-2 Aramaki-cho, Maebashi, Gunma 371-8510, Japan
e-mail: nakano@gunma-u.ac.jp

S. Minato et al. (eds.), *Algorithmic Foundations for Social Advancement*,
https://doi.org/10.1007/978-981-96-0668-9_22

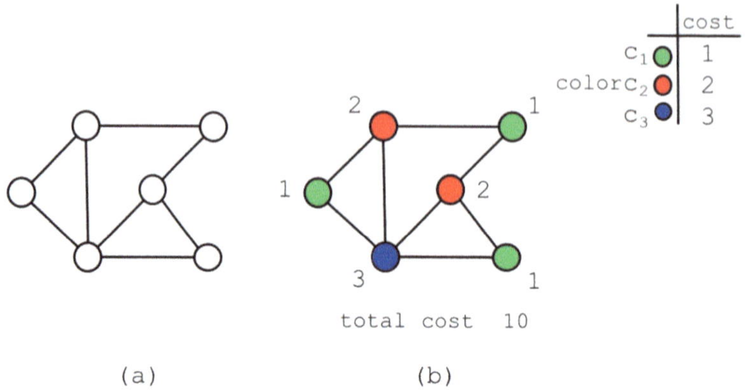

Fig. 1 **a** An example of G. **b** A cost vertex-coloring with the minimum total cost

with the minimum total cost. One can solve the problem by coloring each vertex as above with paying cost each time to color each vertex depending on the color and with the minimum total cost. In Fig. 1, we show an example of graph and its cost vertex-coloring.

Another example is as follows. Assume that we have a set U of classes, a set V of teachers, and a set E of class-teacher pairs. Two class-teacher pairs are in conflict if the pairs share either a teacher or a class. Thus any conflict class-teacher pair cannot be assigned to the same time slot. One can solve the problem by coloring each edge of bipartite graph $G = (U \cap V, E)$ so that any pair of edges sharing an end vertex has different colors. We assign the edges with color i to time slot i. We typically strive for coloring with the minimum number of colors.

Assume that each time slot has different cost. Now our task is to assign each class-teacher pair to one of time slots with no conflicts and with the minimum total cost. One can solve the problem by coloring each edge as above with paying cost each time to color each edge depending on the color and with the minimum total cost. In Fig. 2, we show an example of a graph and its cost edge-coloring. Then an edge-coloring of the bipartite graph corresponds to a time table.

The remainder of this paper is organized as follows. In Sect. 2, we set up definitions and notation. In Sects. 3 and 4, we define cost vertex-coloring and cost edge-coloring and give known results. Finally, in Sect. 5 we conclude the paper.

2 Preliminary

Let $G = (V, E)$ be a graph with vertex set V and edge set E. We denote $|V|$ and $|E|$ by n and m, respectively. Throughout this paper, graphs are simple (no multiple edges) except Theorems 13 and 14, and connected. A *tree* T is a connected graph

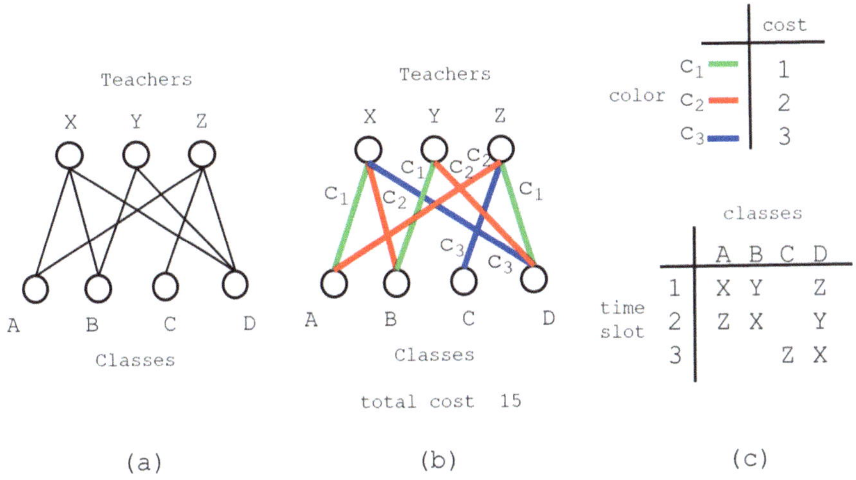

Fig. 2 **a** An example of G. **b** A cost edge-coloring with the minimum total cost. **c** The corresponding time table

with no cycles. The *degree* $deg(v)$ of a vertex v is the number of edges incident to v. We denote the maximum degree of G by Δ.

Let $C = \{c_1, c_2, \ldots, c_q\}$ be a set of colors with q colors. Let $\omega : C \to R$ be a cost function which assigns a real number $\omega(c) \in R$ to each color $c \in C$. One may assume that ω is non-decreasing, that is, $\omega(c_1) \leq \omega(c_2) \leq \cdots \leq \omega(c_q)$.

3 Cost Vertex-Coloring Problem

A *vertex-coloring* $f_v : V \to C$ of $G = (V, E)$ is to color V with colors in C so that any two vertices connected by an edge have different colors. The vertex-coloring is optimal if it uses the minimum number of colors.

The cost $\omega(f_v)$ of a vertex-coloring f_v of $G = (V, E)$ is defined as follows:

$$\omega(f_v) = \sum_{v \in V} \omega(f_v(v)).$$

A *cost vertex-coloring* f_v of G is *optimal* if $\omega(f_v)$ is the minimum among all cost vertex-colorings of G. The *cost vertex-coloring problem* is to find an optimal cost vertex-coloring. Note that using more colors may result in less total cost. See an example in Fig. 3. The (original) vertex-coloring is the cost vertex-coloring with $w(c_1) = w(c_2) = \cdots = w(c_q)$ and additionally minimizing the number of colors.

The cost vertex-coloring problem was introduced by Supowit [15].

Note that the cost vertex-coloring problem is different from the "*Weighted Coloring Problem*" in which each vertex has weight, the cost of a color is the maximum

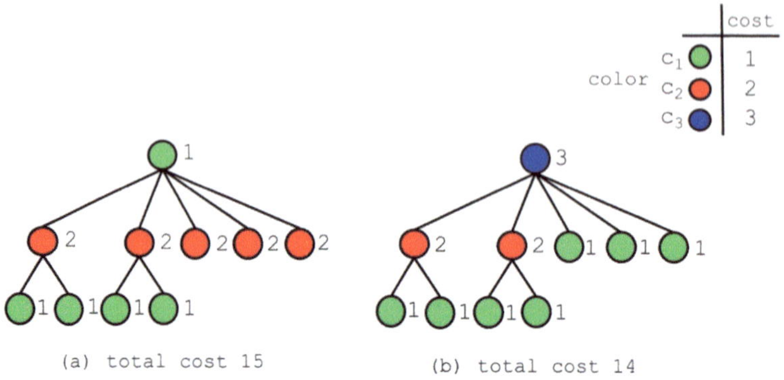

Fig. 3 **a** A cost vertex-coloring with 2 colors and total cost 15. **b** An optimal cost vertex-coloring with 3 colors and total cost 14

weight of the vertex colored with the color, and the cost of a coloring is the maximum cost among the costs of colors.

The cost vertex-coloring problem is NP-hard for interval graphs [9] and bipartite graphs [8]. However, the problem can be solved by dynamic programming in linear time for trees [12] and in polynomial time for graphs with bounded treewidth [8]. Also the problem can be solved in $O(n^2)$ time for bipartite graphs with $\Delta \leq 4$ [6].

Theorem 1 ([9]) *The cost vertex-coloring problem for interval graphs is NP-hard if there are at least four different values for the costs of colors.*

Theorem 2 ([8]) *The cost vertex-coloring problem for bipartite graphs is NP-hard.*

Theorem 3 ([9]) *The cost vertex-coloring problem for trees can be solved in O(n) time.*

Theorem 4 ([8]) *The cost vertex-coloring problem for graphs with treewidth at most k can be solved in* $O(n(\log n)^{k+1})$ *time.*

Theorem 5 ([6]) *The cost vertex-coloring problem for a bipartite graph G with* $\Delta \leq 4$ *can be solved in* $O(n^2)$ *time, using only at most three cheapest colors.*

The *vertex-chromatic sum problem* [10, 12] is the cost vertex-coloring problem with $\omega(c_i) = i$ for each i. Recall that $C = \{c_1, c_2, \ldots, c_q\}$. The following results are known.

Theorem 6 ([12]) *The vertex-chromatic sum problem for trees can be solved in O(n) time.*

For some restricted classes of graphs, the following results are known. A *unicyclic graph* is a connected graph containing exactly one cycle. An *outerplanar graph* is a graph having a planar embedding with all the vertices lying on the boundary of the outer face.

Theorem 7 ([11]) *The vertex-chromatic sum problem for unicyclic graphs can be solved in O(n) time. The vertex-chromatic sum problem for outerplanar graphs can be solved in $O(n^3)$ time.*

Can we efficiently enumerate all the cost vertex-colorings with the total cost less than given constant budget k?

4 Cost Edge-Coloring Problem

An *edge-coloring* $f_e : E \to C$ of $G = (V, E)$ is to color all edges of G with colors in C so that any two edges incident to the same vertex have different colors. The edge-coloring is *optimal* if it uses the minimum number of colors.

The cost $\omega(f_e)$ of an edge-coloring f_e of $G = (V, E)$ is defined as follows:

$$\omega(f_e) = \sum_{e \in E} \omega(f_e(e)).$$

A *cost edge-coloring* f_e of G is *optimal* if $\omega(f)$ is th minimum among all cost edge-colorings of G. The *cost edge-coloring problem* is to find an optimal cost edge-coloring. Note that using more colors may result in less total cost. See an example in Fig. 4.

The (original) edge-coloring is the cost edge-coloring with $w(c_1) = w(c_2) = \cdots = w(c_q)$ and additionally minimizing the number of colors.

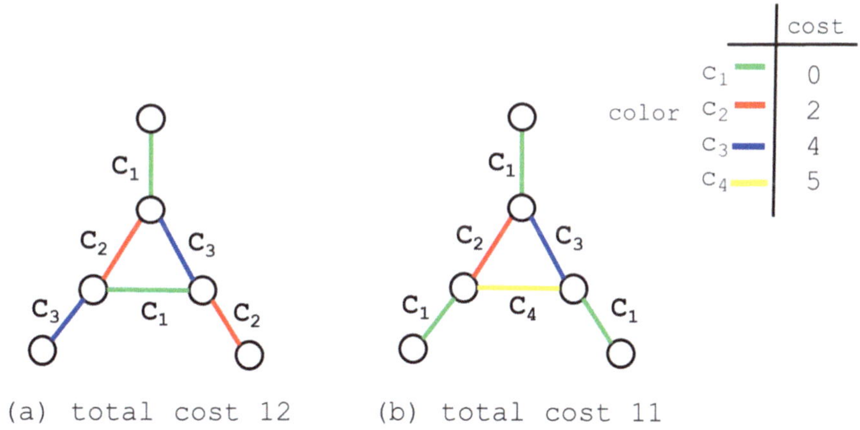

Fig. 4 **a** A cost edge-coloring with 3 colors and total cost 12. **b** An optimal cost edge-coloring with 4 colors and total cost 11

The cost edge-coloring problem is NP-hard for bipartite graphs, because a subproblem of the edge-chromatic sum problem defined below is NP-hard for bipartite graphs [5].

The problem can be solved by dynamic programming in $O(n\Delta^2)$ time [18, 19] for trees. The running time is linear if Δ is a fixed constant.

Theorem 8 ([18, 19]) *The cost edge-coloring problem for trees can be found in* $O(n\Delta^2)$ *time.*

If all the color costs $\omega(c)$ are integers in the range $[-N_\omega, N_\omega]$, then a faster $O(n\Delta^{1.5}\log(nN_\omega))$ time algorithm is known [18, 19].

Theorem 9 ([18, 19]) *The cost edge-coloring problem for trees can be solved in* $O(n\Delta^{1.5}\log nN_\omega))$ *time, if all the color costs* $\omega(c)$ *are integers in the range* $[-N_\omega, N_\omega]$.

The *edge-chromatic sum problem* [5] is the cost edge-coloring problem $\omega(c_i) = i$ for each i. The edge-chromatic sum problem is NP-hard for subcubic bipartite graphs. However, the problem can be solved in $O(n\Delta^{3.5}\log n)$ time for trees.

Theorem 10 ([5]) *The edge-chromatic sum problem is NP-hard for bipartite graphs with* $\Delta \leq 3$.

When restricted to trees, many NP-hard problems can be efficiently solved in polynomial time [1, 2, 16, 17]. The same applies to the edge-chromatic sum problem.

Theorem 11 ([5]) *The edge-chromatic sum problem for trees can be solved in* $O(n\Delta^{3.5}\log n)$ *time.*

For some restricted classes of graphs the following results are known. A k-cyclic graph is a graph with $n + k - 1$ edges. A multicycle is a cycle with parallel edges.

Theorem 12 ([5]) *The edge-chromatic sum problem for* k*-cyclic graphs can be solved in* $O((\Delta + 1)^{k+3.5} m \log m)$ *time.*

Theorem 13 ([3]) *The edge-chromatic sum problem for multicycles can be solved in* $O(n\Delta)$ *time.*

Theorem 14 ([3]) *The edge-chromatic sum problem for multicycles of even length can be solved in* $O(m)$ *time.*

An enumeration algorithm for edge-colorings of a given graph is known [13, 14]. It enumerates all the edge-colorings in $O(n)$ time for each. Can we design an efficient enumeration algorithm for cost edge-colorings of a given graph with the total cost less than a given constant budget k?

In Fig. 5, we give all the six cost edge-colorings of a bipartite graph with the total cost 9.

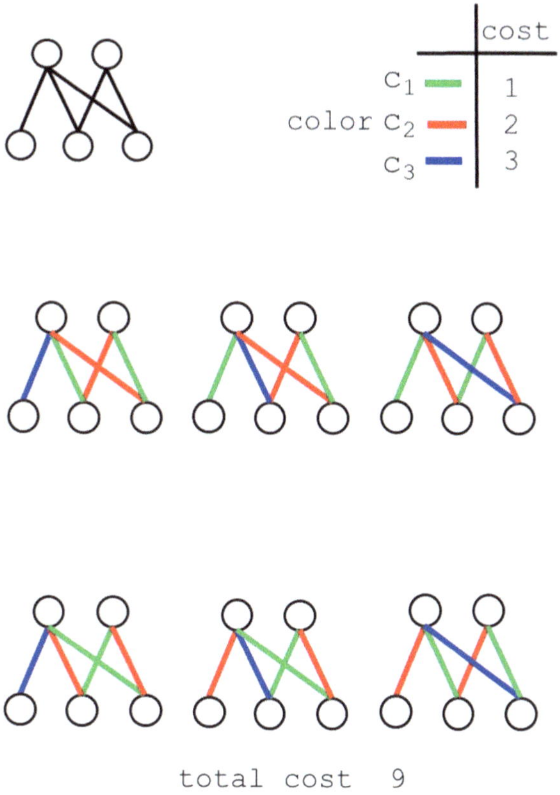

Fig. 5 An example of enumeration of cost edge-colorings on a bipartite graph with total cost 9

5 Conclusion

In this paper, we presented a brief survey of cost graph colorings. We emphasize on the complexity results and algorithmic results.

Acknowledgements This research is partially supported by JSPS KAKENHI grants JP20H05964 and JP20K04973.

References

1. S. Arnborg, J. Lagergren, Easy problems for tree-decomposable graphs. J. Alg. **12**, 308–340 (1991)
2. R.B. Borie, R.G. Parker, C.A. Tovey, Automatic generation of linear-time algorithms from predicate calculus descriptions of problems on recursively constructed graph families. Algorithmica **7**, 555–581 (1992)

3. J. Cardinal, V. Ravelomanana, M. Valencia-Pabon, Minimum sum edge colorings of multicycles. Disc. Appl. Math. **158**, 1216–1223 (2010). https://doi.org/10.1016/j.dam.2009.04.020
4. P. Formanowicz, K. Tanaś, A survey of graph coloring-its types, methods and applications. Found. Comput. Decision Sci. **37**, 223–238 (2012). https://doi.org/10.2478/v10209-011-0012-y
5. K. Giaro, M. Kubale, Edge-chromatic sum of trees and bounded cyclicity graphs. Inf. Process. Lett. **75**, 65–69 (2000)
6. K. Giaro, M. Kubale, A note on polynomial algorithm for cost coloring of bipartite graphs with $\Delta \leq 4$. Discussiones Mathematicae Graph Theory **40**, 885–891 (2020)
7. H. Hajiabolhassan, M.L. Mehrabadi, R. Tusserkani, Minimal coloring and strength of graphs. Disc. Math. **215**, 265–270 (2000)
8. K. Jansen, *Proceedings of ICALP '97*. Lecture Notes in Computer Science (Springer, 1997), pp.727–737
9. L.G. Kroon, A. Sen, H. Deng, A. Roy, The optimal cost chromatic partition problem for trees and interval graphs, in *Proceedings of WG'96 International Workshop on Graph Theoretic Concepts in Computer Science*. Lecture Notes in Computer Science, vol. 1197 (Springer, 1996), pp. 279–292
10. E. Kubicka, The chromatic sum of a graph: history and recent developments. Int. J. Math. Math. Sci. **30**, 1563–1573 (2004). https://doi.org/10.1155/S0161171204306216
11. E. Kubicka, Polynomial algorithm for finding chromatic sum for unicyclic and outerplanar graphs. Ars Combinatoria. **76**, 185–192 (2005)
12. E. Kubicka, A.J. Schwenk, An introduction to chromatic sums, in *CSC '89: Proceedings of the 17th conference on ACM Annual Computer Science Conference. NY, USA* (ACM, 1989), pp. 39–45
13. Y. Matsui, T. Matsui, Enumeration algorithm for the edge coloring problem on bipartite graphs. Combin. Comput. Sci. 18–26 (1995)
14. Y. Matsui, T. Uno, On the enumeration of bipartite minimum edge colorings, in *Graph Theory in Paris: Proceedings of a Conference in Memory f Claude Berge (Trends in Mathematics*, pp. 271–285 (2004)
15. K.J. Supowit, Finding a maximum planar subset of a set of nets in a channel. IEEE Trans. Comput. Aided Des. CAD-6, **1**, 93–94 (1987)
16. J.A. Telle, A. Proskurowski, Algorithms for vertex partitioning problems on partial k-trees. SIAM J. Disc. Math. **10**, 529–550 (1997)
17. X. Zhou, S. Nakano, T. Nishizeki, Edge-coloring partial k-trees. J. Alg. **21**, 598–617 (1996)
18. X. Zhou, T. Nishizeki, Algorithm for the cost edge-coloring of trees, in *Proceedings of the 7th Annual International Conference on Computing and Combinatorics*. Lecture Notes in Computer Science, vol. 2108 (Springer, 2001), pp. 288–297
19. X. Zhou, T. Nishizeki, Algorithm for the Cost Edge-Coloring of trees. J. Combin. Optim. **8**, 97–108 (2004)

Perpetual Scheduling Under Frequency Constraints

Akitoshi Kawamura

Abstract We provide a brief overview of theoretical results to date on perpetual scheduling problems where we want to schedule recurring tasks or agents with minimum or maximum frequency requirements.

Scheduling algorithms and heuristics may prove useful for planning a single execution of a set of tasks for a one-time project, but there are also many situations where we must deal with *recurring* tasks that must be diligently and constantly performed. In this short survey, we consider scheduling problems of this form, in which—for purposes that may include monitoring, maintenance, defense, or replenishing supplies—we wish to perform various recurring tasks, with certain minimum frequencies, in perpetuity. Although the practical relevance of such problems has motivated the development of heuristics and simulation-based analyses targeting a variety of real-world situations, we restrict attention to the mathematically simplest settings and focus on theoretical aspects such as problem structure, optimal solutions, and computational complexity, surveying the progress of research to date and a number of outstanding challenges.

1 The Problem: Pinwheel Scheduling

We begin with the most basic setting, proposed by Holte et al. [22], where we have one agent and k recurring tasks. Each task $i \in [k] = \{1, \dots, k\}$ has a given *period* a_i, meaning that it must be performed at least once every a_i days. We wish to satisfy these frequency requirements by selecting one task to be performed each day. This problem (together with some of its variants we will discuss later) is known as *pinwheel scheduling* [22] or *windows scheduling* [4]. Formally, an instance of this problem consists of a nondecreasing sequence of positive integers $A = (a_i)_{i \in [k]}$, and a solution consists of a *schedule* specifying one of the k tasks to be performed each day. A

A. Kawamura (✉)
Kyoto University, Kyoto, Japan
e-mail: kawamura@kurims.kyoto-u.ac.jp

S. Minato et al. (eds.), *Algorithmic Foundations for Social Advancement*,
https://doi.org/10.1007/978-981-96-0668-9_23

schedule may be thought of as a collection $(S_i)_{i \in [k]}$ of k subsets $S_i \subseteq \mathbb{Z}$, each specifying the days on which task i is performed; this is a valid schedule for A if $S_1, \ldots, S_k$ are pairwise disjoint and, for each $i \in [k]$ and all $m \in \mathbb{Z}$, the interval $[m, m + a_i)$ intersects S_i. An instance for which such a schedule exists is said to be *schedulable*. For example, the instances (3, 3, 3), (2, 4, 8, 8), and (3, 4, 5, 8) are all schedulable, but all become non-schedulable if any one period is decreased. The instance (3, 4, 5, 8) is satisfied by the schedule $\big([0]_8 \cup [3]_8 \cup [6]_8,\ [1]_8 \cup [5]_8,\ [2]_8 \cup [7]_8,\ [4]_8\big)$, where we write

$$[r]_a = \{a \cdot n + r : n \in \mathbb{Z}\} \tag{1}$$

for the residue class of integers congruent to $r \in \mathbb{Z}$ modulo $a \in \mathbb{N} \setminus \{0\}$. This schedule describes a recurring 8-day sequence in which tasks are performed in the order 1, 2, 3, 1, 4, 2, 1, 3.

Pinwheel scheduling may be thought of as a *packing* problem in which the sets $S_1, \ldots, S_k$, subject to the minimum-frequency constraints, must be arranged without overlapping inside the container $\mathbb{Z}$. In Sect. 5, we will consider the dual situation of *covering* problems, in which the goal is to cover all of $\mathbb{Z}$ by subsets subject to *maximum*-frequency constraints. When we wish to emphasize this distinction, we will refer to the case discussed in this and the following three sections as the packing version of pinwheel scheduling, or simply *pinwheel packing*.

2 Computational Complexity

The schedulability of an instance $A = (a_i)_{i \in [k]}$ may be checked via the following procedure [22, Theorem 2.1]. The elements of $[a_1] \times \cdots \times [a_k]$ are called *states* (or *urgency* [18, Section 4.3]); if, at the end of a day, we find ourselves in a state $(u_i)_{i \in [k]}$, this means that task i must be performed no later than u_i days from now. For a task $j \in [k]$ and two states $u = (u_i)_{i \in [k]}$ and $u' = (u'_i)_{i \in [k]}$, we write $u \vdash^j u'$ if

$$u'_i = \begin{cases} a_i & \text{if } i = j, \\ u_i - 1 & \text{otherwise.} \end{cases}$$

This means that if we are in state u on a given day, then performing task j on the next day will bring us into state u'. We write $u \vdash u'$ if $u \vdash^j u'$ for some j. The instance A is thus schedulable if and only if its *state transition graph*, i.e., the directed graph with the relation $\vdash$ as edges, admits an infinite walk, or equivalently, contains a cycle. This, by Savitch's theorem, can be checked in polynomial space [22, Corollary 2.2]:

Theorem 1 *The problem of deciding schedulability of a given pinwheel packing instance is in* PSPACE.

Note that the number of states is in general exponential in the size of the input A. It is unknown whether or not the problem is in NP. It is also unknown whether the problem is NP-hard; however, as we will see in Theorem 5, a slight modification of the input format ensures NP-hardness.

Because our schedules are infinite, some care is required when describing the computational complexity of algorithms for finding a valid schedule (rather than just deciding whether there exists one). From the preceding discussion, it is clear that any schedulable instance has a schedule consisting of a finite sequence of tasks repeated in perpetuity (thus justifying the term "pinwheel" scheduling); however, in general the length of this finite sequence may grow large, and thus we cannot hope to write it out in polynomial time. The question of which alternative criteria should be used to characterize the computational efficiency of schedulers has been discussed already by Holte et al. [22, Section 1]. One (somewhat informal) criterion put forward there for an efficient scheduler is to require that we can, given an instance, generate in polynomial time a *fast online scheduler* (FOLS), which consists of simple instructions that on each day tell us in "constant time" which task to perform.

3 Density

For an instance $A = (a_i)_{i\in[k]}$ to be schedulable, the condition that its *density*

$$\mathrm{D}(A) = \sum_{i\in[k]} \frac{1}{a_i} \tag{2}$$

be at most 1 is clearly necessary [22, Theorem 2.3], but not sufficient. For example, $(2, 3, a_3)$ is non-schedulable for all values of a_3. Nonetheless, there are a number of special cases in which this condition *is* sufficient, as was shown in [22, Theorem 3.1] and [23, Corollary 4.9] (see [26, Theorem 2] for a simpler exposition):

Theorem 2 *A pinwheel packing instance A is schedulable if*

- *the periods in A are pairwise divisible; or if*
- *A consists of at most two distinct period values.*

For example, (2, 4, 12, 12, 24) and (5, 5, 5, 8, 8, 8) are easily schedulable by these criteria. It follows from the first part of this theorem that *any* instance with density $\leq \frac{1}{2}$ is schedulable [22, Corollary 3.2]: simply round down each period to the nearest power of 2, increasing the density by a factor of at most 2. In fact, this bound can be improved, as conjectured by Chan and Chin [8] and confirmed recently by Kawamura [26, Theorem 1]:

Theorem 3 *A pinwheel packing instance A is schedulable if* $\mathrm{D}(A) \leq \frac{5}{6}$.

Note that this value $\frac{5}{6}$ is the best possible, because of the aforementioned non-schedulability of $(2, 3, a_3)$.

Theorem 3 was established by first showing that the problem could be reduced to considering a large but finite number—tens of millions—of instances satisfying certain conditions, and then verifying their schedulability via a brute-force computer program. A proof more amenable to human intuition would be desirable, but remains elusive. Schedulers that arose from earlier efforts toward Theorem 3 [6–8, 16, 30] may prove useful in this respect, although they also tend to involve detailed case analysis.

In the computer experiment for Theorem 3, it also turned out that the only unschedulable instances with densities approaching the bound $\frac{5}{6}$ are $(2, 3, a_3)$ and $(3, 4, 4, a_4)$ (for a_3 and a_4 tending to infinity). It is easy to see that instances of the form $(a_1, a_1 + 1, a_1 + 1, \ldots, a_1 + 1, a_{a_1+1})$ are likewise unschedulable. One could thus propose a revised conjecture that these are the least dense unschedulable instances starting with each fixed value of a_1:

Conjecture 1 A pinwheel packing instance $A = (a_i)_{i\in[k]}$ is schedulable if $\mathrm{D}(A) \leq 1 - (a_1 - 1)/(a_1(a_1 + 1))$.

A weaker conjecture that there is a bound of this form tending to 1 as $a_1 \to \infty$ has been made [7, Section VI] and confirmed [17, Corollary 1], with the bound $1 - 3/\sqrt{a_1}$.

4 Exact Schedulability

We may also consider a modified version of the problem [25, 35, 37] in which, rather than requiring each task $i \in [k]$ in an instance $A = (a_i)_{i\in[k]}$ to be performed *at least* once every a_i days, we instead require that it be performed *precisely* once every a_i days. In this case, each of the sets constituting a schedule $(S_i)_{i\in[k]}$ takes the form of a residue class $S_i = [r_i]_{a_i}$ (see (1)) for some r_i, so the problem is to choose residues r_i such that $[r_1]_{a_1}$, …, $[r_k]_{a_k}$ are pairwise disjoint. If such residues r_i exist, we say that A is *exactly schedulable*. For example, (2, 4) is exactly schedulable, but (2, 5) is not. We refer to the corresponding (decision or search) problem as *exact pinwheel packing*.

The complexity status of this problem is better understood than that of the non-exact version. Two residue classes $[r]_a$ and $[r']_{a'}$ are disjoint if and only if $r \not\equiv r' \pmod{d}$ for the greatest common divisor d of a and a'. This condition can be checked for all pairs of tasks in polynomial time, given an instance $(a_i)_{i\in[k]}$ and a putative solution $(r_i)_{i\in[k]}$; thus, decision of exact schedulability is in NP. The problem is also NP-hard, as was shown by Mok et al. [32, Theorem 1]:

Theorem 4 *Exact pinwheel packing is* NP*-complete, even if the periods a_i in an instance are presented in tally notation, 0^{a_i}.*

As noted in Sect. 2, it is unknown whether pinwheel packing without the exactness requirement is NP-hard. However, Theorem 4 may be used to show that the problem is indeed NP-hard *if* we allow instances to be specified using a concise notation in which, rather than simply listing up the full set of tasks, we describe them in the form

"N_1 tasks with period a_1," "N_2 tasks with period a_2," ..., with N_1, N_2, ...written in binary. This was stated already by [22, Theorem 4.12], but no proof seems to have appeared in subsequent publications (although the essential ideas can be found in [5, Theorem 2.1]), so we present a proof here.

Theorem 5 *The (non-exact) pinwheel packing problem in which the input is written in the concise notation described above is* NP*-hard, even when restricted to instances of density* 1.

Proof The proof proceeds by reduction from the exact pinwheel packing problem of Theorem 4. Given its instance $A = (a_i)_{i \in [k]}$, we set $l = \prod_{i \in [k]} a_i$ (in binary notation), and let A' be the (non-exact) pinwheel scheduling instance obtained by adding $l \cdot (1 - \mathrm{D}(A))$ new tasks, each with period l, to A. This new instance A' has density 1 and can be written in polynomial time in the concise notation. We claim that A' is schedulable if and only if A is exactly schedulable.

For the "if" direction, note that an exact schedule for $A = (a_i)_{i \in [k]}$ repeats every l days, of which only $l \cdot \mathrm{D}(A)$ days are devoted to performing tasks 1, ..., k; thus, we obtain a schedule for A' simply by scheduling each of the new period-l tasks on one of the remaining $l \cdot (1 - \mathrm{D}(A))$ days. For the other direction, suppose that A' is schedulable. Then, as noted in Sect. 2, it admits a schedule consisting of a finite sequence repeated in perpetuity. Because $\mathrm{D}(A') = 1$, each task i in this schedule must be performed precisely every a_i days [22, Lemma 4.1]; thus, simply removing the newly added tasks from this schedule yields a schedule for A. □

Wei and Liu [37] discuss a simple greedy heuristic for this problem. Huhn and Megyesi [25] gave a sufficient condition for an instance to be exactly schedulable (or *harmonic* in their terminology), which was then improved by Sun [35] and Chen [10]. Generalization of exact schedulability to groups other than $\mathbb{Z}$ has been studied [31] in relation to the Herzog–Schönheim Conjecture.

5 Covering Versions

So far we have considered *packing* versions of pinwheel scheduling, but it is equally natural to consider a *covering* version of the problem. We have a single task that must be performed every day, and we wish to determine a shift schedule for sharing the burden of performing the task among several agents. In this case, for each agent i, we are again given a period $a_i \in \mathbb{N}$, but here the constraint is that agent i can perform the task *at most* once every a_i days. A problem instance is again given by a nondecreasing sequence of positive integers, $A = (a_i)_{i \in [k]}$, and we look for a schedule $(S_i)_{i \in [k]}$ (with $S_i \subseteq \mathbb{Z}$ the set of days on which agent $i \in [k]$ performs the task) such that $S_1 \cup \cdots \cup S_k = \mathbb{Z}$ and, for each $i \in [k]$ and all $m \in \mathbb{Z}$, the interval $[m, m + a_i)$ intersects S_i in at most one point. Kawamura and Soejima [28, Section 4], viewing this problem as a version of the patrolling problems, referred to it as "point patrolling," but here we will call it the covering version of pinwheel scheduling, or *pinwheel covering*.

Many of the ideas used to analyze pinwheel packing are also applicable to pinwheel covering. In particular, schedulability can be decided in polynomial space by constructing the state transition graph as in Sect. 2. This puts pinwheel covering in PSPACE, but we do not know whether it is in NP.

The question of necessary and sufficient density conditions can also be discussed, with conclusions dual to those of Sect. 3. In this case, an obviously necessary condition for schedulability is that the density be 1 or greater. This condition is not sufficient—as is demonstrated by the non-schedulability of instances such as (2, 3, 5) or, more generally, $(2^{i-1} + 1)_{i \in [k]}$—but, in analogy to the packing case, *does* become sufficient if we restrict attention to instances with pairwise divisible periods. Hence, rounding *up* every period in an instance to the nearest power of 2 shows that any instance with density 2 or greater is unconditionally schedulable. This threshold can be, again, improved. Using a computer-assisted method similar to that used to prove Theorem 3, Kawamura and Soejima showed [28, Theorem 16] that $\mathrm{D}(A) \geq 1.546$ is sufficient for schedulability, and conjectured [28, Conjecture 18] that this threshold may be further lowered to 1.264... (the best possible value allowed by the counterexample $(2^{i-1} + 1)_{i \in [k]}$ mentioned above). In contrast to the packing case, this gap has not yet been filled.

In analogy to Sect. 4, one can consider *exact pinwheel covering* problems in which agent i must work *precisely* (rather than *at most*) once out of every a_i days. Thus, we are again looking for schedules of the form $([r_i]_{a_i})_{i \in [k]}$, this time satisfying the covering condition $\mathbb{Z} = \bigcup_{i \in [k]} [r_i]_{a_i}$. In contrast to pairwise disjointness that we had here for the packing problem, this covering condition does not appear to be easily checkable for a given putative solution $(r_i)_{i \in [k]}$. Note that it belongs to coNP, and thus decision of the exact pinwheel covering problem is in the class $\Sigma_2^{\mathsf{P}} = \mathsf{NP}^{\mathsf{NP}}$. It is not known whether the problem is Σ_2^{P}-complete. Covering schedules of the form $([r_i]_{a_i})_{i \in [k]}$ are known as *Erdős's covering systems* and have attracted mathematicians' interests [2]. For example, the question of whether, for every N, there exists a covering system satisfying $N \leq a_1 < a_2 < \cdots < a_k$ remained open for more than half a century, until it was recently resolved in the negative [24].

In pinwheel packing and covering problems, we respectively consider instances for which the density $\mathrm{D}(A)$ is *at most* 1 and *at least* 1, as otherwise non-schedulability is guaranteed. If we restrict attention to instances with density *exactly* 1, the two problems—or in fact, the four problems including their exact versions—coincide. Some suspect [28, Conjecture 19] that even this special case is NP-complete.

6 Variants and Generalizations

The problems considered above are only the most basic settings, which may be extended in a variety of ways. An immediate generalization is to allow more than one agent, so that some fixed number of tasks can be performed each day. This is studied both for the non-exact [4, 5] and exact [9, 37] pinwheel packing. Another generalization is to suppose that the time required to perform a task varies from task to task, rather than always being one unit time. This has also been considered for the non-exact [15] and exact [29] pinwheel packing.

We may consider various optimization problems under constraints like those of pinwheel scheduling. Perhaps the most natural optimization version of pinwheel packing is *bamboo-garden trimming* [17]. In a grove of k bamboo plants, plant $i \in [k]$ grows in height at a given daily rate; each day (at a fixed time of day), we select one plant to be trimmed (i.e., reduced to height 0) with the goal of keeping the overall height of the grove as low as possible. This is equivalent to saying that we wish to obtain a pinwheel packing schedule that violates the frequency constraint by as small a factor as possible. Some efficient approximate algorithms (mostly under the complexity criterion mentioned at the end of Sect. 2) have been proposed [17, 21, 26, 36], with [26] giving the current best ratio of $\frac{4}{3}$.

There are problem settings where we optimize other objectives, such as the number of agents for the multiple-agents scenario [4], as well as the long-term average of profit gained by completing a task each time [34] or cost incurred by leaving a task waiting each time [1, 3].

The problem may be combined with geometric aspects. The tasks may be placed in a metric space so that moving between different pairs of tasks takes different amounts of time that are not uniformly one day [11, 17]. One can even imagine that the tasks are distributed continuously over a one-dimensional terrain such as a path or a cycle, so that we have *patrolling* problems [14] where we want mobile agents to visit each point in the terrain with sufficient frequency. There are many studies [12, 13, 19, 20, 27, 28, 33] about the best efficiency with which the agents with limited speeds can patrol the terrain.

Acknowledgements This work was supported in part by JSPS KAKENHI Grant Number JP20H05967.

References

1. S. Anily, C.A. Glass, R. Hassin, The scheduling of maintenance service. Disc. Appl. Math. **82**, 27–42 (1998)
2. P. Balister, Erdős covering systems, in *Surveys in Combinatorics 2024*, ed. by F. Fischer, R. Johnson (Cambridge University Press, 2024), pp. 31–54
3. A. Bar-Noy, R. Bhatia, J. Naor, B. Schieber, Minimizing service and operation costs of periodic scheduling. Math. Oper. Res. **27**(3), 518–544 (2002). Preliminary version in *Proceedings of the Ninth Annual ACM-SIAM Symposium on Discrete Algorithms* (SODA), pp. 11–20 (1998)
4. A. Bar-Noy, R.E. Ladner, Windows scheduling problems for broadcast systems. SIAM J. Comput. **32**(4), 1091–1113 (2003). Preliminary version in *Proceedings of the Thirteenth Annual ACM-SIAM Symposium on Discrete Algorithms* (SODA), pp. 433–442 (2002)

5. A. Bar-Noy, R.E. Ladner, T. Tamir, Windows scheduling as a restricted version of bin packing. ACM Trans. Alg. **3**(3), Article 28 (2007). Preliminary version in *Proceedings of the Fifteenth Annual ACM-SIAM Symposium on Discrete Algorithms* (SODA), pp. 224–233 (2004)
6. S.K. Baruah, S. Lin, Pfair scheduling of generalized pinwheel task systems. IEEE Trans. Comput. **47**(7), 812–816 (1998)
7. M.Y. Chan, F. Chin, General schedulers for the pinwheel problem based on double-integer reduction. IEEE Trans. Comput. **41**, 755–768 (1992)
8. M.Y. Chan, F. Chin, Schedulers for larger classes of pinwheel instances. Algorithmica **9**, 425–462 (1993)
9. Y.-G. Chen, On m-harmonic sequences. Disc. Math. **162**, 273–280 (1996)
10. Y.-G. Chen, A theorem on harmonic sequences. Disc. Math. **186**, 287–288 (1998)
11. S. Coene, F.C.R. Spieksma, G.J. Woeginger, Charlemagne's challenge: the periodic latency problem. Oper. Res. **59**(3), 674–683 (2011)
12. J. Czyzowicz, L. Gąsieniec, A. Kosowski, E. Kranakis, Boundary patrolling by mobile agents with distinct maximal speeds, in *Proceedings of the 19th Annual European Symposium on Algorithms* (ESA), LNCS 6942, pp. 701–712 (2011)
13. J. Czyzowicz, K. Georgiou, E. Kranakis, F. MacQuarrie, D. Pajak, Fence patrolling with two-speed robots, in *Proceedings of the Fifth International Conference on Operations Research and Enterprise Systems* (ICORES), pp. 229–241 (2016)
14. A. Dumitrescu, C.D. Tóth, Computational Geometry Column 59. ACM SIGACT News **45**(2) (2014)
15. E.A. Feinberg, M.T. Curry, Generalized pinwheel problem. Math. Methods Oper. Res. **62**, 99–122 (2005)
16. P.C. Fishburn, J.C. Lagarias, Pinwheel scheduling: achievable densities. Algorithmica **34**, 14–38 (2002)
17. L. Gąsieniec, T. Jurdziński, R. Klasing, C. Levcopoulos, A. Lingas, J. Min, T. Radzik, Perpetual maintenance of machines with different urgency requirements. J. Comput. Syst. Sci. **139**, 103476 (2024)
18. L. Gąsieniec, B. Smith, S. Wild, Towards the 5/6-density conjecture of pinwheel scheduling, in *Proceedings of the SIAM Symposium on Algorithm Engineering and Experiments* (ALENEX), pp. 91–103 (2022)
19. B. Gorain, P.S. Mandal, Approximation algorithms for sweep coverage in wireless sensor networks. J. Parallel Distrib. Comput. **74**, 2699–2707 (2014)
20. B. Haeupler, F. Kuhn, A. Martinsson, K. Petrova, P. Pfister, Optimal strategies for patrolling fences, in *Proceedings of the 46th International Colloquium on Automata, Languages, and Programming* (ICALP), LIPIcs 132, Article 144 (2019)
21. F. Höhne, R. van Stee, A 10/7-approximation for discrete bamboo garden trimming and continuous trimming on star graphs, in *Proceedings of the 26th International Workshop on Approximation Algorithms for Combinatorial Optimization Problems* (APPROX), Article 16, LIPIcs 275 (2023)
22. R. Holte, A. Mok, L. Rosier, I. Tulchinsky, D. Varvel, The pinwheel: a real-time scheduling problem, in *Proceedings of the 22nd Annual Hawaii International Conference on System Sciences*, vol. II, pp. 693–702 (1989)
23. R. Holte, L. Rosier, I. Tulchinsky, D. Varvel, Pinwheel scheduling with two distinct numbers. Theor. Comput. Sci. **100**, 105–135 (1992). Preliminary version in *Proc. 14th International Symposium on Mathematical Foundations of Computer Science* (MFCS), LNCS 379, 281–290 (1989)
24. B. Hough, Solution of the minimum modulus problem for covering systems. Ann. Math. **181**(1), 361–382 (2015)
25. A.P. Huhn, L. Megyesi, On disjoint residue classes. Disc. Math. **41**, 327–330 (1982)
26. A. Kawamura, Proof of the density threshold conjecture for pinwheel scheduling, in *Proceedings 56th Annual ACM Symposium on Theory of Computing* (STOC), pp. 1816–1819 (2024)

27. A. Kawamura, Y. Kobayashi, Fence patrolling by mobile agents with distinct speeds. *Distributed Computing* 28(2), 147–154, 2015. Preliminary version, in *Proceedings of the 23rd International Symposium on Algorithms and Computation* (ISAAC), LNCS 7676, pp. 598–608 (2012)
28. A. Kawamura, M. Soejima, Simple strategies versus optimal schedules in multi-agent patrolling. Theor. Comput. Sci. **839**, 195–206 (2020). Preliminary version in *Proceedings of the Ninth International Conference on Algorithms and Complexity* (CIAC), LNCS 9079, pp. 261–273 (2015)
29. J. Korst, E. Aarts, J.K. Lenstra, Scheduling periodic tasks. INFORMS J. Comput. **8**(4), 428–435 (1996)
30. S. Lin, K. Lin, A pinwheel scheduler for three distinct numbers with a tight schedulability bound. Algorithmica **19**, 411–426 (1997)
31. L. Margolis, O. Schnabel, The Herzog-Schönheim conjecture for small groups and harmonic subgroups. Beiträge zur Algebra und Geometrie **60**, 399–418 (2019)
32. A. Mok, L. Rosier, I. Tulchinsky, D. Varvel, Algorithms and complexity of the periodic maintenance problem. Microprocess. Microprogram. **27**(1), 657–664 (1989)
33. F. Pasqualetti, A. Franchi, F. Bullo, On optimal cooperative patrolling, in *Proceedings of the 49th IEEE Conference on Decision and Control* (CDC), pp. 7153–7158 (2010)
34. J. Sgall, H. Shachnai, T. Tamir, Periodic scheduling with obligatory vacations. Theor. Comput. Sci. **410**, 5112–5121 (2009). Preliminary version entitled "Fairness-free periodic scheduling with vacations" in *Proceedings of the 13th Annual European Symposium on Algorithms* (ESA), LNCS 3669, pp. 592–603 (2005)
35. Z.-W. Sun, On disjoint residue classes. Disc. Math. **104**, 321–326 (1992)
36. M. van Ee, A 12/7-approximation algorithm for the discrete Bamboo Garden Trimming problem. Oper. Res. Lett. **49**, 645–649 (2021)
37. W.D. Wei, C.L. Liu, On a periodic maintenance problem. Oper. Res. Lett. **2**, 90–93 (1983)

MIX
Papier aus verantwortungsvollen Quellen
Paper from responsible sources
FSC® C105338

If you have any concerns about our products,
you can contact us on
ProductSafety@springernature.com

In case Publisher is established outside the EU,
the EU authorized representative is:
Springer Nature Customer Service Center GmbH
Europaplatz 3, 69115 Heidelberg, Germany

Printed by Libri Plureos GmbH
in Hamburg, Germany